IRAN'S CONSTITUTIONAL REVOLUTION

IRAN'S CONSTITUTIONAL REVOLUTION

Popular Politics, Cultural Transformations and Transnational Connections

Edited by
H. E. Chehabi and Vanessa Martin

Iran and the Persianate World

I.B.TAURIS
LONDON · NEW YORK · OXFORD · NEW DELHI · SYDNEY

I.B. TAURIS
Bloomsbury Publishing Plc
50 Bedford Square, London, WC1B 3DP, UK
1385 Broadway, New York, NY 10018, USA
29 Earlsfort Terrace, Dublin 2, Ireland

BLOOMSBURY, I.B. TAURIS and the I.B. Tauris logo
are trademarks of Bloomsbury Publishing Plc

First published in Great Britain 2010
This paperback edition published 2022

Copyright © H. E. Chehabi and Vanessa Martin, 2010

H. E. Chehabi and Vanessa Martin have asserted their rights under the Copyright, Designs and Patents Act, 1988, to be identified as editors of this work.

For legal purposes the Acknowledgements on p. xvii constitute an extension of this copyright page.
The assistance of the Iran Heritage Foundation is gratefully acknowledged.

All rights reserved. No part of this publication may be reproduced or transmitted in any form or by any means, electronic or mechanical, including photocopying, recording, or any information storage or retrieval system, without prior permission in writing from the publishers.

Bloomsbury Publishing Plc does not have any control over, or responsibility for, any third-party websites referred to or in this book. All internet addresses given in this book were correct at the time of going to press. The author and publisher regret any inconvenience caused if addresses have changed or sites have ceased to exist, but can accept no responsibility for any such changes.

A catalogue record for this book is available from the British Library.
A catalog record for this book is available from the Library of Congress.

ISBN: HB: 978-1-8488-5415-4
PB: 978-0-7556-4923-5
ePDF: 978-0-7556-1469-1
eBook: 978-0-7556-1097-6

Series: International Library of Iranian Studies, Vol 28

To find out more about our authors and books visit
www.bloomsbury.com and sign up for our newsletters.

Contents

List of Illustrations	ix
List of Contributors	xi
Acknowledgements	xvii
Glossary of Persian and Arabic Terms	xix
Introduction	
Vanessa Martin and H. E. Chehabi	xxi
Prologue: The Poetry of the Constitutional Revolution	
Homa Katouzian	1

PART I. HISTORIOGRAPHY

1. Whose Revolution? Stakeholders and Stories of the 'Constitutional Movement' in Iran, 1905–11
   Joanna de Groot — 15

2. The Iranian Constitutional Revolution as lieu(x) de mémoire: Sattar Khan
   Anja Pistor-Hatam — 33

3. Introducing Georgian Sources for the Historiography of the Iranian Constitutional Revolution (1905–11)
   Iago Gocheleishvili — 45

PART II. STATE-BUILDING

4. Constitutional Rights and the Development of Civil Law in Iran, 1907–41
   Ali Gheissari — 69

5. The Constitutional Revolution, Popular Politics, and State-Building in Iran
   Stephanie Cronin — 81

6. Municipalities and Constitutionalism in Iran
   Reza Mokhtari Esfahani — 99

Part III. Nation-Building

7. Merchants, Their Class Identification Process, and Constitutionalism
   Soheila Torabi Farsani — 117

8. Tribes of the Homeland: The Bakhtiyari in the Revolutionary Press
   Arash Khazeni — 131

9. Revolution and a High-Ranking Sufi: Zahir al-Dowleh's Contribution to the Constitutional Movement
   Lloyd Ridgeon — 143

Part IV. Intellectual and Artistic Initiatives: Public Awakening

10. The *Rowshanfekr* in the Constitutional Period: An Overview
    Mangol Bayat — 165

11. An Iranian Modernist Project: Ali Akbar Dehkhoda's Writings in the Constitutional Period
    Nahid Mozaffari — 193

12. Readership, the Press, and the Public Sphere in the First Constitutional Era
    Negin Nabavi — 213

13. Writing in Tehran: The First Freedom of Press Law
    Pardis Minuchehr — 225

14. The Constitutional Revolution and Persian Dramatic Works: An Observation on Social Relations Criticism in the Plays of the Constitutional Era
    Ali Miransari — 239

15. National Identity and Photographs of the Constitutional Revolution
    Reza Sheikh   249

PART V. TRANSNATIONAL PERSPECTIVES

16. *Mashrutiyat, Meşrutiyet,* and Beyond: Intellectuals and the Constitutional Revolutions of 1905–12
    Charles Kurzman   277

17. Erin and Iran Resurgent: Irish Nationalists and the Iranian Constitutional Revolution
    Mansour Bonakdarian   291

18. Crafting Constitutional Narratives: Iranian and Young Turk Solidarity, 1907–09
    Farzin Vejdani   319

19. Constitutionalists *Sans Frontières*: Iranian Constitutionalism and its Asian Connections
    Touraj Atabaki   341

20. *Mashruteh* and *al-Nahda*: The Iranian Constitutional Revolution in the Iranian Diaspora Press of Egypt and in Arab Reformist Periodicals
    Kamran Rastegar   357

21. The Iranian Constitutional Revolution as Reported in the Chinese Press
    Yidan Wang   369

22. Japan and the Iranian Constitutional Revolution
    Michael Penn   381

Notes   397
Index   491

Illustrations

1–2.	The orderly and the disorderly revolutionaries. The Bakhtiyari tribal retinues in camp outside Isfahan in 1909. Photographs from Browne, *The Persian Revolution*.	133
3.	'The Victorious Army of the Nation,' a caricature of the Bakhtiyaris' march on Tehran that appeared in the Isfahan newspaper *Kashkul*, Isfahan, 1909.	141
4.	Photograph of Zahir al-Dowleh, taken by Sevruguin. (Reproduced courtesy of the Freer Gallery of Art and Arthur M. Sackler Gallery Archives, Smithsonian Institute. Sevruguin sub-series 1.1.8 negative number 49.3 (675)).	147
5.	Zahir al-Dowleh is second on the right in this photograph taken by Sevruguin. (Reproduced courtesy of the Freer Gallery and Arthur M. Sackler Gallery Archives, Smithsonian Institute. Sevruguin sub-series 1.1.8 negative number 15.2).	157
6.	The Angel Esrafil carries a scroll bearing the words *horriyat* (freedom), *moasvat* (equality), *okhovvat* (brotherhood).	218
7.	The motto at the top of every issue of the weekly *Mosavat* read *horriyat* (freedom), *'edalat* (justice), *okhovvat* (brotherhood).	219
8.	Masthead of *Ayineh-ye Gheyb Nama* (Mirror of the Hidden).	229
9.	Another masthead of *Ayineh-ye Gheyb Nama* (Mirror of the Hidden).	231
10.	A sketch of Malek al-Motekallemin.	235
11.	*Mosavat*'s celebration of the emergence of the press law.	237
12.	'Birth of the Iranian Nation', Photographer: Hojjat Sepahvand, *E'temad-e Melli* Daily Journal, no. 132, 16 July 2006.	249
13.	Posing for the Court photographer.	252
14.	Photography in a public studio.	252
15.	Syndicate of Merchants.	252
16.	A group during the sit-ins.	253
17.	Tabriz resistance to Mohammad Ali Shah's coup.	253
18.	Early manifestations of civil society institutions.	253

19–20.	The constitution, the government, and the sciences.	256
21.	The *mojahedin*.	257
22.	Postcard of an Iranian streetscape.	258
23.	Ethnographic documentation as shown in a postcard.	259
24–5.	Postcards showing events of the constitutional period.	259
26.	Talebov ca. 1910.	261
27.	Public hanging in Tabriz carried out by the Russians on 'Ashura 1911.	261
28–32.	Inscribed photographs from the constitutional period.	262–4
33.	Picture of Tehran *basti*s at the Ottoman Embassy under the Ottoman Flag. *Resimli Kitap*, June 1909, vol. 2, no. 9.	334
34.	The caption reads 'Islamic countries will soon be under the shadow of the unity of these two far-sighted (*del-agah*) kings, protectors of Islam, and attain the highest degree of civilization.' *Kashkul*, year 2, no. 31.	339
35.	Mozaffar al-Din Shah. *Dongfang Zazhi* 1/9 (1904).	370
36.	Mohammad Ali Shah. *Dongfang Zazhi* 4/6 (1907).	371
37.	Ahmad Shah. *Dongfang Zazhi* 8/6 (1911).	373
38.	The two princes: A'lā al-Saltane and his son. *Dongfang Zazhi* 8/6 (1911).	373
39.	Ahmad Shah. *Dongfang Zazhi* 9/9 (1912).	375
40.	The Persian land force. *Dongfang Zazhi* 9/9 (1912).	375
41.	(Left) In front of the Persian telegraph office. (Right) The Persians praying before a war. *Dongfang Zazhi* 9/9 (1912).	376
42.	The current situation of the Persian army. (Upper left) The Persian soldiers. (Upper right) The Cossack Brigade stationed in Persia. (Middle) The hostel of the Persian trade caravan. (Below left) The Persian soldiers as peddlers. (Below right) The Persian artillery. *Dongfang Zazhi* 9/9 (1912).	376

Contributors

Touraj Atabaki is a professor of social history of the Middle East and Central Asia at the University of Leiden and a senior research fellow at the International Institute of Social History. He is the author of *Azerbaijan: Ethnicity and the Struggle for Powers in Iran* (1993) and *Beyond Essentialism: Who Writes Whose Past in the Middle East and Central Asia?* (2003); editor of *Post-Soviet Central Asia* (1998); co-editor, with Erik Jan Zürcher, of *Men of Order, Authoritarian Modernisation in Turkey and Iran* (2004); co-editor, with Sanjyot Mehendale, of *Central Asia and the Caucasus: Transnationalism and Diaspora* (2005); and editor of *Iran and the First World War: Battleground of the Great Powers* (2006), *The State and the Subaltern: Modernization, Society and the State in Turkey and Iran* (2007), and *Iran in the 20th Century: Historiography and Political Culture* (2009). His current work focuses on the historiography of everyday life and comparative subaltern history.

Mangol Bayat is an independent scholar. She has taught at Shiraz (formerly Pahlavi) University, Harvard, MIT, the University of Iowa, and the University of Bonn. She is the author of *Mysticism and Dissent: Socioreligious Thought in Qajar Iran* (1982), *Iran's First Revolution: Shi'ism and the Constitutional Revolution, 1905–09* (1991), and is currently finishing *Iran's First Revolution: The Second Majles* (forthcoming).

Mansour Bonakdarian is a visiting faculty member at the University of Toronto at Mississauga. He is the author of *Britain and the Iranian Constitutional Revolution of 1906–1911: Foreign Policy, Imperialism, and Dissent* (2006), and has published articles, book chapters, and encyclopaedia entries on topics ranging from Iranian women and British suffragists in the early twentieth century to the ideological cross-currents and interactions between Iranian and Indian nationalists from 1905 to 1921, and Iran and the Ottoman Empire at the First Universal Races Congress (London, 1911). His current projects include a collected volume of essays (with Ian Christopher Fletcher) on the First Universal Races Congress, and monographs on the contentious confluences of nationalism, internationalism, and transnationalism in India, Iran, and Ireland, 1905–21; empathy and cross-cultural/cross-racial epistemology in

Edwardian Britain; and global networks of 'anti-imperialist' nationalist solidarities and resistance to European imperialism in the early twentieth century.

Houchang Esfandiar Chehabi is a professor of international relations and history at Boston University. He is the author of *Iranian Politics and Religious Modernism: The Liberation Movement of Iran under the Shah and Khomeini* (1990); principal author of *Distant Relations: Iran and Lebanon in the Last 500 Years* (2006); co-editor, with Alfred Stepan, of *Politics, Society, and Democracy: Comparative Studies* (1995); co-editor, with Juan J. Linz, of *Sultanistic Regimes* (1998); and editor of *Robert Michels, Political Sociology, and the Future of Democracy* by Juan J. Linz (2006). His main research interest is Iranian cultural history.

Stephanie Cronin is Faculty Tutor in the Faculty of Oriental Studies, University of Oxford. She is the author of *The Army and the Creation of the Pahlavi State in Iran, 1910–1926* (1997) and *Tribal Politics in Iran: Rural Conflict and the New State, 1921–1941* (2006); editor of *The Making of Modern Iran; State and Society under Riza Shah, 1921–1941* (2003), *Reformers and Revolutionaries in Modern Iran: New Perspectives on the Iranian Left* (2004), and *Subalterns and Social Protest: History from Below in the Middle East and North Africa* (2007). She is currently preparing for publication *Shahs, Soldiers and Subalterns: Opposition, Protest and Rebellion in Modern Iran* (forthcoming, 2010).

Ali Gheissari is a professor of history and an adjunct professor of political science at the University of San Diego. He is the author of *Iranian Intellectuals in the Twentieth Century* (1998); co-author, with Vali Nasr, of *Democracy in Iran: History and the Quest for Liberty* (2006); editor of *Harfi az hezaran keh andar 'ebarat amadeh: khaterat-e Haj Mohammad Taqi Jurabchi, vaqaye'-e Tabriz va Rasht 1324–1330 HQ* (a memoir of Tabriz and Rasht in the Iranian Constitutional Revolution) (2008) and *Contemporary Iran: Economy, Society, Politics* (2009); and translator into Persian of Immanuel Kant's *Groundwork of the Metaphysics of Morals* (1991). His research interests are the intellectual and political history of modern Iran, and his current research focuses on legal thought and institutions.

Iago Gocheleishvili is a lecturer at the Department of Near Eastern Studies at Cornell University. His current research focuses on the evolution of constitutionalism and the development of the constitutional movement in Iran in the early twentieth century, with a primary interest in exploring the connections of the Iranian constitutional movement with the Caucasus and Ottoman Turkey. His latest publication on the topic is 'Georgian Sources on the Iranian

Constitutional Revolution (1905–1911): Sergo Gamdlishvili's Memoirs of the Gilan Resistance', *Iranian Studies* 40/1 (2007).

Joanna de Groot is a senior lecturer in the History Department and member of the Centre for Women's Studies at the University of York, UK. Her publications include *Religion, Culture and Politics in Iran: From the Qajars to Khomeini* (2007). Her main scholarly interests are in the history of Iran since 1800, in gender and women's histories since the eighteenth century, and in histories of empire and ethnicity.

Homa Katouzian is the Iranian Heritage Foundation Research Fellow, St. Antony's College, and a member of the Faculty of Oriental Studies, University of Oxford. His English books include *Musaddiq and the Struggle for Power in Iran* (second edition, 1999), *Sadeq Hedayat: The Life and Legend of an Iranian Writer* (paperback, 2002), *State and Society in Iran: The Eclipse of the Qajars and the Emergence of the Pahlavis* (paperback, 2006), *Sa'di, The Poet of Life, Love and Compassion* (2006), and *Iranian History and Politics: The Dialectics of State and Society* (paperback 2007). He is the editor of *Sadeq Hedayat: His Works and His Wondrous World* (2008) and co-editor, with Hossein Shahidi, of *Iran in the 21st Century: Politics, Economics and Conflict* (2008). He is also editor of *Iranian Studies*. His current research interests are Iranian history and politics, the comparative sociology of Iranian and European history, and modern and classical Persian literature.

Arash Khazeni is an assistant professor of history at Pomona College. He is the author of *Tribes and Empire on the Margins of Qajar Iran, 1800–1911* (2010). His research is focused on the Middle East since 1500, with an emphasis on the social, cultural, and environmental history of Iran, Afghanistan, and Central Asia, and he is currently working on a history of the Central Asian steppes based on early-modern-period Persian travel narratives.

Charles Kurzman is a professor of sociology at the University of North Carolina at Chapel Hill. He is the author of *The Unthinkable Revolution in Iran* (2004) and *Democracy Denied, 1905–1915* (2008) and editor of *Liberal Islam: A Sourcebook* (1998) and *Modernist Islam, 1840–1940: A Sourcebook* (2002). His research focuses on comparative historical sociology.

Vanessa Martin is a professor of modern Middle Eastern history at Royal Holloway, University of London. She has written three books, *Islam and Modernism: The Iranian Revolution of 1906* (1989), *Creating an Islamic State* (2000), and *The Qajar Pact: Bargaining, Protest and the State in Qajar Iran*

(2005). She has edited two volumes, *Women, Religion and Culture in Iran* (2001), and *Anglo-Iranian Relations since 1800* (2005). She is the series editor and chair of the publication committee of the British Institute of Persian Studies and a co-editor of its journal *Iran*. Her main research interest is in Iran during the Qajar period, and especially the Constitutional Revolution, on which she is currently writing a study of urban popular involvement.

Pardis Minuchehr is lecturer and coordinator of Persian Studies at the University of Pennsylvania. Her most recent publication is '*Sur-e Esrafil* in Exile: Modern Definitions of Monarchy', in *Iranian Studies* (2009). Her current research project is the emergence of the print media in Iran as it relates to cultural and linguistic transformation in early twentieth-century Iran.

Ali Miransari is the head of the Persian Literature Department at the Centre for the *Great Islamic Encyclopaedia*. His book-length publications include bibliographies on Khaju Kermani (1991), Naser Khosrow (1994), Farid al-Din 'Attar (1995), and Nima Yushij (1996), as well as a five-volume reference work on Iran's contemporary literary notables (1997–2004), an edition of the letters of Malek al-Sho'ara Bahar (2001), and *Namayeshnamehha-ye Mirzadeh 'Eshqi* (The Plays of Mirzadeh 'Eshqi) (2007). His main research interest is contemporary Persian literature, and he is also preparing a catalogue of the Persian manuscripts of the Ferdowsi Library, Wadham College, University of Oxford.

Reza Mokhtari Esfahani is an independent researcher. He is the author of *Honar-e Esfahan az negah-e sayyahan* (The Arts of Isfahan as Seen by Travellers) (2006) and *Radio, farhang va siyasat dar Iran (1319–1332)* (Radio, Culture and Politics in Iran) (2008); and editor of *Khaterat-e Mohammad Pishgahi Fard* (Memoirs of Mohammad Pishgahi Fard) (2006). He has also published a number of document collections, such as *Asnadi az anjomanha-ye baladi, tojjar va asnaf* (1300–1320) (Documents on Municipal Councils, Merchants and Guilds [1921–1941]) (2001), *Asnadi az anjomanha va majame'-e mazhabi dar dowreh-ye Pahlavi* (Documents on Religious Societies and Associations in the Pahlavi Era) (2002); and *Gozareshha-ye ayalat va velayat az owza'-e ejtema'i va eqtesadi-ye Iran dar sal-e 1310* (Reports of Provinces and Districts about the Social and Economic Conditions of Iran in the Year 1931–32) (2004). His main research interests are documents from the Qajar and Pahlavi eras and contemporary social history.

Nahid Mozaffari is an adjunct professor teaching graduate courses in modern Iranian and modern Middle Eastern history at New York University. She is the author of *Crafting Constitutionalism in Iran: Ali Akbar Dehkhoda, 1906–*

1956 (2009) and editor of *Strange Times, My Dear: The PEN Anthology of Contemporary Iranian Literature* (2005). Her research interests are focused on social history, including the history of slavery in Iran and the surrounding areas, and the social history of opium in the Middle East.

Negin Nabavi is an assistant professor of history at Montclair State University. She is the author of *Intellectuals and the State in Iran: Politics, Discourse and the Dilemma of Authenticity* (2003), and editor of *Intellectual Trends in Twentieth Century Iran: A Critical Survey* (2003). Her field of research is the intellectual and cultural history of nineteenth- and twentieth-century Iran, and her current project is on the emergence of the public sphere in early twentieth-century Iran.

Michael Penn is the executive director of the Shingetsu Institute for the Study of Japanese–Islamic Relations, an open research institute that examines Japan's connections with the Islamic world from a variety of perspectives. He has published more than twenty articles, including 'Islam in Japan: Adversity and Diversity', in *Harvard Asia Quarterly* (2006) and 'East Meets East: An Ottoman Mission in Meiji Japan', in *Princeton Papers* (2007). He is currently preparing his first full-length book for publication on the topic of Japan and the War on Terrorism.

Anja Pistor-Hatam holds the chair of Islamic Studies at Kiel University, where she is also dean of the Faculty of Humanities. Her publications include *Nachrichtenblatt, Informationsbörse und Diskussionsforum: Akhtar-e Estānbūl (1876–1896) – Anstöße zur frühen persischen Moderne* (1999) and *Iran und die Reformbewegung im osmanischen Reich: Persische Staatsmänner, Reisende und Oppositionelle unter dem Einfluß der Tanzimat* (1992). Her research focuses on modern history (of the nineteenth to twenty-first centuries), especially intellectual history in Iran and the Ottoman Empire and the Shiite pilgrimage to the holy sites in Iraq (*'atabat*).

Kamran Rastegar is an assistant professor of Arabic literature and culture at Tufts University. He is the author of *Literary Modernity Between Europe and the Middle East* (2007) and translator of Mahmoud Dowlatabadi's novel *Missing Soluch* (2007). He researches on topics relating to nineteenth-century Arabic and Persian literatures, as well as the contemporary literary and visual cultures of Iran and the Arab world.

Lloyd Ridgeon is a reader in Islamic Studies at the University of Glasgow. He is the author of *'Aziz Nasafi* (1998) and *Sufi Castigator: Ahmad Kasravi* *and the Iranian Mystical Tradition* (2006) and editor of *Islamic Interpretations of Christianty* (2000) and *Religion and Politics in Iran: A Reader* (2005). He is currently finishing a book on the relationship between *javanmardi* and Persian Sufism. His main research interests include religion and politics in Iranian society and their manifestations in social institutions, such as the *zurkhaneh*, and in Iranian cinema.

Reza Sheikh is an independent scholar in Iranian photohistory and managing director of a development NGO in Tehran. He was a founding member of the 'Akskhaneh-ye Shahr Museum in Tehran, and has published numerous articles on Iranian photography and European photographic depictions of Iran, many of them in the journal *'Aksnameh*.

Soheila Torabi Farsani teaches at the Department of History of the Islamic Azad University at Najafabad. She is the author of *Tojjar, mashrutiyat va dowlat-e modern* (Merchants, Constitutionalism, and the Modern State) (2005) and editor of *Asnadi az madares-e dokhtaran az mashruteh ta Pahlavi* (Documents on Girls' Schools from the Constitutional to the Pahlavi Eras) (1999). She has also published a collection of her translations of articles by Ervand Abrahamian, *Maqalati dar jame'ehshenasi-ye siyasi-ye Iran* (Articles on the Political Sociology of Iran) (1997) and by Ahmad Ashraf and Ali Banuazizi, *Tabaqat-e ejtema'i, dowlat va enqelab dar Iran* (Social Classes, the State, and Revolution in Iran) (2008). Her research interests are economic history, historical sociology, social history of Iran, and women's studies.

Farzin Vejdani is an assistant professor of history at the University of Arizona. He is co-editor, with Abbas Amanat, of *Iranian Identity and Modern Political Culture* (forthcoming 2011). His research interests include Turko-Iranian cultural relations, Iranian nationalist historiography, and the development of language policy and folklore studies in late Qajar and early Pahlavi Iran.

Yidan Wang is a professor of Persian literature in the Institute of Iranian Cultural Studies at Peking University. Her publications include *Tarikh-e Chin az Jami' al-Tavarikh* (History of China and Cathay in *Jami' al-Tavarikh*) (2000), a Chinese translation of *Masnavi-ye Ma'navi*, vol. 4 (2002); and *A Study and Collated Translation of Rashid al-Din's History of China in Jami' al-Tavarikh* (in Chinese, 2006). Her main research interests are cultural exchange between China and Iran in the Il-Khanid dynasty (thirteenth to fourteenth centuries) and the history of the introduction of Persian literature into China.

Acknowledgements

This collection of studies on the Iranian Constitutional Revolution of 1906 arises out of a conference held at the University of Oxford from 30 July to 2 August 2006 to mark the centenary of that event. It began in a series of discussions by an organizing committee comprised of Abbas Amanat, John Gurney, Farhad Hakimzadeh, Mohamad Tavakoli-Targhi, and ourselves, which sought to create an occasion that would provide the widest possible range of subjects and views on the revolution. We would like to thank the other members of the committee for their highly significant input in terms of ideas, expertise, and organization.

The volume is indebted to the Iran Heritage Foundation for the support it provided in promoting, funding, and organizing such a major event, not least through its worldwide connections with those engaged in Iranian studies. The authors would also like to thank the British Institute of Persian Studies for their contribution to the publication of this volume.

An invaluable contribution was made by the Oriental Institute of the University of Oxford, especially through John Gurney, which placed its facilities and university contacts at the disposal of the conference. Further encouragement and support came from the Persian Cultural Foundation, which did much to promote the conference, from Julius Beer (Middle East) Ltd., and from Hassan Khosrowshahi, to all of whom we extend our deepest appreciation.

Hossein Moghadam worked tirelessly to manage the conference, ably assisted by Roham Alvandi, Homa Nasab, David Patrikarakos, Ebrahim Talae, and Omid Uskowi in Oxford as well as Nahid Assemi and Pegah Zohouri Haghian at the IHF in London. We thank them all.

Janet Afary, Abbas Amanat, and Ahmad Mahdavi Damghani helped us with the editing of this volume. They were most generous with their time, and we are most grateful to them. Finally, we thank Marie Deer for the extraordinary care she devoted to the copy-editing of this volume.

Glossary of Persian and Arabic Terms

anjoman: association, club
'Ashura: the tenth of the lunar month of Muharram, the day on which Imam Husayn was martyred in 680 CE
asnaf: guilds (plural of *senf*)
atabak: elevated title occasionally given to the prime minister
'atabat: the four shrine cities of Iraq: Najaf, Karbala, Samarra, and Kazimayn. Twelver Shiites go on pilgrimage to these cities to visit the tombs of the Imans
ayalat: province
Azali: a follower of Mirza Yahya Nuri, Sobh-e Azal (1831–1912), a successor to the Bab
Babi: a follower of Mirza Ali Mohammad, Bab (1819–50), who founded a new religion considered heretical by Twelver Shiites; hence a byword for 'heretic'
baladiyeh: municipal government
Balasari: in Kerman, a Twelver Shiite who is not a *Sheykhi*
bast: sanctuary against government conduct perceived as oppressive
fada'i: devotee of a cause seen as being Islamic
Farangestan: Europe
farrash: deputy of a *kadkhoda* with the task of enforcing order
fatwa: a religious edict issued by a *mujtahid*
fiqh: Islamic jurisprudence
Hadith: the recorded traditions of the Prophet Muhammad
hezar: a currency unit, equal to a rial and a qeran (literally 'thousand')
ijtihad: the exercise of independent judgement on the part of a *mujtahid*
ilkhan: paramount tribal chieftain
Imam: for Shiites, the legitimate successors of the Prophet Muhammad
kadkhoda: headman of a village of urban quarter
kalantar: chief of the traditional municipal administration
khan: title of tribal chiefs and landowners
Lesser Despotism: the period from June 1908 to July 1909 when Mohammad Ali Shah suspended the Iranian constitution
luti: urban ruffian who lives on the edge of legality but is also capable of occasional acts of nobility and self-abnegation or sacrifice
madrasa: traditional Islamic institution of learning
Majles: parliament

Mamalek-e mahruseh-ye Iran: the guarded domains of Iran
marja'-e taqlid: literally 'source of emulation', *mujtahid*s who are consulted by believers on religious matters and to whom the believers pay their religious dues, the highest authority in Twelver Shiism
mashrutiyat: constitutionalism
mohajerat: emigration, exile.
mohtaseb: the regulator of prices in the marketplace
mojahedin: plural of *mojahed*: those who militarily fought for the constitutional cause in 1907–09
monshi: secretary
mujtahid: cleric entitled to exercise *ijtihad*
mullah (*molla*): a Muslim cleric, usually used for lower-level ulema
nayeb: deputy
Nezam-e jaded: new (modern) army; also used to describe a new political order
pishkar: agent
qanun: law, usually non-religious law
qasida: a panegyric poem
qeran: a curreny unit, equal to a rial
rial: a currency unit, equal to a qeran
rowshanfekr: intellectual, member of the intelligentsia (plural: *rowshanfekran*)
rowzehkh^van: a reciter of lamentations commemorating the martyrdom of Imam Husayn
sarraf: moneylender, traditional banker
shabnameh: a tract, usually anonymous, distributed at night
shahi: a currency unit; 20 shahis equals a rial or qeran
Shahnameh: the *Book of Kings*, Iran's national epic, written in the tenth century by Ferdowsi
shari'a: Islamic law, based on *fiqh*
Sheykh al-Islam: most senior religious official in the Ottoman Empire
Sheykhi: member of a Twelver Shiite sect prominent in Tabriz and Kerman
Sufi: a member of an order of mystics
takfir: excommunication
taqlid: imitation or emulation of a *mujtahid* in religious matters
Titles (*alqab*): in Qajar times, distinguished persons and members of the royal family were given a title (*laqab*), most titles ending with *al-Molk, al-Saltaneh, al-Soltan*. They were abolished in 1925.
tojjar: plural of *tajer*, merchants
tollab: plural of *talabeh*, madrasa students
toyul: a type of land tenure analogous to a fief
tuman: a currency unit, equal to 1000 rials
ulema (*'olama'*): plural of *'alem*, Muslim clerics
'urf: customary law

Introduction

The Iranian Constitutional Revolution broke the old order and ushered in a new 'modern' era, making way for new institutions and ideologies. Although it floundered in 1911, its legacy allowed Iran to engage with the world of the twentieth century. It was one of the most complex events in Iranian history, and of its kind anywhere, for it released an extraordinary range of ideals for the future. And in that sense, more than most, it was every person's revolution. The collapse of the state through financial indigence and foreign pressure, which were in the end to consume the new regime itself, created a vacuum, a blank canvas, on which many visions were imprinted. In turn, this rich picture, of which much is still unclear, has stimulated a literature of great imagination, depth of research, and varied expression.

This volume seeks, as did the conference from which it derives, to develop and advance the many existing debates on the revolution as well as to open up new avenues of interpretation. Poetry has always played a major part in the lives of Iranians, and an event as momentous as the Constitutional Revolution could not leave poets indifferent. To set the stage, Homa Katouzian presents poetry from the constitutional era. The Constitutional Revolution saw a flowering of young poetical talents who wrote mostly on social and political subjects and published their works immediately in newspapers and political tracts. Their poetry was unmistakably fresh and modern, often experimenting with modified classical and neoclassical structures. These poets invented new figures of speech and literary devices, and sometimes even used colloquial or folksy words and expressions, which was an innovation. Poetry was the most effective instrument used in popular campaigns for constitutionalism, law, freedom, and even nationalism, and against arbitrary rule, backwardness, and corruption. But it was also in this period that the seeds of pan-Persianist and Aryanist nationalism were sown, an ideology which exploded after the First World War and later became the official Pahlavi creed.

Following Homa Katouzian's prologue, the contributors to this volume address a whole range of themes, which we have grouped into five sections. We begin with historiography. The rich historiography of the Constitutional Revolution, with its multiplicity of perspectives and approaches, is illuminated by Joanna de Groot in 'Whose Revolution? Stakeholders and Stories of the

"Constitutional Movement" in Iran, 1905–11'. She evaluates the processes, practices, and perceptions of the historiography, as its judgements and its scriptures emerged, and argues that individuals have made use of and responded to the shared conditions and concerns of their times. She starts with the accounts of those who were themselves involved in the revolution, such as Nazem al-Eslam Kermani, Ahmad Kasravi, and Yahya Dowlatabadi. De Groot shows how these authors highlighted chosen themes, for example, presenting the story in terms of pro- and anticonstitutionalism. Later, the revolution began to be perceived in more ideological – whether secular radical, religious radical, or religious traditionalist – terms. At this point popular politics and movements from below also became involved. Modernity began to take over the constitutional ethos from progress and enlightenment, and large-scale narratives, contrasting with E. G. Browne's detailed focus, placed the revolution in the context of Iranian modern history. The original drama of the struggle of light and dark was dismantled by a more nuanced and complicated picture, which nevertheless showed power relations implicit in choices to include or exclude, to emphasize or marginalize, and to incorporate cultural, political, and ideological influences of the historian's own. A whole new dimension, and parallel point of reference, has been added by another event, the 'Islamic Revolution' of 1979, which has provided a new framework for thematic discussion. In addition, light has been thrown on little-studied areas, most notably the story of women, in terms both of the emergence of nationalism and the restructuring of individual lives. Debate has also centred on the nation's struggle to define itself and how far that struggle came out of Western-style borders and Western ideologies or, alternatively, out of the complex restructuring of occupational religious and communal interests. De Groot emphasizes the power of choice implicit in historical writings, not so much in placing one individual, such as Taqizadeh, in the limelight, but in studying the subject with a sense of diversity, and of highlighting the range of experience, objectives, activities, and associated individuals. Finally, she pleads for yet greater relativism and greater self-awareness, to elicit all the complexities of the period.

The variety of experiences of the revolution, as encapsulated by de Groot, evokes a rich legacy of memories. In 'The Iranian Constitutional Revolution as *lieu(x) de mémoire*: Sattar Khan', Anja Pistor-Hatam explores collective memory in terms of Pierre Nora's concept of *lieu de mémoire*, composed of two dimensions: a material dimension, defined as space and time, and a symbolic one, defined as memory of the past. To illustrate her argument, she focuses on Sattar Khan as both a symbol of the revolution and a part of the identity-building in its historiography, as well as an example of a mythical personage as *lieu de mémoire*. She asks if he was in reality the bravest of the brave, or a simple bandit. After examining contemporary accounts of his conduct and objectives during the revolution, she concludes that he was both a local rogue and a protagonist of the constitutional cause, particularly for the qualities of leadership he showed during the civil war in Tabriz. His subsequent enterprises were failures, but the special qualities he possessed made him a hero for the ordinary people, and thus a *lieu de mémoire*. She concludes, however, that it was professional and nonprofessional historians, together with the many photographs of him, who actually preserved his place in the pantheon of the revolution.

In 'Introducing Georgian Sources in the Historiography of the Iranian Constitutional Revolution (1905–11)', Iago Gocheleishvili not only examines a new Transcaucasian perspective on the revolution, but also throws light on the involvement of the so-called Caucasian outsiders. While the involvement of Armenians in the Constitutional Revolution has been studied extensively, the role of Georgians has been largely neglected. Gocheleishvili draws attention to the significance of little-studied Georgian sources, not only for the role of the Transcaucasians, but as a source on the Iranian radical, particularly leftist, groups in general. He emphasizes the diversity of views, from Bolshevik, Menshevik, and Socialist Revolutionary (SR) to simply idealist, of those who became involved in the revolution. Most were appalled by the poverty they saw in Iran, some obviously seeing the whole struggle from a class perspective. A rich range of opinion existed amongst the revolutionaries, causing disputes and rivalry both among the Transcaucasians themselves and between them and local Iranian revolutionary groups. To these radicals, the revolution was not only an Iranian struggle, but part of the overall Russian struggle against autocracy. As such, it became part of the agenda of political parties in Georgia and elsewhere in the area.

From historiography we pass to state-building, an outcome of many revolutions. Three contributions explore the much-neglected question of the evolution of the Iranian state between the constitutional and Pahlavi periods, and seek to fill the historiographical chasm from which Reza Shah appears to spring ready-made. Thus the slow but persistent processes of constructing a new order are brought to light and analysed, as are the crucially important evolving concepts of the rights of the state and of the individual under the law.

In 'Constitutional Rights and the Development of Civil Law in Iran, 1907–41', Ali Gheissari begins with a significant clarification of the understanding of rights in the modern legal sense, which he contrasts with their classification in the shari'a. He then argues that the constitutional movement was anti-absolutist, but its pursuit of justice was less centred on civil rights and more on the rights of the nation; as such it was bound up with the emergence of Iranian nationalism. As a result, the Constitutional Laws brought a systematic change in the structure of political authority. The attempts to ratify a standard Civil Law which took place were a manifestation of one of the revolution's major goals, and helped change the status of Iranians from subjects to citizens. However, during the subsequent period the movement towards legal change became subsumed by the drive towards centralization and its concomitant need for uniformity. The approach to law-making in Iran, nevertheless, remained complex, on the one hand still drawing on shari'a precepts, and on the other, institutionalizing through procedures the concept of individual rights.

The continuity of state-building, along with popular aspirations, also forms the subject of Stephanie Cronin's article 'The Constitutional Revolution, Popular Politics, and State-Building in Iran'. She challenges the dominant view that the constitutional period ended in failure and futility in 1911, and that there followed a period of anarchy from which, in her words, Reza Khan rose unheralded, his advent apparently announcing a new era of state-building and modernization. She argues that the constitutional period left two significant institutional legacies, the first being the parliament – the Majles – and the ideals it inspired, and the second, the process of military reform, embodied in the Gendarmerie and the Cossack Brigade. Whilst the Majles provided a focus for political activity, the Gendarmerie and the Cossack Brigade were developing military instruments. The popular forces of the period curtailed the objectives of the great powers, and impeded the rise of Reza Khan, but never succeeded in consolidating the procedures required by parliamentary democracy. As a result, of the two legacies of the constitutional period, it was the authoritarian military reformism embodied in the Cossack Brigade, with its associations with both Qajar absolutism and Russian autocracy, that prevailed. The politics of the urban crowd, however, were never lost, and remerged in 1979.

The endeavour to create and develop new institutions is further explored in Reza Mokhtari Esfahani's article 'Municipalities and Constitutionalism in Iran', which traces the struggle to establish municipalities during and immediately after the revolution. Although the period failed to achieve a complete change in local government structures, and indeed a complete transfer of power, it set significant goals for a new order in terms of civil institutions. The battle over these issues also symbolizes the differing visions of the Court and the old order on the one hand, and the new social forces active in the revolution on the other. At the same time, these issues were at the heart of a skein of other struggles over authority and power between urban, provincial, and central authorities. The movement towards civil engagement expressed itself most notably in the newly formed *baladiyeh* or municipalities, one of the most constructive legacies of the Constitutional Revolution, which were a means of educating the people in civil responsibility. The Municipal Law which established the new bodies aimed at furthering the well-being of city residents and representing their views. However, it met with unrelenting difficulties, not least financial, and never developed organic roots. It was left to the policies of Reza Shah to introduce effective municipal government, albeit with different, centralizing intentions.

From state-building we turn to nation-building, with a section also comprising three chapters. One significant social group which belonged to the popular forces mentioned by Cronin, who sought justice and rights through constitutionalism as a replacement for the non-accountable absolutist system, was the merchants. In 'Merchants, Their Class Identification Process, and Constitutionalism', Soheila Torabi Farsani discusses how the merchants developed class awareness in the years of the revolution and afterwards, and used it subsequently to strengthen their rights in the Pahlavi period. She notes that traditionally, merchants were an integrated part of the bazaar network. However, at this time they gradually disengaged themselves from their former allies, the *sarrafs* (moneylenders), the guilds, and the ulema, and began to develop a sense of 'class-in-itself', the first step, in accordance with the Marxist terms of definition, in the acquiring of class consciousness. Thus they passed out of the old economic order and into the new with a more cohesive and strengthened sense of group identity from the point of view of representing their interests to the state. In this process they founded and used successive organizations, of which the Majles was one, to advance their interests. Meanwhile, the discarded guilds engaged in religious-nationalist activities to represent their needs.

One group which sought an enlarged role in the new world of enhanced political influence and engagement created by the politics of the constitutional period was the Bakhtiyari tribe. Arash Khazeni in 'Tribes of the Homeland: The Bakhtiyari in the Revolutionary Press' finds a new perspective on the Bakhtiyari march to Tehran by looking not only at their bid to become assimilated into the emerging national politics, but also at how their perceived patriotic initiative was reported on and shaped by the revolutionary press, which perceived the Iranian homeland as embracing all the diverse identities of its people. A variety of newspapers proclaimed the Bakhtiyari who marched on Tehran as protectors of the nation. The Bakhtiyari perceived themselves as acting in the same cause as Sattar Khan, the idol of Tabriz, whose values of courage, humble beginnings, and masculine appearance seemed to echo their own. At the same time the press became a means whereby the Bakhtiyari could enhance their status and project their mixed motives as an expression of commitment and devotion to their homeland. Thus whilst apparently integrating into the newly emerging Iran, the Bakhtiyari did not entirely forsake their ancient tribal identity and consciousness.

On the whole, as far as had yet emerged, the religious modernizers did not include Sufis, who tended to otherworldly disengagement. However, one notable group of Sufis was active in the reform movement, as is demonstrated by Lloyd Ridgeon in 'Revolution and a High-Ranking Sufi: Zahir al-Dowleh's Contribution to the Constitutional Movement'. He examines the thought and activities of Zahir al-Dowleh, a Qajar prince, during the constitutional period, with a view to establishing the nature of his brand of Sufism and his general perspective on the constitutional movement. Zahir al-Dowleh's worldview was infused with his Sufism and dedication to reform, but he was not a revolutionary. Nevertheless, his founding of a secret organization, the Anjoman-e Okhovvat, motivated by a sociopolitical agenda, together with a pantomime which ridiculed the Shah, brought down on him the opprobrium of the latter, and his house was bombarded at the same time as the Majles. Zahir al-Dowleh, nonetheless, remained committed to reform.

The section on nation-building is followed by one on intellectual and artistic trends, comprising six chapters. The existing literature on the study of the influence of European ideas of the Enlightenment and the role of an emergent intelligentsia is advanced both by articles on the international current and interaction of ideas and by precise studies of their effect in Iran in terms of the growth of secular modernism and of a public sphere.

The intellectuals who sought to lead Iran out of political, economic, and social backwardness and called for reform in the administration included religious intellectuals and modernizers with a religious worldview, as well as secular reformers. Two contributors, Mangol Bayat and Nahid Mozaffari, look at the role of modernist reformers in the revolution. In 'The *Rowshanfekr* in the Constitutional Period: An Overview', Bayat discusses the evolution of the term *monavvar al-fekr* into the twentieth-century *rowshanfekr* to designate the sociopolitical reformist mind shaped by the Enlightenment. She uses it in a broad sense as the equivalent of 'intelligentsia', to include modernist reformers who were not writers or intellectuals in a contemporary sense. She specifically examines the historical-ideological context of the early 1900s in Iran in comparison with elsewhere to assess the success of innovation in the revolution, which she sees as taking place under the influence of both Freemasonry and the Young Turks. The intelligentsia were faced with the problem of dealing with the ulema's influence in a deeply religious society in achieving the institutional changes they sought, and reinterpreting traditional meanings of words to introduce such terms as 'citizenry' and 'the will of the people'. They, nevertheless, faced considerable opposition from the ulema, notably Fazlollah Nuri, though in fact by supporting the constitutional movement, the ulema were conceding the Fundamental Law, including a division between religious and secular law. As a result, the *mashrutiyat* desacralized political power and altered its structure, many radicals exchanging clerical for lay garb. However, the interests of the great powers did much to undermine the success of the *rowshanfekr* initiative, and in that sense the revolution was of its age.

The impact of the European enlightenment and Russian social democracy is also explored by Nahid Mozaffari in 'An Iranian Modernist Project: Ali Akbar Dehkhoda's Writings in the Constitutional Period'. She discusses the precise evolution of European ideas in their Iranian context in order to trace the interaction between specific Western concepts and their Iranian interpretation/adaptation from text to text, focusing on the newspaper *Sur-e Esrafil* and the *Sorush* essays of Ali Akbar Dehkhoda, one of the principal literary modernists. His purpose was to clarify the meaning of *Mashruteh* at a time when it had many interpretations and to illuminate the meaning of social democracy in particular, and its accompanying Western concepts derived from the Western experience, for an Iranian context and readership. He wrote for both an educated and less educated readership in different styles, using satire for the latter. Thus he promoted secularization, modernization, and democratization, simultaneously attacking the religious order, and evolving as he did so a new political language. His philosophy involved a belief in a kind of natural law whereby different stages required different forms of government, and accordingly each stage involved different mutual rights, and above all general awareness of those rights. The modern era demanded the rejection of absolutist values underpinned by religious endorsement.

The subject of a new political and cultural discourse arising from the impact of modern ideas is also pursued by Negin Nabavi in 'Readership, the Press, and the Public Sphere in the First Constitutional Era', with particular reference to establishing how the proliferation of newspapers led to the formation of a new journalistic culture and to the laying of the building blocks of a nascent public sphere. She focuses on the readers of the newspapers, their expectations, and the innovative elements of their experience, using examples from the period; she also looks at the newspapers' strategies for developing different kinds of opinion, especially from 1907. A notable trend was the quest by the publications for interaction with the readership in terms of explaining the procedures of the emerging political order and its new terms, and asking for engagement, so passive subjects would become members of an active nation. Nabavi shows how even those who could ill afford newspapers found ways to read them, either in coffeehouses or through sharing. Letters to the editor contributed to the emergence of an uncensored public opinion and enabled the airing of grievances, notably by women. Thus the idea of rights in a modern sense was articulated. So the press encouraged a change in the journalistic and political culture, and initiated a nascent public sphere.

The press is also the subject of Pardis Minuchehr's chapter. In 'Writing in

Tehran: The First Freedom of Press Law' she shows that in the months following the triumph of the Constitutional Revolution Iranian journalists fought to obtain constitutional guarantees for the exercise of their craft. They had their first success when the drafters of the Supplementary Fundamental Law included an article guaranteeing freedom to publish anything that was not heretical or contrary to Islam. This was not enough, however, as various editors and writers were subsequently arrested or brought to court by the authorities. The struggle went on, finding a denouement in the country's first press law, in February 1908. In light of the repression that befell Iran a few months later, the promulgation of this law may appear to have been a pyrrhic victory, but it set standards to which all subsequent laws had to live up.

The subject of dramatic works is addressed by Ali Miransari with special reference to social-relations criticism in the plays of the constitutional period. He locates these plays in the evolution of Western-style dramatic literature in Iran, beginning with Akhundzadeh in the 1850s and Mirza Aqa Tabrizi in the 1870s. This tradition had wide influence at the time of the revolution, and as a result a number of playwrights emerged in the constitutional era. Their plays had a chequered history, some being published but never performed, while others were actually staged. The playwrights themselves came from a variety of social backgrounds and occupations and included moderates and radicals. All were particularly concerned with perceived regressive trends in the political situation after Mohammad Ali Shah came to the throne. Four playwrights particularly are discussed by Miransari: Zahir al-Dowleh, Mirza Reza Na'ini, Abbas Ali As'adi, and Mohammad Reza Mosavat. They identified, respectively, the following flaws in the course of the revolution: that the political destiny of Iran was becoming a plaything of feudal landlords and merchants; that the need to eradicate ignorance and superstition was being neglected; that liberty facilitated selfishness and division; and that censorship played a pernicious role in the ill treatment of journalists. All in all, their plays were more works of social criticism than of literature and were meant to encompass all of society. The playwrights were not able to remedy the social wrongs they perceived, but they taught the public that playwriting had a serious purpose.

The question of identity-building and photographs is addressed by Reza Sheikh in 'National Identity and Photographs of the Constitutional Revolution'. He argues that the period was a turning point for Iranian photography as, for the first time, the face of 'the man on the street' was widely and publicly disseminated next to images of the elite, and in unprecedented numbers. Taking identity as an extension of image, he considers that the photographs of the era collectively played a significant role in the building of a 'national self-image', which constitutes a visual historiography. Questions arise, however, as to how Iranians themselves perceived this new collective self-image at the time, and what role the photographs actually played. To answer these questions Sheikh examines five sets of photographs of different origin. He concludes, firstly, that they were iconoclastic in terms of undermining the old order, and introducing new concepts and protagonists; and, secondly, that the taking and making of photographs contributed to nation-building, though it applied in the urban rather than the rural areas. At the same time, they create a common history in the eyes of posterity, linked to the concepts of both struggle and national identity.

The final section of this book contains chapters that discuss the transnational linkages and ramifications of the Constitutional Revolution. The early twentieth century was a period which saw the collapse of old state structures and values and the complex process of the emergence of the new, and the revolution in Iran was part of a wave of such events across the world. The intriguing proximity in time of these revolutions is addressed by Charles Kurzman in 'Mashrutiyat, Meşrutiyet, and Beyond: Intellectuals and the Constitutional Revolutions of 1905–12'. His comparative study of the Ottoman, Russian, Chinese, Portuguese, and Mexican revolutions shows that they followed parallel trajectories and faced parallel obstacles from the great powers. Intellectuals played a significant role in all of them: in fact, the revolutionary period saw the emergence and identification of a new class, that of the modern intellectual, a term which rapidly spread from France round the world, carrying with it an awareness of common objectives and fellow feeling. In a democratic variant of Comtean positivism, this class held that it should be the vanguard in movements for reform and social change. Kurzman sets out to identify the specificities of the Iranian revolution as compared to the others, and notes differences in events and organization, but above all in the intellectual leadership. The intellectuals made careful use of terminology to ally themselves with, rather than oppose, the traditional intellectuals, the influential ulema, by using the term *daneshmandan*. However, over the period, this alliance fell apart, and the pattern of the Iranian revolution reverted to the same trajectory as elsewhere, though the need to propitiate the religious was never entirely overlooked.

Britain was a major player in Iranian affairs, and so it is not astonishing that events of the Constitutional Revolution were reported widely in the British Isles. As Mansour Bonakdarian explains in his chapter 'Erin and Iran Resurgent: Irish Nationalists and the Iranian Constitutional Revolution', within the United Kingdom, Irish nationalists conceived of their island as constituting a British colony, and consequently took an interest in anti-British struggles elsewhere in the world. They established contacts and engaged in collaboration with nationalists in the Empire (India in particular), and also continuously expressed support for many other nationalist and reformist movements, including the constitutional movement in Iran. Some Irish nationalists even went so far as to emphasize a real or imagined common ancestry of the Irish and the Iranians. This solicitude was not reciprocated by the Iranians, however, who interpreted the struggle of the Irish nationalists as a separatist movement that was an internal affair of the United Kingdom.

If the cultural gap and geographical distance between Eire and Iran were too wide for any meaningful cooperation, the opposite situation obtained in the case of the Ottoman Empire and Iran. In 'Crafting Constitutional Narratives: Iranian and Young Turk Solidarity, 1907–09', Farzin Vejdani argues that the rise of Pan-Turkism in the Ottoman Empire during the First World War and the resulting Young Turk designs on northwestern Iran should not obscure the intense cooperation among Iranian and Ottoman constitutionalists that took place in the period 1907 to 1909. Ottoman constitutionalists were encouraged by the success of the Constitutional Revolution in Iran, and two years later, when they gained power shortly after Mohammad Ali Shah's countercoup in neighbouring Iran in June 1908, they assisted their embattled Iranian counterparts by providing a place of exile for Iranian revolutionaries fleeing the government, allowing Iranian constitutionalists to take refuge in Ottoman diplomatic and consular premises, and, even more dramatically, supplying arms, military assistance, and fighters to the most hotly contested battle zone – the province of Azarbayjan. Vejdani then argues that the continued Ottoman military occupation of parts of Azarbayjan has to be seen in the light of the struggle between constitutionalism and autocracy on both sides of the border. He shows that Iranian and Ottoman constitutionalists imagined both revolutions as being part of a phenomenon beyond the borders of their respective states. Constitutional, anti-imperial, socialist, and Pan-Islamic discourses all contributed in varying degrees to a transnational utopian vision through which Iranian and Ottoman constitutionalists articulated their cooperation.

Touraj Atabaki extends this holistic approach to what has been called Turko-Persia by analyzing connections between the reformists and constitutionalists in Iran and their counterparts in the lands north and east of Iran. In 'Constitutionalists *Sans Frontières*: Iranian Constitutionalism and its Asian Connections', he shows that a number of early Persian-language newspapers circulated widely in the area, providing their readers with news from Afghanistan, the Caucasus, Central Asia, and Iran. Moreover, a number of literary genres – dialogue, imaginary travel diaries, plays – were used by progressive writers and intellectuals from the region for didactic purposes to propagate and popularize reform ideas. The common themes and cultural references of these writings testify to the existence of a common high culture that facilitated the intellectual contacts, but that common high culture receded into the background with the triumph of ethnic nationalisms and, in the case of the Russian areas, Communism.

Beyond Turko-Persia, the revolution was also widely reported in the Arab press, as discussed by Kamran Rastegar in '*Mashruteh* and *al-Nahda*: The Iranian Constitutional Revolution in the Iranian Diaspora Press of Egypt and in Arab Reformist Periodicals'. He argues that the nationalist populist tradition of the historiography on the revolution has been too inclined to seek its influences within Iran itself, and failed to take account of influences from outside Iran, especially that of the Iranian diaspora communities, and of the Arab reformist movements. In particular Iranian newspapers, such as *Hekmat* and *Chehreh Nama*, acted as a conduit of ideas between Egypt and Iran in the campaigns of political, social, and cultural reform. Both Arabic and Persian newspapers translated each others' articles, not only on political matters but on subjects such as science, history, and geography. The Arabic newspapers also focused on the newly emerging subject of women, their rights, and their desired role in politics. A quite different characteristic of their reports was the wider perspective and they were alive to the influence of the Ottoman reforms on movements elsewhere. Thus intercultural circulations played an important but neglected role in facilitating the spread and advance of new ideas.

The renown of the Iranian Constitutional Revolution spread far afield, beyond the Middle East and Central Asia, to East Asia, though it did not have the same impact there as in the region itself. Yidan Wang looks at 'The Iranian Constitutional Revolution as Reported in the Chinese Press', noting that the Iranian developments found resonance with contemporaries in China. It also inspired the Chinese revolutionary democrats who later played an important role in the Chinese Xinhai Revolution 1911–12. It was identified with the Chinese revolution and regarded as part of a wave of events which signalled 'the Awakening of Asia'. Well-known constitutionalist sympathizers wrote news reports and discursive articles which analysed the events in Iran for a readership of patriotic businessmen, enlightened gentry, educated persons, and students. The competition of Britain and Russia in Iran, and its effect on the country, was also noted with empathy, in the context of China's own experience and desire to drive out foreign powers.

The revolutions in Iran, the Ottoman Empire, and China were negative examples for the ruler of Siam (Thailand), who drew his own lessons from the demise of the traditional monarchies in these three states. King Vajiravudh (r. 1910–25) reacted unsympathetically to events in Iran, writing: 'The Persian people have been saddled with a parliament that they understand nothing about and do not want, and which has caused the country more trouble than the most incompetent shahs put together.'[1] Unfortunately, however, we were unable to find a historian of Thailand willing to explore to what extent the experience of Iran's and Asia's other constitutional revolutions may have retarded the advent of constitutionalism in that country.

While the events of the Constitutional Revolution were followed closely in China and Siam, there was little interest in it in Japan. As Michael Penn shows in 'Japan and the Iranian Constitutional Revolution', Japan by this time had managed to deflect foreign interference, and, having defeated both China and Russia in battle, its elites did not conceive of their country as sharing in a community of destiny with the other Asian nations. There were regular reports of events in Iran in the Japanese press, but they were brief and cursory, without much analysis or discussion. The Anglo-Russian agreement of 1907, by contrast, attracted more comment, as it had greater bearing on Japan's interests, especially as there was not much trade between Iran and Japan. The Iranians, by contrast, took a considerable interest in Japan as an Eastern power that had successfully modernized, and defeated a European great power in war. The Japanese did not reciprocate the admiration, and looked down on the Iranians as lowly Orientals, a group from which they themselves were now aloof. However, a small group of Japanese adventurers took an interest in the country, and Penn provides a translated account of the travels of one of them, Tei Suzuki.

In the transliteration of Persian words we have opted for a simplified system that reflects the standard pronunciation of Persian as spoken in Iran. To stay out of competing nationalisms, we refer to the Azeri-speaking areas north of the Aras River as Azerbaijan while the Iranian region south of that river is referred to in transliterated form as Azarbayjan.

Vanessa Martin
H. E. Chehabi

PROLOGUE

The Poetry of the Constitutional Revolution

Homa Katouzian

The Constitutional Revolution saw a flowering of young poetical talents who wrote mostly on social and political subjects and published them immediately in newspapers and political tracts. Their poetry was unmistakably fresh and modern, often experimenting with modified classical and neoclassical structures, innovating new figures of speech and literary devices, and sometimes using colloquial, even folksy, words and expressions.

Thus, Persian poetry, having been the main vehicle throughout its long history of literary and social expression, discharging sentiments, moralizing, disparaging, and lampooning, came into its own as the most effective instrument used in popular campaigns for constitutionalism, law, freedom and even nationalism, and against arbitrary rule, backwardness, and corruption. Through their works the poets campaigned for the constitutional movement, opposed Mohammad Ali Shah during the struggle between him and the First Majles, struggled against Lesser Despotism after Mohammad Ali's coup, celebrated the conquest of Tehran and the fall of Mohammad Ali, expressed disillusionment shortly afterwards, and displayed anger and frustration at the Russian ultimatum and the dismissal of Morgan Shuster in 1911. It was also in this period that the seeds of the pan-Perisanist and Aryanist nationalism were sown, which exploded after the First World War and later became the official Pahlavi ideology.

When in 1906 Mozaffar al-Din Shah signed the constitution many poets greeted it with expressions of great joy and gratefulness. Poet-laureate Mohammad Taqi Bahar, then barely twenty, wrote a *qasideh* in praise of the Shah's justice in granting a constitution, and convening a Majles made up of 'artful wise men':[1]

کشور ایران ز عدل شاه مظفّر   رونقی از نو گرفت و زینتی از سر...
پادشه داد گر مظفّر دین شاه   خسرو روشن‌دل عدالت‌گستر...
مجلس آراست کاندرو ز همه ملک   انجمن آیند بخردان هنرور...
احسنت ای پادشاه مملکت آرای   احسنت ای خسرو رعیّت‌پرور...

Shortly afterwards the Shah died and his son Mohammad Ali succeeded to the throne. As usual, elegies were written for the deceased Shah, and eulogies to welcome his successor, since only a small elite were already suspicious of the new Shah's intentions. Bahar lamented the Shah's death and celebrated his son's succession in a *tarji'band*. It began with the distich: A shah arrived and a shah left / Thank God that this came, alas that that went:[2]

شاهی به میان آمد و شاهی ز میان رفت   صد شکر که این آمد و صد حیف که آن رفت
المنّة لله که جهان باز جوان شد   وین شاه فلک مرتبه سلطان جهان شد
جم رتبه محمّدعلی آن شاه جوان‌بخت   کز فرّ وی این ملکِ کهنْ گشته، جوان شد...
بگزید چو بر مسند و اورنگ پدر جای   این گفتِ ملک را به فلک ورد زبان شد
شاهی به میان آمد و شاهی ز میان رفت   صد شکر که این آمد و صد حیف که آن رفت

No sooner were the celebrations over than the conflict of the Shah and the Majles came out into the open and intensified by day. Disillusionment was already setting in when Ali Akbar Dehkhoda, known as Dakhow, wrote a colloquial and humorous *mosammat*, addressed to the common man, Aqa Karbala'i, which title was commonly pronounced as 'Akablai'. Using both satire and irony, he discouraged too much optimism for the country's progress: he poked fun at high hopes and pointed to contradictions between constitutionalism and social reality:[3]

مردود خدا رانده هربنده آکبلای   از دلقک معروف نماینده آکبلای
با شوخی و با مسخره و خنده آکبلای   نز مرده گذشتیّ و نه از زنده آکبلای
هستی تو چه یک پهلو و یک دنده آکبلای
نه بیم ز کفر بین و نه جن‌گیر و نه رمّال   نه خوف ز درویش و نه از جذبه و از حال
نه ترس ز تکفیر و نه از پیشتو شاپشال   مشکل ببری گور سر زنده آکبلای
هستی تو چه یک پهلو و یک دنده آکبلای...
از گرسنگی مرد رعیّت به جهنّم   ور نیست در این قوم معیّت به جهنّم
تریاک برید عرق حمیّت به جهنّم   خوش باش تو با مطرب و سازنده آکبلای
هستی تو چه یک پهلو و یک دنده آکبلای
تو منتظری رشوه در ایران رود از یاد؟   آخوند ز قانون و ز عدلیه شود شاد
اسلام ز رمّال و ز مرشد شود آزاد؟   یک دفعه بگو مرده شود زنده آکبلای
هستی تو چه یک پهلو و یک دنده آکبلای

He also wrote a folksy – as opposed to formal – *masnavi*, depicting the people as a child who is close to death from hunger, and the political leaders as his ignorant and neglecting mother, quite contrary to the prevailing notions of *mam-e mihan* (literally, the county's mother) which depicted her as an old and ailing victim of arbitrary rule:[4]

خاك به سرم بچّه به هوش آمده   بخواب ننه یک سر دو گوش آمده...
إهه إهه، ننه چته، گشنمه   بترّکی این همه خوردی کمه...
از گشنگی ننه دارم جون میدم   گریه نکن فردا بهت نون میدم...
ای وای ننه جونم داره در میره   گریه نکن دیزی داره سر میره...

In a *masnavi*, Bahar resorted to friendly advice combined with admonitions to the Shah not to continue his confrontation with the constitutionalists: 'O' Shah everything you do is wrong / Not to us but to yourself you do wrong':[5]

پادشها چشم خرد باز کن   فکر سرانجام در آغاز کن
بازگشا دیده بیدار خویش   تا نگری عاقبت کار خویش...
پادشها یکسره بد می کنی   خود نه به ما بلکه بخود می کنی...
وای به شاهی که رعیّت‌کش است   حال خوش ملّت از او ناخوش است...
زشت بود یکسره کردار تو   تا چه شود عاقبت کار تو

He followed this by a *mokhammas* which amplified a didactic *ghazal* by Saʿdi. Here he went further and told the Shah to abandon arbitrary rule (*estebdad*), since it would result in nothing but wretchedness:[6]

پادشاها زاستبداد چه داری مقصود
که از این کار جز ادبار نگردد مشهود
جودکن در ره مشروطه که گردی مسجود
«شرف مرد به جود است و کرامت به سجود
هر که این هر دو ندارد عدمش به که وجود»

But he ended the poem by saying that it was useless to try and persuade the Shah to take the right course, since wrong-doing was in his nature:

جز خطاکاری از این شاه نمی‌باید خواست
کانچه ما در او بینیم سراسر به خطاست
مَدَهش پند که بر بدمنشان پند هباست
«پند سعدی که کلید در گنج سعد است
نتواند که بجا آوَرَد الّا مسعود»

When Sheykh Fazlollah Nuri took *bast* in Hazrat-e ʿAbd al-ʿAzim against the Majles, Iraj Mirza, a Qajar nobleman who was characteristically not a political poet, nevertheless attacked him in a *qasideh* and hurled abuse and invective at him: He is a hardened slapper this hero / be careful for he may slap you…If he gets hold of the dandies / he would beat their fart with a stick:[7]

حجّة الاسلام کتک می زند   بر سر و مغزت دگنگ می زند
گر نرسد بر دگنگ دستِ او   دست به نعلین و چُسک می زند...
چک زنِ سختی بود این پهلوان   ملتفتش باش که چک می زند
دستش اگر بر فکلی‌ها رسد   گوز یکایک به الک می زند...
حالا در حضرت عبدالعظیم   شیخ درِ دوز و کلک می زند
إن شاءاللّٰه دو روز دگر   خیمه از آن جا به دَرَک می زند

At the same time, Seyyed Ashraf al-Din, producer-editor of the journal *Nasim-e Shomal*, who, because of his massive as well as passionate outpouring of poetry, could be justly described as the poet-laureate of the Constitutional Revolution, wrote a passionate *vataniyeh* or 'patriotic' in the form of an elegy for the motherland. In it, inter alia, he mourned both for the loss of (true) Islam and constitutionalism, since, like many other constitutionalists, he regarded constitutionalism as consistent with true Islam:[8]

گردیده وطن غرقه اندوه و محن وای   ای وای وطن وای
خیزید و دوید از پی تابوت و کفن وای   ای وای وطن وای...
کو همّت و کو غیرت و کو جوش و فتوّت   کو جنبش ملّت
دردا که رسید از دو طرف سیل فتن وای   ای وای وطن وای
افسوس که اسلام شده از همه جانب   پامال اجانب
مشروطه ایران شده تاریخ زَمَن وای   ای وای وطن وای...
بعضی وزرا مسلکشان راهزنی شد   سرّی علنی شد
گشته علما غرقه در این لای و لجن وای   ای وای وطن وای...
کو بلخ و بخارا و چه شد خیوه و کابل   کو بابل و زابل
شام و حلب و ارمن و عمّان و عدن وای   ای وای وطن وای...
اشرف به جز از لاله غم هیچ نبوید   هر لحظه بگوید
ای وای وطن وای وطن وای وطن وای   ای وای وطن وای

The conflict between the Shah and the Majles finally led to the coup d'état of June 1908. Among the constitutionalists who were rounded up and executed was Jahangir Khan, joint editor of *Sur-e Esrafil*, and a close friend of Dehkhoda, who managed to leave the country. Shortly afterwards when Dehkhoda had reached the safety of Switzerland he saw Jahangir Khan in a dream who told him: '*Hich nagofti keh an javan oftad*' (You didn't at all say that that young man fell). He woke up and wrote his famous *mosammat* with the refrain 'Remember the extinguished light, remember!':[9]

ای مرغ سحر چو این شب تار   بگذاشت ز سر سیاهکاری
وز نفخه روح بخش اسحار   رفت از سرخفتگان خماری
بگشوده گره ز زلف زرتار   محبوبه نیلگون عماری
یزدان به کمال شد پدیدار   وَ اهریمنِ زشتخو حصاری
                  یاد آر ز شمع مرده یاد آر

Thus began the period of Lesser Despotism (*estebdad-s saghir*). Adib al-Mamalek-e Farahani addressed a long and scathing *qasideh* to the Shah, telling him that from that time his days were numbered:[10]

امروز که حق را بی مشروطه قیام است   بر شاه محمّدعلی از عدل پیام است
کای شه به زمینت زند این توسن دولت   کامروز به زیر تو روان گشته و رام است...
پنداشتی از احمد و فضل‌الله نوری   کان خواجه وزیرت شده این شیخ امام است
کارتو تمام است و ندانی که از آن روز   شاهّی تو و دولت و ملک تو تمام است...
و آن شعله که از توپ تو افتاد به مجلس   زودا که برافروختهات در به خیام است...
از زخم تو خون در جگر شیرخدا شد   وز تیر تو آذر به دل خیر اِنام است...
ما بر مَثَلِ آل محمّد شده مقهور   تو همچو یزیدستی و این شهر چو شام است...

Seyyed Ashraf wrote a *mosammat* vehemently attacking both the Shah and Nuri, calling the former a help to the traitors, and the latter, weak in the mind, and adding that as long as these two were up to their mischief 'this caravan could not move until doomsday', a common expression which is used as the poem's refrain:[11]

تا کلّه شیخنا ملنگ است   تا در دل ما غبار و زنگ است
تا پیر دلیل مست و منگ است   تا رشته بدست این دبنگ است
این قافله تا به حشر لنگ است
تا مصدر کار مستبد است   تا دل به نفاق مستعدّ است
تا ملّت ما به شاه ضدّ است   تا شاه به خائنین ممدّ است
جان کندن و سعی ما جفنگ است
این قافله تا به حشر لنگ است
گفتیم قلم شده‌ست آزاد   ایران خراب گشته آباد
مشروطه قوی نمود بنیاد   بس مدرسه‌ها شده‌ست ایجاد
افسوس که شیشه‌مان به سنگ است
این قافله تا به حشر لنگ است...
مشروطه و مشورت خدا گفت   پیغمبر نیز بر ملا گفت
حرّیت خلق را صلا گفت   افسوس که باز شیخنا گفت
مشروطه نمونه فرنگ است
این قافله تا به حشر لنگ است
خر صاحب اختیار گشته‌ست   سگ مصدر کار و بار گشته‌ست
روبَه عظمت‌مدار گشته‌ست   شاپشال خزانه‌دار گشته‌ست
شه مات و به خلق عرصه تنگ است
این قافله تا به حشر لنگ است...

When in January 1909 Isfahan fell into the hands of Samsam al-Saltaneh, Bahar wrote a *qasideh-ye mostazad* saying that it would be useless to talk to the Shah about freedom:

> To talk to the Shah of Iran about freedom is a mistake
>   God help Iran
> The Shahanshah of Iran's religion is other than religions
>   God help Iran:[12]

کار ایران با خداست	باشَهِ ایران ز آزادی سخن گفتن خطاست
کار ایران با خداست	مذهب شاهنشه ایران ز مذهبها جداست
مملکت رفته ز دست	شاه مست و شیخ مست و شحنه مست و میر مست
کار ایران با خداست...	هردم از دستان مستان فتنه و غوغا بپاست
خون جمعی بی‌گناه	پادشه خود را مسلمان خوانَد و سازد تباه
کار ایران با خداست...	ای مسلمانان در اسلام این ستم‌ها کی رواست
نام حق گردد پدید	باش تا از اصفهان صمصام حق گردد پدید
کار ایران با خداست...	تا ببینیم آنکه سر ز احکام حق پیچد کجاست

When the Shah finally sensed the danger and tried to appease the revolutionaries, Seyyed Ashraf wrote a folksy satirical piece making fun of the Shah for his about-turn:[13]

درویش نهنگ پلنگ علی چطو شد؟ آن که می‌گفت بلی بلی چطو شد؟
وِردِ خَفی ذکر جَلی چطو شد؟ آن لُمعاتِ منجلی چطو شد؟
نوری و شیخ آملی چطو شد؟...
آدرویش علم و معرفت صحیح است در همه کار مشورت صحیح است
ظالم قبیح و معدلت صحیح است مشروطه بَهرِ مملکت صحیح است
صحبت کور موصلی چطو شد؟

And likening the Shah to the devil who was up to a new trick, he wrote another poem with the refrain 'Ouch what can I do, what can I do (?), said the villain of the piece':[14]

گشت مشروطه به پا آخ چه کنم واخ چه کنم	گفت شیطان دغا آخ چه کنم واخ چه کنم
معدلت بر رگ و شریان ستم خنجر زد	مرغ مشروطه به گلزار وطن شهپر زد
مستبد گشت فنا آخ چه کنم واخ چه کنم	نام مشروطه به چشم ظَلَمه خنجر زد
مستبدین همه مردند ز غم پیر شدم	من که شیطانم از این غصّه زمین‌گیر شدم
گشتم انگشت‌نما آخ چه کنم واخ چه کنم...	راستی من که ز اوضاعِ جهان سیر شدم
	گفت شیطان دغا آخ چه کنم واخ چه کنم
چه شد آن قتل رعیّت چه شد آن ظلم و عذاب	چه شد آن برّه بریان چه شد آن جام شراب
چه شد آن شربت قند و چه شد آن مرغ کباب	چه شد آن برگ و نوا آخ چه کنم واخ چه کنم
	گفت شیطان دغا آخ چه کنم واخ چه کنم...
از حقوقِ وطن خویش خبردار شدند	اهل گیلان همه یک مرتبه هشیار شدند
شحنه دَر داد ندا آخ چه کنم واخ چه کنم	دزدی امشب نتوان کرد که بیدار شدند
	مستبد گشت فنا آخ چه کنم واخ چه کنم
کارِ تبریز ز سردار به انجام آمد	اصفهان در کَنَفِ حضرت صمصام آمد
رشت بگرفت صفا آخ چه کنم واخ چه کنم	خاک گیلان ز سپهدار نکونام آمد
	مستبد گشت فنا آخ چه کنم واخ چه کنم

On the very day the revolutionary troops entered Tehran, Ashraf attacked Nuri vehemently in a poem as an 'auctioneer' of Iran and Islam, in which he also referred to the support of the great ulema in the *'Atabat* for the revolution:

I'll sell the whole of Iran...
Religion is, of necessity, on sale
Buyers come, it's sale, sale:[15]

حاجی بازار رواج است رواج
کو خریدار حراج است حراج

عرض و ناموس مسلمانان را	می فروشم همه ایران را
بخرید این وطن ارزان را	رشت و قزوین و قم و کاشان را
کو خریدار حراج است حراج	یزد و خونسار حراج است حراج
قاتل زمره احرار منم	دشمن فرقه ابرار منم
دین فروشنده به بازار منم	شیخ فضل الله سمسار منم
کو خریدار حراج است حراج...	مال مردار حراج است حراج
زده چادر به لب شطّ فرات	آن شنیدم که حجج در عتبات
جز حراجم نبود راه نجات	شده عازم به عجم با صلوات
کو خریدار حراج است حراج	دین به ناچار حراج است حراج

When the victory celebrations began, Bahar wrote a *tarji'band* praising God for the victory:

Bring wine since ended the painful time
The country is in peace, God owns the Kingdom:[16]

آسوده شد مُلک، المُلک لله	می دِه که طیّ شد دوران جانکاه
کوس شهی کوفت بر رغم بدخواه	شد شاه نو را اقبال همراه
	شد صبح طالع، طی شد شبانگاه
	الحمدلله، الحمدلله
جان یار غم گشت دل غرق خون شد	یک چند ما را غم رهنمون شد
و امروز دشمن خوار و زبون شد	مام وطن را رخ نیلگون شد
	زین جنبش سخت زین فتح ناگاه
	الحمدلله، الحمدلله
از جا برانگیخت ستّارخان را	چون که خدا دید جور شبان را
تا کرد رنگین تیغ و سنان را	سدّ ستم ساخت آن مرزبان را
	از خون دشمن وز مغز بدخواه
	الحمدلله، الحمدلله
لیکن مراورا غم در کمین بود	بدخواه دین را سدّی متین بود
دشمن که با عیش دایم قرین بود	خاکش به سر شد پاداشش این بود
	اکنون قرین است با ناله و آه
	الحمدلله، الحمدلله
سردار اسعد پاینده بادا	بخت سپهدار فرخنده بادا
ضرغام دین را دل زنده بادا	صمصام ایران بُرّنده بادا
	کافتاد از ایشان بدخواه در چاه
	الحمدلله، الحمدلله
تیریزیان را یزدان نگهدار	ستّارخان را بادا ظفر یار
احرار را نیز دل باد بیدار	سالارشان را نیکو بود کار
	تا جمله گویند با جانِ آگاه
	الحمدلله، الحمدلله

Ashraf too joined the poetical celebrations in his folksy style, thanking God that 'the motherland received its rights':[17]

صد شکر حقوق وطن امروز ادا شد   به به چه بجا شد
هنگام وفا وقت صفا دفع جفا شد   به به چه بجا شد...
می‌خواست ستمگر بکشد نوشِ لبان را   والانسبان را، قانون‌طلبان را
حسرت به دلش ماند و خوش رفت و فنا شد   به به چه بجا شد
این غلغله وین جنبش و این شورش ملّی   این کوشش ملّی وین جوشش ملّی
والله که از بهر حقوق فقرا شد   به به چه بجا شد
ای ملّت تبریز سعادت شدتان یار   ای حضرت ستّار و ای باقر سالار
از همّتتان مات عقول عقلا شد   به به چه بجا شد
تا شد علم نصر من الله نمایان   در خطّه تهران، ای ملّت گیلان
از سطوتتان محو همه ارض و سما شد   به به چه بجا شد
تا شد ز صفاهان عَلَم کاوه پدیدار   شد بخت به ما یار از جلوه سردار
اسعد که مددبخش جنود سُعَدا شد   به به چه بجا شد...
قاطرچی و الدنگ و دبوری به کجا رفت   نوری به کجا رفت
یارو به درک رفت و دبوری کله پا شد   به به چه بجا شد

This was the summer of 1909. Two years later in the summer of 1911 the deposed Shah made a bid to recover his throne. He entered Iran with a military force, but was defeated and driven out. Bahar wrote a satirical *tarji'band* as if it was from Mohammad Ali's own mouth: Why is the universe at loggerheads with me / God be praised, what manner is this (?):[18]

با بنده فلک چرا به جنگ است
سبحان‌الله این چه رنگ است...
بودم روزی به شهر تهران   مولا و خدایگان و سلطان
بستم همه را به توپ غرّان   گفتم که کسی نماند از ایشان
دیدم روزِ دگر که جنگ است
سبحان‌الله این چه رنگ است
گفتیم که خلق حرف مفتند   آخر دیدیم دم کلفتند
خیلی گفتیم و کم شنیفتند   یک جنبش سخت کرده گفتند
بسم‌الله ره سوی فرنگ است
سبحان‌الله این چه رنگ است...
دیدیم به شهر قال و قیل است   حجت ز نگار بی‌بدیل است
و ز ما سخنان بس طویل است   گفتیم که نام ما خلیل است
گفتیم که کار ما شلنگ است
سبحان‌الله این چه رنگ است...
من مَمدلی گریز پایم   با دولت روس آشنایم
تهران تو کجا و من کجایم   خواهم که به جانب تو آیم
کز عشق تو کلّه‌ام دبنگ است
سبحان‌الله این چه رنگ است
امروز ز بخت در گله استم   درگیر شکنجه و تله استم
در کار فرار و ولوله استم   گر بنده امیر قافله استم
این قافله تا به حشر لنگ است
سبحان‌الله این چه رنگ است

At the same time Ashraf also wrote a poem, in a folksy style as usual, as if from the ex-Shah's mouth: 'I am Mamdali [Mohammad Ali], police chief of Anzali – leeks do not make sweets, Mamdali Beg will not be Shah':[19]

چه زبردستی تو	ای فلک این چه بساطی است که چیدستی تو
چقدر پستی تو	دل اعداء وطن را از جفا خستی تو
گوئیا مستی تو	عهد با هموطنان بستی و بشکستی تو
ترّه حلوا نمیشه ممدلی بگ شا نمیشه...	کمترین ممدلی‌م داروغهٔ انزلیم
از فراق یاران	ممدلی اشک همی ریخت مثال باران
همه در خون غلطان	ترکمانها همه کردند فرار از میدان
لعن حق بر شیطان	هدف تیر بلا گشت رشیدالسّلطان
خرقه شولا نمیشه ممدلی بگ شا نمیشه...	گول شیطان خوردم، آبروی خود بردم
وکلا را بکشم	هوسم بود جمیع ورزا را بکشم
عقلا را بکشم	دستخط پاره نمایم علما را بکشم
غربا را بکشم	جمله اصناف و عموم فقرا را بکشم
ترّه حلوا نمیشه ممدلی بگ شا نمیشه	مال مولا را می‌خوام؟ چنته و شولا را می‌خوام

A few months later, a great conflict broke out over the Shuster affair, where following two successive Russian ultimatums the Iranian government was obliged to terminate Morgan Shuster's contract in December 1911. There were large public demonstrations against this decision and the Majles (which was near the end of its term) was shut down by the order of Naser al-Molk, the Regent. 'Aref-e Qazvini wrote a piece which was a combination of poetry and song:[20]

> Shame about a home when the guest leaves the table unfed
> Sacrifice your life to the guest and do not let him leave...
> God let you stay, God let you stay:[21]

جان نثارش کن و مگذار که مهمان برود	ننگ آن خانه که مهمان ز سر خوان برود
ای جوانان مگذارید که ایران برود	گر رود شوستر از ایران رود ایران بر باد
به جسم مرده جانی، تو جان یک جهانی، تو گنج شایگانی، تو عمر جاودانی	
خدا کند بمانی، خدا کند بمانی...	
تو در این مملکت امروز خبیرّ و بصیر	مشت دزدی شده امروز در این ملک وزیر
تو اگر رفتی از این مملکت عنوان برود	دست بر دامنت آویخته یک مشت فقیر
به جسم مرده جانی، تو جان یک جهانی، تو گنج شایگانی، تو عمر جاودانی	
خدا کند بمانی، خدا کند بمانی...	
کور شد دیده بدخواه ز همدستی ما	تو مرو گر برود جان و سر و هستی ما
ناله عارف از این ورد به کیهان برود	در فراغت به خماری بکشد مستی ما
به جسم مرده جانی، تو جان یک جهانی، تو گنج شایگانی، تو عمر جاودانی	
خدا کند بمانی، خدا کند بمانی	

And Bahar wrote a *tarkibband* which accused the Regent (although with no basis in fact) of secret complicity both in the ex-Shah's earlier intrusion and the Russian campaign against Shuster:[22]

ناصرالملك آمد و مسند ربود / با وزیران پیل بازی‌ها نمود
حیله‌ها انگیخت تا خود از شمال / شاه سابق با سواران رخ نمود
شوستر آن والامشیر ارجمند / بهر دفعش دست غربت برگشود
آمد از روسیه اولتیماتومی / سرخ و سبز و ارزق و زرد و کبود
ناصرالملك از طبابت‌های خویش / اینچنین بر خستگان بخشود سود
از دواهایش شفا نامّد پدید / وین مریض از آن کسل‌تر شد که بود
این مریض و این دوا را مولوی / کرده اندر مثنوی خوش وانمود
...«کز قضا سر که انگبین صفرا فزود / روغن بادام خشکی می‌نمود»
«آن علاج و آن طبابت‌های او / ریخت یك سر از طبیبان آبرو»
خائنان زین کار نبوَد ننگشان / کور بادا کور چشم تنگشان
بنده و اجری خور روسَند و بس / از تمدّن‌خواه تا الدنگشان...
اندرین صلحی که کردند این گروه / مولوی گفته‌ست روی و رنگشان
«کز خیالی صلحشان و جنگشان / وز خیالی نامشان و ننگشان»
«این وزیران از کهین و از مهین / لعنت اللّه علیهم اجمعین»

And so ended the highly eventful period 1906–11, which was no less eventful in the development of modern Persian poetry and prose than it was in politics and society, when both of these literary forms became much simpler and – in some cases – folksy, highly political, and much more accessible as they were read out in meetings and published in the press. This period was also one in which the seeds of the later Pan-Persianist and Aryanist nationalism were sown, with occasional poems, virtually all pessimistic, celebrating the past glories and lamenting present failures. Thus Adib al-Mamalek wrote in a *mosammat*:

> We are the ones who took tribute from kings…
> Now we are in sorrow, suffering and pain: [23]

برخیز شتربانا بر بند کژاوه / کز چرخ عیان گشت همی رایت کاوه
از شاخ شجر برخاست آوای چکاوه / وز طول سفر حسرت من گشت علاوه
بگذر به شتاب اندر از رود سماوه / در دیده من بنگر دریاچه ساوه
وز سینه‌ام آتشکده پارس نمودار
ماییم که از پادشهان باج گرفتیم / زان پس که از ایشان کمر و تاج گرفتیم
دیهیم و سریر از کهر و عاج گرفتیم / اموال و ذخایرشان تاراج گرفتیم
وز پیکرشان دیبه و دیباج گرفتیم / ماییم که از دریا امواج گرفتیم
و اندیشه نکردیم ز طوفان و ز تیّار
خاك عرب از مشرق اقصی گذراندیم / وز ناحیه غرب به افریقیه راندیم
دریای شمالی را بر شرق نشاندیم / وز بحر جنوبی به فلك گرد فشاندیم
هند از کف هندو، ختن از ترك ستاندیم / ماییم که از خاك بر افلاك رساندیم
نام هنر و رسم کرم را به سزاوار
امروز گرفتار غم و محنت و رنجیم / در داو فره باخته اندر شش و پنجیم
با ناله و افسوس در این دیر سپنجیم / چون زلف عروسان همه در چین و شکنجیم
هم سوخته کاشانه و هم باخته گنجیم / ماییم که در سوگ و طرب قافیه سنجیم
جغدیم به ویرانه، هزاریم به گلزار

Bahar's piece was less passionate but no less committed. It vehemently expressed his love of 'the great Iran' but painfully mourned 'its present state':[24]

ای خطّهٔ ایرانِ مهین ای وطن من   ای گشته به مهر تو عجین جان و تن من...
دور از تو گل و لاله و سرو و سمن نیست   ای باغ گل و لاله و سرو و سمن من...
دردا و دریغا که چنان گشتی بی‌برگ   کز بافته خویش نداری کفن من
بسیار سخن گفتم در تعزیت تو   آوخ که نگریاند کس را سخن من...
و امروز همی گویم با محنت بسیار
دردا و دریغا وطن من وطن من

Ashraf wrote a poem in which the word 'cock-a-doodle-do' appeared for the first time, long before it was used by Nima Yushij, the founder of modernist Persian poetry in years to come:

> A cock was singing in the cloister, cock-a-doodle-do…
> Where is Bahman, where Rostam, cock-a-doodle-do…[25]

می‌خواند خروسی به شبستان قوقولیقو   می‌گفت که ای فرقه مستان قوقولیقو
کو بهمن و کو رستم دستان قوقولیقو   آوخ که خزان زد به گلستان قوقولیقو
فریاد ز سرمای زمستان قوقولیقو
از سیل ختن شهر وطن رو به خرابی   ما خفته و مدهوش چو مستان شرابی
می‌گفت به مرغان هوا آدم آبی   در شهر بود قحطی انسان قوقولیقو
فریاد ز سرمای زمستان قوقولیقو...
کو بلخ و بخارا و چه شد خیوه و کابل   کو هند و سمرقند و چه شد بابل و زابل
کو نقطه قفقاز و چه شد آن چمن گل   این بحر خزر بود از ایران قوقولیقو
فریاد ز سرمای زمستان قوقولیقو...
هی هی بخروشید که باز اول کار است   شیرانه بجوشید که هنگام شکار است
مردانه بکوشید که دشمن به کنار است   زیر لگد افتاده خروسان قوقولیقو
کافر به کجا خاک مسلمان قوقولیقو...

Finally, a piece by Abolqasem Lahuti – the young nationalist poet who was destined to lead an unsuccessful coup in the early 1920s and flee to the Soviet Union – was innovative by being in the form of a mother's lullaby for her child, although this form had been used before in another context by Ashraf. And incidentally it was a much more prevalent notion than Dehkhoda's symbolic depiction, noted above, of the country's mother as careless political leaders: 'You are a child of Iran, and Iran is your motherland / Your living is to put your good body to work, *balam lai* [lullaby]…' [26]

آمد سحر و موسم کار است بالام لای   خواب تو دگر باعث عار است بالام لای
لای لای بالالای لای لای لای بالالای لای...
تو کودک ایرانی و ایران وطن توست   جان را تن بی‌عیب به کار است بالام لای
تو جانی و ایران چو تن توست لای لای بالالای لای
برخیز سلحشور و تو در حفظ وطن کوش   ای تازه گل ایران ز چه خوار است بالام لای
بس جامه عزّت به بدن پوش لای لای بالالای لای...
نگذار وطن قسمت اغیار بگردد   با آن که وطن را چو تو یار است بالام لای
ناموس وطن خوار بگردد لای لای بالالای لای

Thus the revolutionary movement led to a spontaneous revolution in Persian poetry, whereby, notwithstanding the continuing use of classical genres and structures, there was radical change in the themes, words, and language as well as imageries and other literary devices employed. Virtually all revolutionary poetry was much simpler than in the past in its diction, and this was all the more so in the case of the new and innovative folksy and colloquial verses. And since the revolutionary poetry was almost daily produced and published, it made a substantial contribution to the directing and shaping of public opinion, especially among the urban crowds.

Part I
Historiography

CHAPTER I

Whose Revolution? Stakeholders and Stories of the 'Constitutional Movement' in Iran, 1905–11

Joanna de Groot

'Historians are not in the business of deciding about right and wrong, permitted and forbidden, sinful and good deeds. They should, with the utmost precision, and on the basis of investigation and research, write the truths of events.'
Mohammad Hashem Asef, 'Rostam al-Hokama' (early nineteenth century CE)

'The job of the historian is not to collect all kinds of facts ... . The historian with historical insight marks the most meaningful and important events from that pile, offers the truthful description of that event with its cause or causes, evaluates the logical link in events following one from another, and with analysis offers a most concise and clear picture of the historical events.'
Fereydun Adamiyat (later twentieth century CE)

'Everything which is known is known not according to its own power but according to the capacity of the knower.'
Boethius (early sixth century CE)

Introduction

A century after the events and experiences discussed in this piece, we are heirs to a rich, if problematic, historiography describing, judging, celebrating, and analysing what is often seen as the foundational episode in 'modern' Iranian history. We have also seen some interrogation of that historiography, as historians have begun to produce self-reflexive critiques of such descriptions, judgements, celebrations, and analyses.[1] My text is in the nature of a 'think piece', or a contribution to conversations among historians and readers who investigate, interpret, and reflect on the 'constitutional period'. Its purpose is to raise questions about how we think about the happenings, changes, influences, and dynamics which Iranians in that period made, and were 'made' by, reflecting on the process, the practices, and the perceptions of those who study and analyse them.

By referring to process and practice I draw attention to the ways in which accounts and/or explanations are produced by the activities of historians, who, as Adamiyat puts it, select, organize, and connect evidence and ideas to create narratives/interpretations. His view of historical practice acknowledges a whole series of inputs from historians going beyond the 'investigation and research' proclaimed as the core of good practice by Rostam al-Hokama. While the observations of Adamiyat and Rostam al-Hokama seem familiar, even banal, I have placed them at the head of this piece because I want to centre discussion on what historians, and writers in the 'constitutional' era itself, actually do/did as they made/make the stories told about that era and the explanations of events and developments within it.[2] One does not have to take the view that the past does not exist outside texts which discuss the past to recognize the active role of commentators and analysts in constructing our understanding and knowledge of the past. Reflecting on the practices of historians, and their implications, is thus a more complex activity than is indicated by the familiar discussion of relationships between information and interpretation, or 'research' and 'analysis'. It involves deeper consideration of the contexts, concerns, and influences which shape historians' choices, and of the consequences or effects of those choices to include/exclude or prioritize/marginalize particular persons, themes, information, developments, or problems.

I therefore offer Boethius' observation as a third insight into questions of process and practice. I use his notion of 'capacity' to open up discussion of the practices of individual historians, and to draw attention to the shared sociocultural capital which forms a common resource for historians in particular times and places. Just as accounts of the 'French Revolution' by Lefebvre, Taylor, and Cobban in the 1960s, or by Furet, Outram, and Hunt in the 1990s, incorporated individual uses of, and responses to, the shared conditions and concerns of their times and milieux, so accounts of the 'Constitutional Revolution' in Iran expressed the personal and collective 'capacities' of their authors.[3] The cultural, material, and political conditions within which historians produce their work, like their distinctive individual use of such influences within their texts, are constitutive of that work rather than optional decorative elements. This can be seen in accounts of the period 1905–11 by Kasravi in the late 1930s, as in those by Malekzadeh and Taherzadeh-Behzad in the 1940s and 1950s, Adamiyat and Abrahamian in the 1970s and 1980s, Bayat, Foran, and Afary in the 1990s, or Tavakoli-Targhi and Najmabadi in the early twenty-first century.

A Chronology of Historians' Conversations

The texts mentioned above reveal not just blends of personal and cultural elements in the making of historical narratives and explanations, but ongoing conversations within the historiography of the Constitutional Revolution. The earliest accounts combined autobiographical elements with the first making of meanings for the events and experiences of 1905–11, as former activists incorporated their experiences into narrative interpretations. Nazem al-Eslam Kermani's 1910 presentation of the 'awakening of the Iranians' entwined original texts (telegrams, *shabnameh*s, correspondence) with his own diary/memoirs, and an account of the pro-constitutional politics of an alliance of patriotic and enlightened ulema and reformers from mercantile, official, and intelligentsia backgrounds. By the 1930s and 1940s personal experiences, memories, and ideals were incorporated into larger narratives of struggle, progress, and constitutionalism in the writing of Kasravi and Malekzadeh. Both narratives emphasized chosen themes, whether secularism and the dangers of ethnic and factional division to the 'national' cause (Kasravi), or the role of particular groups and individuals (Malekzadeh). Like the accounts of Nazem al-Eslam and Dowlatabadi, they set events and issues within a powerful framing story of pro- and anti-constitutional politics.[4] The very use of the terms 'constitution/*mashruteh*' and 'constitutional/*mashrutiyat*' in their titles placed that political issue at the core of the story, as it has been in histories of the period ever since.

The emergence of a wider range of materials and methods upon which historians could draw for their accounts and analyses did not so much displace the primacy of that issue as embed it in a range of more specific interpretations and lines of enquiry. The increased availability of newspapers, memoirs, and correspondence from the late nineteenth and early twentieth centuries allowed for more source-based investigation and interpretations. New ideas and methods for the study of politics, social groups, and political cultures in the past became resources for historians' work. One line of enquiry, exemplified in Adamiyat's work, traced the development of 'progressive' ideas and policies as influential forces upon the men and movements of the constitutional period. Another, found in the work of Mangol Bayat, Vanessa Martin, Abdul-Hadi Hairi, and Nikki Keddie, explored the role of various strands of religious thought and political interest in both pro- and anti-constitutional politics. Bayat, like Cosroe Chaqueri, Janet Afary, and Ervand Abrahamian, also investigated the growth of secular, leftist, and grassroots activity within that politics.[5]

However, in the 1980s and 1990s historians began to set their research questions and their stories and analyses of the constitutional movement in larger explanatory and conceptual frameworks, taking concerns which had stimulated participants in the movement as guiding themes. Thus Kermani's and Kasravi's invocations of the '*mardom/mellat* = people/nation' of Iran as both object and agent of constitutionalist politics generated more systematic enquiries into relationships between that politics and nationalistic thought and activism in the work of Keddie and Bayat. The links of constitutionalism with 'progress' and 'enlightenment' asserted by Kermani, Kasravi, and Adamiyat morphed into analyses of the place of the constitutional movement in the larger processes of social and political change often labelled as 'modernity'.[6] In stories told along these lines, constitutional politics is seen as entwined with, or even produced by, transformations associated with administrative, educational, and legal reform, and with the development of 'modern' class identities, economic activities, and forms of politics. Abrahamian in the early 1980s and John Foran a decade later produced large-scale accounts of Iranian history in which the constitutional movement is depicted as a significant specific episode within their grand narratives. Abrahamian's narrative concerned the changing 'social bases of Iranian politics' across the twentieth century framed by the 'two revolutions' of 1905–11 and 1977–82; Foran's story concerned the transformation of societies and politics in Iran by the effects of the capitalist world system, and the emergence of relative dependency within that system between the sixteenth and twentieth centuries.[7]

Such attempts to integrate accounts of the Constitutional Revolution within broad narratives of global change and social analysis coincided with the production of explorations of the complexity of the social and political movements, and of contending or convergent ideas and interests in early twentieth-century Iran. This work complicated and disaggregated some of the established stories of the revolutionary era, which had opposed ulema and government, religion and secularism, or pro- and anti-constitutionalists. The accounts of that era produced by Martin, Bayat, and Afary have entered the canon of Iranian historiography precisely because they offer nuanced and coherent depictions of multi-group alliances, shifting coalitions and conflicts of interest, and complex ideals and motivations. Their achievements express the prevalent ethos of modern history-writing, where the aim of researchers and texts is to critique and modify the work of predecessors, making Oscar Wilde's observation that 'truth is rarely pure and never simple' a guiding principle. While one aspect of this ethos is adversarial, reflecting the competitive modes of academic life, there is also a 'conversational' aspect whereby these authors and texts engage interactively with previous narratives and interpretations. They also provide different kinds of storytelling, informed by scepticism about oversimplified conventional assertions and the desire to restore 'forgotten' or marginalized protagonists and issues to the historical record.

Themes and Debates

For some historians the trend to more complex stories of the Constitutional Revolution raises questions not only about what ought to be added or re-evaluated, but about the provisional and conflicted character of all possible narratives, and the power relations implicit in choices to include/exclude, emphasize/marginalize. Neither Rostam al-Hokama's appeal to research and investigation, nor Adamiyat's to truthful description grounded in analysis, addresses such issues. Both assume, firstly, that truth is 'out there' to be discovered and explained, rather than being made in the process of investigation and interpretation, and secondly, that choices and selections made by researchers and writers in the process of creating historical narratives are exercises in authority, not authorship. They do not consider how research and writing inevitably incorporate the cultural, political, and ideological influences and resources within which their practitioners have been formed and operate. They ignore relationships between the preoccupations and priorities of individuals who create narratives and those of the society and culture within which they operate, which together form their 'capacity' to 'know' the topics which they study and write about.

To take an obvious example, since 1979 writing about the Constitutional Revolution has been informed both explicitly and implicitly by awareness of the 'revolution' which overthrew Shah Mohammad Reza Pahlavi in that year. From the title of Abrahamian's text cited above, to the comments within which Afary, Bayat, and Foran frame their discussions, the modes and meanings of the 1978–82 'Islamic revolution' have formed a parallel paradigm or point of reference for stories of the earlier episode.[8] More generally, concerns with nationalist, anti-imperialist, and patriotic ideas, with religion and secularism, and with the role of multi-group or cross-class political alliances, have moved between narratives of revolution in the eighth decade of the twentieth century and narratives of revolution seventy years earlier.

More challengingly yet, there are now deeper critiques of simplified notions of authoritative/rational/truthful narrative, as historians consider the larger implications of excluding and selecting particular themes and groups as significant features in the story of the Constitutional Revolution. Bayat's and Afary's discussions of religious aspects of the revolution challenge the somewhat undifferentiated views of 'religion', or 'Shiism', or 'ulema', deployed in earlier accounts. They introduce themes of dissidence and hierarchy into their analyses, and shape their narratives around notions of popular (as opposed to privileged or professional) aims and ideas, and of diversity and contingency, rather than uniform orthodoxy, in religious identity and thought. Afary's text not only offers evidence-based accounts of grassroots and popular participation, but seeks to shape the whole story of the Constitutional Revolution around the emergence and vicissitudes of new kinds of radicalism and 'politics from below'. If the *mardom* invoked by Kasravi turn out to be particular groups of merchants and intelligentsia, the protagonists depicted by Afary as politically active and prefiguratively imaginative about a better future are defined by their unprivileged or marginal status (peasants, women, artisans) or their democratic-egalitarian outlook (leftists and radicals). Their presence in the narrative, and the weaving of 'subaltern' analyses through the text as a whole, goes beyond the addition of complexity to reframe the narrative itself as a story of the struggle of popular politics with other forces.[9]

Another important contribution to the redirection of whole narratives has come from those who draw on gender theory and scholarship alongside historical research to challenge gender blindness and gender exclusion in canonical accounts of the Constitutional Revolution. Starting in the late 1970s a slow process of recuperation used early twentieth-century materials to show that there were female as well as male participants in the revolution, and that concern with male–female differences, roles, and relationships coloured the political culture of that time.[10] As with the emergence of narratives of 'history from below', some accounts of gender issues used this work to go beyond mere inclusion and argue for reinterpretation of the constitutional narrative on gendered lines. Afary and Paidar, like Tavakoli-Targhi, suggest that the core projects of constitutional politics – accountable government, the rights of subjects/citizens, 'national' autonomy, social progress, and justice – were inflected with gender concerns which refigured political processes and thinking. Taking that theme further, the work of Najmabadi argues that the restructuring of Iranian genders and sexualities was constitutive of the major shifts in Iranian society, culture, and politics between the mid-nineteenth and later twentieth centuries, often narrated as the onset of 'modernity', with the constitutional era as a significant moment in that story.[11] It explicitly critiques the 'forgetting' of women, gender, and sexuality in mainstream historiography, not just as a scholarly omission, but as a form of epistemic violence reflecting the deeply embedded and unacknowledged gender/heterosexual 'blindness' and discrimination underpinning material, cultural, and political life in twentieth-century Iran, as well as much historical scholarship. This critique voices the concerns of those who have produced informed and reflective work on these themes over three decades, but find that work (mis)treated as a mere 'special-interest' addition to the historical canon, and argues that this canon is thereby rendered deficient.

If arguments for the transformative potential of gendered narratives of the Constitutional Revolution have been made, but not widely recognized or acted upon, narratives of that revolution as 'national' (indeed as the 'foundation myth' of modern Iranian 'national' history) have had even less critical attention. Detailed work by Mostafa Vaziri and Firoozeh Kashani-Sabet makes clear that notions of an Iranian 'nation', and aspirations for its progress and autonomy, were specific to nineteenth- and twentieth-century Iranian political culture. Vaziri's text critiques European and Iranian historiography for misleading uses of ahistorical and essentialist notions of 'Iran', while Kashani-Sabet explores the development of various nationalistic themes and images by writers and politicians, and the significance of the constitutional period in this process.[12] They historicize the context and content of Iranian nationalism without pursuing the case for non-'national' narratives of the constitutional period and movement. Yet informed discussion of local specificities, ethnic variety, and cross-border political and cultural influences by Bayat, Afary, Chaqueri, and Berberian, and the comparative work of Kurzman, suggest that 'Iranian' constitutional politics was defined neither by ethnic homogeneity nor by state borders.[13]

While recognizing that 'national' ideals and aspirations had real significance for many participants in the Constitutional Revolution, as evidenced in journalism, memoirs, and political activity, it is possible to produce scholarly narratives which emphasize other agencies and priorities. Historians have long acknowledged the role of ideas and movements from outside Iran on politically aware and active Iranians of the constitutional era.[14] Moreover, movements in Iran between 1905 and 1911 can be placed in an international spectrum of upheavals including the Mexican Revolution of 1910–14, the Young Turk movement of 1909, the Russian Revolution of 1905, and the Chinese Revolution of 1911. The role of anti-colonial, Pan-Islamic and leftist influences on Iranian activism and thought, and of Armenian and Transcaucasian militants moving between Ottoman, tsarist, and Qajar territories, similarly suggests other trans-border narratives. From another point of view, the importance of diverse ethnic, occupational, religious, hierarchical, and communal interests and affiliations in pro- and anti-constitutional politics indicates that spatial and conceptual frameworks other than those associated with 'the nation' can structure accounts of that politics. Whether or not such accounts emerge rests on the choices of researchers and writers, most of whom, following traditions established by key constitutionalists and their political heirs, whether Pahlavi modernizers or their leftist and democrat opponents, make the story of the constitutional period predominantly a story of 'nation' and nationalism.

Priorities and Protagonists

The issue is not whether particular accounts of the Constitutional Revolution which emphasize either 'national' institutions, resistance to foreign intervention and internal tyranny, international social democracy, and anti-colonial politics, or else regional and localized communal, class, or ethnic politics, are 'right' or 'wrong'. Rather, the discussion here considers the stakeholders in, and effects of, various investigative and interpretative choices made by researchers and writers. Reflecting on the historiography of modern Iran sketched above, and on my own study of regional aspects of the Constitutional Revolution, I examine the politics of ownership of particular narratives of the revolution and of the highlighting/marginalizing of particular participants. From Nazem al-Eslam Kermani and Edward Browne, writing before 1914, to authors in the twenty-first century, the drive to link stories of the revolution to larger narratives and to identify its leading protagonists has been a powerful agenda whose implications merit such consideration.

While tracing its antecedents to the later nineteenth century, canonical accounts of the revolution construct the constitutional period as the foundational episode in the story of 'modern' Iran. Kermani's story of 'awakening', Browne's 'Persian Risorgimento' in 'the cause of Freedom and Reform', and Kasravi's confrontation between government and 'awakened' people, a 'story of seeking justice against oppression, liberty against injustice', are presented as starting points for Iranians' advance towards an enlightened, justly ruled, and prosperous society.[15] In these and later accounts the establishment and defence of the constitution itself are depicted as putting down markers of Iran's emergence as the (potential) equal of other advanced states governed under the rule of law and representative institutions. They are presented as signifiers of the self-assertion of the 'nation' against foreign interference, and quasi-colonial subservience to great powers, as well as against 'backwardness' and arbitrary rule. Furthermore, the creation of constitutional government is presented not just as an end in itself, but as the key to the reforms and self-strengthening associated with 'modern', 'advanced', or 'progressive' and 'just' polities and societies. Lastly, many canonical accounts present the events and experiences of the constitutional period as 'unfinished business' undermined by hostile indigenous elites, by divisions among the 'freedom lovers', and by foreign intervention, which by 1911 had prevented patriotic Iranian reformers and social radicals from achieving their aims. The constitutional period is regularly depicted as setting an agenda, whether successfully or not, for what historians, like politically active Iranians, have seen as key struggles for democracy, independence, progress, and good government continuing through the twentieth century. This tradition might be regarded as an Iranian version of the 'Whig' narratives of political upheaval in Britain and Ireland produced by Thomas Babington Macaulay, James Mackintosh, and their followers. Reza Afshari explicitly refers to Adamiyat as the grand exemplar of Whiggish writing on the revolution, and the practice of placing accounts of 1905–11 at the start of a story of progressive forces thwarted by malevolent opponents still demonstrates its powerful continued appeal in recent work by Ali Gheissari and Vali Nasr, as well as Fakhreddin Azimi.[16]

These narratives also identify specific protagonists, depicted as making their central contribution to the revolution and shaping its course and character. In Kermani's narrative an alliance of enlightened ulema and reformers, educating and leading supporters in political debate and activity and giving direction to popular discontents, demonstrated the capacity of progressive mullas to struggle for the anti-despotic and patriotic cause. For Kasravi the story of the revolution was that of educated and enlightened reformers battling for a 'modern' integrated national polity against both religious conservatism and popular communal sectionalism and violence.[17] Malekzadeh and Adamiyat told constitutional stories of great men ('leaders', heroes, 'freedom lovers') and great ideas (democracy, freedom, progress) constructing memories to celebrate and legacies to inspire.

More recent accounts of the Constitutional Revolution turn their attention to the complexities and instabilities of alliances among constitutionalists, and to the shifting combinations of self-interest, idealism, and group attachments in those alliances. Nonetheless, they too identify protagonists who made key contributions to the constitutional movement. For Abrahamian and Foran, revolutionary successes were gained by coalitions of bazaaris, reforming officials, and intellectuals of varying degrees of radicalism both religious and secular, allied to popular forces, battling with their own conflicts of interest and with the governing elite. Revisiting the story of ulema leadership, Martin produces a narrative which emphasizes the role of collective vested interests, relationships to various supporters, and internal rivalries as much as of ideals or policies. For Bayat the powerhouse of change lay among religious dissidents and leftists with modernizing agendas, and the outcomes of the struggles of 1905–11 are defined by the fragility of those actors' alliances with the merchant, official, and elite classes, in which 'the mobilized masses had little to say'.[18]

In contrast, Afary's text emphasizes 'grassroots' self-generated activism by subordinated and underprivileged groups, who found allies and inspiration among the radical activist intelligentsia but who also 'made' their own ideas and protests. The movements and ideas of peasants, women, and urban protestors are shown to critique and challenge both old and new political classes, and the 'failure' of many progressive policies and aspirations is seen as the defeat of their 'popular' and 'democratic' initiatives. In both Bayat's and Afary's work close and knowledgeable analysis reveals nuances and contradictions in political and ideological activity, but also highlights large issues which underpin the experiences of 1905–11 and which still resonate for the authors. They suggest that the unresolved state of the entangled relationships among the secularist, religious, modernizing, and establishment interests and objectives of the constitutional era influenced later developments, notably the theocratic outcome of a later revolutionary period with the establishment of Khomeini's Islamic Republic. Bayat highlights the inability of a new secularizing elite to address the sociocultural, as opposed to political, implications of the displacement of the old religio-political hierarchy. Afary argues that failure to appreciate the 'multi-cultural and democratic legacy of the Constitutional Revolution' fostered problematic and 'uncritical attitudes towards the ulema in 1978–79'.[19]

To point out the role of selection and exclusion in accounts of the Constitutional Revolution seems obvious, even banal, but has serious implications. As Najmabadi argues with reference to gender blindness, and Afary with reference to grassroots agency, the choices involved do not only express scholarly judgements, but also make silent or invisible those whose significant ideas and activities were marginalized during the constitutional era. Similar arguments apply to the unexplored assumptions behind the many versions of the constitutional narrative as the story of the assertion, or at least first stirrings, of a 'nation' in which local, regional, or transnational elements are allocated secondary or diversionary roles. When the seizure of the 'daughters of Quchan' is forgotten but the killing of *tullab* (religious students) in Tehran remembered, or the radical ideas of educated activists privileged over protests by those who did not write the records, or localized movements judged solely in terms of convergence or conflict with 'national' developments, the consequences deserve attention as acts of cultural power.

Choices and Strategies

Two points are particularly worth making. Firstly, it is important to acknowledge the power implicit in choice and selectivity. Decisions that particular persons and their actions and aspirations are not important flow from the unavoidable judgements made by writers and researchers as they create accounts and interpretations. However, they may also conceal and disregard what was important for such persons and for those affected by their actions and aspirations. The challenge for historians is to sustain coherent narratives and analyses while doing justice to the rich complexity of source material, but avoiding antiquarian shopping lists, or a pessimistic refusal to make sense of diversity. Recent critiques of grand narrative and of knowledge and discourse as forms of power have their limitations and problems; they also show how historians might reflect constructively on the processes of selection and prioritization which are integral to their practice. Rather than ignoring such processes, or justifying any given choice as the only alternative, it makes more sense to recognize that particular choices suit particular purposes, but not others. Just as microbiologists use microscopes and not astronomical telescopes, because the former reveal cells and the latter distant stars, so historians decide the focus and range of a project not as an abstractly or universally 'correct' choice, but as contingently appropriate means to specific ends.

Secondly, there are constructive ways to deal with the challenge of acknowledging varied, complex, even contradictory material from the past while making coherent narratives about that past. Rather than treating such material as evidence of random diversity, it can be used to explore and evaluate the plurality and inconsistency of experience, purpose, action, and viewpoint among the protagonists, movements, and situations of the constitutional period. This allows researchers, readers, and writers to avoid an unhelpful binary opposition of varied evidence to clear narrative, and to consider the period as a field of converging, contending, and cohabiting elements and people.[20] It also establishes the 'constitutional period' not as some pre-existing phenomenon but as a field of knowledge constructed by researchers, readers, and writers who can choose to incorporate notions of plurality and contradiction within their thinking.

One way to convey this perspective is to focus on the playing out of human agency through the negotiation of conflict and contradiction within the ideas, activities, and experiences of Iranians in the period from 1905 to 1911. Accounts of nationalism can depict not so much a single forward-moving story, but rather the cross-fertilization and tension of intellectual and popular ideas and protests, regional and international influences, and secular, religious, and gender agendas, as seen in the writings and actions of those who espoused the 'national' cause and called themselves 'Iranians'. Real contests over new forms of law and government can be shown to be cross-cut with familial, communal, gendered, and class-based concerns. Rather than these complexities being presented as marginal or distracting from a unidirectional analysis of 'national' and 'constitutional' histories, they can be shown as integral to, and constitutive of, such histories.

Another approach would focus on particular groups or individuals. Thus women's contributions to constitutional politics can be analysed as a composite phenomenon characterized by choices, conflicts, and combinations, rather than through an either/or binary of 'gender' versus 'constitutional' or 'nationalist' politics. For educated women from privileged backgrounds who wrote in the constitutional press, opened schools, and formed patriotic women's associations, the language and aims of female interests and agency intersected with those of national regeneration, citizenship, and social progress. They negotiated calls for the recognition and inclusion of women in the new polity both within and against codes of religious authority and propriety, male and family honour, class distinctions, and gender-blind versions of patriotism and citizenship. For unprivileged women who participated in protest in the constitutionalist era, communal and religious affiliation combined with traditions of female networking, popular 'moral economy',[21] and street politics. Their challenges to official oppression, or to insults to 'their' religious leaders, like protest over food shortages or foreign intervention, can be understood as using and combining all these resources, entwining gender politics with the politics of faction, class, and place, just as women's rights campaigners linked it to the politics of nation-making and reform. Histories of constitutional ideas and movements can shape their accounts around the complex intersections and conflicts of these varied elements, rather than posing supposedly more or less relevant elements against one another.

Similarly, a study of a constitutional 'hero' such as Seyyed Hasan Taqizadeh can be presented less through binary alternatives ('principled'/'opportunist', 'radical'/'moderate'), and more as an analysis of interactions of diverse influences and aspects within his experience and career. His exposure to, and use of, political ideas of reform, nationalism, and social justice linked him to liberals and leftists in the tsarist empire and Western Europe, just as it bonded him to Tabrizi associates and organizations who pursued those ideas through the 1890s into the constitutional era. His negotiations of Azarbayjani and leftist connections on the metropolitan stage of the Majles and popular politics in Tehran, and his relationships with supporters or critics within and outside Iran, shaped a political course combining roles as a strong advocate of the constitutional cause and a pragmatic practitioner of alliance politics and compromise. His apparently incompatible links to social democrat revolutionaries, to members of the ulema, to English lobby groups, and to both establishment and dissident politicians, can be depicted as evidence of inconsistency, opportunism, or lack of commitment to the progressive cause.[22] They can equally well be discussed as markers of the inherently many-sided and inconsistent character of political life, in which specific aims and actions are rooted in and flavoured by multiple influences and conflicts of interest. Taqizadeh's career as advocate of high political ideals, broker of alliances, party leader, and reformer can be read as 'declining' from commitment to compromise, or as richly revealing of the varied influences and challenges shaping the political lives of those educated and ambitious young men who became activists during the constitutional era.[23] The latter holistic approach allows historians to establish narratives which follow a story without neglecting the complexities and contradictions within it.

A Case Study

Using another kind of holistic approach, taking a specific framework and considering relationships between developments in one area and those elsewhere, I now explore events and experiences during the constitutional era in the south-eastern region of Kerman at two particular moments. First I examine upheavals in Kerman city in 1905–06, which Nazem al-Eslam and Kasravi incorporate into 'national' narratives of the early stages of the constitutional movement. I then discuss the career of a local leader, Mirza Qasem Khan 'Ref'at-e Nezam', variously portrayed as a brigand, a 'freedom lover', an opportunistic minor notable, and a 'rebel', who figures in various episodes in 1908–09 and 1911–12 which can be depicted as having both local and wider interest. The aim is to compare the effects of different choices about narrative and emphasis.

Accounts by Nazem al-Eslam Kermani and Kasravi of the events leading up to the granting of a constitution in 1906 include descriptions of protest and political conflict in Kerman.[24] A story of overlapping confrontations between local notables and princely Qajar provincial governors, among rival kin groups among those notables, and among different religious sects in the city in 1905–06, intersected with wider popular grievances and emergent anti-regime politics in Kerman and elsewhere. Kermani's narrative of these intersections is shaped by personal connections to Kerman, his city of origin, and to circles around the leading ulema Tabataba'i and Behbahani, who were developing their own brand of oppositional politics at the start of the twentieth century. Kasravi's account, which relies to a considerable extent on Kermani, is shaped by experiences of religion and politics in Tabriz in the constitutional era and by commitment to the promotion of secular centralizing 'national' progress in later life.[25]

Each account establishes its ownership of the story and choice of lead protagonists within those frameworks. Thus Kasravi emphasizes the ambition rather than the piety or reforming ideas of one of the leading ulema participants in the Kerman events, the *mujtahid* Mirza Mohammad Reza, and comments disparagingly on the sectional religious affiliations and conflicts of Kermanis as 'hostility and vengefulness'. Mirza Mohammad Reza appears as a manipulative figure, making use of popular feeling and spinning the story of his mistreatment by government officials to gain support from Tabataba'i. Kermani depicts an alliance between progressive mullahs in both Kerman and Tehran, but also a detailed back story of the competing familial and religious interests shaping Kerman politics and communal life.[26] He develops an account of Tabataba'i's Anjoman-e Makhfi (Secret Society), of which Kermani was a member, emerging as a leader of Iran-wide opposition to tyranny and speaking for 'national' grievances through contacts with centres like Kerman. Ultimately, rather as Kermani's career moved from teaching in Kerman to metropolitan ulema politics, the 'story' of Kerman politics in 1905–06 becomes a tributary feeding the main current of constitutional politics in the capital city, as it is in Kasravi's narrative.

The spotlights shed on the 'Kerman story' by both narratives do indeed illuminate key developments which contributed to political movements whose apex was the Tehran campaign leading to the granting of a constitution in 1906. They also spotlight the role of individual persons depicted as significant actors in the 'Kerman story', from reform-minded activists like Nazem al-Eslam's fellow townsman the journalist Majd al-Eslam, to ambitious Kerman notables, the anti-Jewish preacher Sheykh Barini, prominent *mujtahid*s like Tabataba'i, and Qajar princes. By definition they also, and necessarily, leave other elements in shadow. On the one hand this approach conveys a sense of the interdependence of events and experiences in different parts of Iran in the creation of constitutional politics. Kasravi's account suggests that misreported 'disturbances' (his term) in Kerman provided a means for emergent anti-despotic groups in Tehran to build a campaign against 'oppressive' royal ministers. That of Kermani depicts convergence between anti-despotic politics in Kerman and the growth of the campaign by Tabataba'i, Behbahani, and their associates, a view which may be supported by references in British consular sources to an *anjoman* of mullahs in Kerman. They also present views of particular historical actors in pursuit of their goals, whether establishing Sheykh Fazlollah Nuri (with benefit of hindsight) as a critic of 'progressive' ideas, or depicting the influence (self-interested or otherwise) of Haji Mirza Mohammad Reza in Kerman.[27] On the other hand these choices involve a process of selection, which, however insightful, offers only one perspective on the social bases and culture of politics in Iran in the early twentieth century.

Just as different perspectives on the Tehran aspects of the story might foreground other players than Tabataba'i, or emphasize the ulema's vested interests rather than their ideals, so other narratives of the protests in Kerman might focus on participants and aspirations other than those highlighted by Kermani and Kasravi. Thus, while it may not be possible to individualize the anonymous *ahl* or *mardom* (people) of Kerman referred to in their accounts, it is possible to give them greater attention and analysis, and explore the issues they raise. Other readings of the material may provide a fuller account of the agency of those who appeared on the streets, attended mosques and *rowzeh-kh"ani*s (lamentation sessions for Imam Husayn), and expressed their views during the events of 1905.

Thus one could depict the influence of Haji Mirza Mohammad Reza as created by interaction between the *mujtahid* and sections of the Kerman populace, rather than entirely the product of his manipulation. For crowds of young and old, and 'respectable' women, to meet him on his return to Kerman after fourteen years, as described by Kermani, indicates some degree of interest and choice on their part. So too do his accounts of grievances against the Sheykhi elite, attacks on wineshops, and the fears of protestors faced with armed government troops. While Kermani and Kasravi note how preachers and *mujtahid*s stirred up audiences and followers, they do not consider why such audiences or followers responded to the sermons and exhortations, preferring just to label 'common people' as ignorant, factional, or wicked.[28] Patterns of patronage, worship, and communal solidarity, which sustained the loyalties and enmities which brought people into protest as Sheykhi or Balasari, were created by the active, if unequal, involvement of both the powerful and powerless. Outrage at the beating of a *mujtahid*, or the use of physical defilement of mosques as a weapon, like the Kerman mullahs' boycott of religious duties and the efforts of intellectuals to explore relationships between Islamic and republican ideas (all mentioned in the texts), can be seen as expressions of lively political cultures shaping political action.[29]

Apparently anecdotal references in the texts to gender issues and to protest actions by women can likewise be used to provide a story of Kerman politics in which gender analysis has a significant role. Accounts of anti-Sheykhi mullahs invalidating marriages solemnized by Sheykhi ulema, or rumours of a Sheykhi man killing his Balasari wife, like the specific emphasis on the abuse and killing of women, indicate the power of marital and gender themes as political signifiers for both participants and commentators. Reports of women, both 'common' and 'respectable', taking initiatives to support 'their' chosen mullahs and joining with men in protests, suggest that they can be understood as political actors, just as references to such actions reveal the presuppositions of observers.[30] In a context where existing patterns of female activism and gender distinction in Iran intersected with new views of gender roles, marriage, and political or educational reform, accounts of women's agency and of key gender aspects of political thought and action offer more than depictions of women or men as a one-dimensional 'crowd'.

Unpacking references to 'crowds' or 'people' to consider the distinctive role of local elites, competition for money and office, allegiance to religio-communal identities and hierarchies, interest in 'freedom-loving' politics, and the dynamics of class and gender, makes other stories and protagonists visible. This makes it possible to incorporate *tullab* debating reform with senior ulema, the urban poor resenting price manipulation by notables, and men and women outraged by offences to their sense of sexual honour or to the respect due to men of religion, in a story of Kerman politics as a complex constituent of constitutional politics. Such an approach can be glimpsed in Scarcia's 1963 article on religious sectarianism, which drew on an Iranian narrative published in the 1950s.[31] Such a story opens up the space to appreciate the diverse aims and interests animating these varied contributors and suggests what may have been important to them as well as to later researchers and writers.

Similar possibilities emerge from material about the career of Mirza Qasem Khan Ref'at-e Nezam, from Narmashir, in south-eastern Kerman province, during the constitutional era. This career took him from work as a *monshi* (secretary) and *pishkar* (agent) in Kerman and Bam to a more dissident and/or personally ambitious course of confrontation with khans and 'tribal' leaders in the south-east, and with the provincial government. By 1908–09 his activities converged with conflicts between constitutionalist activists and the government, with Ref'at-e Nezam helping constitutionalist leaders from Kerman while policing or manipulating the rivalries and alliances of Baluch raiders and local landlords. He continued to combine these activities for the next three years, and by August 1911 was governor of Bam, to be found both challenging and enforcing attempts to maintain security on the roads, collect taxes, and control notables. In April 1912 his quarrels with the governor general of Kerman escalated into an alliance with a range of notables in a larger challenge to governmental authority and an armed march on Kerman city, where Ref'at-e Nezam had some support among 'democrats'. By June this alliance had been disrupted, its armed force dispersed, and Ref'at-e Nezam captured and hung.

This compressed narrative draws on references in *Tarikh-e bidari-ye Iraniyan*, on British records, and on recollections of Kermanis collected in the 1950s and 1960s. In the texts from which the references come, narratives of rebellion and constitutionalism are entwined with accounts of opportunism, violence, and double-dealing. It is tempting to adopt a judgemental stance whereby Ref'at-e Nezam's story becomes either that of an ally of the constitutional cause and bold enemy of government oppression, or else that of a disruptive, acquisitive, self-regarding climber using force and cunning to advance his interests.[32] However, the material also allows an analysis which portrays the ambiguity and unstable complexity of political conflict and negotiation in his career.

This unstable complexity is evident in the sources themselves. Just as celebration of Ref'at-e Nezam's 'freedom-loving' commitment also mentions his violent competition with officials and landowners across Kerman, so British reports of his ambition and depredations include references to his 'Democrat' associates and constitutionalist pronouncements. Those who put material together with one story in mind simultaneously provide elements for another. The Ref'at-e Nezam shown burning the wooden staves used to beat peasants also appears as a participant in armed competition with fellow khans in Bam. The Ref'at-e Nezam portrayed as a violent opportunist is also depicted defending constitutionalists. His alliances with Baluch and Narmashiri nomads are reported both as measures to protect the populace from their raiding, and as establishing his personal power base.[33] The twists and turns of his dealings with local leaders and with provincial government indicate simultaneous self-interested calculation and responses to the vicissitudes of constitutionalist politics, and his last campaign can be read in the context of the collapse of his own ambitions as well as of wider constitutional aspirations.

Narratives of this career can thus canvas options beyond the restrictive binary of 'disruptive opportunist' versus 'noble freedom lover'. Arguably it is beneficial to combine stories of the spread of constitutional politics far beyond Tehran, or Kerman city, of local ambitions and rivalries, of how struggles for 'liberty' might slip into 'licence',[34] and of complex relations among nomads and settled communities, or between government centres and their borderlands. Such combinations recognize the range of potential stakeholders and protagonists in the story of events and experiences in Iran in the constitutional period, the many-sided character of political activity and culture, and the varied and contradictory resources on which its participants have drawn.

Conclusion

This abbreviated attempt at a narrative centred outside Tehran could be developed further, and be replicated for other parts of Iran, shifting the presentation of constitutional history from a centre/region format towards a decentred or many-centred picture.[35] Such a rethinking of spatial and political hierarchies might be matched by a similar rethinking of the protagonists and priorities chosen as the focus of constitutional stories, allowing the privileged and powerless, women and men, the famous and the anonymous to openly jostle for, and change, their positions. The concern would be more with the shifting unstable connections between different elements in the story, rather than with what is 'accurate', 'important', or 'correct', since such categories, as Boethius suggests, are relative and context-specific rather than definitive. The energy of the Bam khans, or of pious women and carpetmakers in Kerman city, like that of the Anjoman-e Makhfi, merchants, officeholders, and reformers in Tehran, or *luti*s and leftist intellectuals in Tabriz, inhabited a reality which was specific to each while sustaining fragile but evident connections to one another.

In this discussion I have suggested that the historiography of constitutional movements will benefit from greater relativism and greater self-awareness. In the past the power of many narratives of the Constitutional Revolution came from their arguments for the primacy of particular issues and protagonists. More recently, more detailed research and nuanced interpretations have provided, whether implicitly or explicitly, the basis for a different approach, based neither on unidirectional explanation nor on the mere accumulation of data. If researchers and writers openly recognize the power of selection and marginalization, they can use that power more transparently and responsibly. If they treat their choices as provisional rather than authoritative, they open up possibilities for powerful narratives of many-sided power relations, complex encounters, and the relative autonomy of particular people and circumstances within the field of constitutional history. The reflections offered here are contributed in that spirit.

CHAPTER 2

The Iranian Constitutional Revolution as *lieu(x) de mémoire*: Sattar Khan

Anja Pistor-Hatam

Introduction: Defining *lieu(x) de mémoire*

In 2006, the Iranian Constitutional Revolution of 1906 was commemorated. This hundredth anniversary was celebrated with a number of conferences, attended by scholars who presented their latest research concerning the revolution. In Austria, as in the rest of Europe, Mozart's birthday was also commemorated in 2006, albeit with music instead of scholarly papers. Of course, Mozart was born long before the Constitutional Revolution and these two events are in no way interrelated. What is more, we may assume that there are more people in the world who have heard of Mozart than have heard of the Iranian Constitutional Revolution. However, both events have one thing in common: Mozart and the Constitutional Revolution can be called *lieux de mémoire* or locations of remembrance/*loci memoriae*. Whereas it is easy to recall what Mozart stands for in the cultural and collective memory of Austrians, Germans, Europeans in general, and the many peoples of the world – the musical genius who, as a young boy, already filled his audiences with enthusiasm[1] – it is perhaps more difficult to define the Iranian Constitutional Revolution as a *locus memoriae*. This is especially true for the non-Iranian scholar, whose recollection of the revolution is based neither on childhood memories like texts and pictures in schoolbooks, songs, street names, and so forth, nor on any Iranian nationalist sentiment or adult pride in Iranian history. The foreign scholar has usually formed his or her image of this revolution based on texts read and photos viewed in university classes, at his or her desk at home or in various archives. He or she may have approached the revolution with the help of E. G. Browne's renderings and the abundance of revolutionary photography printed in Ahmad Kasravi's famous history of the revolution.[2]

It was Maurice Halbwachs who first spoke of the importance of the social memory (*mémoire collective*),[3] claiming that the past is remembered, construed, or imagined within a frame of collective representations. According to Halbwachs, historical interpretations and patterns of perception are shaped by a combination of the individual and the social memory.[4] Past events are built into memory by a collective need to create meaning, by the traditions and perceptions coming from different social milieus.[5] Pierre Nora, for his part, argues that the coming to power of 'history' has destroyed and replaced 'memory'. *Lieux de mémoire*, therefore, come into existence because social memory (*milieux de mémoire*) no longer subsists.[6] The main purpose of these *lieux de mémoire*, consisting of museums, archives, graveyards, celebrations, monuments, etc., is to protect the 'collective memory' against decline and against its transformation into 'history'.[7] In order for the 'collective memory' to survive, *lieux de mémoire* unavoidably have to be composed of two dimensions: a material dimension (space and time) and a symbolic memory (memory of the past).[8] According to Nora, *lieux de mémoire* must be reconstructed as well as deconstructed to show that 'memory' has its own history and to bring to light the demystifying potential of the 'history of memory'.[9] Against Nora's claim that history (as a science) is in opposition to memory, even aiming at memory's destruction and suppression, Aleida Assmann sees history and memory as two means of remembrance that do not necessarily suppress and exclude one another. History, therefore, exists as science *and* as memory.[10]

Drawing inspiration from the above-mentioned authors as well as Jan Assmann and Paul Ricoeur,[11] among others, Etienne François and Hagen Schulze in the foreword to their three-volume *Deutsche Erinnerungsorte* (German *lieux de mémoire*) define *loci memoriae* as locations of material as well as immaterial existence.[12] Such *lieux de mémoire* may consist of mythical personages, events, buildings, historical monuments, terms, books, works of art, etc. A location of this kind, therefore, is to be understood as a metaphor or a topos, each one of which is situated in a real, social, political, cultural, or imagined space. *Lieux de mémoire*, the authors continue in a further elucidation of their concept, are created due to the symbolic function they possess. They are long-lasting focal points of collective memory and identity.

'We are what we have become. In our memories we recognize who we are, who or what we want to be, and in which way we are different from other people.'[13] The individual remembers, but not individually. According to Halbwachs, the individual remembers within a framework built by a given social milieu, which marks the shape and content of collective memory. Historical interpretations and perceptions, in turn, follow from the combination of individual remembrance and collective memory. Not every historical event becomes part of the individual or collective memory. Those that do, however, are made into what is to be remembered by a collectively felt desire for meaningfulness.[14] *Erinnerungskultur*, the culture of remembrance, is characterized by the functional employment of the past for current purposes.

Customs of commemoration are used to construct an historically based collective identity.[15]

During the Constitutional Revolution Iranians fought for their existence as a nation. The parliament in Tehran, the Majles, served as a forum for nationalist debates that established new myths, which in the end altered the nation's political landscape.[16] Under the influence of secularism, territoriality, the designation of Persian as the official language, and constitutional or democratic movements, a modern Iranian identity emerged.[17] As a milestone on Iran's route to becoming a nation in the modern sense of the term, the Constitutional Revolution formed part of the historically based collective identity. This was made possible not least by Iranian historiography focused on the Constitutional Revolution. In refining the main populist concepts, metaphors, and myths, contemporary witnesses and historians put this 'fund of knowledge' at the disposal of the Iranian nation.[18] It was the Constitutional Revolution in its entirety that became a long-lasting focal point of Iranian collective memory and identity, but it is also possible to single out particular events, regions, cities, buildings, and individuals that served as symbols of the Constitutional Revolution, its supporters, and its enemies. One such individual was Sattar Khan.

The Life and Deeds of Sattar Khan

When thinking about the Constitutional Revolution, the name of Sattar Khan suggests itself immediately. His is one of the names, his is one of the faces, his posture with his comrades and their rifles is one of the images that come to mind most easily. Sattar Khan has impressed himself on the minds of all those who, in one way or another, are connected with the Constitutional Revolution. One might even say that he gives a face to that particular event, that Sattar Khan embodies the revolution, at least after the coup d'état of 1908. He also presents himself as an example for a mythical personage as *lieu de mémoire*, whose symbolic function has an effect until this very day. Perceived as a local hero in Azarbayjan, Sattar Khan is still remembered as one of the champions of the Constitutional Revolution all over Iran. Schools, streets, municipal districts, and restaurants are named after him. Recently, he has also occupied space on the Internet, in this way also becoming part of virtual reality.

Who, then, was this man? How are his personality and his acts presented to the public? In what way do the descriptions of his life and deeds contribute to the construction of the mythical personage whose image is deeply rooted in the collective Iranian mind? The information concerning Sattar Khan to be obtained from Persian historical narratives ranges from a few occasional remarks, to whole chapters, to the dedication of an entire book solely to him, and the image that emerges when reading the various accounts related to Sattar Khan seems to be contradictory. The question remains whether Sattar Khan was in reality only a simple *luti* (social bandit or rascal) and *rahzan* (highway robber), who by chance was drawn into the revolution, or whether he was the 'bravest of the brave men of Iran' (*shoja'-e shoja'an-e Iran*),[19] who saved the revolution.

Based on this kind of narrative and often one-sided literature, it is admittedly difficult to obtain an unbiased impression of the Constitutional Revolution and those engaged in it. With regard to the above-mentioned concept of *lieux de mémoire*, however, this is not our concern. On the contrary, what concerns us here forms part of the intellectual history of the period under consideration. It is the personal viewpoints and biased opinions of those narrating the events of the Constitutional Revolution that mainly constructed the revolution, its locations, and heroes like Sattar Khan as *lieux de mémoire*. In this way, different aspects of the revolution and the people and places associated with it are transformed into what is to be remembered by a collectively felt desire for meaningfulness. This paper will give an account of Sattar Khan's life and deeds, as it is presented in the mentioned sources, to show how he was established as a *lieu de mémoire*.

Sattar Khan was born sometime between 1867 and 1869 (1284/1285).[20] His father, Haj Hasan Bazzaz Qaradaghi, had two wives and three sons. The eldest, Esma'il, became a highway robber and was executed when Sattar was still a child.[21] Haj Hasan then moved from Qaradagh to Tabriz with his family, where at the age of 17 or 18 Sattar first came into conflict with the law. His father had given shelter to two refugees from Qaradagh who had killed a muleteer during a dispute. To find them a hideout, Sattar was sent with them to the gardens outside Tabriz, where they were soon cornered by the dead muleteer's friends. After some more fighting and the killing of another muleteer, the two men from Qaradagh, along with Sattar, were detained by government troops and Sattar was wounded during the arrest. Whereas the two detainees from the Caucasus were later executed, Sattar was sent to the prison of Narin Qal'eh near Ardabil. After two years of imprisonment, he was able to escape with the aid of another inmate.[22] He then gathered round him a few armed men and turned to highway robbery, with the result that he was subsequently returned to prison on a number of occasions. Finally, he was taken into the services of the gendarmerie and later of Crown Prince Mozaffar al-Din Mirza as a rifleman (*tofangdar*). Sattar, who had been given the title *khan* in the crown prince's service, then went to Tehran and later to Mashhad, where he headed mounted auxiliary troops of fifty, fighting against Turkmen highway robbers. When he returned to Tabriz, he was called 'Mashhadi Sattar Khan'. Again, he turned to highway robbery and had to flee Tabriz to escape imprisonment. This time, in 1894/95 (1312), Sattar Khan went on pilgrimage to the Shiite holy sites in Iraq, where he made the acquaintance of the famous *marja'-e taqlid* Mirza Hasan Shirazi. As conveyed by Amirkhizi, while in Kazimayn, Sattar Khan heard complaints about the servants of the holy shrine in Samarra. When he went there himself, he experienced the Sunni servants of the Shiite site as rude and insulting and witnessed them mocking the pilgrims.[23] Immediately, Sattar Khan called on Mirza Hasan Shirazi and told him about the appalling situation, and Mirza Hasan Shirazi's visible distress moved him to action. Together with a small number of other pilgrims from Tabriz, Sattar Khan went back to the shrine, carrying sticks and whips. The young men beat the servants severely, an attack for which they were, in turn, arrested, although Sattar Khan himself, thanks to Mirza Hasan Shirazi's intervention, was saved from experiencing an Ottoman prison and was instead taken to the Iranian frontier.[24] Back home, however, he continued his unsettled and criminal way of life, spending his time between highway robbery, being on the run, and prison. In 1901/2 (1319), seven years after his first visit to the holy sites in Iraq, he went on the *ziyarat-e 'atabat* again, but on this occasion behaved himself. Finally tired of his exhausting lifestyle, Sattar Khan did penance at the shrine of Imam Ali in Najaf and never again came into conflict with the law. Since he was illiterate and his skills were restricted to gunmanship, his temporary work as a guardian in Salmas quickly ended in 1903/4 (1321). Sattar Khan finally returned to Tabriz, where he joined the local horse dealers; this was still his profession at the outbreak of the Constitutional Revolution in 1906.

In the spring of 1907, Sattar Khan, together with Baqer Khan,[25] became a member of the constitutionalists' police force. He also joined the constitutionalist society Anjoman-e Haqiqat, founded in the Amirkhiz quarter of Tabriz, which later became the centre of Sattar Khan's political and military activities.[26] He made his first public appearance in the midst of a group of *azadikh-vahan*. They were on their way to a garden outside of Tabriz, where riflemen of the former Crown Prince Mohammad Ali Mirza, under the leadership of a certain Akram al-Saltaneh, were hiding. Sattar Khan had volunteered to arrest them but came too late; the men had already fled when he and his men finally arrived on the spot.[27] When the political situation in Tehran deteriorated in 1908, Sattar Khan asked the Anjoman-e Haqiqat to send him, accompanied by fifty men, to Tehran where he would hoist the flag of constitutionalism on the roof of the parliament building.[28] After they had finally left with a large number of fighters (between 150 and 300 men, depending on the source), the *mojahedin* had to return quickly, since simultaneously with the bombardment of the Majles in Tehran on 23 June 1908, war broke out in Tabriz.[29]

For eleven months, civil war prevailed in Tabriz, which was also beleaguered by government troops. During the first stage of the war, in late June and early July, the *mojahedin* were able to prevent the royalist forces from gaining control. Then followed a second stage during which the royalist forces attacked the town from outside but could not conquer it. Eventually, beginning in early February 1909, the government troops besieged Tabriz, causing hunger, disease, and death. The siege was finally brought to an end by Russian troops.[30] Backed by his adviser Amirkhizi and by the leading Sheykhi cleric Seqat al-Eslam,[31] Sattar Khan emerged as *the* military leader of Tabriz, who also played an important role regarding political decisions.[32] When the Russian consul came to see him and, hinting at his hopeless condition, tried to convince him to surrender, Sattar Khan refused. In the 'simple words of the commoner', he replied: 'We do not want peace or posts. We are defending the constitution and will continue fighting until the constitution is restored and the parliament reopened.'[33] Sattar Khan became famous in Iran and abroad when, in a desperate situation where the government forces seemed to have prevailed and the inhabitants of Tabriz, fearing for their lives, had hoisted white banners on all the houses, he went out and took the banners down again. His brave and stubborn resistance in the face of total disaster made Sattar Khan the saviour of the constitution[34] – and, in consequence, of the nation. Due to his selflessness (*janfeshani*), his boldness, and his fearlessness (*shoja'at va reshadat*), he earned himself the title *sardar-e melli*, national commander.[35]

In the face of the advancing Russian troops, Sattar Khan, among others, sought asylum in the Ottoman consulate. He only left his *bast* after Mohammad Ali Shah's abdication on 16 July 1909. Neither the newly appointed governor nor the Russian diplomats and military commanders in Tabriz were eager to cooperate with Sattar Khan and his men. Therefore, he was hastily appointed governor of Ardabil in September 1909.[36] Being wholly incapable of uniting the town in the face of internal dissensions, and defending his own standing against a coalition of strong enemies from outside, Sattar Khan lasted only two months and returned to Tabriz defeated.[37] As described in some of the Persian sources, Sattar Khan, apart from just being unequal to the governorship of Ardabil, also misbehaved, drinking heavily and abusing the population.[38]

The last attempt to relieve Tabriz of Sattar Khan and his comrades' disturbing presence was made in early 1910 (1327/28). They had done their duty during the civil war and now their skills were no longer needed. On the contrary, as *luti*s the *mojahedin* had again turned into a source of unwelcome unrest and disturbance. So, instead of granting Sattar Khan, for services rendered, the garden outside town that he so desired,[39] a coalition consisting of the Russian consul, the governor Mokhber al-Saltaneh,[40] and even the provincial council (Anjoman-e Ayalati), together with the government in Tehran, planned to send him to the capital. He was told that it was in the interest of the people that he should not come back.[41] On 19 March 1910, a large crowd, joined by members of the national army and a band playing music, escorted Sattar Khan and Baqer Khan out of town.⁴² Members of parliament greeted them in Qazvin, and thousands of people awaited them in Mehrabad. In Tehran, both men were welcomed by the Shah and members of his government at the Golestan palace. Soon they were lost in the capital's political turmoil, which they neither understood nor could properly handle. At the same time, the situation in Tehran was becoming increasingly unstable, not least due to the existence of a large number of armed men in the city whom the government could not control. After the assassination of Seyyed Abdollah Behbahani,⁴³ a leading constitutionalist cleric, in July 1910, and two activists of the Democratic party a month later, the Iranian government and parliament agreed to disarm the *mojahedin*. While Sattar Khan and others of their leaders were negotiating the terms of the disarmament with the government, large numbers of discontented *mojahedin* assembled in the Atabak Park. Although a compromise was finally found, hostilities broke out on 8 August 1910. Sattar Khan and Baqer Khan sided with the 1000 *mojahedin* assembled in the park as it was surrounded by 1500 Armenian and Bakhtiyari troops. In the ensuing fights, Sattar Khan was wounded in the leg. He later pleaded to be allowed to return to Tabriz but was turned down by the government. He died in Tehran on 16 November 1914.

Sattar Khan – The Emergence of a National Myth

Based on the historical narratives of eyewitnesses and later chroniclers, Sattar Khan is memorialized as a person in a real political and historical place. At the same time, he is transformed into a *lieu de mémoire* because he possesses a symbolic function that turns him into a long-lasting focal point of memory and identity. In what way do the descriptions of his life and deeds contribute to the construction of the mythical personage whose image is deeply rooted in the collective Iranian mind?

In an article published in 1993, Reza Afshari places the historians of the Constitutional Revolution into three groups: the populists, the elitists, and the traditionalists. Whereas, according to Afshari, populists like Ahmad Kasravi focused on the common people and glorified the *mojahedin* in Tabriz,⁴⁴ elitist historians like Fereydun Adamiyat or Ebrahim Safa'i concentrated on reformers and demystified popular heroes. Traditionalists, among them Nazem al-Eslam Kermani and Mehdi Sharif Kashani, represent a version of the history of the Constitutional Revolution that is more sympathetic towards the leading proconstitutional *mujtahids*.⁴⁵ Many writers of the Constitutional Revolution were storytellers,⁴⁶ not historians in a scholarly sense. They told their respective versions of the occurrences, depicting one or the other of the *dramatis personae* as their hero, be it a renowned Sheykhi cleric like Seqat al-Eslam (Fathi),⁴⁷ an

Armenian Dashnak like Yeprem Khan (Ra'in),[48] or a *luti* like Sattar Khan (Amirkhizi).[49]

As the texts inform us, without exception, Sattar Khan never went to school and, as Amirkhizi puts it, could not tell *alef* from *ba*.[50] He is described as a simple man (*mardi 'ammi*), as dumb (*bihush*) and ignorant but noble (*sharif*), as a zealous (*mote'asseb*) Shiite and a Sheykhi. He seems to have been proud (*maghrur*) and ambitious (*boland-parvaz*), truth-loving (*rastgu*), and trusting (*sadehdel*). How could such a simple, uneducated, and unskilled man, lacking any experience in warfare apart from his proficiency as a highway robber and a gunman, become a hero of the Constitutional Revolution? Even those authors who point to Sattar Khan's flaws in character and expertise admit to his courage and his extraordinary commitment to defending the cause of the constitution. Although it seems that he, like many of his contemporaries, did not understand the meaning and the consequences of a constitution and its implementation, he sided with the constitutionalists and vigorously fought against the government troops.[51]

Some chroniclers of the Constitutional Revolution believe that Sattar Khan joined the constitutionalists because he hoped to avenge himself on the Qajar government for executing his elder brother Esma'il and for his own imprisonment as a young man. According to this version of events, he had been waiting night and day for a chance to fight the despotic government, and when he realized that the Iranian people had had enough of tyranny and despotism, he joined the constitutional forces.[52] Sattar Khan is also assigned, in these accounts, a desire to prove his boldness (*daliri*) and a fundamental belief in the wickedness of tyranny and the superiority of justice.[53] This is not surprising, since justice is, after all, one of the main attributes of good Islamic governance.[54] At the dawn of the Constitutional Revolution, 'justice' ('*adalat*) was demanded by the revolutionaries, the concepts of *mashruteh* or *mashrutiyat* (constitutionalism) being introduced about a year later.[55]

Many of the aforementioned characteristics attributed to Sattar Khan are typical for a *luti*, that is, a social bandit. In his work *Bandits*, Eric Hobsbawm defines 'social bandits' as robbers whom the population does not regard as ordinary criminals.[56] Owing to their image as helpers of the poor and sometimes even 'noble robbers',[57] they are distinguished from those criminals who merely care for their own survival. Although Hobsbawm only focuses on social bandits in rural societies, leaving out the urban equivalent,[58] some of his findings also apply to the kind of urban banditry described as *lutigari* in Iran. Bandits, says Hobsbawm, 'resist obedience, are outside the range of power, are potential exercisers of power themselves, and therefore potential rebels.'[59] Although banditry and rebellion seldom turned into revolution and social bandits hardly directed it, bandits sometimes joined revolutionary movements when they considered its motives to be just. In this case, 'the revolutionaries demonstrated their trustworthiness by unselfishness, self-sacrifice and devotion – in other words, by *their personal behaviour*.'[60]

In Iranian pre-industrial society, social banditry, often concentrated in the competing groups of Heydaris and Ne'matis,[61] was a common urban phenomenon. These bandits had their own code of conduct, they were loyal to the quarter of the town (*mahalleh*) to which they belonged, and committed their crimes mainly in enemy quarters.[62] Although they presumably based their ideals on *fotovvat/futuwwa* and *javanmardi* (movements or groups of young men who represented Islamic and pre-Islamic ideals of manhood), *luti*s quite frequently were ordinary thugs.[63] However, *luti*s could be respectable and disreputable people at the same time,[64] they could commit themselves to social justice and welfare and, simultaneously, engage in gambling and drinking.[65] Iranian *luti*s belonged to the urban poor, they adhered to Shiite Islamic values and related to pre-Islamic Iranian traditions that were based on an epic culture proclaiming virtues such as manliness and heroism.[66]

*Luti*s frequently earned their reputation as men of courage and prowess while fighting against the oppression of those in power. In this combat, they were often used by local high-ranking clerics or notables, for whom they worked as an executing force. It was a common scheme for *mujtahid*s or other local leaders to let the *luti*s cause social unrest and to employ them in civil war against government forces. Once these leaders had achieved their aims with the help of the *luti*s, they more often than not then rid themselves of the fighters[67] – as happened to the *mojahedin* themselves after the end of the revolution. Sattar Khan not only confirmed his talents as a *luti* in Azarbayjan, but also behaved as a typical *luti* when visiting the *'atabat* in Iraq. During the eleven months of civil war in Tabriz, he presumably had a spiritual, maybe even political, guide. Seqat al-Eslam, head of the Sheykhi community in Tabriz and a constitutionalist, allegedly impressed the advantages of a constitution on Sattar Khan and his comrades and is said to have been the leading figure behind the scene.[68] According to Fathi, when Sattar Khan prevented the surrender of Tabriz by taking down the white banners that had been raised by the inhabitants, he acted in agreement with Seqat al-Eslam.[69]

Together with other *luti*s, Sattar Khan took the opportunity provided by the constitutional movement to demonstrate his courage and his fighting skills and to prove himself to other strata of society, such as the middle-class intellectuals and pro-constitutionalist merchants.[70] As 'a successor to several generations of looties whose bravery and defiance of autocratic rule were living legends among the population of Tabriz' and benefiting from the 'looty myth', Sattar Khan was venerated by the masses, who even endorsed him with magical power.[71] However, it is not least due to Iranian intellectuals that Sattar

Khan survived, because they enforced the creation of his myth in their writings. A few examples may elucidate Sattar Khan's transfigured image as it was presented by his middle-class admirers: Kasravi, who as a young man witnessed the Constitutional Revolution, recounts the first time he set eyes on Sattar Khan in Tabriz. His description of the impression Sattar Khan made on him clearly reveals his admiration for the man, which is typical for his whole narrative:

> I remember very well how he cut his way through the crowd and, together with his followers, crossed the Artillery Square (*Meydan-e Tupkhaneh*) with his rifle in his hand and his boots on his feet. It was the first time that I saw him and I greatly admired his manly face (*chehreh-ye mardaneh*), his swiftness of posture (*chaboki-ye raftar*), and his self-control (*kh"ishtandari*).[72]

Malekzadeh describes the legendary hero as a last-minute saviour. At a time when the constitutionalists had lost all hope and the darkness of tyranny had taken hold of the town, one man arose:

> A man of slender build, tall, with a dark face, from among the ordinary people, who was totally unknown, and had earned his living with minor trading activities [sic!]. At the time, when the star of freedom rose above the horizon of Tabriz, he had shouldered his rifle and joined the *mojahedin* to defend fatherland and freedom, with unshakeable belief and pure at heart.[73]

Another ardent admirer of Sattar Khan was his adviser and constant companion Amirkhizi. In his account of his hero's life, Amirkhizi gives a whole list of, as he calls it, 'Sattar Khan's esteemed qualities and blessed manners' (*sefat-e pasandideh va khasayel-e setudeh-ye Sattar Khan*): proverbial were his boldness and bravery (*shoja'at va rashadat*); his determination (*'azm va eradeh*) never relented and he was like an iron mountain (*kuh-e ahanin*) to his comrades; although he excelled in his military command (*maharat dar fonun-e jang*) and was very brave, he never forgot that being considerate (*mora'at*) and cautious (*ehtiyat*) were important; he always spoke the truth (*dorost-qowli*), and distinguished himself by his gratitude (*haqq-shenasi*) and forbearance (*gozasht va eghmaz*), his remembrance of friends (*yad-e dustan*), his zeal (*ta'assob*), his justice (*ensaf*), and his compassion (*morovvat*). Added to these outstanding qualities are Sattar Khan's self-reliance (*e'temad beh nafs*) which helped him to stand firm even if attacked by a gang of 50; his patriotism (*hobb-e vatan*) that led him to idolize Iran; his religiousness (*tadayyon*), and his reliance on God's grace (*e'temad beh rahmat-e khodavand*).[74] This idealized portrait of Sattar Khan contrasts with other narratives that point to his more problematic features. However, although Safa'i, for example, characterizes Sattar Khan as haughty (*maghrur*) and boastful (*boland-parvaz*), he also mentions the fearlessness (*bibaki*), zeal (*ta'assob*), and the truthfulness (*sadaqat*) Sattar Khan showed in his fight for the constitutional cause.⁷⁵ And yet, as Ra'in points out, in spite of all those qualities that turned him into a hero, Sattar Khan was only human. Moreover, we might add, quoting from the reports cited by Browne,

> [t]here is no doubt that Sattár Khán deteriorated sadly during the latter part of the siege and afterwards. [...] But success spoiled him. He began to rob inoffensive citizens; his house was full of spoils; [...] he took to heavy drinking; he took unto himself many wives; he was no longer seen in the firing rank, but rested on his laurels in slothful ease. [...] After the siege his behaviour was disgraceful and he and Baqír [sic] Khán were largely responsible for the prolonged stay of the Russian troops.⁷⁶

These observances too might have been biased. In any case, they were made by an Englishman and, apparently, did not become part of the Persian narrative regarding Sattar Khan.

Conclusion: Sattar Khan as a *lieu de mémoire*

Looking at his biography, we may conclude that Sattar Khan was both local rascal or 'chivalrous brigand'⁷⁷ and a national hero and defender of the constitutional cause. Moreover, we might even say that he could only rise to the rank of national commander in Tabriz because he had, for the better part of his life, lived as a brigand in the hills and as a social bandit in town. Whatever the reasons, in a desperate situation Sattar Khan proved to be a man of exceptional talents and bravery who could convince the people of Tabriz to endure a civil war of eleven months and who was able to convince the *mojahedin* to continue fighting. To all appearances, he seems to have been the man of the hour who took his chances and rose to fame just when a man of his stature and talents – a fearless *luti* – was needed. Afterwards, Sattar Khan lost his glory and his success, apparently letting the less glorious aspects of his personality once again gain the upper hand. Also, when put into difficult situations which demanded political and diplomatic skills he did not possess – one only has to mention his disastrous governorship in Ardabil and his disappointment as a leading *mojahed* in Tehran –, Sattar Khan failed. Yet, the story of his life after the victory of the constitutionalists until his premature death in Tehran in 1914, at the age of 47, does not damage the mythical personage that was created in the collective Iranian mind. Sattar Khan still remained a symbol of the Constitutional Revolution, a long-lasting focal point of collective memory and identity, a *lieu de mémoire* for Iranians and students of Iranian history. The emphasis in the texts on his lowly origins and his illiteracy – a feature common to the majority of Iranians at the beginning of the twentieth century –, together with legends regarding his magnanimity and his protection of the poor and helpless, as well as his being a devout Shiite Muslim, all made him the ideal hero for the so-called masses. Sattar Khan represented masculine Muslim virtues – be they real or imagined – that made it easy for many people to identify with him. In this way, he gave meaning to a revolution whose political and intellectual aims many, among them Sattar Khan himself, could and did not fully understand.

According to Halbwachs, there exists a social milieu which marks the shape and content of collective memory. Regarding Iranian history, particularly the Constitutional Revolution and its significance for the development of Iranian nationalism, we have to take a closer look at the specific social milieu(s) responsible for the way the Constitutional Revolution has been remembered. One such milieu might be the 'ordinary people'. Yet, does what they remember about their involvement in the revolution and their local heroes really influence collective memory in an essential way? Hobsbawm argues that the only reason many bandits were remembered lastingly was that their memory was kept alive by rulers and their chroniclers.[78] In the case of Iran, most of the chroniclers of the Constitutional Revolution did not belong to a scholarly community wanting to 'provide a documentary record of the events'.[79] Instead, their narratives present the personal viewpoints and biased opinions of men who had often participated themselves in the events they describe and who sided with one or the other of the involved personalities or groups. It may well be that some of them began to write down what they remembered because they feared that 'what really happened' would otherwise be forgotten.[80] 'La mémoire ... se définit elle-même, du moins en première instance, comme lutte contre l'oubli', says Ricoeur,[81] so what we remember is merely the remains of a much larger entity.[82] States and their representatives often have an interest in keeping certain periods of history and specific events in the collective mind and in making sure that others are quickly forgotten. They usually try to establish an official or political memory, often based on history books and school textbooks, to assert their own historical version. In this way, some of the characters of an historical event may be remembered while others sink into oblivion. However, the latter may still become part of the collective remembrance if there exists a counter-memory,[83] protesting against the official version of a nation's past. In the case of Sattar Khan, it may be deduced that he counted among those who were and are remembered as heroes of the Constitutional Revolution by Iran's professional and non-professional historians,[84] and that an official memory made sure he was one of the characters to survive. Due to their narratives and not least due to the many photographs published in the relevant books, his face is one of those that represent the revolution.

CHAPTER 3

Introducing Georgian Sources for the Historiography of the Iranian Constitutional Revolution (1905–11)

Iago Gocheleishvili

The establishment of a government system based on a written constitution and an elected parliament that marked the beginning of the twentieth century in the history of Iran was an unprecedented democratic achievement that demonstrated, to use the words of Edward Browne, 'conspicuous advances in public spirit and morality made by the Persians in so short a time ... that parallels will not be easily found.'[1] The adoption of the constitution in 1906 was, indeed, an important milestone not only in the history of this country, but in the history of the Middle East in general. For Iran, it meant the prospect of greater advancements in the political, social, and economic aspects of the nation's life.

However, assembling a Majles and even adopting a constitution, as much as these were phenomena of historic importance, could not and did not bring, by themselves, a solution to the difficulties Iran faced at the time. The ascent of the new Shah, Mohammad Ali (r. 1907–09), took place against a background of continuous and increasing tension between the constitutionalists and the royalists. It was marked by an unsuccessful coup against the Majles attempted by the royalists and an equally unsuccessful attempt by the revolutionaries to assassinate the Shah. Finally, in June of 1908, the Majles was bombarded by the Persian Cossack Brigade, and some of the prominent constitutionalists were executed. Thus, less than two years after the inauguration of the constitution and parliament, the constitutional movement was in a desperate situation, with besieged Tabriz as the new centre of organized constitutional resistance.

The 'Gorjis' and the Transcaucasian Involvement in the Resistance

Unable to sustain the resistance on local resources alone, the Tabriz revolutionaries resorted to their international connections. Technical assistance and manpower requested and acquired from abroad by the Iranian constitutionalists not only played a decisive role in saving the Tabriz resistance from, probably, certain defeat, but it also made the composition of the constitutionalist forces even more diverse, and gave the movement truly international meaning.

The multinational and international nature of the revolution was one of its most striking characteristics. Speaking about the composition of the revolutionary forces, Vlasa Mgeladze (Tria), the Georgian member of the Tabriz constitutional resistance, wrote that the Iranian revolution brought together people of various nationalities and religions – Iranians, Azerbaijanis, Georgians, Armenians, and Jews – and brought them into the service of a common goal: the victory of constitutionalism in Iran.[2]

The Constitutional Revolution in Iran found sincere and passionate sympathy far beyond the borders of the country, but especially in neighbouring Transcaucasia, where anti-royalist revolutionary activities had existed for years. Indeed, the Transcaucasians constituted an absolute majority of the international members of the constitutional resistance movement in both the Azarbayjan and Gilan provinces of Iran.

The interaction of the Iranian constitutional resisters with neighbouring Transcaucasia was based on the historically close cultural and economic interaction between Iran and the Caucasus. By the beginning of the twentieth century, there was a rather large Iranian community in the Caucasus. According to the records of the general census, by the late nineteenth century Iranian subjects constituted 52.8 percent of the foreigners in the county of Tbilisi;[3] in Baku, by 1904, Iranian subjects constituted 22 percent of *all* workers.[4] Many of these Iranians working in the Caucasus and travelling between Iran and the Russian Empire became a live and mobile link that connected the Tbilisi, Baku, Tabriz, and Rasht revolutionary groups, which eventually made it possible for the Iranian resistance to secure continuous assistance from Transcaucasia throughout the course of the revolution. Transcaucasian involvement in the constitutional resistance became particularly active at one of the most crucial points of the revolution – when the Tabrizi resisters found themselves completely besieged by the royalist forces and confronted by the very real prospect of sharing the fate of the Majles. The Transcaucasian assistance to the Iranian constitutional resisters had two significant consequences for the revolution at that stage: (1) it protracted the Tabriz revolt, and, thus, kept the organized armed resistance in Iran alive; and (2) by prompting the takeover of Rasht it created conditions for the emergence of a new revolutionary front and the formation of a revolutionary army in the north of the country, which eventually resulted in the constitutionalists' march on Tehran that, with the support of the Bakhtiyari advance from the south, led to the establishment of constitutionalist control over the capital, Tehran. The Transcaucasian connections have been recognized by modern researchers and by the contemporaries of the events as one of the decisive factors in the progress of the Iranian Constitutional Revolution.[5] To quote Janet Afary, the road that connected Iran and Transcaucasia had become 'the lifeblood of the resistance through which a steady stream of food, supplies, ammunition' and manpower arrived in Iran.[6]

The most important centres of Transcaucasian assistance to the Iranian Constitutional Revolution were in Baku, Tbilisi, and Batumi.[7] In Tbilisi there were several groups recruiting volunteers for the Iranian resistance, including the Committee (or Centre) for the Assistance to the Persian Revolution run by the Iranian subjects who lived and worked in the Caucasus. The reports of the Tbilisi gendarmerie indicate that the principal members of this committee were Iranian subjects, namely the physician Nariman Narimanov, the carpet merchant Sadikhov, the leather merchants Alekperov and Rizaev, the tailor Mashhadi Mahmud, and the fruit merchants Taherzadeh and Akhundov.[8] The committee recruited individuals of different party affiliations as well as volunteers with no political affiliation. Apart from them, the Georgian Social Democrats, the Socialist Revolutionaries (SRs), and the Himmat organization, which was also connected to the Social Democrats, created their own groups of volunteers who consisted of the rank and file of their parties.[9] Groups sent from Tbilisi and Batumi were among the first reinforcement corps that the constitutional resisters in Tabriz received from the Caucasus. They were also most instrumental in the development of the uprising in the northern province of Gilan and in the takeover of Rasht.

The first corps of 'Gorjis' were sent from the Caucasus directly to Tabriz to reinforce the resistance from within.[10] From the end of autumn 1908, however, the Georgian revolutionaries started to arrive in northern Iran as well. As Georgian members of the Rasht resistance point out in their memoirs, after the first groups of the 'Gorjis' went to Tabriz, additional groups were sent to northern Iran with the specific goal of creating a new war front in the province of Gilan and engaging the Shah's supporters in the north of the country in order to prevent further concentration of the royalist army on Tabriz.[11]

The participation of the experienced and well-armed Georgian corps had a very significant impact on the course of the battles in Tabriz and Rasht. Speaking about the arrival of one of the Georgian groups in Tabriz, a contemporary points out that 'out of these hundred Georgians all were gallant fighters' who 'greatly mastered combat skills and methods of war' and 'the arrival of these brave men in Tabriz caused great delight among the *mojahedin*.'[12] The arrival of the Transcaucasians, then, also had a considerable psychological effect. According to another insider of the Tabriz resistance, the appearance of the Georgian Social Democrats at the constitutionalists' barricades in Tabriz inspired those hesitating over active involvement in the resistance and lifted the morale of those who were already participating in the revolution.[13]

Although it has been recognized that the Transcaucasian ties of the Constitutional Revolution and more generally the political influences from the Caucasus played an important role in promoting revolutionary ideas in Iran, especially in its northern provinces, and had a most significant impact on the course of the Tabriz resistance, the topic has, nevertheless, not yet been sufficiently studied in all its complexity. A comprehensive and all-inclusive study of the various aspects of the Transcaucasian connections of the Iranian Constitutional Revolution remains to be written.[14]

Georgian Sources and Their Place in the Historiography of the Revolution

Further attention needs to be paid not only to Georgian involvement in the revolution, but also to the Georgian sources for the historiography of the Iranian Constitutional Revolution. So far, use of the Georgian sources has been almost exclusively limited to use of one report by Vlasa Mgeladze that was published in 1910.[15] That is, however, only a small part of the material related to the Iranian Constitutional Revolution, and the participation of the international revolutionaries in it, which exists in the Georgian language. These materials primarily include:

1. The memoirs of the Georgian members of the constitutional resistance in Iran. Due to the participation of the Georgians in both the Azarbayjan and Gilan resistance movements, these memoirs address both the Tabriz and Rasht resistances, depicting also the takeover of Qazvin and the march on Tehran. Thus, the memoirs of Vlasa Mgeladze, Sergo Gagoshidze, and Davit Japaridze are primarily about the Tabriz resistance. Sergo Gamdlishvili, Apolon Japaridze, and Mikheil Bogdanov-Mariashkin address mainly the Gilan resistance.[16] These memoirs take the form of complete self-contained narratives, sometimes a war diary, that contain detailed and chronological depictions of various aspects of the resistance movement in Iran as well as information about individuals who participated in it.

2. Reports and letters of the Georgian correspondents who were in Iran during the revolution and sent their letters to various newspapers in Tbilisi.[17] These reports are shorter than memoirs and take the form of letters, usually titled 'Letters from Persia', 'Letters from Tabriz', and 'Letters from Rasht'. They are of an informative-descriptive nature and are first-hand and lively descriptions of the political and military developments in various parts of Iran during the revolution. Such letters sometimes cover only one specific event or issue, describing, for example, the opening of a hospital in Tabriz,

the funeral of a Transcaucasian member of the resistance killed in combat, or a demonstration held by the revolutionaries in Tabriz during the siege.[18] These materials are found dispersed in the Georgian printed media of the time through 1912.[19]

3. Newspaper columns titled, usually, 'Persia' or 'News from Persia', that contained information about developments in Iran combined with relatively lengthy editorial commentaries and political-analytical elaborations regarding various aspects of the Constitutional Revolution in Iran. Such columns appeared almost daily, sometimes several of them per issue, in the newspapers of the time – such as *Ali* (Flame), *Akhali Skhivi* (New Ray), *Chveni Sakme* (Our Cause), *Batumis Gazeti* (Batumi Newspaper), *Mertskhali* (Swallow), *Talgha* (Wave), *Isari* (Arrow), *Amirani*, *Chveni Khma* (Our Voice), *Imedi* (Hope), *Chveni Azri* (Our Thought), *Momavali* (Future), *Mnatobi* (Luminary), and others.[20] Numerous newspapers of all political leanings showed a lively interest in the problem of constitutionalism in Iran. The diversity of issues, even those of seemingly only secondary significance, the variety of perspectives, and the geographical range of events related to the Iranian revolution that a reader finds in these newspapers is quite impressive. Thus, the newspapers *Ali*, *Ekali*, *Amirani*, and *Imedi* wrote about international aspects of the revolution under the headings 'Persian Revolutionary Committee in Istanbul', 'Situation of Europeans in Tabriz', 'Sattar Khan and the Committee of the Young Turks', 'Persian Immigrants Protest Against Russia and England', 'Threat from Turkey', 'Reaction in Persia and the Russian Influence', and 'Anjoman Addresses Austria'.[21] These newspapers and others, such as *Droeba* (Epoch) and *Chveni Sakme*, informed people about developments in various places in Iran with articles titled 'Developments in Astara', 'Reasons for the Revolutionaries to Withdraw from Khoi', 'Developments on the Persian-Turkish Border', 'Letter of the People of Julfa', 'Who Controls the Town of Marand', and 'Popular Uprising in Rasht' along with numerous articles about events in Tabriz, Tehran, and other major cities of Iran.[22] Almost all newspapers featured information about announcements, appeals, and declarations made by groups and organizations in Iran and abroad related to the revolution. The newspapers also featured articles such as 'Letter from Women to the Revolutionaries', 'Shah's Message to the Revolutionaries of Shiraz', and 'Letter from the Clerics of Najaf'.[23] The columns appeared from the early stages of the revolution through 1911–12. Besides information and elaborations about Sattar Khan, Baqer Khan, the Shah, and the Transcaucasians operating in Iran, the newspapers featured texts of interviews, memoirs, or simply introductions of other figures involved in the revolution on either

side. For examples, *Ali* published the 'Conversation with Colonel Liakhov', *Sakhalkho Gazeti* published 'Memoirs of Yeprem Khan' and 'Activities of Rahim Khan in Persia', *Ekali* and *Imedi* wrote about the personality and activities of 'Eyn al-Dowleh and his relation to the revolution and the Shah, and *Imedi* even wrote about the governor of the town of Marand.[24]

4. Archival materials. The former 'Party Archive' holds interesting, and previously in part classified, materials about the activities of the Transcaucasian revolutionary groups related to the Iranian Constitutional Revolution. These contain reports about the accomplishment of missions and other documentation that might not have been known and recorded by other sources. These materials also provide valuable information about the identities of various Transcaucasian and Iranian-subject revolutionaries working in Transcaucasia and Iran. Because of persecution, which only increased after the Transcaucasians became involved in the constitutional movement in Iran, many of the revolutionaries at the time had several identities. For example, Apolon Japaridze, the Georgian member of the Rasht resistance, used the name Mikhail Tratiants as his alias, and in many Georgian and Persian sources he is referred to by this name – Misha (short for Mikhail). His real name only became known, even to many of his comrades, years after the revolution.[25] This sometimes makes it extremely difficult for a scholar to identify these individuals, and unfortunately the real names of many of the revolutionaries still remain unknown. Therefore, the materials of the former 'Party Archive' still require further study with regard to this issue.

The other collection of archival materials consists of those preserved in the State Archive of Georgia. These materials contain records of the administrative, military, and police authorities of Georgia of the time. The command of the Russian troops in Iran was supervised by the Viceroy of the Caucasus, based in Tbilisi, and naturally, the administration of the region was taking measures to prevent the Transcaucasians from assisting the Iranian resisters with supplies and manpower. Therefore, the reports of the gendarmerie officers in Tbilisi and other cities of Georgia of the time contain information on the transportation of supplies and ammunition, safe places, names, and activities of individuals, both Russian subjects and Iranian subjects, related to the revolution in Iran. These materials are also a good source for establishing the identities of local revolutionaries and their political and professional backgrounds, which might not have been recorded in the 'Party Archive', especially if the individuals were not members of the Social Democrat Party or the groups affiliated with it. The opening of archives made a wealth of invaluable materials and first-hand participant accounts related to the constitutional movement in Iran available to the scholarly community.

Unfortunately, most of the materials under discussion have not been thoroughly compiled and published in full, even in Georgian.[26] None of them has ever been published in English, and they still are not available to the broad scholarly community.

These sources provide interesting and unique insights regarding the ethnic, confessional, social, and political composition of the Transcaucasian volunteer groups joining the resistance. They represent an invaluable source for understanding who actually was behind the term *Qafqaziyan* (Caucasians), the term used in Persian and foreign sources even in reference to the Iranian migrants returning to Iran together with the Transcaucasian revolutionaries. How different or similar various groups of these Transcaucasians were; what agendas they pursued in Iran; how different or similar their agendas were compared to that of the local constitutionalists; if and how these differences affected the course of the uprising in Azarbayjan and Gilan; what the correlation was between foreign interference and local revolutionary activity in the commencement and progress of the movement in northern Iran: these are some of the questions these sources help to answer. They also allow scholars to look – in a way based on accounts of primary sources, and not based on assumptions – at the reasons and motivations behind the involvement of various Transcaucasian groups in the Iranian resistance and to study whether and how they differed from group to group.

Although most of the more commonly known sources tend to focus on the development of the Tabriz revolt and the events in Tehran, it was the movement in Gilan that eventually led to the victory of the constitutionalists in their battle against Mohammad Ali Shah. Therefore, the study of the movement in northern Iran is of essential importance for the history of the Iranian Constitutional Revolution, and the particular concentration of the Georgian sources on the movement in northern Iran makes them of special value. Emphasizing the differences between the development of the resistance in Azarbayjan on the one hand, and in northern Iran on the other hand, Ahmad Kasravi mentions in *Tarikh-e hejdah saleh-ye Azarbayjan* that 'the Gilan revolt was planned in the Caucasus and was executed by the volunteers' (i.e., the Transcaucasian volunteers).[27] The Georgian sources provide a large volume of detailed accounts that address the Rasht uprising specifically. They describe the arrival of Transcaucasian and international revolutionaries in Gilan, the preparation for the uprising, the takeover of Rasht, and the emergence of the new revolutionary front in the north of the country. Even the facts of the Transcaucasian participation in the resistance recorded in other sources appear in Georgian sources with more details and elaboration. The memoirs of Apolon

Japaridze and Gurji Sergo complete accounts of other Persian and Armenian sources with new and interesting insights into the role of the Transcaucasians in the operation of the joint revolutionary committee in Rasht and their impact on shaping its strategies and priorities. They provide insights into strategies, military force, and the position of various local groups on the possible uprising by the time of the arrival of the Transcaucasians; they also reflect on the relation and collaboration of the local Iranian and Armenian groups with each other and with the Transcaucasians.[28] For instance, Gurji Sergo describes the meeting held between the Iranian, local Armenian, and Transcaucasian revolutionary groups to discuss and finalize the plan for the takeover of Rasht. With characteristic straightforwardness the author describes the escalation of tensions between the parties which resulted in one of the groups leaving the meeting, nearly causing the uprising to fail.[29] The author then proceeds with a detailed depiction of how the takeover of Rasht was executed. He even names the people involved and describes weapons used in two separate attacks launched by the constitutionalists on that day – one on the governor's palace in Rasht, and the other on the governor's residence outside the town.[30] Apolon Japaridze and Bogdanov-Mariashkin, also participants in the Rasht resistance, provide similar descriptions of this event, but with fewer details.[31]

Thus, use of the Georgian sources pertaining to the resistance in Gilan is essential for the study of the progress of the constitutional resistance. As for the accounts of the Georgian resisters regarding the Tabriz revolt, their particular value is that they provide a better understanding of the international aspects of the Tabriz resistance, as they often focus in detail and with particular attention on what other sources only mention or touch on in general. On the whole, these materials shed light on some facts related to the revolution that are unknown from other accounts, and also allow us to look from a new perspective at what has already been described in other sources, perhaps providing an opportunity to re-evaluate some of the existing opinions.[32]

An important advantage of the sources under discussion is that they reflect not only on how Transcaucasian involvement influenced the course of the revolution in Iran, but also on how and to what extent the Iranian Constitutional Revolution influenced Transcaucasia, especially its political organizations and their interaction with each other. Accounts of the Georgian members of the resistance reveal that the slogans and goals of the Iranian revolution had truly reached across political, ethnic, and social divides and made it possible for people of different, sometimes even hostile, political persuasions, social status, and ethnicity, even outside Iran, to come together for the sake of collaboration, which eventually resulted in the formation of one of the most disciplined, serried, and efficient military forces in the resistance, both in Azarbayjan and Gilan, during the revolution. Thus, the memoirs of Apolon Japaridze and other

Georgian participants in the Iranian resistance show that the groups sent to Tabriz and Rasht consisted of Mensheviks like Vlasa Mgeladze, Bolsheviks like Misha Dzagania, and SRs like Grigol Emkhvari; among them were Georgians like Mikheil Asatiani and Lado Dumbadze, Armenians like Vano Karapetov, Azerbaijanis like Pasha 'Bakoeli' (i.e., from Baku), and Jews like Mikheil Bogdanov-Mariashkin; representatives of the nobility like Apolon Japaridze, representatives of the middle-level bureaucracy like Iakob Metreveli, and representatives of the peasantry like Sepe Gabichvadze. The very description of Bogdanov-Mariashkin's arrival in Iran represents an example of successful interparty and inter-ethnic cooperation. Sent to Iran by the Socialist Revolutionary Party, he received necessary arms from the Armenian and Georgian Bolsheviks, travelled to Baku together with western Georgian Social Democrats – most probably Mensheviks –, was met in Baku by Azerbaijani Social Democrat activists, transported into Iran through the efforts of the Iranian constitutionalists, and fought in the Rasht resistance alongside anarchists, SRs, Mensheviks, and Bolsheviks, as well as individuals with no formal party affiliation.[33]

In the realities of the Transcaucasia of the time, torn by recurrent and violent clashes between the Armenian and Muslim communities on the one hand, and escalating political division among the Bolsheviks, Mensheviks, Anarchists, and SRs on the other hand, such collaboration was a striking phenomenon of great significance and symbolism. Contemporaries seem to have well understood its importance, as demonstrated in Tria's essay reflecting on the unifying effect of the Iranian Constitutional Revolution, which states that 'the Persian revolution accomplished a miracle – nations ... united for the sake of peace against the common foe.'[34] This statement, coming from a Social Democrat, gains particular meaning considering the fact that ethnic violence in various places of the Caucasus undermined the very existence of revolutionary parties such as the Social Democrat Party, whose rank and file, as well as its leadership, featured quite impressive ethnic diversity.

The idea of internationalism was not strange to the Transcaucasian organizations of the time, as it had long been promoted and used by the worker groups at oil refineries, railway depots, and various factories in the Caucasus as well as by the local Social Democrat organizations. But it was the Iranian Constitutional Revolution that managed to overcome, at least temporarily, not only the ethnic and social but the political boundaries as well. Not even the common antagonism of the involved parties towards the Tsarist regime had such an impact on their interaction.

However, the impact of the Iranian revolution on the interaction between the Transcaucasian political parties should not be overestimated. Hostility between the political parties and organizations in the Caucasus continued to escalate, especially so between the Bolsheviks and Mensheviks. Its outcome was to determine the political future of the region. The Mensheviks became particularly well established in Georgia. After the split within the Social Democrats, the Mensheviks were rapidly becoming the dominant majority among the Georgian Social Democrats, particularly among their leadership. By the time of the Tabriz revolt, the majority of the Social Democrats in Georgia – the Social Democrat committees of Tbilisi, Batumi, etc. – were of the Menshevik persuasion.[35] The Bolsheviks, on the other hand, who according to their own accounts had been widely defeated in Georgia by the Mensheviks in the battle for popular support, eventually had to move their centre to Baku, where they felt much more confident in their strength.[36] 'Comrade Sergo' (Grigol Sergo Orjonikidze) and his fellow Bolsheviks, such as Lado Ketskhoveli, Avel Enukidze, and Soso Jughashvili (Joseph Stalin), came to power in Georgia only after and as a result of Georgia's occupation by the 11th Red Army of then already Bolshevik Russia. In Iran too the relation between the Mensheviks and Bolsheviks seems to have been rather tense at times. Describing the interaction between the Menshevik Mgeladze and Bolshevik Orjonikidze, two Georgian revolutionaries in Rasht, a contemporary recalls that 'there was not a single evening when discussion between them had not turned into argument, and, every time, I thought they would part as enemies tomorrow.'[37] The confrontation between these two men was to become symbolic with regard to the fate of their motherland, as Mgeladze, the member of the Menshevist government, would lead the independent Democratic Republic of Georgia in 1918–21, while Sergo Orjonikidze would lead the forceful 'sovietization' of Georgia following the Russian Red Army's invasion of the country which abolished the independent republic and forced the Georgian government, including Mgeladze, into permanent exile.

Iran and the Revolution Through the Words of the 'Gorjis'

Particularly interesting are the sources under discussion for understanding how the Iranian Constitutional Revolution was seen by its Transcaucasian participants, and what they deemed to be major peculiarities of the movement in different regions in Iran. Especially interesting in this regard are the memoirs of Gurji Sergo, who starts his narrative with an analysis of the political, economic, and social situation in Iran, the impact of external and internal factors on its current status, and the differences between the revolutionary movements in northern Iran on the one hand, and in Azarbayjan on the other. The author believes, for example, that unlike the Tabriz revolution, which was of an actual popular nature and was driven mostly by dedicated popular figures, the movement in Gilan was shaped under the great influence of local khans and various groups with their own priorities and agendas, and that because of that, before the arrival of international revolutionaries in Gilan, the movement in northern Iran was prevented from developing as rapidly and vastly as it did in Azarbayjan.[38]

Who Were the 'Qafqaziyan'?

The arrival of individuals from the Caucasus continued throughout the course of the revolution. The visible and apparent presence of Transcaucasians in the areas controlled by the constitutionalists is noted not only by Iranian, Armenian, and Georgian contemporaries, but by Russian and British observers as well. A British diplomat travelling from Baku to Tehran recalled that 'on the Tehran road for a hundred miles' he constantly 'found Caucasians reinforcing their positions. There were no barricades, but they had dug trenches... . I counted sixty of them [i.e., Caucasians] on the road, ... and saw an advanced detachment of 30 more people... . They all appeared to be Caucasians', concludes the author.[39] Evgenii Sablin, a Russian official in Tehran at the time, also reported that Russian subjects returning from Iran to Russia asked for the travel documents required by the Shah's authorities only to reach the town of Karaj (a city located about 40 kilometres west of Tehran), as 'after that station they don't have anything to fear' because, as Sablin cited the Russian travellers, '[from] there all the way to Rasht stand our countrymen; it is like travelling in the Caucasus.'[40] Although to locals and to foreign observers these Transcaucasian volunteers might have appeared to be a rather homogeneous group, they differed greatly from each other in their ethnicity, political convictions, and motives for getting involved in the Iranian resistance.[41] As the numbers of Transcaucasians in the constitutional resistance increased, the diversity in the composition of their forces grew as well. The very manner of their recruitment in the Caucasus explains why and how they differed from each other. After the commencement of the Tabriz revolt, the Transcaucasian Regional Social Democrat Committee directly suggested to the local committees that they 'intervene in the affairs in Persia'.[42] Following this suggestion, the local party organizations started a selective process for recruiting, from the party's rank and file, politically reliable and conscious individuals who were 'loyal and experienced workers'. This resulted in the formation of serried groups of individuals charged with the ideology of their parties and driven in their actions in Iran by class consciousness and clearly defined political motives. Individuals such as the Menshevik Mgeladze, the Social Democrat Gurji Sergo, the Socialist Revolutionary Bogdanov-Mariashkin, judging by their memoirs, are very obvious representatives of this group. After the takeover of Tehran by the constitutionalists, and following the exacerbation of political differences between the factions of the

Iranian constitutionalists as well as the development of differences between the Transcaucasian Social Democrats and the Iranian constitutionalists, these revolutionaries left Iran. To use the wording of the resolution adopted by the Georgian revolutionaries, they departed 'in order not to complicate their [i.e., the Iranians'] affairs by our presence here'.[43] Mgeladze, reflecting on the decision of the Dashnaks to take over the financial and police offices under the new constitutionalist government, considers that it was a mistake on the part of the revolutionary group.[44]

Alongside the party organizations of Transcaucasia, the Iranian merchants working in various cities of the Caucasus conducted a recruitment process of their own, resulting in recruitment of a different sort of volunteers for the constitutional resistance in Iran. Among the Georgian recruits, Sergo Gagoshidze is an example of such a volunteer. A former assistant commander of an artillery company in the Russian Tsarist Army, Gagoshidze had a family member affiliated with the Social Democrat Party, but was not himself a member of any political organization and had never participated in underground revolutionary activities.[45] He was recruited by Iranian merchants in Tbilisi because of his artillery skills and military experience. Gagoshidze fought in the Tabriz resistance – and, reportedly, was on close terms with Sattar Khan – but his memoirs, though sympathetic towards the Iranian constitutionalists, lack politically charged statements or critical assessments of the social and political situation in Iran, which distinguishes them in a very apparent way from those of, for example, the Social Democrats Gurji Sergo and Tria. In the case of the Georgians, most of such individuals usually ended up in groups of their countrymen formed and controlled by one of the Transcaucasian political organizations.

Another group of Transcaucasians who started to appear in Iran after the initial successes of the constitutionalists, but differed from the two groups mentioned above in their social composition and in their attitude towards political issues, were the *qochi*s, the roughs recruited in Baku by the Iranian activists operating in the Caucasus. Gurji Sergo, who appears to be very hostile to these 'cut-throats of no political persuasion', reports the arrival of 300 of these men from Baku in Rasht, after the town came under constitutionalist control. He portrays them as a force somewhat similar to the roughs of Tehran, who lacked political commitment and, at various times, worked for different sides during the revolution.[46] The presence of a group like the *qochi*s, though they were at odds with the party-affiliated and politically driven Transcaucasian volunteers, certainly served as a justification for the claims of the Russian authorities that the Transcaucasians had arrived in Iran in search of 'adventure and easy spoils'. Unlike most of their fellow Transcaucasians sent to Iran and controlled by political organizations, the *qochi*s stayed in Iran after the restoration of the constitutionalist governance in Tehran and, unwilling to leave the country, participated in the disturbances and shootouts which erupted in Tehran between factions of the Iranian constitutionalists.

On the Nature of the 'Mission' in Iran

The sources also shed light on how the Transcaucasians saw themselves in the revolution and what they deemed to be their role in its events. Because of the diversity among the Transcaucasian participants in the resistance, the statements of the Georgian sources regarding the feelings and motives of Transcaucasians participating in the resistance do not uniformly apply to all Transcaucasian volunteers in Tabriz and Rasht. Close examination of the writings of the Georgian resisters reveals that their statements mostly reflect the position of their immediate environment within specific groups. Bogdanov-Mariashkin, a Tbilisi SR and member of the 'Gorjis' in the Rasht resistance, wrote in his memoirs that they 'had arrived to render revolutionary help to the Iranian people. Each one of us had an extraordinary sense of responsibility to the Iranian people and to the parties that had sent us. We considered our participation in the Iranian revolutionary movement as our revolutionary virtue, our pride and conscience'. 'Victory or Death' was our motto', adds the author.[47] Another member of the Rasht resistance, the Georgian Social Democrat Gurji Sergo, wrote in 1910 that 'Tabriz's desperate situation, her selfless struggle and plight ... ignites a flame of sympathy ... in the Caucasians' and 'they enrol in corps of fighters and, together with the Azarbayjanis, ... they fight for the good of Iran, fight to save long-suffering Iran from the clutches of the enemy.' 'Many of the Transcaucasians went immediately to Tabriz and Rasht and gave their lives for the movement,' concludes the author.[48] The report of Tria, the Georgian Menshevik and participant in the Tabriz resistance, concludes by assuring the reader that the 'participation of the Caucasian revolutionaries in the Persian revolution is a vivid example of the fraternal help of one nation to another in the fight against oppression.'[49] In fact, the Georgian participants in the resistance in Iran called themselves 'internationalists', implying thus the nature of their presence in Iran.[50] The words of these Georgian sources are echoed in an article published in the Persian newspaper *Mosavat*, which describes in a very explicit way how the people of Tbilisi sympathized with the resisters in Tabriz.[51] Reflecting on the relations between the Iranian and the Transcaucasian revolutionaries in Tabriz, Kasravi also emphasizes the atmosphere of solidarity, mutual respect, and consideration between the Iranian and the Transcaucasian constitutionalists.[52]

Although the Transcaucasians might have deemed their participation in the revolution as simple 'fraternal help' motivated by class interests and solidarity, and only intended to assist the Iranian constitutionalists' struggle, accounts in the Georgian sources reveal that as the number and the influence of the Transcaucasians in Tabriz and Rasht increased, their role ceased to be of a purely tactical and auxiliary importance and nature. The representatives of the Transcaucasians were on revolutionary committees in Tabriz and Rasht, they participated in the meetings where the strategy and tactics of the resistance took shape, and they soon had become a force to be reckoned with. The leadership of the Transcaucasian parties sending their men to the Iranian resisters started to see their representatives in Iran as a medium for influencing the decision-making process in the local revolutionary committees in Iran regarding not only military but also political issues and matters of general strategy. With years of experience in conducting revolutionary activities and with invaluable experience gained in the anti-Tsarist revolt in western Georgia and the 1905 Russian Revolution, the Transcaucasian revolutionary groups perhaps believed that they had a lot to share with the Iranian resisters. For this to be implemented, first, the Transcaucasians needed to have in Iran not simply experienced fighters, but politically and theoretically well-prepared leaders who would work in Iran in accordance with the party programme. Secondly, it required effective coordination among those Transcaucasian volunteers in Tabriz and Rasht who were affiliated with the Transcaucasian political organizations.[53] It did not take the Transcaucasian revolutionary organizations long to take measures towards achieving the goal of establishing control over their corps in Iran, making sure that their activities in Iran were conducted according to the directives from the Caucasus.[54] The Social Democrat Tria stated that besides groups of 'the best technicians and the reservists, who had completed military service' 'the Caucasian Regional Committee [i.e., that of the Social Democrats] sent one of its members in the capacity of a leader of the Caucasian revolutionaries' as the number of Transcaucasians in Tabriz continued to grow.[55] Apolon Japaridze's account reveals that, for the same purpose, a Social Democrat, Valiko (Batumeli), who, according to Japaridze, 'was well-versed and politically prepared', was sent to Rasht.[56] Bogdanov-Mariashkin, who described the activities of the revolutionaries in Qazvin after the takeover of the city, noted in his memoirs that 'groups of fighters and weapons were not all that was sent from Azerbaijan and Georgia', and 'they were sending propagandists as well to work with the people.'[57] What made the coordination of Georgian revolutionaries arriving in Iran from various places in the Caucasus a feasible task was the fact that, due to the language barrier and differences with the local ethnic groups in Iran, they ended up together. At the same time, the arrival of the Transcaucasian revolutionaries in Iran was the result of collaboration between various political organizations, which made the coordination between the Transcaucasians – mostly Azerbaijanis and Georgians – possible.[58]

The arrival of Bogdanov-Mariashkin, the Tbilisi Jewish SR in Gilan, which was arranged through collaboration among the Georgian, Armenian, and Azerbaijani Socialist Revolutionaries, Bolsheviks, and Mensheviks, with the support of an 'inter-party committee which included the Iranian revolutionaries as well', is one such case.[59]

Accounts by the Georgian members of the resistance that describe the participation of the Georgians and the Transcaucasians in the meetings of the revolutionary committees in Tabriz and Rasht not only reveal that the Transcaucasians did intervene in the decision-making process, but they also allow us to glimpse the possible agenda that the Transcaucasian parties attempted to enforce, or at least promote, in Iran. Tria, for example, describes how the Transcaucasian revolutionaries prevented attempts by the Russian consul in Tabriz to persuade Sattar Khan and the Tabriz *anjoman* to engage in negotiations with the royalists.[60] In Rasht, as the accounts of Gurji Sergo reveal, the Transcaucasian revolutionaries, dissatisfied with the passiveness of the local constitutionalists, formed a revolutionary committee of their own and put pressure on the local committee to act according to what the Transcaucasians believed was immediately necessary for the progress of the revolution.[61]

In general, it seems that the Transcaucasians were arguing for a more proactive and uncompromising stance, sometimes more radical than that of the local Iranian and Armenian revolutionaries.[62] Such a position is clearly voiced in the writings of Gurji Sergo, who appears to be one of the most ardent proponents of an active and armed disobedience to the royalist governance in northern Iran. He sought action just like that in Tabriz, which he seems to have seen as an example for other revolutionary forces in Iran to follow. Small-scale revolutionary activities in Rasht and other places in the country – besides Tabriz, that is –, though existent, were usually limited to the formation of secret *anjomans* and the holding of clandestine meetings, which did not seem adequate to the Transcaucasians for the needs of the revolution. They also called for a very cautious and uncompromising approach to the royalists. With their experience dealing with the Tsarist government in their motherland, they were always concerned that any royalist proposition to initiate negotiations was simply an attempt to win time and mislead the resisters. That is why the Transcaucasians were so explicitly and decisively against the negotiations between the constitutionalists and the royalists mediated by the Russian consul in Tabriz, and they made every effort to 'expose the intrigues' of the Russian authorities in Iran.[63]

The mention of Russia and 'the Russian authorities' intrigues' in Tria's essay is not accidental. For many Transcaucasians and other Russian-subject revolutionaries – mostly those who were affiliated with political parties – participation in the Iranian revolution appeared, in a way, as a continuation of their fight against the Russian Tsarist regime. Russian and Iranian royalty were seen as related powers, the impact of the Russian revolutionary uprising on the progress of the anti-royalist movement in Iran was not in doubt, the influence of the Russian Court on the Shah did not seem to be a matter of doubt either, and the activation of anti-constitutionalist reaction in Iran was seen as a consequence of the successes of anti-revolutionary reaction in the Russian Empire. The presence of the Russian factor in the Transcaucasians' argumentation regarding the Iranian revolution and the speculations on the role of Russia in the developments in Iran find their most vivid manifestation in the writings of those Georgian resisters who were party members. These authors invariably condemn the Russian government for its direct interference in Iran's affairs and for its attempt to restore the old order in Iran in order to protect Russia's political and economic privileges in the country. Thus, the Social Democrat Tria and the SR Bogdanov-Mariashkin point out in their memoirs that the Shah's actions against the Majles were consequent on the strengthening of the reaction in Russia, and were the result of the Russian government advising and supporting the Shah in his actions.[64] Tria is indignant at the actions in Iran of the Russian Colonel Liakhov who, in Tria's words, 'destroyed the Majles to the ground and erected scaffolds instead'. He is outraged by how many in Iran 'fell martyr to Russian arms'.[65] Bogdanov-Mariashkin, speaking of Russian enterprises in Iran, compares them to leeches that 'have stuck to the tormented body of the Iranian people and sucked blood out of it.'[66] A close reading of the writings of these revolutionaries leads to a conclusion that after the failed 1905 anti-Tsarist uprising in Russia, they viewed the Iranian revolution as an opportunity to strike again against the same enemy, but this time on a different field. It should not be forgotten that many of these Transcaucasian volunteers were young individuals who had left their families, abandoned their noble privileges, and withdrawn from universities to join the underground revolutionary movement in their motherland.[67] They were imbued with ideas of the universality of the revolutionary process and believed in revolutionary internationalism as the way to its eventual victory. Many among them seem to have hoped that the victory of the revolution in neighbouring Iran would be an important step towards the victory of the revolutionary process in their motherland.[68] Interestingly, this vision was shared by the radical part of Russia's reactionary forces. They saw the events in Iran in a very similar way – i.e., as a preparation for the next uprising in the Russian Empire – and openly urged the Russian government to take decisive measures against the Transcaucasian participants in the Iranian revolution, even if it would mean intervening in Iran's affairs. Many of the Russian reactionaries argued that if the revolution in Iran succeeded, 'the Caucasian convicts' would try to repeat 'their beloved 1905 in their motherland' (i.e., the Caucasus and the Russian Empire).[69]

From the elaborations that are found in the memoirs of various Georgian resisters, it also appears that they saw their collaboration with the Iranian constitutionalists as a struggle against a common class enemy. Many of the Georgian revolutionaries still had fresh memories of the massive peasant uprising in the western Georgian province of Guria, which had led to the formation of the peasant-run independent 'Gurian Republic'.[70] The issue of the peasants and the poor is emphasized in the Georgian sources with regard to Iran as well. These sources invariably dedicate attention to the depiction of the extreme economic plight and lack of rights of the Iranian poor, which they had previously known about from the numerous Iranian migrants in the Caucasus and later witnessed during their activities in Iran. Describing the town of Julfa, on the Iranian side of the border, the Menshevik Vlasa Mgeladze describes 'oppressed and impoverished street sellers and workmen sitting in their clay huts. Nearby, rag-clad and half-naked peasants walk in the street... . Dear God. The khans here have taken everything from them, and enslaved them body and soul. These chains of slavery must be broken, and, yes, it is worth participating in the fight for that', concludes the author.[71] Gurji Sergo also seems to be indignant about the local khans who, in his words, 'even today are the same bloodthirsty feudal lords that they were a hundred years ago.'[72] The SR Bogdanov-Mariashkin, describing Rasht, writes that

> There are numerous huts of the poor in the town. Next to horrific poverty one can observe luxurious villas with splendid pools, wonderful orchards, buildings erected in an oriental style with colourful mosaics. In the town and in the bazaar there are uncountable numbers of poor clad in rags. They beg for alms. It is shocking to see this.[73]

These revolutionaries came to Iran with a clear sense of class distinction and of the difference between the interests of various classes; for them, the revolution was a fight against the ruling classes – royalty and those supporting it, the nobility and the clergy.[74] Although social diversity within the revolutionary forces was not uncommon for the Transcaucasians, the role and place of various social groups in the revolutionary movement they witnessed in Iran was different from their experience in the Caucasus, especially with regard to the role of the peasantry.[75] This was especially so for the Georgian revolutionaries who had witnessed the formation of a 'Peasant Republic' governed by peasant councils in western Georgia, which was in contrast to the situation in Iran, where the peasantry showed relatively lower levels of class-consciousness and activism. Many of the Transcaucasians also looked with distrust and suspicion on the Iranian khans participating in the movement. These feelings of distrust and suspicion were voiced by Gurji Sergo, for whom the feud of these khans with the Shah did not represent proof of their dedication to the complete abolition of the monarchy and the removal of the political and economic privileges of the ruling classes in Iran. Members of the nobility among the Transcaucasian revolutionaries had renounced their noble status, privileges, wealth, and even family connections; they had participated in various activities against the Tsarist authorities; they had been part of the revolutionary underground even though it cost them their well-being and, sometimes, their lives; they had effectively alienated themselves from the ruling class and thus assimilated themselves to the revolutionary masses. The Iranian khans participating in the movement, by contrast, had not abandoned their status and appeared to be fighting not against *how* the country was ruled but just against *who* was ruling the country. Their dedication to the revolution and to the interests of the lower social classes, which they claimed to be protecting, was in doubt, especially in a crucial situation when the survival of the revolution would require these khans to compromise their personal interests. That appears to be the explanation for why the attitude of Gurji Sergo and, probably, of other more radical Transcaucasian revolutionaries towards the Iranian khans participating in the revolution was one of distrust and was different from their attitude towards Transcaucasian noblemen who participated in the revolutionary movement. Thus, almost all of the Georgian sources point out that Sepahdar and Moʻezz al-Soltan, the revolutionary leaders in Gilan, had previously been in the service of the Shah and had only later, because of personal feuds with the royal authorities, joined the revolution. However, given that in Iran the role of the classes as the driving or leading force of the movement often shifted, the Transcaucasian volunteers and commanders had to accept the khans and the clergy as integral parts of the revolutionary movement.

As mentioned above, the Russian revolutionary organizations were rather enthusiastic in getting their rank and file involved in the Constitutional Revolution in Iran. One of the factors that explains this willingness to send their men abroad is the very state of the revolutionary movement in the Russian Empire at the time. Although still alive, the revolutionary movement in most of Russia had been suppressed and driven deep underground by executions and imprisonments. The crisis facing the revolutionary organizations was exacerbated by the growing disillusionment among their members, who had been deserting the parties. Underlining the decline of the revolutionary movement in the Russian Empire, Tria admits in his essay that the invitation of the Iranians to 'help out' the constitutionalists in Tabriz came to the leadership of the revolutionary organizations in Russia – particularly the leadership of the Social Democrats – as a much-needed opportunity to shake up their rank and file, to keep them involved in a movement that still promised to succeed, and to maintain the revolutionary spirit until the opportunity for action in Russia came again. Importantly, it was also a way of keeping their members safe from

Tsarist persecution, although it meant that they were then at a much greater risk of being killed by Russian troops on the border or by Russian Cossacks and Iranian soldiers in Iran.

Although the Transcaucasian revolutionaries had a good understanding of the domestic and international importance of the Constitutional Revolution in Iran, their knowledge of the actual state of revolutionary activities in various parts of Iran other than Tabriz was not particularly accurate, as it was, judging by the sources, mostly gleaned from information provided by the Iranian recruiters which, the Georgian sources claim, was at times neither adequate nor realistic. Gurji Sergo wrote in his memoir that the Transcaucasians arriving in northern Iran were soon forced to realize that, contrary to the words of the Iranian activists operating in the Caucasus, there were no large numbers of armed fighters in Rasht ready for immediate military engagement with the royalists; there were not sufficient weapons to make the uprising feasible, even with the participation of the newly arrived Transcaucasians; and there was no one united revolutionary force in Rasht.[76] Instead, there were two major groups that the Transcaucasians worked with: the group of Iranian constitutionalists led by Mo'ezz al-Soltan and the group of Armenian Dashnaks, who, according to the author, did not necessarily have the same agenda as the former. Gurji Sergo elaborates that the difficulties were further exacerbated by the fact that the information coming to the Transcaucasians from the local Iranian revolutionaries on the one hand, and from the local Dashnaks on the other hand, was contradictory, which caused frustration among the Transcaucasian volunteers, so that many of them soon chose to return to their motherland.[77] The depiction of the problems of the constitutional underground in Rasht might have been exaggerated in Sergo's accounts, but it undoubtedly demonstrates, on the one hand, the lack of preparedness and organization of the constitutionalists in northern Iran at the time of the arrival of the first Transcaucasian corps, and, on the other hand, the unawareness on the part of the Transcaucasians of the actual nature and scale of the revolutionary movement in various places in Iran.

From Tbilisi and Baku to Tabriz and Rasht: Making of the 'Lifeblood of the Revolution'

The revolutionaries in Tbilisi and Baku were repeatedly visited by representatives of the Iranian constitutionalists, such as Heydar Khan and Karim Khan, who are well known from other sources. The accounts of the Georgian sources, especially those preserved in the archives of Georgia, also shed light on the activities of another group of Iranians – those who resided, worked, and had their businesses in Tbilisi, Baku, Batumi, and other places of the Caucasus, and supported the constitutional movement from their bases in Transcaucasia.[78] These Iranians – especially merchants and business owners – played an important role not only in recruiting the volunteers but also in funding their transportation to Iran and in securing the supply of ammunition to the Azarbayjan and Gilan resisters. Gagoshidze, who as becomes clear from his memoirs, was recruited by such individuals operating in Tbilisi, describes a meeting he had with Iranian merchants before travelling to Tabriz.[79] Gurji Sergo too underlines the fact that the Iranians operating in the Caucasus played an important role in 'getting the Caucasians involved in the events in Persia'.[80]

The sources under discussion also contain factual material regarding various technical aspects of the organization and execution of Transcaucasian assistance to the Iranian constitutionalists. For example, the Menshevik Mgeladze, who describes how the recruitment of groups for the Iranian resistance was conducted in Tbilisi, explains why the 'Gorjis', and generally the Transcaucasians, turned out to be such an efficient military force in Iran. His accounts reveal that the revolutionary committee in Tbilisi deliberately conducted a selective process of recruitment and did its best to make sure that the reinforcements sent from the Caucasus would make a real impact on the situation in Tabriz. An expressed willingness by volunteers to join the resistance was not considered a sufficient condition alone for recruitment, and the organization made every effort to compose a reinforcement corps of 'the best technicians and reservists who had completed military service'.[81] Bogdanov-Mariashkin also specifically indicates that his party – i.e., the SRP – also recruited groups from the ranks of 'experienced fighters' and that the 'Gorjis' in Rasht 'were all familiar with making bombs, as they used to do it before coming to Iran'.[82] Various events in Georgia and the Russian Empire which preceded the involvement of the Transcaucasians in the Iranian revolution also explain the high military efficiency of the Transcaucasian corps. Some of the Georgian revolutionaries, for example, were veterans of the Russo-Japanese War (1904–05) – Sergo Gamdlishvili had been a field engineer and Gagoshidze an artillerist on the Manchurian front – and many of them had also participated in the 1905 anti-Tsarist Revolution in Russia. Many of the Georgians who had not been on the front of Manchuria or the barricades in Moscow in 1905 had, instead, participated in the armed revolt against Tsarist authorities in western Georgia. As contemporaries report, these western Georgian rebel fighters were skilled in making and using explosives, erecting barricades, and even listening in on telephone lines.[83] Many of them, like Silovan Ivaniadze, had before joining the Iranian resisters also fought a guerrilla war against the Russian punitive expedition in Georgia after the Gurian revolt was suppressed.[84] Due to their military experience and as a result of measures taken by revolutionary committees in Tbilisi and Batumi, most of the Transcaucasians who joined the

Iranian resistance were already experienced and seasoned fighters. Describing the participation of the Georgian groups in the Tabriz resistance, Kasravi also points out their tactical efficiency and states that these men 'were all gallant fighters who had greatly mastered combat skills and methods of war.' [85]

First-hand accounts of how the revolutionaries secured transportation of people and ammunition across the border, set up safe places, avoided gendarmerie surveillance, and coordinated interaction among the Iranian, Azerbaijani, and Georgian revolutionaries on the Russian–Iranian border in order to deliver assistance to Gilan, are found in the memoirs of Bogdanov-Mariashkin. He recalls his first day in Astara, on the Russian side of the border:

> We rented rooms in a small hotel, the owner of which was Georgian and one of our men. He informed us that the local police were suspicious of us and … they would, for sure, search us. The representative of the Iranian revolutionary committee who had been following us like a shadow since we left Baku … distributed money and train documents to all of us on the same day. Giorgi the 'shoemaker', together with Gogi, 'his master' … 'rented' a building and opened a 'repair shop'. They paid the necessary fees … hired workers and launched a shoe repair shop. I received documents according to which I was a representative of some company and had arrived here to find contractors. Petre and Vaso the lame went to the Leonozov fish factory to 'purchase fish'. All this was done in the morning before the search, and the police faced the fact that Giorgi had already started fixing the rented building; the 'fish merchants' had already purchased the first batch of fish; and I had signed contracts. This continued until the police were convinced that we had, indeed, arrived to do business.[86]

Supplies and reinforcements designated primarily for Tabriz, on the other hand, were transported to Iran at the border town of Julfa, which is described in the memoirs of Gagoshidze. He relates how, dressed in the uniform of a Russian artillery officer, he travelled by train from Tbilisi to Russian Julfa, and from there, led by a guide, swam across the Aras river under cover of night to get to the Iranian side of the border:

> We safely crossed the river, … put our clothes on, but did not put on shoes as we were concerned that their sound would give us away… . We walked until we reached Persian Julfa and entered a building with a wide yard … they prepared for us a carriage with four horses … we set off … and … reached the village of Sophian… . We were stopped by the Shah's soldiers. I stepped down from the carriage, and took off my cloak. Once they saw the shoulder-straps, they backed off… . It was about nine o'clock in the evening when we approached Tabriz … the carrier turned to me and said something in Persian. I did not understand, looked around, and saw some people holding torches and crossing the road. As we approached them, three men armed with guns

appeared on each side of the carriage and stopped it.... . I stood up and called out to them: '*men chaush satar-khan*!'. On hearing that, they responded: '*khosh geldi, qardash*! ... khosh *geldi, gurji*!!! ... *yala yetim*!' ... On the orders of Sattar Khan I was taken to the other Georgians. There were about thirty Georgians.[87]

The Georgian sources do not focus exclusively on the activities of the Georgian revolutionaries during the revolution. They also provide a large volume of accounts on the strategy, political views, military priorities, and agenda of other revolutionary groups, such as the Tabriz freedom fighters, Gilani revolutionaries, Sepahdar's followers, Baku revolutionaries, Dashnaks, Hnchakists, etc., and the peculiarities of their collaboration with each other.[88] The sources provide personal and political characterizations of Sepahdar, Yeprem Khan, Panov, and other personalities the authors had met and known during their presence in Iran. For example, Mgeladze describes his meeting with the governor of Marand, Shoja' al-Saltaneh.[89] The sources mention many Iranian, Georgian, Armenian, Azerbaijani, Russian, and Jewish revolutionaries. Therefore, the Georgian sources, while of especially great use for those who study the issues of the international connections of the Iranian Revolution, are also of particular importance for the general study of the development and progress of the constitutional resistance in Iran. The Georgian members of the Rasht resistance noted in their memoirs, 'we considered our participation in the Iranian revolutionary movement as our revolutionary virtue, our pride and conscience' and 'all the torment, suffering and hardship that the Caucasians, and among them the Georgians, went through in Persia will be recognized by the history of the Persian Revolution, if it is ever written.'[90] The international contribution to the Iranian Constitutional Revolution was one of its most important and interesting aspects, therefore, without a thorough and comprehensive study of all aspects of the Transcaucasian connections of the movement, the history of the Iranian Revolution will not be complete.

Part II
State-Building

CHAPTER 4

Constitutional Rights and the Development of Civil Law in Iran, 1907–41[1]

Ali Gheissari

Preliminary Notes

The discussion of constitutional rights as a core concept of political philosophy gained new momentum in Iran during the Constitutional Revolution of 1906 and was subsequently articulated in the Iranian constitutional laws of 1906–07 and 1909. During the post-constitutional period, however, further debates and elaboration on this concept were not systematically pursued. They were first overshadowed by political crises and preoccupations in the 1910s, and later by prerogatives of state-building and centralization in the 1920s and 1930s. This chapter will examine the development of this concept from its early expressions during the constitutional era to its institutional manifestation in the parliament (the Majles) and the subsequent attempts to ratify a standard Civil Law – which was generally viewed as a necessary first step to creating a new judiciary for Iran and thus fulfilling a major goal of the constitutional movement. It will further be argued that although the twofold task of codifying the Civil Law and reorganizing the judiciary was ultimately achieved during the early Pahlavi period, legal reforms in Iran were, in good measure, procedural and administrative – and that, in spite of the 'secular' ethos of the Pahlavi state, the Iranian Civil Law substantively drew from the shari'a in accordance with Shiite private law.

In the late nineteenth century a number of Iranian intellectuals and members of the elite, such as Malkam Khan (1833–1908),[2] Majd al-Molk (1809–81),[3] and Mostashar al-Dowleh (d. 1895),[4] among others, introduced the discussion of rights to intellectual debates in Iran. Their ideas were influential in the subsequent articulation of constitutional aspirations, which was singularly concerned with rights, in terms of the rights of individuals as well as the rights of the nation vis-à-vis legitimate authority. These notions of rights were included in the Iranian constitutional laws, which clearly outlined the rights and responsibilities of both the individual and the state, and as such redefined Iranians from *subjects* to *citizens* and reduced the scope of the authority of the rulers, making it subject to the interests of the nation and the rights of the citizenry.[5] This also called for change in the structure and function of the state itself – i.e., a transition from the notion of the ruler 'maintaining his state'[6] to the growth of the modern state where the ruler himself, like all other citizens, is part of the state.[7] However, with respect to the traditional and pre-modern context, there were still expectations, as propounded in the tradition of the 'circle of justice' and in many didactic narratives written in the 'mirrors for princes' genre.[8] These were particularly important as part of the discourse in the nineteenth century that presented an element of continuity with tradition. In this respect, suggested reforms could be viewed as almost a natural growth from within – as part of the perennial demands of people throughout the ages for continuity and hence their resorting to tradition as authority.

Right and Rights: Concepts and Criteria

In Iran, as elsewhere, there is a wide range of meanings and connotations associated with the term 'right' (in the singular, *haqq*) and 'rights' (in the plural, *hoquq*): *haqq* means right, and it also means the truth (in both the moral and theological senses of the term) as well as title, fee, and share; *hoquq*, on the other hand, is the generic term for rights which also means wage, salary, fees, and dues.[9] *Hoquq* is closely associated with the general notion of law as well as a general or plural reference to laws – in this sense the modern usage of *hoquq* in Persian includes both matters of private law (*hoquq-e khosusi*) and public law (*hoquq-e 'omumi*). Private law regulates the relationships between individuals and, as such, constitutes the core and substance of the civil law. In general terms, civil law refers to the collective and systematic body of laws which define and regulate diverse areas of private law – that is, the legal relationships between individual members of society. These include, but are not limited to, family law (such as laws concerning marriage, divorce, and inheritance), the law of obligations (including contract law, tort, and the law of civil responsibility), property law, labour law, and commercial law, among others. Public law, on the other hand, regulates relationships between individuals and the state and, as its subdivisions, encompasses constitutional laws, administrative laws (including laws of public order), and criminal or penal law. In Persian constitutional discourse public law was primarily recognized as *hoquq-e siyasi*, or political rights. In fact, in the context of modern Persian legal history, somewhat similar to the French school, the general domain of public law (*hoquq-e 'omumi*) was recognized as part of the subdiscipline of political rights (*hoquq-e siyasi*) and was derived from it.[10]

In this same context, *hoquq-e 'omumi* (public law) should be differentiated from the traditional area of *hoquq-e 'ammeh* (general law) in *fiqh* (Islamic jurisprudence) classification, which regulates matters of personal status (*ahval-e shakhsiyeh*). Shari'a law mainly catered to issues of private law and, although it did talk about community and governance, was by and large quiescent in developing what in the modern constitutional sense is referred to in terms of public law.[11] Also in the modern sense, rights in both public and private law are defined by *qanun* (i.e., the general law of the land), and the boundaries of *qanun* are determined by the collective will – either directly (for example through referendum) or through electoral representation. The authors of the Iranian constitution, and later the Civil Law, shared these various meanings of right and rights.

Constitutional Transformation

The Constitutional Revolution of 1906 was the culmination of changes that Iran had gone through as a consequence of imperialism and the declining power of absolute monarchy. Throughout the nineteenth century, the Qajar dynasty (1781–1925) was perceived by many among its administrative elite as continuously declining in power – a perception that may have been based mainly on a widespread belief in the general backwardness of the east.[12] Unable, in the early nineteenth century, to defend Iran's territorial integrity effectively or protect its economic interests, the Qajar state succumbed to British and Russian pressure, and, by the latter part of the nineteenth century, had become a prisoner of imperial interests. The weakening of the Iranian state created tensions among the monarchy, the merchants in the bazaar, and some of the ulema who no longer saw the shahs as capable of fulfilling their traditional role as defenders of the faith and protectors of their domain and its interests – the function that had thus far justified the ulema's loyalty to the shahs. This trend produced a rupture during Naser al-Din Shah's rule (r. 1848–96), which was both the climax of absolute monarchy and was also marked by the expansion of the Russian and British reach into Iranian economy and politics.

Initially, the central idea of the Constitutional Revolution was the demand for a 'House of Justice' (*'edalat khaneh*). The ideal of justice was expressed particularly in the demands for an end to arbitrary rule, for stability and order, and for the protection of national interests from foreign forces. Justice was then seen as synonymous with the curbing of monarchical power, for the monarchy had become associated with arbitrary rule and injustice – which the people viewed as evident from the concessions that foreign interests received in economic matters. Thus the term 'constitutionalism' was translated as *mashrutiyat* (setting conditions), which implied placing conditions on absolutism.[13]

Subsequently, Iranians expressed this concern with justice and the rule of law by referring to the constitution as the Fundamental Law (*qanun-e asasi*).[14] The Constitutional Revolution was therefore not an anti-monarchist movement, but an anti-absolutist one. It was a movement not only for the protection of *civil rights* but also for the protection of the *rights of the nation*. It was concerned not primarily with empowering the individual (in the sense implied by the notion of liberty), but with placing limits on the arbitrary exercise of state authority and especially on the arbitrary application of law – thus demanding a unified legal system.[15] It was concerned not only with personal entitlements within the boundaries of law, but even more so with curbing foreign interference in the affairs of the country, and with efficient administration, economic progress, and protection of the country's territorial integrity. It therefore enmeshed the idea of political freedom and the administration of justice with goals that were expressed in the language of nationalism (or rather, state-nationalism).[16] The Constitutional Revolution therefore provided a systematic and permanent change in the structure and exercise of political authority: one that would ideally be an alternative to fatwas and assassinations as the means of contending with absolutism.

The ulema had often supported the absolute monarchy, starting in the sixteenth century when the Safavid dynasty (1501–1722) established a Twelver Shiite monarchy in Iran.[17] They had viewed the monarchy as the protector of the Twelver Shiite domain and propagator of the faith. During the Constitutional Revolution some members of the ulema, such as Sheykh Fazlollah Nuri (c. 1842–1909), defended absolute monarchy on those lines.[18] Nuri viewed constitutionalism as a Western idea that would ultimately subvert Shiism and the insular sanctity of the Shiite domain. By contrast, others such as Mohammad Kazem Khorasani (1839–1911) or Mohammad Hoseyn Na'ini (1860–1936), both of whom resided in Najaf, saw no tension between the imperatives of Shiite piety, as well as authority, on the one hand, and constitutionalism on the other; Na'ini in fact produced one of the more articulate accounts of the compatibility of constitutionalism with Islam.[19] Moreover, the ulema had supported monarchical absolutism insofar as it was capable of protecting the interests of the people and the nation – which they had equated with the Shiite domain. If the powers vested in the monarchy were manipulated by foreign interests to the detriment of the nation, and if arbitrary rule alienated the masses and caused instability, then curbing those powers under a constitution was necessary. Therefore constitutionalism was not a threat to the integrity of the Shiite domain but, in view of the new historical conditions, a prerequisite for protecting it. Political reform was sanctioned by the imperative of preserving both the faith and the nation that embodied it. During the constitutional period many among the ulema saw no threat to their religion in constitutionalism, nor did many of the political reformers and advocates of the constitution view religion and its guardians as a threat. The constitutionalists' demand for justice was focused on placing limits – setting conditions or *mashrutiyat* – on the monarchy's powers. In general political terms the advocates of constitutionalism, whether religious or secular, did not see it as being exclusively concerned with the shari'a. They were primarily concerned with the notion of popular sovereignty and justice, not with secularism (in the sense of rejecting religion's role in politics) or personal liberties.[20] In fact, at that juncture most constitutionalists viewed the ulema as a barrier against monarchical absolutism and instrumental in popularizing the movement, and, as such, an important ally in their quest for a constitution.[21] The shari'a was used to protest against injustice and to demand accountability from the monarchy – and it was expected to coexist with a new constitution. Constitutionalism was clearly not a secular ideal, and it was not expected to cut off the individual from the hold of religious law. It was neither anti-clerical nor an expression of Muslim 'enlightenment'. In fact, to the extent that constitutionalism was a demand for the rule of law, it reinforced the writ of the shari'a, whose stance vis-à-vis the monarchy reinforced the demands of the constitutionalists. Eventually, powerful members of the elite, such as Mirza Nasrollah Khan Moshir al-Dowleh (c. 1845–1907), among others, understood the necessity of political reforms and persuaded Mozaffar al-Din Shah (r. 1896–1907) to compromise and agree to grant the constitution.

The new constitution was promulgated in 1906, and a parliament (Majles) was convened for the first time in October of that year. It effectively transferred some of the powers of the monarchy to the legislature, and it provided the people with a forum through which to influence legislation.[22] As a result, the monarchy would recognize the authority of a representative government produced by the parliament. The constitution was less certain in delineating the relations between religion and politics. Viewing control of the monarchy rather than that of the ulema as the objective of the constitutional effort, the architects of the new document agreed in providing broad powers of oversight for the ulema in the new constitution.

The Constitutional Revolution therefore did not draw boundary lines between religion and politics. It saw religion as compatible with the demand for the rule of law and limiting the powers of the monarchy. Regardless of the long-term implications of this omission, its immediate significance was that it included religion in the emerging Iranian conception of democracy and national sovereignty. The reform effort was directed at creating a Shiite democracy as much as it was at creating an Iranian one. The ideal of democracy therefore emerged with a religious component and emphasis on the rule of law rather than demand for liberty.[23]

In addition to introducing the concept of rights to Iranian politics, the constitution also provided the framework for institutionalizing these values through legislation in the civil law which, after several attempts in the 1910s, took place from the late 1920s onwards. Iranian legal reforms in the twentieth century would not have been possible without such a constitutional framework.[24] Nevertheless, from the start, there was a persistent effort to combine different, and at times conflicting, legal paradigms. Fresh ground was broken early in this debate by Mohammad Ali Foroughi (Zoka' al-Molk) in his work *Fundamental Laws*,[25] and a few years later by, among others, Seyyed Mostafa 'Adl (Mansur al-Saltaneh) in his *Constitutional Government*,[26] Nosrat al-Dowleh Firuz in his *General Penal Law*,[27] and Mohammad Mosaddeq in his *Parliamentary Laws in Iran and Europe*.[28]

Drafting the Civil Law

The commission in charge of drafting the Fundamental Law, which was ratified in late December 1906, initially consisted of a group of statesmen such as Hasan Pirniya (Moshir al-Dowleh), Morteza Qoli Hedayat (Sani' al-Dowleh), Mehdi Qoli Hedayat (Mokhber al-Saltaneh), and Mohammad Qoli Hedayat (Mokhber al-Molk). Before the document was made public it was reviewed and endorsed by the two leading and pro-constitutionalist *mujtahid*s of Tehran, Seyyed Mohammad Tabataba'i and Seyyed Abdollah Behbahani. The commission that drafted the Supplementary Fundamental Law, which was ratified in October 1907, included a number of reform-minded courtiers and statesmen (such as Mokhber al-Molk, Sa'd al-Dowleh and Moshaver al-Molk), some active intellectuals (such as Seyyed Hasan Taqizadeh), as well as at least one canonist (Seyyed Nasrollah Taqavi, also known as Sadat Akhavi) and a prominent bazaar merchant (Haj Mohammad Hoseyn Amin al-Zarb Mahdavi).[29] However, they all agreed that any meaningful realization of these constitutional laws would be dependent on subsequent legislation in the civil law, a truly monumental task.

Nevertheless, in 1907 four civil courts were created in Tehran – the Court of Property and Financial Claims, the Criminal Court, the Court of Appeals, and the Supreme Court of Appeals (Divan-e 'Ali-ye Tamiz), the last of which 'existed only nominally, and did not function.'[30] However, since there were no codes for any of these courts to follow, they continued with the shari'a traditions. 'This frequently led to disputed sentences, and appeals were made to the *mujtahid*s, whose interpretations of the law not only often conflicted with the findings of the civil courts, but also differed among themselves. Therefore in 1908 a court was created to settle disagreements between the civil and the shari'a courts.'[31]

Several attempts were also made to codify laws, first and foremost the civil law – but this proved a difficult task. Initially, in 1907, Prime Minister Moshir al-Dowleh formed a judicial committee in the Majles to draft the Civil Law.[32] He also suggested that the proposed bills be first provisionally put into practice and only written into law after favourable results were gained from a period of trial. This was a cumbersome process, and when it produced one draft proposal, regarding the Registration of Deeds and Properties Bill (*Qanun-e sabt-e asnad va amlak*), it was rejected by the council of ministers. In similar fashion, draft proposals for the penal code, and also for procedural law, were prepared in 1910, but they also failed to get approved by the Majles. In 1915 a commission was set up to draft a comprehensive civil law; this commission consisted of a group of top experts in Islamic law and included Seyyed Nasrollah Taqavi, Seyyed Mohammad Fatemi Qomi, Seyyed Mostafa ʿAdl (Mansur al-Saltaneh), Seyyed Mohammad Yazdi, and Seyyed Mohammad Reza Afjeh'i. The draft proposal of this committee also failed to pass through the Majles. This was followed by another commission after the end of the First World War, and yet another following the coup of 1921. Finally, the commission which was selected in 1925 (that is, after the advent of the Pahlavi dynasty[33]) drafted the first volume of the Civil Law (with 955 articles), and succeeded in having it ratified by the Sixth Majles on 8 May 1928. Its members included Sadat Akhavi as chairman, Mohammad Fatemi, Mostafa ʿAdl, Mohsen Sadr (Sadr al-Ashraf),[34] Sheykh Mohammad Reza Eiravani, Mohammad Ali Kashani, and Ali Akbar Davar, who was the minister of justice, as *ex officio* member.[35] Fatemi, Eiravani, and Kashani, in particular, were experts in Shiite jurisprudence. From the vast corpus of Shiite law a number of classical sources were particularly influential in drafting the Iranian Civil Law. These included *Kitab al-Kafi* (That which is Sufficient) by al-Kulayni (d. 941), a collection of Traditions taught by the Prophet and the Imams, generally viewed as a comprehensive guide to Imami Shiite Traditions; *al-Fihrist* (Index) by Sheykh al-Tusi (995–1067), a major guide to Shiite sources and authors; *Sharayi' al-Islam wa al-ahkam* (Laws and Precepts of Islam) by al-Muhaqqiq al-Hilli (1206–77), a standard source of Shiite jurisprudence; *Sharh-e al-Lumʿa al-Dimishqiyah* (A Commentary on *al-Lumʿa*) by al-Shahid al-Thani (1506–58), a classical work on *fiqh*; *Wasaʾil al-Shiʿah* (Shiite [Research] Tools) by al-Hurr al-ʿAmili (1624–93), a major sourcebook for acquiring legal viewpoints; *Jawahir al-Kalam fi sharh-e sharayiʿ al-Islam* (Commentary on *Sharayi' al-Islam*) by Sheykh Muhammad Hasan al-Najafi (d. 1849), a comprehensive register of Shiite Traditions and *fiqh*; and *Kitab al-Makasib* (Book of Commerce) by Sheykh Morteza Ansari (1800–64), a major classical text on *fiqh*.[36] Additional references included *Muʿtaqad al-Imamiyah* ([Imami] Shiite Credence) by Seyyed Mohammad Meshkat (1902–81) and *al-ʿUrwat al-wuthqa* (The Firmest Bond) by Seyyed

Mohammad Kazem Yazdi (d. 1919), on transactions.[37]

The final draft of the first volume of the Civil Law was edited by Fatemi and presented for endorsement to a number of high-ranking ulema, such as Seyyed Mohammad Behbahani and Jamal al-Din Esfahani; they in turn appointed Seyyed Mohammad Kazem 'Assar (c. 1884–1975) and Sheykh Alibaba Firuzkuhi (c. 1871–1948), both of whom had extensive knowledge of *fiqh*, to review the text. It has further been noted that prior to this, Fatemi had independently shown the draft to Ayatollah 'Abdolkarim Ha'eri Yazdi, the founder of the seminary centre at Qom, and had already secured his approval.[38]

In a more or less similar fashion, volumes two (articles 956–1206) and three (articles 1207–1335) of the Civil Law were both prepared and subsequently ratified by the Majles. Membership of the judicial commission which was appointed to prepare the second volume of the Civil Law included Seyyed Nasrollah Taqavi (Sadat Akhavi), Seyyed Mohsen Sadr, Seyyed Mostafa 'Adl, Dr. Ahmad Matin-Daftari, Mirza Javad Khan 'Ameri, Seyyed Mohammad Fatemi Qomi, Sheykh Mohammad 'Abdoh Borujerdi, Seyyed Mohammad Reza Afjeh'i, and Sheykh Asadollah Mamaqani. Of this group, Ahmad Matin-Daftari and Javad 'Ameri had studied modern European law. The final draft of this second volume was completed in the winter of 1935 and ratified by the Ninth Majles on 26 January 1935; volume three was ratified by the Tenth Majles on 30 October 1935.[39]

The final version of the Civil Law was studied in the judiciary and legislative committees of the Majles throughout its Eleventh Session and on 16 September 1939 it was passed by the entire body of the Majles. This code differed somewhat from the long series of provisional codes that had been enacted since 1911 – especially in that it allowed greater jurisdiction to lower courts and increased the powers of the state attorneys and prosecutors. It provided (for the first time) for a special procedure for the trial of foreign nationals, and introduced a scale of priorities designed to minimize the court process. Later, in June 1940, 378 more articles were added to the Civil Law, defining the rights of the state in civil matters such as inheritance and the probating of wills.[40] The final version of the Penal Code, which was provisionally promulgated in 1926, was approved in 1940 by the Twelfth Session of the Majles.[41] The new code was a drastically revised version, 'using as model the penal code of Fascist Italy'.[42]

Constitutionalism and the Question of Public Law

It has often been argued that the Iranian constitutional laws of 1906–07 and 1909 drew on both modern Western sources and Persian traditions (which in turn consisted of the shari'a laws and the corresponding local customs or *'urf*).[43] As a result, the challenge facing the drafters of the constitution was how to reconcile Western ideals of rights with Islamic and Persian precepts that were drawn from shariʻa and *ʻurf*. How the constitution struck this balance became consequential for how the concept of rights manifested itself in Iranian politics and legal debates.

It may further be noted that in Iran, from both the constitutional and jurisprudential points of view, there was no uniform approach to Western concepts of rights. Iranian constitutionalists and legal authors drew on both liberal and collectivist (or *étatiste*) traditions of the West.[44] Therefore the constitution had to strike a balance between the directives of these divergent trends and also to negotiate its own compatibility with the prerogatives of the shariʻa. As a legal framework the constitution determined how basic constitutional values, such as individual rights, representational government, and separation of powers, were to be interpreted and implemented. From a political point of view this constitution called for the transformation of an absolutist state into a constitutional one and, as mentioned earlier, the transformation of subjects into citizens with recognized rights and responsibilities.[45] Whereas the focus in Iranian Studies has often been on how the constitution dealt with rights at the political level, it was in the domain of legal theory and practice (or rather, blueprints for practice) that the debate over rights had a more enduring impact on Iran. In fact the authors of such blueprints for practice aimed to design and implement a modern judiciary, by which they understood a common, clearly defined, and standard (hence centralized) judiciary. Therefore their approach to a 'modern' judiciary was primarily and predominantly *formal*, catering mainly to procedure and implementation rather than to a more substantive set of themes such as debates on civil liberties. Perhaps one reason for this selective approach was that with the rise of the Pahlavi state and its modernization agenda, the political format soon became a dominant concern and, apart from some significant interludes, remained so until the Islamic Revolution. Debates on legal theory and practice, therefore, were viewed as pertaining to the modern state, be it autocratic or democratic. Diverse issues regarding commerce, trade with other countries, urban expansion, and land issues, were becoming more and more complex and needed laws and lawyers of one kind or another to function, hence the new judiciary's need for procedural laws in different areas of legal practice.

It can further be noted that, in the 1920s and 1930s, the generation of Fatemi (1873–1945), ʻAdl (c. 1882–1950), and Davar (1885–1937), as bureaucrats with a task set out for them in a general outline by an authoritarian ruler anxious to build a strong centralized state, approached the question of rights by going beyond intellectual debates to focus on issues surrounding the application and implementation of law – and therefore how rights can be expressed, interpreted, and protected through public law – going from intellectualism to implementation. They provided the necessary bridge from ideas to practice, and as such changed the nature of the debate from what rights are to how to apply them.

In fact the application of rights in public law involved constructing an institutional framework for the judiciary – involving the role of courts, judges, and the legal process as a whole to confirm the boundaries of state power, individual rights, and the collective good. In this context, discussion of rights did not get reflected in demands for liberty; rather, it was expressed through interest in the centralization of state power and modernization. Moreover, it may be argued that as a lawyer and in terms of the 'technical interests'[46] of the discipline of law, Davar (who had studied law in Switzerland) did not embark on a fundamental legal shift in the realm of private law which would replace the shari'a. His legal modernization incorporated *fiqh*, albeit within a new framework and procedural methods which were mostly European.[47] If he came to be at odds with the ulema, the reasons for this tension were sociopolitical rather than jurisprudential. His programme was mainly geared towards ending the ulema's monopoly on the application of *fiqh*, including it instead within the singular jurisdiction and domain of the state – and since he was one of the chief lieutenants of the early Pahlavi modernization policies, this formal and selective approach can further clarify the extent and style of the Iranian legal reforms in that period and beyond, at least with regard to the paradigm of rights within a constitutional framework in general and with regard to the prerogatives of private law in particular.[48]

Davar and his team were particularly important in this regard: as Minister of Justice he was instrumental in defining the shape of Iran's judiciary, which in turn went above and beyond the intellectual discussions of rights and became the medium through which rights manifested themselves in Iranian society and in the administration of justice. In this regard (i.e. the administration of justice and procedure), a few illustrative examples would be: the institutionalization of the concept of appeal in judicial rulings, laws governing the right to legal representation, and the elaborate process of appointing judges. These laws introduced and institutionalized the concept of individual rights – and set the boundaries for collective rights as well. These legal reforms, particularly in the areas of implementation and procedure, parted with the directives of Islamic law, which were based on the absolute primacy of the collective good as expressed by the shari'a and traditionally issued through the rulings of *ijtihad* (independent judgement on shari'a-related questions). These legal reforms also introduced procedures and institutions that were not part of the shari'a law as such, nor did they replicate the relativism of *'urf*.

Conclusion

The issue of rights was an important dimension of political discussions in the constitutional period. These political discussions led to the articulation of the notion of constitutional rights within a new constitutional framework which defined the relation between individual citizens and the state, and as such outlined the domain of public law. Although the Iranian constitutional framework was influenced by modern Western concepts and models, its ad hoc accommodation of divergent trends, such as collectivism and individualism, displayed an eclectic approach to the question of constitutional rights. Furthermore, during the periods that followed the constitutional movement, the question of rights within the domain of private law involved considerable legal discussions which primarily followed the precepts of Shiite private law on the one hand and the demands of administrative uniformity and centralization on the other – the two trajectories which ultimately defined the shape of legal reforms in Iran. However, here, too, modern Western methods and procedures were adopted to facilitate the administration and application of a *fiqh*-based private law, divergent approaches to the question of constitutional rights and the prerogatives of public law notwithstanding. It is therefore in the context of applied law that the concept of rights, in the domains both of private law and of public law, should be further studied and theorized and its place in Iran's judicial system and civil society determined. For the discussion of rights is not a branch of speculative philosophy, or theology, or even ethics, but of jurisprudence; and how a society comes to understand and practise rights derives from its institutional designs as spelled out in its public law. This is an important dimension and legacy of Iran's constitutional experience that deserves systematic attention.

CHAPTER 5

The Constitutional Revolution, Popular Politics, and State-Building in Iran

Stephanie Cronin

The Constitutional Revolution has conventionally been subsumed under the 'catastrophist' perspective which has dominated historical writing on late Qajar Iran. According to this perspective, the revolutionary period inaugurated with the mass protests and the Shah's granting of a constitution and a national assembly in 1906 ended five years later with the closure of the Majles under Russian threats, the turmoil of these years having failed to provide Iran with the means to escape from the coils of an exhausted Qajar political order and having opened the way for increased imperialist intervention, both political and military. This view concludes that the comprehensive constitutionalist defeat ushered in a decade of political anarchy and national collapse which was only ended by the coup of 1921.

Even the periodization which has conventionally dominated the historiography of late Qajar Iran has reinforced the impression of constitutionalist failure and futility. Discussions of the constitutional era almost always end with the defeat of 1911, while the era of authoritarian modernization begins in 1921 with Reza Khan's unheralded, and apparently inexplicable, eruption onto the national political stage, the intervening decade little more then a hiatus of primordial chaos without historical significance.

This catastrophist perspective developed under the influence of at least two separate but related outlooks and has achieved an almost unchallenged dominance over scholarship on the period, whatever the orientation of individual authors – whether sympathetic or hostile to the revolution or to its successor regimes. It resulted, firstly, from the observations of the British diplomatic and commercial establishment in Iran, observations which were lent an especial significance by a general belief that Britain was sympathetic to constitutionalism, at least at first. Whatever the actual degree of British sympathy for what they imagined the objectives of the constitutional movement to be, it did not outlast the accommodation with the Russian Empire reached in the Anglo-Russian Agreement of 1907, and the growing British alarm at the radical direction taken by certain constitutionalist trends. Indeed it was the British dislike of the some of the more chaotic manifestations of the constitutional movement, coupled with their exasperation at the old Qajar aristocracy, which later led them seamlessly into offering their public backing to the new 'man of order', Reza Khan. British fears and anxiety at the exuberance and vitality of the popular politics of the constitutional years led to a growing hostility which seeped into their descriptions of the revolution, and these descriptions formed an important basis for much Western scholarship on the revolution.[1]

The catastrophist perspective was also fostered by another interest. During the 1920s and 1930s the ideologues of the Pahlavi regime itself were eager to present the pre-coup decades as a period of chaos and relentless disaster, as part of the attempt to emphasize Reza Shah's own unique individual claim to the role of national saviour. Both the existence and vitality of a broad constitutional milieu and the achievements of the revolution were systematically downplayed and finally written out of history altogether. These two trends of historical analysis naturally converged and reinforced each other as a result of the political support given by Britain to the emerging Pahlavi order.

The account which follows questions this catastrophist perspective. Such a challenge is important not only because of the need to acquire a more accurate picture of the revolutionary years for its own sake, but also because the gaps and distortions in many conventional depictions of the revolution lead to further, and even more serious, distortions in the broad historical narrative of modern Iran. It especially obscures the process by which the country moved from the embryonic multi-party pluralism nurtured in the space provided by the collapsing Qajar monarchy to the consolidation of a dictatorship which obliterated the developing civil society in the interests of an imagined 'national unity' and 'modernity'. Rather then seeing the constitutional years as barren and without issue, and the early Pahlavi period as discrete, self-contained, and entirely novel, this account stresses the links between the two periods. It seeks particularly to discuss the character and extent of both the revolution's successes and its failures and to analyse their consequences.

The Constitutional Revolution wrought profound changes in the Iranian political landscape, changes that are largely unrecognized or erased by the catastrophist perspective. The revolutionary years were seminal to Iran's subsequent history in terms of ideology and political culture. The period produced the broad agenda for reform adopted by the nationalist elite over many subsequent decades, while the inability of the constitutional authorities to overcome Iran's internal and external problems proved to be a crucible of Pahlavi authoritarianism, predisposing the political class towards succumbing to the allure of a charismatic personality.[2] However, the narrative below argues that the constitutional revolution was of decisive significance to Iran's modern history in other, more specific ways. Firstly, the state-building effort of the constitutional period, far from ending in futility, created institutions of immense significance. Perhaps the most important of these were the Majles, convened in 1906, and the Government Gendarmerie, established in 1910. Both not only survived the Russian ultimatum of 1911 but entered on a period of expansion and vitality, making important contributions to the nationalist struggle during the First World War, stabilizing radical political activity and providing it with a focus and with political and military instruments.[3] Both institutions continued to play important roles in shaping political and military developments in the 1920s, constituting elements of continuity between the state-building efforts of the constitutional and early Pahlavi periods. Secondly, the constitutional period represented a high-water mark in the development of popular politics in Iran, a form of politics which was to be crucial in shaping the domestic landscape, by restricting the space available to the imperial powers before the coup of 1921, and by influencing and contesting the strategies of the new, post-coup, regime in the first decade of its existence, forcing Reza Khan to engage in a protracted struggle with his political opponents over the character of the new state.[4]

The late nineteenth and early twentieth centuries were pre-eminently the era of constitutionalism in the Middle East, and the Iranian revolution took place amidst a flurry of such upheavals across the world.[5] Everywhere intellectuals in countries falling under imperial domination seized on constitutional government as the secret of Europe's political and military strength. Successive revolutionary outbreaks in Tsarist Russia, the Ottoman Empire, and Qing-dynasty China sought to limit or abolish autocratic monarchies and to bring about constitutional reform and national regeneration. Although each movement had its own character and historical context, they shared broad objectives. In 1905 an alliance of middle-class constitutionalists and working-class revolutionaries succeeded in wresting wide-ranging concessions from the Tsar, including a guarantee of civil liberties and a promise of universal male suffrage. In early 1906 the first Russian constitution was promulgated and a consultative assembly, the Duma, convened. This victory, although it quickly succumbed to brutal repression, was of immense symbolic and exemplary significance. In 1908 an uprising sparked by Ottoman army officers fearful of imperial disintegration, economic domination by Europe, and the loss of territories to Russia and to new states in the Balkans, forced the sultan to restore the constitution first granted in 1876 and suspended indefinitely two years later. Parliamentary elections followed immediately. In China, ineffective imperial absolutism seemed to be the harbinger of administrative decay and the cause of Chinese helplessness against Western economic and political control, expressed through unequal treaties and spheres of influence. A combination of secret societies,

Westernizing intellectuals such as Sun Yat Sen, the reformed and modernized military, and provincial merchants and gentry brought about the 1911 revolution, followed by a republic, a constitution, and elections to a national assembly.

During the nineteenth century in Iran, as in the Ottoman Empire and China, the arbitrary and theoretically absolute power of the monarch was increasingly starkly contrasted with a reality in which the state was growing weaker and weaker in the face of internal and external threats. These threats included the economic, military, and political power of Europe and internal centrifugal forces, especially national, regional, or tribal bids for autonomy or independence. In both the Ottoman Empire and China, officers and soldiers from the new modernized army units, who had absorbed ideas of political change along with concepts of military reform, were key in launching the revolutions. In Iran, owing to the generalized failure of modernization projects, this element was absent. Also absent, owing to Iran's economic underdevelopment, were the working class and leftist forces prominent in the 1905 upheavals across the Russian Empire, although from 1905 onwards left-leaning groups began to appear and play an important role, especially in Tabriz, as the revolution moved through its successive phases.[6] In Iran the task of launching a revolution fell to a coalition of social forces and intellectual trends, 'a religious-radical alliance',[7] an anti-imperialist and anti-absolutist conglomeration of clerics, merchants, and dissident intellectuals, sometimes active in secret societies. This coalition had first emerged during the Tobacco Protest of 1891–92,[8] when it had an early and striking success in forcing the Shah to cancel the tobacco concession granted to a British subject, Major G. F. Talbot. It derived its power from the ability of the leadership to mobilize an urban 'crowd', consisting of low-ranking mullahs, theology students, guild artisans, bazaar shopkeepers, and the mass of the urban poor. The Shah was forced to agree to the demand for a constitution by this crowd, active in ever-increasing numbers in three waves of strikes and public protests between the spring of 1905 and the summer of 1906, in Tehran, the shrine of Shah 'Abd al-'Azim, and in Qom. By the time of the great *bast* of 1906 in the British legation, which provided the environment for the formulation of a coherent demand for a national assembly, the revolutionaries had been able to assemble a crowd numbering 14,000, representing nearly one-third of the labour force of Tehran.[9]

The success of this first phase of the revolution was achieved purely by the methods of mass public protest, without resort to arms or violence. Paradoxically, this success was possible partly because of the very weakness of nineteenth-century efforts at reform and state-building. The failure to carry out measures which might have strengthened the institutions of Qajar government, or to create new institutions, particularly a modern army, meant that when the crisis came, the Shah and the social forces on which the monarchy rested had no repressive apparatus at their disposal. On the other hand, of course, in the Ottoman Empire and Qing-dynasty China, sultan and emperor were to be deposed by the very modernized army units they had worked so hard to build up. In Iran, no such units existed. Although the Shah had no modernized army on which he might depend to defend him against the constitutionalists, neither did he need to fear that such an army might turn against him. The Iranian state's weakness at this time was certainly the result of the failure of nineteenth-century reform. Yet the Qajar dynasty's survival for another twenty years after 1905–06 may equally have been the result of this very failure and of the consequent absence of a modern officer corps with sufficient dynamism to seize the political initiative. The very real danger to the Shah potentially represented by army officers may be illustrated by the response to the revolution of Iran's partially modernized cavalry unit, the Russian-officered Cossack Brigade, which had been deeply compromised by the spread of constitutionalist ideas, and the trajectory later adopted by the much more consistently reform-oriented Government Gendarmerie. The last Qajar Shah was indeed eventually deposed by one of his own officers, but this did not take place as an integral part of the revolutionary process, as it had in the Ottoman Empire and China, but only after a struggle for supremacy within the country lasting two decades. It did not, furthermore, result in the abolition of the institution of the monarchy, as had been the case elsewhere, but rather only in a change of dynasty, with profound consequences for Iran's future.[10]

Between the winter of 1905 and the summer of 1906 the Shah could resist the revolutionaries only by the methods of bribery and the sowing of division among his opponents. When these methods failed, he found himself with no choice but to accede to the demands for a constitution and a National Assembly. The Shah lacked coercive instruments, troops and police, with which to defend his autocracy, but the revolutionaries too lacked the means, armed force, to seize and retain real power. Each side launched bids to seize and retain power, including the Shah's coup of 1908 and the constitutionalist recapture of Tehran in 1909. Yet their mutual weakness produced an underlying deadlock which neither side was able decisively to resolve.

Thus, when in 1906 the First Majles convened, the revolutionaries were not truly in power. The constitution had been designed to limit the absolutism of the Shah but the institutions of constitutional government lacked the means in reality to enforce their will within the national territory and to guarantee the survival of the state against its external enemies. The answer to the resulting danger perceived by the new deputies and the ideologues of the constitutional movement was to reactivate the state-building project inaugurated by Abbas

Mirza in the early nineteenth century and continued by Amir Kabir between 1848 and 1851 and Moshir al-Dowleh in the 1870s, a central plank of which had always been the construction of a modern army.[11]

Thus it may be seen that the Constitutional Revolution embodied two quite distinct traditions. The first was a tradition of popular politics, with a strong subaltern dimension, which had begun to acquire a modern agenda and a national dimension in the late nineteenth century and which found its fullest expression in the mass strikes, demonstrations, and *bast*s which led to the granting of the constitution. The second was an elite tradition of state-building, which was represented most clearly by a concern with military reform. These two traditions did not represent a straightforward left-right split. The vision of a strong, modern, and independent Iran was, in many respects, shared by both left and right. During 1909–11 the left-leaning Democrat Party, for example, included in its programme the demand for universal conscription as a means of safeguarding the country and engendering patriotism, a demand eventually implemented by Reza Shah in the 1920s in precisely these ideological terms.[12] Indeed it was Reza Shah's ability to pose as the inheritor of the state-building tradition which, in the 1920s, encouraged many of the constitutionalist intelligentsia, including its leftist components, to offer their support, however conditional, to the new Pahlavi authoritarianism. Nor was this a simple religious-secular split. It rather represented, in different forms and combinations, elite-subaltern, official-popular, and central-local contradictions. Such conflicts may clearly be discerned in, for example, the hostility of the Majles to the provincial *anjoman*s.[13] These two traditions may be seen as broadly embodying two differing conceptions of political organization, represented on the one hand by a modern, 'top-down' secular, and centralizing nationalism, and on the other by local, autonomous, voluntarist, and decentralized movements driven by demands for natural justice, sometimes conceptualized in religious terms.[14] During the early constitutional years these two traditions were not usually perceived as being in any fundamental opposition but, on the contrary, were assumed to be mutually reinforcing. Nonetheless an underlying contradiction existed between them: between, on the one hand, the evolution of popular politics in the direction of democratic government and a vibrant civil society, and on the other, the growing weight of an authoritarian nationalism which found its purest expression in uniform and on the parade ground. This tension continued throughout the constitutional period, was submerged in the struggle for survival characterizing the years during and immediately after the First World War, but came fully to the surface between 1921 and 1925. It was only resolved when Reza Shah succeeded in openly sundering the religious-radical alliance, winning the enthusiastic support of the secular reformers for his version of the state-building project while suppressing the opposition of other loci of power, the clergy, the bazaar, and the tribes.[15]

Popular Politics in Constitutionalist Iran: The Political 'Crowd'

The establishment of the constitution and a formal representative and democratic institution, the national assembly or Majles, was the crowning achievement of the Tehran crowd.[16] In Iran, various social groups, historically lacking formal channels of political representation, had become accustomed to asserting themselves through mass popular actions, as a political crowd, and such crowds were a familiar feature of urban life.[17] Like their counterparts elsewhere, Iranian crowds possessed their own traditions, repertoires of actions, ideological context, and concrete objectives.[18] Their actions ranged from peaceful, even routine, protests designed merely to engage with the authorities and perhaps to change or modify a particular policy, through more determined and prolonged confrontations, to outright mass defiance emphasized by the use of different forms of violence. Urban crowds habitually employed a wide variety of methods in their efforts to influence, manipulate, resist, and sometimes confront local and national authorities. Indeed there existed a repertoire of actions with which both the people and the authorities were intimately acquainted and through which conflict between rulers and ruled could be choreographed. This repertoire was deeply ingrained in the historical experience of broad layers of the urban population, who resorted to it spontaneously and almost instinctively. Among the actions constituting this repertoire, perhaps the best known are the addressing of appeals in the form of petitions and telegrams to the authorities, the use of mosques for political meetings, the taking of *bast*, the guild strike and the closure of the bazaars, the distribution of anonymous and often menacing and intimidatory *shabnameh*s and, when these methods were exhausted, collective bargaining through riot.[19] These actions were, furthermore, ranked in a generally recognized hierarchy, ready to be adopted successively until the authorities responded, and there was a broad expectation on the part of those resorting to protest that the authorities were under an obligation to listen to their grievances and to offer remedies. The authorities themselves, largely lacking any effective coercive power and conscious of the necessity of consensus and consent, were often prepared to heed such demonstrations, especially once they reached a certain pitch.

In the nineteenth century and earlier, popular protests had usually been provoked by localized issues such as resentment at avaricious and oppressive governors. Since the late nineteenth century, however, mass urban protests in Tehran and the provincial cities had increasingly focused on issues of national politics, meeting with a large measure of success. The first victory of national significance came with the 'Tobacco Protest' of 1891–92, when the closure of the bazaars in cities throughout Iran, the mass consumer boycott of tobacco, and demonstrations in the streets of Tehran forced the Shah to cancel his sale of the tobacco concession to a foreigner. In 1905–06 these techniques produced their greatest success when mass *bast*s, bazaar strikes, and street demonstrations provided a context within which revolutionary intellectuals were able to formulate a novel political agenda, the demand for a constitution and a national assembly.[20]

The victory of the revolutionaries in 1905–06 showed the continuing and indeed deepening salience of a repertoire of methods typical of past urban protests. The persistence of such methods, traditional in form but modern in political content, and the readiness of wide layers of the population to adopt them, continued into the 1920s. Urban crowds in early Pahlavi Iran, in both Tehran and the provincial cities, continued to demonstrate their political vitality and to play a key role in the crises which periodically rocked the new regime.[21] In the political and constitutional battles of 1924–25 the Tehran crowd again became a factor of central and sometimes decisive importance. The struggle over republicanism, for example, was decided not in the Majles, nor in the madrasas of Qom, but on the streets of the capital, the actual political victory belonging to the anti-republican Tehran crowd led by Seyyed Hasan Modarres and acting in defence of the constitution.[22]

The power and legitimacy of crowd action, especially in the capital, not only forced the new post-coup regime onto the defensive but exercised a profound impression on Reza Khan as a political strategist. During the mortal struggle inaugurated by the republican movement and culminating in the change of dynasty, Reza Khan translated the lessons drawn from his early observations of Iran's urban politics into a new strategy, with a marked populist dimension. His agenda for radical constitutional change – first a republic and then a change of dynasty – required some form of political backing and legitimacy. Lacking any political party, he resorted directly to the urban crowd, a tactic he adopted, and threatened to adopt repeatedly, in his struggle with Ahmad Shah, finally triumphing after orchestrating a strong anti-Qajar protest campaign in the provincial cities and led by radical Tabriz.

With the stabilization of Reza Shah's new dynasty, the army, and especially the new police force, were to be exclusively the instruments for the imposition and defence of the new order in Tehran; the capital's crowd was silenced. Yet in the provincial cities, where the regime's control was less complete and local leaderships to some extent remained influential, the tradition of urban dissent continued. In 1927 Isfahan and Shiraz were wracked by mass protests against conscription, in Tabriz in 1928 to both conscription and clothing reform, and in Mashhad in 1935 to the 'European' hat.[23] These urban protests, however, were everywhere led by middle-ranking levels of the clergy and the bazaar, and sometimes, as in the case of Mashhad, even by very junior and subaltern figures.[24] Lacking the allies among the modern intelligentsia who had been so crucial during the Constitutional Revolution and who were now wedded to the Pahlavi project, and with the most senior ulema quiescent, these protests were unable to coalesce into a coherent opposition and were relatively easily suppressed. Nonetheless, immediately after the abdication of Reza Shah in 1941, the Tehran street again became an arena of political action and the urban crowd a key player, re-emerging during every political crisis: the years of the oil nationalization, the White Revolution, and most spectacularly between 1977 and 1979.

Popular Politics and State-Building: The Majles

In July–August 1906 the huge *bast* in the British legation culminated in the Shah's granting of the Constitutional Edict, which provided for the convening of the First Majles, and an electoral law was formulated the following month. In the late nineteenth and early twentieth centuries formal ideas of representative government had been confined to a tiny intellectual elite. Yet these notions spread rapidly during the revolutionary months of 1905–06. Over the following years the actual establishment of a representative institution, and the impact on popular consciousness and modes of political activity of repeated elections, left the relationship between authority and people fundamentally transformed. The holding of elections for deputies to the First and Second Majles began to school at least the urban population in the methods of democratic and electoral politics, parties began to emerge, and the press reflected and formed a nascent public opinion. Throughout this period, the Majles became a focus of national political activity, both elite and popular. It was the site for elite opinion-forming debate as well as for decision-making and the actual passage of legislation. But it was also an institution which the mass of the people claimed as their own. Appeals, petitions, pleas for justice, and complaints of oppression poured in, and the Majles grounds were the site of repeated political demonstrations, on local matters as well as on issues of national significance. This popular conception of the Majles as a place where grievances might be aired and wrongs redressed was encouraged by the ideological origins of the institution in demands for a 'House of Justice' ('*edalat khaneh*), an autonomous representative body which might administer justice and secure the rights of the individual against the state.[25]

The Majles was first convened in 1906 and the constitutional era is deemed to have ended with its closure in 1911. Yet, although it was closed under Russian threats in 1911, it did not cease to exist. Elections were again held and a new Majles reconvened in 1914. These elections to a new Majles provided Iran with a legitimate representative institution which proved capable of providing political leadership to nationalist forces battling against foreign intervention and control and a docile and collaborating Shah. The Majles deputies played an important role in the *mohajerat* (the self-exile of part of the government) of 1915, leaving Tehran and establishing a nucleus of authority beyond the reach of the Russian armies. In 1919–20, the appeal to constitutional government and democratic legitimacy was successful in frustrating British efforts to force through the Anglo-Iranian Agreement, this agreement requiring a Majles ratification impossible for Britain to obtain.[26]

In all the popular protests of the post-constitutional and early Pahlavi periods, those concerned with local matters as well as those that had a national political significance, the Majles played a central role. The establishment of the Majles in 1906 had constituted an extraordinarily important development for popular politics in Iran, its immediate acquisition of the status of a place of *bast* indicating the reverence in which it was held. For the Tehran crowd, the Majles, as a new source of legitimacy, constituted the centre of national political life, its buildings themselves the focus of popular political activities and the constitution an ideological lodestar. Protests of every kind were held on the Majles grounds; complaints, demands, and petitions were directed ceaselessly to the deputies; and press and public displayed a profound belief in the legitimacy of this embodiment of constitutional and representative government.

The Majles continued to play an important role until the consolidation of Reza Shah's military monarchical dictatorship foreclosed independent political activity altogether. It was, for example, the Majles deputies who actually took the decision to reject Reza Khan's republican legislation in 1924, although in this they were accepting the view of the Tehran crowd that they were debarred from tampering with the constitution, and were reacting to the pressure from below which had become, momentarily, stronger than the pressure from above.[27] From the mid-1920s the increasingly confident new regime was able to suppress the Majles as an institution of popular political legitimacy. However, Reza Shah never succumbed to the temptation to abolish the Majles altogether, although he clearly possessed the power to do so. Rather, having established total control, he then sustained the Majles's existence, attempting to appropriate some of its charisma.[28] After his abdication in 1941, the institution itself, with all the accompanying panoply of representative and democratic politics, sprang back into life, to occupy again a central role in the intense political struggles of the years of the oil-nationalization crisis.

State-Building and Military Reform in Constitutional Iran

In tandem with their efforts to establish representative institutions, the constitutionalists also grappled with the central state-building question posed by successive generations during the nineteenth century – how could the state enforce its own power, defend itself against its internal and external enemies, assert its authority over all the national territory, and halt the disintegration that threatened Iran's existence as an independent state?[29]

The constitutional movement answered this question by appropriating the state-building project which had been launched by the Qajars a century earlier but which had, during the course of the nineteenth century, been repeatedly frustrated.[30] The new authorities developed two specific strategies. Firstly, they tried to establish their own effective control over the existing military forces, most significantly, the Russian-officered Cossack Brigade. In this they failed. Their second, parallel, strategy, to establish a modern military force of their own, succeeded when the Majles, in 1910, voted for the organization of the Government Gendarmerie. However, although their success with the Gendarmerie was real, it was to be less significant than their failure with the Cossack Brigade.

The constitutional and post-constitutional years provided a new context for the politics of state-building and military reform. Since the early nineteenth century, the Qajar Shahs and their ministers had made repeated efforts at building a modern army on the European model as part of a general programme of defensive modernization. This project had undergone a relentless deterioration, until Abbas Mirza's plan to raise regiments capable of engaging in warfare and defending the country against Iran's enemies had become a simple desire to have troops suitably modern in appearance with which to provide the Shah with the trappings and accoutrements of power and statehood. After the constitutional revolution, the project of army reform and the wider state-building agenda in which it was embedded were wrested away from the Shah and taken up by a new generation of constitutionalist and nationalist reformers. For these circles, the Shah was no longer, if he ever had been, capable of acting as an agent of reform, but was now rather a major impediment to Iran's regeneration.

The nineteenth century had seen a mania across the Middle East for military modernization and the importation of European methods of military organization. *Nezam-e jadid* (new order) regiments sprang up everywhere – in the Ottoman Empire, Egypt, North Africa, and Iran – , the ruling dynasties in these areas embarking on army reform in a desperate effort to strengthen their defensive capacity and to resist growing European hegemony and direct or indirect control, but also to bolster the state, expressed in the person of the ruler, against competing domestic power bases.[31]

The Qajar Shahs and their ministers and, by the end of the nineteenth century, wider layers of elite reforming opinion had become obsessed with the need to establish regular disciplined military forces, and the nineteenth and early twentieth centuries were peppered with attempts to set up a standing army on the European model with the help of foreign officers. In all, nineteenth-century Iran saw three formal French military missions, three British ones, two Austrian, one 'unofficial' Italian mission, and one Russian, as well as a miscellany of foreign adventurers and mercenaries employed on an individual basis. Yet the cumulative result of this obsession was to leave Iran at the beginning of the twentieth century burdened by an immense expenditure on the army but militarily greatly weakened.[32]

By the late nineteenth century, the *nezam* troops were essentially for show, to furnish a 'modern' backdrop for the Shah's power, to indulge the Shah's fondness for what amounted to military fancy-dress, and to provide a conduit through which state money might be channelled into the pockets of elite families. Nonetheless, in the 1870s, one step had been taken which was to have permanent and momentous consequences for the country. In 1879, the first Russian military mission came to Iran to establish the Iranian Cossack Brigade. The Russian military mission of 1879 was a turning point in Iran's experiments with foreign officers. After its arrival, Iran found itself with a regular cavalry force, but one which was permanently lost to Iranian control and which was, in 1908, to overthrow the institutions of constitutional government at the behest of a foreign power.[33]

For most of the nineteenth century, Iranian suspicions of Russia had been too great to allow the Tsar's officers the training of the army. Now the very existence of the Russian military mission and the Cossack Brigade seemed to symbolize Iran's increasing weakness and the demoralization of the Court. Although previous foreign military missions had, formally at least, deferred to Iranian sovereignty, the Russian mission gave up any such pretence and operated independently according to the commandant's interpretation of Russian interests. By giving Iran the Cossack Brigade, Russia only partially succeeded in tying the Shah to itself. It was, however, completely successful in establishing a visible and apparently permanent affront to Iranian sovereignty. For the Russian officers of the brigade, furthermore, the advance of Russian interests was indissolubly linked to the defence of Qajar absolutism. By the late nineteenth century the monarchy had become dependent on the brigade. In 1896, after the assassination of Naser al-Din Shah, it was the Russian Cossack officers and their men who ensured the accession of the new Shah, Mozaffar al-Din (r. 1896–1907). After the Constitutional Revolution, the brigade was drawn ever deeper into domestic political conflicts, not an arm of the state but rather a partisan of the Shah in his struggle with the constitutionalists.

The novel position of the brigade and its commandant was reflected in a new degree of hostility from Iranian opinion. The developing constitutionalist milieu profoundly resented the Russian mission, which it believed to have been imposed on Iran as a result of pressure on a weak and despotic ruler.[34] From 1906, and especially after the accession of the new and fiercely reactionary Mohammad Ali Shah in early 1907, the establishment of constitutional control over the brigade was an imperative for the new authorities. The unpopularity of the brigade was clear from the constant attacks made on it by the deputies in the Majles. The deputies complained that the Cossacks were maintained with Iranian money entirely for the benefit of Russia, and that the officers and men in the provinces were systematically employed in collecting intelligence for the Russian War Office. In fact, a sworn statement to this effect, signed by five Iranian officers of the brigade, was laid before the Majles. Members of the Shahsavan tribal confederation, earmarked by the Shah as recruiting material for the brigade, also complained to the Majles about their position, and 22 Shahsavan officers and 160 men obtained their discharge.[35]

Not only was the brigade viewed with open hostility by constitutionalist opinion, but constitutional ideas had penetrated deeply into the ranks of the brigade itself. During the mass protests of 1905–06 the Iranian ranks of the brigade showed sympathy for the demand for a national assembly, and the Russian commandant expressed himself doubtful about the loyalty of his men. Despite its royalist and pro-Russian traditions, in 1905–06 the brigade did not act. Its Russian officers could not provide the Shah with a coercive instrument to use against the revolutionaries and the brigade's paralysis and the absence of other effective army units meant that the revolution was able to achieve its objectives largely peacefully. The upsurge of national sentiment which accompanied the establishment of constitutional government drove a wedge between the Russian officers of the brigade and their Iranian subordinates. The Russians were unable to maintain their authority and the Iranian officers formed a military council to take control of the brigade.[36]

In 1905–06 the Cossack Brigade was weak and demoralized. Popular hostility was intense and many of the Iranian officers and men sympathetic to the revolution. The Russian mission was in disarray and the military authorities in Russia preoccupied with defeat at the hands of Japan and the suppression of the 1905 revolution. Nonetheless, the constitutional regime was not strong enough to grasp this opportunity to rid itself of the hated Russian military mission. The Russian authorities regained the initiative and, at what was a critical moment for the brigade, both internally and vis-à-vis the wider political situation, a new senior officer, Colonel Vladimir Liakhov, arrived from Russia and assumed command of the brigade. He was determined to reassert

Russian control and succeeded in abolishing the military council and in weeding out Iranian officers opposed to Russian influence. In this he encountered considerable difficulty not only due to resistance within the brigade itself, but also because of continued efforts by the leading ulema, government ministers, and Majles deputies to curb his power. In December 1907, when Mohammad Ali Shah plotted to use the brigade in a coup, Liakhov had to confess that his men could not be relied on for that purpose.[37]

The constitutional regime soon paid the price for its inability to remove or subordinate the Russian officers of the brigade. Throughout early 1908 Liakhov concentrated on consolidating his control of the brigade by purging elements disloyal to his leadership and by the distribution of a special bonus, and in June the Shah succeeded in doing what he had not been able to do the previous December, using the Cossacks to carry out a coup d'état. The brigade, under its Russian officers, made a decisive intervention in the domestic political conflict, bombarding and suppressing the Majles and overthrowing the constitutional government on the orders of Mohammad Ali Shah and his royalist and Tsarist supporters. However, Liakhov had not been able to carry out the Shah's coup without provoking some discontent within the Brigade. At least one Iranian officer resigned in protest at the bombardment of the Majles,[38] while it seems that about 400 men of the brigade simply disappeared quietly, preferring not to remain with their Russian officers. Liakhov himself became military governor of Tehran, using martial law to suppress all constitutionalist activity, but his ascendancy was soon reversed. In July 1909, when the constitutionalists, with tribal military support and revolutionary volunteers, recaptured the capital, the brigade was once again powerless to offer resistance. With the constitutionalists again in power in Tehran, the brigade was once more eclipsed, to re-emerge again only after the Russian government in 1911 forced a second closure of the Majles. In the context of the general defeat suffered by Iranian constitutionalism in 1911, the brigade was once more consolidated into an instrument of foreign control and, later, royalism.

During the revolutionary years, the Iranian officers and men of the Cossack Brigade tended to reflect the prevailing political trends among the wider Iranian population and were swayed by the same considerations as those which dominated civilian political concerns. It was only when Iranian constitutionalism faltered or experienced repression, in 1908 and then after 1911, that the Shah and Russia were able to regain their authority over the Cossack Brigade's Iranian officers and men. Between 1911 and 1917, as a result of constant Russian pressure, the brigade was repeatedly enlarged, eventually becoming a division, with ever greater numbers of Russian officers. But its role as a tool of foreign interests did not end with the Russian revolution of 1917 and the collapse of tsarism. On the contrary, it was simply taken over by the surviving imperial power, Britain, who, in 1920–21, again fashioned it into an instrument capable of carrying out a coup d'état.[39] In the 1920s, the Cossack officers were to provide a bedrock of political loyalty on which Reza Shah secured not just the new regime but also his dynasty.

By the beginning of the twentieth century, all the broad schemes of military modernization under missions of foreign officers had ended in failure, while the establishment of the Cossack Brigade under the Russian military mission had created a new problem of loss of authority without solving the old problem of a lack of effective military strength. By the constitutional period, the issue of sovereignty had become paramount and the state-building agenda had passed from the Shah and his high ministers to a new generation representing new social forces. Iranian constitutionalists argued strongly in favour of the creation of a force which could defend Iran's borders and independence, maintain internal security, collect taxes, and uphold the authority of the constitutional authorities. In government pronouncements, Majles debates, programmes of political parties, and the press, the need for a strong national army was constantly reiterated.

The Majles attempted to assert control over the existing *nezam* troops and the Cossacks but found itself powerless to resist the Cossack Brigade's coup of 1908. Suppressed in the capital by Liakhov's martial law, constitutionalist forces regrouped in the provinces and in 1909 recaptured the capital, their military strength resting on sympathetic tribal forces and on revolutionary irregulars led by the famous Armenian constitutionalist, Yeprem Khan. After 1909, however, the new government remained without an integral military arm and dependent upon a combination of Bakhtiyari horsemen and *mojahedin*. In 1910 the minister of war, Sardar As'ad Bakhtiyari, put forward a scheme for military reform, but this again evaporated without any concrete results. Real progress was only made when, later the same year and as part of a concerted reform drive, the recently elected Second Majles voted for the establishment of a new force, the Government Gendarmerie. The following May the Majles approved a Swedish military mission to lead the force, Sweden being an acceptable source of foreign officers as it had a tradition of neutrality and was considered a minor power.[40]

A mission of three Swedish officers, led by Colonel H. O. Hjalmarson, began its work at the end of 1911.[41] By 1914 seven regiments, all volunteers, had been established in Tehran and throughout southern, south-eastern, and south-western Iran.[42] By 1914 the Gendarmerie had become the first real success in Iranian efforts to build a regular military force and embodied the state-building trend which had begun with Abbas Mirza and was now represented by the constitutional movement. The Swedish mission had been engaged by the Majles and offered no challenge to Iranian sovereignty; on the contrary, it drew its legitimacy from its identification with the constitutional authorities. The Gendarmerie possessed a novel ideological coherence and dynamism and, unlike the Cossack Brigade, was able to employ the motifs of nationalism to attract recruits and ensure their loyalty.[43] It was, in particular, able to assemble a professional Iranian officer cadre which, after the eclipse of the Swedish command during the world war, proved capable of providing the nationalist movement with its most coherent military force and with its only competent military leadership. By 1918 the Gendarmerie constituted one of the few remaining stable structures of the Iranian state and was able to pose as a potential national leadership. Yet it was not the Gendarmerie which finally acted to resolve the crisis engulfing Iran in 1920–21. Drawn into a coup led by elements outside itself, the Gendarmerie was submerged in the new army by a combination of cooptation and repression. Nonetheless, former gendarme officers provided Reza Khan with a human resource, the military expertise and experience, vital to the construction of the new army.

Conclusion

The Constitutional Revolution's failure to establish its authority over a key institution of the Iranian state, the Cossack Brigade, had profound consequences for the future. The Russian officers were left *in situ* and, in the years of reaction and foreign occupation after 1911, were able to strengthen their position. Although the overthrow of tsarism freed Iran from the grip of the Russian military mission, this only created a space immediately occupied by the remaining imperial power, Britain, and opened the way for another Cossack coup, this time British-sponsored.[44] Thus it was the Cossack Brigade, historically identified with anti-constitutionalism, led by an officer, Reza Khan, who had played no visible part in the political and military struggles of the previous decade, which carried out this decisive political intervention. The resulting regime embarked on a state-building project which owed its central features to the programmes of the revolutionary period. Yet the Cossacks had grown to political maturity in an atmosphere dominated by loyalty to autocracy, Russian and Iranian, and hostility to constitutionalism and reform, and the circumstances of the coup and the character of the new national leadership which it produced led to the marginalization of elements more centrally committed not just to the state-building but to the constitutionalist dimension of the revolution's goals. As a result, the way in which the new Pahlavi regime appropriated the legacy of the constitutional revolution was problematic. The new regime's authoritarianism, martial temper, and inclination to resort to force distorted and rendered deeply unpopular many of the reforms long advocated by the constitutionalist intelligentsia. For example, constitutionalist proposals for encouraging and providing protection for women who gradually chose to discard *chador* and *picheh* became unveiling by administrative diktat backed up by force, while the 'tribal problem' was reconceptualized from a problem of historical backwardness into an existential threat to national survival, this threat then becoming the justification for an increasing military hegemony over civil society.[45]

The Constitutional Revolution may best be understood when it is placed within its historical and global context. It was an Iranian manifestation of an international trend, part of a wave of such movements and upheavals which swept across much of the world, including southern Europe, the Middle East, and Asia, in the late nineteenth to early twentieth centuries. At the same time, its precise character, the social forces which it mobilized, its leadership, and its agenda were conditioned by the specific circumstances of Iranian history. The methods employed by the revolutionaries drew on a deep tradition of urban protest. Their objectives, however, were no longer, as in the past, the traditional localized grievances but, in an illustration of the growth of a modern political consciousness, national demands focused on the state. Furthermore, the constitutional revolution itself produced a rapid acceleration of political consciousness, the formulation of new demands for a National Assembly, for example, taking place during the very course of the *bast*s. The mass participation in the revolution, the establishment of the Majles, the holding of elections, the spread of a free press, generated a democratic potential, while the efforts to secure constitutional rule led to the reactivation of an Iranian state-building project which dated back to the beginning of the nineteenth century.

The activists of the constitutional period were unable to transform their experience into the more conventional and orderly repertoire required by parliamentary democracy. In the 1920s the tension between state-building and popular politics was resolved in favour of a strong state with an authoritarian and commandist approach, unwilling to engage in the negotiation and compromise required by popular involvement and typical of the Qajar period. This was exemplified by the fate of the right of *bast*. This practice, so vital to the success of the constitutional revolution, was systematically suppressed by the post-1921 regime in the name of national independence and state sovereignty. Yet the popular politics which had first won the constitution was to re-emerge repeatedly during periods of political crisis and, in 1978–79, the urban crowd, again led by a religious-radical alliance, reappeared to engage in a final confrontation with the Pahlavi state and its army.

CHAPTER 6

Municipalities and Constitutionalism in Iran

Reza Mokhtari Esfahani
Translated by Kouross Esmaeli

Introduction

Although Iran's Constitutional Revolution did not have all the characteristics of a full-fledged revolution, the historical period did encompass many important political, social, economic, and cultural innovations. In the multiple attempts at reform, the various participants in the revolutionary movement were looking to fulfil their interests and goals. But historical accounts assert that goals of structural change were lacking within the revolutionary movement which might otherwise have qualified it as a full-scale revolution, involving 'the rapid and violent destruction of existing political institutions, the mobilization of new groups into the politics, and the creation of new political institutions'.[1] Nevertheless, the presence of new political forces such as merchants, the urban middle class, and guilds and the creation of institutions for these new forces were important by-products of the constitutional movement.

Although the final outcome of the Constitutional Revolution did not entail a complete transfer of power, the revolution was significant in the way that its participants aimed to challenge the old order through civil institutions. The various stages of the constitutional period witnessed struggles between the Court – the main institution of the old order – and the civil institutions, symbolic of the new social forces. These included the newly formed *baladiyeh* or municipalities, one of the most constructive legacies of the Constitutional Revolution.

The *baladiyeh* was one of the institutions created to facilitate the civic participation of city dwellers and to destroy or lessen the rule of non-urban forces over urban lives. In addition to civic participation, the municipalities endeavoured to render the urban forces conscious of their interests.

This chapter traces the formation of the municipalities from the later nineteenth century through the period of the Constitutional Revolution. Firstly, it demonstrates how the municipalities were at the centre of a tangle of rivalries, itself symptomatic of the centrifugal and centripetal forces in Iranian politics. These rivalries included struggles between the old central authorities and the new; between the new central authorities and the new local institutions; and between new provincial and urban local authorities. The subject also encompasses the continuing resistance of the populace to taxation and the disputes between different groups arising from this resistance. Secondly, the chapter aims to show how the municipalities represented the growth of a sense of civic responsibility and awareness, which in turn led to new, more modern, institutions in the 1920s.

Precedents to Municipal Administration

The institution of the *baladiyeh* is a legacy of the Constitutional Revolution. However, there was a traditional precedent to this institution, somewhat modified in the later nineteenth century, as signified by the name that was accorded to the leader of the municipal council: the *kalantar*. Prior to the constitutional period, the term *kalantar* had been used in urban administration to signify the position of the mediator between the government and city residents. At a lower rank than the *kalantar* was the *kadkhoda*, who was responsible for 'public order and security in cities and neighbourhoods'. According to reports in the newspaper *Vaqaye'-e Ettefaqiyeh*, it seems that the intended responsibilities of the *baladiyeh* covered military affairs and security rather than public welfare.[2] According to the same sources, the official hierarchy for urban administration was: ruler, minister, *kalantar*, *kadkhoda*.[3]

There is no specific report in *Vaqaye'-e Ettefaqiyeh* relating to urban sanitation except for a public service announcement on the possible spread of cholera. This announcement, which was submitted by the *kalantar* and the various neighbourhood *kadkhoda*s, informs the public of the importance of 'sanitation in the streets and neighbourhoods'.[4] The announcement shows that, at this point, the cleaning of public passageways and streets was specifically intended to stop the cholera epidemic rather than demonstrating a general acceptance and understanding of the official responsibilities of civil servants.

The hiring of Count Antoine di Monte Forte in 1878, after the travels of Naser al-Din Shah to Europe, ushered in a new era in urban administration in Iran. In effect, the hiring was a result of his European voyage and a new approach to urban administration. Within a year of his appointment as the Administrator for Public Order, the Count wrote a handbook on the various aspects of his administration including security, policing (*ehtesabiyeh*), and judicial and social welfare. In the handbook, the Count is identified as the 'supervisor of all municipal administrations for order, security, and law enforcement'.⁵ It can be argued that in the new laws, security and policing were aligned with social welfare whereas in previous times, the *ehtesabiyeh* and its leader, the *mohtaseb*, had been responsible solely for supervising merchants and the various professions within the bazaar, their responsibility resting mainly on standardizing weights and measures and preventing actions deemed to be against religious values.⁶

In the new laws set by the Count, the police were seen as responsible for enforcing the laws and dealing with criminal offences.⁷ The police were also responsible for various other urban matters, the most important of which was monitoring sanitation, a responsibility that had thus far been that of the *kalantar* and *kadkhoda*. The *mohtaseb*'s responsibilities were now given to the police as well. In this way, religious and lay matters came to be held as the responsibility of the same institution, and with an extra emphasis on protecting the public interest. The laws lent a modern feel to the new urban administration: 'the police have to respect the public and ensure that the public respect each other; moreover, the public is obliged to respect the police.'⁸

Among the police's many other new responsibilities were preventing famine and food shortages, monitoring sanitation, overseeing new construction and street lights, regulating trade and prices, and exercising quality control over meat.⁹ The Count's handbook also identified some specific matters, such as making it illegal to build new houses without permits, and having to register new building and architectural plans with the police. Transgression would be punished by 24-hour incarceration and a fine of one to five tumans.¹⁰

According to E'temad al-Saltaneh, the responsibility for sanitation had initially belonged to the *ehtesabiyeh*, over which Nayeb al-Saltaneh Kamran Mirza presided, but Naser al-Din Shah transferred it to E'temad al-Saltaneh in 1880. The note goes on to explain that the Count had requested control over the position for himself, and a salary of fifteen thousand tumans; the Shah, however, gave the position to E'temad al-Saltaneh. The *ehtesabiyeh* was under the control of E'temad al-Saltaneh for two years before the filthiness of the capital's streets caused open complaints. According to E'temad al-Saltaneh, the Shah was informed of this problem through 'secret newspapers' instigated by Kamran Mirza, and became concerned to the point where he took a personal tour of the streets on 25 December 1881. Upon seeing the disorder, he transferred responsibility to Nayeb al-Saltaneh, who in turn gave the position to the Count.¹¹ E'temad al-Saltaneh did not take the complaints of his detractors well, claiming that the filth in the streets was being blamed on him simply because he was absent, and that he was being used as a scapegoat.¹² E'temad al-Saltaneh did not have a positive view of the Count's administration, claming that his presence simply meant over-expenditure and the hiring of younger, 'Westernized' *kadkhodas* instead of the 'experienced, older, and civilized *kadkhodas*'.¹³

It seems that the continued problems in urban management facing the *ehtesabiyeh* led the Shah to make further changes in the municipal administration. Furthermore, the problem of the cholera epidemic added to the pressures. There is a mention of this fact in an undated letter regarding the travel of Amin Aqdas, the Shah's spouse, to Europe. The letter mentions the ruler's order to form a council for the 'sanitation of the city' comprised of E'temad al-Saltaneh, Count Nazm al-Molk (head of the police), Monsieur Denis (head of the railway), the Minister of Military Affairs, Nayeb al-Saltaneh Kamran Mirza, and the author of the letter, who seems to have been Amin al-Soltan.[14] From E'temad al-Saltaneh's daily journals, the date of the letter can be established as Rabi' I 1307/October–November 1890. Just as on the previous occasions, sanitation was proposed as a solution to the cholera epidemic. According to E'temad al-Saltaneh, on 11 November neither he nor the Count accepted this responsibility, and it remained up to the Shah to decide on a solution.[15] Until that decision was made, the responsibility was to be shared among Kamran Mirza, E'temad al-Saltaneh, and the Count. Finally, seven days later on 18 November, another meeting was held between Kamran Mirza, Amin al-Soltan, the Minister of Military Affairs, the Count, Nayyer al-Molk, and E'temad al-Saltaneh. According to E'temad al-Saltaneh 'the responsibility of urban sanitation was offered to me and I did not accept. I said that no one is better than the Count for this job. The Count accepted out of greed. He wrote a requisition for a transfer of seven thousand tumans to himself so he could get started right away. The requisition was taken to His Majesty. The Shah did not accept. He claimed that the residents should be responsible for their own sanitation.'[16]

A few months later, E'temad al-Saltaneh was able to acquire the title and post of Ehtesab al-Molk for his nephew, Taqi Khan, and according to eyewitness accounts, the Count's handbook on urban administration did not enjoy further implementation.

Municipalities during the Constitutional Period

During the constitutional period, municipalities were aligned with urban forces with the direct aim of giving responsibility for municipal matters to urban residents. The First Article of the Municipal Law states that 'The main purpose for the establishment of the municipalities is to protect the interests of the cities and their inhabitants.' The proceedings of the First Majles also show how the peoples' representatives aimed, through any means necessary, to force the control of the price of everyday necessities such as bread and meat out of the hands of the central government so that the Court would not be able to use these issues as political leverage.

The words of Aqa Seyyed Abdollah Behbahani speak to these concerns: 'We have struggled to free bread and meat from their control. They want to make profits from these matters. The eight people who are made responsible are not allowing a proper solution to this issue. Everyday they create a new game to distress and trouble the public.'[17] However, in the same proceedings, Seyyed Hasan Taqizadeh warned the Majles against intervening in specific issues and suggested that there be a 'municipal council' comprised of members of 'each class and guild' to deal with these matters.[18] It was because of these worries and concerns that Article Two of the Municipal Law identified one of the responsibilities of the council as 'fighting against urban food scarcity as much as possible'.[19] But the Municipal Law did not simply aim to protect the urban population. In what seems to be a translation from Western law,[20] Municipal Law also aimed to educate the urban population in civic matters. This is a matter that had a great influence on the modernization of the urban space. Of course, the agenda went even further than the education of city residents. As can be deduced from the words of Ehtesham al-Saltaneh, the Speaker of the First Majles during the deliberations over this law, it was generally understood that this matter needs 'to be generalized and public awareness needed to be spread to the villages as well'.[21] With this duty in sight, the municipal councils took on the responsibility for public education through 'facilitating the establishment of libraries, reading rooms, and museums as well as the upkeep of mosques, schools, and old buildings'.[22] It is not an exaggeration to say that the establishment of municipalities was intended to educate the urban population and to achieve their entrance into civic and modern life with an eye to their gaining eventual control over power in the new system.

In reality, the *baladiyeh* was an institution meant to give control over urban matters to the urban population. In the history of Iran, urban forces had generally been at the mercy of tribal leaders and the tribal base of governments had meant that various urban classes enjoyed little control over their resources to defend their interests. The Municipal Law aimed to force non-urban power out of the urban centres. As such, one of the requirements for electing and being elected onto the municipal council, other than being an Iranian citizen, was 'paying taxes or owning a house or real estate within the city limits'. This requirement was further limited by the price of the property in question. In large cities the minimum acceptable price was 1,000 tumans, in medium-sized cities 500 tumans and in small cities 300 tumans. There was thus an implicit property qualification, which could be interpreted as representing the interests of the middle social groups so active in bringing the parliament into being. Among civil institutions, it was only educational and philanthropic bodies that were allowed to participate in elections, and that participation was limited to their right to propose a representative and even that on the condition that the group owned property within the city limits. Merchants, on the other hand, had a special status. Even if they owned no real estate in the city, they were still allowed to participate in municipal elections if they owned a shop front or trading post.

The list of those disqualified from elections included felons, criminals, bankrupt individuals, and municipal tax debtors. (Women were also barred.[23]) Thus, the law was calculated to allow participation only by those who had a direct interest in the city and whose interests were tied to the improvement of the city's needs. This inclination to tie the individual representatives' interests to those of the municipality is what distinguished municipal election laws from the laws that governed the national Majles elections.

The new Municipal Law took the further step of barring 'rulers and their deputies', 'police staff', 'military personnel including [those of] the army and navy', and all government employees from serving on municipal councils.[24] It seems as if the lawmakers were intent on lessening the prerogatives of the central government in municipal concerns. This is further proven by the fact that the Majles saw itself as an institution so independent of the existing central government system that it wanted to take responsibility for municipal matters until the formation of the municipal councils. Aqa Seyyed Mohammad Tabataba'i justified this step before the Municipal Law was passed by the Majles thus: 'Once we have municipal and justice councils, it will be important for the Majles to refrain from intervening in specificities [that pertain to municipal matters.] But what are we to do now while we do not have [these councils]?'[25] The deputies believed that the turmoil in various regions of the country was caused by the officials of the old order. When telegrams describing disturbances from various regions reached the parliament, Aqa Seyyed Hoseyn said, 'All this turmoil and noise from all corners of the country such as Rasht, Qazvin, and other regions is a result of the nonexistence of the municipal charters. Passing this law is the overriding priority, so write the municipal charter and send it to the provinces to stop the chaos.' Although Aqa Seyyed Hoseyn was confusing provincial councils with municipal councils,[26] the aim of both of these institutions was to take power away from the officials of the old order and give it to the elected representatives of the people. This enthusiasm can be seen within the populace as well. In Isfahan, for example, one of the mass sit-ins at the telegraph office had the specific demand that the central government send the provincial and municipal charters. The city's top ulema, Mohammad Taqi Najafi and Aqa Sheykh Nurollah, sent a telegram informing the Majles deputies that the disturbances were 'directly related to the passage of the provincial and municipal constitutions'.[27] The letter sent from Tehran to the Isfahan council newspaper announcing the passage and distribution of the municipal council charter promised a solution to the city's problems in light of the new laws: 'According to the charter, a council will be formed for each municipality. For the time being, a temporary council will advise on municipal matters such as street lights, water wells, sanitation drains, water drains, and street cleaning.'[28]

Finally, the Municipal Law was passed, after some debate, by the Majles on 2 June 1907 and signed by the Shah.[29] The law was the basis and origin of the municipal councils which were comprised of representatives from each city's different quarters. In large cities, the council had 30 members, in medium-sized-cities it had 20 members, and in small cities 16 members. The term limit for the councillors was four years.[30] As already mentioned, there was a strong emphasis on independence from the central government. According to Article 64, for example, 'members of the municipal council would not draw a salary from the state or the nation.'[31] It seems as if the law was meant to sever the economic ties between the municipal councils and the central government and to guarantee that the councils did not lose their civic characteristic and turn to corruption and abuse of power. It also ensured that rulers would not have any role in the councils' administration. The head of the council would be elected by a majority vote of the members, although the holder of the position would be formally approved by the order of Shah, in the case of Tehran and provincial capitals, and by the Minister of the Interior in the case of other cities.[32] Within the municipality, power and legitimacy would come from the electoral process of the municipal council so that the head of the council, the *kalantar*, was also considered the chief administrator of the municipality. The *kalantar* would appoint one of the four members of the core municipal administration as his deputy. This appointment was to be approved by the Minister of the Interior. The four administrators were elected by the municipal council members and their term, like the *kalantar*'s, was four years. These four years were organized in such a way that after the first two years, half of the members would leave according to lottery and new members would be elected in their place. If, after the end of any two years, there were members who had already served four years in the municipal administration, they would leave and new members be elected in their place. The municipality, therefore, became a place completely run and administered electorally, with its chief members chosen by the municipal council, whose members in turn were chosen by the electorate. The municipal administration's decisions were valid and enforceable by a majority vote. In case of a deadlock, the *kalantar*, who was directly elected by the people, would cast the deciding vote. The *kalantar*, as the chief of the municipal administration as well as the representative of the municipal council in that office, could veto a decision by the administration if he deemed it 'in the interest of the city and the public' and notify the municipal council of his decision.[33]

The Municipal Law was not completely implemented. In Tabriz, the municipality was organized in such a way that the *beyglarbeygi* (Turkish for *kalantar*) had control of the city and the municipality. The individual neighbourhood leaders (*kadkhoda*) were under his supervision. He had a deputy (*nayeb*) who in turn supervised his own deputies, the *farrash*es.³⁴ The *kadkhoda* was a permanent post whose holder was appointed by the elders of the quarters and considered a middleman between the quarters and government officials.

In Tabriz's city governance, there was a municipal administration and eleven quarters, each with a *nayeb* and several *farrash*es. Before the constitutional movement, the *farrash*es had made their living through blackmail and bribes. However, the Tabriz council brought the posts of *nayeb* and *farrash* into the government bureaucracy as municipal employees. It was decided that they would receive two government-issued suits every year. These suits had 'specific badges and medals' in order to identify the 'neighbourhood *farrash*'. Regulations were enacted to prevent the pre-constitutional practices of the *nayeb* and *farrash*: '… (2) Whoever acts against the civil laws will be accountable to the person in the next highest post. (3) A limited number of government-issued guns and bullets will be distributed so that [these officials] can be in regular control of the order and security of the city. (4) Any wrongdoer from the wider province, even a merchant, military officer, etc., who is [subpoenaed] must be treated with respect and brought to the relevant body by the *farrash*. (5) If the *farrash* disrespects or transgresses the rights of any individual or if he accepts bribes, he will be permanently barred from public service in addition to the appropriate legal punishment.'³⁵ In light of the confusion and disarray in the city, it seems that the Tabriz constitutionalists preferred to rely on the old municipal system rather than create new institutions. They decided to update the old system by creating monitoring rules for the old officials and posts. This was done under the supervision and approval of the Anjoman-e Melli.

Traditionally, the *kadkhoda*s had been chosen by the elders responsible for each quarter, but in the new system established by the Tabriz council, they were now responsible to the council and, in case of wrongdoing, were banned from public service forever.³⁶ There is much to be said about the power and influence of the *kadkhoda*. When there was a political polarization in Tabriz, at the suggestion of Seqat al-Eslam Tabrizi, it was decided that each *kadkhoda* appoint four influential residents of each quarter who would participate in the collective resolution of the problem.³⁷

The first action of the Tabriz municipality in this vein was the by-laws on city sanitation written and submitted to the Anjoman-e Melli of Tabriz by Rafiʿ al-Dowleh, the Tabriz *beyglarbeygi*. This by-law included guidelines for city sanitation as well as hygiene for the trades and guilds. According to the new rules, cows and sheep were to be slaughtered outside of the city, and during the transportation of the meat, care had to be taken so as to prevent contamination. Felt-makers (*namadmal*) were forced to transfer their workspaces to caravanserais and private shops in order to guard against pollution and illness. Storefronts had to have steps that would not obstruct the narrow public passageways. And there were also guidelines for bathhouses, bakers, and arms dealers. The *farrash*es were banned from accepting gifts or bribes.[38] This announcement seems to be the first act that aimed to improve city life passed by any municipality after the ratification of the constitution and the Municipal Law. The Isfahan council newspaper printed an article dated Safar 1326/ March 1908 about the activities of the municipal council in Tehran which is worth considering. The article reports on the erection of city lights in the streets of Tehran and the fact that the municipality 'is in the process of placing tiled numbers on houses and doors. They are starting from the four corners of the city and charging each house a qeran for the tiles, but it seems the tiled numbers are small and misshapen as a result of certain [misguided] money-saving measures.' The reporter makes an important point about this process of naming and numbering Tehran streets and houses: 'Thank God the streets of Tehran are losing their anonymity and acquiring names and numbers.'[39]

A year later (after Tehran had been retaken by the constitutionalists) the Tabriz municipality actually assumed most of the responsibilities that had been accorded to it by law. This meant, in the cultural sphere, such matters as printing, education and educational endowments, and the publication of journals; and in the social realm, issues such as the burying of the poor, the pensions and welfare for the poor, orphans and the relatives of murder victims, and public hospitals. Steps to create more order and to improve the cityscape included 'numbering street carriages as well as shop fronts in and out of the bazaar, affixing city lights and [making] gravelled roads'.[40] These steps show that the municipality was concerned not just with modernizing the appearance of the city but with its social life in general. Social welfare and diminishing the effects of poverty and misery were also matters that the Tabriz municipality took into consideration.

Another important matter was the municipality's right to accept or reject public advertisements and announcements. The urban trades did not have complete control over the publication of their advertisements. For example, in an incident in Dhu l-Qa'da 1327/November–December 1909, Tehran's Farus printing house circulated an announcement by a physician. The municipality warned the printer that he 'must produce the diploma of the said doctor and only then publish his announcement'. The Ministry of Education concurred on this step since the municipal council had the right to prevent announcements that 'are harmful to the public interest'.[41]

At times this modernization of social life was effected through the changing of external aspects of city life, which had a profound effect on the lifestyle of the city dwellers. Through the regulations imposed on them by the municipal council, the citizens gained access to a form of collective social life. For instance, in 1909, as a result of the cholera epidemic which threatened Tehran, the municipal council was forced to stop people from 'relieving themselves' in the streams. It was decided that 'a few toilets would be built using the municipality budget so that people would know that there are places other than streams for this necessity.'[42]

Although they were ostensibly concerned with health and sanitation, the fact is that these regulations caused changes in urban public behaviour. In the announcements issued by the municipal councils one can perceive an attempt to inculcate in the population a new and more sociable attitude, including the idea that public spaces should be shared by all rather than appropriated by individuals. For example, the Tehran municipal council on 10 October 1912 issued a statement regarding the obstruction of public passageways: 'In order to remove all obstacles from public streets and crosswalks and to provide pedestrians with easy passageways, a five-day warning is issued to all shopkeepers to remove all their goods from the front of their stores and steps and to stop selling goods in the streets altogether.'[43] Another announcement dated 6 May 1917 discouraged the selling of goods such as yoghurt, yoghurt drinks (*dugh*), and herbs on pavements since 'it creates a nuisance for pedestrians.'[44] Such regulations aimed to create a more comfortable life for citizens by spreading the idea that public space is not private property and that it should be protected from improper behaviour. It is not baseless to say that the *baladiyeh* was teaching modern and civil life to the urban population and spreading urban values in general.

Municipal Revenues and Disputes with the Ministry of Finance

Article 70 of the Municipal Law, relating to the councils' responsibilities, also speaks of budgetary concerns: 'Easement and taxes to be extracted from the residents of the city for the municipalities' expenditure are to be determined' by the councils.[45]

According to this subsection, the municipal council had the right to determine those taxes that were levied on the citizens according to the law. This responsibility became a source of great tension between the *baladiyeh* and the Finance Ministry. The first tax bill that the municipalities introduced to the Majles was a transportation tax to be levied on carriages, carts, wagons, etc. According to the bill, taxes were to be collected in the following manner:

> Private carriages and coaches: 5 qerans per month or 6 tumans per year
> Commercial carriages and stagecoaches: 25 qerans per month or 30 tumans per year

Carts: 3 tumans per month or 18 tumans per year
Bicycles: 6 qerans per month or 7.2 tumans per year
Ice cream carts: 1 qeran per month or 12 qerans per year
Automobiles: 1 tuman per month or 12 tumans per year
Commercial automobiles: same as above
Wagons: set at 3 tumans per month
Stagecoaches and carts from outside city limits must pay 4 hezars each time they enter the city.'[46]

At the end, after much deliberation, the Majles only passed 'taxes on private carriages and coaches' at 5 hezars (5 qerans) per month.[47] The problem with municipal taxes legislated by the Majles was that they were scarcely taken seriously. For example, the Isfahan municipality, in order to cover its own expenses, had to levy its own taxes on various commodities such as tobacco, opium, barks, and skins that were exported from the city, as well as on coffeehouses of the Meydan-e Shah (the city's main square) and on the weighing of coal and rice which were exported to Yazd and Kashan.[48]

Ledgers at the Tabriz municipality attest to the fact that the municipality in that city had overstepped its legal boundaries in terms of tax collection. The following 15 cases are mentioned: (1) 12 percent of real estate tax, (2) Water taxes, (3) Road tolls, (4) Private and public carriages and coaches, (5) Postal stamps, (6) Merchant permits in city squares, (7) Guild permits, (8) Cash summonses and penalties, (9) Tariffs on transportation tickets, (10) Rents on the armory, (11) Rents on merchants in Saheb al-Amr Square, (12) Scale monitoring in the guilds and bazaars, (13) Notary, (14) Stamping of unofficial tickets, (15) Rents on the Shah's endowed storefronts.[49] Finally, in the Second Majles, the municipalities' interference in the collection of city revenues caused an open conflict with the Ministry of Finance. The Majles committee on municipalities was of the opinion that separate bills were needed to provide for what the municipalities could collect.[50] In the 46th session of the Majles, Matin al-Saltaneh asked if taxes on the sale of farm animals (*suq al-davabb*) and coffeehouses could be levied. Sadiq Hazrat responded that no such taxes had been passed by the Majles and that the *baladiyeh* had collected them illegally. He even informed the deputies that during the incumbency of the Second Majles, the *baladiyeh* had asked to have a hand in all 'city taxes'. In that same session, Morteza Qoli Sani' al-Dowleh, the Minister of Education, proclaimed this to be a grievous error and asked the Majles to remedy it. In his view 'the municipalities and the municipal offices being established in this country believe that whatever is collected in the city must be spent in that city, and because in the city of Tehran the government receives tax income both from real estate and non-real estate, they believe that all these should be spent for the city likewise for other cities.' Sani' al-Dowleh pointed out that there were two kinds of taxes, one of which was to be spent in the same place that it was collected, and the other which had a 'general purpose and had to be paid by all the people in the country.'[51] Sani' al-Dowleh's statement points to the fact that the municipal councils were trying to establish their own independence from the central government and to spread their own influence through social work and development programmes. Finally, in that same session of parliament, taxes on rental carriages were passed as municipal taxes.[52] However, the local taxes levied on transportation vehicles as announced by the *baladiyeh* on 13 June 1910 surpassed the Majles provision, for they included taxes not only on rental carriages but also on coaches, bicycles (both personal and for transportation), hauling crates, numberless crates, hauling carts, numberless carts, carriage horses, handcarts, etc.[53] However, ledgers for the Tehran municipality for the year 1329 (1910–11) show that the municipality had collected taxes not only from rental carriages and bicycles and carts but also from coffeehouses, livestock markets, Mohammadiyeh Square rents, and royalties on oil.[54] The Ministry of Finance constantly objected to the municipality's intervening in various tax collections. For example, the Azarbayjan office of the ministry, in a letter to the ministry headquarters on 10 November 1914, wrote: 'all tax revenues, except for those levied on transportation vehicles are considered a part of the government treasury and do not belong to the municipality.' Another letter from the Ministry of Finance to the Ministry of the Interior, in a complaint regarding the municipality of Savojbolagh Mokri (currently Mahabad), informs us about taxes on livestock: 'In the name of municipal expenses, the Savojbolagh Mokri municipal administration has claimed possession not only of taxes on livestock, which are direct taxes, but also indirect taxes, which in the past were all part of direct taxes to the central government.'[55] In one incident, the Ministry of Finance representative who had objected to some activities of the municipality of Isfahan was 'arrested, beaten, and detained'.[56] Of course, incidents that were the reverse of this were also recorded, such as when the office of the Ministry of Finance in Fars Province took control of the province's transportation administration away from the municipality and thereby deprived it of its only source of revenue. This act resulted in a sit-in at the Shiraz telegraph office by the members of the city's municipal council[57] (10 May 1915). The Finance Ministry was operating under the assumption that any and all taxes must be collected and dispersed under its sole control. The Ministry of Finance, in a letter dated 5 May 1915, pointed out to the Ministry of the Interior that 'the direct meddling of the municipal administration is against the principles and laws of the Ministry of Finance and works against the centralization of revenue collection. This will adversely affect the wages and expenses for such offices as the security forces, hospitals, and other agencies that are dependent on these taxes. The Ministry of Finance deems illegal such irregular meddling by the aforementioned administration.'[58]

The letter is significant for the link that it makes between the Ministry of Finance and budgets for public services such as police and hospitals. The municipal councils had other problems in addition to those with the Finance Ministry over transportation taxes. For example, the *chaparkhaneh*, which was in charge of the postal service, raised objections to paying a transit tax to the municipalities in light of the terrible state of the roads.[59] In one case, the transit tax caused riots in the city of Qom, to the point that the local ulema joined the demonstrators in their sit-in at the Hazrat Ma'sumeh shrine. The protesters were farmers who wanted an exemption from the toll on their animals, which were primarily used for 'farming and manure transportation'. According to the Qom office of the Ministry of Finance, 'a group of farmers formed a council for the purpose of negotiating and reforming local taxes. The council, which even created its own official stamp, intervenes in local financial and political matters and makes unacceptable demands on the local office of the Ministry of Finance.' The same report makes the point that since 'a part of the transportation tax is used for city sanitation and lighting' the residents do not have the right to ask for an exemption from it.[60] If we accept the report of the Qom office of the Ministry of Finance, the class basis of the protests consisted of farmers from outside city limits who were forced to pay transit tax because of their economic ties to the city. But since they did not benefit from the lighting and sanitation of the city, they protested against paying the tax.

In addition to the many problems facing the municipal councils in defining and carrying out their responsibilities, foreign meddling, especially by the Russians, became yet another source of pressure following the occupation of Iran and the closing of the Second Majles in 1911. Russian consulates in various Iranian cities prevented their subjects from paying the transit tax. In one example in Ardabil, the Russian vice-consul claimed that his obstruction of the payment of the transit tax by Russian subjects rested on their demand that 'an honorary representative of the Russian merchants sit on the municipal council at all times.'[61]

As we have seen, then, the municipal council, in fulfilling its most important obligation – setting a budget and collecting revenues – faced problems from the government, various social groups, and foreign powers.

Comparison of the Municipal Council Laws of 1907 and 1930

Much like the rest of the legislation and institutions created during the constitutional period, the Municipal Council Law passed in 1907 did not have a happy ending. Although the municipal councils were to be elected by the populace, in the prime minister's decree of March–April 1921, the leadership of the Tehran municipality was transferred to the prime minister.[62] And then, in many cities, the municipal councils which were supposed to set up the municipalities never got off the ground. With the advent of Reza Shah and increasing centralization, the Municipal Law of the constitutional period lost its relevance. The Majles passed a new law on 20 May 1930, which superseded the Municipal Council Law of 1907. The municipal council thereafter became class-based, and only merchants, guilds, and property owners were allowed to participate in municipal elections.[63] Under the new system, electors chose five times as many representatives as necessary. From this list, the Ministry of the Interior chose and proposed a smaller list of representatives to the cabinet, out of which the cabinet appointed the new council. Those who had received more than 3/10 of the vote had precedence over those who had received less than 3/10.[64] As is clear from the preceding, the municipal council members took part in a two-tiered election process whereby in the second round of elections they were chosen by the government in accordance with the law that openly called this step the 'appointment' of council members. In part three of the regulations of the municipality, the responsibilities of the municipal council were described as 'studying' the proposals of the municipalities and ratifying them.[65] Whereas in the earlier law, the head of the municipal council (the *kalantar*) headed the municipality, in the new law, 'the municipal administration was under the leadership of one person ... who was chosen and appointed by the Interior Ministry.'[66] In reality, it was now the government that controlled the municipality and the municipality became an arm of the Interior Ministry, whereas in the earlier Municipal Law of 1907, the Shah as the highest officeholder in the nation had put his seal of approval to the elected leadership of the municipal council. In the earlier system, the head of the municipal council and the municipality, like the prime minister, was an elected official whose election by the people the Shah merely endorsed. As state power in Iran was centralized, the municipalities came under direct government control, becoming half-elected, half-appointed bodies. But these new institutions were to prove more successful than their predecessors in the task of modernizing the cities.

Conclusion

The *baladiyeh* was born in the constitutional period to voice the interests of city residents within the revolutionary movement. The Municipal Law was a general blueprint for a civil institution aimed at furthering the citizens' control over their lives and environment. Once enacted, however, this blueprint met continuous problems and obstacles to the point where it was never institutionalized. The municipal council was designated as the watchdog and administrator of the municipalities; however, in the implementation of the Municipal Law this institution remained generally neglected or completely ignored. In many cities, the municipal councils were never even formed. Needless to say, at a time when the national parliament itself was constantly threatened with dissolution or dormancy, it was perhaps too much to hope that the municipal councils would meet a better fate. Nevertheless, the municipalities made a noble attempt at improving cultural, social, and living conditions in their cities. Among the contributions of the municipal movement was the formation of a collective atmosphere and a spirit that were evident in the various cities where the *baladiyeh* was active. The municipalities brought modernity to the life and culture of Iranian cities and allowed for those forces that were trying to achieve control over their own local politics to gain a lesson in civic and civil politics ahead of the rest of society. The movement was slow in the beginning, but grew quite influential with time. The municipalities faced problems not only in their formation but also in the continuation of their mission, for example in being allocated inadequate budgets. They aspired to independence from the government, especially from its finance officials, but faced insurmountable hurdles in their quest.

It would seem that the municipalities were perceived as the representatives of each region vis-à-vis the government, perhaps embodying the local populations' yearning for greater autonomy from the central government. The attempt to collect taxes beyond what was stipulated in the Municipal Law was an indication of this trend. For this reason it is fair to say that the changes in the Municipal Law under Reza Shah, especially the substitution of elected bodies by appointed ones, were a reaction to this trend and a move towards centralization.

Finally, the institution of the *baladiyeh* was one of the many aspirations of the Constitutional Revolution. However, their actual implementation fell far short of the aspirations, and in the end, like so many other aspirations of the revolution, they remained unfulfilled for the time being.

Part III
Nation-Building

CHAPTER 7

Merchants, Their Class Identification Process, and Constitutionalism

Soheila Torabi Farsani

In the traditional fabric of Iranian society, merchants could in no sense be called a social 'class-for-itself'. They belonged at the centre of complex bazaar networks and were dependent on other groups, particularly the *sarrafs* (traditional bankers or moneylenders) and the *asnaf* (guilds), to further their interests and to negotiate with the state, as well as to protect the bazaar as a whole against the state's depredations. The hypothesis of this chapter is that a generative process took place between the late nineteenth century and the 1920s whereby the merchants disengaged themselves from their former allies amongst the *sarrafs* and *asnaf* and acquired the characteristics of a 'class-for-itself'. This chapter looks at the period of the Constitutional Revolution as a stage in the formation of the merchants as a 'class-for-itself', and discusses how far they were able to disengage themselves from their allied groups, and what impediments they faced in achieving class awareness and solidarity.

The process of social identification took place over a span of time extending from a few decades before the constitutional movement to the very first years after the end of the First World War. During this period there were both a gradual accumulation of wealth in the hands of merchants and an increasing internal integrity forging individual merchants into a distinct social class with its clearly defined interests. However, the perpetual social unrest, insecurity, financial crises, class weaknesses, and intra-class conflicts of the period of the Constitutional Revolution and the years which followed it were crucial impediments to this class-identification process. Correspondingly close ties among merchants, ulema, and *asnaf* were maintained in the familiar traditional setting of Iranian society, and did not change much even after the victory of the Constitutional Revolution and establishment of modern institutions. By the early Pahlavi period (and outside the remit of this chapter) a substantial degree of class consciousness and class solidarity was emerging, which brought along a deep sense of being a 'class-for-itself', clearly evident in subsequent political skirmishes with state officials, which undoubtedly were of a nature none other than that of a class conflict.

This chapter defines a merchant as one engaged in the wholesale buying and selling of commodities to make a profit. Merchants are divided into three groups by the amount of capital they possess and the scope of their trading: large merchants engaged in export and import trading, medium-sized merchants conducting business within the boundaries of the country itself, and wholesalers (*bonakdar*) acting as intermediaries between other merchants and retailers in the bazaar.[1] The term 'class-in-itself' has been taken from Marx, who applied it to a social group at a stage of development somewhere between class conscientiousness and class consciousness.[2] Class is used in the sense of a cohesive social group whose members have similar economic status and common interests, enjoy a more or less similar social status, and occupy a similar social base, making them self-aware and enabling them to exert a certain amount of power.

Beginning the discussion, therefore, in the late nineteenth century, it may be noted that the merchants had a certain distinct organizational identity in a guild of their own, headed by a *ra'is al-tojjar* (head of the merchants). However, the main function of this body was to negotiate with state officials on the amount of taxes to be levied on merchants, to settle financial claims made against merchants, and to deal with bankruptcy cases. The growth of foreign trade in Iran, particularly from the 1860s onwards, when the first state concessions were given to foreigners, led to an influx of foreign capital into the country. This meant that Iranian merchants found themselves in the midst of fierce competition resulting in the gradual process which was to make them aware of themselves as a distinct social class.

Faced with the intrusion of foreign capital, Iranian merchants tried, well before the advent of the constitutional movement, to improve their situation by establishing trading companies and financial institutions, particularly a national bank; they also made repeated attempts to invest in modern industries and transportation, including trying to obtain state concessions to build and manage road networks and railways. In addition, they aimed to establish a national bank, presumably to replace the Shahi bank.

In the few decades before the constitutional movement, merchants made many attempts to establish trading and financial companies. These included the Kompani-ye Tejarati-ye Iran (Iran Trading Company) in 1885, the Ettehadieh company in 1888, the Naseri company in 1890, the Sherkat-e 'Omumi-ye Tejarati (General Trading Company) in 1894, the Eslamiyeh company in 1898, along with dozens of other companies and merchant houses in and around that time.[3] Merchants also tried to invest in modern industries and transportation networks. For example, Amin al-Zarb founded a silk weaving factory in Rasht and obtained a concession from Naser al-Din Shah to connect Mahmudabad and Amol by railway. Factories were also established in Tehran and a few provincial towns, such as a cotton-cordspinning factory (1857), a gun-making factory (1858), and a crystal-making factory (1867).[4]

At this time, the traditional structures within which merchants dealt with one another and conducted their relations vis-à-vis the state were going through a transitional phase, bringing about a changing order of affairs. The growth in commercial ties with foreign countries, which required travelling to the West and acquiring knowledge of how trading was conducted in advanced countries, and the social prominence enjoyed by their Western counterparts, made merchants more class-conscious, leading them to adopt new strategies to match their newly acquired 'social awareness'. Consequently, in 1883 they established the 'Merchants' Representatives Council' (Majles-e vokala-ye tojjar), their very first association, and actively participated in the anti-tobacco-concession movement of 1890–92, which gave them confidence, as they had managed to turn the tables on state officials and nullify what they saw as policies harmful to their economic interests.

The Merchants and the Moneylenders

As has been mentioned, at this time merchants had close links with another significant group in the bazaar, the *sarraf*s or moneylenders. These moneylenders were engaged in financial dealings and acted as traditional bankers; their sphere of activity was different from that of merchants, though there were some major merchants who, apart from carrying out purely commercial dealings, were also involved in moneylending. Moneylenders sometimes took up commercial commodities or agricultural land as security against the loans they made out. According to documents in the Ettehadieh archives, moneylenders constituted a social group clearly distinguished from that of merchants, a group which was made up of three different layers, i.e., major, minor, and peddler moneylenders.[5]

To conclude foreign transactions, merchants required the financial services of moneylenders, who were dominant in the Iranian money market before the introduction of modern banking services by the British and the Russians. In the face of foreign capital intruding into the country, merchants and moneylenders felt that both groups were, so to speak, in the same boat. Both groups regarded Western capital as their fiercest competitor and took a similar stance against it. Nevertheless, there were occasions on which moneylenders showed signs of differentiation from merchants, and where there seemed to be a conflict of interests.

Economic recession, shortage of bank notes and coins, and sociopolitical insecurity created a situation of financial instability. Volatile markets and constantly changing interest rates would inflict financial loss on both merchants and moneylenders. To decrease the amount of the losses incurred during a crisis, moneylenders were able to convert their money capital into silver coins, but merchants who were engaged in trading commodities made substantial losses when interest rates changed sharply, and thus were inclined to seek stable interest rates.[6] Moneylenders also used the constant change in interest rates to make profits from buying and selling and converting copper coins into silver coins and vice versa, in order to 'add a few nickels to their profit'.[7] Merchants, for their part, interpreted this volatility in money markets as 'gambling'. *Sarrafs* hoarded coins in the hope of converting them at higher rates later. This would lead to a sharp decrease in the amount of money in circulation and a subsequent increase in interest rates, a situation whereby *sarrafs* made great profits and merchants made heavy losses. Whenever there was an increase in interest rates, merchants and *sarrafs* would get into a head-on conflict. Merchants needed credit from *sarrafs* to facilitate their transactions and, thus, whenever there was an increase in the lending rate, they incurred heavy losses.

In a letter in the Ettehadieh archives we read, '*Sarrafs* and merchants are engaged in daily meetings in order somehow to reduce the conversion rate of the qeran.'[8] *Sarrafs* and merchants naturally each wanted to come to an eventual agreement to their own benefit.[9] For example, as Haj Ali Akbar, a moneylender, claims in a letter, 'Merchants made an effort to persuade the *mujtahids* that moneylenders engage in gambling in the midst of the bazaar.'[10] It was also alleged that the merchants were calling financial transactions conducted by moneylenders *qomar-e qonsolot* (consulate gambling),[11] in order to get the upper hand on the moneylenders by agitating the clerical authorities against them.

Although in the years prior to the constitutional movement moneylenders got together and made a number of collective decisions, they suffered from internal disputes. At one stage it was reported that '[Moneylenders] have decided not to accept any money orders [*havalehs*] from bazaar [merchants] and have sealed a petition to that effect ... except for Haj Kazem, who has declined to seal the petition and says he would not bind himself by any such pledges; he would accept money orders at the going rate.'[12] Whenever there was a financial crisis these disputes could turn into open hostility. According to one merchant in October 1898: 'Shortage of cash has reached such an extent that moneylenders seem to be all idle ... fighting one another over the available cash in the bazaar.'[13] It is evident from different sources that the establishment of modern financial institutions and the subsequent change in the structure of the economy had a devastating effect on the status of moneylenders, weakening them so much that by the end of the nineteenth century and the first two decades of the twentieth century they had lost their prominence within the bazaar.

For their part, merchants adopted new strategies, diversified their business activities, got involved in the anti-tobacco concession and constitutional movements, and assumed a more active part in political affairs, trying to conform to the new business environment and in the process developing a sense of 'class-for-itself' consciousness. With the triumph of the constitutional movement, merchants made the Majles an arena in which to pursue their social demands. They saw in the democratic process a chance whereby they could realize their demands through Majles legislation.

The active involvement of merchants in drafting the election law (*nezam-nameh-ye entekhabat*), and their firm stand on the demand for constitutionalism, were such that 'merchants and guild masters and moneylenders in the [British] legation compounds say they would not leave [the legation] unless a Majles is established to their satisfaction.'[14] As a result, merchants and bazaar guild members constituted 41 percent of the deputies in the First Majles.[15] Merchants participated actively in the elections to the First Majles; a majority of the wealthy merchants all over the country were active members of the election-monitoring committees.[16] There were, of course, signs of elections being rigged by merchants,[17] which is an indication of the importance the Majles had for them. They had high hopes and regarded the Majles as an institution which they could use to realize their demands. A review of the proceedings of the Majles and laws passed shows a distinct and effective influence exerted by merchants on the First Majles arising from the importance which they saw in this new institution.

Chamber of Commerce (Anjoman-e Tejarat)

The merchant deputies in the Majles introduced a motion on 17 May 1907 to set up formally a chamber of commerce, which was to be housed in a proper building allocated by the government.[18] There were lengthy sessions dealing with this issue, but there is no clear and positive indication that the chamber was actually established.[19] Nevertheless, newspapers of the day, for example *Neda-ye Vatan* on 29 May 1907, carried news of the establishment of a chamber of commerce in Tehran, where 'zealous merchants' met two days a week to discuss matters like 'the propagation of Iranian products to replace foreign products' and to set up rules and regulations pertaining to financial transactions.[20]

The chamber was a distinctly professional association where the participation of major merchants seemed essential. Thus, merchant deputies in the Majles made every effort to change the legal status of the chamber into a formal, regulated permanent body. In consecutive Majles sessions a motion on a chamber of commerce was discussed, a code (*nezamnameh-ye anjomanha-ye tejarati*) to maintain the chamber of commerce was read to deputies, and there were negotiations pertaining to drafting a 'commercial law'. The Minister for Trade, during a speech delivered in the Majles on 6 January 1908, said the country needed a 'school for commerce'.[21]

Iranian expatriate merchants, too, established their own chamber of commerce in order to conduct their trading in an organized and improved way. Mirza Mohammad Amin al-Tojjar, who headed the Iranian merchants in Bombay, received a third-order *Shir o Khorshid* (Sun and Lion) medal as a reward for his distinguished efforts to promote trade ties. In a speech delivered to Iranian residents in Bombay, he declared that India's commercial success was due to the establishment of a chamber of commerce.[22] Bombay-based Iranian merchants were involved in other associations too: for instance the Anjoman-e Vatankh'ahan-e Irani (Iranian Patriotic Society), founded in February 1907, headed by Mirza Ebrahim Tajer Shirazi. The constitution of this society maintained that Iranian Shiite Muslims were eligible to apply for membership on the condition that they pay a membership fee of one anna a month. It declared one of its main aims to be to support constitutionalism and the Majles in Iran and to promote unity, egalitarianism, and fraternity among its members.[23]

Habl al-Matin, too, reported on 24 June 1907 that Istanbul-based Iranian merchants, in a meeting held at the trading office of Aqa Mirza Aqa (Mojahed) Tajer Esfahani, had made an effort to set up their own chamber of commerce. The Ottoman government had reacted negatively to the idea. After some lengthy negotiations a quasi-agreement was reached maintaining that the chamber would solely engage in the affairs of Iranian merchants based in the Ottoman Empire and would not meddle in the internal affairs of the host country, leading to a subsequent lifting of state restrictions.[24]

The Merchants' Association (Anjoman-e Tojjar)

Politicized merchants, in addition to their active and effective participation in the Majles, and with the hope of benefiting from modern institutions stemming from the constitutional revolution, set up an association named Anjoman-e Tojjar (Merchants' Association), with branches in Tehran and provincial cities. There are no documents left to indicate what the constitution of the association might have consisted of, how the sessions were held and conducted, or who its founding members were. It is not certain how many, if any, of the merchant deputies in the Majles were also active in this association; nevertheless, there are evident indications that this may have been the case. It is known that Haj Mohammad Taqi Bonakdar, a Majles merchant deputy, made a great effort to hold celebrations on the anniversary of the granting of the Majles, at the merchants' association.²⁵

The aims of the Anjoman-e Tojjar are mentioned in a pamphlet entitled 'The association of the order of merchants in Isfahan', published by the Isfahan branch of the association in 1907. These aims included the propagation of Iranian products, the banning of foreign products except those that could be used to expand Iran's industrial base, the expansion of domestic industries in order to have a greater share of the textile market, and the establishment of publicly owned companies.²⁶ The Yazd branch invested 18,000 tumans in founding a company with the ultimate aim of producing textiles. They intended to import the machinery from Russia and employ Russian experts and also ask the ulema to declare foreign textiles to be 'impure'.²⁷

The anti-foreign stance that Anjoman-e Tojjar had taken, resisting foreign capital and propagating domestic products, was in conformity with the spirit of the day, evident in merchant deputies' speeches in the the Majles and in the laws the parliament enacted. In the First Majles there were speeches demanding the dismissal of Belgian advisers on 8 and 27 January 1908,²⁸ a no vote to the idea of borrowing from overseas on 26 and 28 October 1907,²⁹ and a proposal by Mo'in al-Tojjar, a merchant deputy, to establish a national bank on 4 December 1907. On the second issue, Mo'in al-Tojjar delivered a speech in which he proposed that Iranian merchants themselves supply the necessary funds in order 'not to be humiliated by foreigners'.³⁰ Although the proposal proved to be futile, it is an indication of the mentality of the day. One other proposition Mo'in al-Tojjar made was to have a trade commission added to the existing Majles commissions in order to monitor imports and exports to the benefit of Iranian merchants,³¹ but it was to no avail. Despite the fact that merchants were clear about their demands and were also participants in the newly established political order, they failed in many objectives, as there existed a state of dual authority and constant conflict between the Shah and the Majles, along with the resulting political instability, which meant that the Majles was unable to realize some constitutionalist goals in general and those of the merchants in particular. The necessary framework within which this could have been accomplished was only provided in the first years of the Pahlavi era.

The Anjoman-e Tojjar made every effort to support the constitutionalist cause; they gathered funds and made arrangements to facilitate sending merchant deputies from the provinces to the Majles in Tehran.³² On the anniversary of the Constitutional Revolution, they made it customary to raise their association's banner to full mast to celebrate the occasion, to confirm once again their allegiance to the constitutionalist cause. The association invited prominent constitutionalist figures – intellectuals, clerics, government ministers, and Majles deputies – to give speeches at public meetings. In these sessions current affairs and Majles procedures were discussed.[33]

It would seem that major merchants were more interested in Majles proceedings than in the Anjoman-e Tojjar. This was in spite of the fact that there were a great number of influential associations, which imposed their ideas on Majles deputies in a variety of ways, such as by petitioning the Majles and calling for gatherings to be held in front of the Majles building. The Anjoman-e Tojjar was not very active during the life of the First Majles, and it even seemed to be disengaged from political affairs. In March 1908 a merchant member of the Anjoman called it 'the most incapable association in town' and, protesting against its inactivity, went on to write: 'At the beginning we were at the fore … but unfortunately, we are lagging behind everyone else now. We have no policy; our goals are unknown. Not even one useful speech has so far been delivered.'[34] Other sources of the day, newspaper articles included, support this criticism of the Anjoman.

The Guilds and the Merchants

As previously mentioned, the other group, apart from the *sarrafs*, who were closely connected to the merchants in a relationship of mutual dependence were the *asnaf*, or petty traders and artisans. They were an important bazaar grouping who would normally not have direct dealings with major merchants, conducting business via wholesalers instead, but in effect they were in charge of outlets scattered all over the city, selling the goods that merchants supplied.[35] The *asnaf* had a guild for each occupation and a guilds association, the Anjoman-e Asnaf, which had close ties with merchants, playing an important role in every sociopolitical movement where the merchants were at the fore. In the traditional setting of the day, merchants employed their vast financial muscle and their social prominence to rally the masses of petty traders, artisans, and their apprentices in order to achieve whatever demand they might have.

Merchants regarded themselves as socially superior to petty traders. They showed this presumed superiority blatantly, as is even evident from the Majles debates, in which *asnaf* deputies would seldom engage, leaving the floor almost solely to the merchant deputies. Merchants, as a whole, were very influential in the Anjoman-e Asnaf and there were some very prominent merchants who played an active role in that association. They led the petty traders in every event: in the closing or reopening of the bazaar during protest movements, in taking refuge in sacred religious sanctuaries or at foreign missions, in calling for demonstrations, and in holding public celebrations. Merchants provided funds to help petty traders financially on the occasion of bazaar closures or refuge-taking. They were the ones who, using their financial muscle, were influential in bazaar closings and reopenings. This, of course, is not to conclude that the Anjoman-e Asnaf paid complete heed to merchants at all times, as there were occasions on which the *asnaf* resorted to such radical actions, which sprang from a difference in outlook and understanding between the *asnaf* and merchants. For instance, when the Shah's forces were gathering to attack the Majles, Amin al-Zarb refused to provide funds for a sit-in protest, Mo'in al-Tojjar avoided appearing in the Majles, and Eftekhar al-Tojjar called for caution in a speech at an *asnaf* association; however, on the other hand, there were a number of people from the *asnaf* association who were among the defenders of the Majles building.

After the victory of the Constitutional Revolution, the *asnaf*, like the merchants, founded an association. But even then, modern institutions like the Majles and the associations did not replace the traditional ties between merchants and *asnaf*. It was only in the Pahlavi era that the relationship between these two groups weakened, as a direct result of a new economic context as well as of the self-identification process they had already passed through, which had in time altered their use of such traditional alliances.

Merchants had a more extensive range of connections than did the *asnaf*, were wealthier, and were more knowledgeable about the ways of the modern world. They were relatively more open-minded, but could also take more conservative positions, as they had close ties with the ruling elite. Converging ties between merchants and intellectuals allowed the petty traders to invite intellectuals to give speeches at their association. Nevertheless, their limited scope of social connections, coupled with the great influence exerted by senior clerics on their affairs, led to a more traditional stance on the part of petty traders in comparison with merchants. Influential merchants tried to rally the Anjoman-e Asnaf behind them, but also incorporated their brand of conservatism into it.

The *asnaf* also had significant political links with one other social group, and that was the ulema, to whom they looked to represent their grievances and for protection against the state. The *asnaf* were a traditional and pious social group, whose bond with the ulema was particularly strong.[36] It was especially reflected in the Shiite practice of *taqlid* (the imitation of senior clerics in religious matters), but also in the religious and legal services they performed. Many of them looked to the two *mujtahid*s who ostensibly led the constitutional movement, Seyyed Mohammad Tabataba'i and Seyyed Abdollah Behbahani. Unlike the merchants, the guilds, representing as they did the traditional economic sector, were not finally, in the period under question, able to find a more successful alternative to the ulema to represent their interests to the state. During the revolution itself, although they pursued a variety of strategies, they remained essentially linked to the ulema.

The more traditional character of the guilds and the nature of their role in production meant that, unlike the merchants, they were not moving towards a consciousness of 'class-for-itself'. They thus responded differently to the times, and it is useful to study their behaviour in the constitutional period as a means of differentiating between their long-term development and that of the merchants, and in particular the ways in which they diverged.

The Guilds Association (Anjoman-e Asnaf)

The Anjoman-e Asnaf was active on both purely professional and political issues. It made efforts of a political nature by sending telegrams to the Majles or publishing its views in *Bamdad*, its own newspaper, and in other newspapers of the day. A telegram jointly signed by the Anjoman-e Asnaf and the Anjoman-e Jonub (the Southern Association) to the Majles, demanding a ban on the exportation of sheep hide,[37] and on one other occasion a directive sent by them to the shoemakers' guild enjoining them 'not to use materials of low quality',[38] are two examples of their activities.

The Anjoman-e Asnaf followed the two *mujtahid*s who led the constitutional movement, Behbahani and Tabataba'i, and was influential in the decision-making process within the Majles. Its stance was on occasion instrumental in having a motion passed in the Majles or preventing its adoption. This was the result of its ability to call for bazaar closures and street demonstrations. On one occasion there arose a conflict of interest between the Majles speaker, Ehtesham al-Saltaneh, and the *mujtahid* Behbahani in a case where there was a dispute between two noblemen from Zanjan. This led to an open confrontation between these two prominent figures, both trying to win support from influential associations. The *mujtahid* Behbahani succeeded in attracting some influential figures of the Anjoman-e Asnaf to his side,[39] resulting in the association issuing a petition asking for Ehtesham al-Saltaneh's resignation.[40]

On the subject of the national bank proposed by merchant representatives in the Majles, the Anjoman-e Asnaf offered its support and declared that there had already been negotiations to that effect in the association and a fund of 500 tumans had been collected to be used for that purpose. Furthermore, the association persistently demanded to know why the national bank had, to date, not been founded, as there was no definite news of its constitution, founding members, chairman, or the formalities of its establishment. The Anjoman-e Asnaf asked the Majles to clarify the reasons why 'the bank had not been already founded'[41] and proposed a new Majles committee be set up – including fifteen prominent Majles representatives, five top clerics, ten members of the government, two Zoroastrians, two Armenians, six merchants, and ten intellectuals – to make an inquiry into the subject and do whatever was necessary to have the idea of a national bank realized.[42]

One striking feature of the Majles debates was that *asnaf* representatives did not give as many speeches as others, nor did they actively participate in Majles proceedings, which may be attributed to the fact that *asnaf* representatives coming from lower social strata were not educated or confident enough to dare deliver speeches. Where there was some indication that Majles proceedings were monitored by the Anjoman-e Asnaf, even on those occasions when this association sent petitions to the Majles, intellectuals and perhaps even medium-sized merchants can be seen as the instigators of the movement. In our present state of knowledge it cannot be fully established that medium-sized merchants cooperated with the Anjoman-e Asnaf, but the fact that intellectuals were covertly in a leading position can be affirmed by Yahya Dowlatabadi's involvement with the association and the efforts made by him to have the Anjoman-e Asnaf newspaper *Bamdad* published.[43] It is, however, worth mentioning that Dowlatabadi, the source quoted here, might have been trying to enlarge his own contribution.

The stance that the Anjoman-e Asnaf took on purely political matters is also worth mentioning, particularly as it was not always consistent, reflecting the differing views, reformist and more conservative, within the organization. On the subject of the premiership of Amin al-Soltan, Atabak-e A'zam, on 2 February 1907, the Anjoman-e Asnaf was hesitant at first, a position in total contrast to that of the merchants. Major merchants welcomed his return to power and saw him as someone who could balance the opposing interests of the state and those involved in the constitutional movement. Essentially, the merchants wanted stability, and were particularly frightened by the spectre of revolutionary radicalism spreading to more and more social strata. Even the Atabak-e A'zam's otherwise archrival, Amin al-Zarb, was trying to rein in Amin al-Soltan's opponents: he managed to unravel an intrigue orchestrated by a group headed by Movaqqar al-Saltaneh.[44] The Anjoman-e Asnaf held a session to discuss Amin al-Soltan's administration and what his prospective strategy might be; at its conclusion it was decided that the very presence of Amin al-Soltan in the Iranian political arena was the root cause of all problems. A letter was written to ask the prime minister to clarify his policies and to give reasons for what his administration had done so far. The letter was to be delivered personally by Dowlatabadi, who went to meet Amin al-Soltan when he was, incidentally, meeting some prominent merchants. Amin al-Soltan frankly expressed his opinion that the Shah himself was an obstacle to the progressive path of constitutionalism and the Majles.[45] It was only after Amin al-Soltan's assassination that the Anjoman-e Asnaf's views on him came to resemble those of the merchants. The Anjoman-e Asnaf went so far as to call him a constitutionalist in a letter to the Majles, praising his sincere services and demanding punishment for 'the instigators of this despicable act',[46] and calling for the formation of a Majles committee to investigate the matter. This harsh protest made it evident that the Anjoman-e Asnaf had clearly moved away from the extremists who, in a retaliatory move, condemned the association as being composed of agitated lackeys and criticized their regret at the Atabak's assassination.[47]

The Anjoman-e Asnaf held sessions to look into Sheykh Fazlollah Nuri's anti-constitutionalist activities in 1907. The association invited some government ministers, Majles deputies, top clerics, and prominent merchants to discuss the matter and find a way to persuade the sheykh to end his *bast* in Shah 'Abd al-'Azim and return to Tehran in order to avoid further disturbances.

Nevertheless, there was a division of opinion among members of the Anjoman-e Asnaf. On the one hand, although the Anjoman had close ties with Behbahani, many less prominent petty traders, though not the minor merchants, supported Sheykh Fazlollah, demonstrating their essentially conservative nature. However, speeches given by the sheykh's opponents succeeded in persuading some of the bazaaris and other members of the association to take a clear stance in opposition to the sheykh. Behbahani himself attacked Fazlollah harshly, saying that, 'if he does not repent of his actions and is still defiant at what senior clerics tell him to do, ... I will order Muslims to attack his house and mutilate him.'[48] This speech had a definite impact on the Anjoman-e Asnaf, in which support of Behbahani increased, resulting in a clear anti-Sheykh Fazlollah stance.

The Anjoman-e Asnaf subsequently demonstrated its commitment to the Majles itself in December 1907, when the parliament was attached by a mob organized by Sheykh Fazlollah. In a move to challenge the sheykh's followers, constitutionalist associations gathered their forces in the Baharestan square and the Sepahsalar seminary on 15 December 1907. Amongst them, the Anjoman-e Asnaf made arrangements to provide food for the constitutionalists.[49] A telegram was also sent to Najaf, signed by a number of Tehran associations, the moneylenders' association included, criticizing the sheykh's anti-constitutionalism and asking the *mujtahid*s in Najaf to intervene to avoid bloodshed among Muslims.[50]

At the time when the Shah appeared to be gathering a force to attack the Majles in June 1908, the Anjoman-e Asnaf remained loyal to the Majles. Eftekhar al-Tojjar, a merchant who had a record of active participation in the Anjoman-e Asnaf, called for caution at a private session at the association, saying, 'I believe this is the time to remain neutral and avoid any involvement, otherwise we could all be detained.'[51] A few days before the actual bombardment of the Majles, representatives of the merchants', *sarrafs*' and *asnaf*'s associations settled in the Majles compound.[52] Nevertheless, the Majles leaders banned any gatherings by constitutionalist associations in and around the Majles buildings. There were, thus, only a few members of the *asnaf*'s association present in the Sepahsalar seminary, but these few actually volunteered to negotiate with the Cossacks. There is, however, no mention of the three bazaar associations among those associations which offered armed resistance in defence of the Majles buildings.[53]

The three bazaar associations, namely merchants', *sarrafs*', and *asnaf*'s associations, held sporadic common meetings and clearly supported the Majles – so much so that, when on one occasion the moneylenders' association was criticized for allegedly engaging in anti-Majles activity, they responded with a claim that they had only petitioned the Majles against the Ministries of the Interior and of Finance, and were able to refer to the first priority in their association's constitution, which expressed their support for the Majles.[54] The moneylenders' association was not very active due to a lessening of the moneylenders' social prestige in the aftermath of the Imperial Bank operations in Iran.

Conclusion

Merchants were actively involved in the Majles proceedings, an indication of their high hopes for this modern institution. This is the main reason why the merchants' association was not itself very active. All through these years the merchants continued to acquire class consciousness. This played a great role in their understanding of their collective interests, which led to the taking of collective action and thus equipping them with a sense of self-recognition as a distinct social class. It was in effect a process of identification in the social sphere which contained the sociologically familiar pattern of a dichotomy between *us* and *the other*.

Although the merchants' association had connections with merchant deputies in the Majles, major merchants preferred to be involved in the Majles itself rather than in the association. For that reason the association was not a very efficient organization, appearing inactive and cautious compared to the Anjoman-e Asnaf. The merchants' association is mentioned, as a matter of formality, in telegrams sent to different bodies by various associations when they sent congratulations on celebratory occasions or protested against insecurity and disturbances in a province. However, it is worth noting that the moneylenders' association is seldom mentioned at all in such telegrams.

In the aftermath of the conquest of Tehran by constitutionalist forces, the Majles reconvened. The number of merchant deputies in the Second Majles was much smaller than in the first parliament. Although merchants were still capable of having an impact on the election results in urban centres, they had, by this time, become disillusioned with the Majles and taken a passive political position. After a few years, and especially in the aftermath of the First World War, however, merchants strengthened their intra-class structure and established coherent organizations, such as the Hey'at-e Ettehadiyeh-ye Tojjar (the League of Merchants),[55] to protect their class interests. The Hey'at-e Tojjar became a well-established organization with branches in Tehran and the provinces. Merchants now tended to have some influence over the government, asking for their demands to be met by the state itself. The petty traders and artisans who had traditionally supported and followed the merchants gradually fell away as their economic interests diverged, and in the Pahlavi era religious-nationalist political forces took the place of merchants in representing the interests and meeting the needs of petty traders.

CHAPTER 8

Tribes of the Homeland: The Bakhtiyari in the Revolutionary Press

Arash Khazeni

The Constitutional Revolution of 1906–11 marked the beginning of the development of modern representative politics in Iran. Initiated during the reign of Mozaffar al-Din Shah Qajar (r. 1896–1907), punctuated by a civil war, and finally dissolved under the pressure of imperial intervention, the Constitutional Revolution introduced a new social and political order in Iran. Wide sections of the Iranian population participated in the revolution, on both sides of the struggle, and the tribes were no exception. During the Constitutional Revolution, some of these tribes began to become assimilated into the fabric of the emerging nation. Under the electoral laws, the tribes were counted among the inhabitants of their province and given the right to vote, while the Shahsavan, Qashqa'i, Khamseh, Turkmen, and Bakhtiyari tribes were each to send one representative to the national assembly.[1] To these institutional changes were added the revolutionary experiences of these people on the periphery. The encounter between the tribes and the Iranian Constitutional Revolution was reflected in and shaped by the revolutionary press, which defined the Iranian homeland as encompassing different tribal populations. An article in the 5 July 1909 edition of *Habl al-Matin* (The Firm Rope) beckoned the tribes to join the revolution: 'O lucky Bakhtiyari, O persevering Qashqa'i, O brave Shahsavan, O Poshtekuhian, O Kalhorian – rise up [*barkhizid*]. Unite for Islam and the nation. Put aside your differences and drive away the foreigners from the sanctuary. Don't stand content while your country's independence is blown to the wind.'[2] The nationalist press thus identified Iran's tribal subjects and called on their support in the constitutional movement.

Among the tribes in Iran, none played a more significant role in the Constitutional Revolution than the Bakhtiyari, a tribal confederacy from the Zagros Mountains. Marching on Isfahan and Tehran in support of constitutionalism (*mashrutiyat*), the Bakhtiyari were fondly portrayed in the revolutionary press as tribes of the homeland, appearing prominently in the pages of *Habl al-Matin*, *Chehreh Nama*, *Sorayya*, and *Hekmat*, as well as the local press of Isfahan, including *Kashkul*, *Zayandeh Rud*, and *Jahad-e Akbar*, among others. In *Habl al-Matin* the Bakhtiyari were presented as 'the protectors of the people' (*hami-ye mellat*) from despotic rule and Western imperialism.[3]

The story of the Bakhtiyari's place in the movement has lived on in the historiography of the Constitutional Revolution. Some authors have interpreted the role of the Bakhtiyari in the revolution as that of nationalists. In *The Persian Revolution* (1910), Edward G. Browne hailed the Bakhtiyari tribes as supporters of the constitutional cause, calling them 'the brave and hardy Bakhtiyaris who so often played a part in Persia's endless wars'.[4] Others, however, have pointed out that the Bakhtiyari had tribal, not national, interests in mind when they entered the constitutional movement. Ali Akbar Dehkhoda, the writer for the newspaper *Sur-e Esrafil* (Trumpet Call of Esrafil), feared that the Bakhtiyari were supporting the constitutional cause as a pretext for ascending the throne and warned that they were 'a lot more dangerous than the weakened Mohammad Ali Shah'.[5] In his articles for *The Times* of London and in *Persia and Turkey in Revolt*, David Fraser portrayed the Bakhtiyari as chaotic and still committed to nomadic ideals of liberty. Fraser's reports in *The Times* tended to portray the Bakhtiyari as 'completely indifferent to the Constitution, and as actuated solely by tribal ambitions, innate love of fighting, and hatred of a dynasty at whose hands they had suffered much.'[6] According to Fraser, the Bakhtiyari tarnished the revolution and in turn the revolution corrupted them – the tribesman had been 'carried into the vortex of city life, given pay in cash, tempted and seduced by new delights', becoming 'a gambler, a tavern haunter, and a convert to crime in the city'.[7] Still others have suggested Bakhtiyari collusion with the British as a prelude to their emergence in national politics, citing the simultaneous British exploration in the Bakhtiyari oil fields as their sole evidence.[8] While the Bakhtiyari took part in the revolution without abandoning their tribal consciousness or their sense of place, using revolutionary symbols to further tribal goals, ambitions, and interests, the tribes were in turn influenced by their participation and experience in the constitutional movement – nor were they the only ones to enter the fray for the chance of quick gain.

Surprisingly, the existing scholarship in English has yet to provide a full account, employing the available sources, of the Bakhtiyari's fateful participation in the Constitutional Revolution. The most detailed account appears in Gene Garthwaite's groundbreaking *Khans and Shahs: A Documentary Analysis of the Bakhtiyari in Iran* (1983), which explores the subject through the lens of British diplomatic sources and is focused on the political machinations of the elite khans, Sardar As'ad in particular.[9] This chapter, by contrast, examines the social and cultural history of the tribes in the constitutional period through a reading of previously unexplored textual sources, including revolutionary print

1. & 2. The orderly and the disorderly revolutionaries. The Bakhtiyari tribal retinues in camp outside Isfahan in 1909.

and *Tarikh-e Bakhtiyari*, the tribal narrative of the revolution.

Through a reading of the constitutional press, this essay argues that Iran was defined as encompassing different tribal confederacies and ethnic groups. Drawing upon revolutionary print sources, this essay follows the Bakhtiyari as they marched from the Zagros Mountains to Isfahan and Tehran in support of the constitutional movement and the restoration of the parliament (Majles), ending with their desertion of the constitutional cause in 1911. The following pages explore some of the narratives that emerged about the tribes in the constitutional press. In well-known constitutional journals such as *Habl al-Matin*, as well the local newsletters of Isfahan – *Kashkul, Jahad-e Akbar,* and *Zayandeh Rud,* among others – the Bakhtiyari khans appeared as commanders of the people. What is more, as the following essay reveals, revolutionary print became a medium for the Bakhtiyari khans to project their power through expressions of their commitment to the constitution and the patriotic homeland.

In Praise of Brave Men: The Bakhtiyari Tribes in the Constitutional Press

Narratives about the tribes in Qajar Iran did not emerge suddenly during the constitutional period. Nineteenth-century Persian gazetteers, chronicles, and geographical histories provided narratives and depictions of the different ethnicities and cultures in 'the guarded domains of Iran' (*mamalek-e mahruseh-ye Iran*). These texts include the mid-nineteenth-century chronicles *Nasekh al-tavarikh* by Mirza Mohammad Taqi Lesan al-Molk Sepehr and *Rowzat al-safa-ye Naseri* by Reza Qoli Khan Hedayat, as well as Mohammad Hasan Khan E'temad al-Saltaneh's geographical dictionary, *Mer'at al-boldan*, and his official history, *Tarikh-e montazam-e Naseri*. Narratives about the tribes (*tayefeh, tavayef, il*) appeared in Iran's first official newspaper, *Ruznameh-ye vaqaye'-e ettefaqiyeh* and in Mirza Abol-Hasan Sani' al-Molk Ghaffari's illustrated gazetteer *Ruznameh-ye dowlat-e 'alliye-ye Iran*. These historical and geographical texts set a precedent for Qajar representations of the tribal groups on the margins and the frontiers of the empire.[10]

The significant shift that occurred with the advent of the constitutional press in Iran was that tribal societies no longer appear as subjects of the empire but as tribes of the homeland. An edition of *Habl al-Matin* from December of 1908, just before the Bakhtiyari's entry into Isfahan, calls on the tribes of the Zagros Mountains to recognize the advantages of involvement in a national movement:

> We ask that the Bakhtiyari and the Qashqa'i should understand that nationhood (*vataniyat*) and the constitution are the will of God. So far, the Qashqa'i have remained neutral and have not taken part in oppression. And the Bakhtiyari, who call themselves Iranians, would not act against the nation. … Because anyone with pure Iranian blood [*khun-e pak-e Irani*] in their body would not take part in the oppression of Iran. … One hundred Bakhtiyari and Qashqa'i tribes, if they opposed this movement, would become defeated and filled with regret.[11]

Habl al-Matin appealed to the tribes to become involved in the revolution and to embrace the Iranian homeland. In the revolutionary press, tribal khans and headmen were no longer regarded simply as the chieftains of their respective confederacies and tribes but as the commanders of the people (*sardaran-e melli*).

The values of the Bakhtiyari chimed with those of Sattar Khan, the hero of Tabriz and icon of the revolution, whom they much admired and, as folk revolutionaries, sought to emulate.[12] Tribal populations such as the Bakhtiyari found appeal in Sattar Khan's humble origins, his bravery, and his appearance of rustic masculinity. Clad in arms and rifles and accompanied by his retinues, Sattar Khan provided a revolutionary image and a brave-man myth palatable to the Bakhtiyari. In *Tarikh-e Bakhtiyari* Sattar Khan is lauded as the commander of the people (*sardar-e melli*) and is credited for inspiring the Bakhtiyari's entry into Isfahan and the Constitutional Revolution. According to the tribal history, 'due to the example of the resistance of Sattar Khan, the commander of the nation in Azarbayjan, and the defeat of the government troops, most of the lands of Iran have become mobilized.'[13] This theme was registered in the revolutionary press in newspapers such as *Habl al-Matin*, which counted the Bakhtiyari khans as among the *sardaran-e melli*, lauding the bravery of their men (*mardan*) with slogans following their entry into Isfahan: 'Long live Haji Ali Qoli Khan Sardar As'ad/Everlasting the endeavours of men/Uplifting the people of Iran.'[14] Other slogans linked the Bakhtiyari to Sattar Khan and the insurgents of Azarbayjan: 'Long live (*zendeh bad*) Samsam al-Saltaneh and Sattar Khan who raised up the great name of Iran.'[15] Circa 1909, *Habl al-Matin* and other nationalist newsletters depicted the Bakhtiyari khans, like Sattar Khan, as brave men and commanders of warlike revolutionary armies.

The Bakhtiyari's entry into the Constitutional Revolution in 1909 was caused by several factors, including news of the insurgency in Tabriz, the protests in Isfahan against the bombardment of the parliament, and the appointment of the reactionary prince-governor Eqbal al-Dowleh, and out of consideration for inner-tribal rivalries.[16] The Bakhtiyari's capture of Isfahan was described in the local newspapers; the pages of *Jahad-e Akbar* (The Greater Striving) detailed the fighting in Isfahan.[17] Seeking a military force to withstand the government troops, the Revolutionary Society (*anjoman*) of Isfahan, led by the town's influential cleric Aqa Najafi and by Aqa Nurollah Seqat al-Eslam, called on the Bakhtiyari tribes, known enemies of Mas'ud Mirza Zell al-Soltan, to rid the city of the Qajar governor, sending a messenger to deliver a Qur'an to the *ilkhan* (paramount chief) Samsam al-Saltaneh, along with an invitation for the Bakhtiyari to enter Isfahan.[18] In January of 1909, Ebrahim Khan Zargham al-Saltaneh, an influential khan from the Ilbaygi branch of the Duraki Haft Lang and cousin of Samsam al-Saltaneh, captured

Isfahan with roughly one hundred horsemen, defeating the government troops in the Meydan-e Naqsh-e Jahan, following a battle that left the blue-domed city square covered with dust. When the tribesmen reached Naqsh-e Jahan and moved towards the Masjed-e Shah, they were fired on by government troops entrenched all around the square. It is told that near the mosque, Zargham al-Saltaneh selected twelve khans and *khanzadeh*, as there were twelve Shiite Imams, instructing them to begin the fight against the roughly two hundred royalist troops stationed in the city. By noon, the sound of cannons had ceased and the city was under the control of the Bakhtiyari, leading Eqbal al-Dowleh to seek refuge in the British consulate, while many more of his scattered troops became uncontrollable and turned to pillaging the bazaar.

Word of the capture of Isfahan was sent to Samsam al-Saltaneh and on 5 January 1909 the *ilkhan* entered the city at the head of a thousand Bakhtiyari horsemen, becoming acclaimed as a national hero. He declared in public that he was 'not a governor [*hakem*] and had only come to establish the constitutional government', adding also that he had no intention of bringing an entourage of servants and footmen (*farrash va shater*) to Isfahan.[19] *Habl al-Matin* and other nationalist newsletters reported the event and depicted the Bakhtiyari *ilkhan* as a national hero. In *Habl al-Matin*, there was speculation that Samsam al-Saltaneh had one hundred thousand Bakhtiyari horsemen (*savaran*) behind him who could capture Tehran if they marched on the capital, bringing 'woe to the clan of the Qajars'.[20] The Bakhtiyari uprising, it was thought and hoped, would lead the Qashqa'i to act in Fars and the Kalhor Kurds to rise up in Kermanshah.[21] *Chehreh Nama*, a Persian newspaper printed in Cairo, published photographs of Bakhtiyari revolutionaries and hailed Samsam al-Saltaneh as a 'unique pioneer of freedom [*horriyat*]' and the preserver of the kingdom and its people (*molk va mellat*).[22] In the pages of the constitutional press, the Bakhtiyari entered nationalist culture with Samsam al-Saltaneh emerging as a grassroots symbol of revolutionary Isfahan.

Taking control of the telegraph house, Samsam al-Saltaneh began sending news of the Bakhtiyari's victory in Isfahan all over Iran, as well as to constitutionalists taking refuge in the Ottoman Empire.[23] From Isfahan, he wrote to *Habl al-Matin*: 'The city is in order, the *anjoman* in place, the people safe, awaiting comrades [*montazer-e hamrahi*].'[24] He sent a telegram to the revolutionary hero of Tabriz, Sattar Khan, addressing him as fellow sufferer (*hamdard*) and brother (*baradar*), recounting the sacrifices made by his tribes for the nation (including coming to Isfahan at a time of year when the rest of the tribes were in the *garmsir* or winter quarters).[25] Telegrams honouring him and applauding the efforts of the Bakhtiyari soon arrived from the ulema of Najaf, including Mohammad Kazem Khorasani and Abdollah Mazandarani, the provincial *anjoman* of Tabriz, and constitutionalists in Istanbul.[26] The ulema addressed the Bakhtiyari *ilkhan* with the utmost respect as 'the greatest and most glorious excellency' (*jenab-e ajall-e akram*) and praised him for 'helping the seekers of Islam [*eslam kh^wahan*] and disposing of the oppressive government.' The success of the revolutionary society and the *mojahedin* of Isfahan had caused the ulema the maximum of joy and it was acknowledged that the heroism and 'manliness' (*fotovvat*) of the *ilkhan* and the Bakhtiyari had protected and backed the public ('*omum-e ahali*).²⁷ The message from Tabriz to the Bakhtiyari *ilkhan* was similar, with the exception that it perhaps stressed the nation more than Islam: 'your support for friends is like medicine for our life and soul [*dava-ye del va ruh*] and sent from the Imam [*emam ferestadeh*].'²⁸ After thanking the *ilkhan* for defending the 'homeland' (*vatan*) from the 'oppressive sultan,' the revolutionary society of Tabriz proposed saving the other parts of Iran and stirring the uprising (*qiyam*) of Gilan, Mazandaran, and Astarabad.

Ultimately, the constitutional press provided a medium to narrate the encounter between tribal consciousness and national culture. In an interview that appeared in a February 1909 edition of *Habl al-Matin*, Samsam al-Saltaneh articulated his aims and provided a laudatory narrative of the history of the Bakhtiyari and Iran:

> I have no other aim apart from answering the call of the oppressed [*dadresi-ye mazlumin*], putting an end to chaos [*harj o marj*], and preserving this holy nation of ours. The purest blood of Iran [*paktarin khun-e Irani*] from the time of the Sasanians until today has been in the bodies of the Bakhtiyari, who have throughout history preserved this nation and served the state [*saltanat*]. The Bakhtiyari have always, without obligation, been there to assist the state of Iran and their dear nation. Even though the Bakhtiyari tribes have always regarded themselves a partner of the Iranian state [*sharik-e saltanat*], they have offered their services during the reign of every Shah. Without thoughts of sensual gain and due to their inborn love of the homeland [*hobb-e vatan*], they have worn the shield on their chests and come to the rescue every time the independence of Iran has seemed in harm. ... This city, which for centuries was the seat of Iran's throne, invited me to participate in the constitutional government. Still my vote is but a single vote. ... What Isfahan wants is the same thing that Azarbayjan, Astarabad, Gilan, Mazandaran, Khorasan, Kerman, and Larestan want and that is the proclamation of popular elections [*entekhabat-e melli*], the restoration of the parliament, and the establishment of the rule of law.²⁹

During the course of the interview, Samsam al-Saltaneh obviously highlights the noble intentions of the Bakhtiyari as patriotic and 'pure-blooded' tribes of Iran. This is in line with the Bakhtiyari's belief in their descent from the ancient Persians: that they are Iranian tribes, as opposed to, for instance, the Turkic Qashqa'i confederacy of Fars Province.

According to the tribal history *Tarikh-e Bakhtiyari*, the Bakhtiyari tribes were the heirs of the people of ancient Persia. The lowland winter pastures of the tribes (*qeshlaq*) abounded with ruined monuments of the past, and the authors of the *Tarikh* imagined the Bakhtiyari to be descendants of the heritage of Elam, which included an ancient language and kingdom in southwestern Iran that thrived as early as 2200 BCE. In close vicinity to the Bakhtiyari tribal stronghold of Malamir could be found the ruins of the Elamite capital of Susa, as well as the rock reliefs and cuneiform inscriptions nearby, in the caves of Shekaft-e Soleyman and on the cliffs of Kul-e Farah. In their tribal history, the Bakhtiyari khans thus imagined cultural continuities with the seemingly distant Persian past: 'The native tongue of the Bakhtiyari is Old Persian (*farsi-ye qadim*), their customs and culture are the customs of ancient Iran, their women still wear the costumes of Sasanian times.'[30] What is more, Samsam al-Saltaneh's interview in *Habl al-Matin* reveals a shrewd understanding of the nationalist language of the times and suggests that the revolution had reached the tribal khans. In the press, Samsam al-Saltaneh and the Bakhtiyari retinues that stood behind him emerge as brave men and warlike tribes who raised the call of *mashrutiyat* in Isfahan.[31] Through their participation in the constitutional movement, the Bakhtiyari entered the national narrative, which perceived the Iranian homeland as being constituted by not merely the people of the heartland, but also the tribes and confederacies on the country's periphery.

Kashkul of Isfahan and Other Local Newsletters

During the Constitutional Revolution, the people of Isfahan could choose from a number of newsletters that were published in the city. The flowering of the revolutionary press in Isfahan overlapped with the presence of the Bakhtiyari in the city following 1909, and consequently the local press published many stories about the activities of the tribes. The Bakhtiyari khans, moreover, used the press as a means of communication and a forum to express their commitment to the constitutional cause. The local press is thus a unique and previously unused source on the role of the Bakhtiyari tribes in the revolutionary politics of Isfahan.

The modern Persian press in Isfahan may be traced to the publication of the official Qajar gazette *Farhang* (Culture), which ran from 1879 to 1891 and was edited by Mirza Taqi Khan Sartip, the head physician (*hakimbashi*) of Mas'ud Mirza Zell al-Soltan, the prince-governor of Isfahan.[32] This official gazette often included reports and news about the Bakhtiyari tribes and the periphery of Isfahan. By the constitutional period, Isfahan could boast of a number of newsletters and papers. The first examples of the constitutional press in the city included *Anjoman-e Esfahan* (The [Revolutionary] Society of Isfahan), established in 1906 and edited by Seraj al-Din Sadr al-Musavi, and *'Ali Jenab* (Excellency), first printed in 1906 and edited by Haji Mirza Seyyed 'Ali Jenab. The following year, in 1907, there appeared *Jahad-e Akbar*, edited by Mirza Ali Aqa Khorasani, *Anjoman-e Baladiyeh* (The [Revolutionary] Society of the City and Region), edited by Aqa Mirza Nur al-Din Majlesi, and *Esfahan*, edited by Mirza Hoseyn Khan E'tela' al-Dowleh. By 1909, the year of the Bakhtiyari's arrival in the city, the following weeklies appeared: *Zayandeh Rud*, edited by Mirza 'Abd al-Hoseyn Khonsari; *Naqus* (Bell), edited by Aqa Masih Tukizgani; *'Orvat al-Vosqa* (The Firmest Handle), edited by Jalal-al-Din Meyhani Mo'ayyed al-Ashraf; and *Parvaneh* (Butterfly), edited by Seyyed Hasan Mo'menzadeh. In the same year, Majd al-Eslam Kermani revived the popular satirical newsletter *Kashkul* (Mendicant's Bowl), formerly printed in Tehran before the Lesser Despotism of Mohammad Ali Shah, in Isfahan.[33]

The image of the Bakhtiyari tribes that emerged in the local press of Isfahan, echoing that of *Habl al-Matin*, was defined by bravery and honour. In the long-running newsletter *Zayandeh Rud*, poems lauded the Bakhtiyari and their defence of the homeland, some drawing meaning from Samsam al-Saltaneh's title, the 'Sword of the State':

> When the sword was raised from its sheath
> The people's struggle became complete.
> Long live the Bakhtiyari, essence of zeal (*gheyrat*),
> Long live the flourishing chief of retinues![34]

Moreover, revolutionary print became a means for the Bakhtiyari khans to project their power and profess their love of the homeland. Local newsletters and gazettes portrayed the confrontation between the loyalist and pro-constitutional Bakhtiyari tribes to be imminent and printed rumours that government troops were on their way to subdue the revolutionaries in Isfahan. They capture the mood of the city after its 'liberation'. Isfahan was bracing itself, as Samsam al-Saltaneh and the growing ranks of the revolutionary Bakhtiyari constructed trenches and barricades (*sangar*) outside of the city, stockpiled arms, and practised firing their rifles. It soon became clear that the Bakhtiyari tribes, with Ali Qoli Khan Sardar As'ad returned from Paris, where he had been receiving medical treatment for his failing eyesight since 1906, had become unified behind the constitution and were seriously contemplating a march on Tehran.

In June of 1909, eight hundred Bakhtiyari horsemen rode from their summer pastures in the Zagros Mountains towards Tehran to restore the Majles and the constitutional movement in Iran. In the local press of Isfahan, the Bakhtiyari moved from the mountainous edge of the city into the heart of the nationalist culture. Incendiary letters from Sardar As'ad appeared in the pages of *Kashkul, Zayandeh Rud*, and *Jahad-e Akbar*. In June 1909, the following letter from Sardar As'ad appeared in the Isfahan newsletter *Kashkul* as the Bakhtiyari were on their way to Tehran:

> I would like to remind all that the headmen of the Bakhtiyari are not thinking about government [*hokumat*] and monarchy [*saltanat*] and live content lives. And I was in Europe for fun and treatment but when I kept hearing for ten months about the behaviour of the Shah and his court in Iran, and when I heard from the sources of emulation [*maraja'-e eslam*] and Europeans that the only way to save Iran was through constitutionalism [*mashruteh*], I decided to do what I could for the sake of my religion and country. ... And nothing can frighten or stop me. I am not worried at all about the military camp at Kashan. The only way I will stop and return is when I hear the news of *mashrutiyat*. So send the news to our brothers in Azarbayjan and Gilan, and the people of Tehran, that we will be at Baharestan. Long live the people of Iran! Long live freedom! A willing martyr for the people of Iran [*Zendeh bad mellat-e Iran! Zendeh bad azadi! Fada'i-ye mellat-e Iran*], Ali Qoli Khan Bakhtiyari.[35]

Here, on the pages of *Kashkul*, Sardar As'ad invokes the Bakhtiyari headmen's patriotic love of the homeland and their brave commitment to upholding the constitution. The satirical cartoon below parodies the weakness of the Shah's troops in the face of the bold and daring tribal horsemen of the Bakhtiyari. The Bakhtiyari are honoured as 'The Victorious Army of the Nation' (*Qoshun-e zafarnemun-e melli*) while the government troops are lampooned as deserters fearful of even the thought of confrontation with the tribes. In the caricature, they are seen shouting cowardly statements as they drop their rifles and flee from the advance of Sardar As'ad's retinues, one of them seeking a mousehole (*yek surakh-e mush*) in which to hide from the warlike tribes.[36] The revolutionary press of Isfahan, thus, came to define the Bakhtiyari as tribes of the homeland.

On 12 July, a 1200-man Bakhtiyari cavalry, joined by the nationalist *mojahedin* from Gilan and the Caucasus, entered Tehran from the hills north of the city and then moved to make their headquarters at Baharestan, the site of the old parliament bombarded by the forces of Mohammad Ali Shah in 1908.[37] In less than a week, the number of Bakhtiyari tribesmen in the capital had swollen to nearly 2000, forcing the Russian-led Cossack Brigade to surrender and compelling the Shah to seek refuge in the Russian legation.[38] The Revolutionary Committee chose the eleven-year-old Ahmad Shah as his father's successor and 'Azod al-Molk was appointed regent. Despite the enthronement of the young Qajar heir, the Bakhtiyari tribes had attained the greatest influence in the land as a revolutionary army, defending the country from the forces of counterrevolution on numerous occasions. Bakhtiyari prestige extended beyond their military prowess, as Sardar As'ad became Minister

3. 'The Victorious Army of the Nation,' a caricature of the Bakhtiyaris' march on Tehran that appeared in the Isfahan newspaper *Kashkul*, Isfahan, 1909.

of the Interior, Samsam al-Saltaneh became governor-general of Isfahan, and various other khans rose to provincial governorships. Following the Qajar practice of appointing members of their tribe to high office in the provinces, the Bakhtiyari had suddenly become the most dominant group in the national government. Under the banner of constitutionalism, the Bakhtiyari tribes had emerged in the political culture of Iran.[39] These developments were unceremoniously brought to a close in 1911, when the Bakhtiyari khans accepted the Russian ultimatum and closed down the Majles, bringing an end to the constitutional period in Iran.

Conclusion

During the Constitutional Revolution, the Bakhtiyari maintained their tribal consciousness, resulting in complex and often contradictory political behaviour.[40] The Bakhtiyari were never firmly united behind the constitutional cause, with some seemingly ready to back off from their role as defenders of the revolution. Crimes committed by the Bakhtiyari in the cities and on the roads revealed a tenuous commitment to constitutionalism and the rule of law. For many of the tribal rank and file, the Constitutional Revolution may have been inconsequential, irrelevant, and distant.[41] In his memoirs, Haj Sayyah recounts travelling with Sardar As'ad's Bakhtiyari retinues to Tehran in 1909.

Upon asking one of the Bakhtiyari horsemen if he knew where he was going and what he was taking part in, Haj Sayyah received the following reply: 'No! We obey and follow the commands of the Sardar.'[42] By the winter of 1911, perhaps out of their disdain for the newly created tax-collecting gendarmerie, the Bakhtiyari had effectively deserted the constitutional cause as the khans opted not to resist the Russian occupation of Qazvin and accepted the Russian ultimatum to close down the Majles. When Sardar As'ad, so instrumental in steering the tribes to the defence of constitutionalism in the past, returned to Iran from Europe in late 1911, some expected him to mobilize the tribes behind the constitutionalists again, but instead he urged the acceptance of the Russian ultimatum's terms, seeking to avoid the occupation of Iran.[43]

After the revolution, the Bakhtiyari fell from grace in the pages of the constitutional press. In *Habl al-Matin*, they were blamed as the cause of anarchy and insecurity (*na amni*); while they had given lives to restore the constitution, they did not follow any of its laws (*dar hich qanuni nemiravand*).[44] It was reported that in Isfahan, the retinues of the various khans had swollen and that Bakhtiyari rebels (*ashrar*) had burned and looted the constitutional assembly. The people of the city demanded that Aqa Najafi, who had invited Samsam al-Saltaneh and the Bakhtiyari to enter Isfahan in 1909, ask the tribes to return to their mountains.[45] In the Azeri newsletter *Molla Nasreddin*, a cartoon portrayed the tribes as devils and condemned the 'injustice of the Bakhtiyari in Tehran' (*Tehranda Bakhtiyarilarak zolmi*).[46]

The history of the Bakhtiyari in the Constitutional Revolution shows that, despite the persistence of tribalism in Iran, the late Qajar period was a time of social and cultural transformation. The Bakhtiyari's participation in representative politics during the Constitutional Revolution presents a strange moment in the narrative of the making of modern Iran, for here were pastoral nomadic tribes who, at least for a time, made up Iran's revolutionary armies. This seems difficult to reconcile with a historiography that has privileged the urban classes, the natural carriers of nationalist sentiments, and has often dismissed the tribes as the enemies of a unified, independent, and modern Iran.[47] While distance certainly marked the frontier between centre and periphery, the tribes had also long served as retinues of the 'guarded domains of Iran'. This duality between autonomy and assimilation can also be seen in the Bakhtiyari's actions in the Constitutional Revolution. As read on the pages of the Persian constitutional press, during the revolution the Bakhtiyari khans, with their retinues behind them, embraced the homeland even though they did not entirely relinquish their traditional tribal motives nor leave their tribal consciousness behind.

CHAPTER 9

Revolution and a High-Ranking Sufi: Zahir al-Dowleh's Contribution to the Constitutional Movement

Lloyd Ridgeon

Introduction

During the reign of Naser al-Din Shah, many intellectuals believed that Iran was economically, politically, and intellectually backwards in comparison with Western nations, such as Britain and Russia. As a result the intellectuals called for reform of the Iranian administration as well as a change in the cultural and religious worldviews of Iranians. The latter included both institutionalized Shiism and the Sufi tradition. There is a reasonable quantity of literature to demonstrate the nature of the criticisms of institutionalized Shiism, such as that contained in the writings of Malkam Khan (1833–1908)[1] and Mirza Aqa Khan Kermani (d. 1896);[2] however, there has been very little scholarly activity upon the intellectual responses to Sufism in the years leading up to the Constitutional Revolution. Akhundzadeh (d. 1878) and Mirza Aqa Khan Kermani were among the pro-reform intellectuals who were critical of the Sufi tradition, aspects of which were also condemned by many clerics.[3] Dislike of Sufism was focused on both Sufi belief and practice; distaste for the former was due to the perception that Sufis advocated pantheism, typified in the doctrine of annihilation (*fana*), while the practices that were considered reprehensible included begging, drinking wine, taking opium, homosexuality, and fatalism. Such criticisms were perpetuated by some among the succeeding generation of scholars who lived through the constitutional movement. These included Ahmad Kasravi (d. 1946) who, as a virulent opponent of the Sufis, claimed that during the Constitutional Revolution many people came to the conclusion that Sufism had caused Iran so much misfortune because the Sufis advised people against engaging in worldly affairs. However, according to Kasravi, since most people saw through the 'evils' of the Sufis, the latter began to change their perspectives and promoted activity in the world.[4]

It is difficult to assess the role of the Sufis during the Constitutional Revolution because their critics left only vague and general examples of Sufi 'evils', so it is unknown what the attitudes of the Sufis actually were regarding important concepts such as equality, gender, and democracy. The usual sources for the Constitutional Revolution[5] are silent on the role of the Sufis (which may be attributable to either the absence of a Sufi presence in the revolution, or else the desire of authors to foreground other groups or individuals). Only one of the major Persian works on the constitutional period focuses upon Sufism in any depth, and that is Safa'i's *Rahbaran-e mashruteh* (Leaders of the Constitutional Movement).[6] As its title indicates, Safa'i's book does not concentrate on the rank and file but rather on those who earned a name for themselves, and he includes one chapter on Zahir al-Dowleh, who was the leader of the Anjoman-e Okhovvat (Society of Brotherhood), one of the influential Sufi groups during this period.

This chapter will examine the thought and activities of Zahir al-Dowleh during the constitutional period, drawing specific attention to aspects of his brand of Sufism and his general perspective on the constitutional movement.[7] It will draw on the older sources of the Constitutional Revolution as well as utilizing the more recent material that has been published. Of the traditional sources, Safa'i's work is the most laudatory, but there is a need to be circumspect with his work because of his connection with Sufism.[8] More critical of Zahir al-Dowleh was Mehdi Malekzadeh, who wrote: 'Zahir al-Dowleh was a practising dervish and a gnostic. He and his disciples were seekers of freedom and reform, and they expressed their disgust at the conditions [of the time]. However, just as it is in the way of the dervishes, their actions never went beyond words.'[9] Malekzadeh included Zahir al-Dowleh among a group of Court officials who, despite desiring reforms, were a little fearful, selfish, and lacking the sentiment of self-sacrifice, and who only revealed their beliefs to a select few.[10] Finally, one should mention the opinion of the virulent anti-Sufi, Ahmad Kasravi, whose antipathy towards Sufism may have prejudiced his perspective of Zahir al-Dowleh. Zahir al-Dowleh is mentioned on only one page in Kasravi's *History of the Constitutional Revolution*, and he receives similarly scant attention in *The Eighteen-Year History of Azarbayjan*. Kasravi remarked, 'Everyone knows this man who is the leader of the Sufis, or in his own words is "the servant of the master". His presence in Rasht has greatly increased the troubles of the freedom fighters [*azadikh^vahan*].'[11] In a footnote, Kasravi explained that Zahir al-Dowleh made a mistake with some dates in a note to the Foreign Ministry, 'and this' exclaimed an exasperated Kasravi, 'is an example of the work of a governor!'[12]

There is, then, no real consensus among the traditional Iranian scholars of the constitutional period on Zahir al-Dowleh's position in the constitutional movement. These scholars had their own particular agendas which coloured their attitudes towards Zahir al-Dowleh. Of course, no study can be completely dispassionate and all writing is loaded with a certain amount of baggage, and even a chapter written by a non-Sufi, non-Iranian, one hundred years after the Constitutional Revolution still carries its own presumptions and prejudices. The present study is assisted by the fact that more sources have been published in recent years. These include Zahir al-Dowleh's own memoirs, which were edited by Iraj Afshar and published in 1972.[13] Other useful works include Bamdad's *Sharh-e hal-e rejal-e Iran* (Description of the Circumstances of the [Important] Men of Iran)[14] and Mo'ayyer al-Mamalek's *Rejal-e 'asr-e Naseri* ([Important] People of the Naseri Period)[15] (although both of these works refer all too briefly to Zahir al-Dowleh). More recently, Mohammad Hoseyni has published two analytical articles that discuss Zahir al-Dowleh and the Anjoman-e Okhovvat.[16]

This chapter will adopt a chronological approach, commencing in the period in which Zahir al-Dowleh served as Minister of Ceremonies to Naser al-Din Shah; it will then investigate the nature of the Anjoman-e Okhovvat (the Sufi organization that Zahir al-Dowleh established on a legal basis), the period in which he served as governor of Hamadan (June 1906 to November 1907), the brief time that he stayed in Tehran when he had his pantomime performed (which was highly critical of Mohammad Ali Shah), the period of his governorship of Gilan in 1908, and, finally, the bombardment by the Shah's forces of Zahir al-Dowleh's house in Tehran. To anticipate the conclusion, what emerges from such a chronological approach is Zahir al-Dowleh's firm attachment to the constitutional movement – firm and yet always tempered by a commitment to education and not violent revolution.

A pertinent question at this point is whether it is possible to bracket off Zahir al-Dowleh's Sufism from his political and social life. In other words, did his Sufism contribute, shape, or determine his sociopolitical worldview, or, rather, is it possible that the two spheres of politics and religion were completely isolated from one another, with neither sphere influencing the other? It is often observed these days that 'Islam is a way of life' as if Islam were unique in this regard among religious traditions. If religion is understood as an amalgamation of ultimate meanings held by an individual (who may or may not participate in communal rites and customs, or may manifest individual practices), then ultimate meanings such as belief in God, justice (*'edalat*), morality (*akhlaq*), etiquette (*adab*), etc., influence to greater and lesser extents all aspects of life. Therefore, the Sufism of Zahir al-Dowleh, as an ultimate source of reference, was an integral element of his politics and the goals that he pursued in the constitutional movement. His form of Sufism, to be discussed below, mirrored his 'reform rather than revolution' perspective on politics, and this was no doubt influenced by the changing sociopolitical circumstances of the late Qajar era, when Western ideas and norms were penetrating into Iran.

Zahir al-Dowleh's Early Years

Ali Khan Qajar was born in 1864 into one of the leading Qajar families; he was the son of Mohammad Naser Khan Qajar, who served in a number of important state positions, including Minister of Ceremonies and governor of Khorasan, and was also appointed to various posts in the ministries of justice and war.[17] Following his father's death in 1877, Ali Khan was given both his title, Zahir al-Dowleh, and his position as Minister of Ceremonies. Moreover, two years later, in December 1879, he married one of Naser al-Din Shah's daughters, Tuman Agha (who was later known as Forugh al-Dowleh, and then Malekeh-ye Iran).[18]

From his own writings, it would appear that Zahir al-Dowleh had a favourable opinion of his father-in-law, Naser al-Din Shah. Indeed, in a short work about the assassination of the Shah which Zahir al-Dowleh wrote in 1314/1896 (the same year the Shah was assassinated), he commented, 'In the history of Fars and 'Ajam there have been few more benevolent, long-suffering, nurturing, progress-seeking and well-wishing kingships, possessing mercy, wisdom, and compassion, without being short-tempered, than [that of] Naser al-Din Shah Qajar'.[19] Zahir al-Dowleh continued by describing the developments that had occurred in Iran during the Shah's reign, including the creation of sugar-processing factories, glass factories, railways, the mint, the arsenal, the tramway, electric lighting, the telegraph, photography, and the phonograph, and he concluded that there were benefits accruing to Iran from the Shah's reign but that they remained unrecognized or else the subjects were ungrateful for them.[20] These views are surprising from a contemporary perspective, especially as Naser al-Din Shah is not commonly associated with the kind of adjectives used by Zahir al-Dowleh in the above description. Amanat's argument is more typical of recent histories:

> The Shah's success in achieving relative tranquility went only so far as to guarantee his survival at the center of his own universe. The same balance between chaos and order observable in domestic affairs was at work in the Shah's treatment of the central administration. In an endless game of chess-like maneuvers and counter-maneuvers, dismissals, reinstatements, grants of royal favor, infliction of royal wrath, exiles, secret murders ... palace intrigue, bribery, annual auctioning of offices ... extortion in the guise of gifts and estate taxes imposed on deceased members of the government and court, and compromise and coercion, the Shah was able to walk a tightrope.[21]

4. Photograph of Zahir al-Dowleh, taken by Sevruguin.

Only a few years after writing his flattering comments, Zahir al-Dowleh was to become a champion of reform (if one accepts the views of Safa'i) during the constitutional movement, which was generally aimed at limiting the arbitrary powers of the monarch. It is interesting to speculate on the reasons why Zahir al-Dowleh joined the movement for reform, especially when it is difficult to argue that Naser al-Din Shah possessed qualities and attributes that made him a more worthy monarch (by constitutional standards) than his successors, Mozaffar al-Din Shah and Mohammad Ali Shah. Zahir al-Dowleh's writings about Naser al-Din Shah may reflect a certain consideration for the sentiments of his wife (the Shah's daughter), and perhaps, as Minister of Ceremonies, he felt an obligation to write a few panegyric lines for his deceased employer, and indeed, he had a precedent to follow, as Safi Ali Shah (see below), his own spiritual mentor, had expressed a similar opinion about Naser al-Din Shah.[22] Zahir al-Dowleh's support for the reform movement may also be attributed to the changing sociopolitical context of Iran between Naser al-Din Shah's death and 1905. In 1900, as Minister of Ceremonies, he had the opportunity to travel to Europe, accompanying Mozaffar al-Din Shah on one of his medical trips.[23] Such first-hand experience of the West, his observation of Western technology and science, and the chance to become familiar with European sociopolitical administration may well have contributed to Zahir al-Dowleh's commitment to reform. Moreover, the possibility of discussing the amelioration of the Iranian system increased due to the domestic policies that were initiated by the new Shah, which included the relaxing of censorship and association, resulting in the mushrooming of new societies which advocated reform.[24] Typical of such societies was the Anjoman-e Okhovvat.

The Anjoman-e Okhovvat

One of the leading Sufis of late nineteenth-century Iran was Safi Ali Shah, who was a disciple of several Neʻmatollahi sheykhs, before he established his own line of Neʻmatollahi Sufism. He gathered around him a number of followers at his *khanaqah* in Tehran, and attracted the attention of the Shah as a result of the animosity of some clerics who were highly critical of his Persian versification of the Qur'an, which, however, was subsequently sanctioned by a fatwa from the leading cleric in Iraq, Mirza Hasan Shirazi. Among the devoted followers of Safi Ali Shah were princes, nobles, and Court officials,[25] and due to this popularity Naser al-Din Shah sent Zahir al-Dowleh to see what was happening at the *khanaqah*. Ironically, Zahir al-Dowleh himself was attracted to this Sufi master and became his disciple in 1885.[26]

It is reported that Safi Ali Shah had established a secret organization that was to be called the Anjoman-e Okhovvat.[27] It was only after Safi Ali Shah's death in 1899, when Zahir al-Dowleh became Safi's successor, that royal assent was given to establish this society on a formal basis. The Society of Brotherhood was created with 110 members, all of whom were personally selected by Zahir al-Dowleh, and he also created the 'Consultative Council' (*he'yat-e moshaver*) of 12 individuals in 1899. When a member of the Consultative Council passed away, his successor was elected by the remaining 11. Many of the original 12 members had titles (*laqab*), such as Entezam al-Saltaneh, Nazem al-Dowleh, Yamin al-Mamalek, Nezam-e Lashgar, Nosrat al-Soltan, and Mokhtar al-Molk, a fact that reveals their connection to the Court, which bestowed such titles.[28] The structure and composition of the Anjoman-e Okhovvat manifests a high degree of elitism and hierarchy; indeed, it has been claimed that 'the Society of Brotherhood was as centralized an organization as many Sufi orders'.[29]

Even though the *anjoman* may have represented a form of Sufism for the reformist tendencies at Court, it was ultimately to the benefit of all. The aim of the society was most probably an attempt by Zahir al-Dowleh to promote a particular type of Sufism. Safa'i reports that he said a 'dervish ... must serve society, assist the oppressed and support independence and freedom'.[30] One can speculate that the requirement for the dervishes to serve society began at the very top, even in the royal Court, and that the benefits of this would trickle down to the less fortunate in society. In fact, one might see this version of Sufism as reform from above, where the elite provided guidance and served as exemplary models; the dervish should have the right character traits or morals, which would be manifest in his actions within society. In the words of Safa'i, 'Zahir al-Dowleh turned the *anjoman* into a school (*maktab*) for moral teachings and a stronghold for freedom and liberality.'[31] Zahir al-Dowleh taught:

> The purpose is that there is nothing worth bothering about in this world and the afterlife except good character traits (*akhlaq-e hasaneh*) and correcting evil ones. This can only be done by following the dervish path. Understand what I am saying. I speak of being a dervish, not ... blowing the [Sufi] horn. The dervish also must perform service without being negligent – he must pay attention. My *pir* [Safi Ali Shah] said, 'A dervish must not have anything in his bag that when opened will cause him embarrassment in company.'[32]

The commitment to aiding the less fortunate was very strong in Zahir al-Dowleh, and this contrasts markedly to the general criticisms (outlined above) that were levelled at Sufis by their opponents. This commitment was an integral part of his Sufi perspective, and as argued above, this Sufi worldview was not neatly folded away, only to be made visible during Sufi devotions and rituals. Some of the ways in which Zahir al-Dowleh expressed his support for reform may be considered more explicitly Sufi, such as the performance of the pantomime condemning those who robbed Iran of its wealth (which was acted out within the headquarters of the *anjoman* (see below), which made it a 'Sufi' event). Zahir al-Dowleh's other activities were equally directed towards ameliorating the conditions for the poor and hungry, and while not necessarily outwardly relevant to Sufism, such behaviour reflects the Sufi altruistic ideal of the need to serve others, which has been the backbone of much Sufi literature in the Persian tradition.[33] Zahir al-Dowleh's reaction to the grain-hoarding that took place in Hamadan when he was governor there is a good example of this. Appalled at the plight of the hungry people of Hamadan, he gathered them together, castigated the grain-hoarders, and instigated the masses to save themselves and their families by raiding the stores of grain. One may consider his explicitly and implicitly Sufi-inspired activities as the *zaher* and *baten* manifestations of his Sufism.[34]

The difficulty of determining the precise nature of the *anjoman*'s Sufism in the early constitutional period is due to a lack of documentation: most material derives from a later period (such as its constitution of 1910). However, many of the points in the constitution of 1910 reflect the advice given by Safi Ali Shah to Zahir al-Dowleh, such as wearing everyday clothing and having a profession,[35] which points to an emphasis on ethics (*akhlaq*), proper Sufi etiquette (*adab*), and correct human relations.[36] The constitution of 1910 that was written by Zahir al-Dowleh does not contain any specific mention of mystical vision, and has only passing reference to God and the Sufi *zekr* ritual, while greater attention is paid to relations among the dervishes. This stress on the human dimension of the Society reflects Zahir al-Dowleh's aim in its creation: it was meant to attract the influential and aristocratic members of society, especially the princes, nobles, and the aristocrats at the Court, and 'he wanted to bring their behaviour and actions in line with reform and the movement for humanity.'[37]

Although these aims are not overtly political, Zahir al-Dowleh and the Anjoman-e Okhovvat have been associated with Freemasonry, which for many Iranians is perceived to have promoted certain political aims. Indeed, the Anjoman-e Okhovvat has been termed by Hamid Algar a 'pseudo-Masonic organization' that attempted 'to promote the cause of constitutional government', and also 'relinquished the traditional structure of a Sufi order in favour of one drawn from Freemasonry.'[38] With respect to the latter claim, Algar also appears to be referring to the trappings that the society adopted, including its emblem ('a pair of crossed battle-axes from which hung a rosary and a *kashkul*, actually an adaptation of the level, compasses and chip-axe used in Masonic emblems'[39]), and other modern elements including written rules, the practice of sitting on chairs, rather than on the floor before the master, and the use of membership cards and a register.[40]

However, it would be incorrect to consider Zahir al-Dowleh's apparent

Freemasonry as implying any form of subservience to Western powers. Even his opponents recognized him as an individual of moral integrity in this regard; as Kasravi states, as governor of Gilan, Zahir al-Dowleh 'was not polluted and gave no leeway to the Russians'.[41] His form of patriotism is also evident in his remarks about the Alliance school in Hamadan, which he claimed had four hundred young boys and eighty girls, most of whom were Jews, and who were taught to speak French.[42] Zahir al-Dowleh indicated that some of the students had lost their ability to speak Persian,[43] and he remarked to the teachers:

> 'You are the scholarly army of the French nation. You teach French language and manners as best as you can to children and youths who do not yet have an insight for patriotism (*vatan-parasti*), national enthusiasm, or prejudice, without [using] the sword or violence or conquest. It is clear that when these children leave your school they will not be Iranian, but they will be French.' He [one of the teachers] laughed and agreed. *All the same, I did not leave the school feeling happy.*[44]

Although various dimensions of the *anjoman* reflect sociopolitical considerations, it is also true that the Society engaged in what may be termed the more traditional Sufi activities. For example, distinctly religious activities took place during the months of Muharram, Safar, and Ramadan, when members observed lamentations and recited religious poems in the *khanaqah*. Moreover, the members celebrated the births of Muhammad and Ali, and the latter's appointment as the Prophet's successor at Ghadir.

Governor of Hamadan (June 1906–November 1907)

The commitment of Zahir al-Dowleh to constitutionalism and the eradication of arbitrary and despotic rule can best be witnessed in his actions as governor of Hamadan from June 1906 until November 1907. Only four days after entering Hamadan, Zahir al-Dowleh declared that it should establish the first elected assembly in Iran, and he made arrangements to meet representatives from the trade guilds and the city's notables. He wrote in his memoirs that the meeting was made up of 'fifty-two or three individuals from the ranks of the merchants, guilds, the Jews and Armenians, and more than fifty leaders, notables, and deputies of the princes'.[45] Given the controversy that was to erupt over the inclusion of non-Muslims in the national Majles,[46] the inclusion by Zahir al-Dowleh of Christian and Jewish representatives in this assembly (named the *majles-e fava'ed-e 'omumi*)[47] is highly significant, yet it was part of his attempt to have all sections of society represented in the assembly. Zahir al-Dowleh notes with some pride that all groups in Hamadan came to lay their bricks in the construction of the assembly, including the Jewish schoolchildren[48] and the *luti-bashi* (head *luti*) of Hamadan; even the monkeys and bears of the street entertainers brought bricks in their paws to the construction site.⁴⁹ The inclusive nature of the Hamadan Assembly, the stress on unity, is a theme that occurred with increasing frequency at the time. For example, the famous clerical supporter of constitutionalism, Seyyed Mohammad Tabataba'i delivered a sermon in June 1906 (the month before the establishment of the Hamadan Assembly) in which he discussed the need for a *majles-e 'edalat* (Assembly of Justice) in which 'the Shah and beggar would be equal before the law'.⁵⁰

The first public meeting of the assembly, on 7 July 1906, occurred a month earlier than the proclamation issued by Mozaffar al-Din Shah to establish a National Assembly, four months prior to the creation of a provincial assembly in Shiraz, and five months earlier than that of Isfahan.⁵¹ For the first six months, the assembly was to meet every ten days. The deputies were composed of artisans and notables. Zahir al-Dowleh believed that as governor, he was entitled to preside over the proceedings, but for the first six months he delegated that authority to Haji Abol-Fath Khan, a local notable.⁵² He wanted to show Iranians concerned with politics the values and benefits of democratic methods in the administration of affairs of a geographical region.⁵³ Although Zahir al-Dowleh was the first to establish such an assembly, it should be noted that calls for the creation of an assembly of one sort or another had had a reasonably lengthy history in Iran. There had been calls for an *'edalat khaneh* since the time of Malkam Khan in 1860, and this had developed by 1905 in various ways, including 'a system of tribunals under the Ministry of Justice with the function of watching over the provincial authorities and obtaining redress of grievances against them'.⁵⁴ It is in this sense that Zahir al-Dowleh envisaged the assembly that he set up. In his speech of 7 July he said:

> So for each one of the governors, such as the state representative, the policeman of the subjects, and the security official, it is necessary that he always consult with the notables of that region on important matters of order, security, methods of reform, deterioration in the subjects' affairs, and in their manifest and non-manifest progress and wealth ... the result of each topic [debated will be decided] by majority vote and will be executed at the appropriate time.⁵⁵

Even if Zahir al-Dowleh was not the first to discuss such an assembly, this should not belittle his achievement in its actual creation. However, it is not clear how Zahir al-Dowleh perceived the potential clash of interests between the demands of the Shah (and his representatives) on the one hand and the interests of the people of Hamadan. His commitment to decisions based on majority vote left the Shah's representative in a potentially awkward position. That the assembly was apparently created without a careful consideration of the potential conflicts is not at all surprising, especially when reflecting on the deliberations that were later to take place surrounding the constitution and the Supplementary Fundamental Law. It may be the case that the creation of the Hamadan Assembly during the reign of the comparatively weak (or liberal) Mozaffar al-Din Shah may have blinkered Zahir al-Dowleh to the possible reality of harsher, less tolerant policies that were to be adopted by his successor, Mohammad Ali Shah. Was Zahir al-Dowleh too idealistic or naïve? Did he not see the conflict between a system based on the word of the Shah and one based on popular will? A similar question may be asked about Tabataba'i's speech of 1906, in which he foresaw no conflict between secular law and divine law in establishing a *majles-e 'edalat*. As Vanessa Martin comments, 'It is unlikely that Tabataba'i really understood the conflict that might arise under the constitutional system between a law based on the word of God and one based on popular will.'[56]

Regardless of the *potential* troubles for the Hamadan Assembly, it did score some notable successes; an example of this is the episode of some members of the assembly complaining to the manager of the Shahanshahi Bank in Hamadan, which was taking too much of a commission on some of its transactions. When the bank manager finally agreed to end this practice, Zahir al-Dowleh wrote in his memoirs, 'Well done, the Provincial Assembly of Hamadan which has done this! For many years in Tehran they wanted to say this to the bank manager, but they couldn't and he wouldn't accept [their criticism].'[57]

Aside from creating an assembly for the people, Zahir al-Dowleh's attempts to promote justice and accountability may also be witnessed in the establishment of a 'complaint box'.[58] This was set up on 16 June 1906, and in his own words, Zahir al-Dowleh said, 'Tonight Zahir al-Mamalek carried a table, box, and signboard into the courtyard of the Imamzadeh Yahya [shrine], and whoever has a grievance and cannot do anything [about it] can put his written complaint in that box, and after one night he will receive a reply.'[59] The location of this box is another indication of Zahir al-Dowleh's commitment to limiting arbitrary power, for had the complaint box been positioned at the site of the assembly, it would have been in full view of those in authority, whereas with the complaint box at the shrine, those with a grievance would be able to record their complaint in reasonable safety.[60] In an amusing episode, it is revealed that the box was indeed used, and that Zahir al-Dowleh took the responsibility of responding to the comments and criticisms of the people seriously. He wrote:

> Today in the papers in the [complaint] box we had a very unusual letter that had to be read. One 'Abd al-Karim ... had written in a cordial manner that 'for nine months I have been thinking about someone. I have become enamoured and lovesick with him/her[61] to the extent that it has driven me crazy. ...

Whatever I have done in these nine months, from seeking remedies and medicines, only increases my suffering. ... I looked for an augury in the Qur'an, and so I am now presenting the case to you, that you will instruct me with a prayer, or a [certain] *zekr* in order to drive this love and madness out of my head or else that will make this person behave kindly towards me.' We gathered together and laughed in astonishment at this letter. I asked for the address of his beloved and asked that she/he should be kind to him.[62]

Zahir al-Dowleh's support for constitutionalism is not in question, but the method of achieving lasting reform was a topic for debate. His perspective on the issue whilst he was governor of Hamadan can be gleaned from an analysis of the telegraphs and journal entries that he made. Of particular interest are his comments about the role and policies advocated by the pro-constitutionalist cleric, Seyyed Abdollah Behbahani. In June of 1906 Behbahani was instrumental in encouraging Iranians to take sanctuary in the British legation in Tehran,[63] and Zahir al-Dowleh rejected this course of action unreservedly. He wrote:

> This policy is completely mistaken and wrong. It is just as if someone gives the front-door key of his house to his thieving neighbour, with his own hand. They [Behbahabi and Tabataba'i] sent a reply [to me, saying], 'We won't do this anymore.' I spit on this cowardice and self-interest [*naf' parasti*].[64]

These remarks are intriguing and are open to speculation. It may well be the case that Zahir al-Dowleh perceived that the policy of taking *bast* in the British legation would be seen as playing into the hands of the British (or at least offering the British a chance to become more involved in the crisis). Perhaps Zahir al-Dowleh believed that an increasing level of British involvement would certainly antagonize the Russians and Iran's pro-Russian camp, including the future Shah, Mohammad Ali. It appears likely, therefore, that Zahir al-Dowleh's comments reflect not so much a lack of commitment to the constitutional movement as a desire that the foreign powers should be kept out of the dispute, as British or Russian involvement would only exacerbate the crisis. Such a view conforms to the argument that Zahir al-Dowleh was a staunch nationalist and patriotic Iranian, and that contrary to arguments from the likes of Kasravi, Sufis did not undermine the country because of their 'evil' teachings.

Zahir al-Dowleh's reserve towards the politics of Behbahani and Tabataba'i is revealed most explicitly in his comments about his meeting with Tabataba'i on 24 December 1906, when he observed that Mohammad Tabataba'i 'spoke very confidently. He has a good political head, and his manners and behaviour are also pleasant. It is a shame that he is a little radical (*tond*) and fearless (*bi-bak*).'[65] Even though Zahir al-Dowleh had some reserve towards Tabataba'i, the latter had a favourable opinion of the Sufi. Tabataba'i wrote to him, 'Your Excellency was the first in establishing an assembly of justice. I wish there were several others in Iran like Your Excellency to comfort the people.'[66]

Zahir al-Dowleh's reticence about direct political action (such as taking *bast*) seems to stand in contrast to the establishment of the assembly in Hamadan. Yet the successful creation of this assembly appears to have shocked even Zahir al-Dowleh himself, for on addressing crowds during the construction of the Hamadan assembly on 6 September 1906, he said, 'If you knew how much this building is contrary to your habits, you would never have embraced it.'[67] Zahir al-Dowleh's perspective became apparent a month later, on 14 October, in his reaction to reading a newspaper article about the reforms demanded by the Chinese that were directed at the Emperor. When they asked for an assembly and constitutional rule, the Emperor replied, 'You do not have the wisdom and knowledge for an assembly and constitutional government. It may be possible in ten years, for I will order a school, based on Western plans, to be built in each city and village. You will get educated there, and after ten years, once you have all become wise, I will entrust the empire to you with great pleasure and satisfaction. You will be able to do exactly as you please.' The Chinese people accepted this offer with much happiness, and the Emperor immediately gave the order to commence the building of schools in all the country's cities and villages. On hearing all of this, Zahir al-Dowleh remarked, 'May God bless the Emperor of China for being such a wise man! In my opinion, if he lives for ten more years and the Chinese people become wise and appreciate his beneficence and fatherly care, they will increase [the country's] independence and power more than before.'[68] In assessing Zahir al-Dowleh's perspective on constitutionalism, it is instructive to compare him with his contemporaries. Parallels in the thinking of Zahir al-Dowleh with that of Tabataba'i have already been made (regarding the powers that influence constitutional bodies), yet more striking is the similarity on the need for education first. Zahir al-Dowleh's reflection about the Chinese situation may well have mirrored his opinion about the conditions in Iran, and likewise, Tabataba'i is reported to have commented in 1906 that the people of Iran 'have not yet reached the necessary level of education and are not capable of constitutionalism.'[69]

Zahir al-Dowleh's cautious approach to reform was probably not due to any personal cowardice, as he was quite prepared to tackle leading authorities in Tehran. A particular example of this is his exchange of telegrams with the Shah's prime minister, Mirza Nasrollah Moshir al-Dowleh Na'ini, concerning the famine that the people of Hamadan were experiencing, which was caused in part by grain-hoarding. Zahir al-Dowleh sent a telegram to Moshir al-Dowleh, asking for powers to help the people.[70] Moshir al-Dowleh's arrogant response reflects the insensitivity of Tehran to peripheral areas: 'I am busy eating venison kebabs. I wish you were here. I will forward your request for special powers to His Majesty, and then give you an answer.' Zahir al-Dowleh shot back a telegram that did little to conceal his anger: 'The scent of your kebab has reached Hamadan and has incited the hungry people even further. If you do not give me special powers within three days, I will not take [any] responsibility [for what may happen].' Moshir al-Dowleh ultimately gave Zahir al-Dowleh the special powers to ensure that the people of Hamadan could obtain bread.[71]

Before leaving Hamadan and Zahir al-Dowleh's duties there, it is important to mention that throughout 1907 many regions in Iran witnessed major uprisings and disturbances in the wake of the granting of a National Assembly and of the attempts of the new Shah, Mohammad Ali, to undermine the institution. Zahir al-Dowleh was not immune to these troubles, as the Shah's brother, Salar al-Dowleh, lay claim to the throne and, supported by his Lur followers, estimated at several thousand,[72] commenced a march on Tehran. The Majles did not support Salar al-Dowleh's move for power, affirming its loyalty to Mohammad Ali's right to the throne,[73] and Salar al-Dowleh was defeated by the monarch's forces in June 1907. He escaped to Kermanshah and sought refuge in the British consulate. However, Zahir al-Dowleh persuaded him to surrender and sent him to Tehran under arrest.

The Pantomime

In November 1907, Zahir al-Dowleh was recalled to Tehran, where he stayed for a couple of months before being sent as governor to the province of Gilan (February 1908). It was probably during this period in Tehran that Zahir al-Dowleh had the members of the Anjoman-e Okhovvat perform a pantomime that he had conceived. This pantomime must be seen in the context of the increasing penetration and influence of foreign powers in Iran: the Ottoman Turks were attacking Iran's border near Urmia, and the Anglo-Russian Agreement of August 1907 had divided Iran into spheres of influence. It may be that Zahir al-Dowleh believed that the political situation had deteriorated so much that he felt increasing measures needed to be taken to respond to the new circumstances. Certainly this would help to explain the controversy surrounding the pantomime.

The pantomime was performed by members of the Anjoman-e Okhovvat in a theatre within Zahir al-Dowleh's property (located in 'Ala al-Dowleh Street, now Ferdowsi Street), behind the society's headquarters. The performance attracted most of the leading figures of the day, including some from the European legations. When the curtain rose, an individual who was recog-

5. Zahir al-Dowleh is second on the right in this photograph taken by Sevruguin.

nizable as Mohammad Ali Shah was seen sitting on his throne, while a body in rich clothes, and adorned with a crown and gold and silver, symbolizing the nation of Iran, lay at his feet. At this point the 'English ambassador', with the permission of the 'Shah', appeared on the stage and stole the crown from the prostrate body, upon which he departed. Then it was the turn of the 'Russian ambassador', who ran off with jewels that he took from the body. Following this, several Iranian political representatives and plunderers took some of the clothes, the watch, and rings from the body, while the 'Shah' remained unaware. Then some well-wishing individuals, who loved both the Shah and the nation, entered the scene and made the monarch aware of the state of the nation at his feet, and when the 'foreigners' and 'Iranian thieves' returned to steal more, the 'Shah' and his supporters drove them away.[74]

The real Mohammad Ali Shah was livid when he was informed of the contents of the pantomime, and he was determined to seek revenge.[75] While the pantomime did not explicitly blame the Shah for the backward state of Iran (the curtain did descend on a Shah who had been awakened to the dangers of foreign and internal exploitation), it certainly must have positioned Zahir al-Dowleh in the ranks of the constitutionalists, whether he liked it or not, and as an opponent of the Shah. His connections and friendship with radical advocates of reform (such as Malek al-Motakallemin, see below) must also have increased this perception. Further evidence of this stance is offered in Zahir al-Dowleh's expulsion of Mohsen Khan Mozaffar al-Molk from the Anjoman-e Okhovvat for overseeing the execution of Seyyed Jamal Va'ez Esfahani.[76]

Governor of Gilan (February–August 1908)

Gilan was also engulfed in the struggle for the constitution, as revolutionary groups were active in Rasht and Anzali. Between 1906 and 1908 these two cities had become centres of secret coordinating committees for the Organization of Social Democrats. This organization espoused liberalism and nationalism, and while critical of the conservative ulema, supported Shiite religious traditions.[77] In addition, there were other revolutionary organizations in the province with similar ideologies, such as the Secret Centre, which created a volunteer army that had branches in both Rasht and Anzali.[78] Another revolutionary group of significance was the Sattar Committe of Rasht, whose military commander, the Armenian Yeprem Khan, was being encouraged to lead an uprising in Gilan by other revolutionaries in Tabriz.[79] Ever since the start of the revolutionary fervour, there had been strikes by the fishermen of Anzali. These strikes were supported by many sympathizers in other locations, who boycotted Russian goods. By June 1907 some people tried to break open the grain silos of a local tribal brigand, and this was followed by a general strike in Rasht.[80]

It was in these turbulent circumstances that Zahir al-Dowleh was appointed governor of Gilan. Safa'i claims that the military commander in Rasht was pocketing the revenues that were due to Iran under a fishing concession in the north that had been given to several Russians.[81] As governor of Gilan, Zahir al-Dowleh sent his son, Zahir-e Hozur, to Anzali to restore order. The situation in Gilan became more enflamed as news emerged from Tehran of the Shah's attempts to undermine the National Assembly. When Behbehani and Tabataba'i invited the provinces to prepare for battle with the Shah, the people of Gilan took control of the arsenals, and the National Guard in Rasht put on their military uniforms and set off for Tehran.[82] It seems that Zahir al-Dowleh tried to prevent them,[83] an argument that accords with his philosophy that genuine and lasting reform could only come through education. Yet, others have argued that Zahir al-Dowleh supported the revolutionaries in Rasht who had established a military base there.[84] The suspicions held by Mohammad Ali Shah and his Court concerning Zahir al-Dowleh's sympathies with the revolutionaries are apparent in a telegram that Moshir al-Saltaneh[85] sent to Zahir al-Dowleh on 23 June 1908, in which he comments on a report that had reached the British embassy that one of the societies (*anjomans*) in Gilan desired to purchase 12,000 rifles which had appeared in Anzali, that the state had ordered. Moshir al-Saltaneh was alarmed that the rifles might fall into rebel hands. In his reply, Zahir al-Dowleh maintained that the reports received by Moshir al-Saltaneh were just a rumour.[86]

The Ransacking of Zahir al-Dowleh's House

The bombardment of the National Assembly on 23 June 1908 temporarily curtailed the constitutionalist movement. Even though the events concerning the bombardment are well documented, there remains some confusion concerning the subsequent attacks on the houses of leading personalities in Tehran. Zahir al-Dowleh was informed that after the Majles had been destroyed his house had been ransacked and plundered.[87] Furniture, golden items, jewellery,[88] and thousands of valuable manuscripts from the library were taken, and Zahir al-Dowleh's wife, daughter, and servants were treated in a fashion that was unbecoming for aristocratic members of the Qajar elite.

Various explanations have been offered for the attack on Zahir al-Dowleh's house. The first is that the circumstances of the bombardment of the Majles and the subsequent general confusion were used by Moshir al-Saltaneh and Qavam al-Dowleh[89] in an attempt to gain the upper hand with Zahir al-Dowleh in a land dispute. In a letter from Malekeh-ye Iran to Zahir al-Dowleh dated the same month in which the house was ransacked, it is possible to piece together the following story. Qavam al-Dowleh had claimed the right to some land in Varamin, outside of Tehran, that Zahir al-Dowleh argued was his own (as he held the deed of endowment).[90] Malekeh-ye Iran reports that Qavam al-Dowleh even attempted to send someone to steal the endowment from Zahir al-Dowleh's library. Moreover, she adds in her telegraph to her husband, 'Now, I swear this hostility [the ransacking of their house?] has been instigated by Qavam al-Dowleh. The Shah and Nayeb al-Saltaneh[91] said that without a doubt this was the case.'[92]

The second explanation was offered by Kasravi, who stated that the ransacking of the houses after the bombardment of the Majles was tactical, and aimed specifically at Zell al-Soltan, a potential rival for the throne. Kasravi commented, 'The only houses that they plundered were those that the Shah ordered. Today they only ransacked the houses of Jalal al-Dowleh – the son of Zell al-Soltan, and Zahir al-Dowleh (the husband of Zell al-Soltan's sister). ... Mohammad Ali Mirza's hostility was directed at Zell al-Soltan more than anyone else.'[93] This explanation seems more plausible than the first, especially in the light of Zell al-Soltan's ambitions (and that of other members of the royal family, such as Salar al-Dowleh, who had made a move on the throne.)

The third explanation, which was given by the Cossack leader, Colonel Liakhov (who led the ransacking of Zahir al-Dowleh's house), was that it was an attempt to destroy the powerbase of the Anjoman-e Okhovvat which was located within Zahir al-Dowleh's house, because the Shah associated the society with the other *anjoman*s that were espousing radical reforms.[94] Liakhov's explanation was echoed by Mo'ayyer al-Mamalek, who argued that the attack was due to the perception that people held that Zahir al-Dowleh was the innovator in the creation of the societies that mushroomed during the constitutional period, and this perception naturally influenced the Shah.[95]

This third explanation certainly seems plausible, as the Anjoman-e Okhovvat did have certain radical individuals, such as Nosrat al-Soltan (a member of the First Majles), who had close links with Malek al-Motakallemin, a vocal critic of the policy of taking foreign loans and also a member of one of the most radical secret societies, the Revolutionary Committee.[96] Other radical individuals who must have been associated with Zahir al-Dowleh's house would have included Zahir al-Soltan (son of Malekeh-ye Iran and Zahir al-Dowleh), who was one of eight individuals whose expulsion from Tehran the Shah had requested in the days prior to the bombardment of the National Assembly.[97] Zahir al-Soltan was a member of a number of radical societies, including the Anjoman-e Beyn al-Tolu'eyn, whose affiliates included Seyyed Hasan Taqizadeh and Heydar Khan Amuoghli.[98] Zahir al-Soltan's life was spared as a result of his mother's intercession; she wrote a letter begging for leniency to Amir Bahador Jang (who aside from being Minister of War also headed the Royal Guards).[99] Browne also reports that Zahir al-Soltan's life was spared by the Shah since the former's mother said she would kill herself if he were put to death.[100]

Whether or not the third explanation be the most credible, it is certain that the Shah was worried that the members of the Anjoman-e Okhovvat would retaliate against the destruction of Zahir al-Dowleh's house and their headquarters. He asked Malekeh-ye Iran to

> 'do something so that the dervishes don't do something [in revenge]. The Cossacks destroyed their master's house, but one of them killed [some] Cossacks.[101] There may be a riot, and it would be embarrassing for me.' I [Malekeh-ye Iran] said 'I will write your request to Entezam al-Saltaneh.[102] I will ask him.' He replied, 'Write [to him] now, in front of my eyes, and say that [the Shah] says to all the dervishes, "I have the utmost regard for Zahir al-Dowleh, and I very much regret this terrible event. I was unaware that they destroyed his house. It was something that just happened. I will pay for all the damage to the property of Malekeh-ye Iran and Zahir al-Dowleh. They [the dervishes] can all rest assured."' I wrote this in front of the Shah.[103]

Malekeh-ye Iran's telegrams to her husband suggest that she believed the Shah's claims. 'Know that His Majesty was unaware [of the events]. Showing utmost kindness to me, he has sworn all oaths [to this effect].'[104] She also states that the Shah was furious with Liakhov and Amir Bahador Jang.[105]

That there must have been much confusion is clear from Malekeh-ye Iran's portrayal of events (which are dramatic to say the least, especially her description of how she and her daughter escaped from the Cossacks by climbing over the roofs of neighbouring houses).[106] But the fact that the operation was overseen by the head of the Cossack Brigade, Colonel Liakhov, might suggest that the Shah knew more than he was willing to concede.

The response of Zahir al-Dowleh to all of these events reveals the dilemma in which he found himself. As a supporter of the constitutional movement, although one not so radical as his son or others such as Taqizadeh, he must have been distraught. Yet as a representative of the Shah in Gilan, and perhaps clinging to the ideal of reform rather than revolution, he followed the royal command that all the societies should be closed. He ordered a band of Cossacks who were with him to carry out their task and close the *anjomans*. This was done without much opposition, although three Cossacks were wounded and two members of an *anjoman* were killed. A week later, Zahir al-Dowleh was relieved of his post in Gilan and sent to neighbouring Mazandaran as the new governor.[107] Yet he must have felt deep resentment at Mohammad Ali Shah, and perhaps later came to believe that he was the instigator in the destruction of his house. In a poem addressed to Mohammad Ali, dated 1910, he wrote:

> If you destroy the house of an innocent person
> Know for sure that your house will be ruined.[108]

And when in 1918, Mohammad Ali Shah's own house in Odessa was ransacked by the revolutionary Bolsheviks, Zahir al-Dowleh repeated the same lines in a poem that he addressed to the exiled Shah.[109]

Conclusion

Zahir al-Dowleh's commitment to the constitutional movement from 1906 onwards cannot be questioned. Prior to this date, especially before the turn of the century, there is no indication of his commitment to reform. However, perhaps as a result of his trip to Europe and the different context of Iran following the death of Naser al-Din Shah, his support for constitutionalism becomes clear. He believed that reform must be concomitant with education, and in this, he shared similar views with some of his contemporaries, such as Tabataba'i. The latter may be considered a moderate reformist, and given Zahir al-Dowleh's remarks about Tabataba'i being 'a little radical and fearless' and also his criticism of supporting the *bast*, one may speculate that Zahir al-Dowleh was rather conservative. However, as I have argued, Zahir al-Dowleh's opposition to supporting the *bast* was probably due to his desire to limit the influence of the foreign powers. His remarks about Tabataba'i being radical are difficult to unfold, as the context is not discussed within his writings. It may be that Zahir al-Dowleh was considering just one aspect of Tabataba'i's views (support of the *bast*); on the other hand, it may also be that he really did consider Tabataba'i as too radical. In this case, no definite conclusions can be drawn. What is clear, however, is that Zahir al-Dowleh and Tabataba'i did have much in common, such as the belief that education was a necessary condition for lasting reform.

In considering the three different perspectives on Zahir al-Dowleh that have been offered by three of the major historians of the Constitutional Revolution (summarized in the introduction to this chapter), it is clear that Kasravi's criticisms and failure to give due credit to the efforts of Zahir al-Dowleh are unjust. Malekzadeh's remark that 'just as it is in the way of the dervishes, their actions never went beyond words' fails to consider Zahir al-Dowleh's activity in Hamadan and also disregards the courage that he showed in presenting the pantomime in Tehran. Safa'i's treatment of Zahir al-Dowleh appears, therefore, to be the most constructive and accurate. This aristocratic Sufi remained committed to constitutionalism and to his idealist vision of democratic government in Iran, as several years after the bombardment of the National Assembly he reflected sadly, 'I don't suppose that we will have a really good Parliament and constitutional state within one hundred years, but [even so], I do hope we shall have one, God willing.'[110]

Zahir al-Dowleh's commitment to the constitutional movement should not be doubted, although he perceived that lasting reform should be organic, and nurtured through education, filtering down from the elite to the masses. In some ways this stance parallels his form of Sufism, which was elitist and hierarchical. As leader of the Anjoman-e Okhovvat he selected the first 110 members and appears to have led the Consultative Council from the beginning. Yet the ultimate goal was one of reform: to initiate more members and educate them in the ways of his version of Sufism, which was neither radical nor antinomian, as it emphasized the need to cultivate traditional Sufi etiquette (*adab*) such as humility and the need to work for one's living and to perform one's daily functions in ordinary clothes. Although it is clear that this Sufi, who was a high-ranking member of the Court, was committed to reform, more research needs to be undertaken to determine the nature of the Sufi contribution to the constitutional movement, especially among the 'rank-and-file' Sufis.

Part IV

Intellectual and Artistic Initiatives: Public Awakening

CHAPTER 10

The *Rowshanfekr* in the Constitutional Period: An Overview

Mangol Bayat

Throughout the constitutional period the revolutionary discourse was dominated by the terms *monavvar al-fekr* and *'oqala*, used to distinguish the emerging nationalist-modernist leadership from the established religious guardians of traditional values and sociocultural institutions. While *monavvar al-fekr* ('enlightened thinker' in Arabic) was also applied to some of the reform-minded ulema who actively supported the constitution, the term *'oqala* (from *'aql* in Arabic, meaning intellect or reason) was specifically used to contrast the lay modernists from the ulema in general. Gradually the Persian version *rowshanfekr* was coined and increasingly gained currency to the point of displacing both *monavvar al-fekr* and *'oqala* in twentieth-century Iranian vocabulary. It acquired a secular, liberal meaning, in contrast to its Arabic equivalents which had retained a semblance of Islamic legitimacy, if not authenticity. All three terms were European-inspired neologisms to designate the Iranian counterpart to the Central European and Russian intelligentsia, reflecting the sociopolitical ideals of eighteenth-century Enlightenment. For the purpose of the time frame of this chapter, I shall use the term *rowshanfekr* in a broad sense as the equivalent of 'intelligentsia', to include modernist reformers, bureaucrats, and politicians who were not writers or intellectuals in a contemporary sense, as well as publicists, journalists, and writers in general.

As agents of change with a self-imposed mission of nation-building, the intelligentsia also aimed at modifying the collective consciousness and organizing new modes of sensibility. The formidable obstacles they encountered in the process determined the meandering paths they had to follow to attain their goals. Therefore, a discussion of the activist ulema's role in the constitutional movement and its consequences is needed here, in order to, first, explain how the religious leaders lost the political authority and prestige that had defined their status in society for centuries and, second, provide a sociopolitical context for the *rowshanfekran*'s adopted strategies. The revolution constitutes a large, multicoloured tapestry formed from a variety of interwoven threads. Two essential components so far not adequately discussed, Freemasonry and the Young Turk Revolution, deserve attention. The focus on these two outside sources of support for the constitutionalists is by no means intended to give them more weight in shaping the revolutionary movement than is given to other equally involved groups. It is a supplement to my earlier analysis of the religious dissidents', the social democrats', and the moderate reformers' contributions, which are not discussed here in order to avoid repetition. Finally, the *rowshanfekran*'s political gains were not to last: an analysis of the domestic and international power politics of the time is also necessary for a better understanding of their political failure.

During the past three decades, champions of cultural and religious authenticity throughout the non-Western world and even in Europe, not to mention the United States, have tended to delegitimize the secular legacy of the Enlightenment. Such an onslaught is noticeable in some studies of the Constitutional Revolution written with the 1979 revolution as a subtext in mind, obscuring or downplaying the strong underlying secularist trends that characterized the very nature of the constitutional movement. Undoubtedly most of its champions at that time referred to Islamic texts and laws in defence of their ideas and programmes. However, the Islamic rhetoric by no means displayed a genuinely innovative trend originating from within the ulema's ranks and distinct from the lay modernists' argument. It merely adopted modernist views, accommodating them to religious principles. In fact, the *mujtahid* Fazlollah Nuri and other ulema who actively opposed the constitution, regardless of their respective motives, represented the sole contemporaneous authentic voice of Islamic jurisprudence. Thus, it is necessary to take into account the true historical-ideological context of the early 1900s in Iran in comparison with the rest of the world, in order to reach a comprehensive assessment of the revolution's successful or unsuccessful innovations. Here, a brief comparative study of the emergence of the intellectuals as a social group in Western Europe may help in understanding how peculiarly Islamic the situation of pre-modern Iranian thinkers was.

From *Clerc* to *Rowshanfekr*

In his classic study of the European intellectuals in the Middle Ages, Jacques Le Goff traces their origins to the monastic *clerc*.[1] He accounts for the gradual disengagement of speculative thought from theology with an analysis of the *rapports de force* among the church, the university, and the reigning dynastic power. From the twelfth through the fifteenth century Christian scholastic and humanist thinkers emerged from within the monastic ranks, and they in turn gave rise to the Renaissance intellectuals. The latter group, Le Goff argues, proved to be the fiercest adversary of scholasticism, striking a final blow in the universities and ushering in the secular humanists of the sixteenth century. The eighteenth-century Enlightenment then helped consolidate the status of the modern secular intellectual.

Le Goff substantiates his argument with a detailed analysis of the gradual but periodically stormy evolutionary development of autonomous institutions of higher learning from within the broader sociopolitical contexts. The disengagement of European thought from theology followed a long, painful, and haphazard process, often leading some scholars, such as Daniel de Morley of England or Abelard of France, to seek refuge in Muslim Spain, where each could 'live in peace ... as a Christian in the midst of the enemies of Christians'.[2] The intellectual crusade of the dissidents in the twelfth century provoked controversies and ignited street fights. For teaching was an ecclesiastical function under the bishops' control, and culture was deemed a matter of faith. The university was also engaged in a struggle against expanding monarchical power, which attempted to expropriate its rich endowments. The struggle ended with the university forcing both the secular and ecclesiastical authorities to acquiesce to its demands for autonomy. Ironically, as Le Goff explains, it was the Pope in Rome who helped the universities acquire this autonomy in order to better 'domesticate' them and bring them under papal control.[3] The final disengagement of speculative thought from theology was facilitated in the fourteenth century by the war waged between church and state, when dynastic powers mercilessly struggled against papal claims to temporal authority. The war ended with the emergence of the absolutist monarchy, its state founded upon the separation of the law from ecclesiastical jurisdiction, though with the church conferring upon the monarch an aura of religiously legitimacy.

This peculiarly Western European tradition of warfare between church and state did not occur in pre-modern Iran, or elsewhere in the pre-modern Muslim world. Periodically, there were individual religious leaders who denounced some government officials as corrupt and even shunned any association with the state. But these were exceptions rather then the rule. Through the nineteenth century, high-ranking religious leaders living in Iran gained wealth and social status as members of the ruling elite. In the Qajar period they formed a privileged class, rich and powerful, often with hereditary rights for their sons to succeed to their high-ranking clerical positions. Some engaged in the power politics of their time as individuals, joining a political faction of their choice, in alliance with lay politicians. Personal motives rather than doctrinal considerations tended to determine their choice. In fact, political clout consolidated the activist ulema's status and influence within the religious institutions in Iran proper. Despite the divisive character of the political cabals, the Islamic traditional social order remained intact, preserved by this close working relationship between the two mutually dependent centres of authority, state and religion. The religious leaders taught the law and presided over the religious courts of justice, but the enforcement of God's law was under state jurisdiction. The Shah was not granted doctrinal legitimacy, but he was regarded as an integral and necessary part of Islamic society and referred to as 'the Shadow of God on Earth'. Originally a pre-Islamic Persian attribute of the monarch, the title was revived by the Sunni Abbasid Caliphate of Baghdad (750–1258). As Fazlur Rahman, the late scholar of Islamic theology and philosophy, explained, for the ulema this title 'meant a point of cohesion against chaos and lawlessness, but in the popular belief, influenced by the ancient Iranian idea of kingship, this phrase assumed literal truth.'[4]

The traditional Qajar power structure positioned the sovereign's rule, *saltanat*, as transcending, and hence distinct from, the royally appointed government, *dowlat*. Popular revolts and even the ruling elite's discontent would generally be directed at government officials, rarely holding the monarch responsible for the officials' wrongdoings. Thus, unlike the European experience in the High Middle Ages, the religious-political climate prevailing in Iran up to the late nineteenth century deprived speculative thinkers of any strong institutional backing in their struggle to free themselves from theology. Iranian reformers even lacked the military institutional backing that the Young Turks enjoyed in Ottoman Turkey, where modernization of the armed forces had produced a new nationalist leadership. Theology continued to monopolize the whole field of metaphysics and would not allow rational investigation of the nature of the universe and of man. Knowledge was defined as knowledge of the divine, with no distinction made between the sacred and the profane, the religious and the secular. God's Law was the law of the realm, as taught and executed by its guardians, the *mujtahids*. Shiite mysticism in all its variety experienced an even deeper tension between the discipline of the law and a powerful messianic impulse, which the *mujtahids* combated.[5]

The intellectual in pre-modern Iran thus remained a *clerc* in Le Goff's sense of the term. It was only in the last two decades of the nineteenth century, as a result of European economic and political intervention in domestic Iranian affairs and of greater Iranian awareness of Europe, its knowledge, its institutions and political systems, that those dissident thinkers found the historic opportunity and the political means to detach themselves from religious institutional authority. It is important to note here that the Iranian *rowshanfekr* missed both the centuries-long evolutionary process and the necessary socio-economic and scientific conditions that facilitated the social maturing of his Western European counterpart. However, he benefited from the well-marked trail European innovations had set: modern technology and communication, modern science, and modern educational institutions offered a tested model, a breakthrough path that enabled an accelerated process of change outside Europe. Moreover, again unlike his European counterpart, the Iranian *rowshanfekr*, who initially threw away his *clerc* mantle at the turn of the twentieth century, emerged as a political activist clamouring for modern reforms. The failure of nineteenth-century Shiite schools of thought and religious movements that had been deemed heretical to leave any lasting impact on institutionalized religion dissuaded the activist intellectual from further pursuing the quest for change in this direction.[6] Politics then dominated his debates and programme of action, committed as he was to the belief that social and political problems were the central issues of life. Declaring that the truly religious person was no longer interested in the mystery of life, seeking instead pragmatic solutions to particular problems, he distanced himself from Islamic theology and mysticism, deemed 'ancient', and looked to Europe for a source of inspiration and emulation. The source of the profound schism that was later to occur between modern Iranian thought and its centuries-old Shiite intellectual heritage goes back to this period.

No historical figure better symbolized this transition from the *clerc* to *rowshanfekr* than Seyyed Jamal al-Din Asadabadi, known as al-Afghani (1838–97). Though much has been written about his Islamism and Pan-Islamist activities, Jamal al-Din was *essentially* a man in revolt against institutionalized religion and its hierarchical order, fighting for the intellectual 'renewal' of Muslim societies. Reared in traditional madrasas, he was more attracted to Islamic philosophy and dissident schools until, charged with heresy, he was forced into exile. Travelling to Muslim colonized countries and then Europe, he became acquainted with modern ideas and institutions. A man of paradoxes, contradictions, and shifting political alliances, he thereafter remained constant in his call for a change in the Muslims' attitude towards the 'new learning', that is, European thought and science. 'Science', he wrote, 'is not connected to any nation', and he persistently maintained the view that 'men must be related to science, not science to men'.[7] It would be no exaggeration to state that Jamal al-Din had in fact initiated the process of desacralization of the concept of knowledge, no matter how haphazard, confused, and obscurantist his rhetorical argument and action often were. He thus helped to open wide the intellectual frontier which, he claimed, had been artificially erected by the ulema. Just as the European *clerc* of the High Middle Ages had initially won his battle against the dynastic power by winning the support of the Pope, Jamal al-Din seized the occasion of the 1890–92 Tobacco Concession Affair to call for revolt against the Qajar Shah and mobilize the *mujtahids*' backing. He appealed to the doctrine of the Imamate, the sole legitimate source of authority, of which, he reminded them, they were the guarantors. Sheer political expediency lay behind this paradoxical move. It proved to be a formidable, though unprecedented, strategy to forge a broad national coalition in opposition to government policies. He did not live long enough to witness the outbreak of the Constitutional Revolution. But his strategy was to be emulated by the Constitutional Revolution's major players in an even more successful coalition that forced the Shah to grant a constitution to the nation. It was also a strategy that bore inherently fatal weaknesses with lasting consequences, leaving unresolved secular/religious tensions.

The secularist leaders who wished to undertake radical social and cultural reforms through a political revolution were unable to disengage their programme and the vocabulary used to promote it from the prevailing religious norms. The normative vocabulary of their time exerted a powerful restraint on their actions, limiting their freedom of manoeuvring to what could be justified by and rendered seemingly compatible with religious principles; hence the complexity of the debates on constitutionalism. All groups involved adopted the innovative term *mashrutiyat*, which provided a common leitmotif for their respective diverse and, in many cases, irreconcilable objectives. All had therefore to confront the same dilemma: how to justify resistance to the 'Shadow of God' and the *mujtahid*s while proclaiming belief in the Islamic sanctity of the prevailing sociopolitical order. Hence, their right to resist tyranny was legitimized through reference to the time-honoured Shiite tradition of dissent as much as through imported modern European concepts. The strategy initially bore fruit, as it successfully mobilized many high-ranking ulema to their cause. The ulema's active participation in the events, however, precipitated the destruction of the very old power structure within which the strategy was originally situated.

The *Rowshanfekran* and the Ulema

The ulema, whether they were supportive of or opposed to the constitution, upheld the traditional distinction of *saltanat* transcending *dowlat*. In their communication with the Shah they never failed to address him in the customary respectful tone of 'those who pray for His Highest, Most Holy Majesty', the Shadow of God, the King of Islam and the Muslims, putting the blame for the crisis on corrupt elements within his government. At the early stage of the movement, lay leaders followed their example, sparing the 'affectionate father of the nation'[8] from any responsibility for official wrongdoing. In his response, Mozaffar al-Din Shah (r. 1896–1907) would call upon the ulema's duty to pray for his royal well-being, reminding them of their obligations to the throne and the government. He would insist on his royal prerogatives and the authority bestowed upon him by divine grace. 'Certainly, our responsibility to safeguard the pure shari'a exceeds that of other people.'[9] When he first decreed the constitution in August 1906, he referred to his 'royal self' as the 'protector of all rights of the people of Iran, our true subjects', and expressed his 'royal desire' for government reforms to be enacted by a 'national consultative assembly'.

Most ulema, including the conservative *mujtahid*s who had conveniently joined the movement when it gathered nationwide momentum, perceived the Majles as a means to check abuse of government power and protect religion. The Shah believed it would act as the 'guarantor of our justice' and ensure the application of the holy law.[10] At the opening ceremony of the Majles, speakers made repeated references to 'Mozaffar's justice' and expressed the people's gratitude for the solicitude of the compassionate Shadow of God, the Shah of Islam.[11] Because of the highly visible part the constitutionalist ulema, led by Seyyed Abdollah Behbahani and Seyyed Mohammad Tabataba'i, had played as nominal leaders of the movement, and the seemingly predominant aura of religious legitimacy it acquired, the Shah mistakenly believed he was witnessing the erosion of kingly power and, conversely, the ascendancy of ulema power in political affairs. Terminally ill, the Shah confided to the ulema that he was taking off his shoulders 'this heavy iron yoke' of responsibility, placed there by his ancestors, and handing it to the ulema, for them to assume it fully.[12] British officials in Tehran tended to reinforce this impression, which they manipulated as leverage over the Shah's weakened willpower. Neither the moderate secularists nor the radical revolutionaries initially involved in shaping and directing the movement wished to dispel this illusion, at least not at this early stage. The newly crowned Mohammad Ali Shah's open hostility to the constitution, his Court intrigues against the Majles, and his support of the anti-constitutionalist ulema finally released the virulent energy of the radical wing of the movement from these self-imposed tactical constraints.

The intelligentsia, whether moderate or radical, aristocratic or middle-class, by then viewed the prevailing fragmentation of society by tribalism, sectarianism, and ethnicity as a formidable obstacle to their reforms. They still conceded hereditary rights to the Qajar dynasty, including the right to appoint the heir apparent. However, they understood that institutional changes had to be carried out in order to build a modern state. Such a state would claim sovereignty and demand loyalty from all citizens, no longer regarded as mere subjects, and to whom civic rights and equality before the law would be granted, regardless of their social status, their tribal, or their religious affiliation. The term *ra'iyat*, traditionally meaning the subjects of the sovereign, was reinterpreted to mean 'citizenry'. However, the constitutionalist pamphlets of the time preferred a more populist terminology: *mardom* (people) and *mellat* (nation), as distinct from *saltanat* and *dowlat*. An unprecedented conception of the 'will of the people' began to take root, decisively aiming at eroding the theological premises of Iran's political power structure. The old conception of *saltanat* itself was redefined, as radicals began to challenge the Shah's 'most holy' authority. Night letters circulating in Tehran and Tabriz reminded him of the fact that his rule depended on the nation's right to confer it upon him. The people of Iran, he was told, 'are no longer the same as they were five or six years ago. ... It is now evident to all that your power ... rests on the nation. ... By God, if there is no nation, there is no government; if there is no government, there is no Shah!'[13] Mohammad Ali Shah, now enjoying the full support of the conservative ulema turned reactionary, resisted any new legislation that curbed his royal prerogatives and urged the official replacement of the term *mashrutiyat* (constitutionalism) with *mashru'iyat* (based on the shari'a), which he deemed more compatible with the traditional Islamic political order. However, moderate elements of the intelligentsia did not hesitate to refer to the traditional crown-ulema balance of power, to dissuade him from such a drastic reactionary step. *Mashru'iyat*, he was warned, would allow 'others' (meaning the ulema) to call for a *shar'i* government, hinting at the ulema's potential claim to rule on the basis of their being the sole guarantors of the Islamic law.[14] The Shah withdrew his demand.

The chronicles of the Constitutional Revolution amply show how the ulema, even those who had espoused it from the start, formulated neither its concepts nor its objectives. They were willing to concede in theory, though not always in practice, to the Fundamental Law (*qanun* as distinct from *fiqh* or Islamic jurisprudence) jurisdiction over matters pertaining to *'urf* (political-public affairs traditionally kept under Court authority), provided the law in those cases was compatible with Islamic principles and values. In fact, radical pamphlets widely circulating at the time stressed the importance to be given to such a distinction: between the rules of the Qur'an and the Imams for religious affairs and the Fundamental Law for worldly matters, urging the ulema to limit their functions to theology and worship. A tiny faction from among the radicals, who included some middle-ranking dissident members of the religious institutions, attempted to target the ulema directly. But they were compelled to remain underground and mute their radicalism. Periodically, sparks of fire they ignited would be swiftly extinguished and the 'arsonists' forced to tone down their rhetoric.[15] Nonetheless, the constitutionalist ulema's role in drafting the Fundamental Law was increasingly reduced to the mere giving of a seal of approval.[16]

The ulema's initial acceptance of the constitution and the later defection of those who came to realize the true nature of the entire movement underscore the personal motives of their participation in one camp or another. Beneath the highly visible role they collectively played in these fateful events lay considerable differences in temperament, ambition, and personal ability to comprehend the enormous implications of the term *mashrutiyat*. In a manner reminiscent of old Qajar political cabals, but with graver repercussions for the nation at large, activist ulema took sides for or against the government then in office. The government, however, even though it was composed of members of the old political elite, was now accountable to the Majles and no longer to the Shah, and its officials were men who, genuinely or expediently, supported the constitution. Publicly, the constitutionalist ulema's social status, clout, and financial support suffered no loss for as long as the Majles–Shah power struggle tilted in favour of the Majles.[17] Conversely, their star was tarnished and Sheykh Fazlollah Nuri's would shine once Mohammad Ali Shah was ready to strike a severe blow to the Majles. Thus, the individual fate of the activist ulema depended on the worldly political cause each espoused and on the fate of that cause's lay sponsors, just as it was with the old cabals. In other words, the *rapport de force* between the two ulema camps was determined by the corresponding *rapport de force* between political factions outside the religious institutions.

Sheykh Fazlollah and his fellow conservative ulema represented mainstream Shiite jurisprudence; Seqat al-Eslam, Tabataba'i, and others who rose in defence of the constitutionalists stood for an updated Islamic tradition of dissent. Both trends, often at war with each other, have enriched Islamic cultures in all their diversity through the centuries. However, the activist ulema became victims of their partisanship, drawn as they were to power politics which, at the time of the revolution, had become too complex for them to survive unscathed. They proved to be useful instruments for their respective factional leaders. Sheykh Fazlollah Nuri, executed in 1909; Behbahani, assassinated in 1910; and Seqat al-Eslam, executed by the Russians in 1911; paid for their activism with their lives. Similarly, by granting their support to the movement, the constitutionalist ulema were in fact conceding their acceptance of the concept of a Fundamental Law, *qanun*, pertaining to matters of worldly affairs, as distinct from the shari'a. In practice, this concession allowed a greater delineation of the worldly from the religious realm, *donyavi-dini*, than had the traditional *'urfi-shar'i* jurisdictions. Furthermore, the destruction of Qajar absolutist power brought about a severe erosion of the ulema's political prestige and cultural influence in society. The traditional balance of power based on mutual dependence and accommodation between state and religion in Shiite Iran would suffer irreversible consequences.

The *mashrutiyat* irrevocably desacralized the nature of political power and altered its structure. This inevitable consequence of the Constitutional Revolution and the legislative reforms of the Majles would, in turn, hasten the secularization of the vital social institutions which had, until then, remained under the ulema's jurisdiction. The *clerc* and the turbaned *monavvar al-fekr* would give way to the modern intellectual. Many of the clerical exiles, along with the dissidents who had stayed in the country during the period of 'Lesser Despotism', took off the clerical garb they had worn until the coup. Seyyed Hasan Taqizadeh and Seyyed Sadeq Tabataba'i (Mohammad Tabataba'i's son) were among many, mostly middle-ranking, ulema or sons of *mujtahid*s, who thus symbolically expressed their distancing from the religious institutions. The stage was, indeed, set for a new breed of Iranian secular nationalists to take over the task of shaping public opinion and constructing the 'new Iran,' ushering in modernity.

The *Rowshanfekran* and Freemasonry

Eugen Weber, the late historian of modern France, argued that French identity was a relatively recent creation. In his celebrated book *Peasants into Frenchmen*, he showed how the country which was largely rural and a mixture of cultures, was transformed in the half-century after its defeat in the Franco-Prussian War of 1870–71. France until the nineteenth century, he commented, was largely a Parisian political project rather than a national reality.[18] In 1790 only three million people could speak French; as late as 1893 about a quarter of the population of 30 million still had not mastered the national language. It also took *La Marseillaise* almost a century to emerge from a Strasbourg drawing room in 1792, where it was the battle song of the Rhine Army, to become the French national anthem. Nationalism in this formative French period was a humanitarian, Enlightenment-based movement. One should add here that, broadly speaking, the process of forging a national identity, as it developed at different stages elsewhere in Europe, the United States, Asia, and the Middle East, did not differ much from the French process just described. The issues defining the times, though originating in Western Europe, spread widely to other continents.

Modern nation-building in Iran was the self-appointed mission of its intelligentsia that had thus emerged at the start of the twentieth century. Though they never were a cohesive group, personally or ideologically, they came as a wave that challenged the traditional socioreligious base of the political power structure. They all shared a conviction rooted, paradoxically enough, both in the Iranian Shiite tradition of dissent and in the philosophy of the Enlightenment, that the ulema's functions in society had to be curtailed. Like their counterparts in other parts of the world, they identified modernity with secularism, and they sought in French and British secular institutions the models they wished to emulate. The vehicles for the transmission of European knowledge and political concepts have already been studied in numerous publications devoted to various aspects of modernization, including my own.

One other important organization for the spreading of modern Western European ideas, Freemasonry, needs to be studied here. For, by 1905–06, most of the prominent constitutionalists, be they of aristocratic or middle-class background, were already affiliated with European Freemasonry. Babis, nihilists, revolutionaries, Freemasons! These were the defamatory epithets hurled, often interchangeably, at the most militant constitutionalists. Thus, unsurprisingly, some historians developed conspiracy theories that, in their most extreme versions, viewed Masonic activities as part of the imperialists' plot to destroy national culture and sovereignty.[19] Other narratives opted to overlook, cover up, or totally omit any mention of the constitutional movement's Masonic aspects. One question has never been raised: why were the Iranian intelligentsia so attracted to Freemasonry? This question has to be addressed here.

Modern Freemasonry emerged fully defined and structured with the 1723 so-called Anderson Constitution, named after its main author. A Scottish Calvinist minister, Anderson had partly disengaged Masonry from esotericism and imposed administrative rules and regulations, assuming the right to universally proclaim what constituted correct ('regular') Masonry. With the second edition, in 1738, the constitution was accepted worldwide and non-Protestants were allowed to join the lodges. The constitution particularly emphasized the concept of universalism based on a shared faith in one God, the 'Grand Architect of the Universe'. As a non-Mason historian remarked: 'Mecca and Geneva, Rome and Jerusalem are identical. There are no Jews, no Mohammedans, no Papists, and no Protestants; there are only brothers who have sworn to God, common to all, to remain brothers for all.'[20] In theory, though seldom in practice, all religions were deemed equal. Humanist values transcended religious parochialism, imposing an ecumenical framework resting on the basic principles of tolerance, pluralism, and freedom of worship. Honour, loyalty, practising good and shunning evil, and a strong belief in humanity as one and indivisible were, again in theory, lofty ideals uniting all in a common bond. Eighteenth-century Freemasonry fully absorbed the philosophy of the Enlightenment, its faith in human reason, human perfectibility, science and progress and, above all, liberty. By the end of that century Freemasonry increasingly identified liberty with patriotism and freedom with national independence and sovereignty. It forged networks in Europe and the Americas, and came to play a dominant role in both the American and the French Revolutions. In France, Freemasonry continued its active participation in all subsequent national and international events and government policies. In the nineteenth century, appropriating the revolutionary slogan of liberty, equality, and fraternity as if it were their own creation, Masonic orders extended their activities to the Balkans and the Middle East. They came to shape political events and social movements, often enjoying the full support of successive Paris governments that used them as instruments to penetrate colonized, or semi-colonized, societies. It would be no exaggeration to state that Freemasonry was one of the most important agents of modernization in the Middle East, serving not only the interests of colonial powers but also those of the rising reform-minded regional elites, which did not necessarily coincide.

For various reasons the Grand Orient de France acquired a predominant role in the Constitutional Revolution. Chief among these reasons was this order's particularly aggressive promotion of its political agenda at home and abroad. Of all the orders in Europe it emerged as the most combatively secularist organization, imbued with Auguste Comte's positivism based on an absolute faith in reason and science. It was by no means immune to ideological and political dissension, often tearing apart its leadership; nonetheless its power survived internal schisms well enough to be labelled the 'godmother of the Third Republic'[21] following the humiliating 1871 defeat in the Franco-Prussian War. In fact, French historians generally refer to Freemasonry as the church of the Third Republic. In 1877 the Supreme Council of the Order of the Grand Orient officially revoked articles regarding the existence of God and immortality of the soul, replacing them with the affirmation of morality independent from religion; in short, proclaiming freedom of religion for all members. By 1886 it called for an official separation of church and state, engaging in a fierce political-religious struggle that involved the Catholic Church in France and the Vatican. Identified with the middle class, its members occupied important positions in the executive and legislative branches of consecutive French governments, translating into practice the principles of the Declaration of Human Rights, which, reportedly, many Masons had helped formulate.[22] With Jules Ferry, one of the Grand Orient's most famous 'brothers', in charge of national education from 1879 to 1884, the entire public education system was secularized, allowing the lodges to claim paternity for those laws.[23] In 1905 France was definitively declared a secular republic, with laws enacted to separate church from state. By all accounts, this legislation, considered the Grand Orient's greatest contribution, marked the apogee of its political influence.

The order played an equally important part in the government's *mission civilisatrice* in the non-European world, popularizing the universalized ideals and slogans of the French Revolution and using its vast networks and social ties with the ruling elite of the targeted countries. Although it did not establish in Iran an official lodge of its order prior to the outbreak of the Constitutional Revolution, the Grand Orient attracted to its various lodges in Paris and Istanbul many reform-minded Iranians. These 'brothers' found highly inspirational the concepts of freedom, rule of law, national representative government, sovereignty of the people, human rights, modern science and technology, and public secular education, which they viewed as essential to national renewal. Almost all were well-born, well-connected Qajar high or middle-ranking officials: many helped in founding, administering, and teaching at Dar al-Fonun, the first school offering a modern curriculum in Tehran.

Founded in 1851 by Amir Kabir, one of the first reform-minded Qajar ministers, Dar al-Fonun emerged within half a century as the best institution of higher learning in Iran, emulating European education and educating children of the political elite and the wealthy. Its staff and directors belonged to Masonic lodges in Europe; so did its European, mostly French, instructors. The Masonic connection was consolidated with the establishment in 1889 of French cultural centres in Tehran and Shiraz, affiliated with the Alliance Française. The predominant objective of this Paris-based national institution was the propagation of French culture and language as part of the government's *mission civilisatrice* programme abroad. It worked closely together with French Freemasonry, in particular with the Grand Orient. Joseph Richard, a Frenchman who had spent decades in Iran and was a member of the Dar al-Fonun faculty, was appointed the first director of the Alliance school in Tehran; its first secretary was Paul Henri Morel, another instructor at Dar al-Fonun. A supervising committee included Alphonse Nicolas, the French Orientalist expert in Persian language, religion, and culture; Julien Bottin, a French engineer; Jean-Baptiste Lemaire, musical director at the imperial Court and son-in-law of Dr. Joseph-Désiré Tholozan, the Shah's French physician; and many other European and Iranian diplomats, businessmen, educators, and other professionals. The French ambassador was the honorary chairman. Within three years of its foundation the Alliance's ties with Dar al-Fonun were consecrated with the Shah's personal approval and financial backing. The Alliance came to share Dar al-Fonun's classroom facilities and faculty. The Alliance's activities developed further when Dr. Justin Schneider assumed its directorship in 1899. A French physician who had come to Tehran in 1894 to join the circle of royal doctors, Schneider expanded the centre's educational role and led it to acquire great influence on the Anjoman-e Ma'aref, a private Iranian educational and library association run by reform-minded politicians. In 1899 the central committee of the Alliance Française in Paris also sponsored and financed a bilingual Franco-Persian school in Tabriz, the Loqmaniyeh, directed by Zeyn al-'Abedin Loqman al-Mamalek, a French-educated physician. Reportedly, it was virtually run by the Alliance. Similarly, the Roshdiyeh School, first founded in Tabriz in the early 1900s by Mirza Hasan Roshdiyeh, another reform-minded educator, received Alliance support. Other Roshdiyeh schools were later established in Tehran. In 1900 Joseph Vizioz was brought from Istanbul, where he had been teaching for years, to direct the Alliance school. Under his guidance, the school's student enrolment increased and its academic standards were raised considerably.[24] Bottin, Lemaire, Morel, Vizioz, and Schneider, all Freemasons in good standing affiliated with the Grand Orient, played a pivotal role in organizing, recruiting, and planning the Réveil de l'Iran or Bidari-ye Iran lodge, the sole officially recognized European lodge that existed in the country for the entire duration of the revolution.

According to the archival sources at the Grand Orient library in Paris,[25] on 29 November 1906, Lemaire invited several French and Iranian Masons to his house to discuss the need for a lodge in Tehran. A group of ten individuals met that evening, includeding Bottin; Ebrahim Khan Hakim al-Molk, a French-educated physician; Mirza Fazlollah Lava' al-Molk, a high-ranking military official; Mohammad Hasan Sheykh al-Molk Sirjani, a publicist who had spent some years in Paris; Haj Sayyah Mahallati, a middle-ranking mullah turned publicist; Haj Hoseyn Amin al-Zarb, the prominent merchant; Entezam al-Saltaneh, a government official; and Ahmad Khan Vazir Hozur, another Court official later known as Qavam al-Saltaneh, whose brother, the important politician Hasan Khan Vosuq al-Dowleh, would join the Bidari lodge only in 1910. The group agreed on the need for a lodge to organize Masonic activities in Tehran. Three days later it met in Hakim al-Molk's house and unanimously decided to have the lodge affiliated with the Grand Orient de France. According to the list of the earliest members filed at the order's archives, most were already members of either the Clémente Amitié or the Sincère Amitié, two lodges of the Grand Orient most favoured by non-European Masons and most prone to recruit non-Christians, especially from the Middle East. The Bidari lodge opted for the Scottish rite, however, which, in contrast to the Grand Orient rite, continued to enforce the belief in the Supreme Being Creator of the Universe and in the immortality of the soul. On 28 December 1906, the newly elected committee, headed by Lemaire as its *vénérable* (Worshipful Master), as the presiding officer of a lodge is called, wrote to the Paris headquarters requesting official recognition. It took almost a year for Paris to grant its consent, and Bidari-ye Iran was not incorporated as a legitimate lodge until November 1907. However, from the start, the Bidari-ye Iran acted as a fully fledged chapter of the order. When Lemaire died in February 1907, Morel replaced him as Worshipful Master. Indeed, by all accounts, it was Morel, the energetic torchbearer of Freemasonry in Tehran, who determined its policies, committing it even more to the constitutionalist cause. The close contacts with the Iranian intelligentsia and the ruling elite he had cultivated through the long years spent in the capital enabled him to provide the lodge with moral support and influence in shaping public opinion. His home was a safe house and a discreet meeting place for the brethren, though a rented house was their official address.

The Bidari-ye Iran lodge included among its membership government officials turned constitutionalists such as Nasrollah Khan Moshir al-Dowleh and his two sons, Hasan Khan and Hoseyn Khan; reform-minded aristocrats such as Momtaz al-Dowleh, whose brother, Samad Khan Momtaz al-Saltaneh, was then Persian ambassador in Paris; and Qajar royalty such as Zell al-Soltan, Salar al-Dowleh, Sho'a' al-Dowleh and Movaqqar al-Saltaneh, a brother-in-law of the Shah. It also included more members from the middle-class intelligentsia who came to play a prominent part in the revolution: Hasan Taqizadeh, Ali Akbar Dehkhoda, Malek al-Motekallemin, Jamal al-Din Va'ez, Mirza Jahangir Khan, Mirza Aqa Tabrizi, the Tarbiyat brothers, Seyyed Nasrollah Taqavi, Mo'azed al-Saltaneh, Zoka' al-Molk Foroughi, and Adib al-Mamalek Farahani, as well as the *mujtahid* Seyyed Mohammad Tabataba'i and his son Mohammad Sadeq.[26] By 1910 the list would read like a Who's Who of prominent constitutionalist figures, ideologically disparate, ranging from radical through moderate to conservative.[27] Here one must note that, in its lack of ideological cohesiveness, the Bidari-ye Iran lodge did not differ from many of its French counterparts, notorious for their internal power struggles.[28] Members were told to spread the Masonic message through personal instruction, lectures, publications, gatherings, and the establishment of new schools and newspapers in order to inform the public of the benefits of its principles: tolerance, liberty, the freedom to pursue knowledge, humanism, and universalism. They were urged to replace divisive personal conflicts with unity and accord, and to combat self-complacency and passive surrender to the status quo. 'Awake from the slumber of ignorance' constituted the universal Masonic slogan. News of the formation of the lodge was received enthusiastically in Paris. The Worshipful Master of the Clémente Amitié wrote to Adib al-Mamalek, the poet and one of its first members, to congratulate him. 'It is time to show to the modern world that [Iran] is worthy of [renewed] life. ... Cry out loudly: we want to attain spiritual and material liberty, equality of all before the law, and fraternity of all.'[29]

Here, another pertinent question needs to be raised: Was Nazem al-Eslam Kermani's secret *anjoman*, founded by the *mujtahid* Tabataba'i and his son Mohammad Sadeq, both members of the Bidari-ye Iran lodge, an unofficial auxiliary? To be sure, the *anjoman*'s first meeting, on 7 February 1905, predates that of the Bidari by some ten months; but the future members of Bidari were already affiliated with European lodges and were thoroughly familiar with Masonic goals and strategies. More importantly, the *anjoman*'s structure was modelled on a typical Grand Orient lodge, and the repeated slogan: 'Awake from the sleep of ignorance' recalls that of the Freemasons. In fact, Nazem al-Eslam's famous chronicle of the revolution is titled *History of the Awakening of Iranians*. *Réveil*, awakening, *bidari*: one identical key code of the Grand Orient throughout North Africa and the Middle East. Furthermore, the *anjo-*

man's programme significantly reflected Masonic principles and concepts. It promulgated the Masonic rendering of the French revolutionary concept of patriotism, the idea of a nation, a sense of people's transcendence of their individual self-interest to achieve national interest, all resting on the new concept of citizenry. Another secret *anjoman* formed at about the same time by Malek al-Motekallemin and Jamal al-Din Va'ez, the two famous orator-preachers of the revolution who mobilized the public at mosques and religious gatherings, resorted to identical slogans, programme, and strategy. Its membership list overlaps the Bidari's, and its meetings were also often held at Hakim al-Molk's house. The secret *anjoman*s 'persianized' French revolutionary ideals as popularized by the Freemasons. However, one must stress that these ideals were similarly upheld by all major players, regardless of their ideological affiliation to one group or network or another. In fact, many individuals belonged to several different groups simultaneously, as they shared identical primary objectives and a common vision for the future of Iran; their tactics, though, and often their rhetoric, differed.

While it is possible to trace the networks and the intellectual origins of their ideas, it is much more difficult to gather solid information on the Freemasons' political activities. Archival materials are scarce. As noted by other researchers on the subject, the archives keep their secret. However, Bidari correspondence with Paris sheds enough light to reveal some less secretive deeds favouring the constitutionalists. Morel's letters confirm his participation on their side. Following the Shah's coup, he intervened on behalf of Taqizadeh, Dehkhoda, and Mo'azed al-Saltaneh with the secretariat of the Grand Orient, organizing their safe departure to Europe and requesting the order's help for the three certified brethren. The exiles were helped in organizing their opposition and publishing their articles. The coup forced Morel to declare the lodge 'dormant' (*mise en sommeil*); this did not mean that its committee ceased all activities. The letters, official or private, document its discreet interventions to promote the constitutional cause. Morel pleaded with the Paris secretariat to call on the Minister of Foreign Affairs Stephen Pichon, a member of the Grand Orient, to request the appointment of Freemasons to the French legation in Tehran who would be favourable to the constitutionalists; the ministry accepted the request.[30] In Tabriz, where fierce battles against royal forces determined the constitutionalists' fate, Alphonse Nicolas, honorary chairman of the Alliance Française committee, was appointed French consul in October 1906. He established a close collaboration between the Alliance and the Anjoman-e Azarbayjan, the Tabriz political organization that played a decisive role in the revolution. Nicolas regularly attended the *anjoman*'s meetings, where he was often requested to lecture on the French Revolution.[31]

The *Rowshanfekran* and the Young Turks

The Iranian Freemasonic experience mirrors that of the revolutionary Young Turks in the Ottoman Empire. Prior to the 21 July 1908 coup that brought them to power, the Young Turks formed several loosely tied opposition groups, all styling themselves modernist and in favour of radical political, cultural, and institutional transformation of society. The leadership then was generally freethinking, promoting a single goal: 'to replace religion with science'; and denigrating any effort to reconcile Western civilization and science with Islam and traditional values.[32] Ahmed Rıza, a leader of the Committee of Union and Progress and a proponent of August Comte's positivism, had publicly commented in 1897 in a French newspaper interview that religion is a matter of private concern and not of the state.[33] Other CUP leaders expressed their religious beliefs less openly and concealed their true ideology. Such cautious tactics also characterized Iranian dissidents. Dehkhoda met the prominent Young Turk leader Ahmed Rıza in the autumn of 1908 in Paris at an Ottoman-Iranian society, La Fraternité Musulmane, frequented by expatriate Young Turks and Iranian constitutionalists.[34] Duly impressed, he labelled him the Ottoman Voltaire of their time. Though neither Ahmed Rıza nor his close collaborator Nazem Beg were Masons, they had close contacts with the Grand Orient, which honoured them with a grand reception in Paris a few months after the Young Turks' Coup. At the banquet, Nazem Beg expressed his government's gratitude for the order's help and inspiration. 'Our peaceful revolution is more your achievement than ours; you gave us the ideas, and we resorted to your methods and means. ... We followed your way to emancipate ourselves from the yoke obstructing our path to progress, and have accepted the separation of church from state.'[35]

Many Iranian reformers, moderate and radical alike, had forged close ties with the Young Turk leaders in Istanbul or in Paris as 'brothers' in various lodges. Once in power in 1908, the Young Turk government gave its full political and financial support to the Iranian constitutionalists who had fled the coup. Istanbul became the centre for the exiles, with the Anjoman-e Sa'adat staging and coordinating the resistance to the restored Qajar absolute rule, planning and disseminating a centralized programme of action. In the late spring of 1909, Dehkhoda came to Istanbul to assume the editorship of a new, Young-Turk-financed Persian paper called *Sorush*, the *anjoman*'s official organ. The exiles saw in the Young Turks' success a major source of inspiration and guiding principles; and the Young Turks referred to them as their own brothers-in-arms, the *Jeunes Persans*, a self-identifying label often found in some Persian constitutionalist private papers and pamphlets. In its first issue of 30 June 1909, *Sorush* eulogized the Young Turks as path breakers to freedom and independence, a source of inspiration for the Iranian exiles' own struggle, and acknowledged with gratitude their support. The paper borrowed from the Young Turks the slogan 'unity, accord, and progress'. Leading articles developed the themes of modern civilization, insisting on the primacy of an intellectual revolution to lay the ground for a political revolution. The French Revolution, it argued, was successful because of the philosophy of the Enlightenment that intellectually revolutionized France. Iran, it stated, must follow the same path and go through a 'general intellectual revolution', otherwise the Constitutional Revolution would have no lasting effect.[36] Similarly, in a fiery nationalist editorial addressing the constant threatening presence of Russian troops in the north of the country, Dehkhoda proudly proclaimed that Iranian 'warriors' had been fighting to attain independence and to 'create anew the history of France in the heart of Asia'.[37] Issues of national sovereignty, independence, and territorial integrity filled many pages, calling on the Iranians, who were now fully conscious of their 'Iranian-ness' (*iraniyat*) and aware of their rights, to assume their national responsibility.[38] Most of these moralizing, occasionally self-critical essays echoed themes developed by earlier generations of Persian nationalists; the tone, however, was by far more intransigently secular-nationalist, with concrete targets and objectives. In a highly colourful article, written on the day Tehran fell to the constitutionalist forces, the publicist Hoseyn Danesh, an Iranian-born Ottoman subject, dramatically stated that Iran was now a playing field where the ideas of the 'enlightened civilization' were clashing with 'our three-hundred-year old tradition of superstitions', a battlefield where forces of Light were combating forces of Darkness, and where the 'sane Aryan nature' was fighting the 'frightening nonsense of alien countries'.[39] Who will rescue Iran, he asked? Which model of expertise, which kind of statesmanship would the nation choose? Published at a time when great efforts were being exerted to forge a 'national reconciliation' on all fronts, the paper also subdued the Transcaucasian-influenced political radicalism which had initially characterized the Anjoman-e Saʿadat.

During his European exile, Dehkhoda had vehemently and relentlessly rejected any idea of cooperation with the old aristocratic and tribal elites, especially the Bakhtiyari khans, as part of the effort to restore the constitution. In his days of European exile he believed that the leadership of the resistance should be entrusted to the intelligentsia, the 'brain-trust of the nation,' and not to Sardar Asʿad Bakhtiyari or those 'would-be-ministers',[40] those 'al-Saltanehs and al-Dowlehs'. Sardar Asʿad and people like him, he wrote, could be useful to the cause merely as instruments, a means to attain the goal; otherwise, they should be kept deliberately in the dark as to the intelligentsia's objectives, and compelled to collaborate through coercion and intimidation. He had worked for the resumption of his paper *Sur-e Esrafil* first in Paris and then in Yverdon, Switzerland. His old column *charand parand* appeared in the first issue, dated 23 January 1909, where he passionately refuted the concepts of a hereditary right to rule and the sacred authority of the monarch. He categorically dismissed the institution of monarchy as contrary to the Islamic doctrine of monotheism, for belief in the 'Shadow of God on Earth' amounts to polytheism.[41] Though many of his associates and other fellow-exiles agreed with him, the new *Sur-e Esrafil* drew fire from many quarters, thus underscoring the ideological divides within the constitutionalist ranks. Publication ceased after the third issue of March 1909, when Dehkhoda prepared to leave for Istanbul, where political circumstances forced him to considerably rein in his radicalism.[42]

Even before his departure, Dehkhoda had written a letter to the Anjoman-e Sa'adat leaders, expressing his willingness to work in unison with them towards the common desired goal and calling on all to overcome their ideological differences. Setting aside his earlier mistrust of the aristocracy, he recognized the effective role they played as spokesmen with British officials. Anticipating the objections to his views that 'some individuals' within the *anjoman* would bring up, he admitted: 'The fact is the time of war is over. To resist Russian intervention we have no choice but to resort to *politique* (in transliteration in the text)'; and politics, he acknowledged, is what could best draw English attention. He insisted on the need to consolidate national unity with only one programme of action, one platform enunciating collective objectives, with the Anjoman-e Sa'adat forming one party rallying all groups under one umbrella. He argued that the old tactics of threat and intimidation which had been pursued so far must give way to acceptance of all who joined the national cause, including tribal leaders; and he cited Ahmed Rıza and the CUP as models of leadership to follow, pointing admiringly to their 'miraculous achievement'.[43]

The pages of *Sorush* amply display this newly acquired political moderation within the framework of a constitutional monarchy, accompanied by radical social-cultural reforms. The 'would-be-ministers' had taken over the national reconciliation movement, and a united front of all exiles in alliance with the Bakhtiyari khans had won the support of the Foreign Office in London. The radicals' hope to stage their return to power on their own terms had waned. Once the Second Majles was inaugurated, power politics severely divided the ranks of the intelligentsia. Indeed, the crisscrossing alliances and rivalries prevailing among the dominant players informed the intellectual debates and decision-making.

Party-Games (*partibazi*)

In the winter of 1909 the repeated threat of imminent Russian military occupation forced all constitutionalists involved in the resistance from within and abroad to tone down their rhetoric and reduce their demands. In Tabriz, where the most radical elements were engaged in a fierce battle against the royalists, the local *anjoman* began to send conciliatory telegrams to Tehran, promising that 'the nation shall stand behind the Shah' if he restored the constitution.[44] The Shah, on the other hand, finally giving in to concerted Anglo-Russian pressure, signed a decree on 2 May 1909 proclaiming the restoration of the Fundamental Law and its supplement.[45] By that time, Sadeq Khan Mostashar al-Dowleh, the prominent Tabriz deputy of the First Majles who, together with Taqizadeh, had led a group advocating the most secularizing legislative reforms, assumed the position of chief royal adviser for constitutional affairs and liaison with the constitutionalists in the provinces and abroad. It was then safe for him to contact Taqizadeh directly through the government-controlled telegraph line.[46] Taqizadeh began to pursue secret negotiations through separate channels, embarking on an episode that would seriously tarnish his reputation as national leader in many chronicles, including Ahmad Kasravi's.

The 1908 coup had demonstrated to the activists how vulnerable they were to foreign intervention. Unlike Dehkhoda, the man of the pen, Taqizadeh was foremost a political activist, whose talent for national leadership had already been tested in the First Majles. A rising star in the nascent nation, he had enjoyed freedom and power before being brought down to earth as a result of foreign-power intervention on behalf of the despised monarch. He now chose to adopt a dual radical-moderate role, striving to ride the revolutionary tide whenever possible but also to avoid being once more wiped out when it reversed course. Thus, he maintained close ties with the Transcaucasian and Iranian Social Democrats while simultaneously maintaining his membership in the Bidari lodge and negotiating with moderate constitutionalists, adapting his rhetoric to correspond with that of his different interlocutors. E. G. Browne and his Persia Committee and, indirectly, the Foreign Office believed him to be 'on the side of moderation';[47] at the same time, his revolutionary contacts in Tabriz, Rasht, and Baku viewed him as their natural leader, commanding respect and allegiance. Upon his return to Tabriz in December 1908, which Browne and the Persia Committee had sponsored, he coordinated the local *anjoman* activities with the *mojahedin* troops in Qazvin while engaging in secret talks with the Shah's commander in Azarbayjan.[48] In the capital, Mostashar al-Dowleh, too, acknowledged Taqizadeh's leadership status, affectionately labelling him the 'soul of Iran'.[49]

Intransigent in his negotiations over the selection of new cabinet members and governors of the provinces, Taqizadeh, put under severe pressure by the moderates in Tehran, ended up compromising his alliance with the *mojahedin* and radical constitutionalists. The moderates in the capital bore the brunt of the concerted Anglo-Russian effort to prevent the 'reformist', 'nationalist' movement, as they persistently perceived the constitutional struggle, from degenerating into a revolution. Barely three days after the restoration of the constitution, Gilan's *mojahedin*, together with Armenian, Georgian, and other volunteers from the Caucasus led by Yeprem Khan, conquered Qazvin. All waited for Taqizadeh's signals for the final assault on Tehran. At this point Taqizadeh's notorious *volte-face* took place, confusing the radical comrades who had trusted his leadership. Once more fearing Russian occupation, he counselled moderation; many agreed, but many others refused. Undoubtedly worried about the potential long-term consequences of any drastic action taken at this fateful moment, he decided to give up a revolutionary victory through military means in order to ensure freedom from foreign intervention in internal affairs. Iranian negotiators in Tehran and London were at that time alarmed by European press accounts of an ongoing Anglo-Russian programme aimed at establishing their supervision over Tehran's political decision making: over the appointment of cabinet ministers, foreign loans and concessions, and the overall administration of the various ministries. In a long, apologetic message to the *mojahedin* in which Taqizadeh tried to explain his decision, he asserted his conviction that a revolution following the model of an advanced nation like France, or as accomplished in the Ottoman Empire where a Europeanized military existed, could not succeed in Iran. Iran lacked modern institutions, he argued; the population was uneducated, a third of this population consisting of marauding tribesmen, leading him to warn against prolonging the bloody war. War, he concluded, would be tantamount to suicide.[50] Subsequent events proved him right. With the *mojahedin* advancing from Qazvin and the Bakhtiyari amassing in Qom in preparation for an assault on Tehran, the Russian legation informed the government that it was sending its troops to Qazvin. On 7 July 1909, eight hundred Cossacks landed in Anzali and marched southward to Qazvin, threatening Tehran should troubles occur there. But on 9 July the *mojahedin* took Tehran without a battle.

The fall of Tehran was, indeed, swift but orderly, despite occasional acts of violence in some quarters. The constitutionalists were eager to form their government and reopen the Majles, giving top priority to institutional reforms. The task was daunting as both the victors and members of the old elite turned constitutionalist acquired important positions in the new cabinet. The *mojahedin*, ethnically and ideologically diverse, inexperienced in the finer art of the military yet armed to the teeth, began to spread a climate of fear and intimidation. From his exile in Russia the deposed Shah fomented political plots to destabilize the country, receiving support from Russia, which still occupied parts of the country. France and Britain, despite outward official support, watched the unfolding events with great scepticism bordering on cynicism. All three powers had their proxies in the government and in the Majles, acting to preserve their respective interests. In a dispatch to Paris the French envoy described the dire situation prevailing in Tehran, predicting the new regime's ultimate failure to accomplish any lasting reforms. Only Taqizadeh, he wrote, 'personifies the idea of revolution', endowed with a 'real democratic spirit', determined and audacious, not content with the timid programme of 'timid revolutionaries'. Should he succeed in consolidating his power, the 'mediocre revolution of the palace' could 'melt away' and a profound transformation of the nation would then take place. Wishing to soften the blow of such a 'grave prognosis', the diplomat hastened to declare: 'We are, after all, in Persia, where solid virtues are rare, where means to soften them are numerous.' Even in the event that Taqizadeh persisted in pursuing his objectives, and despite his activities as an 'apostle' and his moral values and principles, he might fail; the 'mediocre *arrivistes*' that filled the ranks of the government 'would eliminate that threat'.[51]

The constitutional monarchy was restored in Iran, but the government was by no means any longer democratic. Successive cabinets that barely lasted a few weeks saw the same individuals occupying different posts, with each reshuffling playing out the same game of musical chairs. Diplomatic caution and an outward eagerness to maintain intact the 'national coalition' of disparate forces failed to conceal deeply entrenched personal rivalries and mistrust. Two political parties emerged officially, the Democrat and the Moderate, marking a fragmentation of the constitutionalists' ranks that defies any ideological definition. Democrat leaders very quickly distanced their party from the old Social Democrat faction both in name and ideologically, despite their continuous though secretive ties to former fellow activists. Neither their programme nor their official organ, the *Iran-e Now* newspaper, displayed any concrete socialist trends, despite numerous articles devoted to the plight of the peasants and workers in Iran and calls for the improvement of their economic condition. Moreover, neither Taqizadeh nor any of his fellow party members officially active in government or the Majles was promoting radical economic policies, busy as they were in restoring political, social, and financial order in the country and confronting multiple existential challenges to their power. Their task was daunting, and they needed all the support they could get from within and abroad. Their cohesive programme of action attracted so-called radicals, chief among them the Tarbiyat brothers, Hoseyn Qoli Khan Navvab, Soleyman Mirza, and Vahid al-Molk, whose ties to West European sympathizers were closer than to Caucasian revolutionaries. However, Amin Rasulzadeh, the Baku-born editor of *Iran-e Now*, who was still affiliated with the Caucasian Muslim Social Democrats, and Heydar Khan 'Amuoghli, the Russian Azerbaijani revolutionary activist, as well as several genuine Iranian and Armenian socialists residing mostly in Tabriz, cast their 'radical' shadow over the rest of the Democrats. Taqizadeh navigated the often tense line between a predominantly Christian/Armenian-run party and a suspicious Iranian intelligentsia. Though he was in theory its leader, in fact, the Democrat Party consisted of two separate wings, one composed of more 'pragmatic' politicians and the other of ideologues who wrote the manifesto and programme and secretly engaged in written or militant activism away from government and Majles circles. Perhaps a serious cause of detachment between the politicians and the ideologues was that the latter still remained revolutionary comrades, striving to exercise power that continued to be beyond their reach.

The Moderate Party, on the other hand, was controlled by its leading politicians in or out of government; all sources generally agree its creation was meant to offer a 'moderate' counterpart to the Democrats' programme. It constituted a disparate group, including the old Qajar elite and genuine activist constitutionalists such as Mostashar al-Dowleh, Mo'azed al-Saltaneh, Momtaz al-Dowleh, Nasrollah Taqavi and, most surprisingly, Dehkhoda. Similarly, Yahya Dowlatabadi, the Azali Babi turned constitutionalist, chose to work more closely with the Moderates and keep his distance from those he perceived as 'revolutionaries' or 'extremists', despite the fact that he candidly admitted his own affinity with the radicals. They were more 'genuine freedom seekers', he wrote, in contrast to the Moderates who were 'willingly or unwillingly, the despots' instruments'.[52]

Both party programmes shared much more in common than conventionally admitted, reflecting the nation-building nationalism so typical of their historical era. Both supported progressive reforms modelled upon the European liberal social, political and military, institutions deemed necessary for successful national development. Both stated concerns for the urban and rural poor, and enunciated their intention to curb the abusive power of masters and landlords alike. Both promoted universal education, including for women. The tension between the two parties intensified over the issue of religion and its place in the reformed nation. The Moderates pushed for gradual change to be undertaken from within the existing social and moral order, in full compliance with the spirit of Islam. The Democrats unequivocally called for a total separation of religion from politics, which the Iranian Social Democrats active in the First Majles had never explicitly included in their programme. For Taqizadeh and other Democrats, the freedom that the constitutionalists so vigorously defended meant freedom of thought, which entailed freedom of conscience; without it, there could be no modernizing reforms, no 'new

Iran'. The social liberalism that defined their party upheld an ideal of tolerance and equal justice that transcended religious identity. They believed that the separation of state and religion was the only possible guarantor of the successful institutionalization of modernizing reforms. Therein lay the 'extremism' their detractors, including equally reform-minded Moderates, charged them with. In the context of the politics of the Second Majles, religion was mostly discussed as if the main argument were between believers and non-believers. In fact, the most important disagreement was between religious people who valued the secular character of Western European politics, which they saw as the founding stone of modernity, and religious people who viewed it as impious. Many genuine constitutionalists in the Moderate party failed to make the argument for secular values, fearing to offend the religious conservative element in their party: Dehkhoda, the staunchly secular *rowshanfekr* who had inexplicably joined the Moderate ranks, is perhaps the most notorious of them all. Party politics triumphed over ideological policy and principle.

Both the Democrats and the Moderates openly experimented with the European multi-party system, each offering its own rules and programme, giving a distinct political identity to its members, and insisting on loyalty and devotion to their respective cause. This political innovation, however, was either partially or not at all comprehended by the public at large. Conservative detractors began to ridicule the whole idea, denigrating it with the coining of the term *partibazi*, or party-game playing. Rival politicians used the same term to accuse one another of personal abuse and downgrading the system. (The term as originally conceived in this period had a different meaning from its current usage as having the right influential connections.) Party leaders and their supporters were thus compelled to explain themselves and justify the system as an essential component of representative government. Rebutting their critics, they argued that *partibazi* was an incorrect term since it referred to the factions and cabals that flourished in despotic times. A democratic political party, they insisted, does not play games, nor does it constitute a private party. Its ideological programme transcends personal interests. In reality, though, power-politics was also about personalities, their temperament, their personal beliefs, their social circumstances. Taqizadeh, the dominant and domineering figure, rallied around him loyal fellow radicals, relentless in fighting the cause they believed in and, thus, attracting envy, hostility, or mere disagreement over tactics. Taqizadeh and his group were 'radical' or 'extremist' in their fight against the old elite, both lay and clerical. Appointing members of the old regime to government posts, Taqizadeh often asserted, would not serve the purpose; only worthy *Jeunes Persans* could be entrusted with the great tasks lying ahead.[53] He swiftly took over power by forming a committee composed of twelve close collaborators to oversee the executive branch and the

Majles. The cabinet increasingly lost ground as his committee, referred to as the *directoire*, turned into a powerful centre of decision making, even though the membership lists of the two bodies overlapped. Party politics rather than national interests defined many of the players' actions, deepening the climate of mistrust among the constitutionalists.

Determined to reform the prevailing power structure, Taqizadeh believed in the importance of modern education for the emergence of a new class of responsible citizens capable of building the nation anew. Liberal papers such as *Sorush* and *Iran-e Now* regularly published articles calling for the formation of a new middle class of modern educated professionals. To this end, the government should send students to study in Europe and employ them upon their return. In a long letter full of advice, Browne, the liberal constitutionalists' mentor, specifically counselled Taqizadeh to select students from the middle class and not from among the wealthy grandees,[54] a view shared by many constitutionalists. This called for the institutionalization of secularist programmes in laws affecting national education and the judiciary. Of all the major players of the Second Majles period, practically none were opposed to institutional reforms aiming at modernizing Iran. Significant changes were generally deemed essential to balance religious power in politics. In fact, the ulema's traditional prerogatives and authority in public affairs had few staunch defenders in the government or Majles. Nonetheless, as Dowlatabadi pointed out, many politicians adopted a religious tone in reaction to the radicals' rhetoric. 'The sword of religion', he remarked, was a useful weapon for waging war against rivals and undermining their credibility.[55] Taqizadeh and his group were adamant in denying the ulema any political role similar to that they had played in the early phase of the revolution and in the First Majles. His detractors conspired to denounce him to the ulema in Najaf, urging them to declare him a heretic. The assassination of the *mujtahid* Behbahani by lawless *mojahedin* elements from the Caucasus provided them with a well-timed pretext. Rumours were spread that Taqizadeh had masterminded the murder; Najaf issued a fatwa to declare him a heretic (*takfir*). Taking a leave of absence from the Majles, Taqizadeh left town and, eventually, the country. The political demise of Taqizadeh deprived the constitutionalist movement of its fiercest champion of secular nationalism and, as the French consul had predicted, the 'timid revolutionaries' were left without genuine leadership.

Each of the two political parties had its role: distinct, yet, paradoxically, so identical in their fundamental objectives. Neither the Democrats nor the Moderates, who, reacting to their competitors, had also adopted a tone of concern for social issues, gave priority to socioeconomic reforms. They were in fact complementing each other in their common effort to transform the nation's political and cultural institutions. But in the party game each group played in its respective turf, with competing claims, they indulged in fighting small battles in the midst of a bigger war involving royalist and foreign intrigues. Taqizadeh, like his fellow Democrats and many Moderates, was a novice in the art and ways of exercising power in a parliamentary setting, itself a novelty. Entrenched old-style Qajar politicians were more experienced than the reformers of either party. They knew how to play the game better. More importantly, Taqizadeh and fellow Democrats lost as a result of their radical wing, whose verbal extremism by far outweighed the actual facts on the ground. That wing was in no position to implement any socialist programme. Ironically, that 'extremism', so ineffectual in reality, carried weight exceeding its political significance as it provided the necessary target and pretext for the assault on the Second Majles in late 1911. Thus, on the rhetorical level, those 'extremists', so insignificant in number, overpowered the secular nationalists.

Conclusion

The period of the Second Majles constituted an era in which the tension between secularizing and religious impulses flared into open warfare, which was then fuelled by political factions, domestic and foreign, with divergent vested interests. The constitution, and the political philosophy behind it, were still too alien as concepts for their detractors to concede defeat without a struggle. Indeed, national and international politics rendered the *rowshanfekr* vulnerable to manipulation and intrigues. British and French individuals involved in promoting the constitutionalist cause, whether they were Freemasons or liberal champions of the *rowshanfekr*, proved powerless to stop their respective governments from damaging Iranian sovereignty and independence. The European balance of power on the eve of the First World War took precedence over commitments to fellow constitutionalists or 'brothers' in Iran, resulting in a betrayal of those very universal values of human rights and liberty that Europe upheld. Setting aside some individual exceptions, the Iranian intelligentsia were no docile agents of European imperialism acting in the guise of Freemasonry. However, British, Russian, and French officials exploited their vulnerabilities and abused their eager readiness to follow the European model of development. To a large extent the history of the Constitutional Revolution is part of the history of the age, inextricably linked to its time. It must be seen against a dense pattern of factors that conditioned, promoted, impelled, and sometimes braked its course.

The tragic collapse of the power of the Majles following the 1911 Russian ultimatum, marking the political failure of the Constitutional Revolution, overshadows its two main achievements: the desacralization of political power and the far-reaching changes in the balance of ulema influence. In that sense it followed a common pattern with all nineteenth- and early twentieth-century revolutions that were modelled after the French Revolution and its ideology. (Later Marxist-oriented or, by the turn of the present century, ethnic or religious revolutions belong to different historical eras). These were the contributions of the *rowshanfekran* that reshaped Iran's political culture, lasting till the advent of Ayatollah Khomeini in the late twentieth century. The *rowshanfekran* had provoked a social explosion with fatal consequences for the Islamic social order.

CHAPTER 11

An Iranian Modernist Project: Ali Akbar Dehkhoda's Writings in the Constitutional Period

Nahid Mozaffari

Introduction

The impact of the European Enlightenment and Russian social democracy on the small but influential group of middle-class secular intellectuals of the Iranian Constitutional Revolution has been researched and documented by several historians.[1] But efforts to explore the precise trajectory of these European ideas in their Iranian context and to map the discourse between specific Western concepts and their Iranian interpretation or adaptation from text to text have been rarer. My focus will be on the *Sur-e Esrafil* and *Sorush* essays of Ali Akbar Dehkhoda (1879–1956), one of the principal figures of the literature of revolt that accompanied the Constitutional Revolution.[2]

As editor and one of the main writers of the influential paper *Sur-e Esrafil* and later *Sorush*, Dehkhoda set out to contribute to what he considered to be a primary task of the educated intellectual of the time, namely, the elaboration of the meaning of constitutionalism (*takmil-e ma'ni-ye mashrutiyat*). Aware that constitutionalism and other concepts such as liberty, freedom, and the social contract were Western concepts not grounded in the historical experience of Iran, Dehkhoda and his colleagues believed that their precise meaning had to be constructed through discussion, dialogue, and adaptation to Iranian conditions and contexts.

What did Dehkhoda and his colleagues identify as the core elements of constitutionalism? How did Dehkhoda, as a prime example of the 'men of the pen', articulate new and alien ideas to his various audiences? How did he combine the unfamiliar new constructs with the more familiar ways of thinking to communicate with large audiences? What did he identify as the main obstacles to their vision for the future? What role did language play in this discourse?

In this chapter, I shall try to answer these questions by providing an analysis of some of Dehkhoda's essays written in *Sur-e Esrafil* (Tehran and Yverdon) and *Sorush* (Istanbul).

Dehkhoda and the Historical Context

Born in 1879 in Tehran, Ali Akbar Dehkhoda was descended from a family of minor landowners from Qazvin. He received his early education under the tutelage of Sheykh Gholam Hoseyn Borujerdi, from whom he learned Arabic and the 'formal sciences' (*sarf, osul-e feqh, kalam,* and *hekmat*) and from Haj Sheykh Hadi Najmabadi, whose house and gatherings he frequented as a youth. Dehkhoda continued his education at the School of Political Science in Tehran, where he studied the 'modern' sciences of world history, geography, international law, political science, and French language. After completing his studies, Dehkhoda was employed by the Iranian Ministry of Foreign Affairs and given a post as a junior diplomat serving under Ambassador Mo'aven al-Dowleh Ghaffari, who was based in Bucharest and Vienna. While serving in the Balkans, he continued to study the European sciences and the French language.

When he returned to Iran in 1905, he was briefly employed by Haji Hoseyn Aqa Amin al-Zarb to serve as translator to the Belgian engineer who was charged with building the Khorasan roadway. By this time, the constitutional movement was well under way. Through his contacts with Amin al-Zarb and the entourage of Sheykh Hadi Najmabadi, Dehkhoda found access to the web of dissident intellectuals who had organized secret societies and were active in recruiting followers and organizing protests. He was invited to join the Revolutionary Committee as a young recruit. Shortly after the success of the revolution, Dehkhoda joined Mirza Jahangir Khan, a social democrat and a prominent constitutionalist,[3] and Mirza Qasem Khan, a constitutionalist merchant from Tabriz, to publish *Sur-e Esrafil*, one of the most vocal, radical, and popular newspapers of the constitutional period. Each issue of *Sur-e Esrafil* consisted of an article about a current political or social issue written by Dehkhoda, several articles of current news and analysis written by Mirza Jahangir Khan and others, and, finally, the popular column of satire written by Dehkhoda entitled *charand parand* (gibberish, poppycock).[4]

In the first constitutional period, from May 1907, when the first issue of *Sur-e Esrafil* came out, to the absolutist coup on 23 June 1908, Dehkhoda focused on explaining the social democratic project to the people, to the educated by writing political and philosophical essays, and to the less educated population through the *charand parand* column. The main brunt of his attacks at this time, the main objects of his critique, were the absolutists and the conservative ulema – a group he referred to as *kohneh-parastan* (reactionaries). In the second period of his writing, the period of the Lesser Despotism and exile when he wrote in *Sur-e Esrafil* in Paris and Yverdon, and in *Sorush* in Istanbul, Dehkhoda focused on a tougher stance against despotism but became more accommodating towards religion. This was because the constitutionalists relied on the (Tehran and Najaf) ulema's influence on public opinion to undermine the nominal legitimacy of Mohammad Ali Shah. In the third period, when he returned to Iran as a Majles deputy and joined the Moderate Party (*E'tedaliyun*), Dehkhoda observed, mostly in silence, the conservatism of the landowners, ulema, and the conservative elements of the bourgeoisie, the radical politics of the Democrats, the volatile international situation, and the unceasing manipulations of Britain and Russia. This was the beginning of his period of disillusionment with politics. He wrote very little in this period, and shortly thereafter, during the First World War, conceived of the *Loghatnameh*, a monumental lexicon of the Persian language finished long after his death, as a long-term continuation of his efforts to pursue the Enlightenment project in Iran. The focus of the present paper will be on the first period of *Sur-e Esrafil*, on Dehkhoda's attempts to engage an ongoing discussion on the meaning of *mashrutiyat* from the social democratic perspective.

During the years 1907 to 1908, as Dehkhoda became completely immersed in the post-constitutional politics of the First Majles, many factors led him to select Iranian social democracy and its project for society as the one he identified with most. His background in the urban middle class and exposure to economic hardship, his training in both traditional and modern education, his knowledge of Arabic, Turkish, and French, his sojourn in Europe and interest in European revolutionary history, his experience of state corruption, imperialist meddling, and arrogant profiteering by some foreigners, his realization of the severe economic and political injustices suffered by the largely helpless and illiterate masses – all contributed to this choice. His exposure to the entourage of Sheykh Hadi Najmabadi in adolescence and his association with Amin al-Zarb as a junior employee exposed Dehkhoda to the circles of influential intellectuals, reformers, and critics who came to regard despotism and conservative religion as the major obstacles to reform in Iran.

Though we know that Dehkhoda was a member of the Revolutionary Committee, we have no record of his particular contribution within that body. The primary evidence for Dehkhoda's immersion in politics comes in the form of his own written work in *Sur-e Esrafil* and from a number of political pamphlets that have been attributed to him.[5] In his political essays, he was a fiery and passionate advocate of parliamentary democracy, socioeconomic justice, and the modernization and rationalization of culture that coalesced into a movement in Iran after the Constitutional Revolution. To promote parliamentary democracy, he focused on crafting the definition of constitutionalism in its Iranian context (*takmil-e ma'ni-ye mashrutiyat*) and on defending the Majles against its religious and secular foes. To promote economic and social justice, he proposed a programme of land and tax reform, and the reorganization of all institutions according to rational principles.[6] The modernization of culture (secularization, rationalization, democratization) was the most complex and difficult agenda, and in retrospect, the one in which Dehkhoda made the most important and lasting contribution to Persian culture. To define and promote this task, he launched a critique of religion as it was interpreted and practised, advocated a modern secular education and justice system, and advocated the direct participation of the people, particularly the disadvantaged, in determining the agenda and setting the priorities of state and society. Towards this latter goal, his particular utilization of language to expose the ills of society and to give a voice to the people was one of his greatest achievements.

It is important to note that during this period, Dehkhoda was a revolutionary whose aim was not only to educate, but to mobilize. This made him acutely aware of the different groups which made up his audience in *Sur-e Esrafil*. Street poetry, anecdote, satire, and complex essay genres and forms were all used to appeal to different audiences.

The Crafting of Constitutionalism: The Political Dimension

There was no one 'true meaning' of *mashruteh* in the early constitutional period. Through discussions and interactions in the Majles, the *anjoman*s, and the newspapers, the leaders, the intellectuals, and the general population were attempting to arrive at a workable definition of constitutionalism acceptable to the precarious political alliance that had made the revolution possible.

The articulation of the first goal of *Sur-e Esrafil* – the 'completion' of the meaning of constitutionalism – itself demonstrates intellectual and political sophistication on the part of Dehkhoda and his associates. They understood that constitutionalism was originally a European word, a European concept, and in some cases a European reality. The exact meaning in its Iranian form had to be constructed through democratic interaction and dialogue and adapted to the conditions of Iran. Dehkhoda was acutely aware both of the ambiguity associated with the word *mashruteh* in the way it was understood in Iran and of its immediate Western origin:

> The Muslims of Iran have been speaking of constitutionalism openly for a year and a half and secretly for thirty to forty years, and as we have observed, they are willing to risk their lives and property to achieve this worthy end. But without a doubt, as the knowledgeable ones (*'oqala*) among them attest, they still have not realized the importance of this desire, nor its substance,

prerequisites, and implications, such that we are compelled to explain today that the transformation from a despotic to a constitutionalist monarchy is not, for example, like the simple exchange of authority from one leader to another in a village. Constitutionalism is a particular construct which has forsaken the Islamic world since the period of the first four caliphs; for over one thousand and two hundred years, we have forgotten the fundamentals of constitutionalism. We have lost and abandoned its name in all of Islamic history, let alone the principles, conditions, and knowledge associated with it.

A constitutional monarchy has a different set of characteristics, principles, structures, and body of knowledge that set it apart from a despotic monarchy. Even though it[s precepts are] in harmony with the commands of the Qur'an and the just precepts of Islam, because of the time factor, and the fact that Muslims have no memory of it, we are compelled to use terms from foreign languages, since they have been engaged in developing them for a long time. As mentioned before, any set of principles or specific structure has its own specialized knowledge, and the expression of any specialized knowledge necessitates the use of special words and expressions. You cannot call a train conductor (*vagonchi*) a camel driver (*sareban*), or a telegram (*telegraf*) a certificate (*parvaneh*) or message (*barid*). If we do [i.e., use imprecise words], we have not succeeded in conveying the proper meanings and intentions, and we will forever continue to remain as vague and confused as we are today. In other words if we want to establish a modern (*mostahdeseh*)[7] constitutional monarchy today, we need to use modern words.[8]

Dehkhoda clearly announced the fact that constitutionalism was a Western phenomenon; that Europeans had had the experience of constitutionalism and therefore had the right words, which Iranians would have to borrow until such time as they too could apply their own meaning, their own significance for the words. This demonstrates to what extent Dehkhoda was conscious of the significance of words and their meaning, and felt compelled to explain the connection of the word to the experience and the context, in order for it to acquire meaning. Accordingly, throughout his essays, he often used the Persian transcription of the French words *constitution*, or *politique*, when attempting to be precise. He also went to great lengths to explain these words, often using anecdotes, rather than simply assigning them a Persian equivalent, since his goal was to debate and discuss these concepts with his audience.

From the very first essay, Dehkhoda associated with constitutional monarchy the notions of loss of fear (of authority), happiness (*sa'adat*), progress (*taraqqi*), renewal and rebirth, freedom (*horriyat, azadi*), equality (*mosavat*), and honour (*sharaf*).[9] Other words linked to this cluster are rights (*hoquq*), unity (*vahdat*), love of country (*hobb-e vatan*), and humanism (*adam-parasti*). According to Dehkhoda:

historical experience, the commands of the prophets and leaders, and the secret laws of nature indicate to us that nations of the world, like individual people, go through periods of infancy, childhood, adulthood, and maturity. The total and ultimate authority of the guardian (*vali*) over the possessions and deeds of the minor are valid whilst the child has not reached a mature age. But when [the child] reaches that stage, as the immutable laws of the world and the firm commands of the religions attest, these rights (*ekhtiyarat*) revert to the one who has matured. This is such a natural matter that not even the most conniving minister, the most powerful and valiant warrior, or the most magnificent and forceful king can prevent it from happening.[10]

Dehkhoda went on to explain that often it was disastrous when this natural process was not respected, which usually happened through the faulty advice of a traitor prime minister, who had not properly identified the nation's correct stage of growth and maturity.[11]

Whereas a person with a full stomach may desire more food due to lack of self-control, or a rich person may desire more money due to excess greed, never, in no period in history, has a nation demanded more rights and responsibilities than its corresponding level of growth and maturity.

He exhorted Mohammad Ali Shah to 'compare the current state of [his] people and subjects to the mature period of other nations and [he] will see that the attitudes and acts of this nation, which [Amin al-Soltan would have us believe] is "unprepared for such [parliamentary] debates",[12] are identical to those of the Romans in 509 BCE, the British in 1649, and the French in 1793.'[13] Aside from the audacity of this manner of addressing the monarch – 'get in line with the times, or your people will kill you' – here, we get a glimpse of Dehkhoda's social and political philosophy, which contains a belief in natural law *combined* with a theory of cultural and political relativity. There existed certain immutable laws of nature; different times and different stages demanded different forms of government. His essay discussing 'rights' (*hoquq*) further illuminated this vision, while continuing to demonstrate his interest in words. With characteristic wit and humour, he wrote:

When hearing the word 'rights' in Iran, the bureaucrat understands it to mean 'salary', or the due compensation for his double-crossing and bungling inefficiency. The theological student perceives its meaning as 'fidelity' and 'loyalty', and the average person ('*avamm*) confuses its meaning with 'delinquency'.[14]

However, he contended, all substances of the natural world from mineral to animal to human, behaved according to an invisible law (*qanun-e nama'lum*) from which they derived their duties and took advantage of their rights (*ekhtiyarat*). Human beings were dependent upon each other for mutual survival and protection. Dehkhoda called this dependence, along with the necessity for the division of labour, a natural contract (*kontrat-e tabi'i*) made 'without the command of a leader, without permission of a *mujtahid*'. Living with others entailed many benefits and certain sacrifices – to produce and progress together, and to protect each other from dangers, we know that we have to refrain from antisocial behaviour:

> Elements of this natural contract have been written on clay, rock, skin, or paper, in some order or other, and have been called the rights of man. In Iran, Arabia, Mesopotamia, Syria, and Palestine, these rights and duties have been articulated through prophets and are called the commands of God.[15]

The harmony emanating from these natural laws became disturbed, Dehkhoda continued, as it was in the Iran of the time, when people did not know their rights: thus, ignorant kings and conniving ministers prevailed, and oppression and injustice were perpetuated.[16] Dehkhoda left it unclear why it was that in Iran and the other areas mentioned above, the local conditions and requirements had produced a (predominant) religious law, while natural law applied everywhere else. What was the relation between natural law and religious law, and how were they articulated differently in Europe? As we observed in the comment about the prevalence of 'constitutionalism' at the time of the four rightly guided caliphs (*kholafa-ye rashedin*), a certain vagueness regarding the position of religion within this worldview creeps up in Dehkhoda's formulations again and again. I believe that these issues are deliberately left vague to avoid offending the religious sensitivities of the ulema and the people, and also to allow for a cultural/religious connection – no matter how vague and contrived – between historical memory and the new concepts. This was the longtime habit of all reformers in the nineteenth century, such as Malkam Khan and Mirza Aqa Khan Kermani. Furthermore, whenever the issues were *not* put vaguely by Dehkhoda and others in *Sur-e Esrafil*, an uproar from the ulema ensued: *Sur-e Esrafil* was forced to stop publication five times, Dehkhoda's life was threatened, and he was brought to trial in front of the Majles. Because of their precarious alliance with some of the ulema, the secular intellectuals were constantly testing their limits during this period.

In another essay, Dehkhoda discussed the meaning of the word 'unity' (*ettehad*).[17] Giving credit to Darwin's ideas, he stated that human beings had once been indistinguishable from animals, but gradually distinguished themselves through unity, which they derived from their natural sense of sociability (*qovveh-ye ons*). This sense of sociability drew humans together, caused them to learn from each other, to cooperate, and achieve progress, such that families and tribes, nations, and eventually governments were formed. The sense of sociability was the drive for the establishment of civilization; it was what made humans human.[18] Dehkhoda wrote that in the countries that had nourished and encouraged this drive – the United States, Britain, France, Germany, Japan – there had been immense progress, whereas in China, the Ottoman Empire, Afghanistan, and Iran, where division and differences had been dwelt upon, there had been constant conflict and little progress.[19]

Besides sociability, or the urge to cooperate, freedom was the other condition for human progress. In an essay that got Dehkhoda into deep trouble with the ulema, he posed the question, 'Is there any limit to human progress?' He then proceeded to point out that the only limits were the obstacles set by people who believed in a limited, inflexible vision of human perfection based on the past:

> According to the opinions of the reactionaries (*kohneh-parastan*)[20] of the land, or those people who hold on to their esteemed fathers' imaginings, no matter how sordid, and who consider it among their sacred duties to maintain them, the height of human achievement began a few years before Ya'reb ibn Qahtan[21] with the conquest of herds of sheep and camels and the migrations of the tribes of the Mesopotamian region, and ends with the illness, laziness, sloth, and the state of infirmity of contemporary Iran. ... But according to those whose opinions respect the stature and dignity of humankind, and believe in at least a slight advantage of man over earthworm, the point of destination ... is doubtlessly connected to the endless and limitless knowledge of God. ... Human knowledge and achievement cannot be limited to the opinions of Socrates, or the ideas of Aristotle or the knowledge of Spencer or Kant. ... Whichever level humanity reaches, the wall of ignorance should not be an obstacle to [further] progress. The progress of humanity has no rational limit. ... All the necessities and tools for the achievement of progress and completion already exist in every human being, as does the natural will to progress, improve and complete the self. The help of no sovereign, the leadership and direction of no leader, the guidance and initiative of no moral guide, is worth a pea in the quest and preparation for the means of progress and human perfection (*kamal-e bashari*). It is sufficient to allow each human being to pursue his/her own path to progress and self-fulfilment. The only favour that must be asked of every spiritual and corporeal leader is that from now on, it is not necessary for you to introduce us to our desired method of progress and self-fulfilment through the force of the baton, or the struggle of argument, or the whip of religion.[22] Just allow us the right to identify and determine our own [path to progress]. ... The meaning of the new word freedom ... is precisely this – that the claimants to the leadership of this graveyard that is Iran should not limit [the quest for] human perfection to their definitions alone, but to grant permission for human beings to use their own innate powers to determine their path to progress and perfection and to pursue it without fear.[23]

He continued to write that much blood had been shed in the world throughout the centuries in order for people to achieve freedom, which consisted of the right to define, select, and pursue one's own path to progress and perfection. With freedom, one attained the status of a subject, in charge of one's destiny, but without it, one was only an object, the property of the powerful, like their furniture, or their horse. The only limit to the freedom of one person should be the freedom of other people. Dehkhoda was careful to point out that freedom was not contrary to the teachings of Islam and added, rather vaguely, that much of the material in the Qur'an and in the teachings of the prophets and other religious leaders consisted of efforts to determine the limits of freedom. He then provided a number of examples to demonstrate to the reader that freedom consisted of the right to hold opinions, beliefs, and choices that might be different from the majority, but as long as the different beliefs and acts did not hurt anyone or limit the freedom of anyone else, then neither the 'Protectors of Islam'[24] (the ulema) nor the Protector of the Realm (the king), had the right to interfere with that right.[25]

The distinction between *kohneh-parast* and what he, on several occasions, calls *adam-parast* (humanist) is of seminal importance in understanding Dehkhoda's political philosophy. For Dehkhoda and other constitutionalists, the reactionaries consisted of both lay and clerical anti-constitutionalists; in other words, those who looked towards an ideal in the past as the basis for their value system and their model of an ideal society. *Kohneh-parast* was coined by Mirza Malkam Khan as the Persian translation of the word 'reactionary' and Dehkhoda used the word when he wanted to make a connection, as he often did, between the characteristics of the absolutists and the anti-constitutionalist ulema. But apparently, the word was in use as a designation for 'reactionary' amongst other writers as well, particularly in the circles of journalists and activists of the Caucasus region. One such article, from the journal *Ershad*, was translated and reprinted in *Sur-e Esrafil*. The article enjoined Muslims in Russia to participate in the political process and explained the five main political parties, their political positions, their positions towards the various nationalities and religions, and their economic viewpoints. According to this article, the followers of the *kohneh-parast* party (*chernosotniki*) preferred the absolute power of the Tsar and his agents (the police) and were virulently antisemitic and against Muslims, Armenians, intellectuals, and workers. They believed that the Bible should be the only source of education and morality in society.[26] This definition is consistent with Dehkhoda's discussion of the *kohneh-parast* position in the Iranian context mentioned above, except that dated and ignorant interpretations of the Qur'an and shari'a replace the Bible as the source of morality. Also, virulent antisemitism was more a characteristic of Russian than Iranian absolutism, although a not-so-virulent form of antisemitism did exist in Iranian culture at large.[27]

Dehkhoda mentiontioned *adam-parast* and *adam-parasti* less frequently, and when he did it was always in reference to the progressive and modern way of thinking that was consistent with the demands of the modern period and the rule of law. *Adam-parasti* would be the guiding philosophy of a modern society, and its adherents, which implicitly included constitutionalists, were forward-looking, rational beings who believed in the potential of human reason and unlimited human progress. On one occasion, Dehkhoda invited his readers to contemplate the future of Iran through 'the ideas of Jean Jaurès, the leader of world humanists'.[28]

If according to Dehkhoda, the conditions for human progress were sociability, unity, freedom, an awareness and understanding of the laws of nature, a belief in human reason, and the will to progress, then the political construct of constitutionalism – or the rule of law – was the most amenable political arrangement to nurture it. In other words, if each period had its own conditions and subsequently compatible laws, then for secular intellectuals like Dehkhoda, 'the laws of the modern era'[29] would ideally beget a government of law responsible to its citizens through representative institutions. The word *mashruteh* or *mashrutiyat*, which meant so many things to so many people, had this meaning for Dehkhoda. From the statement of intent in the first issue of *Sur-e Esrafil*, to its repetition in every issue of the newspaper thereafter, *mashruteh* referred to the political construct and the cultural state of mind that would enable the process of transition from *kohneh-parasti* to modernity.

The similarity of this construct to Enlightenment thought, particularly that of Montesquieu, is striking. Indeed, Dehkhoda was well versed in the discussions of constitutionalism in Europe. He had translated Montesquieu's *Considérations sur les causes de la grandeur et de la décadence des Romains* (1734) and *De l'esprit des lois* (1748) when he was a student at the School of Political Science at the turn of the century. He was further aware of European ideas through his familiarity with the work of Kermani, Mirza Abd al-Rahim Talebov,[30] and others, and through reading about the Ottoman reforms and the efforts of reformers and revolutionaries in Russia.[31]

Let us focus for a moment on the influence of Montesquieu's *The Spirit of the Laws* on the thought of Dehkhoda.[32] Hailed as 'a feast of reason and decency',[33] *The Spirit of the Laws* contended that there existed certain immutable laws of nature, based on the way human beings were made. These laws had a variety of manifestations, based on *physical* differences such as climate, soil, and size of country, and on *moral* differences like culture and religion. Using a 'scientific' approach, Montesquieu's paradigm suggested that one has to determine what the universal laws are on the one hand, and to understand their particular manifestation in each situation, on the other. That is why he has been credited with being the first major thinker to focus on cultural relativism.

For Montesquieu, each nation, at any particular time and place, had a distinctive pattern of laws which he set out to define and analyse. In the classification of the types of rule – (democratic or aristocratic) republics, monarchies, and despotisms – what is striking is not the characteristics of the categories of rule that were delineated, but the discussion of the underlying principles pertaining to each. The underlying principle or, as Montesquieu would have it, the 'soul' of a democratic republic is public spirit, and that of an aristocratic republic is moderation (to control the excesses of the nobility). Honour and fear are the principles of monarchy and despotism respectively.[34] Thus, he looked behind the forms and their obvious characteristics to understand the forces that made these institutions function effectively or fail. According to this paradigm, social or political change occurred when the underlying principle was 'corrupted':[35]

> Just as democracies are ruined when the people strip the senate, the magistrates, and the judges of their functions, monarchies are corrupted when one gradually removes the prerogatives of the established bodies or the privileges of the towns. In the first case, one approaches the despotism of all, in the other, the despotism of one alone.[36]

He then asserts that 'the principle of despotic government is endlessly corrupted because it is corrupt by nature', and adds that despotism 'can maintain itself only when circumstances, which arise from the climate, the religion, and the situation or the genius of the people, force it to follow some order and to suffer some rule'.[37]

Reviewing Montesquieu's schema brings Dehkhoda's worldview into sharper focus: in their belief in natural law and cultural relativity, Dehkhoda's essays mirrored Montesquieu, and, faithful to his concept of cultural relativism, he adapted these ideas to the situation of Iran. Dehkhoda constructed his philosophy, as had Montesquieu, on the premise of the uniformity of human nature and the diversity produced by environment and culture. The tension between the two elements of this construction remains in the work of both thinkers.[38]

Voltaire said of Montesquieu's *The Spirit of the Laws* that 'throughout, he battles despotism, makes financiers hateful, courtiers contemptible, monks ridiculous'.[39] This could be said verbatim (replacing monks with reactionary ulema) of Dehkhoda's entire œuvre. Inspired by Montesquieu, Dehkhoda placed much emphasis on the importance of law and the adaptability of laws to the particular conditions of each people at a given time. Based on this paradigm, despotism was depicted as archaic and unjust, a system of government that could only survive in an atmosphere of excessive force, ignorance, and injustice.[40] Change in Iran from despotism to a constitutional monarchy with a functioning parliament representing the people, a body of law, and an educational system compatible with the demands of modern times was deemed inevitable. Those who resisted it were depicted as reactionary, ignorant, self-serving, and superstitious.[41]

The influence of Enlightenment thought (Montesquieu and Rousseau) is further apparent in Dehkhoda's discussion of the nature of monarchy, which appeared in the three issues of *Sur-e Esrafil* published in exile after the coup. In an essay entitled 'What is the Nature of Monarchy?' he argued that neither pure reason, nor faith based on 'untainted *shar°*,[42] would tolerate the consideration of despotism or tyranny as divinely ordained or sanctioned. People had given divine qualities to earthly power due to ignorance, weak reason, and a sense of powerlessness when faced with overwhelming natural phenomena like floods and disease.[43] To survive in the face of natural threats and menacing human enemies, they entrusted one from among themselves who was abler, braver, and more intelligent with power and obeyed his commands. In effect, kingship was a contract, whereupon the king would assume power and legitimacy based on the qualities of courage, higher intelligence, and ability. However, this system became corrupted as the concentration of power brought with it pomp and circumstance and, above all, hereditary succession.[44] Dehkhoda then gave the historically creative example of Nader Shah Afshar, who laid bare the incompetence and corruption of Shah Tahmasb II one evening in the camp in Isfahan. Tahmasb's men, having observed the piteous state of their king, withdrew their loyalty from him and chose Nader instead. Thus, he argued that with the growth of man's knowledge, he gained a sense of control over his environment, and began to see kingship for what it was: a contract between two parties, which like the relationship between a landlord and tenant would be null and void if one of the parties did not respect the terms of the contract.[45]

In the context of this essay, Dehkhoda was trying to undermine the legitimacy of Mohammad Ali Shah's rule, through the argument that he had broken his contract with his people by not honouring the constitution. However, his argument about the social contract as the basis for legitimacy would apply to any ruler, at any time.

The Crafting of Constitutionalism: The Cultural Dimension

Dehkhoda was well aware that the political and economic project of constitutionalism could not succeed without addressing important issues that pertained to the culture at large. Much of what he wrote between the first issue of *Sur-e Esrafil* in 1907 and the coup in 1908 – and indeed for much of his career as a journalist and essayist – fits into the category of cultural critique. As we observed above, he interpreted many of the problems of his time in political and economic terms, but a look at the whole body of his writings indicates that he considered these political and economic problems as inextricably woven into the fabric of history and culture. For example, he considered the imperialist meddling of Britain and Russia to be a major source of the problems and inimical to the welfare and progress of his country. But, although he took every opportunity to condemn this encroachment, he dwelt more on the critique of 'self': on the attempt to dissect and analyse the problems within his own society that rendered it so vulnerable to despotism, poverty, and the manipulation of others. In this regard, the editorials and satirical *charand parand* essays provide a map, or an epidemiology, of culture which is fascinating to study.

Dehkhoda's critique addressed the different elements of a culture of servility (*farhang-e ta'abbod*), which he considered to be the greatest obstacle to the establishment of a modern culture. The culture of servility was sustained and nurtured by the alliance of reactionaries or *kohneh-parastan* – an ignorant self-serving despot, a corrupt Court, oppressive governors, and leaders in collusion with the reactionary ulema, which he called *'olama-ye su'* (malignant ulema), promoting a backward-looking religion. As a glimpse of Dehkhoda's views on kingship and despotism have been provided above, let us focus for a moment on Dehkhoda's critique of religion in the context of his epidemiology of culture.

Dehkhoda's understanding of religion and its role in Iranian society was extremely complex and seemingly contradictory. At times, he attacked and ridiculed it relentlessly; in other instances, he quoted the Qur'an and hadith at length, used the logic of religious arguments to legitimate his own positions, and pleaded for the support of the ulema against the monarchy. On occasion, we witness an awkward dance between secular content and religious form – secular projects framed in religious terms.[46] There are in many of Dehkhoda's essays seemingly opportunistic uses of religion to make new ideas either comprehensible or acceptable to the public. Careful consideration of his position indicates that he was most assuredly a secular thinker. His vision of society, of its problems and solutions, was a humanist one. He had the 'modern' penchant to relegate to religion a useful function in the rational organization of society – that of providing a moral and spiritual bond among its members.

In a series of essays on monotheism and superstition which he wrote as a response to the religious anti-constitutionalist discourse, Dehkhoda disclosed his definition of religion:

> Religion (*din*) is the guardian of laws and the fulfilment of the morals of all the nations in the world. All the past prophets and great men of wisdom and intelligent men of religion know the benefit of religious belief to be this: and the miraculous words 'I have been anointed to complete noble morals' leaves no room for sophistry.[47]

Thus religion became internalized as conscience, or our 'internal secret police' as Dehkhoda called it, and it assured our good behaviour and good deeds, but only as long as we were dealing with one prevailing authoritative source. Once the sources became plentiful and diffused, confusion and corruption ensued. That is why, Dehkhoda maintained, the prophets and leaders insisted so often on *towhid* (the unity of God) and the denial of *sherk* (polytheism). To back up this claim, Dehkhoda listed no fewer than ten quotes from the Qur'an about the benefits of *towhid* and the detriments of *shefa'at*, or appealing to any authority other than God. His discussion of *towhid* in this manner and context led to the suggestion that Islam as practised in his day, under the auspices of the ulema, had resorted to *sherk*. His argument seemed to point to the Qur'an as the ultimate source of law and authority – as the constitution for morality, so to speak – and to consider all other authorities as conducive to confusion and corruption.

This sociological view of religion does of course have a great deal in common with Montesquieu's views on religion in *The Spirit of the Laws*. Though Montesquieu paid lip service to the 'Christian religion as the first good',[48] he went to great lengths to establish that differences in 'climate, laws, mores and manners' gave rise to different kinds of religions and that therefore, each religion was compatible with the physical and cultural characteristics of the areas where it originated or was practised.[49] Montesquieu also differentiated between the aims and functions of human laws and those of religion, and Dehkhoda definitely agreed. His view of the ideal society was one where the affairs of men and women were governed by rational laws, and their conscience by religious law. He wrote, 'A rational Muslim is asked, what is the divine purpose behind the sending of prophets and holy books, or, what benefit or harm does the Almighty derive from the faith or denial of people?' His answer as that rational Muslim was: 'Only *our* need for the existence of an inner conscience within our hearts has led the Source of all Wisdom to send books and prophets such that we would come to recognize His Unique Essence.'[50] In this rational world where elected representatives would govern political and economic affairs through rational laws, and religion would be relegated to the role of the guardian of morality, Dehkhoda's partiality to *adam-parasti* (humanism), mentioned above becomes clearer. Linguistically, in Persian, *adam-parasti* (human-worship) was a word that was created as the translation of 'humanism'; but it was modelled after the word *khoda-parasti* (God-worship), which distinguished monotheism from *bot-parasti* (idol worship). In effect and meaning, *adam-parast* is an apparently deliberate creation of a contradistinction to *khoda-parast*, putting the human being, as it does, at the centre of concern. It could be interpreted as a daring declaration of secularism.

The first openly and systematically critical article about the contemporary practice of religion that appeared in *Sur-e Esrafil* was the editorial entitled *Zohur-e jadid*, which was published in *Sur-e Esrafil* dated 20 June 1907. This essay touched such a sensitive chord in the religious establishment that it led to Dehkhoda being pronounced a heretic (*takfir*) by the Society of Religious Students (*tullab*) and to the closing of *Sur-e Esrafil*. With characteristic wit, Dehkhoda wrote:

> If you say to an Iranian Muslim, O Man of Faith, clean your nose, O Holy One, clean your ears, O Enemy of Mu'awiya, pull up your socks, such simple tasks prove to be too burdensome and difficult for the poor bloke. But if you say, O Seyyed, Become a Prophet! O Sheykh, Make claims to Imamhood! O Hojjat al-Eslam, Be the Shadow of the Imam on Earth, in a flash, our noble man fixes his stunned eyes on a distant object and assumes a forlorn countenance. He begins to mumble softly. He juts out his breast as a shield of protection against the nefarious arrow of hidden enemies, hypocrites, and violators. In other words, every atom in the man's being becomes ready to receive revelation and inspiration. At first, he just hears noises – the movement of ants or the buzz of bees – but after a few days, in his mind's eye, he sees the angel Gabriel at the height of his majesty.

> It is strange. Although all the advantages of the pure religion of Islam are as obvious and plain as sunshine to all the world ... although all those firm *aya*s and clear *akhbar* point to the fact that since the Prophet Muhammad is the final prophet, revelation has ended; even though belief in these tenets is basic to our religion, still, all these false prophets, fake *imam*s and phony leaders have ignored the rest of the world and have descended their holy selves right into this small piece of land which is the centre of the true religion of Islam. A First Point (*Noqteh-ye owla,*) A Blessed Step (*Jamal Qadam*), an Eternal Morning (*Sobh-e Azal*), He whom God shall Manifest (*Man Yazharuhu Allah*), a Fourth Pillar (*Rokn-e Rabe'*)[51] – none of these useless good-for-nothings appear in any of the mountains of Europe or any of the villages in America,[52] because of the rule of law and widespread education. And [there] even if Gabriel tries to anoint [someone] to prophethood and issue a direct command a thousand times, they will not hear of it. But *mashallah*, the bountiful soil of Iran produces a fresh prophet, a new imam, even, Allah help us, a new God every hour. And stranger still is that their efforts take root and their movements spread. What is the reason for this?

> Whatever the stimuli for the imagination of the pretenders, the reasons for the acceptance of the people and receptivity of the Iranian populace are no more than two: one is ignorance, and the other, the habit of servility (*'adat beh ta'abbod*). In the duration of one thousand and three hundred years, with so many *aya*s of proof (*ayat-e bayyenat*), with so many direct commands (*avamer-e sariheh*), and with such *aya*s as 'those who use tricks and plots against us ... ' (Qur'an 54:5), they have enslaved us and forced blind acceptance of the

fundamental and subsidiary elements of our religion to such an extent, they have so blocked the development of depth and focus and the development of new ideas, that today, in the vast world of Islam there exists not one religious student, not one jurist who can have an orderly discussion based on the laws of logic with a Christian priest, a Jewish rabbi, or a hashish-using Sufi, without raising the stick of *takfir* – which is the final tool in defeating the enemy or opponent.[53]

Dehkhoda blamed the ulema for not knowing and not imparting the 'truth' of Islam. The body of religious knowledge which they studied and taught was convoluted and mixed with superstition, and they were more interested in power than in truth and morality. As a consequence, the community of believers as a whole was ignorant and susceptible to fear and superstition. The power of the ulema could only be maintained and regenerated through the habit of servility that they encouraged amongst the believers. This was a general critique against the institution of religion and its members, but it has also been interpreted as undermining the whole Shiite concept of *taqlid*.[54]

In another *Sur-e Esrafil* editorial, we get a definite indication that the politics of the constitutional period had an important cultural dimension, and that along with the political struggles in the parliament and the *anjoman*s and in the streets, there was also a struggle between different views of history, identity, and morality. This was where Dehkhoda first mentioned the term *'olama-ye su'*, which he defined as 'malignant ulema, and the faith-selling jurists who do not believe in anything but the [British] Pound and the Imperial [a gold coin], and in return for bills and Manat [Russian currency], would consider [selling] this world and the next.' The ulema's ample influence on the people, Dehkhoda continues, was based on 'the enormity of their stomach, the length of their beard, the size of their turban and the width of their trousers, regardless of their knowledge or faith.'[55]

'Olama-ye su' is a familiar term in hadith literature, used negatively to describe those clerics who preferred to seek wealth and power and enjoyed this life rather than looking to the next. According to al-Ghazzali, they would be severely punished on Judgement Day.[56] Closer to Dehkhoda's own time, his mentor Sheykh Hadi Najmabadi had used this term in his critique of the ulema.[57] Dehkhoda's use of the term *'olama-ye su'* (later also employed by Taqizadeh) was designed to help the people (*mellat*) to differentiate between the 'righteous' constitutionalist ulema and the 'malignant' anti-constitutionalist ulema. According to Dehkhoda and *Sur-e Esrafil*, the 'malignant' ulema spoke against the legitimate rule of law and parliament, agitated against the abolition of *toyul* (a type of fief) and tried to turn the minds of the people and the ulema in Najaf against the constitutionalists. They organized *anjoman*s (*Hemmat*, *Amr beh ma'ruf*) to fan discontent and create disorder against constitutionalist

rule; they insulted the parliament and constitutionalist preachers by disseminating rumours and falsehoods, accusing them of being Babis. 'Righteous' ulema such as the *mujtahid*s Tabataba'i and Behbahani, and the radical preachers Seyyed Jamal al-Din Va'ez and Malek al-Motekallemin, were in agreement with constitutionalism, the rule of law, the progress of humankind, and all that those entailed, such as the pursuit of modern knowledge and education.

In Dehkhoda's writing, other elements of the culture of servility included illiteracy, ignorance, the lack of enlightened education leading to poverty and superstition, and the oppression of women and minorities. The people, *mellat*, were often portrayed as ignorant and unmotivated (symbolized by the image of the opium addict, the *taryaki*). The stark division between rich and poor, the powerful and the powerless, led to the regular perpetuation of injustice. The culture of servility could not tolerate the freedom of critique or expression, which meant that intellectuals could not freely function in it.[58] In contradistinction, modern culture was characterized by the rule of law, where the interests of the *mellat* were fairly represented in an elected parliament, where modern education produced bright, energetic, honest, and competent men and women. The gap between rich and poor shrank. The pursuit of modern culture meant the recognition of women as productive members of society, and the improvement of minority rights; it would, in time, lead Iran out of economic, social, and political backwardness. Modern, enlightened society would make Iran more confident and tolerant of freedom of expression; intellectuals could freely use their pens as the instruments of justice and right – as the collective conscience of the community.[59] A modern enlightened Iran would be less susceptible to the manipulations of the imperial powers.

Educating the people about the culture of servility, and fighting against it, was an important goal not only for Dehkhoda and *Sur-e Esrafil* but for many other newspapers, such as *Tarbiyat*, *Majles*, *Mosavat*, and *Habl al-Matin*. The secular intellectuals saw themselves as the facilitators of this process of transformation from the culture of servility (*farhang-e ta'abbod*) to modern civilization (*tamaddon-e jadid*). In order to accomplish this, they understood that they had to capitalize on the sentiments and the associations that had been mobilized during the constitutional revolution. They needed the active participation of the *mellat* for this project to succeed. They utilized the power and influence of the constitutionalist ulema, though they knew that the ulema failed to grasp many of the contradictions between democratic institutions and religion. Their most formidable cultural rival was conservative anti-constitutionalist religion. All the sustained argument and writing by Dehkhoda and others about the conservative ulema and the backwardness of their ideas was underscored by an implicit unspoken fear of the power that they wielded over the *mellat*.

Dehkhoda and Satire

Since Dehkhoda wrote to promote a social democratic modernist project (*tamaddon-e jadid*), reaching as wide an audience as possible was extremely important. Anecdote, satire, Western and Islamic philosophical argumentation, were all used to appeal to different audiences. For the most part, Dehkhoda wrote in three voices, each with its own audience, style, and logic of argument. Within each voice, he was acutely aware of the reader in his choice of words, images, and line of reasoning. In his political and philosophical essays, which were written in complex and difficult language, Dehkhoda addressed the educated, secular intellectuals, the ulema, and their students. In the essays addressed to the secular intellectuals, he used Western political and philosophical terms and transcriptions of French words. In the essays addressed to the ulema and their supporters, he used his traditional religious education to make his points understood through language fraught with Arabic terms and Qur'anic quotes. In his satire, using rhythmic street poetry, anecdotes, popular aphorisms, and jokes, he addressed the largest category in his audience, the literate as well as the masses of semi-educated and illiterate people whom he was anxious to draw into the political process.

Many of the aforementioned critiques and situations appeared as vignettes in the *charand parand* columns where Dehkhoda analysed the state of mind and the types of practices which he deemed unjust or obstructive to the successful transformation of culture from backwardness to modernity. Selecting and setting up certain absurdities, he then attacked those whom he deemed responsible for the absurdity, thereby undermining their legitimacy. Dehkhoda's cast of characters, such as *Kabla'i Dakho, Berehneh-ye khoshhal, Nokhod-e hameh ash, Khar Magas, Sag-e Hasan daleh*, all inhabit a world of heightened absurdity reflecting real problems and injustices. *Kabla'i Dakho*, who appears often, is a traveller who learns a lot from the sciences in the course of his travels. He exposes corruption and the double-crossing of the people by the state and the ulema. This character represents Dehkhoda himself, the knowledgeable observer, who is honest and courageous in the face of power to the point of stupidity. Most of the satirical pieces are written from his point of view. *Khar Magas* (horsefly) is a facilitator – he sells Iran to the foreigners (and exposes the wealthy merchant Malek al-Tojjar doing the same). *Nokhod-e hameh ash* (the peas and beans in every soup) is the common man/woman and an opportunistic observer. *Sag-e Hasan daleh* (greedy Hasan's dog) is ignorant and easily manipulated. *Damdami* (wishy-washy) is one who blows with the wind. *Khadem al-foqara Dakho Ali Shah* is an ignorant dervish who spreads superstition. *Molla 'Eynak Ali* is an ignorant low-ranking mullah and *Ra'is-e anjoman-e lat o lutha* (chief of the association of riff-raff) is an ignorant member of the excitable rabble. Through these characters, and the situations they are put in, injustices are accentuated to the point of arousing common indignation. The *charand parand* articles seen as a whole create a pageant, a carnival of the absurd, allowing the breakdown of hierarchies as well as fear. The presence of many poor people and the constant, almost exaggerated, use of street language and popular colloquialisms reflect both Dehkhoda's social democratic sensitivities and the desire to be a voice for those who did not possess one.

Conclusion

The trajectory of ideas from the European Enlightenment and Russian social democracy to the Iranian revolutionary context can be mapped in Dehkhoda's writing in *Sur-e Esrafil* and *Sorush* during the early constitutional period. There was no one 'true meaning' of *mashruteh* at this time; through the discussions and interactions of the Majles, the *anjoman*s, and the newspapers, leaders, intellectuals, and the general population were attempting to arrive at a workable definition of constitutionalism acceptable to the precarious alliance that had made the revolution possible.

It was a time of social upheaval, where fragments of diverse discourses – doctrinal clashes, political and economic rivalries, and various Western paradigms – were coexisting not only at the level of discussions among intellectuals, but also in the public sphere through the distribution of newspapers and discussions in mosques, schools, and *anjoman*s. In this situation of flux, *words*, their specific usage and meaning, gained a particular significance. Whether due to political, cultural, or religious considerations, the different players felt that they could not express their ideologies and goals openly; in this context, their choices of words and what significance was attached to them often offered clues to the contending ideologies and paradigms.

As part of the small group of secular intellectuals, Dehkhoda meant to communicate his social democratic vision to the public and to create shared critiques, shared symbols, and shared solutions. The main features of this vision, which was inspired by the concepts and terminology of the European Enlightenment and some elements of socialist thought (Russian social democracy, Jean Jaurès) were: the construction and defence of a Majles (parliament) through elections, the promotion of economic and social justice, and the modernization of culture.

To promote parliamentary democracy, he focused on crafting the definition of constitutionalism in its Iranian context (*takmil-e ma'ni-ye mashrutiyat*) and on defending the Majles against its religious and secular foes. To promote economic and social justice, he proposed a programme of land and tax reform and the reorganization of all institutions according to rational principles. The modernization of culture (secularization, rationalization, democratization) was the most complex and difficult long-term agenda. To define and promote this task, he launched a critique of religion as it was interpreted and practised, advocated for a modern secular education and justice system, and called for the direct participation of the people, particularly the disadvantaged, in determining the agenda and setting the priorities of state and society.

In the translation and transformation of European concepts and terms into ones which would fit the Iranian cultural, social, and political context, Dehkhoda introduced or popularized new words such as *kohneh-parast* (reactionary), *adam-parast* (humanist), and *farhang-e ta'abbod* (the culture of servility) and redefined old ones, such as *azadi* (freedom), *mosavat* (equality), *sharaf* (dignity), and *towhid* (unity of God). Like other secular intellectuals, he sometimes utilized a language with religious form and secular content – secular projects framed in religious terms. These opportunistic uses of religion can be interpreted in the context of their immediate political goals – speaking in terms comprehensible to the general public, keeping the constitutionalist ulema on their side, and not providing further ammunition for the supporters of the anti-constitutionalist ulema. Furthermore, keeping Islam as an ethical and cultural part of the discourse of the modernist project in Iran differentiated Iranian Enlightenment thought from the mere blind imitation of Europe, of whose negative and imperialist aspects intellectuals like Dehkhoda were painfully aware.[60]

The visibility of the small group of radical and secular intellectuals like Dehkhoda during the constitutional period, and their presence on the political scene, did not accurately reflect their power base or their actual level of political organization. The failure of the revolution attested to that fact. However, throughout the rest of the twentieth century and the beginning of the twenty-first, Iranian intellectuals have continued to grapple with the different versions and interpretations of the Enlightenment project championed by Dehkhoda and his colleagues.

CHAPTER 12

Readership, the Press and the Public Sphere in the First Constitutional Era

Negin Nabavi

The Constitutional Revolution (1906–11) has been widely regarded as a milestone in the history of modern Iran. Not only did it result in the establishment of institutions like the National Assembly, but it also laid the grounds for a new political and cultural discourse in general. While on the one hand, the advantages of constitutionalism and the rule of law became hotly debated issues of concern, on the other, progress, and the role that learning in general and the printed word in particular played in bringing it about, gained increasing resonance among a growing number of people. In such a context, it was perhaps no accident that in the year that followed the promulgation of the constitution by Mozaffar al-Din Shah, newspapers proliferated in an unprecedented way, as did reading rooms that made both books and newspapers increasingly available to the public.[1] Although we do not have definitive figures for the number of books that were published or the number of reading rooms that were opened at this time, we do have some idea about the number of newspapers. According to a recent study, whereas in the previous 70 years put together (that is, from 1837, when the first short-lived newspaper, *Akhbar*, was published), at most 91 publications had been issued in Iran, in the one year that followed the constitution alone, 99 new newspapers saw the light of day.[2] While this newly emerging constitutional press has long been recognized by historians as an invaluable source for the study of the Constitutional Revolution, one question that has not received much attention is the impact that it may have had in formulating a new journalistic culture and in laying the building blocks of a nascent public sphere. My aim here is to delineate the broad outlines of this changing journalistic culture by focusing on the question of readership and the role of newspapers. Just who read these newspapers? What did they expect to get out of their papers? How did the papers, in turn, see their task, and what class of reader did they cater to? How was this experience different from what had come before? And finally, can one talk about the emergence of a public sphere at this time, and, if so, what part did the press play in its reconfiguration? I will discuss some of these questions by giving examples from three newspapers that were published in Tehran, and which have come to be widely regarded as among the most influential and popular in the history of constitutionalism in Iran. These are the Tehran *Habl al-Matin* (Firm Cord), *Sur-e Esrafil* (The Trumpet of Esrafil), and *Mosavat* (Equality). Whereas *Sur-e Esrafil* and *Mosavat* were weeklies that first appeared in May and October 1907, respectively, the Tehran *Habl al-Matin* was a daily that appeared in Tehran a little earlier, in late April 1907.[3] By focusing on these three newspapers, and comparing them with a reputable semi-independent newspaper that had been published earlier, my aim here is to show the process through which a new journalistic culture, which also included a change in readership, gradually took shape.

Subjects, Citizens, and an Emerging Public Sphere

Following the royal decree that was issued by Mozaffar al-Din Shah Qajar in August 1906, granting permission for the establishment of a National Consultative Assembly or Majles, an end was brought, even if temporarily, to the many restrictions on the press. That is, until then, most newspapers published in Iran had been state-sponsored, which meant that the Ministry of Publications had direct supervision over the articles and material that were printed in their pages. In other words, whereas the triumph of the constitution led to a proliferation of some 99 newspapers in the country, in the decades that preceded it an independent press had found it, by and large, difficult to develop inside the country. Having said that, however, there was one newspaper that had tried to inspire reform and further the cause of progress in spite of the restrictions within the country. This was *Tarbiyat*, a privately owned weekly that was published in Tehran between December 1896 and March 1907, and which gained the respect of many for providing substance at a time when other publications were little more than mouthpieces for the Qajar state.[4] That such a venture was even possible had much to do with the standing of its publisher, Mirza Mohammad Hoseyn Khan Zoka' al-Molk, a literary man who, himself, had already had much experience as secretary and translator to Mohammad Hasan Khan E'temad al-Saltaneh, the official in charge of the Ministry of Publications and of censorship in previous years.[5] In other words, Zoka' al-Molk's close familiarity with the workings of the Ministry of Publications, together with the rumoured liberalism that surrounded the early years of Mozaffar al-Din Shah's reign, was what had enabled the former to walk the tightrope of both appeasing the sensitivities of the authorities of the time and offering an element of novelty that differentiated his weekly from the others that were published at the time.[6] As he explained quite candidly in the last issue of his paper, in March 1907:

During the time that I published *Tarbiyat*, among the [various] means of protection that I had set up [for myself] was that every six months to a year, at an appropriate time, I would compose a *qasida* in praise of the king and his sort. I hoped that in this way, I could carve out a benefactor and protector, whose support I could rely on [in order] to talk about the good of the country and nation.[7]

In other words, in the unpredictable circumstances in which Iran was in the years that predated the constitution, having friends in high places and convincing the establishment of the harmlessness of one's intentions was part and parcel of what was required to run a respected weekly such as *Tarbiyat*. In fact, over the course of the years, Zoka' al-Molk made a point of stating that his sort of journalism was of the positive kind. He reassured his audience that he would publish all sorts of 'news, from within and without, provided they were advantageous to the readers.'[8] Newspapers, in his view, had the task of 'reassuring people, not adding an extra burden to their [already existing] load of hardship'.[9] As a result, the content that was featured in the pages of *Tarbiyat* was primarily educational and informative. It included discussions of the Iranian past, matters of hygiene, the advantages of schooling and education, the new schools that had opened, and developments in the outside world. There was little that was directly political or meant to lead to immediate action. As Tarbiyat wrote in one issue:

> Imagine that we, the people of Iran, are not men of action, that we put aside deeds and spend our dear lives talking. Is there any harm if we become correctly informed of the realities and the intricacies of worldly matters and ... find out where things lead to? [For example] how have those who have got somewhere realized their aim ..., and [of] those nations and peoples that have stagnated and declined, why have some stood still and others waned?[10]

While on the one hand, the points above hint at some of the challenges that a newspaper editor would have encountered in pre-constitutional times, on the other, they can also serve as a counterpoint to what comes after. For by the time the first of our three newspapers appears in Tehran, times had changed. A constitution had been granted, an electoral law written and ratified, elections were held, and deputies voted in. Press restrictions had been lifted, newspapers had begun to appear, and so all matters were considered public and open to debate. In short, there was an atmosphere of hope and possibility.[11] In fact, if Zoka' al-Molk, the publisher of *Tarbiyat*, decided to publish his last issue in March 1907, it was in part because his style of journalism seemed no longer appropriate to the times. As he put it in the same issue,

> Before this, newspapers had nothing to say other than to tell people why they

were sitting unaware and idle, and why they remained uninformed about the responsibilities of the day and so on. As a result of the restrictions, we would not enter into the circle of politics. ... Even if the newspapers wrote something about the politics of government, firstly, no one would have understood, and secondly, it would have been of no use. ... But now times have changed. There are so many things that must be said. ... Now is the time for journalism and work, it is the time for discussion and exchange of ideas.[12]

In fact, the new journalism that emerged in 1907 distinguished itself from the old in a number of ways. In the first place, the background of the individuals who set up our three newspapers could not have been more different from that of Zoka' al-Molk. Seyyed Hasan Kashani, Mirza Jahangir Khan Sur-e Esrafil, and Seyyed Mohammad Reza Mosavat, the publishers of the Tehran *Habl al-Matin*, *Sur-e Esrafil*, and *Mosavat*, respectively, were not only from relatively modest backgrounds but could also be regarded as activists of sorts, since they had each been involved in secret pro-constitution societies of one kind or another in the years preceding the granting of the Fundamental Law. Mirza Jahangir Khan Sur-e Esrafil, together with Seyyed Mohammad Reza Mosavat, had been members of the Association of Free Men (*Majma'-e azadmardan*), which was set up to fight autocracy, and Seyyed Hasan Kashani had been affiliated to a secret society that was active against the prime minister, Mirza Ali Asghar Khan Amin al-Soltan.[13] Secondly, following the establishment of the Majles, there was a great deal of optimism and enthusiasm about the way that lay ahead. There was a sense that people had changed, that their 'eyes and ears had become opened',[14] that they had become aware of their rights and that they would not let themselves be trampled upon by anyone.[15] Inasmuch as newspapers had to strike a chord with these new times, their aim had to extend beyond merely broadening the parameters of learning, as had been the case with *Tarbiyat*. Instead, they became actors; that is, they were not satisfied with simple reporting of news; rather, they took the side of the underdog and the common man and aimed to promote the concepts that were thought essential to these new times, namely 'freedom, equality, and brotherhood' (*horriyat, mosavat, okhovvat*). *Sur-e Esrafil* famously included the motto as part of its insignia (with the angel *Esrafil* carrying a scroll bearing these words), *Mosavat* published the maxim at the top of every issue, albeit with a slight modification (adding justice or *'edalat* to the list), and *Habl al-Matin* expressed its support for these principles in the editorial of its first issue (see Figures 6 and 7).[16] This did not mean that they were alike in the stance that they took with regard to all issues. *Mosavat* was probably the most radical of the three. Its tone was blunt and its articles unabashedly critical of the establishment. *Habl al-Matin*, celebrated for its anti-imperialist stance and enjoying a daily circulation of 4,000 to 5,000 copies,[17] acted as the most moderate and cautious of the publications, and *Sur-e Esrafil* seems to have been the most popular of all, with a reported circulation of 5,500, in part due to its use of colloquial language and the satirical columns written by Ali Akbar Dehkhoda.[18] However, what all three shared was the importance that they placed on the role of the common man in bringing about change. In its first issue, *Habl al-Matin* wrote:

> today our nation's need for independent newspapers, especially dailies, is clearer than daylight since no nation (*mellat*) can preserve its rights and be vigilant towards the actions and inactions of its trustees and representatives unless it is constantly alert and attentive. ... Let me be more clear: [It is only] when the nation is fully awake and watchful ... and mindful of the acts of the leaders from afar ... that it will be able to distinguish between the good and the bad.[19]

This excerpt was part of *Habl al-Matin*'s statement of purpose, and its emphasis on the wakefulness (*bidari*) of people was no new idea. However, if there was an element of novelty here, it was the active role that people were encouraged to play in the political process. The questions of rights, of vigilance towards representatives, of law, of the meaning of Majles and constitution, were part of the new political discourse that was put forth by much of the press at this time, and which had the common man at its centre. Whether it was through articles explaining the practical procedure that was involved in running the Majles or the numerous editorials calling for unity between the people and the state (*mellat* and *dowlat*),[20] the constitutional press saw its role as transforming former passive subjects into the active members of a nation. At the same time, however, when the combination of rising expectations with persistent disorder and chaos across the country led to despondency about the political process, newspapers had no qualms about appealing directly to the people to take action. While these two attitudes may appear contradictory at first, what they point to is a belief shared by many at this time, namely that people had the ability to sweep despotism away provided they took on some *gheyrat* or strength of conviction.[21] As *Habl al-Matin* argued in an article:

> Our comfort, dignity, constitutionalism, freedom, and everything else are dependent on [our] strength of conviction (*gheyrat*). If we don't have conviction (*gheyrat*), we will not protect our country (*vatan*) [and] we will throw away our honour and dignity. If we do not have conviction, we will become enslaved and weak. If we do not have conviction, we will continue to need foreigners, and will not [be able to] get rid of the despots and tyrants.[22]

Furthermore, inasmuch as newspapers both reflected and shaped public opinion, they reinforced this sense of identity and purpose.

6. The Angel Esrafil carries a scroll bearing the words *horriyat* (freedom), *mosavat* (equality), *okhovvat* (brotherhood).

While what has been said until now has had to do with the intention of newspapers,[23] what it also points to is the question of the intended audience: the readership that the constitutional papers catered to was a nation that itself was in the process of being forged. In other words, to the extent that the subject matters that they wrote about were designed to appeal to a wider public in order to involve them in a political process, or at times, in revolutionary action, these publications imagined their readers to be far more representative than a narrow group of the privileged and literate sectors of society, which had been the primary audience of Zoka' al-Molk's *Tarbiyat*. That the constitutional papers also made conscious efforts to make themselves more affordable and easily available to a larger public further reinforces this point. While they could all be obtained through annual subscriptions, they also adopted a deliberate policy of selling single issues on the streets and in public places, and at a price that was competitive and at times less expensive than *Tarbiyat*, for example, had been nine years earlier. [24]

Readership and Letters to the Editor

In dealing with the issue of readership, another important and perhaps more difficult question is to see how newspapers were received, how they were read,

7. The motto at the top of every issue of the weekly *Mosavat* read *horriyat* (freedom), *'edalat* (justice), *okhovvat* (brotherhood).

and of whom this readership actually consisted, given the absence of any hard facts such as lists of subscribers that would allow us to speculate on the number or the social identities of readers.[25] It is of course always difficult to measure the impact of newspapers on readers, especially at a time when rates of literacy in urban areas are not thought to have extended beyond five percent. However, memoirs, diaries, and newspapers themselves can help us draw some conclusions. A letter in *Mosavat*, for example, tells of how people spent all their money on newspapers,[26] another of how people awaited the post with enthusiasm in order to get the latest copies of newspapers.[27] Other accounts talk of how newspapers changed hands and were passed on to others who could not afford to buy their own copies.[28] As for those who could not read, they would gather in coffeehouses to hear newspaper articles read aloud. A correspondent who was based in Tehran at the time writes how 'in many of the *qahvehkhaneh*s [coffeehouses], professional readers [were] engaged who instead of reciting the legendary tales of the *Shahnameh*, regale[d] their clients with political news.'[29] Even in rural areas, according to one source, 'peasants, even if illiterate, bought newspapers, taking them back to their villages, where they could find someone to read the newspapers to them.'[30] In short, the impression that emerges is of the prevalence of newspapers among common people, especially in the months that followed the establishment of the constitution. People were keen on newspapers for all sorts of reasons; some, in order to follow the parliamentary debates that were covered in a number of dailies;[31] others so as to see whether their own letters had been published, or their town mentioned in print;[32] and many because there was the general belief that newspapers were essential for progress and acted as 'mirrors reflecting the opinions of the people' (*ayeneh-ye 'aqideh-nama-ye mardom*).[33]

Another way of measuring the impact of newspapers and of gaining some insight into the people that constituted their readership would be by considering the contents of the letters that were sent and published in the pages of newspapers. To take the examples of *Habl al-Matin*, *Sur-e Esrafil*, and *Mosavat*, in the course of their columns, a series of letters was published from groups as well as individuals – men and women – writing from different towns and provinces across the country, with a range of demands and grievances. Some were addressed to the editor, others acted more as open letters. Rarely were they in reaction to the articles that had been published in the newspapers, although interestingly enough, on occasion, they tended to be in response to other letters. In other words, not only did the publication of these letters provide an opportunity for people to be heard by a larger readership that also included members of parliament and government, but it further contributed to an exercise in the expression of uncensored public opinion. When people did not receive their fair share of justice, they would send their story to be published in newspapers; when they became impatient or angry at the slow pace of change, they would use the pages of newspapers to communicate their sense of disappointment and outrage. Some wrote in to clear their names,[34] others to find sympathy and, if they were lucky, a solution to their problems.[35] People did not hesitate to complain about officials who had persevered with their autocratic ways, despite the promises of the constitution, even if they were long-term governors or advisers to the king. In fact, the letters, at times, constituted the most blunt and challenging section of the newspapers, and one could say that in a way, they provided the editors with an added pretext of publishing material that might otherwise have been considered too risky. Consider, for example, the following letter by a woman addressed to Sheykh Fazlollah Nuri, the celebrated and controversial conservative cleric who opposed women's education. This was published in the Tehran *Habl al-Matin* in September 1907.

> Your Excellency, Hojjat al-Eslam Sheykh Fazlollah: In the newspaper that you have published and sent to Tehran, these words feature: 'Learning for women is against religion and faith.' Since, I, the humble writer of this letter, am an ill-educated woman and do not understand these words ... I thought it necessary to ask you to explain them to me. If what you meant was that women should not learn anything and remain unthinking beasts until they die and that this is God's decree, please state in which part of the Qur'an and Hadith God Almighty has said such a thing. And if this is correct, could you please explain the reason behind God's unkindness towards women.[36]

In fact, at this time, there were several instances of women writing in to newspapers demanding that their grievances be heard and that they be given more rights in these new times. That they had taken part in a constitutional movement but had not gained much recognition for it meant that they had to take matters into their own hands and speak out if they wanted to improve their lot. Writing in the press was one way of 'going public' and 'claiming new space' for themselves.³⁷ As one explained in her letter, 'Strength of conviction (*gheyrat*) and commitment are essential [qualities] for all humankind. It does not matter whether it is a man or a woman!'³⁸ It would not be an exaggeration to say that as a result, women's letters were among the most forthright letters published. Another such example, also published in *Habl al-Matin*, was when a woman's letter was not at first published as she had expected, and she wrote in not only to protest but also to threaten further action in the event of it not being published. Addressing herself to the publisher of *Habl al-Matin*, she wrote:

> Why haven't you published the letter that was sent to you a few days ago in the name of a woman? You said [that you would publish it] either on Saturday or Sunday. Today is Monday, and there is no mention of it in the newspaper. What are you waiting for? Do you think that women aren't worthy or do you think that what I have written is a lie? It is either that you don't have any love of the homeland (*gheyrat-e vatan*) or that we women don't have any right to speak in our own country. Seriously – you will either publish it or else I will distribute it as a night letter (*shabnameh*), and curse your name forever.³⁹

For our purposes, however, and for the sake of determining the question of the actual readership by means of letters, several observations can be made. In the first place, there is the problem of authorship in the sense that the letters were not always signed; at times, signatures were withheld, and at others, the letters were published anonymously or under a pseudonym. Even when the name of the author did appear, it was not necessarily accompanied by any information regarding the individual. As a result, categorizing the readers in a conventional manner is not an easy matter. However, the fact that such details were absent is in itself significant and telling of a changing journalistic culture. This becomes all the more apparent when one compares these letters with those that were published in *Tarbiyat*. In the case of the latter, letters were often accompanied by a preamble about the writers. This not only included the name but also the writer's position in society and, at times, the name of the person's father.⁴⁰ (That the writers often had titles was indicative of the fact that the readership of *Tarbiyat* tended to consist mostly of members of the social elite.) On the occasions when the letter contained what could have been perceived as controversial opinions, much space was devoted to praising the credentials of the letter-writer, presumably in an attempt to reassure the audience of the respectability of the latter and the consequent lack of any malice.⁴¹ Furthermore, when the letter-writer was not known personally to Zoka' al-Molk, the background information that had been learnt through hearsay was still included.⁴² Therefore, the fact that the constitutional papers neither followed such an elaborate procedure, nor felt the need to identify each and every one of their letter-writers, points to the fact that they may have wanted to be inclusive, appeal to broader sectors of society, and encourage more people to speak out, get involved and interested in newspapers. The more letters they published, the more their chances grew of boosting their readership, a segment of which bought newspapers primarily to learn about the sentiments and experiences of their fellow citizens.

Furthermore, as has been mentioned, the writers of the letters published seem to have come from quite diverse backgrounds. They sent in letters from different parts of the country. They consisted not only of women but also of members of religious minorities, of widows who had lost husbands and property by violent means, and of people who felt that they had no other recourse to justice than to make their case known to their fellow readers, in the hope of generating compassion and some positive response. Of course, one cannot overlook the fact that the letters that were featured in the newspapers would have undergone a process of selection and modification by the editors, who may have been more prone to publish those letters that were consistent with their viewpoint. It is also possible that in some instances, particularly in cases where the letters were written in a tone that was perhaps overly blunt and scathing for the times, the editors may have indeed been the original authors. This, however, does not diminish the fact that in many cases, the letters probably did represent an outpouring of genuine opinion on matters of public interest. Furthermore, that more and more such letters were published between April 1907 and June 1908, when a coup d'état by the Shah put an abrupt end to the first constitutional era and closed down all newspapers, points to the growing popularity of such expressions of individual predicaments. Hence, in the aftermath of the constitution, it seems that the function of newspapers changed in the eyes of the public. Newspapers were not only considered as agents of change and progress, or even conveyors of information and learning, but increasingly also as a forum that could potentially serve both as a conduit between state and society and as a means – to paraphrase Benedict Anderson – that would enable 'people to think about themselves in relation to others'.[43]

It is often argued that the constitutional movement, by virtue of propagating the concept of a representative government, promoted the idea of the people's participation and thus reinforced the point that the people were henceforth citizens and not mere subjects.[44] However, as has been argued here, an important factor in enabling this process of transformation was the press. Whether by calling on their readers to act according to their sense of conviction or by giving voice to a range of readers' grievances, the constitutional press played a significant role in both defining this new politics and broadening the classification of who could take part in it. Furthermore, in giving recognition to formerly marginalized sectors of society by publishing their letters, the newspapers put forth a new sense of possibility, one where readers' complaints and criticisms would be considered equally valid, regardless of the readers' societal rank and position. Finally, the letters that were published in the pages of the constitutional press attested to the fact that the idea of rights as something that one was entitled to had become accepted, or at least articulated. In other words, the fact that readers no longer saw themselves as mere passive recipients of information, but as active participants with expectations, could be seen as an indication that the press constituted not only an effective exercise in encouraging a change in the journalistic and political culture but also as the groundwork for a nascent, if limited, public sphere.

CHAPTER 13

Writing in Tehran: The First Freedom of Press Law

Pardis Minuchehr

'A nation that has not witnessed the growth of open and free newspapers is an orphan nation', wrote Mirza 'Abd al-Rahim Elahi, the printer-editor of *Oqyanus* (The Ocean), a constitutional-era newspaper published in Tehran. He likened newspapers to a flame with three characteristics: light, darkness, and heat. If handled well, he averred, a newspaper's light could illuminate the path to bliss, its light could dispel the gloom from the face of the state and the nation, and its heat could secure one from the harm which ignorance's frigidity brings with itself.[1] Elahi did not stand alone in idealizing the new press of the constitutional era – in fact, many other writers of his time perceived the act of writing to be one of their main tasks in enlightening, informing, and engaging a larger public. Writing and publishing inflammatory content, exposing evil-doers, revealing the chaotic state of affairs, and emancipating the masses were all part of the innovative communications war waged by newspaper writers and correspondents.[2] On the opposite side of this ideological stance stood the Qajar state, the monarch and his appointees, who became the subjects of multiple attacks during this period as those who tried to stop the unfettered, unbridled, and unrestrained medium. Given the new nature of this social and cultural tension, the parties involved needed to find ways to resolve the escalating conflict. This early social and cultural tension accompanying the unfolding of constitutionalism in Iran has received relative scant attention. Therefore, it is the aim of this chapter to open up this inquiry and examine how early constitutionalists addressed and tried to resolve these new cultural, intellectual, and social tensions during the first constitutionalist era, a critical historical juncture.

From very early on, it became clear that no explicit laws protected the press, a new communicative medium which skilfully appealed to popular sentiment to accomplish its goals. Oddly enough, the original Fundamental Law of 1906, based on French and Belgian models, was devoid of any provisions to protect the press, regulate state control over it, or monitor the new-found freedom of expression. Newspapers could not defend themselves against arbitrary lawsuits by offended officials, nor could administrators protect themselves from capricious slander and libel. Under these circumstances, it seemed indispensable to enact a law that would conceptualize different points of tension and confrontation and at the same time provide a framework of reference for legal procedures. It is to this aim that the early constitutionalists drafted Article 20 of the Supplementary Fundamental Law, ratified on 7 October 1907, which stated unequivocally:

> All publications, except heretical books and matters hurtful to the perspicuous religion [of Islam] are free, and are exempt from censorship. If, however, anything should be discovered in them contrary to the press law, the publisher or writer is liable to punishment according to that law. If the writer be known, and be resident in Persia, then the publisher, printer, and distributor shall not be liable to prosecution.[3]

However, this brief legal paragraph did not suffice, and it was not until a few months later, as the result of extensive discussion in the Majles and the commencement of a national debate, that the Press Law, with its detailed provisions, was ratified on 10 February 1908.[4] This new Press Law (*Qanun-e matbu'at / enteba'at*) included provisions for the printed media as well as bookstores and book distributors. It also addressed such issues as accusatory violations, the foreign press, advertisements, newspaper peddlers, the reading out loud of announcements and newspaper articles in social gatherings, individual violations, offensive and impertinent statements about foreign political personalities and rulers, and prohibited matters, and laid down guidelines for trials and the closing down and confiscation of newspapers.

This seminal law, on which all future press laws were based, came about largely as the result of the activities of zealous early constitutionalist writers and the public debates they triggered. As Sa'idi Sirjani maintained, 'In the end the conflicts between unrestrained journalists, on one side, and the government, elected representatives, and the conservative Shiite clergy on the other, led in the autumn and winter of 1907–08 to extended debates in the Majles on a press law, which was passed on 10 February 1908. It was more libertarian than any subsequent press law in Persia, although the most extreme reformers and journalists had hoped for even more.'[5] It is therefore necessary to examine how early constitutionalist newspapers forged a language that defied the dominant order and at the same time created an idealist model for the new constitutionalist state. Furthermore, it is important to note that the discourse that evolved during this early constitutionalist period set the stage for the advancement of a culture of modernity, one that would try to negotiate between the public and private throughout the twentieth century. Hence, in the following section, I will analyse this early writing and the sociopolitical and cultural tensions that it encountered on the way to the emergence of the first Freedom of Press Law in the winter of 1908.

The 'Sacred Press': Perceptions and Presumptions

In issue after issue of the early constitutionalist publications we find detailed passages in which authors define themselves as 'newspaper writers of the sacred press'. Having quickly flourished in the public sphere as an effective and accessible communicative medium, the new press felt it necessary to justify and explain its indispensability in a 'constitutionalist state'. Ostensibly, the new journalists endorsed a free press that would document the 'chaotic condition of the homeland', record the 'administrative deficiencies' of the Qajar government, and highlight the critical 'cultural backwardness' that contributed to the dysfunctional state of affairs in Iran. As such, they rejected the 'compromising stance that selectively ignored many Iranian ills'. Following the example of Majd al-Eslam Kermani, one of the prominent editors of the constitutionalist era who took the moral high ground by stating that it was 'better to speak up rather than to hide',[6] other constitutionalist writers carried on the public debate. In the course of one of his ambitious articles in the daily paper *Neda-ye Vatan*, Majd al-Eslam Kermani argued that 'if [newspapers] disregard telling the truth, [they] have not fulfilled their *farizeh* (religious duty), and those not fulfilling their *farizeh* are traitors.' By employing religious language (perhaps only in a tactical way) to redefine the significance of the culture of print in the early constitutional period, the canny editor set journalists up as having high moral stature in their role as 'objective' and 'truthful' reporters.[7] The duty referred to here is not only a patriotic one, but also has a religious dimension; Iranian and Islamic identities are thereby blended.

Many other newspaper editors shared Majd al-Eslam's view on this matter, and insisted on analyzing, exposing, and criticizing the current situation, trying to understand what was plaguing Iranian towns and citizens. For instance, the editor of *Oqyanus*, 'Abd al-Rahim Elahi, believed that the members of a family or a country would fare better once they were aware of what plagued the other members of that family or country. If a disease afflicted any one of them, they would rise against the challenge 'together'. 'Therefore', he argued, 'a service to the homeland should be publicized in the same way as a betrayal'. Elahi went on to list the functions of writing as '[providing] prescriptions for the maladies of nations', '[taking] responsibility for the community's morale', 'guaranteeing people's bliss', 'preserving the foundations of justice and the principles of humanity', 'disseminating science and industry', 'emancipating [people] from the bondage of slavery', and 'guarding public etiquette'.[8] Similarly, *Habl al-Matin* contended:

> Newspapers should be written with the pen of truth. They should be devoid of libel and slander, for taking a pen in hand and accusing everyone and blaming others for this and that without adequate evidence is not just. What do we newspaper people say and what do we claim? We stipulate that the press be the reformer of morality and traditions. The press is the mirror that reflects the truth. The press should reflect the truth as truth and falseness as falseness. The press is the guide to the oasis of civilization and humanity, and the leader to the abode of magnanimity and bliss.[9]

In the same vein, newspaper publishers also believed that they were responsible for relaying the true news of injustice in the provinces, where the rule of law was least upheld. To this aim, they published pieces on the perils of life in various parts of Iran, essentially blaming the appointed aristocratic governors for the unrest. These reports were effective: Qavam al-Molk, for instance, was dismissed from his office as governor of the province of Fars due to these *ad hominem* attacks, and Asef al-Dowleh, the governor of Khorasan, was interrogated by the Majles for his policies with regard to slavery on the border with the Turkmens.[10] Similarly, Amir A'zam, the governor of Gilan, was summoned to a criminal court to respond to legal inquiries with regard to his abuse of power.[11]

Gradually, it became evident that the 'truthful representation' of the plights and predicaments plaguing the Persian lands was leading to increased tension between citizens and the central government. In order to overcome the split between the citizens and authorities, editors began to outline their role as mediators between the government and the citizens, and listed their function as serving both, with the objective of improving the desperate circumstances afflicting the 'beloved homeland'. Not all authorities, however, viewed the situation in the same way; nor did they all react in a similar manner. Even the Majles representatives were not unified in this stance. In the course of the legislative deliberations in the First Majles, while most deputies agreed about the indispensability of the publication of newspapers, there were others who vehemently opposed them and the new mode of writing they had ushered in. The latter claimed that since there had been no newspapers in the age of the Prophet, there was no need for them now either. As one cleric put it, 'if newspapers were necessary, the Prophet himself would have said so.'[12] In response to some Islamic traditionalist Salafists who sought to legitimize their positions of the basis on the Prophet's saying and deeds, Majd al-Eslam Kermani resorted to a language embedded in the discursive practices of Islam. In January 1908 he raised the issue of the well-known Qur'anic precept of *al-amr bi l-ma'ruf wa al-nahy in al-munkar* (enjoining good and forbidding evil) and claimed

8. Masthead of *Ayineh-ye Gheyb Nama* (Mirror of the Hidden).

that a newspaper did both, as it commanded the good and dissuaded from the wrong.[13]

In the same vein, many newspaper editors considered the role of their publications as complementary to the function of the new Majles. Just like the nation's representatives, these editors believed it to be their duty to echo the voices of those silenced throughout Iranian history. Characterizing their role as 'objective', 'truthful', 'non-selective', and 'all-embracing', early newspapers went beyond merely relaying news as they forged a dynamic social atmosphere for debate and negotiation. Eventually, this new atmosphere of debate empowered the common man to speak directly to the rulers, to object, to demand assistance, and to anticipate a direct response, begetting a new non-hierarchical relationship with the sovereign that defied the traditionally accepted and taken-for-granted role of individuals in Iranian society. Furthermore, early newspapers quite often considered themselves to be the 'mirror of the nation', and not of the rulers. A satirical illustrated paper, *Ayineh-ye Gheyb Nama* (Mirror of the Hidden), even named itself after this metaphorical expression, illustrating its masthead with two commoners holding a mirror to their faces, one of them representing beauty (*hosn*) and the other faults and flaws (*'eyb*) (see Figure 8). As such, being a truthful representative of people's voices and discussing the advantages of constitutionalism and the drawbacks of despotism developed into an essential objective for many of the emerging written media.

Furthermore, many newspapers viewed their own existence to be a crucial element necessary for progress and advancement, alongside the constitutional assembly. As *Habl al-Matin* asserted, 'it is not possible to attain a level of civilization without newspapers. In Egypt there is no national consultative assembly, but they are much more advanced in wealth and civilization because they enjoy a free press; the pen and expression are free. Whoever thinks a nation can progress without newspapers is making a big mistake.'[14]

Another example is provided by Mahmud Eskandani, publisher of the Tabriz paper *Eblagh* (Herald). In an article titled 'The Benefits of the Written Media', published in the paper's inaugural issue, he wrote that his main objective was to accelerate the nation's progress, so that the publication could be beneficial to both the nation and the government. *Eblagh* considered the first and foremost step for procuring progress and reform to be the pursuit of knowledge, not only theoretical but also practical. Not coincidentally, Eskandani shared a belief with many other constitutionalists that the written media would be beneficial only when people learned to read and gain knowledge. In his article, he adduced examples from countries with already advanced newspaper cultures. 'In the rest of the world', Eskandani contended, 'this medium has contributed to people's advances by allowing them to gain greater insight into the affairs of the world, thus paving the way for them to advance toward civilization.' He further suggested that for Iranians to develop like the rest of the world, they needed to seek knowledge of a kind that was also practical and could take them out of the island of ignorance.[15] As is clear from Eskandani's opening remarks, he considered newspapers to be an essential step in the modernity project: they began by pointing out the existing faults in the society, the lack of functional institutions, the absence of the rule of law, and the lack of industrialization and of knowledge and science. He further argued that it was the sum of these deficiencies in Iranian life that required immediate attention, and that change could be advanced through constitutionalism, where people gain rights and increase their knowledge for their own betterment. By pointing out how Iran compared in newspaper publishing with the rest of the world, he demonstrated his apprehension that Iran was lagging behind on the global level.

Oqyanus, with its characteristic literary language and metaphorical style, compared the emergence of newspapers to 'the first rays of civilization' and to the 'reflection of the Goddess of Progress', where they constituted the 'first blossom of education'. In the same vein, they represented 'a blessing that opened up the treasures of science and mysticism', and 'broke the spell of ignorance' by informing the nation's members of each other's well-being.[16] Hence, it was not astonishing that some constitutionalist writers viewed the publication of newspapers as the holiest and the best service for their country, a 'sacred' weapon aimed at unifying the powerful forces of the nation with those of the

9. Another masthead of *Ayineh-ye Gheyb Nama* (Mirror of the Hidden).

government. The tension between the press and the state escalated even more as the constitutionalist newspapers exposed more moral and social injustice. At the same time, state control also became more stringent as more uninhibited reports of social and political unrest, and at times vicious attacks aimed at administrative authorities, and even the Shah himself, were published.

The 'Sublime Purpose': Freedom of Expression and the Restriction of State Control

For most constitutionalist writers, who expressed their idealism in public, the very act of writing constituted a 'sublime purpose'. They therefore aimed at ensuring that their writings could be published with the least amount of state control – a situation that did not obtain. Ultimately, pre-publication control by the state emerged as one of the thorny issues early constitutionalist writers faced. The licensing process could take days and even then there were no guarantees that permission to publish would be granted, as the officers reviewing the paper could impose arbitrary criteria for permitting or forbidding its publication.

According to Mojir al-Dowleh, it was the members of the Anjoman-e Golestan, a group of highly educated intellectuals, graduates of both domestic and foreign schools, who were mainly responsible for the advocacy work on behalf of the press and, ultimately, for the passing of the Press Law in the Majles. Mojir al-Dowleh recounts in *Neda-ye Vatan* that the members of this intellectual *anjoman* reckoned freedom of the press to be an essential prerequisite for the solidification of constitutionalism, for a guarantee of the enactment of its laws, and for limiting the role of the central state. By printing tracts and disseminating them to a larger audience in front of the Majles entrance in Baharestan Square, Anjoman-e Golestan lobbied aggressively for the ratification of the first Freedom of Press Law. This *anjoman*, which met regularly at the house of Prince Mohammad Ja'far Mirza, deemed its revolutionary quest for press freedom a 'sublime purpose', and in order to accomplish its task, sought the alliance of young and new Majles members, especially the active Azarbayjani ones.[17] Ultimately, it was with the assistance of those young members that the Anjoman-e Golestan succeeded in persuading the Majles to add the provision on press freedom to the Supplementary Fundamental Law. This marked a turning point in the relationship between the press and the state, as papers such as *Neda-ye Vatan* no longer had to be sent to the Office of Publications (*Edareh-ye Enteba'at*) but could go directly to the publishing house. They could also take the word *azad* (free) off their mastheads, for, paradoxically, that term had identified Persian constitutionalist papers not as free to publish whatever they wanted but as papers that needed to obtain that special permit by the state for their publication.[18]

The short paragraph on press freedom in the Supplementary Fundamental Law, however, was as general as it could get, and soon the constitutionalists pushed for more detailed laws for publishers.

Censorship: Regulated or Not

'A poet-philosopher was once asked, "How long are you going to criticize people?" He responded: "As long as they do evil, I will reveal their evil and as soon as they do good, I will declare that". We journalists, the true observers of the nation – from prince to pauper – we do not fear the Shah and we will not deflect our attention from the poor. The entire nation, from prince to paupers, should be able to see its own visage in this mirror.'[19] Thus wrote the passionate Sheykh Ahmad Torbati, known as Soltan al-'Olama Khorasani. His moral stance of publicly exposing wrongdoers and revealing their corruption in public landed him in deep political hot water. In the course of his short writing career as editor of *Ruh al-Qodos* (Holy Spirit), he exposed the corrupt state, discredited government officials, and most importantly, disgraced the Shah himself, calling him a 'butcher' of innocent people and the one person responsible for the mass bloodshed occurring throughout Persian territories.

It did not take long for this young constitutionalist cleric to be summoned to court on account of his personal attacks on the governing authorities Eqbal al-Saltaneh, Amir Bahador, Jahanshah Khan, on Ottoman officers, and on the Shah himself.[20]

As his court date became imminent, the adventurous editor argued aggressively that no matter what, he would not attend a closed trial. He requested that a jury pass judgement upon his case, rather than him being charged in a court where the presiding judge acted as both judge and prosecutor. Furthermore, he demanded to know the identity of the person who had filed the complaint, as well as the potential fine and sentence that his alleged violations would incur. All of the above points raised by Soltan al-'Olama with regard to his court case revealed the legal deficiencies in handling press violations, such as the lack of a jury, the anonymity of plaintiffs, the absence of an indictment, and the lack of legal clauses on the sentencing criteria for a libel case. Soltan al-'Olama's legal case was therefore significant, because it set the stage for further intellectual discussion of the utter necessity of a Press Law in the new constitutionalist state.

Despite his written reaction to the court summons, Soltan al-'Olama in fact attended the court session and listened to the indictment formulated against him. However, as arbitrarily as the court case against him had been formed, his pardon also came in the same manner shortly thereafter. Apparently, the head of the Office of Publications appealed to Haji Sedq al-Molk, the head of the criminal court (*Ra'is-e mahkameh-ye jaza*), for Soltan al-'Olama's pardon,[21] and *Ruh al-Qodos* regained its publishing licence. Soltan al-'Olama, however, continued to undermine with his writing the presumed infallibility of the monarch, Mohammad Ali Shah. The fact that this criticism might lead to fines, imprisonment, or even execution did not deter him. Sadly, his name remains in history as one of the first martyrs of Iranian journalism, as he was finally arrested, tortured, and executed after the bombardment of the Majles.

Like *Ruh al-Qodos*, several other popular newspapers also experienced short-term arbitrary bans and summonses to the criminal court prior to the enactment of the Press Law. Interestingly, *Mohakemat* (Trials), a paper also published by Majd al-Eslam Kermani, relates some of the ongoing press trials of this period, amongst them those of *Sur-e Esrafil*,[22] *Ruh al-Qodos*, *Tanbih*, *Habl al-Matin*, and *Mosavat*.

Not all forms of encroachment upon press freedom were state-sponsored, as in Soltan al-'Olama's trial; many of the punishments originated, in fact, from divergent groups of people, especially from various radical and fanatic *anjoman*s. In the case of the editor of *Hadid* and *Mojahed*, Seyyed Mohammad Shabestari, known as Abozziya' (Abu al-Ziya'), he was beaten and bastinadoed in Tabriz for authoring 'a letter from Najaf' in which he compared

Seyyed Kazem Yazdi, one of the prominent Najaf ulema and at the time an anti-constitutionalist, to Ebn-e Moljam, the assassin of Imam Ali and formal enemy of the Shiites. For this, according to Edward G. Browne, he 'incurred the hatred and vengeance of certain fanatics'.[23] In response to this article, the Anjoman-e Eslami of Tabriz, a radical *anjoman*, first composed a long letter against Abozziya' and published it in *Anjoman*, the official paper of the city council of Tabriz. Abozziya' was then severely bastinadoed and subsequently expelled from the city. Shabestari had been a devoted colleague of Haji Mirza Aqa Boluri on the newly established paper *Mojahed* (Tabriz), and according to Boluri, the Shahsavan soldiers in town might have even killed Shabestari if it had not been for Boluri's interference. Ultimately, Seyyed Mohammad Shabestari arrived in Tehran, where after the constitutionalist victory in the summer of 1909 he became (if only nominally) editor, with Mohammad Amin Rasulzadeh, of one of the most prominent papers of the second constitutionalist era, *Iran-e Now*.[24]

As with Mohammad Shabestari, at the eastern end of the *Mamalek-e Mahruseh-ye Iran* (The Guarded Domains of Iran), in Mashhad, angry mobs seized and beat up the editor of *Khorshid* (Sun) in the holy city. In this case, the members of Anjoman-e Hemmat, a radical Islamic *anjoman*, dragged the paper's editor, Mirza Sadeq Khan, out of his house in the middle of the night and accused the Mashhadi editor of having offended the theology students of Sabzevar in his paper.[25] Outraged at *Khorshid*'s lengthy article about the events of Sabzevar and the depiction of the wanton behaviour of the theology students in the city, this radical anti-constitutionalist *anjoman* gave itself the liberty of meting out justice. Mirza Sadeq Khan was beaten on the streets of Mashhad and publicly punished for the content of his writing.

Other newspapers did not remain silent against such cases of injustice and outright brutality, and showed a great degree of solidarity with their colleagues. *Sobh-e Sadeq* in Tehran, for instance, wrote in support of *Khorshid* and its editor, Sadeq Khan, condemning such vicious and malicious acts of vengeance undertaken without the knowledge of proper authorities. Tehran's venerable *Habl al-Matin* also had a tradition of supporting other constitutionalist newspapers against the threat of being closed down. In a letter in that newspaper, an anonymous writer protested against the ban on Urmia's daily paper *Faryad*. Founded by Mirza Habib Orumiyeh and run by Mahmud Ghanizadeh Delmaqani and 'Abd al-Ali Hariri Delmaqani, *Faryad*, which believed in 'national progress' for the comfort and bliss of the average fellow citizens, had an international distribution in Russia, Turkey, and even Europe. It had been shut down by the members of the Anjoman-e Orumiyeh, due to their belief that the paper did not fully protect the reputation of the *anjoman*'s high officials. The issue under contention was whether outsiders should know what was going on in

10. A sketch of Malek al-Motekallemin.

Urmia, and whether the corruption and chaos there should be publicized. The Urmian officials asserted that the hidden secrets [of the city] did not need to be revealed elsewhere. Others also claimed that 'whatever happens in our city, we all know ourselves! There is no need for it to be repeated in written form and be revealed everywhere else.'[26] The Anjoman-e Orumiyeh prevailed in shutting down the paper so that it could no longer publicize their ills. *Habl al-Matin*, however, made it a point to publish accounts of injustices against constitutionalist papers such as Urmia's *Faryad*.

A great degree of solidarity was especially demonstrated with the seventy-year-old Afsah al-Motekallemin, the editor of *Kheyr al-Kalam* and *Sahel-e Nejat*, both published in Rasht. The Tehran paper *Tamaddon* published a letter from the shareholders of the two papers' printing house, who had protested against the arrest of Afsah al-Motekallemin and the closing down of the papers. In *Tamaddon*, the old man described in detail his own arrest and flogging and how he was wrongly accused of being a member of the Anjoman-e Abolfazl.[27] In a later issue of *Tamaddon*, seventeen signatories from the northern town of Anzali wrote in support of Afsah al-Motekallemin, detailing what had happened to him from their own point of view.[28] Afsah al-Motekallemin later prepared a seventeen-point complaint against Amir A'zam, the governor of Gilan, and took it to the judiciary – no longer denying his links with the Anjoman-e Abolfazl, which Amir A'zam despised. Interestingly enough, his letter of complaint against his aggressors was written only a few days after the Press Law passed in the Majles, and therefore it was one of the very first cases to be processed after this new law came into effect.[29]

Astonishingly, even prior to the ratification of the Press Law in the newly established Majles, the criminal court (*mahkameh-ye jaza*) had already begun to prosecute journalists based on this law. In *Habl al-Matin*'s court case, the editor of the paper was fined for a disrespectful article published against the Russian government and its dignitaries.[30] In spite of the editor's apology, the court decided to fine the constitutionalist daily paper, based on the soon-to-be-ratified Press Law, 50 tumans, over 40 times the paper's annual subscription rate. *Habl al-Matin*'s editor also agreed to pay a fine based on the sentencing guidelines of a future law. *Habl al-Matin* had been supportive of the law to the extent that in one of its editorials, it had stated 'when we [journalists] put pen to paper, we should imagine that the court is present and views our words one by one. Newspaper reporters who present themselves as defenders of the law, should not transgress even one step from the lines of law. They should not jot down a word that they cannot substantiate.'[31] Therefore, in the court case against it, *Habl al-Matin* obeyed the law with no objection, even before it was officially ratified, and paid the fine.

The Celebration of the Emergence of the Press Law

It is no surprise that the constitutionalist newspapers referred to the Press Law as an event to be celebrated; some even referred to it as *Eyd-e zohur-e qanun-e matbu'at* (The Celebration of the Emergence of the Press Law).[32] In *Mosavat*'s

11. *Mosavat*'s celebration of the emergence of the press law.

illustration, we see a glorification of the Press Law, invoking a divinity with the visual image of two angels sitting on either side, holding long quill pens in their hands, and looking at the radiating star with '*ya hu*' engraved on it. Below the star, on a white slate, printed letters herald the *Eyd-e zohur-e qanun-e matbu'at* (see Figure 11).

The freedom of the press had propelled a national debate, and the ratification of this law on 10 February of 1908, subsequent to the Supplementary Fundamental Law, marked the culmination of these debates.[33] Constitutionalists had begun to view press freedom as essential to the functioning of the government, as it would act as a check on governmental abuse of power and at the same time allow citizens to scrutinize government action and, if necessary, take necessary social and political action. Hence, Iranian intellectuals considered freedom of the press integral to preserving the desired relationship between the people and their government.

The murky language of the constitution's provisions allowed for broad and/ or narrow interpretations of them. For instance, in the case of banning the press, it was still permitted to shut down a paper if it had published material that did such things as 'opposing the religion of Islam', 'disrespecting the monarchy', 'revealing the army's secret plans', 'inciting public unrest', 'inciting people against the country's official forces', or 'publishing profane and vile illustrations'.[34] Nonetheless, the constitutionalist newspapers viewed Article 20 as a restraint on the arbitrary banning that had taken place prior to the law's ratification. For instance, a separate advertisement was printed in *Ruh al-Qodos* by the head of the Shahanshahi publishing house in Tehran, Abdollah Qajar, who wrote, elated: 'According to law, the banning of newspapers has been banned.'[35] He expressed the hope that from now on there would no longer be any reason that the weekly Tuesday issues of *Ruh al-Qodos* should not be distributed, adding that if it did happen, readers needed to inform the publisher immediately. Unfortunately, such elation was short-lived, and the episode of the bombardment of the Majles, in June 1908, eventually put an end to almost all constitutionalist papers.

Conclusion

This first Freedom of Press Law, rudimentary in its early version, nevertheless became the premise upon which future, more sophisticated, press laws were drafted and promulgated in Iran. For us, looking back at the nature of writing and the culture it propagated, the early constitutionalist period points to a lingering problem in modern Iranian society, i.e., the dilemma posed in determining the limitations and restrictions of the public versus the private spheres. The underlying challenge of modernity in Iran, I would like to conclude, lies in how people, administrators, and the central power have regulated the new public sphere, and allowed – or not – for its transformation and expansion.

As this chapter has intended to show, Iran's first freedom of the press did not come into being in a vacuum, but within a verbally adroit and culturally complex political and social space. Multiple intellectual and cultural public discourses ensued, launching the country on the road to modernity.

CHAPTER 14

The Constitutional Revolution and Persian Dramatic Works: An Observation on Social Relations Criticism in the Plays of the Constitutional Era

Ali Miransari
Translated by H. E. Chehabi

The six-year period here considered begins with the command to draw up a constitution issued in 1906 and comes to an end with the closing of the Second Majles in 1911. During this period a number of plays were written by Iranian intellectuals containing social criticism. Like all dramatic works, these plays are multifaceted in the sense that they can be considered from at least three aspects: artistic, literary, and social. But since the social aspect of these plays overshadows their literary and artistic features, we will consider them from the social perspective to examine how Iranian playwrights used drama to critique social relations in early twentieth-century Iran. At the time of the Constitutional Revolution, Western-style drama was a relatively recent cultural import into Iran, for which reason we begin with a brief look at the emergence of Western-style playwriting in Iran.

The Emergence of Western-Style Dramatic Literature in Iran (1850–55)

Western-style dramatic literature emerged in Persian nearly six decades before the Constitutional Revolution in Iran. In 1850, Fath-Ali Akhundzadeh, a turkophone resident of Russian Caucasia who considered himself Iranian, published his first dramatic work, titled *Molla Ebrahim Khalil the Alchemist*, paving the way for the reception of the Western playwriting tradition in Iranian culture. Between then and 1855 Akhundzadeh wrote five other dramatic works in the Turkish language and subsequently published all of them in Caucasia: *Monsieur Jordan the Herbalist* (1850), *The Story of Vazir Khan Lankaran (Mirage)* (1850), *The Adventure of the Bear which Beat the Thief* (1852), *The Story of the Stingy*

Man (1852), and *The Tale of the Defence Lawyers in the Quarrel of Tabriz* (1855).

Akhundzadeh's plays had two main features which turned him into a role model for later Iranian playwrights. In terms of structure, Akhundzadeh totally avoided following the principles of traditional Iranian religious drama, *ta'ziyeh*,[1] basing his work instead on the principles of Western playwriting, which he had learned in nineteenth-century Tbilisi. With regard to subject matter, he detached his works from the traditional Persian narration or fable and legend, and critically examined social relations. For him social criticism would lead to what he termed 'ethical refinement' (*tahzib-e akhlaq*): 'It is believed that this art [playwriting] leads to ethical refinement. It is obvious that each nation has its swindlers, rogues, and idiots. The manner and behaviour of these people are satirized through drama so that others will draw the appropriate lessons.' He asserted that the wise and the philosophers understood that the only thing that could cure human defects was ridiculing them. Elsewhere he asserted that the most famous and effective compositions used the honourable medium of drama, whose result was the refinement of ethics. He added that 'until today this art has not been known among Muslims'.[2]

In his critique of social relations, Akhundzadeh concentrated on what for him were the most significant issues, namely ignorance and superstition. This is particularly reflected in his plays *Molla Ebrahim Khalil the Alchemist* and *Monsieur Jordan the Herbalist*. Beginning in 1855, Iranian intellectuals, who were living under the autocracy of Naser al-Din Shah, started receiving the dramatic works of Akhundzadeh, who was labouring under Tsarist censorship in the Caucasus. These works arrived in the cultural field of Persian speakers through two channels. The first channel was Akhundzadeh himself, who endeavoured to send his plays to his many friends in Iran. Together with the plays, he would send letters in which he explained his views on and interpretations of playwriting and social criticism: 'I sent many of my works to Iran so that those who shared my ideas (*hamkishan-e man*) would familiarize themselves with the honourable trade of drama, i.e., theatre.'[3] The second channel consisted of the translations of these works, which had been made by Mirza Ja'far Qarachehdaghi at the request of Akhundzadeh himself and which were published in Tehran in 1874.[4]

Akhundzadeh's letters make it clear that only a very limited number of his friends had access to his dramatic works.[5] It is not quite clear how many Iranian intellectuals beyond Akhundzadeh's friends had the opportunity of reading these works. It would seem that the only recipient of Akhundzadeh's letters who was able to relate to his plays culturally and pen a few plays in the same vein was his friend Mirza Aqa Tabrizi.[6] In the years 1870–71 Mirza Aqa Tabrizi wrote a number of plays that established him as the first Persian-language playwright. The titles of some of these plays were *Ashraf Khan, the*

Ruler of Arabistan; *The Tale of Shah-Qoli Mirza's Pilgrimage to Karbala*; *The Way Zaman-Khan Borujerdi Rules*; and *The Romance of Aqa Hashem Khalkhali*'.[7]

At the time when Mirza Aqa Tabrizi decided to start creating dramatic works, Iranian society was living under the despotic rule and the strict censorship of Naser al-Din Shah. As Mirza Aqa saw it, this society had two main characteristics: the corruption of the Court and ignorance and superstition among ordinary people. Mirza Aqa Tabrizi reflected these two characteristics in his five works and criticized them. He saw his plays as a means of strengthening the nation (*mellat*) in the face of the challenge posed by the Western imperial powers.[8] Like Akhundzadeh, he realized that it was only through defining and representing the weaknesses of Iranian society that there could be any hope for reform. As Shiva Balaghi notes, the strong sense of nationalism (*melliyat*) in the theatre of Akhundzadeh and Mirza Aqa Tabrizi represented a significant break from more traditional forms of Iranian theatre like the *ta'ziyeh*, where the actors and the audience were participants *qua* Shiites.[9] By using theatre as a medium for edifying the nation, Akhundzadeh and Mirza Aqa Tabrizi were in the process constructing the very nation with which they were communicating.[10]

Mirza Aqa Tabrizi constitutes the link between Akhundzadeh and the playwrights of the constitutional era; it is through him that the playwriting traditions and the social criticism of Akhundzadeh found their way to the constitutional era. Tabrizi's plays were published for the first time by Seyyed Hasan Taqizadeh from 1906 to 1908 in Tehran and Tabriz, and found a wide readership.[11] It should be pointed out, however, that the plays were published without Mirza Aqa Tabrizi's name and the reading public was unaware of his authorship. In 1921 three of these plays were published in Berlin from a copy belonging to a former German ambassador to Iran, Friedrich Rosen, naming Mirza Malkam Khan as the author.[12] But then A. E. Ebrahimov published the manuscripts, documents, and letters of Akhundzadeh, and in the papers of Akhundzadeh four plays by Tabrizi were discovered in Tabrizi's own handwriting, and thus it became clear that what Rosen had published had been authored by Mirza Aqa Tabrizi.[13] Of course, translations of European plays, like the works of Molière, which had started at the beginning of Naser al-Din Shah's reign, contributed to this process of acquainting Iranians with drama and theatre, but the issue of the influence of translated Western plays on the development of playwriting in Iran is outside the present discussion.

The Constitutional Era: 1906–11

In this era the social awareness of the Iranian people and the behaviour of their political rulers were utterly different from that in the times of Mirza Aqa

Tabrizi. After the assassination of Naser al-Din Shah, the weakness of the state under his successor Mozaffar al-Din Shah allowed for a certain limited amount of freedom. Under the new conditions modern education spread, intellectuals inside and outside Iran were able to interact with each other, the Iranian press grew both qualitatively and quantitatively, Persian publications from the Caucasus, the Ottoman Empire, India, and Cairo could be imported to Iran, the political writings of modernists such as Talebov, Mostashar al-Dowleh, Malkam Khan, and Akhundzadeh became available in the country, and intellectuals were able to interact freely with common people. The result was a general improvement in the political sophistication of the people.

In contrast to these developments, the next ruler, Mohammad Ali Shah, was influenced by pre-constitutional times and did not intend to share his power with institutions like the cabinet and the parliament. He threatened the parliament, insulted the cabinet, and lost no time chipping away at personal and social freedoms, gradually paving the way for the return of the former leaders. He then started to harass the members of Naser al-Molk's cabinet (14 December 1907), banned the press (21 June 1908), ordered the bombardment of the Majles (23 June 1908), nullified the constitutional order (19 November 1908), and finally organized a coup d'état which resulted in the incarceration and execution of many constitutionalists, starting a year of oppression known as the 'Lesser Despotism'.

Play-Writing in the Constitutional Era

Under these conditions, Iranian intellectuals (including Iranian playwrights) very soon understood that Mozaffar al-Din Shah's constitutional order notwithstanding, the sociopolitical climate of the country was regressing back to despotism and, step by step, society was moving away from the ideals of the Constitutional Revolution. They now had to engage in their social criticism by whatever means they had. Journalists began to write political articles, poets began to compose sociopolitical *qasida*s, and playwrights, who regarded themselves as the inheritors of the methods, plays, and ideas of Akhundzadeh and Mirza Aqa Tabrizi, decided to pen new plays that would criticize the new social relations. At least seven authors emerged as the first generation of playwrights in the constitutional era: Ali Khan Zahir al-Dowleh, Mirza Reza Na'ini, Habibollah Shahrdar, Abbas Ali As'adi, Mohammad Reza Mosavat, Abd al-Rahim Talebov, and Mirza Rahim Mohammadzadeh. The literary output of these writers consists of nine plays, of which only some are available today. The plays include *Political Drama* and *The Nightmare of Autocracy* by Ali Khan Zahir al-Dowleh, *Sheykh Ali Mirza, the Governor of Tuyserkan* by Mirza Reza Na'ini, *Mohseniyeh Association* by Abbas Ali As'adi, *The King's*

Garden by Habibollah Shahrdar, *New Theatre* by Mohammad Reza Mosavat, *A Description of the Iranian People's Miseries* by Talebov, and *Islamic Society* by Mirza Rahim Mohammadzadeh.

These plays differ greatly not only in essence but also in terms of performance and publication. Only *The King's Garden*, *Political Drama*, and probably *The Nightmare of Autocracy* were actually staged, the latter two at the author's (i.e. Zahir al-Dowleh's) home.[14] There were a number of reasons why the other plays were never performed. To begin with, the other playwrights did not have the wealth and facilities of Zahir al-Dowleh. Furthermore, Zahir al-Dowleh's relations with the Court and his membership in a powerful Sufi order provided him with the immunity that allowed him to stage plays criticizing Mohammad Ali Shah's political behaviour under the ruler's very eyes. Finally, at the time there was no official theatre for performing plays, and it was only after the end of the Lesser Despotism that the second floor of the Larousse publishing house in Teheran was set up for performing dramas.

The publication of these plays also varied. While Zahir al-Dowleh's plays were performed, they were never printed, but all the other plays of this era were published. As'adi's *Mohseniyeh Association* was published independently, while *Sheykh Ali Mirza, the Governor of Tuyserkan* by Na'ini and *New Theatre* by Mosavat were published in two newspapers, *Tiyatr* and *Mosavat*, respectively, assuring them a wider reading public.

The Playwrights' Critical Views

The playwrights of the constitutional era were in full agreement that Iranian society was moving away from the ideals of the Constitutional Revolution, but they differed in their diagnoses of why this was so. They saw the evidence for Iran's move away from its constitutionalist ideals in the following developments: the Qajar Court, Mohammad Ali Shah in particular, ignored the national interest; personal and social freedoms were being suppressed; the old landlord class continued its dominance by pretending to have become pro-constitution; local governors were acting tyrannically; people were prone to ignorance and superstition, and believed in magic and alchemy; there were too many political groups and associations; the members of the pre-revolutionary despotic establishment were returning to the political and social scene; and journalism was being restricted while journalists were being threatened.

All the above developments are reflected in the plays of the constitutional era. But if one asks why the playwrights diverged in their approach to the problems, their different sociocultural backgrounds may furnish the answer. Zahir al-Dowleh belonged to the upper class of society and was related to the Qajar Court, whereas the other playwrights were situated in various strata of middle-class society. Mirza Reza Na'ini and Abbas Ali As'adi had received a Western-style education as propagated in Russian, French, and American schools in Iran, and Talebov had become acquainted with modern education in the schools of the Caucasus, while Ali Khan Zahir al-Dowleh and Mohammad Reza Mosavat lacked such a background. Then, being journalists and newspaper publishers, Mirza Reza Na'ini and Mohammad Reza Mosavat had considerable personal experience in relating to the public, an advantage Zahir al-Dowleh and As'adi, as enlightened as they were, did not enjoy. Abbas Ali As'adi and Mohammad Reza Mosavat had been members of political parties, the Democrat party in particular, and Zahir al-Dowleh and Shahrdar were members of the Sufi Anjoman-e Okhovvat, but Na'ini never joined any cultural or political group.[15] And finally, Zahir al-Dowleh, Talebov, and Na'ini were moderate revolutionaries, while Mosavat had taken a radical and extremist stance. Let us now turn to the playwrights themselves, to examine how the issues listed above are dealt with in their plays.

The Playwrights of the Constitutional Era

Ali Khan Zahir al-Dowleh

Zahir al-Dowleh was the first playwright of the period who saw the evidence of a deviation from constitutional ideals in the trampling of the national interest and the continued political dominance of the big land owners. As a courtier, he witnessed the innermost circles of the state from close at hand and drew a connection between what he saw as an indifference to the national interest and the practices of the Court, especially on the part of Mohammad Ali Shah himself.[16] Consequently, in his first play, he criticized the Qajar Court and directly attacked Mohammad Ali Shah.

Zahir al-Dowleh's first dramatic work was a pantomime called *Political Drama* and was first performed at his own home before the coup d'état of Mohammad Ali Shah. We do not know who exactly the performers were and who was in the audience, but we do know that Zahir al-Dowleh himself directed it. Given that the pantomime was performed first at his house and later at the meetings of the Anjoman-e Okhovvat, it stands to reason that the actors and the audience must have been members of the association.[17]

Zahir al-Dowleh's second play was the three-act *The Nightmare of Autocracy or the Sinners*, which illustrated the political atmosphere of Iran after the Constitutional Revolution. In this play Zahir al-Dowleh analysed the emergence of a new class of land owners and the despotic ruling style of local governors and suggested that this new class had been able to accede to a position of leadership under the auspices of the new local governors appointed by the Court after the revolution. In creating the character of Haji Aqa, Zahir al-Dowleh suggested that the political destiny of Iran had become a plaything in the hands of the feudal landlords and merchants. In his play, Zahir al-Dowleh equally criticized the autocrats, false supporters of the Constitutional Revolution, and local governors connected to the Court. The three main characters in this play are:

1. Haji Aqa, a merchant and land owner who supported constitutionalism and had even spent some of his money to help it triumph. He represents a new social class, one which has changed its nature and modus operandi a little bit, but now wants special privileges and immunities.

> Haji Aqa: This is something new again. A landlord should not be able freely to dispose of his peasants? Don't you remember that I myself killed two of my own peasants last year and nobody could say a word? Of course I lost 3,000 tumans, but so what. I earn 100,000 tumans from my properties each year, so it's no big deal to lose 10,000 tumans [for blood money]. Are you saying peasants are subjected to oppression? Haven't you heard that cows and donkeys obey only when they are beaten with a stick? The peasants are our donkeys and cows. ... The situation has changed since the time of the old autocracy. Under the new constitutional government, the state has no right to incarcerate and insult a credible and honest merchant like me who owns one million tumans. ... If the situation is going to be the same as in the old times, what was the purpose of all these controversies, bloodlettings, and sacrifices?[18]

2. The Chamberlain, who is the representative of the local governor and a middleman for receiving bribes, in other words the one who continues the traditions criticized by pre-constitutional playwrights.

> The Chamberlain: So no, please write down the money order for my lord who ... is waiting for me to be informed of the details after your departure.[19]

3. The Prisoner, who symbolizes the craftsman in Iranian society after the Constitutional Revolution, a man oppressed by the governing khan who has jailed him. It seems that Zahir al-Dowleh intentionally gave him an ironical name: Mashhadi Azad (Free):

> My name is ... Mashhadi Azad. I'm a druggist. ... Without asking me a single question or allowing me to say a single word, the khan ordered them to beat me. They beat me so much that I fainted three times ... then he ordered them to take me to a warehouse. Every other day they give me bread and some water, and much as I beg, no one listens to me.[20]

It seems that with his plays Zahir al-Dowleh incurred the wrath of Mohammad Ali Shah, for after the coup d'état his home was attacked by agents of the Shah and destroyed, his furniture was plundered, and all actors and spectators were persecuted.[21]

Mirza Reza Na'ini

A graduate of the American school in Tehran, Na'ini played a major role in the Constitutional Revolution. In 1908 he began publishing *Tiyatr*, the first Persian newspaper to focus on theatre. In the course of Mohammad Ali Shah's coup his home, too, was looted.[22]

In the first issue of *Tiater*, Na'ini presented his views on drama and playwriting and explicitly asserted that the didactic principle of ethical improvement should be the basis of social and political criticism. The continued prevalence of ignorance, superstition, and belief in magic and alchemy constituted proof that the ideals of the Constitutional Revolution had not taken hold in society.

> Our aim is to describe the behaviour and manners of kings, governors, and people who refuse to struggle (*qa'edin*) ... so as to [relate] the issues, as in foreign theatre performance ... in the form of question and answer. We hope to present the problems of the autocratic era in a simple and understandable way so that people will become aware of the blessings of constitutionalism. We hope that our theatre will help the other newspapers to gradually refine the ethics of the nation so that blessing and redemption will be achieved. It is therefore obvious that the doctrine of this newspaper is the refinement of ethics.[23]

On the basis of this notion of theatre, Na'ini wrote the play *Sheykh Ali Mirza, the Governor of Tuyserkan*, in which he criticized ignorance, superstition, and belief in sorcery and alchemy on the one hand, and the despotic behaviour of local governors on the other. The play's action takes place in the context of the administration of a provincial governor who is a member of the imperial family, the point being to show that ignorance and superstition could be found at all levels of society. The story begins when one of the sons of Fath-Ali Shah, who is the ruler of Tuyserkan and Malayer, develops the ambition to rule over the entire country after his father's death. For this purpose he seeks the help of a sorcerer and an alchemist. The man asks for and gets a lot of money, but then does nothing for the prince. Worse, after appropriating all the prince's wealth, he flees from Malayer. The play was published in twelve consecutive issues of *Tiyatr*.

Abbas Ali As'adi

Born in 1888 in Tabriz, As'adi received his education at the Alliance School in Tehran, where he became familiar with the works of Molière and Shakespeare.[24] Like the other dramatists of this era, As'adi was conscious of society's deviation from the ideals of the Constitutional Revolution, but unlike the others he found the source of this deviation in the return of the elements of the previous autocracy to the political and social scene of the country, and in the variety and multiplicity of political groups. While he did pay some attention to ignorance and superstition in his plays, he equated these with simplemindedness and naïveté.

As'adi presented his ideas on the events following the Constitutional Revolution in a play titled *Mohseniyeh Association*. This play, written and published two years after the establishment of constitutional order and one month before the coup d'état of Mohammad Ali Shah, is one of the most significant and yet unknown dramatic works of that time. As'adi's penetrating observation of society had led him to view the new freedoms with a certain scepticism, for which reason he chose to publish his work under the pseudonym of 'Eyn Alef. In spite of this precaution he felt unsafe in Tehran after the coup d'état and fled to Tabriz.

The play is about a profit-seeker named Abbas Qoli Khan who is one of the members of the previous regime and after the Constitutional Revolution has been deprived of all his interests:

> Abbas Qoli Khan: This constitutionalism thing has totally ruined me. My hands and legs have been tied up and put into a nutshell. ... There is no money, no capital, no income. How the devil am I supposed to live? What am I supposed to do? After all, I used to have a carriage and things, and was always able to pay for it all. ... Why do we need constitutionalism? I kept telling them to stop this nonsense and not make so much fuss. What do we need laws for? What use is a parliament?[25]

And so Abbas Qoli Khan tries to work out a solution for his problem:

> Abbas Qoli Khan: We must think of something. We must have a plan. These times are totally different from previous times. Now we must move in such a way that people will not find out. The people of our neighbourhood are making a nuisance of themselves. Everyone has an association (*anjoman*).[26]

In the end, Abbas Qoli Khan makes use of the proliferation of associations and founds one of his own, which he calls Mohseniyeh. He gets people to believe that many of the fundamental events of the Constitutional Revolution had been secretly orchestrated by his association, and declares that he now wants to establish it as a public centre (*markaz-e ʿalani*). He thus inveigles the naïve into joining, and then absconds with the membership dues.

Mohammad Reza Mosavat

Mosavat was a constitutionalist activist who had been a member of the Majmaʿ-e Azadmardan before the revolution and became a journalist after the revolution.[27] His experience in the constitutionalist struggle and his journalistic activities made him realize very early that Iran was deviating from the revolution's ideals, but he looked at this deviation from a different angle: for him it was embodied in the ill treatment of journalists and official censorship. He presented his critical views on this issue in a play consisting of six short acts, titled *New Theatre*. Its story is based on the trial of Mosavat himself. He had published an article titled 'How is the Shah doing' in his newspaper, *Mosavat*, in which he had directly criticized the Shah, whereupon he had been called to appear in court and his newspaper banned. The play was the first dramatic work to assess critically the situation of journalism and protest against censorship.[28]

Conclusion

In conclusion, I should like to make five points about the playwrights of the constitutional era. Firstly, they wrote in the tradition of social and political criticism of Akhundzadeh and Mirza Aqa Tabrizi, but unlike the earlier writers expanded their perspective to encompass all of society. Moreover, they touched upon a certain number of problems which their predecessors had either not noticed or not been able to express. Secondly, they did not approach dramatic works in artistic or technical terms. For them, plays were an instrument which could be used to engage in social relations criticism. Thirdly, they succeeded in gaining an extensive audience comprising members of the elite, intellectuals, and ordinary people by performing their plays or publishing them as independent books or as *feuilletons* in the press. Fourthly, the function of drama changed. Before the constitutional era, some traditional plays and a few comedies by Molière had been performed at Court, but after the constitutional revolution the staging of plays at the house of Zahir al-Dowleh brought about two changes: the Court lost its monopoly, and people no longer viewed drama as mere entertainment, realizing that plays could be used to analyse social relations. Fifthly, while the playwrights succeeded in laying bare what ailed Iranian society, they were not able to suggest remedies. They took the first steps, and for that they deserve our respect.

CHAPTER 15

National Identity and Photographs of the Constitutional Revolution

Reza Sheikh

> Beyond style and technique, the images become and reflect figures from our collective imaginary history, a history constructed from empathy and identification with the portrait subjects and that same instinctual desire to partake of the records of a past.
>
> John Bloom[1]

It has become widely accepted that the contemporary concept of the 'Iranian nation' took root during the years of the Constitutional Revolution. Iranian photography arrived at a turning point in its history during this period and for the first time 'the man on the street' found his face registered and disseminated within public visual space next to the faces of the elite in unprecedented numbers. This chapter is concerned with the visual aspects of the historiogra-

تولد ملت ایران

12. 'Birth of the Iranian Nation', Photographer: Hojjat Sepahvand, *E'temad-e Melli* Daily Journal, no. 132, 16 July 2006.

phy of this period and the concept of 'identity' as an extension of 'image' when applied to the particular genre of photographic portraiture, which was the dominating genre. The photographs of this period became icons of 'self-image' for the individual and collectively, they played a decisive role in the consolidating of the 'national self-image' whose latent effect can be detected to this day. Just as the common Iranian's 'awakening' found a place within the narratives of history recounted by Nazem al-Eslam Kermani[2] at first and years later by Kasravi,[3] the man in the background wrote his micro-history in the form of poems on photographs and messages on postcards which have reached us today. This chapter intends to expound upon how the Constitutional Revolution was visually recorded and remembered during the last two decades of Qajar rule as the watershed archive of what has been handed on to later generations.

Following a brief introduction on the evolution of photographic portraiture in Iran as the medium became public through a trickle-down process from within the walls of the royal palaces and houses of the elite, we embark on the task of trying to piece together the puzzle of how the image of a nation was formed in the minds of the contemporaries of the Constitutional Revolution through the medium of the photograph. The argument that is set forth in the following paragraphs therefore concentrates on publicized photographs. In order to avoid bias in our selection of such photographs, three photo collections that were assembled by contemporaries within the time frame of this study, along with a random set of inscribed photographs from the same period and the first photographically illustrated book on the revolution, have been consulted and are described here separately for the reader. With these photographs in mind, I engage in a conceptual discussion of how Iranians, from the elite to the less educated, 'saw the Iranian nation' during and in the aftermath of the Constitutional Revolution, the emphasis being on the revisiting process and the temporal distance of the viewer from the actual event itself.

Photographs and National Identity

National identity is a difficult subject to tackle. It is neither fixed in time nor grounded in a fixed set of perceptions assembled within a fixed period of time. It is a concept with ill-defined boundaries, a fuzzy notion that dwells in the human mind; a terrain which evades precise cartography. It can be narrated according to the political discourse of those in power or the particular thesis of a scholar who is mapping his way through this maze. In essence, this chapter is an *inquiry* into that part of the construct of national identity which is image-based, particularly the mental image of 'nation' that finds expression in photographs.[4] I am not seeking the 'Iranianness' or the 'Englishness' of a photograph, but rather what roles a photograph and the act of photography can play in forming national identity.

I would like to stress the word inquiry, as this is a work in progress and part of a greater picture. Iran has a history of photography that spans over a century and a half: over 60 years of Qajar rule,[5] the entire 53 years of Pahlavi rule, and 30 years since the Islamic Revolution. Iranian national identity has evolved during this period, and so has the role played by the photograph and film within this sphere. By focusing on photographs of the constitutional period we are concentrating on the last 25 years of Qajar rule. There is, however, more to this argument than mere historical chronology. If we are to speak of photographs and *national* identity, we must focus on those photographs that have found their way into the public domain or visual space, which again leads us, from a different direction, to the last 25 years (1900–25) of Qajar rule. Even though revisiting the photographs is a process that goes on to this day, it will, however, be shown below that the last quarter century of Qajar rule is indeed the most pertinent to our discussion.

This was a period where new concepts and notions were being injected into the vocabulary of Iranians: *Iran* (rather than *mamalek-e mahruseh-ye Iran*); *melli, mellat,* and specifically *mellat-e Iran; dowlat, qanun, haqq/hoquq, mosavat, azadi* and *horriyyat, vakil,* and *majles.* These are words that represent concepts that people hear and/or read. A photograph helps them to *see*. It juxtaposes an image next to a concept. Shahrokh Meskub argued that in order for

> a group of dispersed and scattered people to *acquire a face* and to feel common feelings and as such *acquire a body* (become organic) – to become a *mellat* – there is no better device than language, though it is not the only tool which can be instrumental in shaping a nation. Next to folklore, myths, and religion there are the arts: dance, painting, sculpture, architecture ... however as Muslims, other than in architecture, Iranians were deprived of these tools to create and establish their national identity through such media.[6]

The Persian words he used fit very well the notion of placing an image on national identity: *suratmand va andamvar nemudan* – for the nation 'to acquire a face and a body' respectively.

There was and is, however, the agency of the photograph, whose relatively massive proliferation in Iran coincided with the constitutional period and which has not received proper attention by the scholars in the field. An additional (remarkable) nuance is that the dominating genre of photography throughout the Qajar period was portraiture. We are thus brought immediately to the doorsteps of self/group image and representation through the photography of the period. Basically, the ritual of a 'knowing sitter and a purposeful cameraman'[7] was repeated at length in and outside the photographic studio all across the country during this period.[8] Portrait photographs, if examined individually, are physical records of framed identity. If examined as a whole within a specific time frame or a historical period, they can place an image on a social class or even a nation.[9] This conjecture can be grounded in portrait photographs of the Qajar elite in the mid-nineteenth century, where each picture stands as a representation of the self-image of the human subject matter in an age where the camera was still an oddity, and to be photographed was a ritual that bestowed recognition. We see that the self-identity of this privileged class evolved, from being eclipsed by the virtual presence of the monarch when these elite Iranians were ordered to pose for the Court photographer within the royal atelier ('*Akkaskhaneh-ye mobarakeh*, see Figure 13, ca. 1865), to soliciting the services of a photographer in a public studio (Figure 14, ca. 1875), culminating in group photographs to commemorate a rise in status recognized by officialdom (Figure 15, 'Syndicate of Merchants', ca. 1885).

13. Posing for the Court photographer.

14. Photography in a public studio.

15. Syndicate of Merchants.

National identity invokes collective historical consciousness; therefore underlying all that is stated here is the notion of how history is recorded through photographs. During the constitutional period Iranians found themselves on the public stage in unprecedented numbers and photographers were there to record this mass upstage: from the early excitement and curiosity of appearing in front of the lens as a group during the sit-ins (Figure 16, grounds of British legation in Tehran 1906), to purposefully posing as individuals rebelling against the monarch – the erstwhile Pivot of the Universe, *qebleh-ye 'alam* (Figure 17, Tabriz resistance to Mohammad Ali Shah's coup 1907), and finally early manifestations of civil society institutions (Figure 18, ca. 1915).[10]

16. A group during the sit-ins.

17. Tabriz resistance to Mohammad Ali Shah's coup.

18. Early manifestations of civil society institutions.

As these photographs entered the public visual space and as Iranians revisited them through the years, they assisted them as a 'nation' to acquire a face and a body. Our inquiry is a revisiting process on its own that is taking place a century after that seminal period in modern Iranian history. The challenge lies in trying to piece together the puzzle of how 'the nation' was seen through the eyes of those who lived through the events during the time when the concept of 'nation' itself was taking root within the Iranian collective conscience.

The Photographs

Portrayal of the history of photography is as much a conceptual exercise as it is a chronological one.[11] Our inquiry is of the first kind. Within this realm, it is therefore of the utmost importance not to impose present-day interpretations upon photographs from the past. There is always the risk of 'selecting' photographs, 'connecting' photographs to concepts, 'reading' photographs according to pre-conceived notions and pre-formulated hypotheses, resulting in what Carlo Ginzburg calls 'physiognomic' readings.[12] The challenge is thus not to rummage through photographs of the past only to select and to link images to ideas we have conceived today.

How, then, are we to research the photographs of the constitutional era in order to find the answer to our main question of how (if at all) these photographs have affected Iranian national identity? The answer lies in photo collections that have reached us intact from some time in the past. Five sets of photographs constitute the photographic image base of this chapter, and I have assigned a name to each collection. The first four of these five sets are: (a) four photo albums (*One Hundred Days of Dar al-Fonun*) containing nearly 400 photographs, submitted by Yahya Dowlatabadi to the First Universal Congress of Races (1911) in London; (b) a collection of nearly 200 postcards sent to Istanbul by a Turkish merchant residing in Tehran ca. 1915 (*Merchant of Istanbul*); (c) a photo album (*Curio Shopping*) bought in Tehran in 1912, comprising 'popular' themes depicted in 100 photographs; and (d) a set of popular photographs carrying inscriptions (ca. 1915), which I randomly compiled and have called *Loss, Despair, and Nostalgia*. Most of the photographs of the constitutional period that have reached us today through public channels or private collections have 'messages' inscribed upon them. Many have been published in books with the inscriptions. The collection of inscribed photographs gives us a trace of a revisiting process, a glimpse into the interaction of the public with the event as they look back in time. The fifth set comprises the photographs published in Ahmad Kasravi's illustrated book on the Constitutional Revolution that was published thirty years after the event, a collection I have entitled *The Man in the Background*. Kasravi's work was the first determined effort by a scholar to combine first-hand text and photographs (scholastic revisiting) in order to document the event after a considerable passage of time.

Ultimately, as we trace the common thread through these photo collections, we construct an archive of publicized images which entered the Iranian public visual space after the Constitutional Revolution, thus contributing to the visual memory of the 'nation'. The five sets of photographs are presented below. A brief enumeration of the photographs in the two sets of photo albums is presented separately in the annex. It is recommended that the reader take the time to read this list. It will be an exercise in revisiting through words rather than images.

One Hundred Days of Dar al-Fonun

The First Universal Congress of Races was convened in London in the summer of 1911. Yahya Dowlatabadi was invited to represent Iran in the conference. Back home, the Second Majles had been inaugurated, and Naser al-Molk was the regent as the child king Ahmad Shah was being groomed for his coronation at a later date. The exiled Mohammad Ali Shah was making one last attempt to regain his throne by attacking Iran from the Caspian, for which endeavour he had obtained the support of his brother, Salar al-Dowleh, who was launching raids into Kurdistan. Dowlatabadi presented an article and a showcase of four photo albums containing nearly 400 photographs.[13] His memoirs indicate that he had spent 100 days at Dar al-Fonun to write his paper and gather his photographs.[14] Some of the photographs were from the Dar al-Fonun photo archive, but the majority had to be collected from outside photographers. He went to great lengths to collect data, photographs, and information from around the country. The four albums are presently archived at the Majles Library in Tehran.[15]

Though the Constitutional Revolution was not the main topic of Dowlatabadi's presentation, the social upheavals accompanying it were the main theme of both the text and the photographs. Dowlatabadi had given names to each of the four albums, which carried around one hundred photographs each:[16]

a. Monarchs, elite, and a number of public buildings (*salatin, rejal va ba'zi banaha-ye dowlati*)
b. Some of the provinces, public goods, industries, and such like (*ba'zi ayalat, favayed-e 'ammeh, sanaye' va gheyreh*)
c. Holy sites and ancient relics (*amkaneh-ye moqaddaseh va asar-e qadimi*)
d. The constitution, the government, and the sciences (*mashruteh, nezam, va ma'aref*) (Figures 19 and 20, ca. 1910).[17]

19. & 20. The constitution, the government, and the sciences.

What 'image of Iran' comes through these categorized photographs? The *history* of Iran is depicted through the holy sites and ancient relics, along with the chronology of monarchs since the Safavid period. The *people* of Iran find exposure through numerous photographs of the *mojahedin* (Figure 21, 1908) in a separate category that also includes the political elite (prime ministers, ministers, and members of parliament) and monarchs: a category in which there is no overbearing presence of a king or, for that matter, any figure. The *country* of Iran is depicted through photographs of natural settings and cities. While palaces are presented as public buildings, public goods and industries are seen in the form of bridges, a few factories, and the only railway line then operating, which ran south from Tehran to the shrine of Shah 'Abd al-'Azim.

Preparing an album of photographs is a selection process. The question is: what photographs were not selected? The deserts, the man on the street going about his daily life, his simple adobe dwellings, the bazaar and its winding alleys, the citadel and moat of Tehran, the tribal men and their way of life, and women with their *hejab*. Dowlatabadi is thus presenting an (his) ideal image of Iran: the location of Iran is pristine and abundant; the people are united, having made sacrifices and having risen to obtain their rights; the political elite are charismatic and possess poise; the King and his Crown Prince are young and innocent; the government is standing firm, and the Majles is there to be reckoned with.

21. The *mojahedin*.

The Merchant of Istanbul[18]

Souvenir of Iran (*yadegar-e Iran*), souvenir of the Constitutional Revolution (*yadegar-e mashruteh*), souvenir of Tehran, Rasht, Anzali, or even '*Ashura* (the tenth of the month of Muharram, the day of Imam Husayn's martyrdom in Kerbala in 680 CE), these were the words inscribed in Ottoman Turkish on many of the postcards sent home by a Turkish merchant residing in Tehran around 1910. He repeatedly instructed the recipient to preserve the postcards, as he intended to publish a book upon his return. Clearly, he was impressed by the range of images and the fact that at the time they were the only sources of images of Iran of their kind in the world. There is much information that can be extracted from these short communications, this self-contained collection of postcards and these micro-historical records of an ordinary man in the wake of the turbulent times of modern Iranian history. We, however, will concentrate on the photographs, which became postcards.

The postcard industry took root in Iran within the last 25 years of Qajar rule, with a strong market being established as of 1910.[19] There is, however, something atypical and peculiar (within the tradition of the industry) about Iranian postcards of this period. While a wide range of images, such as cityscapes (Figure 22) and what may be categorized as ethnographic documentation (Figure 23), were printed on postcards, a vast majority carry photographs of the events of the constitutional period (Figures 24 and 25).

Téhéran, Boulevard Chamsol-Emaret.

22. Postcard of an Iranian streetscape.

23. Ethnographic documentation as shown in a postcard.

24. & 25. Postcards showing events of the constitutional period.

The postcards carry informal handwritten Persian inscriptions and/or formal Persian, French, or Russian captions. There appears to have been no selection process, and all available photographs were deemed fit to be turned into postcards. Photographs from the Tabriz siege, many of which were smuggled out and found their way to Europe during the actual blockade, are particularly prominent.[20] Setting aside monetary compensation, the main reason may have been that postcards were the only medium available to photographers to expose their photographs. A very limited number of the few journals that existed printed photographs; those which did were Persian newspapers printed outside of Iran, which carried a single photograph on the front page. There was also a market for and therefore a demand to see the images of the recent events: the violence and the protagonists.[21] Most of the photographs of the constitutional events selected by Dowlatabadi for his aforementioned four photo albums can also be found as postcards. Indeed, not only did these postcards taken as a whole give public exposure to the images, they also became a venue of 'preservation' for future generations. The fact is that many of the photographs from this period that have been available to the public to this date have been in the form of postcards. Through the years, the rare books (including that of Kasravi) that have actually printed photographs of the period have also used these postcards.

Curio Shopping[22]

In terms of shape and size, this is a photo album like any other. The inscription on the opening page indicates that it was 'bought in Tehran 1332 (HG)' [1912]. Each page carries one photograph that has been fixed in place with photo corners. Interestingly, most are albumin prints, a printing technique outdated in Europe by then. Many are photographs of photographs, which is an indication of a concerted activity of amassing an image bank and selling it to a paying public.

There are nearly 180 photographs. We may group them into the following categories: (a) portraits of Iranian kings, (b) portraits of 'celebrities' (Figure 26, Talebov ca. 1910), (c) people and events of the Constitutional Revolution (Figure 27, public hanging in Tabriz carried out by the Russians on 'Ashura 1911), and (d) portraits of women (identified by name) as 'objects of desire'.

Loss, Despair, and Nostalgia

What are the reasons for writing on photographs? Depending on the text, it could be for the purpose of setting the date of the event depicted, identifying those photographed, explaining the context within which the photograph was

26. Talebov ca. 1910.

27. Public hanging in Tabriz carried out by the Russians on *'Ashura* 1911.

taken, or invoking a feeling. Many of the photographs of the constitutional period that have reached us today are inscribed. People and events have been identified, while verses of poetry are also prominent and are commonly used to invoke feelings of loss, despair, and nostalgia. These words are the handprints of a public that is reaching out to a momentous event in the past. This is no longer *taking* pictures, it is *making* an image. In making the image we are revisiting the picture, revisiting the event and leaving a trace of oneself interacting with one's past. Below are a select number of such inscribed photographs:

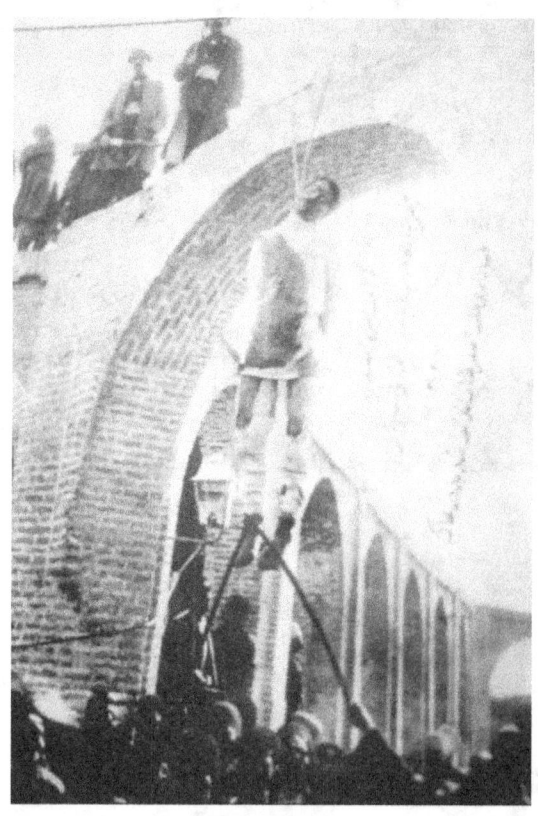

28. (1907)[23]

چه خوب ایندم خود را بر سردار فنا دیدم
خود را سربلند و عالمی را زیر پا دیدم
یک آزادی طلب ۲ صفر ۱۳۲۷ طناب انداخته شد بدون محاکمه

29. (ca. 1910 date of collage, photo in circulation since 1906)²⁴

این نقش وجود تو که در اینورق است
جانیست که آرایش این ما خلق است
عکس رخ تست تافته در عالم
زین است که جمله عالم اندر شفق است

30. (1907)²⁵

خواهی که دادت بر درد صد سلسله بیداد را
منت بکش گردن زنجیر استبداد را

31. (ca 1915)[26]

این سرکه نشانه سرپرستی است
امروز رها زقید هستی است
با دیده عبرتش ببینید
این عاقبت وطن پرستی است

32. (date of collage ca. 1915)[27]

اولین رجال با سیاست و آگاه کنندگان ملت و شهدای راه حریت و مجاهدان طریق انسانیت

Malek al-Shoʻara Bahar wrote these verses during the first constitutional period:

شاه مست و میرمست و شحنه مست وشیخ مست
مملکت رفته زدست
زین سیه مستان به هر سو فتنه و غوغا بپاست
کار ایران با خداست

The inscriptions depict a sense of chaos and loss of control, a state of affairs which has come about because of the 'drunken behaviour' of the King and his entourage, and consequently 'the country is lost and it is only left to God to help'. This overall sense of despair and disillusionment, which is reflected on the inscribed photographs, is repeated throughout the period, in particular during the last decade of Qajar rule, as the country slipped further into chaos after the beginning of the First World War. When juxtaposed, text and photographs combine the linguistic and iconic messages to create a final image, which in the words of Roland Barthes carries its own 'rhetoric'.[28] Each image thus needs to be treated separately, but for the most part the rhetoric is that of commemoration, protest, or defiance.

The Man in the Background

Nazem al-Eslam Kermani began publishing his records of the events leading to the Constitutional Revolution in the immediate aftermath of the victory of the *mojahedin* and the exile of Mohammad Ali Shah (1909). He called his work *Tarikh-e bidari-ye iraniyan* (The History of the Awakening of Iranians), publishing it in the form of weekly newsletters with the aim of introducing the main protagonists.[29] It is not astonishing that these newsletters did not carry any photographs, a feature they shared with the majority of the secret pamphlets and newspapers of the time. As mentioned above, those newspapers which did print photographs were published outside of the country and at most had one picture on the front page. Caricatures and hand-painted lithographs filled this image vacuum in the print media. After a 30-year lull in the historiography of the events, Kasravi stepped forward with his book entitled *Tarikh-e mashruteh-ye Iran* (History of the Iranian Constitution).[30] His professed aim was 'to make sure the real protagonists were not forgotten and due credit was given to all the anonymous *mojahedin* who through enormous sacrifice stood up for their rights and the rights of the nation.'[31] Kasravi used 284 portrait photographs in his attempt to place a face on as many protagonists as possible. This book is the only book on the Constitutional Revolution to this date that has made use of such a wealth of images.[32]

Kasravi was 16 years old during the siege of Tabriz.[33] He was in his early- to mid-forties when he began working on his book. Many of his readers, like Kasravi himself, had vivid memories of the Constitutional Revolution. Their response to the first edition of his book was to supply him with photographs, newspaper clippings, and relevant dossiers.[34] *Tarikh-e mashruteh-ye Iran* was published during the last years of Reza Shah's rule (1935), a time when nearly two decades of concerted effort by the government to depoliticize the population had left the 'awakened Iranians' numb. It became the most popular history book in Iran. Over the span of 25 years prior to the Islamic Revolution, more than 13 editions were published. In a country where there is no copyright, the photographs published by Kasravi became the main source of images for other authors through the years.

As Kasravi oscillates in his story between the national and local spheres, the non-celebrity and local actors and stakeholders take the front seat, and it is their photographs that abound in this book. As an eyewitness to the events in Tabriz, and with his particular literary pen and historiography, Kasravi was instrumental in immortalizing the Constitutional Revolution as a 'popular movement'. His use of portrait photographs was instrumental in this endeavour. The poor quality of the printed photographs did not do justice to his valiant goal, yet the final effect is a fuzzy image bank of faces and names of individuals who would otherwise have been lost to the passage of time, illustrating his intention to demonstrate that the revolution was indeed borne on the shoulders of the common man – from the back alleys of cities to the battlefields, by men who went from a normal life one day (as depicted by studio photographs) to toting guns the next.

The Final Image

The nature of the photographic medium is such that it lends itself to multiplication and circulation. If there is a demand, photographs will find a way to become public, and as such, photographs of any period have dynamics of their own within the recipient society. The photographs of the constitutional period are the first vestiges of photo documentation in Iran that was carried out spontaneously and without a royal decree.[35] Photographers with no previous experience within this domain of photography left their props and the controlled environment of their studios to capture the unfolding events on the streets. One of the direct outcomes of this focused drive to capture 'reality' was that the ordinary man was photographed, and thus the 'Iranian masses' were visually born. Later, as an archive was amassed, the photographs found their way to the public. Two distinct reasons for public exposure (two specific uses) of these photographs can be pinpointed:

a. evidential: used as documents / visual evidence / journalism
b. economic: supply of the pictures as a commodity to meet public demand (for those who could afford it).

Books, newspapers, calendars, flyers, and mounted individual photographs are objects that can be collected, handled, and passed on from one hand to another. The pictures that were popular or perhaps became popular because of increased exposure through their printing as common items were of 'celebrities':[36] Abbas Aqa Tabrizi (alive in the studio and then as a dead body stretched on the pavement after his fatal shooting of Amin al-Soltan), Mirza Reza Kermani (the assassin of Naser al-Din Shah), Seyyed Jamal al-Din Afghani, the three clergymen of Najaf who endorsed the movement, Sattar Khan and Baqer Khan, Ayatollahs Tabataba'i and Behbahani; and portraits of martyrs: shackled activists and members of parliament awaiting their sentence on the grounds of Mohammad Ali Shah's palace, Sur-e Esrafil, Malek al-Motekallemin, Seyyed Jamal al-Din Va'ez, Mirza Kuchik Khan Jangali, Mohammad Taqi Khan Pesiyan. The poster and postcard of members of the First Majles (all in one picture) and the photograph of the signed constitution in the hands of famous merchants in Tehran are also among the pictures that found greater circulation. There are also a great number of photographs depicting scenes of violence, including dead bodies of reactionaries strewn on the battlefield or hanging from scaffolds after the surrender of Tehran to the constitutionalists in 1909. The photographs that found the widest exposure were those of the victors, i.e., the constitutionalists, while the vanquished royalists were rarely depicted.

The collections examined in this chapter can shed light on the dynamics of the exposure of the constitutional photographs over the course of time. Dowlatabadi represented a class of intellectuals who were active in the movement from the early days (though he was less directly involved during the second constitutional period). His selection of photographs as evidence of the what, where, and who of the events, for an educated foreign audience that was keenly aware of the revolution, is a direct manifestation of the state of mind of this influential group of Iranians. The importance of this representational activity is further magnified when one considers the fact that this elite group was responsible for promoting the national discourse at the outset of the movement, which led to the official recognition and inscription of the term 'Iranian nation' within the constitutional law. His idealized photographic representation of Iran, when juxtaposed with his memoirs (as he travels outside the country and returns) and the article presented at the congress, acutely underlines the 'distance' between his mental image (desire) and the reality on the ground – a predicament which continues to haunt many Western-educated Iranian intellectuals to this day as they travel from the West to Iran, from the centre to the periphery.

The collection of postcards and the photo album are commodities sold on the market. While postcards became collectables, many of the same photographs were printed and pasted in albums and sold that way. The juxtaposition of the photographs of women as objects of desire with those of the constitutional events has concocted a strange amalgam of images. However, it is vivid evidence of the types of images that were in demand by the public who had the means to purchase. If stripped to their bare essence, they are images of celebrities, violence, and sex.

The collection of inscribed photographs is a corner of this market. It is evidence of how the public absorbed, felt, and chose to remember the events in the wake of the tumultuous years of 1905–09. The photographs fall within the realm of solidarity and empathy, where emotions combine with imagination to create objects that are reflective of the public's recently acquired self-image. This is an image that is not eclipsed by that of the *qebleh-ye 'alam*, the Pivot of the Universe. The photographs are of new faces risen to the forefront, crowding the public visual space.

A comparison of the collections discussed above indicates that they all carry several similar photographs, either originals, copies, or postcards (see the annex). It appears that most of the photographs of the constitutional period have reached us today and that practically all have received public exposure. Postcards played a key role in 'preserving' the images by keeping a tangible trace of events (in the form of an object) within the reach of the public. Perhaps they played their most crucial role during the strict Reza Shah era, when they kept memories alive 'unofficially', while in the possession of individuals and families.

The social tremors and movements which came to be known as the Iranian Constitutional Revolution took place in the years 1905 to 1909. In London in 1911, Dowlatabadi exposed to the world an ideal image of Iran and Iranians in photographs, while presenting a more critical image in words in the form of an article. Back home, around the same time, a public interested in purchasing photographs found a market of postcards and photo albums at its disposal in the main cities of the country. Revisiting the events through these images at this point in time is basically reliving the events.

Within the next 15 years, up to the change in dynasty in 1925, as the country reeled further and further into chaos, portrait photographs played their most elemental role as souvenir objects and agents of commemoration for an increasing number of city dwellers. Chronologically and from a photohistorical vantage point, the last decade of Qajar rule coincided with the early years of the popularization of the photographic medium among Iranians.[37] With the increasing threat of disintegration of the country, the national discourse (as spelled out in the newspapers) changes from nation-building to nation-saving, to be carried out by a 'benevolent dictator'. Fifteen years later, the *Tarikh-e mashruteh-ye Iran* broke the silence and the public was reminded of the revolution. Thirty-five years had passed. From here on revisiting became an exercise in distinguishing between myth and memory. I resort to the American novelist and photographer Wright Morris to describe this mental journey:

> I ... press my nose to memory's glass to see more clearly, the remembered image grows more elusive like the details of a pointillist painting. I recognize it, more than I see it. The recognition is a fabric of emotion, as immaterial as music. In this defect of memory do we have the emergence of imagination? If we remembered both vibrantly and accurately – a documentary image rather than an impression – the imaginative faculty would be blocked, lacking the stimulus to fill in what is empty or create what is missing. ... Precisely where memory is frail and emotion is strong, imagination takes fire.[38]

As such, the fuzzy and at times out-of-focus photographs in Kasravi's book are brought into focus in the readers' mind, as they are juxtaposed with the images induced by the depiction of events in different literary sources and texts, while complemented by other photographs seen elsewhere.

For a photograph to illustrate certain passages in a text satisfactorily, it needs to adjoin the text, so that the eye takes in the words and then moves to the visual image which confirms or amplifies the sense. This is not the case with most of the photographs in Kasravi's book. 'Even if a photograph can play second fiddle to the text, the relationship between words and image is seldom that simple.'[39] Kasravi's book can be viewed as a kind of biography of the men in the background of group portraits, a narrative of the common soldier on the battlefield rather than only on captains and generals. As a biographer, Kasravi needed every trace of the real that he could find.[40] Barthes in addressing the synergy between text and photograph referred to the dual function of the 'linguistic message', which he categorized as 'anchorage' and 'relay'.[41] Kasravi's use of photographs and their captions is of the first kind, which is the most frequent function (while the inscribed photographs are of the second kind): it is most commonly found in press photographs and advertisements. The majority of the photographs do not appear on cue. They are inserted with a delay, or at random, or modifying or fine-tuning the reader's mental image of the events that are being depicted by the text. The fact that all the photographs are portrait photographs, fixed single appearances, amplifies the sense that the Constitutional Revolution was indeed the revolution of the common man.[42] For a culture that has always been preoccupied with the notion of martyrdom and for Kasravi's readers who are looking back in time, these 'portrait photographs are not only reminders of death but are, in their arrested movement, or even in a succession which conveys movement, death itself.'[43]

From a present-day vantage point, the photographs of the Constitutional Revolution ultimately do not undermine the historical text on the subject. They clearly are evidence of the popular nature of the movement.

The Final Word

We began this article by posing a question that was to form the thrust of this inquiry: What role can a photograph and the act of photography play in forming national identity? This is a general question that can be grounded in different cultures and nations. Our inquiry is not yet at the stage where we could disengage our answer from the locality where the grounding occurs and pronounce universal observations. What follows is an attempt to evaluate the above Iranian case study.

It is very difficult to assess the extent of dissemination of the constitutional photographs during the later years of Qajar rule. Over two-thirds of the Iranian population lived in rural areas as villagers or tribesmen during this period. Tehran, Tabriz, Kerman, Shiraz, Isfahan, Rasht, and Mashhad were the main urban centres, with Tabriz having the greatest population – over 300,000. The prevailing issues of economics, available technology, and sheer logistics at the time are the constraining factors which prevent us from delving into arguments about photographs and their effect on visual culture in Iran during the last two decades of Qajar rule. If we cannot speak of a visual culture, we can, however, assess the collective power and representational value of the assembled set of photographs that addressed the whole of society.

The Constitutional Revolution in Iran democratized photographic portraiture and as such inaugurated a period dominated by portrait photographs. It gave the people a new way of seeing themselves, 'the response to which was primarily individual as long as the photographs remained private'.[44] Viewing a portrait photograph triggers a personalized response. Looking into the eyes of the subject of a portrait taken within the context of an historical event involving a group of people with a common past unleashes a sense of common identification. The function of these portrait photographs within the public domain appears to have been symbolic. As these photographs could not have been detached from the constitutional events, neither then nor now, the viewer responds more directly to the images than to the subjects themselves (who are not present or no longer living). As such the value attached to the subject of a portrait is often transferred to the photograph itself in a way that allows the photograph not only to reflect attitudes or feelings but to affect them in terms of what we see and *how* we see it.[45]

Within this realm, if we are to take the Iranian nation as our overarching concept (symbol), the photographs of the constitutional period:

a. were iconoclastic, contributing to the decline of the royal image through the flooding of the public visual space with images of mass protests and rebellious plebeians (*ro'aya*);
b. promoted new icons: in the absence of long-standing institutions, men and their actions became the subject matter of history, aspirations find human embodiments, and portrait photographs became ideals objectified;
c. reinforced a sense of the ideal through a black-and-white world of good versus evil;
d. placed a face and a body on new concepts and protagonists; and
e. immortalized a sense of 'struggle' by highlighting the sacrifices, violence, destruction, and commemorating the 'martyrs'.

Furthermore, within the nation-building paradigm, and underlying it all, is the actual *act of photography* and the partaking in the purposeful ritual of being photographed that contributes to the mental visualization of the nation: *taking* photographs and *making* photographs of a *nation*, interacting with images – selecting, retouching, creating photo collages, exposing photographs through different media, and finally *revisiting* the past through the agent of a photograph.

The so-called 'nation-building project', which began with the constitutional period in Iran and was promoted by the leaders and intellectual elite of the movement, along with the photographic documentation that occurred in parallel and spontaneously, were both city-based phenomena. The photographs of this period may not have reached the whole country, but they succeeded in connecting with the city audience and the interlocutors in the prevailing discourse. With the changing discourse of nationalism that accompanied the rise of the Pahlavi dynasty, photographs assumed a new and different role in promoting the new identity and image of the 'new nation'.[46] The photographs of the constitutional era were sidetracked in the process, until Kasravi published his book. However, by then the 'constitutional movement' no longer constituted the cornerstone of Iranian national identity.[47]

In his treatment and critique of text that narrates a nation, Homi Bhabha emphasizes its temporal dimension. He clearly states that a 'focus on temporality resists the transparent linear equivalence of event and idea that historicism proposes; it provides a perspective on the disjunctive forms of representation that signify a people, nation, or a national culture.'[48] I propose that photographs can be treated as one such disjunctive form of representation and that they can 'concretize and make visible the national time'.[49] If we consider possessing a common historical consciousness to be a pillar of national identity, then photographs, by entering the public visual space, help delineate 'national time-space and nation space'[50] simultaneously. The visualization of time rather than photographs must have been on Bhabha's mind when he so eloquently stated that 'The recurrent metaphor of landscape as the inscape of national identity emphasizes the quality of light, the question of social visibility, the power of the eye to naturalize the rhetoric of national affiliation and its form of collective expression.'[51] Yet, photographs are agents of visualization and can be treated as such when we are concerned with the spatialization of historical time in confronting national identity.

Within the discourse of nation-building, photographs have a lifespan of their own. As the discourse changes, so does the functional value of the photographs within that realm. What is unique about the photography of the constitutional period is that it was carried out spontaneously and that the eventual public exposure did not follow an agenda, as opposed to what transpired in later years and has continued to this day in Iran.[52] The power of the stark reality of the sudden changes depicted by these photographs was confined to the eye of the beholder, and their effect on Iranian national identity at the time was thus very straightforward and direct: as portrait photographs of the protagonists of the movement, they simply became the portrait of 'Iran and Iranians'. Within the national landscape, the *pictures stood for these words*, nothing more, nothing less. They gave the nation a face and a body, while the stage was the country.[53] However, the image was that of protest, defiance, sacrifice, and violence cloaked within an aura of loss, despair, and a sense of failed ideals. It was within these circumstances that the Iranian nation found its visual birth through the agent of portrait photographs.

At the crossroads of the macro and the micro stand the Iranians who look back at their history and, depending on their position on the timeline extending from the events that structure their history, respond to the photographs differently. There is a sense of immediacy in photographs which dissipates with time, while direct identification with the subject matter gives way to empathy and emotional resonance. Since national identity is in essence a conceptual phenomenon and thus susceptible to images, the act of revisiting historical events through photographs plays a very significant role in either forming or fortifying our mental images of concepts – images that have formed in our minds about a common history through other means: our storytelling, readings, or public education. Those who stand in front of photographs of the Constitutional Revolution in a gallery in Tehran today (Figure 12, beginning of chapter) possess a notion of the event in their mind. Revisiting through photographs triggers a cycle of seeing, connecting, empathizing, resonating, and finally fortifying the original notion by filling the gaps with imagination.

On the occasion of the centennial of the Constitutional Revolution, commemorative events took place and conferences were held within and outside Iran. In the months running up to the centennial, Iranian newspapers dedicated entire sections to that auspicious day in midsummer. So I ask: why do Iranians continue to feel empathy for those faces? Could it be that they are still striving for the same ideals? Or is it that the photographs symbolize the concept of struggle: (in this case) the struggle for rights and justice, which is simultaneously a key concept engrained in their national identity as Iranians and a universal and timeless discourse, no matter what the prevailing national discourse may be and no matter where the nation stands on the face of this earth.

Annex: List of the photographs in each of the two sets of photo albums

1. The four albums of Yahya Dowlatabadi

a. Monarchs, the elite, and a number of public buildings (*salatin, rejal va ba'zi banaha-ye dowlati*): Shah Tahmasb and Shah Abbas; Nader Shah and Karim Khan Zand; all of the Qajar monarchs; Ahmad Shah and his Crown Prince, Mohammad Hasan Mirza; both regents, namely 'Azod al-Molk and Naser al-Molk; prime ministers such as Amir Kabir and Sepahsalar Tonekaboni; Bakhtiyari tribal leaders; cultural figures like Mo'ayyed al-Eslam, Talebov, Mirza Ali Khan Parvaresh, and Mirza Mahmud Khan Zoka' al-Molk; most of the palaces and few of the houses of the elite.

b. Some of the provinces, public goods, industries and others (*ba'zi ayalat, favayed-e 'ammeh, sanaye' va gheyreh*): waterfalls, springs, rivers, the Alburz mountain range, Mount Damavand, numerous bridges, ancient trees, the Caspian forests, a swan and a porcupine, camels, Za'faranlu and Turkmen tribes, a single photograph of two girls, carpets and jewellery, mosaic and plaster works, rock reliefs, calligraphy and sculptures, vessels, paintings of Kamal al-Molk and Reza Abbasi, a painting of Nader Shah crowning the Indian sultan, Sani' al-Dowleh's textile factory, a soap and perfume factory, the railway from Tehran to Shah 'Abd al-'Azim, a turquoise mine in Khorasan, a French pharmacy on Lalehzar Avenue in Tehran, and scenes of the cities of Qom, Qazvin, and Barforush (present-day Babol).

c. Holy sites and ancient relics (*amkaneh-ye moqaddaseh va asar-e qadimi*): Persepolis and Taq-e Bostan, mosques, mausoleums, and various shrines (*emamzadeh*) in Tehran, Qom, Qazvin, Khorasan, and Mazandaran.

d. The constitution, the government, and the sciences (*mashruteh, nezam va ma'aref*): Festivities of the first anniversary of the Constitutional Revolution, members of the First Majles, the ceremony of the prime minister, ministers, and the committee of merchants taking the constitution to the Majles, the *mojahedin* of Gilan and Azarbayjan, Sattar Khan and Baqer Khan, Seyyed Jamal al-Din Asadabadi, Tabataba'i, Behbahani, Mirza Malkam Khan, Jahangir Khan Sur-e Esrafil, Malek al-Motekallemin, Seyyed Jamal al-Din Va'ez, the three clergymen from Najaf who endorsed the constitution, Sheykh Fazlollah Nuri, Liakhov and the Cossacks, the entrance to the parliament before and after the bombardment, Mohammad Ali Shah and his entourage after the bombardment, prisoners after the coup held in chains along with Mohammad Ali Shah's inscription cursing and condemning them, the office of the governor of Gilan in Rasht before and after the bombardment, Mohammad Ali Shah's script condemning the constitution, the hanging corpses of those executed, violence in the wars of Azarbayjan, the destruction of buildings, the assassination of Amin al-Soltan, the 'modern' army performing gymnastics and fencing, medical students of Dar al-Fonun, pupils of different schools in Tehran and Qom, Mohammad Shah's decree with regards to sending five students to Europe, the Qur'an, and the mausoleum of Hafez.

2. *The curio photo-album bought in Tehran*

a. Portraits of Iranian kings: drawings of Shah Ismai'l and Shah Abbas, Nader Shah, Karim Khan Zand, Aqa Mohammad Khan Qajar, Fath-'Ali Shah, Abbas Mirza Nayeb al-Saltaneh, Mohammad Shah, and photographs of Qajar rulers from Naser al-Din Shah to Ahmad Shah Qajar and Crown Prince Mohammad Hasan Mirza.
b. Portraits of political celebrities: the regents 'Azod al-Molk and Naser al-Molk, Amin al-Soltan, Bakhtiyari chieftains, Mohammad Vali Khan Tonekaboni, Hoseyn Pasha Khan Amir Bahador, Zell al-Soltan, Kamran Mirza, Sho'a' al-Saltaneh, a few princes, Sattar Khan and Baqer Khan, 'Ala' al-Dowleh, Zahir al-Dowleh, and Talebov (Figure 26, ca. 1910).
c. The Constitutional Revolution: group portraits of *mojahedin* during the siege in Tabriz, *mojahedin* in Kerman and Rasht, upon entry into Tehran, members of the First Majles, Tabataba'i and Behbahani, Abbas Aqa Tabrizi before and after assassinating Amin al-Soltan, Naus (the Belgian Customs Official wearing a turban and posing as a mullah), various scenes of public hangings ranging from Mirza Reza Kermani (assassin of Naser al-Din Shah) through Movaqqar al-Saltaneh and Sheykh Fazlollah Nuri, hung by the *mojahedin* in Tehran, to Saqat al-Eslam in Tabriz hung by the Russians (Figure 27, 1911), beheaded Turkmen, Sur-e Esrafil, Malek al-Motekallemin, Armenian *mojahed*s including Yeprem Khan.
d. Portraits of women: over eighty photographs of 'objects of desire'.

Part V
Transnational Perspectives

CHAPTER 16

Mashrutiyat, Meşrutiyet, and Beyond: Intellectuals and the Constitutional Revolutions of 1905–12

Charles Kurzman

Every country's history is unique. However, not every aspect of every country's history is unique. Only a comparative perspective allows one to distinguish which features of an event such as the Iranian *mashrutiyat* are specific to the country's history and culture, and which are manifestations of broader transnational phenomena. As it happens, a comparative perspective for the *mashrutiyat* was provided by a series of similar events that occurred in a variety of countries during the same time period, beginning with the Russian Revolution of 1905 and continuing with the Second Ottoman Constitutional Revolution of 1908 (known in Turkish as the İkinci Meşrutiyet), the Portuguese Revolution of 1910, the Mexican Revolution of 1910–11, and the Chinese Revolution of 1911–12.[1]

These constitutionalist revolutions underwent parallel trajectories and faced parallel influences from the great powers of the day. In addition, they were organized and led by an emerging class of modern-educated intellectuals that defined itself as distinct from traditional religious scholars. Only in Iran, however, were the intellectuals careful to draw the boundaries of their class broadly enough to include seminarians, identifying themselves as *daneshmandan* rather than using more exclusively Enlightenment-tinged terms such as *'oqala* or *monavvaran al-fekr*. This attempted alliance ultimately fell apart, and by the end of the *mashrutiyat* period intellectuals came to refer to themselves as *monavvaran* and to shut religious scholars out of power.

Parallels

Transnational influences on the Iranian *mashrutiyat* are no secret. Edward G. Browne's classic account, for example, quotes a British diplomat in Tehran as writing that 'the Russian Revolution [of 1905] has had a most astounding effect here. Events in Russia have been watched with great attention, and a new spirit would seem to have come over the people. They are tired of their rulers, and, taking example of Russia, have come to think that it is possible to have another and better form of government.'[2] Mehdi Malekzadeh's account similarly comments, 'The founding of the Duma [parliamentary] assembly in Russia ... was exhilarating good news for Iranians, and the participation of the Russian nation in making its own destiny announced happy news to intellectual Iran.'[3] Iranian constitutionalists themselves spoke openly at the time about the parallels with Russia. To pick just one example, *Habl al-Matin*, the prominent Iranian newspaper, urged Muslims in 1906 to 'adopt the peoples of Russia as a model'.[4]

It is not so widely known that the Russian Revolution of 1905 and the Iranian *mashrutiyat* of 1906 were part of a broader wave of revolutions. Ali Gheissari has translated a highly amusing article which appeared on this subject in 1907 in the satirical Iranian newspaper *Majalleh-ye estebdad* and took the form of a letter from the baby parliament in Iran to his older brother, the Russian Duma, expecting further siblings in other countries. 'I've heard our father ['Edalat al-Dowleh, or State Justice] has recently taken a wife in India as well, and the wife is pregnant. ... Another thing that I've heard is that from India 'Edalat al-Dowleh intends to go to China, [and] I don't know where he will go first, the Ottoman country or China [?], undoubtedly he will not stay [put] in India; I know my father, wherever he goes he takes a wife and as soon as his wife becomes pregnant he leaves that country. [So] if you [happen to] know where he is going after India [please] write to me.'[5] As it turned out, India's *swadeshi* movement of 1905 did not result in major democratic reforms, but the article was accurate in anticipating revolutions in the Ottoman Empire and China. These and similar events encompassed more than a quarter of the world's population by the First World War. International observers at the time noted the flurry of uprisings. V. I. Lenin, the Russian Social Democrat, lumped several of these events together as 'bourgeois-democratic revolutions'; James Bryce, the British liberal, called them misguided attempts to 'set a child to drive a motor car'; British positivists noted that positivism played 'so great a part' in them.[6] In the decades since, however, knowledge of these democratizing experiments has receded and become the province of area specialists. Plenty has been written about the individual cases, but a comparative perspective is rare. Exceptions include works by John Foran, John Mason Hart, Don C. Price, Ivan Spector, and especially Nader Sohrabi – plus Farzin Vejdani's chapter in this volume – which deal with subsets of the constitutional revolutions considered here.[7]

I propose that a comparative perspective is particularly useful for these constitutional revolutions because they constitute a single international event, an interlinked 'wave' of democratization.[8] Moreover, the individual revolutions featured events that were eerily parallel to one another. These parallels set the events apart from other movements of the same period and from later movements of the same type. The specificities of the Iranian *mashrutiyat* stand out against the backdrop of these parallels.

Each of these revolutions of 1905–12 emerged unexpectedly in the context of a long-standing autocracy, though state capacity varied greatly. There were hazy precedents for constitutional governance in all of these countries but Iran: the gentry's provincial parliaments in Russia and China, the Ottoman constitutional interlude of 1876–77, and the corrupt electoral systems of Mexico and Portugal. Still, just a few years prior to the revolution, movements for democratizing reforms could rightly be considered fringe movements – a handful of idealistic activists operating largely underground or in exile, whose dreams of power struck many observers as futile.

The revolutions were triggered by relatively minor events: the shooting of pro-tsar labour demonstrators on Bloody Sunday in early 1905, the bastinado of merchants in Iran, a military investigation into secret societies in Ottoman Rumelia, the theft of a presidential election in Mexico, the assassination of a leading republican in Portugal, a mutiny in Wuchang, China. Yet within a year – within a week in Portugal, within a month in the Ottoman Empire – the autocracy had given way, allowing free elections, free speech, free assembly, and other liberties. Monarchs retained their thrones, at least initially, in Russia, Iran, and the Ottoman Empire; dynasties were ended in Portugal and China; and the Mexican president was chased into exile.

The new regimes all held elections, though with limited suffrage. Women were not permitted to vote in any of these new regimes – just as women were not permitted to vote in countries that were considered democracies at the time, including France, Great Britain, and the United States. These elections were unprecedentedly competitive, if not perfectly free and fair by today's standards, and the parliaments that resulted were unusually diverse and outspoken. At the same time, popular mobilizations surged under the new constitutional order. Strikes broke out in many places, especially in the more industrialized sectors of each country's economy. Agrarian rebels claimed land rights in each country. Popular associations mushroomed, claiming to represent the interests of the masses, by force if necessary: *anjoman*s in Iran, *soviet*s in Russia, multiple local Committees of Union and Progress in the Ottoman Empire, the *Carbonária* in Portugal, the *Porra* in Mexico, secret societies in China. The new regimes all struggled with disorder, and the states failed in numerous instances to uphold the rights and freedoms that they proclaimed. Nevertheless, these interludes represented a distinct break from the practices of the previous regimes, and from the autocratic regimes that would follow them.

The constitutional period did not last long. In Russia, the tsar dismissed the first two parliaments after only a few months each, and then changed the electoral law to ensure a more compliant legislature. In Iran, the first two parliaments were dismissed within two years each. The Ottoman parliament was subdued in less than a year, after the military and the Committee of Union and Progress used the excuse of the '31 Mart' mutiny to march on the capital and declare martial law. Mexico's democratically elected president was ousted in a coup after a year and a half, and the president of China purged the opposition after two years. By the end of 1913, democratic institutions persisted, if feebly, only in Portugal, where they survived several attempted coups before succumbing to fascists in 1926.

In several cases, constitutionalism got a second chance. In Iran, the pro-democracy forces survived the coup of 1908 and managed to retake Tehran in 1909 before parliament was dismissed a second time in 1911. The Mexican pro-democracy movement defeated General Victoriano Huerta in 1914 and held a constitutional convention in 1916–17, but elections were generally manipulated by the ruling party until the late twentieth century. Portuguese democrats withstood an attempted coup in 1915, staging a second revolutionary uprising in May of that year. In Russia, intellectuals led the brief transitional government in 1917 that abolished the monarchy, but this second democratic interlude lasted only a few months before the Bolshevik revolution. The Ottoman Empire witnessed only an isolated instance of democratic competition during a by-election in 1911, which was won by an opposition candidate, and the authoritarian Committee of Union and Progress was temporarily ousted from the cabinet in 1912–13, but this and other changes in government continued to be determined by force rather than democratic procedures. China still has not recovered competitive elections, except on the island of Taiwan.

A second parallel among these revolutions, in addition to their shared trajectories, is the role of the great powers. These constitutional interludes occurred in countries that had not won a war in many years, and during the period of imperial expansion their politics was haunted by the possibility that they might be colonized by European powers, as many of their neighbours had been. This was no idle threat. Months after parliament began to meet in Iran, for example, Britain and Russia agreed to recognize zones of special influence in southern and northern Iran, notifying the Iranian government several weeks later with an understated cover letter: 'I have the honour of sending you the enclosed text of the Agreement of August 18/31, 1907, entered into by Great Britain and Russia, inasmuch as this agreement treats matters that might interest the Persian Government.'[9] Both countries soon sent troops into Iran to protect their special rights.

The great powers were internally conflicted about the new regimes. On the one hand, all of them were flattered by the imitation of their own political systems – except for Russia, a regional power whose monarchy played a consistently reactionary role in neighbouring countries. 'I can't tell you how refreshing it is to hear the Persians [Iranians] talking about their new liberties and the things they are ready to do for their country,' a British diplomat confided to a colleague around the time that the British chargé d'affaires allowed protesters to take sanctuary on legation grounds.[10] In addition, some great-power officials saw economic or geopolitical advantages in supporting democratic reforms. It is worth noting that most of these revolutions relied at least in part on well-timed assistance from one or more great powers: the sit-in at the British legation in Iran, the postponement of loans to the Russian and Chinese governments, the US government's willingness to look the other way while Francisco Madero organized his pro-democracy rebellion from Texas. In Portugal, the British helped the revolution simply by doing nothing, refusing to summon British warships to protect the king of Portugal despite the 'fixed idea at the [Portuguese] Court that if a revolutionary movement were attempted we [British] should intervene.'[11]

On the other hand, government officials in the great powers frequently shared the racist belief that non-Europeans were unsuited for constitutional forms of government. A US official in Iran suggested that 'As a matter of fact, the [Iranian] people are not in a condition to appreciate the benefits of a constitutional form of government, and are much less fit to govern themselves than are the Filipinos.'[12] A US diplomat held that the Chinese 'are not endowed with the intellect to enjoy the blessings of a free government, the principles of which are wholly unknown to the great majority of the people.'[13] The German ambassador in Mexico wrote, 'The cardinal error lies in his [President Madero's] ... belief that he can rule the Mexican people as one would rule one of the more advanced Germanic nations. This raw people of half-savages without religion, with its small ruling stratum of superficially civilized mestizos can live with no regime other than enlightened despotism.' Kaiser Wilhelm of Germany noted in the margin of this last report: 'Right!'[14] British ambassador Arthur Hardinge, who had served in Iran and the Ottoman Empire before coming to Lisbon, described the Portuguese as midway between Iranians and Europeans on the scale of intellectual development: unlike more civilized people, he wrote, the Portuguese tend to be 'inaccurate persons – I have erased a harsher word' (the word 'liars' is crossed out). At the same time, when compared with Iranians, the Portuguese have 'developed a greater appreciation of the merits of strict accuracy', and their behaviour is therefore more culpable than that of 'my Persian friends, whose mendacities were more naive and childlike'. Hardinge characterized the Portuguese as 'not everyday Europeans': 'I believe that if you found yourself face to face with this inert and corrupt mass you would be the first, now and then, to use the goad.'[15] In addition, some great-power officials were hostile to the economic nationalism promised by some constitutionalist leaders.

Great-power policy could go either way, for or against constitutionalism. As a result, politicians on all sides paid almost obsessive attention to slight cues of support from the great powers. For example, British journalists reported snidely that in Iran, 'The educated Nationalists seemed to feel – mistakenly, as time showed – that the issue of the struggle depended neither upon the efforts of the Shah nor upon those of his enemies, but upon the actions of the British and the Russian governments. Wherever one went brilliant talk reigned upon the subtler points of British and Russian diplomacy.'[16] The Russian democracy movement plastered Paris with handbills protesting against a proposed French loan to the tsar; the monarchy had the French government plaster posters over them.[17] In Mexico, the US ambassador got rival military leaders – each in control of hundreds, if not thousands, of troops – to coordinate their coup plans by threatening to bring in a small number of US Marines.[18] In China, constitutionalist forces offered to cede the province of Manchuria to Japan; to adopt Japanese currency for use in China; even, the next year, when their internal support had been destroyed, to be 'Japan's India'.[19] Japan, with the encouragement of Britain, refused to assist them. Instead, Japan participated in the decisive multilateral loan to the new military ruler. The evening that the loan was concluded, opposition leaders searched Beijing for the location of the signing ceremony. They found it, managed to gain entrance, and made a small speech on the unconstitutionality of the loan – all in vain.[20]

Similarly, the anti-constitutionalist forces checked with the representatives of the great powers before they carried out their coups. In Iran, for example, as he undertook his coup in 1908, Mohammad Ali Shah asked the tsar of Russia 'to accept Persia under [his] patronage' and said he considered Iran to be in 'the same relations to Russia as the emir of Bukhara' – that is to say, a semi-colonial relationship.[21] The tsar wrote back noncommittally, but the Russian-controlled Persian Cossacks helped to carry out the coup. In 1911, the Iranian prime minister visited the Russian and British ambassadors to seek their opinion of his planned coup d'état.[22] Both foreign ministries telegraphed their implied assent: 'we certainly cannot encourage [a] coup d'état,' wrote the British foreign minister, 'but [we] have no more intention of interfering with a Bakhtiari coup d'état than with previous coups d'état in Persia.'[23] (The usual nod towards non-interference in the internal affairs of a sovereign state was particularly insincere in this case, since the British government was at the same time actively engaged in preventing a coup d'état by Mohammad Ali, the former Shah.) The Russian foreign ministry was more honest, hewing to the British line of non-encouragement but instructing the ambassador 'not to repulse the Bakhtiyaris and not to impel them to give up energetic actions against ... the parliament desirable from our point of view.'[24] The coup took place the following month.

A third parallel, in addition to trajectory and the role of the great powers, involved the social basis of the constitutional revolutions of this period: the emerging class of modern intellectuals. The term 'intellectuals', as a collective self-identification, was popularized in 1898 during the Dreyfus Affair in France, in which a Jewish military officer was wrongly convicted of treason. News of the Dreyfus Affair was followed intently by educated people around the world. Thousands wrote letters of support to Dreyfus and his family.[25] A decade later, an Iranian newspaper would comment, 'Of course, the Dreyfus Affair is implanted in [our] memories.'[26] In the Ottoman Empire, the sultan was reportedly concerned that the scandal might encourage the opposition.[27] Indeed, many educated people, drawing inspiration from the mobilization of their French comrades, adopted the activist identity of 'intellectuals'. In Spain, where virtually 'all the literate men' of Barcelona signed a manifesto in support of Dreyfus, the term *intelectuales* gained currency almost immediately.[28] In Egypt, a prominent Islamic modernist reported on the difficulties of the French *'uqala*, an Arabic term for rational intellectuals, as contrasted with religious scholars.[29] In Iran, the terms *daneshmandan* (knowledgeable ones) and later *monavvaran al-fekr* (people of enlightened thought), borrowed from Ottoman Turkish, became popular terms of self-identification among those with modern education (see below), as did the term *ziyalilar* (enlightened ones) in Central Asia.[30] In Russia, the older term *intelligentsia*, previously used to refer to alienated, radical youths, changed in meaning to encompass the broader meaning of 'intellectuals'.[31] China, by contrast, lacked a specific term for intellectuals at this time, as evidenced by the use of the descriptive phrase 'people of education and knowledge' to translate the Russian word *intelligentsia* in 1906.[32] Only in the late 1910s was the term *zhishi jieji* (knowledge class) adapted from Japanese.[33]

This emerging class of modern intellectuals identified itself with a democratic variant of Comtean positivism. This ideology held that modern-educated individuals were the appropriate heirs of pre-modern aristocracies, both because of their scientific expertise and because of their purported lack of self-interest: unlike other classes, they argued, intellectuals acted only on the interests of society as a whole. Several prominent revolutionary leaders were outright followers of Auguste Comte, including Pavel Miliukov in Russia, Ahmet Rıza in the Ottoman Empire, and Teófilo Braga in Portugal. Others picked up the ideology indirectly, tapping into currents of positivist liberalism that were in the air at the time, sometimes through Masonic connections.[34] Comte himself had been no fan of popular sovereignty, but the elitism of early twentieth-century intellectuals was combined with a belief that ordinary people, once permitted to choose their leaders freely, would recognize the value of the intellectuals and elect them to office. As it turned out, this belief was not mistaken. Other social groups acceded to the leadership of the intellectuals during the constitutionalist movement: in Iran, for example, merchants and artisans at the sit-in at the British legation invited intellectuals from modern schools to lecture them on good governance and to negotiate a parliamentary system with the Shah (discussed further below). When the revolutions brought elections, intellectuals came to be hugely overrepresented in parliament. In Russia, a hostile Tsarist official characterized the first parliament as 'the dregs of the Russian "intelligentsia"'.[35] In Portugal, less-educated republicans complained that all the best government jobs were going to youths whose sole qualification was 'having spent years of their youth eating sardines and strumming guitars alongside the learned teat of the University.'[36] In Mexico, young intellectuals 'picked up the plums of office, while the real captains of the revolution' – the non-intellectuals who had actually fought against the dictator's army – 'were fobbed off with, at best, lowly commissions in the *rurales* [gendarmes].'[37] In the Guangdong province of China, where the constitutionalist movement was most entrenched, foreign-educated men occupied 'practically all the important government posts for the province'.[38]

In all these countries, the intellectuals used power not just for the public interest, but also for their particular class interests: reducing censorship, which may have been good for the country but was especially good for writers and publishers; raising taxes for positivist social programmes such as educational expansion and public-health projects, which particularly benefited teachers and doctors; attempting to reform the legal system and public budgeting processes to give a greater role to modern-educated lawyers and accountants. These moves cost the intellectuals the support of the groups that had helped them come to power, and intellectuals found themselves isolated when authoritarian movements threatened the new regime.

After the coups, intellectuals despaired. In Russia, a famous poet worried: 'Already, as in a nightmare or a frightening dream, we can imagine that the darkness overhanging us is the shaggy chest of the shaft-horse, and that in another moment the heavy hoofs will descend.'[39] A poet in Iran brought his audience to tears with the lament, 'These ruins of a cemetery are not our Iran. These ruins are not Iran, where is Iran?'[40] An Ottoman author opined: 'My friend, sometimes the environment is like a bad omen, like a graveyard. What intelligence, what wisdom, what talent can survive there?'[41] A well-known Mexican novelist came to the 'basic conviction that the fight is a hopeless one and a thorough waste.'[42] In Portugal, after the coup of 1926, the journal *School Federation* warned, 'Black days await us. Days of hunger threaten us. Days of slavery await us.'⁴³ A Chinese writer offered this extreme metaphor: 'Imagine an iron house having not a single window, and virtually indestructible, with all its inmates sound asleep and about to die of suffocation. Dying in their sleep, they won't feel the pain of death. Now if you raise a shout to awake a few of the light sleepers, making these unfortunate few suffer the agony of irrevocable death, do you really think you are doing them a good turn?'⁴⁴

The class project of the intellectuals shattered along with hopes for constitutionalism. Some turned to religious identities, such as anti-democratic versions of Russian Orthodox Christianity or Shiite Islam, exemplified by Ayatollah Mohammad Hoseyn Na'ini's attempt to have copies of his treatise, the era's most extensive Islamic defence of democracy, destroyed in 1914.⁴⁵ Others turned to various secular authoritarian trends of the left and the right. Instead of ruling in their own name, intellectuals served other masters.

Iranian Distinctiveness

Against the backdrop of these parallels, numerous features of the Iranian *mashrutiyat* stand out. The use of the extended sit-in as a method of pressure, for example, appears to be unique to Iran during this period, applied not only at the British legation but also in telegraph offices and other settings throughout the constitutional era. The interlude known as the Lesser Despotism, following the coup of 1908, has no direct parallels in the trajectory of the other revolutions of the period. The remainder of this chapter, however, will focus on one distinction in particular: the definition of the intellectuals. Ali Gheissari has noted that Iranians borrowed the term for intellectuals – *monavvaran al-fekr*, or people of enlightened thought – from Ottoman usage.⁴⁶ He cites a source from 1911, and some authors have applied the term *monavvaran al-fekr* to the entire period of the *mashrutiyat*, including the events of 1906.⁴⁷ However, Gheissari's 1911 source may well be the first published use of the term in Iran, though a Persian-language book published in Istanbul used the term in 1910.⁴⁸ The phrase seems to have been strongly identified with modern education and Dreyfusard-type intellectuals. For example, activist Yayha Dowlatabadi later recalled that religious scholars objected in 1906 to constitutional plans coming from people who 'were clearly nineteenth-century Babis, that is, the *monavvar al-afkaran* of the nation, that is, renovators, atheists, and superstitious people, since true Muslims would not enter parliament, because they would consider doing so to be harmful to the [religious scholars'] leadership [of the community].'⁴⁹

In 1906, however, activist intellectuals seem to have been careful not to identify themselves as *monavvaran*, or for that matter as *'oqala* – another, older term constructed from the root for 'rationality', which was used in the nineteenth century as a contrast with religious scholars (*'olama*/ulema).⁵⁰ Indeed, they explicitly attempted to ally themselves with, not distinguish themselves from, seminary-educated religious scholars. One of the organizers of a secret constitutionalist meeting explained that 'Power in this country is in the hands of two classes, the state officials and the religious scholars, and up to now they have colluded with one another to rule the country.' In order to change the regime, the movement would have to win over Islamic scholars 'without letting them know of our real goals', according to Article 7 of the by-laws ratified at the meeting. Article 10 urged activists not to publish material 'related to the laws of Islam, or anything that would hand the weapon of excommunication to ill-wishers'.⁵¹

Perhaps in an effort to play down their distinctiveness, modern intellectuals most often described themselves at this time instead as *daneshmandan*, or knowledgeable ones. The term was distinct from 'religious scholars' – in 1898, for example, the educator Zoka' al-Molk listed 'our *daneshmandan*, our *'olama*' as separate groups,⁵² and in 1902 the traveller Mo'in al-Saltaneh referred to Christopher Columbus – after viewing his statue in a Philadelphia park – as 'that intellectual sage' (*an hakim-e daneshmand*).⁵³ However, this older term had no particularly Western connotations and could subsume people with either modern or traditional educations, both of which categories were active in underground constitutionalist organizations. The first meeting of one such group opened with this term in 1905: 'O gentlemen, O *daneshmandan*, O patriots, O supporters and reformers of Islam, O zealous ones, are you sleeping or are you awake?'⁵⁴ An open letter later in the year used the term as well:

> A hundred to 150 thousand tumans of Iranian money go into the pockets of French and German teachers annually, and the *daneshmandan* of Iran are forced to go hungry. ... It should also be mentioned that Belgians were hired in the customs service and the post office and given 800 thousand tumans while educated, experienced Iranian youths were left unemployed. In any case, although the existence of these students was of no use to the state, it was of great use to the nation. Among other things, they who had seen the condition of the French and English state [in their studies abroad] gradually became offended by the deplorable conditions of oppression and dictatorship in Iran, and laid the foundation for complaints about this and stories about that, and awakened the people.⁵⁵

It was modern-educated intellectuals who turned a reform movement begun by merchants, tradespeople, and religious leaders into an overtly constitutionalist movement in the summer of 1906. The famous sit-in at the British legation, which forced the Shah to declare a constitution and an elected parliament, began as a protest against recent arbitrary oppressive actions of the monarchy. Within days, a delegation of teachers, graduates, and students from modern schools joined the sit-in and set up their own tent alongside those of the various guilds of the city, popularizing European customs such as clapping after speeches.[56] ('We're not Europeans. We don't clap,' Seyyed Mohammad Tabataba'i reprimanded members of parliament the following year. 'Say, "Bravo to you" [*ahsant*]' instead.)[57] 'Since those who took refuge in the [legation] had absolutely no concept as to what a constitution was or what it required, a special group kept them informed and instilled in them its own ideas', according to a socialist pro-democracy activist who identified himself in his memoirs with modern-educated intellectuals (using the terms *'aleman* and *ashkhas-e 'alem*, or knowledgeable people).[58] 'One could say that the legation had turned into a school, what with people sitting around under every tent and in every corner while a politically knowledgeable student [*yek nafar 'alem-e siyasi az shagerdan-e madares*] or someone else gave lessons. That is, the people heard contemporary things that up to now nobody had the courage to say.'[59] A contemporary described the scene: 'Every night they study lessons in law. Everyone has become an expert on politics and law, and they say things which leave one astonished', including the idea that 'when the nation no longer wants a Shah he is not recognized'.[60] Intellectuals dominated the sit-in's negotiating committee and inserted a constitution and elected parliament among the protest's demands.[61] They convinced various groups not to leave the sit-in as negotiations continued over these demands.[62]

Religious scholars also participated in the constitutionalist movement – Jamal al-Din Va'ez was one of the movement's earliest and staunchest activists, for example, and Tabataba'i not only sympathized but encouraged its mobilization.[63] Some of the leading ulema of Najaf famously telegraphed their support.[64] However, the bulk of the ulema had different goals and saw themselves as distinct from the intellectuals. They did not use the term *daneshmandan* to bridge the identities of the two groups. During the parallel sit-ins in July to August 1906 – the ulema in Qom and the constitutionalists at the British legation in Tehran – the religious scholars described their goals as an unelected assembly composed of government officials, merchants, 'several representatives of the knowledgeable ulema of goodwill and intelligence, and certain of the intellectuals [*'oqala*], the learned [*fozala*], the nobles [*ashraf*], and people of intelligence and knowledge [*ahl-e basirat va ettela'*]'.[65] An open letter attributed to Hojjat al-Eslam Mazandarani, one of the pro-constitutionalist scholars of Najaf, also used different terms for modern intellectuals and religious scholars and noted the leading role of the intellectuals in the *mashrutiyat*: 'What has been communicated and written to me about the meaning of *mashruteh* is that intellectuals [*arbab-e 'oquli*, or possessors of reason] would be chosen to protect and secure the rights of the state and the subjects.'[66]

After the constitution was declared, modern intellectuals continued to use the term *daneshmandan* in its dual sense of Western-oriented intellectuals, on the one hand, and also educated people in general, both modern and traditional, on the other. In an early session of parliament, one intellectual used the term *daneshmandan* to refer to ulema supporters of constitutionalism.[67] Similarly, a Tehran newspaper labelled a constitutionalist religious scholar as 'one of the *daneshmandan*'.[68] More commonly, however, the term referred to the modern-educated. A constitutionalist newspaper insisted that 'Today the greatest *daneshmandan* of Iran must be present in the special royal cabinet.'[69] Another newspaper reported on efforts to form a government commission 'composed of *daneshmandan*',[70] by contrast with a more conservative member of parliament's suggestion that the commission be made up of 'knowledgeable persons and proofs of Islam' (*ahl-e 'elm va hojaj-e eslam*).[71]

The term *daneshmand* quickly became the stuff of satire. One newspaper started a Molla Nasruddin story on the subject:

> I'm a *daneshmand* and wise (*kheradmand*) man. I'm aware of what's going on everywhere, and I keep current from Saturday to Friday. ... Wait, I wrote some notes on a piece of paper so I wouldn't forget to ask you. I've lived among the *daneshmandan* for 60 years and I never heard these words until this year. Now if I don't know them, the kids will laugh at me. I have to know them. So tell me what these are – I'll read them from the paper: first, *mashruteh* [constitutional or democratic]; second, *parlaman* [parliament]; third, *qanun* [law]; fourth, *azadi* [liberty]; fifth, *hoquq* [rights].[72]

The meaning of these terms was contested. While most intellectuals sought to derive these terms from Islamic sources and norms, Mohammad Ali Khan, a professor at the School of Political Science in Tehran, openly equated *mashrutiyat* with European democracy: 'In any case, the state is either dictatorial, that is, *absolu* [transliterated from French], or *mashruteh*, that is, *représentatif*. ... Therefore the *mashrutiyat* system is also called the representative system, or *régime représentatif*.' In earlier eras, one person or one group ruled absolutely, in some countries claiming divine right to rule. 'But for more than a hundred years, *hokama* [sages] and *daneshmandan*, and perhaps also the majority of the people, have turned away from this position, believing that one person or one group never has the right to control a people or a nation. The nation must control itself and run its own affairs. In the recent expression, the nation is the only absolute monarch.' However, the professor was unwilling to grant this control to all members of the nation. 'Of course, universal suffrage is the fundamentally correct system, but this system is advisable only when a people has progressed in political affairs and has completed its training. In many countries of Europe, suffrage is still limited in elections.'[73]

Opponents of constitutionalism accepted this characterization of *mashrutiyat* as equivalent to European political systems, and objected strongly to the idea that such systems were applicable to Iran.[74] After the coup of 1908, the already uncertain alliance between the two types of intellectuals began to come apart. Some constitutionalist ulema were executed by the Shah's government, and others shifted towards more cautious political positions. Modern-oriented intellectuals, for their part, became more openly critical of religious scholars. In 1907, the masthead of the constitutionalist newspaper *Sur-e Esrafil* visualized the alliance between modern and traditional intellectuals with an engraving of a group of men with hats (the moderns) and a group of men with turbans (the seminary scholars) both greeting an angel's message of 'freedom', 'equality', and 'fraternity'. Between them lay an inert mass of people sleeping unaware.[75] By 1911, this optimistic alliance was no longer possible – and this appears to have been the moment when the intellectuals shifted from the more inclusive identity of *daneshmandan* to the more exclusively modern identity of *monavvaran al-fekr*.

Modern-educated intellectuals also shifted their political project during the same period. In 1907, they had valued the alliance with religious scholars enough to incorporate a panel of ulema into the Supplementary Fundamental Law, to ensure that the new man-made laws conformed to the religious scholars' understanding of divine law; this document also envisioned separate and equal secular and religious court systems (an original draft had abolished the religious courts entirely). In 1908, parliament created a new state court to adjudicate disputes between the two court systems; in 1910, an attorney general's office was founded; and in 1911, the entire legal system was reorganized, subordinating religious courts to state courts.[76] Similarly, in the field of education, the Supplementary Fundamental Law of 1907 envisioned a secular state school system alongside religious schools. In 1910, parliament reorganized the Ministry of Science and Arts, placing the school system more firmly under state control. In 1911, parliament required all school curricula to be planned by the ministry, and all teachers to pass state examinations. Islamic schools were granted a partial exemption from these rules, but traditional religious schools were subordinated to modern-educated government officials, even to the extent of selecting texts for study.[77]

This shift brought Iran into line with intellectuals in the other constitutional revolutions of the period, who had treated traditional religious scholars all along as a class of competitors who were outside of the category of 'intellectuals'. In Russia, despite a reform movement within the Orthodox Christian church,[78] it was widely recognized that 'church and intelligentsia are deeply divided'.[79] Among the first decrees of the revolutionary government in Portugal was the expulsion of the Jesuits and the substitution of civic education for Christian teaching in primary schools.[80] In Mexico, intellectuals were suspicious of clergy-run schools, which struck them as 'making the cat the butler of the grease', a Spanish phrase roughly equivalent to the English phrase 'putting the fox in charge of the henhouse'.[81] Chinese intellectuals pushed to shut down traditional Confucian *sishu* schools.[82]

Ottoman intellectuals were the closest parallel to Iran in the matter of religion. In both countries constitutionalist movements sought to project Islamic legitimacy onto their intellectual identity.[83] For example, a pro-democracy Ottoman newspaper, *Meşveret*, included a Qur'anic quotation on the masthead of its Turkish-language edition (along with the positivist calendar on the French-language edition): 'And consult them in the matter,' a constitutionalist interpretation introduced to modernist Islamic discourse by Namık Kemal a generation earlier.[84] The title of the newspaper, meaning 'Consultation', drew on this Qur'anic reference, and the editor stressed that 'Consultation is the most important aspect of Islamic law.'[85] Some argued later that the concern for Islam was the undoing of the movement: 'The mistaken starting point of the constitutional revolution, which bound its feet like fetters, was the concern that every movement and plan be consistent with the shari'a, the fear that they would be seen in the country as opposed to religion, and the politics of respecting and protecting public opinion, or more precisely, the guild of religious scholars.'[86] At the same time, some Ottoman intellectuals were bolder than their Iranian colleagues in asserting an identity distinct from seminary-trained religious scholars. A major constitutionalist newspaper, published in Paris, identified its supporters (in Turkish) as the 'Sorbonnes, Tolstois, and Hugos' of the Ottoman Empire.[87] The newspaper later editorialized, 'Thus whether the people get upset about something – for example, whether or not they will oppose despotism – depends on the intellectuals of the nation. ... In sum, it may be said that if a small rudder can by itself steer a ship ten or twenty thousand times its size, the intellectual notables can similarly manage the ordinary masses, steering them forward or backward. ... The people of Istanbul endures its most sacred rights being trodden upon, and the shame that derives from this belongs not to the masses but to the intellectuals of Muslim society.'[88] Opponents of the constitutionalist movement echoed this theme, deriding its leaders as 'Turkish Dreyfuses'.[89]

These considerations are intended to offer a bit of the global context within which the Iranian *mashrutiyat* emerged, in an effort to counteract the geographical blinders that country and area specialists tend to develop. Constitutionalist activists at the time did not wear these blinders. Their newspapers covered developments in other revolutions of the period, and they saw themselves as part of a global phenomenon, the 'caravan of civilization'.[90] To view the Iranian *mashrutiyat* in comparative perspective is to recover something of the perspective of the *mashrutiyat* itself.

CHAPTER 17

Erin and Iran Resurgent: Irish Nationalists and the Iranian Constitutional Revolution[1]

Mansour Bonakdarian

Introduction

The Iranian Constitutional Revolution of 1906–11, directed against both the native autocracy and imperialist intervention in Iran's domestic affairs by Russia and Britain, occurred during a period of intensified anti-colonial nationalist and/or parliamentary-democratic struggles around the world. These ranged from the parliamentary revolution in Russia in 1905 to the dissolution of Norway's union with Sweden (1905), the Egyptian struggle for independence from Britain (particularly in the aftermath of the 1906 Dinshawai incident – see below), Finland's struggle for autonomy from Russia, varying Indian nationalist campaigns (both militant and petitional) either for self-government within the confines of the British Empire or for absolute independence – particularly after the 1905 partition of Bengal –, the Young Turk Revolution of 1908, the Mexican Revolution of 1910–11, and the Chinese Republican Revolution of 1911–12, among many other examples. During the Iranian revolution, Iranian constitutionalists/nationalists expressed support for, and solidarity with, some of these other struggles and received varying degrees of assistance from nationalist and reformist movements around the world.[2]

In Ireland, the years 1900 to 1914 happened to be a time of reinvigorated 'nationalist' politics with a countervailing 'unionist' commitment to the preservation of the union of Ireland and Great Britain under the rubric of the United Kingdom, with an assortment of nationalists and unionists simultaneously involved in Irish cultural and Gaelic 'Revival' movements.[3] Following the introduction of the Irish Home Rule Bill in the British parliament in 1912 (passed into law in May 1914, but postponed and never fully implemented), Ireland was beset by unionist versus nationalist disturbances and heightened sectarian communal tensions prior to the outbreak of the First World War, as the militant wings of the unionist opposition to Home Rule and various Irish nationalist organizations began arming themselves in preparation for an anticipated civil war.

Ireland's status within the British Empire was an ambivalent one, not only because it comprised one of the oldest English colonial possessions (settler plantations) outside 'Britain' and was a European territorial possession of Britain (not forgetting Britain's other European territories in the Mediterranean Sea, the Irish Sea, the North Sea, and the English Channel), but, among other factors, Ireland was also an atypical British imperial dominion in so far as it was incorporated into the United Kingdom of Great Britain and Ireland in 1801 and the Irish Home Rule nationalists enjoyed organized partisan representation in the British parliament in Westminster after 1873. The main nationalist platforms in Ireland in the years just before the outbreak of the First World War were those of the Irish Parliamentary Party (IPP; a.k.a. Irish Home Rule party *or* Irish Nationalist party),[4] advocating self-government for Ireland within the British Empire (in the form of a separate Irish parliament in Dublin) and enjoying parliamentary representation in Westminster at the time; as well as the much smaller militant and clandestine Irish Republican Brotherhood (IRB),[5] which was committed to the complete dissolution of all political ties with Britain; and the Sinn Féin ('ourselves') movement/party founded in Dublin in 1905 by Arthur Griffith.[6] At the time, similar to the IPP, Sinn Féin too favoured self-government for Ireland in the form of a separate Irish parliament within the confines of the British Empire; however, the party lambasted the IPP and adopted an abstentionist platform opposed to the participation of Irish nationalist MPs in the British parliament in London. Sinn Féin also strongly advocated a programme of Irish economic and cultural self-reliance, shared by the IRB and some other nationalist groups, and paralleling the Indian nationalist *Swadeshi* boycott of British products and institutions in the aftermath of the British partition of Bengal in 1905. There were also smaller Irish nationalist groupings, the activities of some of which overlapped with those of other nationalist organizations, including William O'Brien's All-For-Ireland League (1909), the IPP-affiliated Young Ireland Branch, which also advocated women's suffrage and included an amalgam of socialists and non-IRB republicans in its ranks, the sectarian (anti-Protestant) Catholic nationalist organization of the Ancient Order of Hibernians, and various small labour and socialist organizations, such as James Connolly's Socialist Party of Ireland (1909).

Given the sizeable population of the Irish diaspora (outside the British Isles itself) – particularly in the United States –, Irish nationalist politics and organizations also operated at a diasporic level, with competing nationalist diaspora press and groupings advocating the respective platforms of the different nationalist tendencies. The Irish 'nationalist' diaspora, raising funds and publicizing the cause of various nationalist groups, was of particular significance in these years to the militant IRB – as in the case of the IRB's affiliated American organization, the Clan na Gael, based in New York and with regional branches throughout the United States – particularly given the fact that the IRB, declared illegal by British authorities, could not openly operate or publish newspapers or pamphlets in Ireland or Britain.

This essay briefly examines the tortuous intersection of the Iranian constitutional and nationalist revolution with Irish 'nationalist' politics in the years following the outbreak of the Iranian Constitutional Revolution of 1906 and up to the final suppression of the Iranian revolutionary movement in late 1911, as well as the manifold Irish nationalist constructs of 'Iran', both contemporaneous and historical. Iranian and Irish nationalist politics in this period crisscrossed with an amalgam of other nationalist and reformist struggles.[7] The Iranian Constitutional Revolution drew expressions of support and solidarity from different corners of the world and Iranian constitutionalists/nationalists, in turn, repeatedly expressed support for a host of nationalist and reform movements in other parts of the globe, those in India and Egypt (both within the British Empire) in particular.[8] Some Iranian nationalist circles, inside Iran as well as in émigré communities, also directly collaborated, or were in contact, with nationalist and revolutionary groups in other countries, while nationalist, socialist, and anarchist volunteers and mercenaries from other territories (chiefly Armenians, Georgians, and Azerbaijanis from the Russian Caucasus, and Bulgarians) participated in the Iranian constitutionalist/nationalist armed confrontations with the Iranian autocracy and the Russian forces in the north of the country.[9]

Irish nationalists of different platforms not only had long been engaged in direct contacts and collaboration with nationalists in some other parts of the British Empire – India in particular[10] –, but continuously expressed support for many other nationalist and reformist movements worldwide, although different Irish nationalist groups tended to privilege or downplay particular aspects of these other struggles. These contacts included gatherings at the India House (founded in London in 1905) and participation at the Egyptian Congress in Brussels in 1910. Direct militant, republican Irish nationalist participation in armed activities in support of other 'nationalities' was a more recent development. Such armed campaigns before the First World War ranged from the roughly five hundred Irish and Irish-American volunteer fighters joining the Boer resistance against British forces during the Boer War of 1899–1902 in southern Africa (Irish Transvaal Brigade/Irish Commandos/MacBride's Brigade, named after John MacBride, the leader of the volunteers) to the failed joint Irish–Indian attempt to rescue the militant Indian nationalist Vinayak Damodar Savarkar from British police custody in May 1910.

This chapter focuses on Irish nationalist advocacy of, and broader commentaries on, the Iranian revolution, provisionally also exploring, among other things, the multifarious contemporary and historical influences and referential frameworks that underlay Irish nationalist representations and imaginations of 'Iran', which are indicative of the confluences as well as divergences of certain anti-imperialist nationalist positionings and alignments and the manifold globalization processes under way at the time, as reflected by the contours of varying political/cultural discursive deployments of 'Iran' in Irish nationalist commentaries, despite the general Iranian 'nationalist' silence on the Irish Question. Moreover, the essay tangentially outlines the ways in which representations of Iran by various Irish nationalists paralleled and diverged from some of the Iranian ('modernist'-nationalist) self-imaginings and self-representations at the time. Sporadic Irish nationalist (and some other Irish) historicizations and contemporary representations of 'Iran' point to additional examples of extra-Iranian imaginings of 'Iran' at large (both sympathetic and denigrating) which did not entirely correspond to manifold Iranian 'national'-historical self-imaginings at the time, and also lacked any corresponding degree of cross-nationalist dialogic Iranian imaginations of Ireland and failed to produce the same scope of cross-nationalist exchanges as, for example, between Indian and Irish nationalist platforms since the nineteenth century or the direct exchanges between Indian and Iranian nationalists during the Constitutional Revolution and the First World War.[11] Not only were Iranian nationalists evidently unacquainted with the wide-ranging (instrumentalist and otherwise) representations of Iran by Irish nationalists, but, in addition, despite the parliamentary and press advocacy of the Iranian revolution in Irish nationalist circles and some direct contacts between a number of Irish nationalists (e.g., John Dillon or William J. Maloney) and Iranian nationalists, these contacts stopped short of the sort of exchanges between various Irish nationalist and Indian or Egyptian nationalist groups (keeping in mind the shared, albeit differently administered, colonial status of Ireland, India, and Egypt within the British Empire).

Of course, Irish nationalist commentaries on, and imaginings of, Iran at the time[12] cannot entirely be divorced from the more general manifold Irish (including unionist), British, and broader European and American (multivalent and contentious) 'orientalist' perspectives or from the even more general global 'modernist'/'anti-modernist'/'counter-Western modernist' discursive positionings, or from the internationalist or transnational liberal-reformist/ nationalist/socialist/anti-imperialist and other platforms (either in terms of being influenced by these trends and/or in reaction to them). Yet a salient feature of Irish nationalists' commentaries on Iran during the period was their identification, in varying forms, with the Iranian struggle for territorial and national sovereignty following Iran's division into British and Russian spheres of influence under the Anglo-Russian Agreement of 1907 (even if the concept of Irish 'national' sovereignty prior to English rule in Ireland was an invented construct).[13] Furthermore, also present in many of the Irish nationalist commentaries were the varying deployments and applications of the particular genre of 'Irish Orientalism'[14] which militated against imperialist and hierarchical 'West'-centred modes of orientalist discourse. This was a politically and culturally calculated 'self-orientalizing' gesture by some Irish nationalists contra the denigrating modes of Western orientalist commentaries, closely identifying Ireland with the Orient both as an expression of anti-British (anti-imperialist)[15] solidarity and, in the case of India in particular, as a means of establishing an (invented) historical-racial 'Aryan' link for advancing a platform of joint Indo-Irish nationalist resistance to British rule, while also privileging 'Ireland' as the earliest Aryan settlement in what had become the United Kingdom, thereby according Irish Gaelic culture the privileged 'historical' role of the transmitter of 'civilization' to the British Isles prior to the gradual English occupation of Ireland beginning in the twelfth century (despite simultaneous emplotments of 'Greek' or other origins of the Gaels by some nationalists).

Irish Nationalists and the Iranian Constitutional Revolution

A number of Home Rule Irish Parliamentary Party MPs, John Dillon in particular, emerged as the most resolute critics in the United Kingdom of the Iranian consequences of the 1907 Anglo-Russian Agreement and London's subsequent policy of rationalizing Russian aggression in Iran in opposition to the Iranian constitutional/nationalist movement; with IPP MPs holding roughly 82 seats in parliament after the general elections of 1906 and 1910. In late 1911, Dillon and another IPP MP, Stephen Lucius Gwynn (also a journalist, poet, and cultural critic), finally joined the Persia Committee, formed in London in late 1908 to advocate the Iranian constitutional movement as well as the Iranian nationalist resistance to the Russian aggression which enjoyed London's *public* acquiescence.[16] Dillon, who had assisted the committee all along even before joining it, was widely acknowledged in Britain, Iran, and elsewhere as a leading critic of the British Liberal foreign secretary Sir Edward Grey's Iranian policy (with the Liberal Party in power from December 1905 to the end of the First World War).[17] Another Irish Home Rule nationalist (though not an MP), who joined the committee well before Dillon and Gwynn, was the positivist-rationalist Shapland Hugh Swinny, also the president of the London Positivist Society and the treasurer of the Nationalities and Subject Races Committee,[18] while the IPP leader John Redmond and other IPP MPs, such as Richard Hazleton, periodically alluded to the 'Persian Question'. Dillon and Gwynn, inside and outside the parliament, and Swinny, outside the parliament, would be among the leading Irish Home Rule champions of the Iranian constitutionalist and nationalist movement.

Despite the resolute support of the Iranian revolutionary camp by Irish Nationalist MPs such as Dillon, and their reluctance to publicly criticize the miscarriages and failures of Iranian constitutionalists before and after the latter's victory in the Iranian civil war of 1908–09, which ousted the autocratic Mohammad Ali Shah (r. 1906–09) from the throne, the *Freeman's Journal* published in Dublin and serving as a mouthpiece of the Irish Parliamentary Party was by no means uncritical of Iranian constitutional authorities. For example, in its 28 January 1910 issue, months after the constitutionalist/ nationalist victory in the Iranian civil war, under the caption of 'Barbarous Scene in Teheran', the paper was highly critical of the manner in which the Iranian constitutionalist authorities had carried out the public execution of a 'well-known Reactionary', adding: 'A very strong feeling exists in the European community [i.e., those residing in Iran] owing to the barbarous clumsiness of the execution.'[19] Among the Irish papers of varying nationalist platforms, the *Freeman's Journal*, which enjoyed the widest circulation, provided the most regular coverage of Iranian developments after the conclusion of the Anglo-Russian Agreement in 1907, but these reports were generally verbatim reproductions of reports from other sources, chiefly from Reuters, and devoid of editorial commentary. In effect, the paper was not directly utilized by the Irish Parliamentary Party as a propaganda weapon in criticizing Grey's handling of Iranian affairs, even if it provided accounts of the activities of Grey's critics in the Iranian debate.

It is also noteworthy that, with very few exceptions, the leading foreign-policy dissenters in the Iranian debate in Britain, many of whom were advocates of Irish Home Rule, and the Irish Nationalist MPs themselves, refrained from directly alluding either to the current situation in Ireland or to the history of British imperial rule in Ireland in their criticisms of London's and St. Petersburg's policies in Iran or in their general commentaries on the Iranian revolution; this despite many of these same individuals making ample references to, or drawing parallels with, the nationalist movements in Egypt, India, the Ottoman Empire, Finland, and elsewhere in their separate commentaries on Ireland *or* on developments in Iran.[20] This overall reluctance on the part of the pro-Irish Home Rule critics of Grey's Iranian policy in Britain to mix Iranian and Irish nationalist politics in their public statements was in part due to the fact that many British foreign-policy dissenters belonging to, or affiliated with, the multi-party Persia Committee sought to attract Grey's Conservative/ Unionist and Liberal-Imperialist critics to their ranks, and the principal members of the Persia Committee included Liberal-Imperialists and Unionists, such as the Liberal-Imperialist Henry Finnis Blosse Lynch, a co-founder of the committee who was of Irish descent, as well as the Unionist Lord Lamington, the committee's president.[21] Among the rare examples of public allusions by these individuals to Ireland in debates on the Iranian question was this oblique reference by John Dillon in a letter to the editor in the *Manchester Guardian* of 22 January 1909:

> I have read with the keenest interest and sympathy the statement on the Persian Question by Professor Browne published in your issue of January 18. I trust that the appeal of the Persian Nationalists set forth in the conclusion of Professor Browne's statement will be responded to by all Liberals in England who are faithful to true Liberal and radical principles in foreign policy.
>
> ...
>
> During an experience extending over 25 years I have never known the House of Commons treated so contemptuously and so completely denied information as it has been in connection with this question of Persia by the present Secretary of State [i.e., Grey]. ... Meanwhile, so far as it was possible to gather from the information accessible to the general public, the country was being committed to a policy utterly inconsistent with the principles of Liberalism and, so far as I can judge, opposed to the conviction and feelings of the majority of the Liberals of England.
>
> We Irish are outsiders in all these matters. We have no affiliation with any English party, and our views carry no weight with English members on questions of foreign politics. But ever since I entered Parliament I have felt it to be a duty, whenever I was convinced that any nation struggling against oppression was unjustly treated by the Government of England, to speak out against the injustice, no matter how ineffective my protest might be.[22]

Edward Granville Browne, the prominent Cambridge orientalist and the leading British critic of Anglo-Russian policy in Iran at the time (and vice-chairman of the Persia Committee), and a supporter of Irish Home Rule among many other anti-colonial struggles, made only one, indirect, allusion to the situation in Ireland in his 1910 book *The Persian Revolution of 1905–1909*:

> Most of those who watched the Persian constitutional struggle were struck by the rare phenomenon of a popular movement in which the Clergy played so prominent a part, since this movement, if successful, could hardly fail to deprive them of a large part at least of their influence and power. It must be remembered, however, that like the Irish priests, the Persian *mullâs* are an essentially national class, sprung from the people, knowing the people, and, if suspicious of administrative innovations, yet more suspicious of foreign interference.[23]

As for the non-IPP Irish nationalist groupings, the initial reception of the Iranian Constitutional Revolution by the more radical and militant Irish nationalist press was cursory and indifferent, or even dismissive. It was only after the summer of 1907 that many of these organizations and individuals intermittently began to devote attention to Iranian developments, and even then first at a very slow, incremental pace. Under the false impression that, in keeping with its past policy of rivalry with St. Petersburg, London had sponsored the Iranian constitutional movement – given that the demand for a constitution was advanced by Iranian protesters taking sanctuary (*bast*) at the British legation in Tehran during July and August 1906 – (the Clan na Gael) *Gaelic American* (New York, edited by John Devoy and George Freeman), which ardently championed Egyptian, Indian, and many other nationalist movements around the world, wrote in September 1906: 'The British Government has been encouraging the agitation for "constitutional" government in Persia. If it is so good for the people of Persia, why should not the British Government give it a trial in India?'[24] Arthur Griffith's *Sinn Féin* (Dublin), which also devoted considerable space to other nationalist movements around the world, at first simply disregarded the outbreak of the Iranian revolution, offering no account of Iranian developments. This lack of interest, juxtaposed with the paper's regular coverage of nationalist activities and the miscarriages of British rule in India and Egypt, may appear on the surface to be self-explanatory, given that Ireland, Egypt, and India were part of the British Empire. Additionally, various groups of Irish nationalists had long taken up the banner of Indian and Egyptian self-rule or independence and there were regular contacts between varying groups of nationalists in these territories. Nonetheless, the coverage of Iranian developments in *Sinn Féin* during the first year and a half of the Iranian revolution not only was less frequent than the coverage of the activities of the Young Turks – which may be attributed to the Ottoman Empire's pivotal role in the European balance of power as well as the relevance of Ottoman politics to certain groups in the nationalist circles in Egypt and India –, but *Sinn Féin*'s reports on the Iranian question certainly did not even match the paper's keen interest in the political situation in Afghanistan, another country affected by the 1907 Anglo-Russian Agreement and bordering British India (similar to Iran), or its subsequent enthusiastic endorsement of the Chinese Revolution, among other examples.

To a large degree this early position of radical Irish nationalist groups stemmed not only from a resolute anti-British stance and confusion about the developments in Iran, but was also the outcome of bitter rivalries among Irish nationalist camps dedicated to different nationalist platforms and tactics. For example, even before the Iranian Constitutional Revolution, when it was first learned by the public that London and St. Petersburg were conducting negotiations to settle their differences over Iran and Central Asia (eventually resulting in the 1907 Anglo-Russian Agreement that resolved British and Russian differences over Tibet, Afghanistan, and Iran), the republican

Gaelic American had launched an attack on the Irish Parliamentary Party MP William Redmond for his concern with extra-Irish matters, notwithstanding the paper's own ample coverage of extra-Irish developments: 'What on earth has Mr. William Redmond to do bothering himself about an agreement there may or may not be between Great Britain and Russia about Tibet, Persia and Afghanistan, that he should rise in the British Parliament to ask a question of that sententious prig, Sir Edward Grey, on the subject? Hasn't he got enough to do looking after the affairs of his own plundered country, or if he must mind other people's business, why doesn't he ask about what is going on in Natal [in British-administered South Africa]?'[25] Yet the following month the paper did not consider the parliamentary queries of another Irish Parliamentary Party MP, John Dillon, concerning the British execution of Egyptians charged with inciting the Dinshawai incident at all out of place (the Dinshawai incident was an attack by Egyptian villagers on British soldiers after the soldiers had opened fire on the angry villagers whose pigeons the soldiers had been hunting).[26]

Nevertheless, reports of Iranian developments in the radical Irish nationalist press gradually increased after the conclusion of the Anglo-Russian Agreement on 31 August 1907 and became more frequent after the outbreak of the Iranian civil war in the summer of 1908, which pitted the constitutional/nationalist forces against the Iranian royalist forces backed by Russia (with the British foreign secretary publicly rationalizing Russian actions). Reports of Iranian news in these radical Irish nationalist papers further multiplied after the Russian-instigated closure of the Second Majles in late 1911 and the subsequent Russian atrocities committed against Iranian constitutionalists/nationalists. For example, by early 1912, after the termination of the Iranian revolution under Russian duress with London's collusion, the *Gaelic American* would write:

> One would naturally expect to see the governments of those countries which enjoy constitutional rights extending the hand of sympathy and, where necessary, affording material assistance to those fighting for liberty, and none more readily than the country that boasts of being the 'Mother of Parliaments', England. Yet the contrary is the case. So far from aiding any of the countries that are trying to establish their freedom and independence on a constitutional basis, not only are the self-governing countries withholding their support, but they have actually joined the most reactionary government in the world, the Russian, in suppressing or nullifying the efforts of those in revolt against tyranny.
>
> This is peculiarly true in the case of Persia.[27]

This article also included some garbled information on the United States' alleged covert cooperation with Britain and Russia in Iran and the accusation that William Morgan Shuster, Iran's American treasurer general (1910–11), appointed by the constitutional authorities, whom the paper (renowned for its anti-Jewish sentiments) mistakenly identified as a Jew – in keeping with St. Petersburg's anti-Jewish allegations against Shuster –, was part of a deliberate plan to stage a confrontation between the constitutional authorities in Iran and Russia in order to hasten a Russian military clampdown in Iran.[28]

The outbreak of the Iranian civil war (June 1908–July 1909) and the subsequent continued Russian military aggression in Iran, with British acquiescence, were important factors contributing to increased radical Irish nationalist attention to the Iranian question. By 1911, the radical Irish nationalist interest in the Iranian question had at least become recurrent enough so that in an article on 'True and False Imperialism', in the *Irish Review* of August 1911, Griffith could write that 'Mr. Birrell and Lord Aberdeen, and other gentlemen who govern us, are undoubted Britons, but Archbishop Crozier, Mr. William Moore, and the Grand Master of the [Unionist] Orange Order have no more claim to the title than the Shah of Persia.'[29] In fact, after the royalist coup of June 1908 in Iran, which inaugurated the civil war, the *Gaelic American* would even quote from, or reproduce articles by, Grey's chief critics in Britain affiliated with the Persia Committee as well as the Irish Parliamentary Party MPs engaged in the Iranian debate. For example, the paper reproduced the appeal from Sattar Khan and Baqer Khan, two leaders of the Tabriz constitutionalist insurgency during the Iranian civil war, that appeared in the London *Labour Leader* in the summer of 1909,[30] or Browne's letter appearing in the London publication *Egypt* on 'Russian atrocities in Persia' following the closure of the Second Majles in late 1911.[31] *Egypt* had been founded by Wilfrid Scawen Blunt, the conservative British champion of 'Egypt for Egyptians' and a supporter of Irish Home Rule and the Iranian constitutionalist/nationalist movement, among other nationalist struggles. The paper was edited by the remarkable Irish socialist and nationalist committed to internationalism, Fred Ryan (d. 1913). Ryan, also a principal critic of Arthur Griffith and Irish anti-Semitism, was a well-known advocate of Egypt's independence and by this time was additionally distinguishing himself as a defender of Iran's territorial sovereignty and the Iranian parliamentary and reform movement (see below).[32]

The initial marked transformation in the stance of the *Gaelic American* and *Sinn Féin* on the Iranian question should, in part, be attributed to the attention devoted to the Iranian developments by Indian and Egyptian nationalists, Indians in particular, among other nationalist groupings whose struggles were championed in the pages of these radical Irish nationalist papers. However, we should not discount the pro-German stance of both the *Gaelic American* and *Sinn Féin* by 1907 (with *Sinn Féin*'s Arthur Griffith having conveniently transferred his former admiration for the Tsar to the German Kaiser with the mounting tensions between London and Berlin even before the Anglo-Russian Agreement of 1907 – à la 'the enemy of our enemy is our friend'). It was widely acknowledged that a primary objective of London in pursuing the Anglo-Russian Agreement was to check Germany in the European military and imperial balance of power. Moreover, both papers generally held nationalist militancy and physical force (with strong appeals to nationalist cults of 'masculinity') in much higher esteem and were often critical of moderate nationalist groupings in other parts of the world, just as they were highly critical of the Irish Parliamentary Party, even if *Sinn Féin* was technically committed to nonviolent political, economic, and cultural transformation at this stage, while increasingly infiltrated by IRB activists. With Iranian constitutionalists resorting to armed struggle in defence of their political rights and the independence of their country after the summer of 1908, it appears that they finally were regarded by radical Irish nationalists as nationalists worthy of the name.

The frequency of references to Iran by other anti-colonial nationalist groupings helped augment the significance of the Iranian revolution in the pages of radical Irish nationalist papers. In fact, one of the rare favourable early commentaries on Iranian developments after the revolution in the *Gaelic American* (September 1906), under the heading 'Persians' Eyes Open', was based on a report from the Lahore *Panjabee*. This was a report on a public appeal by the high-ranking Iranian Shiite clergy in Isfahan to the Iranian public to avoid purchases of imported cloth, a nativist-nationalist campaign which the *Panjabee* equated with the tactics of the Indian *Swadeshi* boycott of British goods.[33] Given the *Gaelic American*'s simultaneous advocacy of Irish self-reliance and the Indian *Swadeshi* tactic, this report offered an instance of proximity between the Iranian 'anti-imperialist' (and 'anti-foreign' in this context) campaigns and the radical Irish nationalist call for the boycott of foreign-made products. Another early passing reference to Iran in the *Gaelic American* shortly after the Iranian revolution occurred in the text of an appeal by the militant Indian nationalist Vinayak Damodar Savarkar to Indian Muslims: 'Wake Up, Sons of Islam.'[34]

In *Sinn Féin*, too, the early allusions to Iranian developments generally appeared in the form of reports from Indian and other nationalist sources. In March 1907, for example, in an article reprinted in *Sinn Féin* from the Lahore *Panjabee*, it was mentioned 'But has not Persia to-day a Constitution which India, in spite of the benign rule of the sublime bureaucrats, lacks ... ? Truly tribulations produce their fruit – in the lives of Nations as in the lives of individuals.'[35] In October 1908, after the Iranian civil war had got under way, the paper printed an article from the Pune *Mahratta* on the 'general political awakening of Asia', which, among other examples, referred to the Iranian revolution: 'Persia, with the inspiring traditions of a glorious past, was the first

Mahomedan country to feel the force of the new moral impact. In the closing months of 1906 … the Persian people demanded representative institutions.'[36] The organized activities of various Indian groups, be they Indian nationalists or Muslim nationalists, in support of Iran's independence also resonated with the more radical Irish nationalist press – regardless of the highly critical attitude of the *Gaelic American* and *Sinn Féin* towards the Muslim nationalist platform of the All-India Muslim League, founded in late 1906 and loyal to British imperial rule in India until the December 1911 annulment of the partition of Bengal.[37] In a 1910 article under the heading 'The Partition of Persia', Griffith reported in *Sinn Féin*: 'On the afternoon of 2nd November I was present at a meeting which was to my mind deeply significant and interesting. The meeting in question was one convened by Mohammedans resident in London as a protest against the recent action of the British Government in landing a naval force in Southern Persian territory, thereby conveying the impression all over the Mussulman world that the partition of Persia was about to be carried out by both England and Russia.'[38] This meeting was organized by prominent members of the All-India Muslim League in Britain and attended, among others, by a number of leading British critics of Sir Edward Grey's Iranian policy, including members of the Persia Committee and W. S. Blunt.[39]

Over the following years, references to Iran also appeared in the radical Irish nationalist coverage of revolutionary and/or nationalist developments elsewhere, or in the context of 'great power' politics or reports of international and/or anti-imperialist gatherings such as the Nationalities and Subject Races Conference in London in 1910, the organizer and treasurer of which happened to be the Home Rule Irish nationalist Shapland Hugh Swinny of the London branch of the Positivist Society and a member of the Persia Committee. Nonetheless, as late as 1911 the *Gaelic American* still continued to regard Iranians as a less admirable nation than the Afghans and others in their ability to defend their country's sovereignty, stating shortly before the closure of the Second Majles in December 1911 under Russian duress: 'The Persians, lacking all the qualities of the Afghans[,] have had their country divided into two spheres of influence.'[40] On the other hand, on the topic of the 'national' characteristics of Iranians, a peculiar 1910 article by the novelist Louise Kenny in *Sinn Féin*, which began with a parable about arbitrary justice in Iran and concluded with Iranian social attitudes towards women, stated:

> The Persians are supposed to be the only Mohammedan people who have a gift of gaiety, and all Mohammedans are valiant. But Persian historical memories go a deal further back than Mohammed's advent; the people never forget that their country was once the seat of one of the four great Empires of the ancient world; moreover, they have the utter pride of being a native white race in the East. So, naturally, they cherish the Nationalist notion that they would like to

keep Persia for the Persians. Meanwhile, both the Russian Bear and the British Lion have mouthed down some of the fence rails and slicked inside.⁴¹

This article in *Sinn Féin*, alluding to Iran's pre-Islamic ancient past and 'Persian' 'racial' identity, touches on other dimensions of Irish nationalist imaginations and representations of Iran beyond merely the 'political' struggle underway in Iran at the time. During this period, there was a corresponding Irish literary and cultural interest, both nationalist and otherwise, in Iranian history and literature, beside the more extensive interest in Indian culture and Hinduism. In addition to other factors, this interest emanated from two intersecting intellectual tendencies, both with varying degrees of 'Aryan' racial undercurrents: first, the phenomenon of 'Irish Orientalism' [42] emerging in the late eighteenth and early nineteenth century, which, in contradistinction to imperialist and/or civilizationally denigrating trends in orientalism, fed into Irish currents of cultural nationalism, such as the late nineteenth-century 'Irish Literary Revival' movement embraced by many Irish political and cultural nationalists (the latter also including some Unionists); and, second, the advent of the theosophical movement in the late nineteenth century, which influenced a number of prominent Irish nationalist authors and poets, ranging from William Butler Yeats to James and Margaret Cousins.⁴³

'Iran' in Irish Nationalist Imaginations: History, Racial Theories, and Mysticism

Since the nineteenth century, 'Iran', in its various *territorial* and *cultural* historical designations and manifestations, had variously appeared in Irish nationalist poetry and literature, in addition to the more general Irish works of literature – although there were much earlier English-language travel and literary accounts of Iran available to Irish readers. For example, the Irish poet and writer Thomas Moore's (nationalist-inspired) 1817 'narrative poem' *Lalla Rookh*, in its second section, 'The Fire Worshippers', romantically celebrated the failed Zoroastrian resistance to the Arab-Muslim conquest of Iran in the seventh century, with the Zoroastrian struggle serving, among other things, as an allegory for Moore's own identification with the ongoing Irish resistance to English occupation (and the post-sixteenth-century Catholic resistance to Anglican discriminatory (anti-Catholic) penal laws in Ireland). Alternatively, in the mid-nineteenth century, the Young Ireland nationalist poet James Clarence Mangan's works included poems which he claimed to be 'translations from Persian', although they were actually his own creative inventions.⁴⁴

Aside from Moore's castigation of Islam in *Lalla Rookh*, it should be pointed out that the more stereotypical, binary orientalist distinctions between the 'Occident' and the 'Orient' were also not entirely absent from utterances by Irish nationalists. For example, in July 1912 the socialist and feminist Irish nationalist and co-founder of the Irish Women's Franchise League (1908), Hanna Sheehy Skeffington, wrote in an article on the 'Women's Movement' in Ireland: 'An Irishwoman, who has travelled much, told me once that Ireland of all Western countries came nearest to Orientalism in its disregard of woman, its exclusion of her in all public occasions, its scarcely veiled contempt of wifehood, while, with regard to motherhood, the Orientals were ahead of us; for in the East the old woman is venerated, while in Ireland the term is synonymous with imbecility.'[45] Similarly, there was still a great deal of confusion concerning (the manifold) Iranian cultures and historical identities, so that the celebrated Irish nationalist poet and dramatist Padraic Colum's poem on the twelfth/thirteenth-century Iranian poet Sa'di appeared under the title 'Arab Song' in *Sinn Féin*.[46]

Yet, more generally, Irish nationalist 'orientalism' appealed to a more positive identification between Ireland and the Orient. 'Irish orientalism' and certain trends in Irish literary and cultural 'Revivals' were also interlaced with anti-imperialist currents of Irish Aryanism and Pan-Aryanism.[47] Even in the early stages of the emergence of the late eighteenth-century theories of Indo-European (later 'Aryan') languages, following William Jones's philological researches in the Indian subcontinent – which in the nineteenth century assumed clear European 'racial' and civilizational overtones –, there had been attempts to link Ireland to the 'Orient', including Iran, historically, linguistically, and 'racially'.

Sadeq Hedayat, one of the leading Iranian literary figures of the twentieth century, in his *Tup-e morvari* (The Pearl Cannon), written in 1947 but not published until 1979, long after his death, would satirize those he considered to be crank Iranian etymologists of the Persian language by including among his deliberately hyperbolic examples of such unsound etymological claims the following: 'Aran and Iran come from the Magian root 'a'ir' which later appears as Éire and is recorded as Ireland. For this reason it is believed that the Irish have migrated from Iran to their own homeland and have advisedly retained this name.'[48] While this example, among others, was intended by Hedayat as a patently fabulous and unreasonable proposition, what Hedayat and his intended Iranian readers evidently were unaware of was that this statement would not have sounded so entirely fabulous and irrational to some in Ireland itself from the late eighteenth century until the early years of the twentieth century. Part of the 'European debate' on Gaelic culture after the late eighteenth century had been the question of the 'racial' origins of the Gaels, with the Protestant English military officer and amateur linguist Charles Vallancey, who resided in Ireland, as the chief proponent of the contested theory of 'Persian origins'.[49]

By the early part of the nineteenth century, Vallancey's theory was definitively surpassed by a mélange of alternative theories of the Eastern origins of the Gaels with competing (Iranian-speaking) Scythian, (Semitic-speaking) Phoenician, and Carthaginian variations of the Milesian ancestry of the early Gaelic settlers in Ireland. Nonetheless, in Irish political and cultural nationalist usage the Milesians were ultimately traced back to an 'Aryan' origin. Irish nationalist claims concerning the origins of the Gaels were intended both to establish the 'Aryan' origins of the Gaels and to insist on their arrival in Ireland prior to the Anglo-Saxon settlements in the British Isles, thereby privileging the Irish as the earliest harbingers of 'civilization' in the westernmost region of Europe.

Although after the 1880s the Indo-Iranian-Caucasian theories of the origins of the so-called Aryan race were vehemently challenged by a number of scholars who argued in favour of the European origins of the Aryans,[50] the Indo-Iranian 'Aryan' theory, with the German scholar Friedrich Max Müller in Britain as the staunchest proponent of Indo-Iranian origins at the time, continued to hold sway. Moreover, by the early twentieth century, new 'cultural links' between Ireland and the 'Orient' – including Iran – were being brought to light. In March 1908, the *Gaelic American* published an article, 'Finn and Oisin: An Ossianic Version of the Celebrated Persian Story', based on the work of the German Celtic scholar Kuno Meyer at the Royal Irish Academy.[51] The Ossianic cycle of heroic epic poems, 'purported to be translations of the works of a third-century Scottish bard, Ossian', were originally published in the 1760s by the Scottish Protestant poet James Macpherson.[52] The Ossianic epic poems, which immediately after their publication generated controversy in Ireland and Scotland as to the 'true' Celtic identity of Ossian, with most Irish scholars contesting Macpherson's and his supporters' claim of Ossian's 'Scottish' Celtic identity, became immensely popular throughout Europe as a Celtic equivalent of the Homeric epics. However, by the late nineteenth century, literary scholars would prove indisputably that Macpherson's 'translation' was a forgery and that the poems had been Macpherson's own inventive creation, partly based on earlier Gaelic sources.[53] According to Meyer's study, reported in the *Gaelic American*, 'That particular version of the story, which in old Irish literature is embodied in the tale of the fight between Chuchulain and his son Conla, is ultimately derived, both in its main features and in all important details, from the Persian story of Rustem and Sohrab.' Meyer added: 'This occurs as an episode in the Shah Nameh of Firdusi, a poet of the tenth century, who worked by older legends. Long before his time, however, it had passed from Persia Westward. ... It seems most likely that it was the Anglo-Saxons who handed it on to the Irish sometime during the seventh or eighth century.'[54]

(It should be noted that the original publication of Macpherson's Ossianic epics coincided with the late eighteenth-century surge of interest in Western Europe in Celtic languages and cultures, a development that would subsequently impact the Irish literary and cultural Revivals of the late nineteenth century. Among other leading contributors to the eighteenth-century interest in Celtic studies was the already-mentioned Charles Vallancey. In fact, based on his faulty etymological-linguistic approach and his insistence on the Persian origins of the Gaels, in response to Macpherson's claim of the Celtic origin of the Ossian poems, Vallancey, too, had insisted that the poems were 'Persian in origin'.[55])

Particularly among the more radical Irish nationalist groupings during the period covered in this study, the common origins of the Gaels, Indians, and Iranians – albeit with much greater stress on the shared origins of the Irish and Indians, given the extent of collaboration and solidarity among the nationalists from both of these territories within the British Empire[56] – were deployed as an ideological counter-hegemonic narrative in opposition to mainstream British hierarchical civilizational/racial constructs and as a means of bolstering the anti-colonial Irish-Indian nationalist solidarity against British rule. Additionally, the broader Irish interest in the Aryan theory of racial origins at the time needs to be framed within the context of the 'racial' *whitening* of the Irish in British (hierarchical) racial discourses of the late nineteenth century, when the Irish (Catholics in particular) were gradually being transformed from lesser/darker/degenerate whites to the status of more-equal whites in the imperial hierarchy; while simultaneously in the United States the Irish themselves were actively engaged in shedding their appellation of 'white nigger' in order to become 'white'.[57] In Iran too, at the time, Aryan racial theory was utilized in certain predominantly secular circles as a political-historical nationalist discourse. However, this Iranian discourse of Aryanism, in contradistinction to Irish nationalist appeals to Aryanism, stressed the racial affinity of Iranians with the populations of Western European *imperialist* countries, the British in particular. For example, at the 1911 gathering of the First Universal Races Congress in London, the veteran Iranian nationalist/constitutionalist Yahya Dowlatabadi emphasized the 'racial' affinity and intrinsic civilizational proximity of Iranians with Western Europeans in a hierarchical and Perso-centric delineation of Iranian 'racial' identity that underscored the ostensible racial-civilizational aptitude of the Iranian 'nation'. According to Dowlatabadi, 'a categorical denial may be offered in the sense that there is not, and never has been, among our people any natural hostility to Europeans, who are, after all, of one and the same race with ourselves.'[58]

The *Gaelic American* was most enthusiastic about Pan-Aryanism as an anti-colonial project that could expedite Indian and Irish nationalist collaboration and independence. It regularly reported on the meetings and activities of the short-lived Pan-Aryan Association, founded in 1906 in New York City by the militant revolutionary Pan-Indian nationalist Maulavi Abdul Hafiz Mohammad Barakatullah and Samuel Lucas Joshi, with the assistance of Clan na Gael Irish nationalists (notably George Freeman of the *Gaelic American*). In February 1907, Barakatullah presented a lecture at the Brooklyn Gaelic Society. Appealing to the ostensibly common racial identity of the Irish and Indians in further fostering an anti-colonial cross-nationalist platform of solidarity, he maintained that 'Ireland should ally herself with India now. There is a racial question involved. The Irish and the old Aryans of the East are of the same race. Their racial characteristics are the same.'[59] The *Gaelic American*'s reports of the activities of the Pan-Aryan Association included a meeting of the organization in the spring of 1907, with Barakutullah as the guest speaker. At this gathering Barakatullah 'spoke on the situation in Persia', stating that 'Of all the Oriental lands, India and Persia have always exercised a charm on the American mind. The Pan-Aryan Association has been formed in New York with the object of creating a bond of sympathy and good will between the peoples of those lands and of America.'[60] However, what is noteworthy is that those Iranian nationalists who resorted to the Aryan racial theory consciously steered away from anti-colonial Pan-Aryanism, instead preferring to be associated with the 'imperialist' European Aryan races.

In essence, the distinct variations of Aryanist discourse in Indian and Irish nationalist platforms, on the one hand, and in Iranian nationalist platforms, on the other hand, were tied to broader *civilizational* discourses, frequently serving as countervailing instrumental strategies (by no means devoid of their own inherent racist hierarchical inferences) apropos Western/European hierarchical imperialist and hegemonic claims of racial superiority and civilizational maturity and 'modernity'. What these different utilizations of racial mythology underscore is the contemporaneous dissonant instrumentalist adherence to, and deployment of, the myth of Aryan origins, variously incorporated into nationalist discourses of Indians, the Irish, and Iranians.

The trend of Irish nationalist recourse to the myth of the Aryan origins of the 'Gaels' (which by the late nineteenth century had been elided with the generic category of the 'Irish') also assumed more mystical, as well as 'anti-rationalist' or anti-colonial 'modernist', dimensions in the purviews of those Irish nationalists who embraced theosophy, which among other Eastern religions (such as Hinduism and variants of Buddhism) also drew inspiration from some teachings and concepts of Zoroastrianism.[61] This was the case with William Butler Yeats (1865–1939), the Irish nationalist poet and playwright and a major figure of the early twentieth-century Irish Literary Revival, who practised hermetic occult ritual magic and had joined the Dublin Theosophical Society in 1887.[62] But Yeats's worldview was not solely shaped by magic and theosophy or his political and literary interest in India. The fourteenth-century Iranian mystic poet Hafiz was also a crucial influence on Yeats. In Hafiz, too, Yeats discovered the 'mystical cult of achieving union with the absolute through the senses'.[63]

'Iran' in Irish Nationalist Imaginations: History *Beyond* Race and Mysticism

It is important to stress that not only did the differing Irish nationalist discourses of Aryanism, or theosophy and mysticism, not impede the strong sense of common cause and collaboration between Irish nationalists and nationalists elsewhere, as in the case of the Irish nationalist advocacy of the Egyptian struggle for independence from British rule, for example, but that not all Irish nationalist commentators resorted to the Aryan mythology in their claims of cultural-civilizational sophistication vis-à-vis Britain or in their representations of Iran during these years. There were alternative discourses of civilizational antiquity – not always synonymous with the ancient 'golden age' versus subsequent degeneration – that appeared in some Irish nationalist commentaries on Iran's historical and cultural significance.

The parliamentary Home Rule Irish Nationalist John Dillon, a long-time champion of Indian self-rule and Egypt's independence, was among the earliest and most persistent defenders in the United Kingdom of the Iranian revolution and Iran's independence. At the end of a 1912 Persia Society[64] lecture on 'The Literature of Persia' by E. G. Browne – a co-founder and vice-chairman of the Persia Committee and a member of the Persia Society –, Dillon spoke on Iran's continual historical contributions, couched in a bifurcated 'cultural'/'spiritual' v. 'material' paradigm of counter-'Western modernities':

> My interest in that country was aroused some years ago by the writings and the speeches of Professor Browne, and my interest to it was attracted because I have all my life thought that one of the greatest outrages against humanity that can be perpetrated is to kill the soul or the civilisation of any nation. ... I am afraid that in these modern days the vast majority, at all events in Western Europe, have set up a false standard for the guidance of their own judgement as to what is really valuable in the civilisation of to-day. We in Western Europe are so handed over to materialism that we seem to think the amount of manufactures produced and the wealth realised is really the only standard by which you can judge a people, or that a nation like Persia, or many other nations who are no longer warlike [*sic*], wealthy, or able to defend themselves very well, do not matter; and that it is no loss to mankind if they are wiped out of existence and forgotten.
>
> ...
>
> When I learned from Professor Browne that there was a nation with so great a historic past, so great and so well-founded a national pride, and a nation

who had contributed so enormously to the spiritual wealth of mankind by its arts and by its literature, in the condition that Persia is to-day, all my deepest sympathies were aroused.

...

Another thing is perfectly plain: that we in the West have inflicted great injustice and injury on many of the Eastern races.

...

I confess that my sympathies go out to all these races. My sympathies go out to Morocco and to Egypt, and to all these races ... who have a historic past, a national self-consciousness, which in my opinion is the necessary seed-bed of great achievement; and though it may appear somewhat of a paradox, I say that my sympathy goes out especially to those countries which still have succeeded in resisting the introduction of railways. ... I venture to offer my advice ... if you allow railways to be laid down without paying for them yourselves, your country will pass into the hands of others.[65]

Dillon's counter-'Western modernities' model of civilizational maturity, based on a distinction between so-called material and cultural/civilizational realms, was not an exclusively 'Western' or Irish paradigm and had contemporary counterparts in 'oriental' and other reactions to Western imperialism and/ or claims of civilizational grandeur and modernity.[66] Dillon was not the only Irish nationalist whose views on Iran and whose estimation of Iran's continuous cultural/civilizational contributions to the world at large were shaped by Browne. The positivist-rationalist Fred Ryan, a socialist Irish nationalist journalist with an internationalist proclivity and an associate of W. S. Blunt, also was influenced by Browne's writings and public statements on Iran (not discounting the impact of Ryan's residence in Cairo from 1908 to 1909 as the co-editor of the *Egyptian Standard*, along with another internationalist Irish nationalist, William J. Maloney, and Ryan's espousal of and collaborations with other anti-colonial nationalist struggles).[67]

Both the *Gaelic American* and *Sinn Féin* frequently printed reports from the *Egyptian Standard*.[68] The *Egyptian Standard* (Cairo) was founded by the Egyptian nationalist leader Mustapha Kamil in 1907 and was funded by W. S. Blunt as the English-language edition of *al-Liwa* (the Standard). After its first year of publication, the paper (appearing as a daily for the first two years and then as a weekly) was edited by William J. Maloney and Fred Ryan, until it ceased publication in 1909, a few months after Mustapha Kamil's death. With the cessation of the *Egyptian Standard*, Blunt launched a successor English-language journal in London called *Egypt*, which was edited by Ryan until his early death in 1913. The *Egyptian Standard* along with, of course, its original Arabic edition *al-Liwa*, as well as the French edition of the paper, were known in Iranian nationalist circles, with the Iranian constitutionalist/nationalist press periodically reproducing Persian translations of reports appearing in these papers. In February 1908, for example, the Tehran constitutionalist paper *Majles* published a long article on 'Islamic Affairs', in which the paper devoted ample space to Mustapha Kamil's activities and mentioned that *al-Liwa*, not content with its Arabic-language edition and desirous of disseminating its views in Europe, had launched both English- and French-language editions of the paper, adding that the paper provided abundant coverage of news related to Iran and Iranians and expressing gratitude to Mustapha Kamil.[69]

Besides working and writing for the *Egyptian Standard* and *Egypt*, in the case of Ryan, and working for the former and occasionally writing for the latter, in the case of Maloney, both of these Irish nationalists endorsed the Iranian revolutionary movement in other forms. After leaving Egypt, Maloney would briefly report for the *Manchester Guardian* from Istanbul a few months after the Young Turk Revolution, before being stationed in Iran in the spring of 1909 as the Reuters correspondent, providing sympathetic accounts of the Iranian constitutionalist/nationalist camp until he left for England in autumn of 1911 (c. October), and assisting the Persia Committee through communications with Browne and others.[70] Ryan, on the other hand, would write a number of sympathetic articles on Iran, some of them in the form of book reviews, including highly favourable reviews of E. G. Browne's 1910 *The Persian Revolution* in the *Irish Review* (August 1911) and W. Morgan Shuster's *The Strangling of Persia* in *Egypt* (September 1912). Quoting two passages from Browne's *The Persian Revolution* on the role of the clergy in the Iranian revolution (including the passage quoted earlier in this essay), Ryan concentrated on what he considered to be the contemporary cultural and political proximity between Iran and Ireland, while debunking all self-aggrandizing racial theories and denigrating trends in Western orientalism and instead advocating a universalist discourse of 'humanity'. He concluded his review of Browne's book with the following observations:

> How entirely intelligible, one had almost written, how Irish, it all is. Between the issues raised in the controversy over the 'Ne Temere' decree and these domestic questions in Persia what a little way, after all, separates us! The secular and democratic forces standing for the equal rights of all Persians, irrespective of religion, the high clerical party clinging to special privileges for Muslims, and yet amongst the clergy, again, those whose love of national independence, or perhaps more correctly, hatred of what in Ireland is often called 'infidel foreign influences', made them valuable champions of the popular cause.
>
> There are many lessons of worth to be drawn from this story of Persia's heroic effort at self-regeneration. With nations as with individuals, reform cometh from within. ... In the case of Persia, also, we learn the essential unity of the human problem under all its different phases and the futility of the philosophy of Western despots who, anxious to dominate and exploit the East, set up the

pleasant doctrine that the peoples of the East love despotism, and thus fundamentally differ from the peoples of the West. The laws of human nature are not suspended east of Suez, and there is not a single political struggle in the East to-day that has not its counterpart either in the recent history or the contemporary convulsions of the West. It is in this realisation of human kinship, this shattering of the pride of race and the pride of power and the pride of religion, as well as in the wealth of social experience which now opens before humanity that there lies the greatest hope of moral advance, alike for the Eastern and the Western world.[71]

In another article on the 'Persian Crisis: An Irish Parallel' in the Dublin *Irish Independent*, only days after the Russian-instigated Bakhtiyari putsch against the Second Majles in December 1911 and the inauguration of the Russian 'reign of terror' in northern Iran, Ryan wrote:

Professor Browne of Cambridge, who has done so much to support the Persian cause and to put the case of the Persian nation before English readers, once wrote to me that he always thought there was a considerable likeness between Ireland and Persia, Erin and Iran, both countries having gone through the tragedy of manifold national defeat and invasion, yet both always clinging to an ideal of nationality and striving after that ideal through dark and evil days. One of the myths about the East current in Europe is that the idea of patriotism and national independence is unknown there. It is, of course, a convenient myth enough for those who desire to annex rich slices of Eastern countries, but it sometimes leads to sad accidents, as in the Italian raid on Tripoli. The Oriental people may not have heard of the myth, and may stupidly try to defend their country against the invader.

The Persian movement towards national regeneration is, perhaps, the most striking, with one exception [i.e., Egypt], of these revivals in the East which have been such a feature in the world history of the past two decades. [72]

Ryan was locating the Iranian revolution in a universal historical framework without recourse to racial theories or spiritual/mystical formulations, although he was at the same time grossly misrepresenting not only the notion of a historically continuous and uniform sentiment of a collective 'Iranian' identity but also Irish and Iranian historical attachments to 'nationality'. Nor did his universalization of 'nationality' as an ideal quality elucidate the advantage of nationalism over alternative modes of identity/belonging, other than casting imperialism as a malignant and deleterious force.

Irish Nationalist Commentaries on Iran after the Constitutional Revolution

With the outbreak of the First World War in 1914 the Irish Parliamentary Party supported the British war effort – in the hope of London's fulfilment of the Irish Home Rule Act of 1914 after the war –, while the radical and militant Irish nationalists condemned the British war effort. Commentaries by the latter groups, including those in the *Gaelic American* and *Sinn Féin*, after the British entry into the war in September 1914 (with *Sinn Féin* suppressed by British authorities in late 1914) and after the end of the war in 1918 – including during the 1919–21 'Irish War of Independence' – indicate both the continued interest of these nationalist circles in Iran's independence and their instrumentalist utilization of Iran's fate following the Anglo-Russian Agreement of 1907 as a means of underscoring Britain's continued imperialist complicity around the globe.

Following the outbreak of the First World War in 1914, Iran also assumed a new position in the commentaries of Irish nationalists. It was no longer ancient history, a myth of origins, or contemporary political developments in Iran that in various ways appeared in these commentaries. Iran had now also entered the realm of Irish nationalist 'political memory'. For example, a few weeks after the start of the First World War, the socialist Irish nationalist labour leader James Connolly, who later would be one of the chief architects of and participants in the 1916 Easter Rising in Ireland and subsequently executed, wrote sardonically:

> The 'war on behalf of small nationalities' is still going merrily on in the newspapers.
> ...
> The Russian Government and the British Government stand solidly together in favour of small nationalities everywhere except in countries now under Russian and British Rule.
> ...
> This vicious and rebellious memory of mine will also recur to the recent attempt of Persia to form a constitutional government, and it recalls how, when that ancient nation shook off the fetters of its ancient despotism, and set to work to elaborate the laws and forms in the spirit of a modern civilised representative state, Russia, which in solemn treaty with England had guaranteed its independence, at once invaded it, and slaughtering all its patriots, pillaging its towns and villages, annexed part of its territories, and made the rest a mere Russian dependency. I remember how Sir Edward Grey, who now gushes over the sanctity of treaties, when appealed to stand by and make Russia stand by the treaty guaranteeing the independence of Persia, coolly refused to interfere.[73]

Sinn Féin – edited by the then pro-German leader of the Sinn Féin party, Arthur Griffith –, in its explication of why the war had broken out, blamed London for instigating the conflict, condemning, among other factors, London's pre-war sacrifice of Iran's independence in its attempt to win Russia's friendship in the European balance of power against Germany: 'Russia saw her opportunity and seized it. Before she came in she exacted a price from England, which England reluctantly paid – the chief part of that price was Persia – a country whom England was bound by her honour to protect. Her honour!'[74] In his 1915 *The Crime Against Europe: A Possible Outcome of the War of 1914*, the republican Irish nationalist and former British diplomat Sir Roger Casement (executed by British authorities on 3 August 1916 on a charge of treason for attempting to smuggle weapons from Germany into Ireland and allegedly abetting the Easter Rising), alluded to the Anglo-Russian 'spheres of influence' in Iran.[75]

In 1920, after the end of the First World War and following the abortive 1919 Anglo-Iranian Agreement, which was intended to impose British dominance over Iran, and coinciding with the Irish War of Independence following the declaration of the Irish Republic, Eamon De Valera, the president of the declared republic, stated at the conclusion of a speech at the gathering of the Friends of Freedom for India in New York: 'Our cause is a common cause. We swear friendship tonight; and we send our common greetings and our pledges to our brothers in Egypt and in Persia, and tell them also that their cause is our cause.'[76]

The Enigma of the Iranian Silence on the Irish Question

Not only did Iranian nationalists and constitutionalists appeal to a different range of Aryan mythology and historicization than the politically crafted Pan-Aryanism of militant Irish and Indian nationalists during the time of the Iranian Constitutional Revolution, but what remains a seeming enigma is the absence of commentaries on the 'Irish Question' by Iranian nationalists during the revolution. While the Iranian constitutional press certainly were familiar with Indian and Egyptian nationalist commentaries on Ireland, in addition to the coverage of Irish developments in other international press – particularly since Iranian constitutionalist newspapers frequently reported from Indian, Egyptian, and other sources that also happened to cover various dimensions of Irish nationalism –, the absence of commentaries on Ireland in the Iranian constitutionalist press and the dearth of Iranian references to Irish commentaries on Iran (historical, cultural, or political) remains seemingly inexplicable, even as the Iranian constitutionalist press recognized the Home Rule Irish Nationalist MPs John Dillon and John Redmond as among the leading defenders of Iran's independence in Britain (at times mistakenly assigning the IPP leader, Redmond, more credit than Dillon). In addition, as a Reuters reporter in Iran who was sympathetic to the Iranian revolutionary cause, the Irish nationalist Maloney was known to some Iranian nationalist circles.

This is not to suggest that all nationalist movements reciprocated the assistance or advocacy of other nationalist movements. For example, Iranian revolutionaries (other than some Iranian Armenians) did not advocate the Armenian nationalist cause, despite the presence of Armenian nationalists from the Caucasus in the ranks of Iranian constitutionalist fighters during the civil war of 1908–09 and later,[77] leaving aside the competing Armenian nationalist agendas. There were a number of reasons contributing to this lack of advocacy, among them the potential effect of Armenian nationalism on Iran's own Armenian population, the recent tensions between Azeri and Armenian communities in the Russian Caucasus (with both Azeri and Armenian populations also living in Iran, the former in much larger numbers), and the more extensive assistance of Russian and Iranian émigré Azeris in the Caucasus to the Iranian revolutionary camp, as well as the fact that the Iranian province of Azarbayjan was a primary centre of Iranian constitutional resistance to the Russian-backed Iranian autocracy during the civil war. Moreover, there were concerns with the Ottoman reaction to any Iranian sponsorship of the Armenian nationalist cause, with Ottoman Armenian territories a primary focus of the Armenian nationalist activities (particularly because Iranian nationalists hoped for tangible Young Turk support of their own cause and Ottoman military forces continued their occupation of Iranian soil even after the Young Turk Revolution of 1908). In the case of Irish nationalist (Home Rule, Sinn Féin, or various republican groups) endorsement of the Iranian revolution, the lack of a mutual Iranian promotion of any of the Irish nationalist platforms stemmed from very different sets of considerations.

The absence of Iranian nationalist commentaries on Ireland elicited an explanation from two Irish journalists who covered the Iranian revolution during the civil war of 1908–09. In their 1910 book, *Persia in Revolution*, Joseph Maunsell Hone and Page L. Dickinson indicated a sense of unease among Iranian nationalists of being in any way associated with Irish nationalist politics, maintaining that this was due to the fact that some Iranian nationalists believed that even their very designation as 'nationalists' in Britain could harm efforts by Iranian constitutionalists to generate British public support in opposition to Grey's Iranian policy:

> Several Nationalists were at pains to point out that the term was an unfortunate one. Being in bad odour owing to 'those Irish', it would not attract the sympathy of English people. The point was brought before us by the [Persian] correspondent of the *Times* among others. Curiously enough at this very

moment an Irish M.P., under misapprehension that the *Times* had dismissed this gentleman from its service, asked a question on his behalf in the English House of Commons. This gentleman's use of the phrase 'those Irish' and his anxiety lest a parallel should be drawn between the Irish and Persian Nationalists were, in the circumstances, unkind. The ingratitude was of course unconscious; the English newspapers containing the Irish M.P.'s question and the *Times*' explanation of the facts had not yet arrived in Teheran.[78]

While Hone and Dickinson were ultimately correct about the Iranian nationalist reticence in alluding to the Irish Question, there are a number of problems with their explanation, leaving aside the authors' many sensationalist details in the book, which received a highly critical review from Fred Ryan. The Iranian constitutionalists/nationalists visiting Britain during the Iranian civil war (who also met with John Dillon – the 'Irish M.P.' who had inquired into the dismissal of 'the [Persian] correspondent of the *Times*' – among Grey's other critics) were actually apprehensive of being portrayed as 'revolutionaries' in the British press, given the mixed connotations of this term in Britain and in the context of the British Empire, particularly since the British critics of Grey's Iranian policy included stalwart Unionists, and Browne for propaganda purposes was determined to dissociate the Persian Question in British public debates from inferences that developments in Iran might set another precedent for the revolutionary movements in India and other parts of the British Empire, choosing instead to focus on worldwide Muslim outrage at British policy towards Iran, including by Indian Muslim nationalists affiliated with the All-India Muslim League, which at the time advocated loyalty to the British Empire. In fact, the Iranian constitutionalists visiting Britain preferred to be labelled in the British press as 'nationalists' instead of 'revolutionaries'.[79]

Moreover, inside Iran itself, Iranian nationalists did not shy away from alluding to and even applauding militant Indian, 'Egypt for Egyptians', and other nationalist struggles – with the rise in militant Indian nationalist violence after 1905 in some ways paralleling the late nineteenth-century Irish Fenian campaigns of violence.[80] Yet references to Ireland in the Iranian constitutionalist press, including to the moderate parliamentary Irish Home Rule campaign, were nominal at best even in regular reports of world events. There had been very limited direct contact between Iran and Ireland up to that point.[81] This, however, does not denote an absolute lack of familiarity with Irish history, British rule in Ireland, or the broad range of Irish nationalist activities among educated Iranians and others,[82] as jumbled as differing Iranian imaginations of Ireland may have been.[83] Iranian constitutionalist newspapers frequently reported on parliamentary, nationalist, and imperial developments in other parts of the world and copiously commented on British imperial policy elsewhere, and various Iranian nationalists (primarily the secular-oriented) publicly alluded to historical and contemporary developments and parallels with the Iranian nationalist struggle in other parts of the world. But Ireland rarely featured in such reports.

The 'Irish lacuna' in Iranian nationalist references to worldwide nationalist struggles was actually due to the particularities of British rule in Ireland, while also indicative of the limitations of Iranian internationalisms. It was a calculated, instrumentalist Iranian nationalist strategy (hinted at by Hone and Dickinson) that ultimately privileged the Iranian revolution above other nationalist causes (in a manner different from mere preoccupation with the 'self' and similar to the early dismissive stance of the radical Irish nationalist press on the Iranian revolution, and also present in Arthur Griffith's castigation of Fred Ryan's transcendent internationalism). The fact that Ireland had been a constituent part of the United Kingdom since 1801 and had parliamentary representation at Westminster, including the representation of the Irish Home Rule party (and keeping in mind that the majority of Iranian revolutionaries were committed to a parliamentary constitutional monarchy, with only a minority of republicans in their ranks), the Irish Question was regarded not so much as a nationalist concern but, rather, as an internal political matter in the United Kingdom to be resolved through parliamentary and electoral decision making (with the latter process in keeping with the IPP platform).[84] In effect, in this characterization of the body politic of the United Kingdom, Irish republican nationalists would have been cast as 'separatists' or, in the Iranian political parlance of the day, as 'anarchists' (i.e., 'extremists') – keeping in mind also the existing unionist population of Ireland. There also were no major nationalist-unionist disturbances in Ireland during the time of the Iranian revolution akin to the Zulu uprising in Natal (South Africa) in 1906, which attracted press attention in Iran; with communal conflict in Ireland soaring only after the passage of the 1912 Home Rule Bill by the British parliament.

Moreover, not only did the Irish (of various Protestant denominations and Catholic) serve in the British imperial military (in a manner distinct from the imperial use of native Indian forces by Britain), but the Irish also participated in administering the empire. Furthermore, given the concerted efforts by Iranian revolutionaries to bring British diplomatic pressure to bear on St. Petersburg in defence of the Iranian constitutional movement in the aftermath of the 1907 Anglo-Russian Agreement, with Russia as the chief *outside* culprit in suppressing the Iranian constitutional camp, any advocacy of the Irish nationalist platforms was bound to frazzle the British Liberal-Imperialist foreign secretary Sir Edward Grey and prove detrimental to the Iranian constitutional camp. In effect, Iranian self-preservation trumped internationalism. Even after 1907, Iranian nationalists had not completely abandoned hope of courting London as a potential regional counterweight to St. Petersburg's Iranian policy, regardless of London's continued *public* rationalization of Russian aggression in Iran. While Iranian nationalists did not shy away from accepting the assistance of armed mercenaries and volunteers from Russian territories during the 1908–09 civil war, which was bound to further infuriate St. Petersburg, and simultaneously welcomed the support of Armenian or Bulgarian *nationalist* fighters while reaching out to the Young Turks after 1908 (even as the Ottoman occupation of Iranian territories continued unabated), London's potential diplomatic leverage over Russian policy was considered far too critical to relinquish in pursuit of maintaining Iran's existing limited sovereignty. The 'worlding' of the Iranian revolution by Iranian nationalists[85] and cross-nationalist solidarity had their limits.

While India and Egypt, too, were part of the British Empire, there were major differences with Ireland, even aside from the much greater Iranian historical familiarity with the former territories. Egypt, formerly an Ottoman province, was part of the 'Islamic' world that had come under European imperial control in 1882 (regardless of the Shiite–Sunni divisions among Muslims). India, on the other hand, not only bordered Iran to the southeast, but had been a leading factor in the evolution of British policy towards Iran since the start of the nineteenth century. Furthermore, much of the Indian subcontinent prior to British imperial ascendancy had been ruled by the (Muslim) Mughal dynasty, and Iran and 'India' had various ties and exchanges dating back to ancient times, with a sizeable Iranian émigré community in India as well as close collaborations among Iranian nationalists, Indian Muslim nationalists, and Pan-Indian nationalists during the Iranian revolution. In addition, the financial support of India's Zoroastrian Parsi community for the Iranian constitutional camp certainly was not negligible.[86] Ireland, on the other hand, was a geographically, religiously, and culturally far-removed and lesser-known territory for Iranians, while too close to home to Britain and generally understood by Iranians as historically a component of 'British' territory. Therefore, Irish nationalism was a more readily dispensable cause, even if it were recognized as a valid 'nationalist' cause, in the multiple Iranian nationalist matrices of safeguarding Iranian (or Muslim) interests first and foremost – notwithstanding the manifold Irish nationalist advocacy of the Iranian revolution –, and any potential loss of Home Rule Irish nationalist support for the Iranian revolutionary camp would not entirely have hampered 'British' criticisms of Grey's Iranian policy variously spearheaded by the Persia Committee and a few staunch Unionists outside the committee, such as Lord Curzon, the former viceroy of India (1899–1905). Thus were the Iranian configurations of worldwide 'nationalist' struggles and *nationalism above internationalism* at the time, including among many socialists in contact with the International Socialist

Bureau (to which James Connolly's Socialist Party of Ireland belonged). The outbreak of the First World War, and especially the formation of the German-backed Iranian nationalist committee in Berlin, with Berlin also sponsoring militant Irish and Indian nationalists, would inaugurate greater Iranian nationalist awareness of, interest in, and identification with, the Irish Question.[87]

CHAPTER 18

Crafting Constitutional Narratives: Iranian and Young Turk Solidarity 1907–09

Farzin Vejdani

The years 1906 and 1908 witnessed the emergence of two constitutional regimes in the Middle East: the first in Iran and the second in the Ottoman Empire. These twin revolutions were part of a broader global wave of constitutional movements.[1] Current scholarship on these two revolutions rarely takes into account how the two movements informed and shaped one another. This paper makes the revisionist claim that the brief period of 1907–09 witnessed intense cooperation among Iranian and Ottoman constitutionalists, culminating in the construction of shared constitutional narratives. These shared constitutional narratives were messianic in tone: both envisioned the imminence of a golden age of constitutionalism in the Islamic world, signalling the end of absolutist monarchs on the one hand and of foreign imperial domination on the other. But these shared narratives neither appeared in a vacuum nor were they static in light of events on the ground. Throughout the course of the two eventful years from 1907 to 1909, Iranian and Ottoman revolutionaries modified and re-scripted their shared constitutional narratives, reacting to revolutionary victories and setbacks experienced by both groups.

Three crucial turning points determined the shape of this constitutional narrative. First, there was a concerted effort by exiled Ottoman constitutionalists to express their solidarity with their Iranian counterparts while at the same time distancing themselves from the aggressive posturing of Sultan Abdülhamid II along the Iranian–Ottoman border. This was done through letters, manifestos, and the dispatching of Ottoman emissaries to Iran seeking crucial allies and bases of operation from which to launch revolutionary activities in Eastern Anatolia. The Iranian constitutional revolution expanded the horizon of possibilities for the Ottoman constitutionalists: just as the Japanese victory over the Russian Empire in 1905 had demonstrated how an Asian nation could defeat a European power, the Iranian revolution demonstrated how constitutionalism could take root in an Islamic nation, thus contributing to a hope among Ottoman constitutionalists that their country was next.

The second phase of Iranian–Ottoman interactions was marked by two nearly simultaneous events: the fall of the first constitutional regime in Iran in June 1908 and the rise to power of the Young Turks in July of the same year. These two events were crucial in shaping Iranian and Ottoman self-understandings in relation to one another. The devastation felt by Iranian constitutionalists at the Shah's bombing of the Majles was quickly followed by a glimmer of optimism with the triumph of the Young Turks. For the Young Turks, the defeat of the Iranian constitutionalists had the opposite effect: initial Ottoman euphoria was tempered by the sobering possibility of their own monarch heading a similar counterrevolution, a possibility nearly realized in the 'March 31st' incident, but ultimately ending in the fall of Sultan Abdülhamid. Iran and the Ottoman Empire had reversed roles in the constitutional narrative. The Ottoman constitutionalists now assisted their embattled Iranian counterparts by providing a place of exile for Iranian revolutionaries fleeing the government, extending their diplomatic representations as places of refuge and resistance against the Shah's forces, and, much more dramatically, supplying arms, military assistance, and fighters to the most hotly contested battle zone – the province of Azarbayjan. The Iranian constitutionalist march on Tehran and the fall of Mohammad Ali Shah in July of 1909 marked not only a moment of triumph for the Iranian constitutionalists, but also a moment of fulfilment in the shared Ottoman–Iranian constitutional narratives: for the first time, both Iran and the Ottoman Empire simultaneously had constitutional governments. But with messianic fulfilment came new challenges to Iranian–Ottoman relations, particularly with respect to the border question and the rise of Pan-Turkism – challenges that would remain a source of political contention into the 1920s.

The Iranian Constitutional Revolution, the Border Crisis and CUP Solidarity

The 1906 Iranian constitutional revolution had a profound impact on the Ottoman Committee of Union and Progress (CUP) members in Paris. The CUP viewed the Iranian constitutional revolution, preceding as it did the 1908 Young Turk Revolution by several years, as an emerging trend against autocracy in the Islamic world – an event that only emboldened the CUP in their activities against Sultan Abdülhamid II.[2] Since news of the revolution was censored by Abdülhamid, it was the CUP in Paris who were initially most vocal in their support for the Iranian constitutionalists.[3] History, as they saw it, was now on the side of the constitutionalists. The CUP members in Paris who were most intent on building contacts with Iranian constitutionalists represented leaders from different trends within the movement, including

Prince Sabahaddin, Bahaeddin Şakir, and Ahmed Rıza.

Two challenges the Iranian constitutionalists faced almost immediately shaped the shared narrative of Ottoman–Iranian constitutional solidarity: Abdülhamid's border incursions into Iran and anti-government uprisings in Eastern Anatolia. In response to the Constitutional Revolution, Sultan Abdülhamid sent troops into the Iranian province of Azarbayjan, attempting to seize supposedly disputed border lands near Urmia and Savojbolagh (today's Mahabad).[4] This prompted the CUP to contact Iranian ministers and diplomats and various constitutionalist organizations. Their statements on the border issue reveal an attempt to disassociate the Ottoman nation (*millet*) from the Ottoman government, stressing that while the former was constitutional and supportive of the Iranians, the latter was not. The CUP examined Abdülhamid's aggressive actions against Iran within an Islamic and anti-Islamic context: by attacking Iran, the Sultan was undermining Islamic unity and strengthening European imperial designs.

Beyond their negative consequences for Islamic solidarity and anti-imperial efforts, the CUP considered the border incursions to be a deliberate strategy of containment: the Sultan's immediate fear was the spread of constitutionalism from Iran to the Ottoman Empire. A series of uprisings in Eastern Anatolia only added to the Sultan's concerns for the explosive possibility of constitutional ideas emanating from Iran mixing with the powder keg of internal Ottoman unrest. It was this unsettling possibility which struck fear into the heart of the Sultan while simultaneously giving hope to the Young Turks that their revolution was just on the horizon. In the same letter, Şakir mentions that the CUP had sent out manifestos to the Ottoman border guards imploring them to avoid divisions among Islamic countries.[5]

Iranian commentators on the border conflict had a similar reading. One Iranian journalist viewed the uprising in Eastern Anatolia as not merely a reaction to over-taxation, but more importantly as an expression of constitutional aspirations.[6] Another article, by the journalist Asef, used medical tropes in describing the Sultan's 'crazed actions' (*harakat-e majnuneh*). He suggests that the illness afflicting the Ottoman governing body was neither cholera, typhoid, nor influenza. Instead, it was the advent of the Iranian constitution that coincided with 'confusion and trembling' (*herasan va larzan*) in the Ottoman body politic. The immediate outcome of this affliction was a desire to react in a desperate manner – in this case, it included the Ottomans illegally attacking Iran, confiscating newspapers and correspondence, turning their back on governmental agreements, and violating the rights of Iranians as a whole. In addition to these allegations, Asef accused the Ottomans of paying anti-constitutional mullahs to create disturbances inside Iran. Meanwhile the Sultan repressed writers within his borders, although he was unable to stop the free press in Egypt. Asef's reading of the border situation reflects that of his Ottoman counterpart: Abdülhamid's border incursions were more than a land grab, they were an attempt to stop 'dangerous' ideas of constitutionalism from spreading through contagion from an infected revolutionary Iran to its Ottoman neighbour. Asef saw the solution to the Sultan's 'crazy actions' as simple: a 'contagious cure' (*dava-ye mosri*), meaning 'justice' (*'edalat*). This 'contagious cure' apparently 'returns the nation to its spiritual nature and creates a hospital (*dar al-shefa'*) that will cure the diseases afflicting the nation'. According to Asef, Iran has began treatment – the Ottoman Empire is in need of a similar cure – a 'spiritual' (*ma'navi*) cure that is not containable by 'material and tangible means'. Ideas, in other words, cannot be stopped by military troops.

Asef's article frames the Anatolian uprisings with a similar eye to the future, warning the Sultan to fear the 'clouds of revenge', implying an imminent fall of his regime and its replacement with a constitutional government.[7] The degree to which both Young Turks and Iranian constitutionalists expected the imminent fall of Abdülhamid, and of Islamic autocratic regimes in general, was a central aspect of the shared utopian narrative that developed during this period. In a telegram sent to the Iranian Majles in December of 1907 from a Young Turk congress, Prince Sabahaddin and Ahmed Rıza Bey articulated this expectation most explicitly, stating that 'after the establishment of a constitutional administration in the Ottoman government, the two neighbouring countries can strengthen their friendship and render service to Eastern civilization.'[8] Once again, the utopian constitutional script points to a certain sense of inevitability – the Iranian Constitutional Revolution had swept aside despotism, and soon the Ottoman Empire would have its turn. The envisioned change would mean that Iranian and Ottoman constitutional governments, both members of 'Eastern civilization', could usher in a new era of resistance to Western imperialism.

The sympathy of the CUP leadership did not end with mere pronouncements and letters expressing pious hopes of future cooperation, however. The CUP decided to dispatch a group of emissaries led by the poet and preacher Ömer Naci from Paris to Azarbayjan in order to deliver a CUP declaration to the national committee (Anjoman-e Melli) in person. Aside from this task, the emissaries were charged with several other duties: first, they were to assess the nature of constitutionalism in Iran; second, they were to forge links with Iranian constitutionalists; and third, they were asked to contact Armenian groups operating within Iran with the hope of garnering their support against Abdülhamid.

Naci's Mission to Iran, Sa'id Salmasi, and the Ottoman *mojahedin* in Azarbayjan

Ömer Naci's mission to Iran demonstrates how, prior to the Young Turk revolution, Iran served as a base for organizing CUP activities in Eastern Anatolia in addition to fostering alliances with the Armenian Dashnaks. Naci, a prominent CUP preacher and poet, fled the Ottoman Empire after having been charged with publishing subversive material.[9] In Paris, Naci identified with the 'minority' faction of Ahmed Rıza and against the 'majority' faction of Sabahaddin, with whom he had many disagreements.[10] From Paris, the CUP decided to dispatch Ömer Naci with the task of further fuelling uprising in Eastern Anatolia, seeking out Armenian allies in Iran, and forging links with Iranian constitutionalists.

Iran, as a constitutional country bordering the volatile Eastern Anatolia region, became a potentially useful ally for the CUP, who could use it as an ideal launching pad for CUP operations. Entering Eastern Anatolia via Iran, Naci attempted to join the uprisings in Van and Erzurum, but found that the government had suppressed them.[11] Hoping to stir up opposition in Eastern Anatolia, Naci had come to Iran in large part to find support for such a programme among Armenians. The Dashnak attended the Ottoman liberal congresses in 1902 and 1907, and shortly after the second congress, where it was decided that armed resistance was a legitimate means of overthrowing Abdülhamid, they were coordinating with the Young Turks in carrying out terrorist activities.[12] After 1907, it is not surprising to see that Ömer Naci was entrusted with the mission of forging closer ties with the Dashnak organization operating within Iran. As a transnational organization with a sizeable membership on both sides of the border, the Dashnaks were an ideal conduit through which the CUP could pursue its goal of toppling Abdülhamid in the eastern domains of the Ottoman Empire. The Dashnaktsutiun welcomed closer ties with the CUP who were their natural allies against Abdülhamid, particularly in the aftermath of the 1894–96 massacre of Armenians.[13] Naci was involved in similar activities in Iran. Shortly after Armenian uprisings in Van, Naci contacted M. Samsun, a prominent Dashnak leader in the border village of Kalesr, hoping to coordinate further subversive actions in the Ottoman Empire. Some of these uprisings were planned for the spring of 1908.[14] Although these alliances did not lead to the hoped-for insurrection that would eventually topple the government, the Dashnaks continued to be a major ally of the CUP in the immediate aftermath of their rise to power, despite an underlying sense of ambivalence.

Naci's search for allies in Iran brought him into contact with Sa'id Salmasi. Salmasi's school and journal, both named *Sa'idiyeh*, provided a convenient cover for Naci to pursue his activities without drawing the unwanted attention of the local Ottoman consul.[15] Naci, posing as a teacher, was secretly making contacts for the CUP, among both the Dashnaks and other local *anjomans*. While much of Naci's work until this point had been geared towards finding allies for the CUP against Abdülhamid, the course of events on the ground in Iran changed the nature of his mission, as well as the tone of Iranian–Ottoman narratives that made sense of it.

On 23 June 1908, Mohammad Ali Shah gave the order for the Cossack Brigade, commanded by the Russian Colonel Liakhov, to bomb the Majles in Tehran, thereby ending the first constitutional period. This was the beginning of what came to be known as the Lesser Despotism (1908–09). Many of the leaders of the constitutional movement in Tehran were rounded up and executed. In the provinces, including Azarbayjan, the position of the royalists was strengthened. The pro-royalist Eqbal al-Saltaneh Maku'i and his forces capitalized on the coup by directly engaging the constitutionalists in battle, particularly in Salmas.[16] Naci was not unaffected by the course of events – in fact his position in Iran was altered radically. No longer was he in a sympathetic constitutional country where he could freely make contacts for the CUP. And while Naci had previously relied on Salmasi for assistance in carrying out his CUP activities, now both men were desperately fighting for their lives. In response, they formed an armed militia (*çete*), composed of both Iranians and Ottomans, and retreated to a nearby mountain. Almost overnight Naci and his Ottoman companions had gone from emissaries of the CUP to *mojaheds* caught in the grip of a counterrevolution. The royalist forces were sent into the mountains to defeat the militia – Salmasi escaped unharmed but Naci was incarcerated and sentenced to death.[17]

Changing Places: The Lesser Despotism and the Young Turk Revolution

The situation seemed bleak. Naci and his Ottoman associates had hoped a constitutional Iran would make a perfect haven for the CUP to resume oppositional activities against Abdülhamid. But a twist in the political fortunes of the Ottoman Empire had a direct bearing on Naci's fate and the Iranian constitutional movement as a whole. On 24 July 1908, the Young Turk Revolution led to the restoration of the Ottoman constitution. For constitutionalist morale, still reeling from the trauma of the Shah's coup a month earlier, the news of the revolution across the Iranian border was a major boost. Pro-royalist Iranian tribes temporarily sought peace with Tabriz constitutionalists, fearing the Ottoman troops on the border would intervene on the side of the latter.[18] The arrival of Iranian constitutionalist exiles in Istanbul coincided with the Young Turk Revolution, meaning that the Ottoman Empire now became a haven for exiled Iranian dissidents and activists.[19] Iran and the Ottoman Empire had switched roles – it was now a constitutional Ottoman Empire that was in a position to assist Iranian constitutionalists seeking to oppose the forces of autocracy.

Naci, a man already condemned to death, was given a second chance. The Young Turk Revolution meant that the Ottoman ambassador and consul, his erstwhile enemies, intervened on his behalf, alongside the Iranian constitutionalists, ensuring his release from prison.[20] The news of the Young Turk Revolution also emboldened militias to come down from their hiding places in the mountains to engage the government forces in battle. Naci and Salmasi reunited and headed for the Ottoman Empire, marking a new chapter in Iranian–Ottoman interactions.[21]

While Naci had already made allies in Iran and observed its constitutional government, it was now Salmasi who would actively seek allies in Ottoman domains and draw inspiration from Ottoman experiences. Naci, who was accompanied not only by Salmasi but also by two Dashnak militiamen, Ashnuk and Murad, was given a hero's welcome in the Ottoman town of Mush. Shortly thereafter, Naci and Salmasi proceeded to Erzurum, where they were invited to speak at a CUP conference attended by Iranian, Ottoman, and Armenian constitutionalists. While Naci spoke on Namık Kemal Bey and notions of 'freedom, justice, and equality', Salmasi was asked to speak on how the Iranians had gained a constitution and lost it to the forces of despotism.[22] Salmasi's speech constitutes a clear instance of how shared constitutional narratives were rewritten in light of major changes on the ground.

The Ottomans were keen to understand events in Iran. Having recently obtained a constitution, the prospect of having their government revert to an autocracy like Iran was a great source of anxiety. In fact, Abdülhamid, delighted by the bombing of the Majles prior to his own fall, encouraged the Ottoman press to cover this event as a warning of things to come for the constitutionalists in his own country.[23] The bombing of the Majles brought into question the shared grand Iranian–Ottoman constitutionalist narrative, while at the same time, paradoxically, reinforcing it. Despite the bombing, the ultimate triumph of constitutionalism was still largely considered an inevitability; but there was still a potential for throwbacks. Ottoman constitutionalists, therefore, sought to learn the lesson of history (*'ebrat*) from events in Iran in order to avoid a similar fate in the Ottoman Empire. Since Abdülhamid was still on the throne, the possibility of a counterrevolution loomed large.[24] Salmasi's speech illustrates how Iranian and Ottoman constitutionalists learned from one another's revolutionary experiences.

Throughout his speech, Salmasi draws explicit parallels between Iranian and Ottoman experiences with the intent of averting 'the same disaster that befell Iran' in the Ottoman Empire. He considered Ottoman constitutionalists to be the torch-bearers of the movement of the oppressed, which included Iran. In a bold statement, he declared, 'Turkey is my second homeland (*Türkiye de benim için ikinci bir vatandır*)' and went on to identify himself with 'all downtrodden nations', clearly an indication of his socialist tendencies. For him, the Iranian and Ottoman revolutions occurred on a continuum not limited to an Islamic or Eastern phenomenon, but as part of a broader international socialist one.

Salmasi's re-scripting of shared Ottoman–Iranian constitutional narratives along socialist lines comes through in his characterization of khans, governors, and *mujtahid*s as feudal opponents of constitutionalism. Comparing these figures with the Ottoman Empire, he concluded that the Iranian 'feudal lord' (*derebey*) – an apparent reference to the Iranian khans and governors – unlike the Ottoman *derebey*s or *ağa*s, were considered to be relatively unrestricted in terms of their powers, both worldly and religious. His speech takes on a radically anti-clerical tone. The *mujtahid*s, according to Salmasi, 'had more power than the Caliph religiously and had unlimited religious authority' since in the Ottoman Empire at least, '*ijtihad* was not unrestricted'. Salmasi tended to see the conflict between the royalists and the constitutionalists as a conflict between religion and secularism: after the death of Mozaffar al-Din Shah, he claims, 'Iran broke into two: the religious and the secularists/irreligious (*dinsizler*)'. Salmasi's heart-rending description of massacres carried out by these religious-royalist forces against the constitutionalist moved his diverse listeners – Iranians, Turks, and Armenians – to tears.[25]

Like many Iranian dissidents before and after him, Salmasi eventually ended up in Istanbul, a haven for Iranian dissidents since the nineteenth century.[26] No longer beholden to the whims of the Sultan, the Iranian constitutionalists made full use of their new pro-constitutionalist hosts' sympathy. In November 1908, Salmasi delivered a speech in Istanbul, this time at a conference organized by the Anjoman-e Saʿadat, an association of Iranians residing in Istanbul advocating on behalf of the constitutionalist cause during the years 1908–12, and presided over by the CUP leader Prince Sabahaddin – the same leader who wrote many earlier telegrams and declarations to the Iranian Majles and was head of the pro-Armenian decentralist camp within the CUP.[27] Sabahaddin's patronage of Iranian efforts suggests that members of various persuasions were eager to court Iranian allies even after having gained power. The conference, held in the Beyoğlu district of Istanbul, included speakers from the Ottoman, Iranian, Armenian, Kurdish, and European communities; each speaker presented in his own language, expressing solidarity with the Iranian constitutionalists. On the day of the conference, Yahya Dowlatabadi, a prominent Iranian constitutionalist, joined a procession of Iranians carrying the flags of the Ottoman Moon and Crescent and the Iranian Lion and Sun and walking from Valide Hanı, the mainly Iranian-inhabited neighbourhood of Istanbul, to the Tepebaşı theatre, where the conference was being held.[28] After speeches by the Armenian representative Khachatur Malumian and a Kurdish representative whose name was not preserved, in which both pledged that their communities were committed to the cause of freedom in Iran, Dowlatabadi elaborated on Islamic arguments for constitutionalism, revealing how, for this Azali-Babi, Pan-Islamic rhetoric was the discourse through which he articulated Iranian–Ottoman constitutional solidarity.

In Salmasi's lecture, we once again see his socialist proclivities: 'We want a peasants' and farmers' constitutionalism, not the constitutionalism of owners, landlords, and other rulers and governors. We are socialists.'[29] We also see, in contrast to Dowlatabadi, a much more aggressive stance towards the ulema. Salmasi makes no effort to distinguish between pro- and anti-constitutional ulema. Instead, he lambastes the clerics as particularly complicit in encouraging the governors and those in power to characterize the constitutionalists as Babis (and thus heretics) to the people. He gives the examples of Seyyed Jamal al-Din al-Afghani, Mirza Reza Kermani (the assassin of Naser al-Din Shah), and others who were sent to Tabriz for execution in the late nineteenth century. He has harsh words, once again, for the governors and 'traitor' (*kha'en*) clerics who essentially preserved 'tyrannical rule'.[30] Dowlatabadi and Salmasi's speeches, when read together, reveal the simultaneous articulation of shared narratives of Iranian–Ottoman solidarity – from the Pan-Islamic to the socialist. Just as there were various tendencies within each constitutional movement, so too was there a spectrum of possible transnational ideological bases for Ottoman–Iranian solidarity.

The Border Issue Revisited: Young Turk Betrayal?

After the emergence of the Young Turk government in 1908, Ottoman troops remained in Iran. On the surface, this appears to have been a Young Turk betrayal of their promise to collaborate with the Iranians once in power.[31] How then, can the continued Ottoman occupation of Iranian borderlands be understood in light of other evidence suggesting Iranian–Ottoman cooperation? The answer lies in understanding the relationship between the Young Turk government and Mohammad Ali Shah. During the month prior to the Young Turk Revolution, when Abdülhamid and Mohammad Ali Shah both held autocratic power, Abdülhamid began to take measures to withdraw from the Iranian border, proving that for Abdülhamid, the border issue had been more about undermining the constitutional regime than anything else.[32] When, in July 1908, the Young Turks seized power, the occupation of Iran continued, but this time it was not against a *constitutional* Iran, but rather an autocratic one. Continued Ottoman presence in Iran meant that the CUP could provide, should they so desire, military and logistical assistance to the Iranian *mojahedin* who were locked in intense fighting with the royalists in Azarbayjan, while simultaneously diverting royalist troops away from their internal opponents. Ottoman troop presence was now a destabilizing force for Mohammad Ali Shah's regime rather than for the constitutionalists.

Elements within the Ottoman army in Iran had been sympathetic to the Iranian constitutional cause. As early as 1907, the CUP in Paris was issuing manifestos to Ottoman officers stationed along the Ottoman–Iranian border, urging them to support the Iranian constitutionalists.[33] These manifestos in all likelihood had some effect, given the popularity of the CUP among Ottoman officers. After the declaration of the Young Turk regime, pro-royalist tribes on the Ottoman–Iranian border sought peace with Ottoman forces, fearing that they would come to the aid of the Iranian constitutionalists.[34] Royalist fears were not unfounded. Several Ottoman officers stationed along the Qotur river near the Ottoman–Iranian border joined the constitutionalists after witnessing first-hand their struggle with the Shah's royalist forces.[35] The most striking example of Ottoman officers lending assistance to Iranians in Azarbayjan, however, was a group of Ottoman *mojahed*s dispatched by the CUP to Iran in order to fight alongside the Iranian *mojahedin*.

The Forgotten Ottoman *Mojahed*s of Azarbayjan

Salmasi delivered several important speeches during his time in the Ottoman Empire for mixed Iranian, Ottoman, and Armenian audiences. But Salmasi was not a speech-maker by temperament – he was a revolutionary. Events in Salmasi's native province, Azarbayjan, led him to abandon activism in Istanbul and instead focus on engaging the Shah's troops in battle. In the intervening period, the Iranian constitutionalists had asked the CUP for military assistance. The CUP designated Enver Paşa's uncle, Halil Bey (later Halil Paşa), to lead a group of approximately thirty Ottoman *mojahed*s, including Naci and Salmasi, to fight on the side of the Iranian constitutionalists against the royalists.[36] By February 1909, they had joined constitutionalists in Dilman and Salmas.[37] Even prior to their arrival, an Ottoman commander on the frontier near Urmia had relayed a message to Sattar Khan, the leader of the constitutionalist resistance in Tabriz, stating something to the effect of '[the] Turks are ready to support the nationalists.'[38] The mixed Ottoman–Iranian troops' military engagement with the Shah's troops was not only a concrete instance of Iranian–Ottoman solidarity, it became a defining event in their shared constitutionalist narratives.

After arriving in Dilman, near Salmas, the Ottoman *mojahed*s met with local Iranian revolutionaries, and then proceeded to Hashrud, where they eventually engaged the Shah's troops.[39] According to one account, there was also an Armenian division alongside the Iranian and Ottoman ones, suggesting that Armenian cooperation with the CUP continued well after the Lesser Despotism.[40] Part of the mission of this group of Ottoman *mojahed*s, in addition to helping the constitutionalists militarily, was to provide ammunition and arms for local fighters.[41] Halil Paşa supervised three divisions that were led by three Ottoman officers: Ibrahim Bey, Mustafa Bey, and Yakup Bey respectively. From Saʻdabad the mixed Ottoman–Iranian contingent crossed the Qotur river before reaching Hashiyeh Rud, the site of battle with the royalist forces.

Battle cries in both Persian and Turkish reveal how constitutionalism became the rallying point of these mixed troops. Saʻid Salmasi remained true to his revolutionary temperament. He taunted retreating royalist forces for being cowardly (*bi gheyrat*) and stirred the *mojahed*s by saying 'Brothers, attack, do not fear, our blood-ransom is for the constitution. Our good names will be recorded in history.' Halil Paşa played a similar role in inspiring the troops, crying 'Friends, do not be afraid, attack! Long live the constitution (*yaşasın meşrutiyet*)!' In preparation for battle, the troops would also cry out 'long live Sattar Khan the National Leader (*zendeh bad Sattar Khan sardar-e melli*)!'[42] What these shared Iranian and Ottoman battle cries point to is the degree to which what captured the collective imaginations of these fighters was not a specific monarch but the disembodied notion of a constitution (*meşrutiyet* or *mashrutiyat*), a new institutional ideal grounded in a text rather than a sovereign with a divine prerogative. When this ideal was embodied in an individual, it was Sattar Khan – the one who defends the constitution against its enemies. This subtle discursive shift points to how language which had previously been reserved to describe an Islamic monarch was now being employed for a political concept – one which was seen as part of a newly constructed and shared Iranian–Ottoman vision.

In the course of the battle itself, the Ottoman and the Iranian *mojahedin* were badly outnumbered. Despite this, they defeated the Shah's troops with relatively few casualties on their side, while the approximately 100 royalists who were killed 'at the banks of the Qotur [river]' caused its 'colour [to be] changed'.[43] But the young Salmasi, who had played such a crucial role in forging links between Iranians and Ottomans, died in battle and was memorialized as a 'martyr' (*shahid*), a mere two months before he would have seen his dream of the constitution restored in Iran.[44]

The Iranian press of this time memorialized the battle of Hashrud, infusing it with a shared genealogy of constitutional martyrs:

The bullets rained down upon the enemy's heads. The Zahhak-worshipping tyrannical troops of the enemy stayed awake all night in fear of the liberals (*ahrar*). At the break of dawn, each was sleeping in a corner and the sound of fire and the holy cry of 'Freedom, Justice, and Equality' filled the earth ('*alam ra fara gereft*). And from the wafting of the morning wind came the sounds of 'Well done! Bravo!' from the luminous graves of the martyrs of the path of freedom – Haji Mirza Ebrahim Aqa, Malek al-Motekallemin, Mirza Jahangir [Sur-e Esrafil] – which reached the ears of the constitutionalists and which strengthened the hearts of the *mojahedin*.[45]

The Ottomans were similarly praised:

Here we cannot describe the bravery of our fellow party members (*ham maslak*) the Young Turks, which neither the pen can describe nor the tongue do justice to. It was for some time that Enver Bey and Niyazi Bey were observing this brave movement of the liberals and were ready, and said that from each drop of blood of Midhat Pasha the martyr, thousands of brave youth will enter the 'circle of humanity' (*da'ereh-ye ensaniyat*) and will assuredly turn towards uprooting tyranny.[46]

The language used in memorializing this moment reveals the tensions in constitutional rhetoric: the juxtaposition of Iranian 'martyrs' of constitutionalism like Mirza Ebrahim Aqa, Malek al-Motekallemin, and Mirza Jahangir with an Ottoman one, Midhat Pasha, reveals how hagiographical language usually reserved only for Shiite martyrs was mixed with the more humanist and reformist language suggested by terms like 'the path of freedom' and 'the circle of humanity'.

Naci is surprisingly absent from accounts of the battle of Hashrud, although we know that Halil Paşa sent Naci back to the Ottoman side of the border to obtain more ammunition. Naci eventually sent ammunition but failed to return himself, noting in his telegram that confusion had broken out in Istanbul and it was best if Halil Paşa returned to Van soon.[47] The Battle of Hashrud coincided with a setback for Ottoman constitutionalists. The 'March 31st Incident' according to the Julian (Rumi) calendar used in the Ottoman Empire (13 April 1909, according the Gregorian calendar), when conservative elements threatened to reinstate Abdülhamid's autocracy, aroused fears among Ottoman constitutionalists that a reactionary coup of a similar nature to Mohammad Ali Shah's was upon them. But the CUP, having learned from the Iranian example with counterrevolution, was determined to avoid reliving Iran's recent past – the counterrevolution was crushed in its infancy and Abdülhamid deposed.

Taking Refuge with the Ottomans: The Tehran and Tabriz *Bast*s

Military engagements were not the only form of Ottoman support for the Iranian constitutionalists during the Lesser Tyranny: the Ottomans also provided refuge for Iranian constitutionalists during the *bast*s at the Ottoman embassy in Tehran in 1908 and at the Ottoman consulate in Tabriz in 1909. The controversies within the Ottoman Empire over whether or not to grant refuge to Iranian constitutionalists highlighted the divisions within the newly formed constitutional state between the Sultan and segments of the official diplomatic establishment on the one hand, and the pro-Iranian CUP on the other. The *bast*s themselves were important in terms of their timing – in the case of Tehran, it was part of a growing peaceful resistance against the Shah's power and in Tabriz, it came at a crucial moment at which Sattar Khan, the leader of the national resistance, was in danger of being captured by the occupying Russian forces in Azarbayjan.

Both *bast*s should be understood in light of the 1907 Anglo-Russian agreement. With Britain and Russia no longer keeping one another in check, the Russians were given a free hand to pursue their interests in northern Iran, often to the detriment of the Iranian constitutionalists and to the benefit of the royalists. The 1907 Anglo-Russian entente meant Iranian constitutionalists could no longer take refuge at the British legation since the British made it clear that they no longer wished *bast*s to be organized for 'political purposes'.[48] The Ottoman embassy emerged as one of the few alternatives. But unlike other European legations, it had the added advantage of being Islamic. The 1907 Anglo-Russian agreement therefore had the unintended consequence of fortifying Ottoman–Iranian solidarity. Casting the struggle for constitutionalism as an Islamic one took on further rhetorical strength, particularly in Tehran where the constitutional ulema played a leading role.

The Tehran *bast* at the Ottoman embassy began in late December 1908 within the larger context of protests against the Shah.[49] While numerically less significant than the 1906 *bast* at the British legation, the 1908–09 *bast* at the Ottoman embassy, led by constitutional ulema like Sadr al-'Olama and Mohammad Iman, marked a shift away from identification with liberal England as Iran's constitutional ally to an identification with a constitutional Islamic country (Figure 33).[50] This shift in strategy, however, should not be seen in purely religious terms. Abo l-Qasem Tabataba'i, the son of the famous constitutional cleric Seyyed Mohammad Tabataba'i, suggested that Iranian refugees at the Ottoman embassy should attempt to take refuge at the British legation instead since it was safer.[51] Pragmatic politics therefore, as much as Pan-Islamic solidarity, was a consideration. But the British and Russian rapprochement having deprived them of the British option, the Iranian constitutionalists were thrust into the arms of the Ottoman Empire.

The *bast* began with a group of approximately forty people around Sadr al-'Olama taking refuge at the Ottoman embassy on 21 December 1908. Within a few days their numbers had ballooned to nearly three hundred.[52] The composition of *basti*s included 'merchants, guildsmen, and officials who, having received no salary, saw no point in supporting the existing regime'.[53] The constitutionalists, pessimistic at the prospect of Mohammad Ali Shah calling an election, took refuge with the Ottomans as an act of defiance.[54] The royalists in turn surrounded the embassy, arresting anyone who tried to enter or provide provisions.[55] During this protracted struggle, the royalists blamed the *basti*s for conspiring with the Ottomans against them beyond the confines of Tehran. 'Eyn al-Dowleh, the governor of Azarbayjan, sent a cable blaming the *basti*s for Ottoman troops which had crossed the border into Iran, demonstrating how the royalists saw refuge at the embassy as inextricably linked to Ottoman troop movement along the border.[56] Two senior pro-constitutional ulema in Najaf, Mohammad Kazem Khorasani and Abdollah Mazandarani, issued a declaration couched in the rhetoric of Pan-Islamic support for the *basti*s, stating '[i]t is incumbent upon all the believers to aid them in every way possible in order to cut the root of tyranny.' [57]

British and Russian imperial pressures quickly came into play. They collectively applied pressure on the Ottoman government for allowing the politicization of the *bast*. The British Foreign Secretary Lord Edward Grey argued that using the *bast* for political purposes constituted an 'abuse of the custom' and therefore 'the bastis [should] be compelled to leave the Turkish Embassy'.[58] By the end of December, the Ottoman foreign minister Rifat Paşa bowed to British and Russian pressure and prepared to order the expulsion of the *basti*s from the Tehran embassy.[59]

Had this been the end of the story, perhaps historians would be justified in relegating the *bast* at the Ottoman embassy to a footnote in Iranian constitutional revolutionary history. Ensuing events, however, demonstrate perfectly the degree to which Ottoman policies in Tehran as to whether or not to support the Iranian constitutionalists were closely linked to struggles between various factions within the Ottoman Empire. Before the Iranian constitutionalists could be expelled from the Ottoman embassy, the Anjoman-e Sa'adat in Istanbul caught wind of the impending expulsion through a coded message sent via merchant channels. At this point, Dowlatabadi convinced the Ottoman *şeyhülislam/sheykh al-Islam*, Mehmet Cemaleddin, that the expulsion of the *basti*s from a fellow Islamic nation would be a major blow to Islam as a whole. Meanwhile, the Anjoman-e Sa'adat contacted Talat Bey (later Talat Paşa), a member of the CUP and a parliamentary representative for Edirne, who brought forward an Iranian petition for deliberation. During this deliberation, the *şeyhülislam* argued that since the *bast*is had taken refuge as Muslims at a Muslim embassy, he considered them to be taking bast at the 'House of Islam' (*khaneh-ye eslam*) and not the 'House of the government' (*khaneh-ye dowlat*); therefore their fate was under his jurisdiction and not that of the foreign minister. By threatening to resign, which would have meant the dissolution of an already unstable cabinet, the *şeyhülislam* ensured the continuation of the *bast*.[60] The Sultan had been pushing for the expulsion of the constitutionalists from the Ottoman embassy, but his downfall in late April 1909 ensured their continued presence.[61]

The Tabriz *bast* of May 1909, which took place immediately before the fall of Mohammad Ali Shah, shared some salient features with the Tehran *bast*. Like the Tehran *bast*, it too was internationalized, with Britain and Russia pushing for the expulsion of the *bast*is, leading to another confrontation in the Ottoman parliament. There were, however, several important differences. Tabriz was the site of intense fighting between royalists and constitutionalists, and was further complicated by the presence of Russian troops. The composition of the *bast*is also differed: instead of the ulema, merchants, guildsmen, and officials taking part, this was the *bast* of Sattar Khan, Baqer Khan, and the Iranian *mojahedin*. Finally, appeals to Pan-Islamism were relatively absent in the Tabriz *bast*. The significance of the Tabriz *bast* should be seen in the broader context of fighting in Azarbayjan – Sattar Khan represented the national resistance against Mohammad Ali Shah during the Lesser Despotism while most other provinces were still incapacitated by the shock of the counterrevolution. While the eventual toppling of Mohammad Ali Shah was the culmination of forces not restricted to Azarbayjan, the possible Russian arrest and incarceration of Sattar Khan at such a crucial stage would have been a huge blow to the overall morale of the Iranian constitutionalist cause, thereby making the Tabriz *bast* all the more significant.

The *bast* in Tabriz took place despite the stated Ottoman policy of neutrality when it came to Iranian domestic affairs.[62] But this supposed neutrality should be seen within the larger context of CUP activities in Azarbayjan. While the official diplomatic channels might have sent instructions barring their local representatives, particularly in Tabriz, from interfering in local Iranian affairs, the activities of the CUP appear to have been a different matter.[63] The Ottoman Grand Vizier, for instance, was apparently unaware of CUP military activities in Azarbayjan.[64] At the same time, lower-ranking Ottoman officials, employed in consulates throughout Azarbayjan, were willing to disobey the official diplomatic line. This was certainly the case with the Ottoman consul-general who granted protection to Iranian revolutionaries in Tabriz.

The Russians were the most vocal critics of Ottoman and German military officials supplying Sattar Khan and the *mojahedin* with munitions and

33. Picture of Tehran *basti*s at the Ottoman Embassy under the Ottoman Flag.

tactical support, and in light of the battle of Hashrud, their suspicions were well-founded.[65] The immediate causes of the *bast* were Russian claims that the *mojahedin* were disrupting trade along the Julfa road. Dowlatabadi saw this as merely a Russian pretext for disarming the partisans of Sattar Khan.[66] A British report suggests that the *bast* took place because the Russians had arrested a local *feda'i* and had the house of his brother demolished.[67] In any case, the motivation for the *mojahed*s wanting to take refuge at the Ottoman consulate is clear: Russian forces threatened their physical well-being and therefore could jeopardize the entire movement.[68] But what were the Ottoman motivations for granting refuge to the Iranian *mojahedin*? Here the story is once again more complicated than it may at first appear. Ahmad Kasravi suggests that a common religion, a common border, and the triumph of the CUP in the Ottoman Empire were the main reasons for Ottoman support in the form of a *bast*.[69] E. G. Browne also points to a common religion, but adds a broader strategic reason, namely Ottoman fears of Russian domination of its eastern frontier.[70]

While both these accounts are in many ways accurate, they fail to capture the complexity of Ottoman behaviour towards Iran. As with the Tehran *bast*, the Ottoman policy of granting refuge to Iranian constitutionalist was filled with ambivalence. The *bast* once again became the subject of heated contestation between various segments of the Ottoman state. The Ottoman consul in Tabriz, Mehmet Ali Bey, extended his repeated invitation for the Iranian *mojahed*s to take refuge at the consulate.[71] Ottoman diplomatic correspondence reveals the annoyance of the minister of foreign affairs, Rifat Paşa, and the Ottoman ambassador in Russia at having to admit that the Ottoman consul in

Tabriz had acted without official sanction.[72] The Tabriz *bast*, then, constituted a clash of wills: a renegade Ottoman consul in Tabriz took it upon himself to support Iranian constitutionalists against the wishes of the royalists, and particularly against the wishes of the Russians, while high-ranking old-guard Ottoman diplomats and the foreign affairs minister felt the heat of Russian diplomatic pressure leading them to pursue a more cautious approach. A stark difference of approach emerges therefore between Ottoman officials serving on the ground in Iran, witnessing events as they unfold, sympathetic with the constitutionalist cause, and career diplomats and civil servants serving in Istanbul, St. Petersburg, and elsewhere who saw support for the constitutionalists as a liability in light of overwhelming Russian and British diplomatic pressure.

But sympathies towards the Iranian constitutionalist cause were not only drawn along these lines – once again, the *bast* became a topic of debate in the Ottoman parliament, with CUP members, led by Talat Paşa, representing the Iranian constitutionalists' interests, clashing with Rifat Paşa, who called for the expulsion of the *bast*is.[73] The *bast*is were proactive in lobbying the Ottoman government for their support.[74] While Dowlatabadi portrays the Ottoman foreign minister in a very negative light (perhaps somewhat unfairly), even Rifat Paşa was not beyond expressing sympathy for the Iranian constitutionalists when corresponding with his Russian counterpart, Isvolsky:

> If it was the intention of Your Excellency to allude, in his discussion, to the sympathy that the Persian liberal movement finds among us, this is hardly but a very natural sentiment vis-à-vis a people who are fighting for liberty, and toward whom public opinion, in Russia as in England, is most favourable.[75]

At the end of the parliamentary discussions, however, unlike with the Tehran *bast*, those who supported Iran were not able to prevail – at least not explicitly. A compromise was reached with the British and Russian pressure to have Sattar Khan and Baqer Khan deported to the Ottoman Empire: if they refused, then the Ottoman consulate would no longer provide refuge for them.[76] But Ahmed Rıza Bey and other CUP members were able to delay these deportations until events in Tehran made it apparent that the constitutionalists would prevail.[77] The CUP had effectively avoided both the arrest of Sattar Khan and Baqer Khan and their deportation – events which would have been major blows to the Iranian constitutional movement. These stalling tactics bought time for Sattar Khan and Baqer Khan to wait and observe the course of events in Tehran – events which ultimately led to the fall of Mohammad Ali Shah and the restoration of the constitution. Both the Tehran and the Tabriz *bast*s illustrate the durability of Iranian–Ottoman solidarity in the face of imperial opposition during the Lesser Despotism.

The Second Wave of Pan-Islam: Utopian Constitutional Narratives

At various stages through the 1907–09 period, Pan-Islamic rhetoric was a hallmark of Ottoman–Iranian solidarity. Like its nineteenth-century predecessor,[78] it too was markedly anti-imperialist. But central to the more recent articulation of Pan-Islamism was the centrality of constitutionalism as its defining feature. When an Islamic monarch – Iranian or Ottoman – is praised by Ottoman and Iranian constitutionalists, it is often insofar as the monarch is a constitutional monarch. In other words, constitutional monarchs functioned as foils to despotic ones during this crucial period which witnessed a 'constitutional' Mozaffar al-Din Shah followed by a 'despotic' Mohammad Ali Shah in Iran, and a 'despotic' Abdülhamid followed by a 'constitutional' Mehmet V Reşad in the Ottoman Empire. Iranians and Ottomans who referred to one another's monarchs in glowing terms were mainly doing so rhetorically. A good 'constitutional' monarch was ideally also politically irrelevant. Instead, Pan-Islamism in the Iranian–Ottoman context during this period attempted to indigenize the notion of constitutionalism as an Islamic ideal, one which would inevitably triumph over despotism. The Pan-Islamic rhetoric that served as a vehicle for constitutional solidarity permeated pronouncements, letters, and poetry of this period.[79]

Pan-Islamism was used during the period from 1907 to 1909 by numerous individuals and groups, often for very different purposes. CUP pronouncements prior to the party's rise to power stated that 'Today the real enemies of Iran and the Ottoman Empire are the English and Russian governments. Instead of these [i.e., Sultan Abdülhamid's] occupations and invasions, we should be working to create a united military force.' They proceeded to claim that Islam's independence worldwide depended on the success and cooperation of constitutional movements in Iran and the Ottoman Empire.[80] After the Young Turk rise to power, the Russians were cautiously monitoring CUP activities – particularly the dispatch of emissaries – in Iran, fearing (rightly) that they could be a force that would cooperate with the Iranian constitutionalists. The Russian foreign minister Isvolsky while describing Young Turk activities in Tabriz in December 1908, accused these emissaries of promoting 'a Pan Islamic liberal union'.[81] The fact that Isvolsky qualified Pan-Islam as being 'liberal' suggests his awareness that this was a new phenomenon: the 'union' had little to do with the caliphal pretensions of Abdülhamid and everything to do with constitutional solidarity among two 'Islamic' countries collectively threatened by Russian imperialism.

Among Iranians too, Pan-Islamism was a popular rhetorical device to justify Iranian–Ottoman cooperation. In Tabriz, once again Pan-Islamism was deployed – this time the 'constitutional' Abdülhamid (post-Young Turk

Revolution) acted as a foil to the 'despotic' Mohammad Ali Shah. Placards were placed on mosques demanding that the local ulema settle the question of constitutionalism in Iran, or the 'Sultan would be as good a sovereign for them as [the] Shah'.[82] In other words, some, at least rhetorically, preferred a constitutional foreign head of state to a despotic Iranian one. Another similar instance in which Sultan Abdülhamid was held up as a just king, a foil to Mohammad Ali Shah, is in a remarkable petition attributed to the high-ranking pro-constitutionalist ulema of Najaf. In a petition sent to Abdülhamid, the Sultan is asked for assistance in protecting Iranian Muslims against Mohammad Ali Shah, who had reneged on his sworn oath to fulfil the wishes of the nation by not implementing the constitution. Even more striking is the reference to the Sultan as *amir al-mo'menin* (commander of the faithful), a term traditionally reserved for the Shiite Imams and certainly not used for a Sunni Sultan. According to the British consul-general in Baghdad, this petition was in effect an authorization for the Sultan to occupy Azarbayjan.[83]

This petition begs the question of why the pro-constitutionalist ulema in Najaf were appealing to a Sunni caliph, who was known as a despotic monarch, after the declaration of a constitution in the Ottoman Empire. One possible answer is that the letter was altered. Abdul Hadi Ha'iri suggests that the term *amir al-mo'menin* was added by someone trying to gain more sympathy from the Sultan.[84] Mangol Bayat suggests that the epithet may have been added by a middle- or lower-ranking student in Najaf.[85] In any case, the fact that the petition may have been altered or written by lower-ranking or middle-ranking ulema sympathetic to the constitutional cause does not change the fact that there were such Iranian elements operating, and perhaps more significantly, that the higher-ranking *mujtahids* took no steps to correct the terminology used in the petition.[86] If this is true, it may be further evidence of the ways in which lower- and middle-ranking ulema were able to influence the political positions of the *mujtahids*, just as had been the case in the Tobacco Rebellion.[87] We know the Najaf *mujtahids* were in contact with the Sultan's enemies, the CUP, through Sheykh Asadollah Mamaqani, their representative in Istanbul.[88] Since at this point the Sultan was still on the throne and the CUP did not have full control of the government, it is likely that the Najaf *mujtahids*, or those under them, appealed to the Sultan in order to cover all potential bases of support for their cause against Mohammad Ali Shah. Part of this was no doubt the instability of the situation in the Ottoman Empire – there was no guarantee that the CUP would be victorious, especially since they might face setbacks similar to those faced by Iranian constitutionalists.

Representing Abdülhamid as a truly constitutional monarch was not restricted to Iranian constitutionalists: the Sultan himself, ironically, appears to have embraced the role after the Young Turk Revolution. In an attempt not to lose face, Abdülhamid claimed he had been deceived into suspending the constitution from the time of his rise to power until 1908.[89] This might explain why various Iranians invoked his name as a foil – while he may have been autocratic prior to 1908, at the onset of the Young Turk Revolution he made an effort to appropriate constitutionalism in a desperate attempt to cling to power. His remarkable about-face reveals itself in a letter he wrote to Mohammad Ali Shah during the Lesser Despotism, in which he (perhaps somewhat cynically) embraced his new role as a constitutional monarch. In the letter, he expresses surprise that the Iranian ulema had ruled that the constitution was contrary to the shari'a.[90] Abdülhamid hoped that the declaration of an Iranian constitution would finally silence them. His comments, while certainly somewhat ironic, are consistent with the ways in which Abdülhamid attempted to refashion himself as a constitutional monarch who simultaneously harboured deep hostility towards the constitution.

The Constitutional Vision Fulfilled: July 1909

The fall of Mohammad Ali Shah was all the more significant since it signalled the first time that both Iran and the Ottoman Empire were run by constitutional governments. During various stages since 1907, when the two movements had begun collaborating with one another, the Iranian and Ottoman constitutionalists alternated between holding and momentarily losing power in their own nations. A careful examination of the sources demonstrates that Iranian and Ottoman constitutionalists not only cooperated with one another in a number of meaningful and concrete ways – diplomatically, militarily, and ideologically – they also looked to one another's experiences to make sense of their own revolutionary present and, perhaps equally importantly, to anticipate and prepare for their possible post-revolutionary future. It was this spectrum of interpretations that contributed to a utopian vision of the shared destiny of the Iranian and Ottoman constitutional revolutions: one that was characterized by an overwhelming sense of optimism punctuated with moments of profound anxiety over the possibility of the re-emergence of autocracy.

Mohammad Ali Shah's defeat in July of 1909 generated a shared sense of euphoria among Iranian and Ottoman constitutionalists. In Istanbul, various chapters of the CUP sent telegrams congratulating the Iranians on having overthrown Mohammad Ali Shah and lamenting the loss of Iranian 'martyrs' for freedom.[91] The Anjoman-e Sa'adat marked the occasion with festivities in Istanbul. Among the well-wishers were familiar figures: the former Ottoman *şeyhülislam*, Cemaleddin, and the minister of foreign affairs, Rifat Paşa, were among those in attendance. A group of Bulgarian students delivered a speech on Iranian constitutionalists (*azadi-kh^vahan*) and read a statement on behalf of

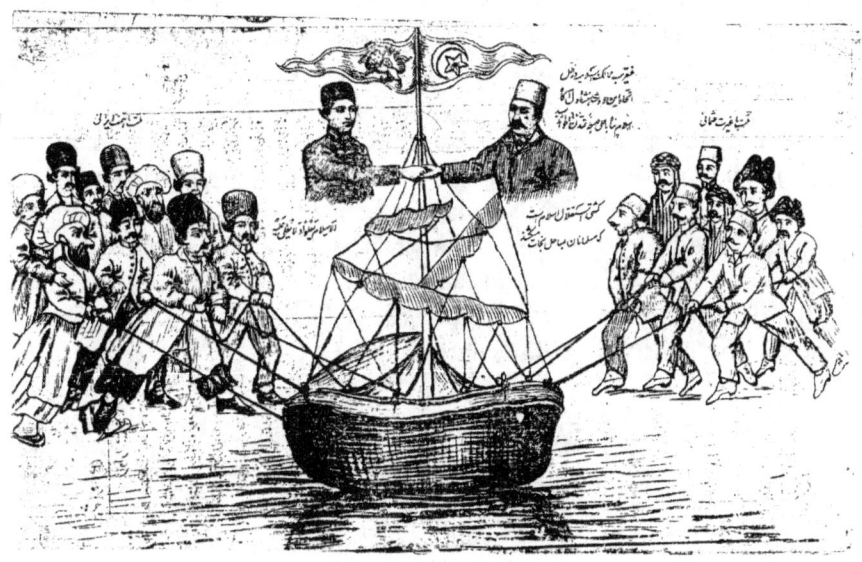

34. The caption reads 'Islamic countries will soon be under the shadow of the unity of these two far-sighted (*del-agah*) kings, protectors of Islam, and attain the highest degree of civilization.'

the Bulgarian committee. The writer covering this event captured the central message of Iranian–Ottoman camaraderie by stating, 'Long live freedom (*horriyat*), long live the Iranian and Ottoman nations (*mellat*), and let the two stars of prosperity of the two exalted kings Sultan Mohammad and Sultan Ahmad Shah shine.'[92] A group of Ottoman students also gave a speech for the Anjoman-e Sa'adat, congratulating Iran and proclaiming: 'From here on let us be united and [as] one being.' This unity, according to the students, was built on the fact that these were 'two great Asian and Islamic nations'. Iran is further described as the 'beloved and blessed brother' of the Ottoman nation.[93] In the Iranian newspaper *Kashkul* (Figure 34), the message of Iranian–Ottoman solidarity along Pan-Islamic lines was visually represented: beneath the Iranian and Ottoman flags, Ahmad Shah and Mehmet V Reşad shake hands while the 'industrious nation of Iran' (*mellat-e ba hemmat-e Iran*) and the 'zealous Ottoman nation' (*mellat-e ba gheyrat-e 'osmani*) pull the ship of 'Islam's independence' to the 'shore of salvation' (*sahel-e nejat*).

While nation-centred narratives of the Iranian and Ottoman constitutional experiences of the early twentieth century provide an account of what these experiences meant to those within the country's borders, they fail to capture how Iranian and Ottoman constitutionalists imagined both revolutions as being part of a phenomenon beyond the borders of the state. Constitutional, anti-imperial, socialist, and Pan-Islamic discourses all contributed in varying degrees to a transnational utopian vision through which Iranian and Ottoman constitutionalists articulated their cooperation. While the subsequent Ottoman occupation of Iran and the rise of Pan-Turkism as the CUP's dominant ideology did much to undermine Ottoman–Iranian solidarity – particularly during the First World War – there is a danger in reading events from this more ambivalent period of Iranian–Ottoman relations back into the early constitutional period.[94] By taking a transnational perspective, we can better understand the regional processes that shaped the trajectories of both the Ottoman and the Iranian constitutional revolutions.

CHAPTER 19

Constitutionalists *Sans Frontières*: Iranian Constitutionalism and its Asian Connections[1]

Touraj Atabaki

Introduction

In the historiography of Iranian constitutionalism and the Constitutional Revolution (1905–09), the reformist movement is treated as a receptive movement crafted by ideas originating chiefly in nineteenth-century Western Europe or Russia, with hardly any attention given to connections with Asia and North Africa other than the well-known linkages with constitutionalism in the Ottoman Empire and the Caucasus.[2] In the case of the Ottoman Empire, the study of the cross-border link has until recently been largely limited to the nonreciprocal impact that the movement for change and reform in the Ottoman Empire had on late nineteenth-century and early twentieth-century Iran, with no investigation of any possible impact that Iranian constitutionalism might have had on the Young Turk Revolution of 1908.[3] In the case of the Transcaspian connections the historiography of Iranian constitutionalism has been content to mention a few nonreciprocal links between Iran and the lands to its north, with the Caucasus in charge of producing revolutionary literature or dispatching revolutionary agents to the south in order to save the constitution from being overpowered by Qajar despotism. References to the publication of periodicals such as the satiric *Molla Nasr al-Din* of Baku or to the camaraderie of Caucasian social democrats and their support of the Iranian constitutionalists in restoring the revolution are the most common topoi.

Similarly, Soviet historiography generally treated the reformist movement of the early twentieth century in the Caucasus and Central Asia as an isolated, self-contained movement confined to Baku, Tbilisi, and Bukhara, or at most to the borders of Turkistan and Transcaucasia. Soviet historians endeavoured to show that reformist movements in the southern regions of the Russian Empire were all inspired by contemporaneous movements among Russians and, at most, Tatars.

What brings constitutionalist historians of Iran to a conclusion analogous to that drawn by historians of the reform movement in the former Soviet south is their exclusive approach to the practice of modernity as a European phenomenon rather than a global project. Studies of political modernity are predominantly influenced by the Weberian assumption that modernity is a product of occidental rationality, with a general mandate regarding its applicability irrespective of geography, time, environment, social order, or practice. Such a perception of modernity, which crafted European historicism, 'posited historical time as a measure of cultural distance (at least in institutional development) that was assumed to exist between the West and non-West'.[4] Accordingly, non-Western societies were doomed to linger in history's 'waiting room' to adopt the European model of modernity. Such historicism, as Dipesh Chakrabarty argues, is 'what made modernity or capitalism look not simply global but rather as something that became global *over time*, by originating in one place (Europe) and then spreading outside it'.[5] The 'first-in-Europe-then-elsewhere' structure of global historical time chiefly manifests itself as Eurocentrism and comes into focus in examining studies of modernity and the process of modernization in non-Western societies.

In this chapter, while not overlooking the consequences that the social and political changes in Europe – Russia – had on the reformist movement in Iran, the Caucasus, and Central Asia, I will also examine the impact that the Iranian constitutional movement and literature had on early twentieth-century reformism in the Caucasus and Central Asia. Sketching the main routes that made such an impact possible, I will highlight historical examples at specific moments rather than adopting a structured and linear description.

Newspapers and Journalism

The early contact between reformist individuals in the Emirate of Bukhara and their fellow thinkers on the other side of the Caspian Sea, namely Iran, dates back to the last decade of the nineteenth century. According to a report by a British agent in the region, in the late nineteenth century the newspaper *Akhtar* (Star) was widely circulated in Central Asia and enjoyed an enthusiastic readership.[6] *Akhtar* was one of the early prominent reformist Persian periodicals that issued outside Iran. Edited by Mohammad Taher Tabrizi, the first issue of *Akhtar* was published in 1875 in Istanbul, and it continued to be published until 1894. The radical reformist partiality of *Akhtar* soon made it one of the most influential voices for promoting social justice in the region where Persian was spoken.[7]

Another influential Persian periodical distributed in Central Asia was *Qanun* (Law). According to an account published in the Russian periodical *Turkistanskie vedomosti* of 1898, *Qanun* had been broadly circulating in Turkistan, causing some anxieties for Russian authorities.[8] Edited by the dissident Iranian statesman Mirza Malkam Khan Nazem al-Dowleh, the first issue of *Qanun* was published in 1890 in London, and within the fifteen years of its existence it became one of the most anti-establishment reformist popular periodicals in the Persian language. Among the various subjects Malkam Khan treated in *Qanun* were the protest against conditions of lawlessness, the need for a grand national assembly, and even Malkam Khan's belief that it would be necessary to retain and apply Islamic jurisprudence in any future just society.[9] *Qanun*'s call for change and reform soon found its way to Central Asia. Of the varied routes for a publication like *Qanun* to reach Bukhara, including the route from Baku via Krasnovodsk (on the eastern shore of the Caspian Sea) to Bukhara, one must not forget the Indo-Afghan passage from Calcutta via Kabul and Termez to Bukhara. Persians had resided in India since the sixteenth century, constituting one of India's prosperous and learned communities. One of the most conspicuous icons of this community's activities was the publication of the periodical *Habl al-Matin* (Firm Cord) in Calcutta.[10]

Edited by Seyyed Jalal al-Din Mo'ayyed al-Eslam Kashani, *Habl al-Matin* launched its publication in 1892 and soon became one of the major sources of analytical information for reformist circles in Iran, Tsarist Central Asia, and Afghanistan. In addition to covering the news and analyzing the political situation in Iran, *Habl al-Matin* paid considerable attention to Russian policy in the occupied Caucasus and Central Asia. Life in the Emirate of Bukhara was a topic that *Habl al-Matin* often tackled in its editorials. With a circulation of seven thousand in the Tsarist empire, *Habl al-Matin*'s critical stance on Russian policy in the Caucasus and Central Asia eventually led to its prohibition, and circulation came to an end in the empire's entire territory.[11]

On its route from Calcutta to Kabul, Herat, and Mashhad, *Habl al-Matin* reached the learned circles of Afghanistan and was welcomed by the country's elites in their pursuit of change and reform. The history of constitutionalism in Afghanistan dates back to 1905, when a group of Afghan constitutionalists urged Amir Habibollah Khan (r. 1901–19) to consent to the founding of a reformist society, Anjoman-e Seraj al-Akhbar. The new society was associated with a new reformist school, Madreseh-ye Habibiyeh, which had been founded some years earlier. The members of the society as well as the teachers and students of the school followed political developments in both Iran and India. The wide circulation of such Persian newspapers as *Habl al-Matin* and *Sur-e Esrafil* (Trumpet of Esrafil) attests to the cross-border connections educated Afghans maintained with their neighbours. Among the subscribers of *Habl al-Matin* in Kabul was Amir Habibollah himself. When the ruler finished reading his copy, it was then handed over to Mohammad Vali Khan, a high dignitary, who then lent it to the Court, to learned princes, nobles, and notables. The newspaper's editorials on the situation in Iran were among the most sought-after columns in Afghanistan at that time.[12] According to Mir Qasem Khan, an active constitutionalist and a teacher at the Habibiyeh school, *Habl al-Matin* and *Sur-e Esrafil* not only enlightened the Afghans with new ideas but also acquainted them with the notion of constitutionalism as formulated in neighbouring countries.[13] Besides *Habl al-Matin* and *Sur-e Esrafil*, one finds traces of the following periodicals in Afghanistan at the time: *Ayeneh* (Samarkand), *Hamdard* (Delhi), *'Amm* (Lahore), *Azad* (Kanpour), *Chehreh Nama* (Egypt), *Rafiq* (Delhi), *Vatan* (Lahore), *Mellat* (Lahore), *Madineh* (Bojnurd), *Moshir* (Morad-abad), *Now Bahar* (Mashhad), *Turan* (Bukhara), *Sahifeh* (Bojnurd), and *Vaqt* (Edinburgh). In a popular poem circulating among the learned circles, an Afghan poet 'Abd al-Hadi, known as Davi, who was a member of the editorial board of *Seraj al-Akhbar*, composed a poem in which he named most of the periodicals published in Afghanistan at the time:

> The *Mirror* of reflection is the *News*
> The *Sympathizer* with you and us is the *News*
> *Popular* everywhere is the *News*
> *Free*, a guiding light, is the *News*
> The *Revealer of secrets*, call the *News*
> The *Companion* in all places, consider the *News*
> The *Homeland*'s true ally is the News
> The *Nation* is its garden, jasmine is the *News*
> *Conscious* of the *Medina*'s hostility is the *News*
> The *Guide* to all of us is the *News*
> *Saviour* of the *World* is the *News*
> The *Great Radiance* is, too, the *News*
> The *New Spring* of Iran is the *News*
> Greeter of the hearts in Damascus and *Turan* is the *News*
> Read thoroughly the *Daily* of the *News*
> Respect all the *Time*, the *News*
> *Guidance* is the path of the *News*
> *Wisdom* is the word of the *News*
> The *East* and West are all exposed in the *News*
> The *Evening* and *Morning* for the friends is the *News*
> Beneficial to every *Muslim* is the *News*
> For *Afghans* in particular is the *News*
> With traders, craftsmen and *Landowners* is the *News*
> Supportive of the *Merchant* and the Scholar is the *News*
> But for everyone the *Torch* is the *News*
> So *Treasured* and sincere is the *News*
> In love with *Unity* is the *News*
> Oh beloved fellows! Filled with the *Knowledge* is the *News*

Affectionate guidance is aspired by the *News*
Superior is the trustworthy pen of the *News*.[14]
(For the original text see the appendix)

By the end of the nineteenth century, journalism had established itself as a new genre in Persian literature. In Iran, the Caucasus, and Central Asia a wide range of periodicals were published that soon crossed the borders, reaching neighbouring countries. *Ershad* (Guidance), and *Molla Nasr al-Din*, both published in Baku, soon became two of the most popular periodicals. While *Ershad* regularly commented on political developments in Iran and Turkistan, *Molla Nasr al-Din* often portrayed, through its critical caricatures, the social and political life of Iran and Turkistan. For example, in 1909, when the Astanqul Beg, the emirate's *qush begi* (the regent, chief minister), on the request of clerics and with the approval of the emir, closed down the Tatar modern school in Bukhara, *Molla Nasr al-Din* filled its pages with caricatures of all known reactionary clerics of the region and, above all, the Bukharan clerics.[15]

The Iranian Constitutional Revolution and its aftermath were a main concern for many of these periodicals. Topics included the temporary setback of the revolution, known as the Lesser Despotism (*estebdad-e saghir*); the restitution of the revolution; the inauguration of the Second Majles in Tehran; and, later, the Russian ultimatum of 1911.

In neighbouring Afghanistan, Mahmud Tarzi (1865–1933) began publishing his *Seraj al-Akhbar* (News Torch) in Kabul in 1911. The new newspaper was reformist and anti-colonialist, emphasizing its regional ambitions with the heading 'Asia for Asians'. It soon expanded its political influence far beyond the boundaries of Afghanistan, and within two years it claimed to have some fifty to sixty subscribers in the cities of Bukhara and Samarkand.[16] It seems that the favourable reception of *Seraj al-Akhbar* among the learned circles of Central Asia ultimately caused Russian authorities to outlaw circulation of the paper in both Turkistan and the Emirate of Bukhara.[17] However, according to some accounts, clandestine circulation of *Seraj al-Akhbar* continued in the region until it ceased publication in 1918.[18]

In the early years of its publication, *Seraj al-Akhbar* covered the news from Iran extensively, but not always approvingly.[19] Mahmud Tarzi, long trained in the Ottoman Empire and associated with the Young Turks, never appreciated any social change from below. His prescribed authoritarian modernization made him sceptical of the Iranian Constitutional Revolution. When he was asked by a correspondent of an English newspaper, published in India, if Afghanistan was following the same path as Iran in establishing a constitutional government, Tarzi made the following remarks: 'The inauguration of the constitutional government [*hokumat-e showra'i*] in Iran is not a model for

Afghanistan to follow but rather it is an event from which we should learn our lesson. For almost four years [following the Constitutional Revolution], there has been nothing but devastation and confusion; and still there is no sign of the promised liberties. There is no sign of progress either. Ultimately, all this chaos has paved the way for the intervention of foreign powers.'[20]

In Bukhara, by 1912, the rather ambivalent political environment in the emirate had convinced many reformists that the moment had come to launch their own regular publication. Through the intermediary of a Russian political agent, they urged the ruler to secure the publication of a Persian-language newspaper. In March of that year, *Bokhara-ye Sharif* (Noble Bukhara) was born in Bukhara. Its editor, Mirza Jalal Yusufzadeh, was an Azerbaijani who was brought in from Baku. Before departing for Bukhara, Yusufzadeh, as a veteran journalist, had been the editor of *Haqiqat* (Truth), a weekly periodical published in Baku. *Haqiqat*, calling itself a 'Turkic-Muslim gazette', covered a wide range of political, literary, social, and economic issues. In *Bokhara-ye Sharif*, Yusufzadeh focused on the same issues as in *Haqiqat*, by covering local, regional, and international news. Furthermore, he called on all local intellectuals to join his campaign of 'disseminating information and knowledge among people' by sharing their news and views with others through the pages of *Bokhara-ye Sharif*:

> Until now, there [has] existed no newspaper in the national and Islamic language in the Emirate of Bukhara, with its three million inhabitants, or in Turkistan and Transoxiana with their 9–10 million-strong population. ... With the assistance of some honourable freethinking Bukharans [Mirza Mohy al-Din Mansur, Mirza Sarraj Hakim, Haidar Kh'ajeh Mirbadal, Sadr al-Din 'Eyni, and 'Abd al-Ra'uf Fetrat], *Bokhara-ye Sharif*, as the first Persian newspaper published in the national language of Bukhara, [has] endeavoured to raise Bukharans' awareness and contribute to the development and prosperity of our ancestral homeland/fatherland.[21]

During the ten months of its publication, *Bokhara-ye Sharif* often tackled issues such as individual and social liberties and the need for change and reform in Central Asia.

One of *Bokhara-ye Sharif*'s main concerns was the launch of an educational campaign to combat illiteracy in the region. It also claimed that this could be achieved only through establishing modern schools with reformed curricula. The importance of education is shown by the fact that *Bokhara-ye Sharif* addressed the need for educational reforms in almost every issue. Although the editor was extremely careful not to jeopardize his already vulnerable relations with the Russian authorities, the emir, and the local clerics, the newspaper's existence as a source of information proved in the end to be intolerable to the pro-Russian establishment, and in January 1913, after 153 issues of the newspaper had appeared, the emir banned the publication of *Bokhara-ye Sharif* at the instigation of the Russian political agent in Bukhara.

In the course of its short life, *Bokhara-ye Sharif* pursued its measured approach to reformism by resorting to a literary device that was novel in the context of journalism, i.e., dialogue. Two examples of this genre were the *Mosahebeh-ye molla va tajer* (The Dialogue between a Mullah and a Merchant) and Yusufzadeh's own *Mosahebeh-e 'elmiyeh* (The Scholarly Dialogue).[22]

Dialogue

Dialogue, variously rendered in Arabic, Persian, and Turkic as *al-hiwar, muhawara (mohavereh/mühavere), mukalama (mokalemeh/mükaleme), munazara (monazereh/münazere)*, or *musahaba (mosahebeh/müsahebe)*, was a literary device in classical Greek literature and is believed to have been introduced by Plato in his *Republic*.[23] In Turco-Persian classical literature, *dialogue*, as a literary form, was almost unheard of. The closest genre to dialogue in the Persian literary tradition was *so'al va javab*, or 'question and answer'.

The earliest traces of this genre are found in pre-Islamic Pahlavi literature, both oral and written. Unlike in dialogue, at least in principle, participants in the question-and-answer format are not on an equal footing; instead, a pupil respectfully poses questions to an accomplished master. Thus any spirit of challenge, often an important component of the dialogue, is absent from the question-and-answer format. The dialogue was introduced into Persian and Turkic political discourse by reform-minded intellectuals only in the latter part of the nineteenth century.[24] *Monazereh* (disputation) offered unhampered and forthright discussion facilitating the airing of participants' concerns in the face of social hardship and arbitrary rule. Next to the idea of anti-despotism, the main feature of such dialogues was often profound discussions of anti-clericalism, aiming to challenge the clerical establishment in the region. Among such dialogues, one may single out Malkam Khan's work, which was as influential as it was far-reaching when his words found a new audience in Turkistan.

In a fictitious conversation titled *Rafiq va vazir* (The Comrade and the Minister), Mirza Malkam Khan initiated the dialogue method to simplify his best known-treatise, *Daftar-e tanzimat ya ketabcheh-e gheybi* (The Book of Regulation, or The Unseen Booklet). In the *Ketabcheh-e gheybi*, penned in 1859, Malkam Khan asserted that the government was 'smitten with plague' and was hopelessly underdeveloped. While he had already put forward a preliminary draft of the future constitution, to facilitate the popular reception of this essay, Malkam Khan felt that it would be more constructive to present his stance in another genre. In the dialogue of *Rafiq va vazir*, *rafiq* (the comrade) is an advocate of political reforms that aim to promote law and order, and *vazir* (the minister) is a conservative who embodies the traditional statesman of unlawful wealth attained by theft, bribery, fraud, and corruption of different kinds who is firmly set against any kind of social change and reform. The individuals engaged in Malkam Khan's *mokalemeh* represent the opposing political camps.

In another dialogue, titled *Sheykh va vazir* (The Sheykh and the Minister), written in 1870 while he was in Istanbul, Malkam Khan adopted the same genre to present a fictitious conversation between a reactionary sheykh and a reformist vizier. While the primary focus of this dialogue is the reform of the Persian/Arabic alphabet, the underlying issue is Malkam Khan's cardinal idea of adopting the achievements of Europe. He writes that Europeans had spent ten times as much effort on developing their countries as they had on inventing the telegraph, and since there was no point in reinventing the telegraph, 'just as we cannot build steam ships and telegraphs ... without the principles of their civilization, it will never be possible for us to attain for our countries the same level of development that they have reached. Either we have to give up on attaining European [levels of] progress and power, or we have to attain them on the basis of the same principles that they did.'[25]

Rafiq va vazir and *Sheykh va vazir* were not the only works that Malkam Khan chose to write in the form of a dialogue. Realizing the popularity of his adopted genre, Malkam decided to employ the dialogue method often for his short polemical editorials, which appeared in his *Qanun*. The circulation of these essays soon became the central project of the regional intellectuals.

Malkam Khan's adoption of the dialogue form was emulated by other writers, the most prominent of whom was Mo'ayyed al-Eslam, the editor of *Habl al-Matin*. Some years before launching his periodical, he had published books and pamphlets in Calcutta, publications which, like others mentioned earlier, reached Central Asia through different routes. One of his writings was *Mokalemeh-ye sayyah-e irani ba shakhs-e hendi* (A Dialogue between an Iranian Traveller and an Indian Individual), published in Calcutta in the early 1890s.

The dialogue genre pioneered by Malkam Khan and Mo'ayyed al-Islam was well received by the Caucasians and the Central Asians, especially by those who lived in exile. In 1909, 'Abd al-Ra'uf Fetrat Bokhara'i (1886/87–1938) published in Persian his work *Monazereh-ye modarres-e bokhara'i ba yek nafar farangi dar Hendustan* (A Dialogue between a Bukharan Religious Scholar and a Western Traveller in India), in which he successfully adopted the dialogue method in presenting his political discourse.[26] In 1913 Mo'in b. Shokrollah Samarqandi translated Fetrat's *Monazereh* into Uzbeki and published it in Tashkent.[27]

Unlike the traditional genre in Persian literature, the *monazereh*s of Mo'ayyed al-Eslam and Fetrat both lack introductions. In Mo'ayyed al-Eslam's work, the dialogue takes place between an Iranian and a learned Indian, while in Fetrat's dialogue a religious scholar from Bukhara meets a Westerner who has some knowledge of Islam. The dialogues, both of which take place in India, blame the 'corrupt clerics' for diminishing the country's social and economic status. Furthermore, the Westerner/Indian argues that in order to resolve the issue one may need to review the causes of the present crisis. He refers to the clerics' malicious beliefs and behaviour, which are further exacerbated by a very traditional educational system. Finally, he concludes that the remedy for all that ails society can be summarized in one word: *qanun* (the law).

This idea, and the rhetorical device used to express it, had of course a famous antecedent in the region. In 1870 Yusef Khan Mostashar al-Dowleh had published a well-known book on politics in Iran titled *Resaleh-e mowsumeh beh yek kalameh* (A Treatise Titled One Word), in which he had stressed the importance of introducing written laws.[28] Mostashar al-Dowleh was followed in Bukhara by Ahmad Danesh, who in 1874, following his return to Bukhara from his third and last trip to St. Petersburg, met Emir Mozaffar al-Din and entreated him to implement a series of fundamental reforms in the emirate. Later that year, Danesh revealed his proposed reforms to the public in a long essay titled *Resaleh dar nazm-e tamaddon va ta'avon* (A Treatise on the Organization of Civilization and Cooperation) and presented it to Emir Mozaffar al-Din. Central to Danesh's treatise was the need to introduce and implement new laws in the emirate. Although in the end nothing came of these attempts at reform, the idea of executing reforms survived and decades later another group of enlightened political activists such as Fetrat once more highlighted it in their reformist campaign.

In Fetrat's dialogue, on occasion, the *farangi* becomes furious and openly challenges the *modarres*, turning the dialogue into a hostile confrontation. This rather belligerent dialogue is an obvious departure from the Turco-Persian literary tradition, in which the dialectic interaction between two opponents rarely leads to new insight into the underlying problems. While Socrates could exploit a fierce opponent's attack and turn it into an opportunity for clarifying or promoting his own view (for instance in the opening book of the *Republic*), Turco-Persian political-literary discourse had little place for real debates. Traditional discourse is underlined by the notion of the disciple-master relationship (*morid va morad*), according to which knowledge is conveyed from *pir*, *morshed*, or *morad* (wise man) to the humble truth seeker. Such knowledge is the product not of a natural learning process of interaction but of independent minds, and it is often conceived of as *vahy-e monzal* (divine revelation) with no *chun-o-chera* (how and why, or questioning).

Fetrat is, however, aware of the absence of an established literary paradigm within which to challenge directly an opponent's political views on intellectual grounds. He strives to initiate a dialectical atmosphere, believing that such a model would encourage open debates on political questions. However, despite his good intentions, the dialogue degenerates into a rather irrational, pseudo-intellectual confrontation, during which the *modarres* accuses the other debater of naïveté and ignorance. At the final stage of the dialogue, the *modarres* eventually demonstrates his conviction by praising the *farangi*, not only for showing the causes of Bukhara's backwardness and its dimensions, but also for offering remedies, which are nothing but the reforming programme of the new Jadidist movement.[29]

Fetrat's *Monazereh* ends with a somewhat lengthy epilogue, also known as *khatemeh*, which does not appear in the Uzbeki translation. As mentioned earlier, those writers who adopted the dialogue approach avoided both lengthy introductions and epilogues. Customarily, both parties involved in the process were expected to part upon the completion of the dialogue. Nevertheless, Fetrat remained unconvinced and added an epilogue to his *Monazereh* to help the reader better understand the nature of the dialogue.

While Fetrat, in his *Monazereh*, blames the ruler's advisers, especially the clerics, for overlooking Bukhara's real needs and delaying the process of political reform, he consciously exempts the ruler himself from any wrongdoing. However, in the epilogue, Fetrat pleads with the emir, or *pedar-e mehraban-e Bokhara'iyan* (the compassionate father of Bukharans), to implement the necessary reforms, especially the educational ones, throughout the country. According to Fetrat, if the ordinary Bukharan subjects are not aware of their right to demand change, that is understandable, since they have been kept in the 'dark'.

By contrast, the behaviour of those, including the emir, who see the necessity of reforms implemented across the world, especially in neighbouring nations, but do not act at home, is unacceptable. Furthermore, Fetrat beseeches the emir and the learned circles in the emirate to bow to this reality and introduce measures in order to elevate Bukhara from its 'enslaved' condition. Finally, he issues an ultimatum, demanding a swift response before it is too late, 'when all mosques are turned into churches and the Bukharans become slaves to their adversaries':

Zaman, zaman-e taraqqi; jahan, jahan-e 'olum, / Olurmi jahl ile qa'il baqay-i jam'iyat? (The era is the era of progress; the world is the world of knowledge, / how then is it possible to survive with ignorance?)[30]

Another treatise written in the dialogue model is the *Mosahebeh-e Iraniyeh* (The Iranians' Dialogue). Its author lived in the Caucasus, most probably in Baku, and failed to obtain permission from Tsarist authorities to publish his work. The treatise remained in the Russian police archives for several years and was permanently buried in the former Soviet Azerbaijan Manuscripts Library. No reference is made to the author in the manuscript itself, and the library's published catalogue gives the author as 'anonymous'. In the library's card catalogue, however, the author's name appears as Mirza Abdollah Ghaffarzadeh. No activist by this name appears elsewhere during this period in Iran or the Caucasus, but it is very likely that the author was in fact Mirza Asadollah Ghaffarzadeh, who was active in the Caucasus around that time. Perhaps those who compiled the new catalogue made a mistake in recording his name.[31]

As with the dialogues mentioned earlier, Mirza Asadollah's work has no introduction. The discussion takes place between Mirza Abdollah and Mirza Sadeq, both of whom are obviously representatives of the middle class, that is, the Iranian intelligentsia, of the late nineteenth century. Mirza Abdollah complains about the chaotic sociopolitical conditions in Iran. Similarly, he blames the 'oppressive rulers' and the 'corrupt clergy' for having reduced the country's economy to such a dire state. He points out that it is absurd that almost all basic commodities are imported from *Farangestan* (Europe). Worse yet, the poor-quality Muscovite products are replacing the better-quality domestic ones.[32] In response, Mirza Sadeq reiterates that he belongs to the same political camp as his interlocutor. Adding a historical dimension to the conversation, he argues that 'ever since the Turkmanchai Treaty was implemented, the Iranians have been in a state of political oblivion from which the trumpet of Esrafil [*sur-e Esrafil*] cannot awaken them.'[33]

The anonymous author of the *Mosahebeh-e Iraniyeh* is aware of the absence at the time of an established literary pattern in Iran for challenging an opponent's political views on intellectual grounds. Therefore, the dialogue turns into a confrontation during which, similar to Fetrat's dialogue quoted earlier, the two Mirzas accuse each other of being naïve and ignorant. After these mutual accusations the dispute quickly subsides.

This 42-page manuscript is written in eloquent Persian, using the elegant *nasta'liq* style. The decision made by the Russian chief of the Inspection Committee appears at the top of the first page saying, 'On April 22nd, 1904, in conformity with Article 102, the Inspection Committee prohibits the publication of the *Mosahebeh-e Iraniyeh*.'

Securing the necessary permission to publish written works was not the main concern of authors living in Iran, the Caucasus, and Central Asia. In a region where literacy rates were very low, the circulation of information among people could be facilitated through intermediary channels, such as private gatherings or coffeehouses. A reader read newspapers aloud while the public listened, and a debate usually followed. Such practices for addressing the illiterate public paved the way for using other literary genres for political objectives. One such genre was the travel diary.

Imaginary Travel Diaries

Like periodicals, imaginary travel diaries found their way across borders. *Siyahatnameh-ye Ebrahim Beyk* (The Travel Diary of Ebrahim Beg), by Zeyn al-'Abedin Maragheh'i (1837–1910), was one of the earliest essays to reach Iran and Central Asia from Baku. The first volume of *Siyahatnameh* was published in Cairo in 1888 and soon became the manifesto of Iranian and Caucasian reformists. In his book, Maragheh'i, a native of Iranian Azarbayjan who spent much of his adult life in Yalta and Istanbul, gives a critical analysis of the sociopolitical order of turn-of-the-century Iran through the fictitious travelogue of a certain Ebrahim Beyk. Once it had reached Central Asia, 'the social order upon which he [Zeyn al-'Abedin Maragheh'i] dwells at length reminded Bukharan intellectuals of their own society and structure.'[34] Moreover, the narrative genre that Maragheh'i employed in his travel diary had its roots in Persian literature; one can therefore assume that the familiarity of Maragheh'i's literary style was one of the reasons his story received regional recognition.

Maragheh'i's book was probably the model for Mirza Seraj al-Din Haji Mirza 'Abd al-Ra'uf Hakim-e Bokhara'i, a.k.a. Mir-Khan Doktor Shaber (1877–1913/14), whose *Tohaf-e ahl-e Bokhara* (Gifts of the People of Bukhara) contains a traveller's account of a voyage to Europe, in the course of which he contrasts what he observes there with the medieval conditions in Afghanistan and the struggle of Iranians against Qajar despotism.[35]

Both the content and the diffusion of these works testify to the supranational scope of many influential reformers' thinking. However, it was another newly adopted literary genre that proved to be more influential yet in disseminating reformist ideas throughout the region.

Modern Drama

After dialogues and fictitious travel diaries, modern drama was another popular genre welcomed by commoners in the area. Modern drama was introduced to the region in the early twentieth century. Judged by today's standards, no trace of professional drama can be found in Iran, the Caucasus, and Central Asia in the nineteenth century, although there existed a long tradition of performances by folksingers, dancers, storytellers, folk humorists (known as *maskharehbazi*), and popular marionette players (in Tajikistan, *zochabozi* or *lukhtbozi*).[36] Mirza Fath-Ali Akhundzadeh (1812–78), the enlightened Azerbaijani reformist, novelist, and dramatist, was the pioneer of drama performance in the East. While living in Tbilisi, he became acquainted with Russian literature and adapted some Russian dramas into Azerbaijani and Persian. However, it was his early compilation of plays known as *Tamsilat*, or the *Six Comedies*, that earned him recognition not only in Iran but also in the Caucasus and Central Asia.

Akhundzadeh's comedies were written between 1850 and 1855, and their technique and structure are, of course, derived from European models; Akhundzadeh is known to have been acquainted with the plays of Alexander Griboedov and Nikolai Gogol, as well as those of Shakespeare and Molière. But he carefully applied Western methods to the creation of characters drawn from local communities. He may be regarded as the first and most successful playwright of the Islamic world in the nineteenth century. In a number of letters to his close friends, Akhundzadeh 'made it clear that his purpose as a playwright was social and didactic; through exposing corrupt, ignorant, and superstitious figures to ridicule on the stage, he hoped that his audience would draw the obvious conclusions and gradually acquire what he regarded as a progressive and enlightened outlook.'[37]

Before long other Azerbaijani dramatists followed in Akhundzadeh's footsteps, among them Najaf bey Vazirov (1854–1926), 'Abd al-Rahim Haqqverdiev (1870–1933), Nariman Narimanov (1870–1925), Jalil Mohammad Qolizadeh (1866–1932), and Ja'far Sarraj Jabbarli (1899–1934). These authors used historical themes for their works, for they believed that one had to learn from history so as to avoid making the same mistakes. Haqqverdiev's *Aqa Mohammad Shah Qajar*, Narimanov's *Nader Shah Afshar*, and Jabbarli's *Naser al-Din Shah*, all historical dramas, were based on the lives of the three Iranian kings. These were among the best-known historical dramas in Turco-Persian literary history.

Written in 1899, the drama *Nader Shah Afshar* was performed in all the major cities of Central Asia and soon became Narimanov's best-received work. Narimanov takes the audience back to the Isfahan of 1717 and portrays the wretched rule of Shah Soltan Hoseyn, the last ruler of the Safavid dynasty. Inspired by romantic nationalism, Narimanov blames the corrupt Court of the last Safavid Shah for the calamities experienced by Iranians. Yet he shows no hesitation in paying homage to Nader, who, according to Narimanov, resisted Ottoman pressure and successfully put all the pieces of the Iranian territorial jigsaw puzzle together again. Nevertheless, Narimanov's story *Nader Shah Afshar* does not end with the new Shah's triumph. By portraying the entire reign of Nader, he demonstrates what is known as the cycle of centralization and decentralization of political power in the East. In a society with high social mobility, assuming power and, hence, restoring order was a viable option for the semi-bandit Nader. Nevertheless, it did not take long for Nader himself to act as an arbitrary ruler, establishing an absolute state, which eventually led to his own downfall. The story of *Nader Shah Afshar* is yet another enactment of the cyclic historical process of centralization and decentralization.

It was in the aftermath of the Russian revolution of 1905 that such pieces were performed in Baku, Tbilisi, and other major cities in Transcaucasia. The move towards the other side of the Caspian Sea began as early as 1909, when the first modern play by the Azerbaijani Haqqverdiev was performed at Fereydun High School in Ashgabat.[38] The title or content of this play remains unknown, but when the same play was performed in Merv it faced an angry reaction from the city's clerics.[39] Following its performance in Ashgabat, the Azerbaijani company moved to other cities in Central Asia, including Samarkand, Kokand, and Charjew. Headed by Ahmad Gamerlinski (Ahmad Hashim oqlu Melikov) (1880–1952), and with renowned actors such as Sidqi Ruhullah (1886–1959), Yunus Narimanov, and Huseyn Arablinski (Huseyn Memmed oqlu Xalafof) (1881–1919), the company performed Narimanov's *Nader Shah Afshar*, or *Nader Shah fajiesi* (The Tragedy of Nader Shah); Vazirov's *Yaqishdan chiqdiq, yagmura dushduk* (Coming out of the Rain, Falling into the Squall); Haqqverdiev's *Aqa Mohammad Shah Qajar*; and *Mosyu Zhordan ve Dervish Mast-'Alishah* (Monsieur Jordan and Dervish Mast-Ali Shah) and *Haj Qara ya sargozasht-e mard-e khasis* (Haji Qara, or The Story of the Avaricious Man) both by Mirza Fath-Ali Akhundzadeh.[40]

The outbreak of the First World War prevented Azerbaijani theatre from continuing its venture in Iran and Central Asia. The early dramatic performances, with their well-rehearsed critiques of the sociopolitical situation in the Tsarist empire's southern region and in neighbouring countries, were gradually replaced with more entertaining musical plays. The highly lyrical and humorous plays of Uzeir Hajibekov (1885–1948), such as the lyric *Leli ve Mejnun* (Leyli and Majnun) and *Asli ve Kerem* (Asli and Karem), or the successful comedies *Arshin Malalan* and *Mashdi Ibad*, were among the most popular performances in the region. Although Hajibekov's comical performances, blended with folk songs and street melodies, remained appealing to many, nevertheless, the political message in these musical performances was not communicated as explicitly as in his earlier plays.

In the early months of the war, other Azerbaijani dramatists such as Khan Talishinski and Rezayev staged their work in different cities of Central Asia. According to the journal *Ayneh*, in 1914, in the Muslim Theatre Hall of Samarkand, Talishinski preformed his *Eski Türkiye* (The Olden Turkey), or what is called in Turkistan *Kohne Türkiye fajiesi* (Tragedy of the Olden Turkey) and Rezayev his *Jahalat* (Ignorance). However, Iran and its past and present were still one of the main concerns of the enlightened circles in Central Asia; Narimanov's *Nader Shah Afshar* was still one of the most popular performances of the time.[41]

Conclusion

When ideas of constitutionalism and reform appeared in the lands surrounding the Caspian Sea in the second half of the nineteenth century, the intellectual elites of Iran, the Caucasus, and Central Asia still partook of a common high culture. The Persian language was the lingua franca of the educated, its rich literary heritage providing cultural references which were accessible to all, native speaker or not. Moreover, Iran's long state tradition furnished a font of historical references whose relevance to current politics was widely understood. These cultural bonds facilitated intellectual exchange and borrowing.

Towards the end of the First World War, the common political culture based on aspirations to constitutionalism declined. Under the combined impact of the Bolshevik revolution in Russia and late Ottoman Pan-Turkism, constitutionalism, with its emphasis on reining in the state, establishing the rule of law, and empowering the individual, lost its centrality in the ideology of reformist intellectuals, who increasingly turned to collectivist preoccupations with the state, the nation, and class. New cultural and political organizations were founded that prompted strong calls for change throughout the region. In Samarkand, Iranians and Tatars formed the *Musalman Musiqi ve Dram Jamiyati* (Muslim Music and Drama Society), and in Tashkent the *Karl Marx Drama Destesi* (Drama Group) was set up. Khan Talishinsky performed his *Hurriyat Qurbanlari* (The Freedom Martyrs) in Samarkand and Tashkent to help raise funds for *Ishtrakiyun Party* (the Communist Party).[42]

The formation of new political parties inspired by socialism, communism, or nationalism crafted a new brand of activism in the region.[43] While some veteran constitutionalists had been affiliated with Pan-Turkism, Pan-Turanism, or Pan-Iranism, others joined the ranks of the socialist and communist parties. The emergence of a new political culture severely undermined the old call for individualism, public presentation, political participation, and constitutionalism. Instead, it was socialism, communism, and the linguistic or ethnic nationalistic patterns upon which the region began to stand. By then the final chapter of reformist constitutionalism had ended.

Appendix

همدرد شما و ماست اخبار	آئینه قدنماست اخبار
آزاد چه رهنماست اخبار	عام است به هر کجاست اخبار
هم در همه جا رفیق دانش	هم چهره نمای راز خوانش
ملت چمن است و یاسمن اوست	غمخوار حقیقی وطن اوست
هم خاص مشیر تو و من اوست	واقف ز مدینه تاختن اوست
هم نیر اعظم است اخبار	هم منجر عالم است اخبار
احوال ده از دمشق و توران	فصلی است ز نوبهار ایران
هر وقت ورا عزیز می دان	هر نکته و هر صحیفه اش خوان
اقوال وی است جمله حکمت	ارشاد وی است کل نصیحت
هر شام و صباح بهر یاران	از مشرق و مغرب است گویان
اخبار خصوص بهر افغان	خوب است برای هر مسلمان
با تاجر و عالم است همکار	با کاسب و صانع و زمیندار
بسیار عزیز و راست گفتار	لیکن ز همه سراج الاخبار
از جام معارف است ای یار	دلداده اتحاد و سرشار
زان افضل و کامل است نامی	وعظ است نکات او تمامی

CHAPTER 20

Mashruteh and *al-Nahda*: The Iranian Constitutional Revolution in the Iranian Diaspora Press of Egypt and in Arab Reformist Periodicals

Kamran Rastegar

There is little dispute over the complexity of historical factors surrounding the advent of the Iranian Constitutional Revolution. Recent studies have shed light upon a wide range of subjects and approaches to the topic that had previously been marginalized in historical scholarship.[1] Despite these important contributions, as M. Reza Afshari has shown in his study of Iranian historiography on the Constitutional Revolution, the predominant mode of historical writing on these events in Iran is best termed as fitting a nationalist populist mode.[2] This mode of historical representation, while presenting challenges to both elitist and traditionalist tendencies, is marked by its largely naturalized conception of the history of constitutionalism as a purely nationalist history.[3] This approach to the revolution serves to marginalize not only perspectives that do not fit a populist framework, but just as importantly, those that do not easily fit a nationalist framework as well.

However, it will here be proposed that the form of political and cultural modernity that the Iranian Constitutional Revolution represented was in part produced outside of Iran's borders, a fact that has not been well recognized by the nationalist populist historiographical tradition. I do not wish to revisit the question of the extent to which this movement was influenced by the West, an issue that has already been attended to in studies on modern Iranian intellectual history.[4] Instead, I intend to show that this form of modernity was not purely the fruit of internal Iranian domestic efforts and aspirations, but that the contributions of the Iranian diaspora communities of that period were of some significant importance to this movement; in great measure this was because these diaspora communities also allowed for the development of links and contacts with reformist movements outside of Iran.[5] This study examines points of contact between Arab and Iranian diaspora periodicals in the Iranian

Constitutional Revolution era, offering a preliminary assessment of the possible links and threads of influence that criss-cross the social landscape between Iran, the Iranian diaspora, and Arab *Nahda* and reformist movements.[6] While historical and literary scholarship has directed some important attention to the role of exilic Iranian publishing in the development of political and cultural reformist and revolutionary discourses central to the Iranian Constitutional Revolution, much of this work has focused on Istanbul, and to a lesser extent on Western Europe.[7] Very little research has focused on the active Iranian press in the Arab world (which in this study will largely be limited to Egypt), despite the presence of a vibrant Iranian community and its active diaspora press.

The Iranian Diaspora Press, the Arab *Nahda* and Egyptian–Ottoman Reformism

The late nineteenth-century and early twentieth-century Iranian diaspora press played an important role within the Iranian community in Cairo.[8] While data on this community is rather scant, we have some indications from which a general image may be developed. The community of Iranians in Cairo comes into focus in the latter years of the nineteenth century, at the apex of Qajar failures to improve Iran's dire economy and at the same time as the spread of famine and disease. The community, however, was never as sizeable as those of some other regions (such as Istanbul); for example, the Egyptian census recorded 1,385 Iranian residents of the country in 1907.[9] In 1938, an Egyptian-based Persian-language newspaper estimated the population at 3,500.[10] As members of Iran's mercantile classes emigrated to neighbouring regions during the late Qajar period, some made their way to India, eventually obtaining status as British colonial subjects. Then, after the British occupation of Egypt in 1882, Iranian merchants from India began to emigrate to Alexandria and Cairo and enjoyed favourable treatment due to their status under British jurisdiction.[11] For example, as British subjects they were accorded special legal standing and were not subject to judgements of the Egyptian native courts, instead enjoying capitulation rights until 1928.[12] Undoubtedly the community also comprised emigrants who arrived directly from Iran, but it would seem that the British link enabled the expansion and consolidation of an Iranian community in Egypt in a manner that would otherwise have been unlikely. Yadegari comments that Iranians in Egypt comprised a striated community with wealthy elites, common merchants, and a poorer working class, and argues that the elites were nearly entirely made up of arrivals via India. Over the decades, this community began to develop various institutions – including charitable and cultural organizations and schools.[13] While for years the community appears to have generally fared reasonably well in Egypt, in the period shortly before and after the 1952 revolution in Egypt some returned to Iran, joining other ethnic minorities (such as the Greek and Italian communities of Egypt) in finding the future uncertain and somewhat precarious. Among these numbered many of the elite traders and industrialists who by the 1940s began to find themselves in stiff competition with an expanding domestic bourgeoisie (which often used nationalist sentiments to its own advantage). Others, perhaps most, chose to assimilate fully into Egyptian society and took Egyptian citizenship, a process accelerated by widespread intermarriage with Egyptians, as in the marriage of Tahia Kazem, from an Iranian family, to Jamal 'Abd al-Nasir.[14]

Despite the relatively small number of Iranians in Egypt, the periodicals published by the Iranian community in Egypt were nonetheless influential, given both the prosperity of Iranians in Egypt and the centrality of Cairo and Alexandria as economic and cultural centres within the region. Because of their diasporic settings, these publications were well-situated to establish networks and relationships with local institutions and groups in their host societies. However, despite an ostensible priority on addressing the questions and reflecting the concerns of the diaspora community, these publications also served readerships inside Iran. This dual audience is palpable in the range of subjects found in these publications and in the particular treatment of these subjects by the writers of these periodicals.

Several Persian-language periodicals were published in Egypt in the years leading up to and shortly after the Constitutional Revolution. These publications were very fundamentally emanations of what we may call the Iranian diaspora culture of the period: they focus very closely on reporting on and discussing events inside Iran; however, they do so within a frame of reference that is informed by their own social and cultural context – that of turn-of-the-century Egypt and the Arab *Nahda* movement. This context does not determine the content of the periodicals, but does affect the manner of analysis and often provides an inherent comparative framework for discussing Iranian issues. In some cases, hints within the Persian-language press betray direct references to Arab *Nahda* sources, referring to Arabic periodicals and publications that may be seen to have contributed to the *Nahda* movement.

Hekmat, the first Persian-language periodical in Egypt, was published in Cairo from 1893 to 1910 by Mirza Mehdi Khan, Za'im al-Dowleh.[15] *Hekmat* was widely known and well respected in Iran, and is cited favourably in Ahmad Kasravi's *Tarikh-e mashruteh-ye Iran*,[16] to no small extent because of its close pursuit of details relating to domestic political issues in Iran and its nuanced support for constitutionalism. However, *Hekmat* also positioned itself very consciously as an Egyptian publication, with a commitment to reporting on matters domestic to Egyptian politics and society. A recurring section heading in *Hekmat*, '*Akhbar-e Dakheliyeh*' (Domestic News), relayed news on policy decisions made by the Egyptian Khedivate, state visits to Egypt and the like. The same section would also often report on the activities of the Iranian community in Egypt – for example, one 1898 issue reports on celebrations in Cairo of the anniversary of the ascendance of the Ottoman Sultan Abdülhamid II to the throne. After relating news of the celebrations generally, the author focuses on the participation of Iranian merchants in the Khan al-Khalili quarter in the same events, relating that the Iranian flag was hung in the market alongside the Ottoman ensign, and that celebratory sweets were offered to passersby from Iranian-owned shops.[17] In this way *Hekmat* presents a picture of an Iranian diaspora community largely assimilated into Egyptian–Ottoman society, eager to present itself as a fully participating group within this society.

While *Hekmat* rarely explicitly referenced Arabic-language periodicals or *Nahda*-related personalities, it at times engaged in criticism of shortcomings in Iranian governance through references to Egyptian state policies, especially when discussing reforms or innovations. For example, in one article reporting on the results of the 1898 census in Egypt, the author offers a plaintive question, 'Will we [Iranians] some day have the same idea of becoming aware of the quantity [of the population] and the conditions of our country, or not?'[18] In *Hekmat*, discussions of both Ottoman and Egyptian governmental reforms often presented opportunities for subtle or explicit criticism of the relative lack of receptivity to institutional reforms to be found in the Qajar Court.

While *Hekmat* at times made oblique references to Arab *Nahda* and political reformist contexts from which to articulate a criticism of governance and social progress in Iran, another Persian-language publication based in Egypt, *Chehreh Nama*, would make much more explicit its references to Arabic sources in its critical writings. *Chehreh Nama* was published in Egypt between the years of 1904 and 1966: an astonishing longevity, which must place this title among the longest-running periodicals in the Persian language to date.[19] While the offices of *Chehreh Nama* moved to Cairo from Alexandria during the first two years of the journal's run, everything else about the publication is a testament to the stability and diligent commitment of its owner and publisher, Haji Mirza 'Abdol-Mohammad Khan Irani, also known as Mo'addab al-Soltan, who was later replaced by his son as the journal's publisher.[20] Perhaps one reason for the longevity of *Chehreh Nama* – especially in comparison with other publications established in the constitutional era – was the fact that the newspaper was at once a critical voice calling for political and cultural reform in Iran, fulfilled a role for the Iranian diaspora community living in Egypt, and positioned itself as an Iranian publication dedicated to both Pan-Islamic and international issues. So while, for example, the 14 October 1909 issue's front page was dedicated to a discussion of the new cabinet for the re-established constitutional government, '*Kabineh-ye jadid-e vozara-ye Iran*', on page 3 we find a report on the Iranian School of Egypt, '*Madreseh-ye kheyriyeh-ye Iraniyan dar Mesr*', lauding a philanthropist among the Iranian community of Egypt, Mirza Mohammad Ali Beyk, for his support for the school. This attention to local issues was not limited only to strictly social and political issues, but also included cultural and literary content relating to Egypt and the wider Arab world – this is an important point that distinguishes *Chehreh Nama* from some other diaspora newspapers. For example, in the issue cited above, we find on page 15 a review of the Egyptian scientific newspaper *al-Muqtataf*, with information on how readers may subscribe to it. It is this fascinating intersection that should merit our attention – the combination of political commentary concerning Iranian domestic conditions with local reportage of interest to the Iranian diaspora community of Egypt, along with an unself-conscious association of this Persian-language periodical with those Arabic-language periodicals promoting a similar set of political, social, and cultural reforms.

Another innovation of *Chehreh Nama* was that in the constitutional period, the publication served to bring together within its pages the voices of Iranians from a wide variety of geographical locations; it did so largely through the innovative use of telegraph reports sent to the periodical from locations as diverse as India, Syria, Europe, and the Americas, not to mention from within Iran itself. In doing so, *Chehreh Nama* presented a deterritorialized conception of its readership as well as its subject. Yet, given its location in one of the major urban centres of the Arab world, the periodical is not self-conscious in its use of references to the discourse of political and cultural reform promoted by certain Arab thinkers. For example, in the tenth issue of the periodical, in the year 1909, we find reviews of books by two major Arab *Nahda* thinkers – Jurji Zaydan's *Kitab tarikh al-adab al-lugha al-'arabiyya* and Shibli Shumayyil's *Falsafa al-nishu' wa al-Irtiqa'*; two issues later we find a letter from the publisher of the Beirut publications *al-Muntaqid* and *al-Balagh*, expressing camaraderie with and support for *Chehreh Nama* and its programme, which indicates that the periodical was read in Beirut in this period. While the aforementioned reviews are relatively brief and only generally outline the contents of the books, they do offer a measure of the value accorded to these authors and their intellectual projects. These references are but a few of the many that appear in the pages of *Chehreh Nama*, marking a level of social and cultural affinity between the Iranian diaspora press and that of the Arab *Nahda* movement. Furthermore, *Chehreh Nama* often translated and published articles from these other publications – *Chehreh Nama* is no different from other diaspora Iranian publications in that it sometimes did not credit the original source of these translations, a matter that led to a complaint in *al-Hilal*'s first 1906 issue to the effect that Persian-language journals were copying its articles without attribution.²¹ However, frequently translations in *Chehreh Nama* were indeed credited, and translations from the vanguard of the Arabic *Nahda* press were a long-standing feature of the publication.²² Indeed, so great was *Chehreh Nama*'s interest in *Nahda* thinkers that in 1910 it featured an article on Jurji Zaydan (the publisher of *al-Hilal*), including a large photographic portrait, a poetic elegy to Zaydan in Arabic (with Persian translation), his biography, and a full bibliography of his written works.²³

Iran's Revolution in the Arab Reformist Journals *al-Hilal* and *al-Muqtataf*

While examining the traces of influence by Arab *Nahda* and Egyptian reformist thought upon the Iranian diaspora press gives evidence of resonances across social and national boundaries, the influence of the Iranian constitutional movement on cultural or ideological developments in the Arab world was also not negligible. The representation of the Iranian constitutional struggle in Arabic publications such as Jurji Zaydan's *al-Hilal* or Yaqub Sarruf and Faris Nimr's *al-Muqtataf* shows that the development of these ideas, in both the Arab and Iranian contexts, was contingent upon the cultural and political influence and inspiration of other regional struggles.²⁴

Published in Cairo from 1876 to 1900, *al-Muqtataf*'s range of topics roughly approximated those of *al-Hilal*, while giving somewhat greater coverage to scientific matters where the latter journal excelled in political and literary analysis.²⁵ In a six-page article published in February 1907, titled 'Mozaffar al-Din Shah and the Iranian Nation', the authors of *al-Muqtataf* offer strong approval for the Constitutional Revolution through their discussion of the impact of Mozaffar al-Din Shah's reign.²⁶ The first sentence of the article reads, 'This just king took power after granting his nation [*ummatahu*] constitutional governance. He carried out what the majority of other constitutional kings did not carry out, other than under the threat of the sword, so may the best thoughts be granted him by his people.' While this introduction pays tribute to the Shah's (rather questionable) role in promoting constitutionalism, the authors later make clear that the reformist project leading to the Constitutional Revolution had been promoted from outside the Court. 'It became apparent to us in discussions with some Iranians that they were working for the reform of their country, unhappy with its conditions continuing as they had; especially those who were from the merchant classes [*ahl al-tijara*] ... knowing what would be beneficial to the country and what would be detrimental.'²⁷ The narrative continues, describing the progression of the Constitutional Revolution as largely an effect of agitation carried out by this same social class, eventually convincing the Shah of the merits of constitutionalism. The section continues further with a description of the illness and eventual demise of the Shah, before the article changes focus to a genre of writing found commonly in *al-Muqtataf*, that of geographical and historical article about a particular country, in this case Iran. As *al-Muqtataf* identified itself as a scientific journal rather than a political or literary one, it often would couch its political analyses of current events within articles that were presented as geographical studies or as general surveys of certain countries in the world.

What is perhaps most interesting in this article is the reference the author makes to the Iranian diaspora members as sources of information for his or her analysis. Given the large number of merchants and traders among the Iranian community in Cairo, it may not be surprising that the *al-Muqtataf* author gives such heavy emphasis to the role of the merchant classes within the revolution. But the merchant classes (*ahl al-tijara*) are not the only sector of Iranian society of apparent interest to the editors of this journal. A separate discussion on Iran appears in *al-Muqtataf* in the following year, 1908, in an article titled 'The Iranian Woman and Her Influence upon the Men of Reform in Iran'.[28] The article provides long excerpts written by a Russian commentator concerning the social status of Iranian women, said to have been published in an unnamed French journal. On the basis of this commentator's observations, the article advances a thesis that the Constitutional Revolution was greatly advanced by changes to the social status of Iranian women. While much of the article is not the work of the authors of *al-Muqtataf*, their framing comments clearly signal their approval of the thesis and their interest in the argument it advances concerning the role of women in social and political reforms.

The focus put on the role of Iranian women by the editors of *al-Muqtataf* follows, generally, on the emphasis given by many Arab *Nahda* thinkers to the importance of social reforms, including a reconsideration of the position of women within Arab societies. It is clear that to the readers of the journal, the Iranian constitutional movement would be viewed with a great deal of sympathy – to attribute to women a significant role in this movement was one manner by which the editors could advance a larger discussion on the social role of women in Arab societies. This comparative method is very similar, in fact, to the kinds of comparisons Iranian diaspora publications were making between Iranian and Egyptian governmental reform, as discussed above.

In the following year, 1909, *al-Muqtataf* returns to the issue of the Iranian Constitutional Revolution in a further article, 'Iran and its Future'.[29] While the article is again styled in the genre of a country profile, containing details about Iran's economic output, geography, and history, it presents this information within the frame of a question about how the return of constitutionalism will affect Iran's future, comparing Iran's reforms favourably to the Young Turk

Revolution. The comparison with the Ottoman constitutional movement is, as I will discuss in greater detail below, a common point of departure for Arab commentators after 1908–09. The events in Istanbul may not have had direct repercussions for Arab *Nahda* thinkers within Arab–Ottoman domains, but, again, the Iranian Constitutional Revolution provided an important comparative context for discussions of how to reform the Ottoman polity.

In addition to *al-Muqtataf*, other Arabic publications also showed great interest in the Constitutional Revolution – perhaps none more than *al-Hilal*. This may not be surprising given that several books by the journal's editor, Jurji Zaydan, had already been translated into Persian – in following years, Zaydan's novels would come to be among the most popular translations published in Persian in the early twentieth century.[30] As a testament to the recognition of *al-Hilal* among Iranian diaspora intellectuals, the publication carried an announcement of the beginning of the publication of *Chehreh Nama* in its 1 November 1904 issue, showing that *Chehreh Nama*'s publisher had sent details of that journal and its first issue to *al-Hilal* even at that early stage, recognizing the need to maintain relations with and accrue legitimacy from the Arab *Nahda* press.

Al-Hilal itself displayed an enduring interest in Iranian history and culture, as well as in the current affairs of the country, especially during the period of the Constitutional Revolution. In the early stages of the Constitutional Revolution, several articles followed the career of Mozaffar al-Din Shah with guarded sympathy. The periodical carried an obituary for him in 1907 that was not entirely unfavourable, viewing him as an admirable reformer for his eventual concessions to the constitutionalists. Later, during the reign of Mohammad Ali Shah, *al-Hilal* pursued a more passionate tone in defence of the constitutional reformers. For example, in the seventh issue of the journal in 1908, an article appeared discussing Mohammad Ali Shah's shelling of the Majles, describing the event as 'the victory of oppression' and explaining that as a consequence, 'power has come to be in the hands of the Shah, and he arrested the proponents of freedom, among them the highest of men of knowledge and liberty.' In the following year, *al-Hilal* picked up the issue of Iranian constitutionalism in its 1 October 1909 issue, celebrating the abdication of Mohammad Ali Shah and the ascension of the young Ahmad Shah to the throne. This article in part presents a narrative of the events between June 1908 and September 1909 in Iran, but quite interestingly presents them against the backdrop of the Ottoman constitutional movement of 1876, and the 1909 ouster of Sultan Abdülhamid II in Constantinople. The article argues that the two events are not at all isolated but that each offers an example and inspiration to the other. The *al-Hilal* article begins this narrative by saying:

This [the struggle against Mohammad Ali's 1908 disbanding of the Majles] took place during the events of the reactionary [*irtija'iyya*] movement in Istanbul, where the anti-reformist campaigners turned the constitution upon its head and ousted the members of the movement of unity and progress. Then those seeking freedom gained the upper hand, entering Istanbul in force, and removing Sultan Abdülhamid from the throne, placing his brother in his place ... and this inspired the Iranians, and they wished to take the Ottomans as an example for themselves, although they had suffered in their way more than the Ottomans had.[31]

This narrative sees the history of Iranian constitutionalism as a fraternal movement to the Young Turks' challenge to Abdülhamid's despotism. The historical narrative gives an emphasis to the idea of a direct linkage, between Abdülhamid's defeat by the reformist Young Turks and the defeat of Mohammad Ali Shah by constitutionalists, that may seem unfamiliar to those steeped in either Iranian or Turkish nationalist historiography. But for the author of the article, the question is not that of the Ottoman events simply inspiring the Iranians, but rather that of a chain of events that are mutually edifying. This is clear when the author states, 'They [Iranian constitutionalists] inspired Ottomans and non-Ottomans and gave them hope with their love of liberty and opposition to oppression, with the courageous correctness within their hearts.'[32] The author gives special mention to the Tabrizi fighters for 'showing to the world that they are men of courage.' This, the article argues, is a reflection of Tabriz's long history as the most progressive city of Iran, noting that the first printing press was established there in 1825, as well as the first newspaper. These developments, *al-Hilal* argues, are the foundation upon which the Tabriz resistance to Mohammad Ali Shah was founded, as these are developments that expanded knowledge and science, and so, 'it is not strange that the residents of Tabriz would show themselves to be set on the path of truth and that they would struggle for freedom, because knowledge [*'ilm*] is the brother of freedom and the enemy of tyranny.'[33] So for *al-Hilal* the material bases for cultural modernity – educational institutions, printing presses and newspapers – are central to understanding the events of 1908–09 in Iran.

The article continues by describing the flight of Mohammad Ali Shah with Russian support, celebrating his departure into exile. It ends with the following sentiment: 'This is how the Iranian freedom-seekers won the constitution, and how they sacrificed in its pursuit more than the Ottomans had sacrificed in terms of lives or what they endured in terms of pain. And so the national parliament was returned to work giving Iranians a sense that their constitution was ensured to continue in their victory.'[34] While this article from *al-Hilal* gives us a broad sense of the lens through which the Arab reformists who were the primary audience for this influential journal may have viewed the events in Iran during the course of 1908–09, I would like to suggest that what this article signifies is more than simple reportage from an Arab perspective. The Arab reformist movements had by now gone through various ideological orientations, in particular the Pan-Islamic orientation perhaps best represented by Jamal al-Din al-Afghani and his student Muhammad 'Abduh, an orientation that often envisioned the Ottoman caliphate as a framework for a reinvigoration of social, cultural, and political life in the region.[35] While it may be an overstatement to articulate the ideas of al-Afghani or even 'Abduh as comprising a coherent programme, the views of Arab intellectuals inspired by these and other reformers indicate that for them the Pan-Islamist project involved a rejuvenation of the concept of the caliphate while eliminating the ethnic particularism practised by the Ottoman leadership, especially where it affected the development of regional – non-Turkish – literary and cultural life. By the period in question, however, this project was under serious re-evaluation, as the antagonism of Sultan Abdülhamid towards the progressive forces in the Ottoman capital began to disillusion the progressive reformists, such as those who wrote for and read *al-Hilal*, from the possibility of rejuvenating the caliphate around the decaying Ottoman polity. Within this context, what this article shows is the continuing importance of the Iranian Constitutional Revolution in the development of reformist and revolutionary political discourse in the Ottoman Empire, in particular for the Arab reformers of the turn of the century.

These excerpts from *al-Muqtataf* and *al-Hilal* provide but a hint of the larger impact of the Constitutional Revolution within the Arab *Nahda* context. *Al-Muqtataf*'s citation of Iranian diaspora sources in its reporting and *al-Hilal*'s exchanges and contacts with the Iranian diaspora press show – if only partially – the intermediary role of the Iranian communities of the Arab world in promulgating contacts between *Nahda* discourse and Iranian constitutionalism. To address this issue in greater depth would require a wider examination of these and other sources, but as has been shown, a survey of some of these publications shows clearly that the Iranian Constitutional Revolution was deemed very significant by the Arab *Nahda* press, and that at the same time, Arab *Nahda* intellectual discourse was significant for the Iranian diaspora press in Egypt, which itself played an important role in the development and distribution of constitutionalist discourse both in Iran and within the Iranian diaspora.

Conclusion: Nationalist Historiography and Intercultural Contacts

This chapter has examined how and to what extent diaspora communities were effective in translating and communicating reformist discourse from their host societies for use in an Iranian context. A further step in this area of enquiry would be the question of what impact the Iranian reformist discourse had on the reform movements of these host societies. Unfortunately these and similar questions have not been adequately addressed in the available scholarship; perhaps as a result of certain limitations in the conceptualization of much of the research that has been carried out about the Constitutional Revolution. These limitations are most apparent in historical and cultural studies carried out through a narrow nationalist lens, a framework that has exerted a great influence in much of our thinking concerning Iran's cultural history in the nineteenth and early twentieth centuries. A different approach to the history of the Constitutional Revolution may be predicated on the emergence of certain innovations – literary and cultural, as well as political – that raise questions about the presumption that what was to be codified as Iranian nationalism and the revolutionary ideals of *mashrutiyat* were naturally coterminous. Where nationalist modernities have emphasized a return to linguistic purity, empowering the conceptions of territorial and geographic boundaries, and so on, an alternative history of the Constitutional Revolution may propose to emphasize exchanges and interactions across social and ultimately national boundaries instead, looking to the manner in which local events inside Iran were influenced by and influenced other contexts such as the Arab world, India, and Central Asia. The diaspora press is one important setting for the exploration of these cross-cultural contacts often not given voice in nationalist historiography.

What is clear from this examination of interactions between the Iranian diaspora press in Egypt and that of Arab *Nahda* thinkers is that reformist and revolutionary social and political movements in Iran and in the Arab world were quite organically influenced by one another. These conclusions would suggest that certain dimensions to this complex historical episode that as yet have not been the subject of sufficient scholarly attention – questions such as the possible influences of, for example, Indian anti-colonial thinking on the Iranian constitutional movement, or the impact of other non-European engagements with modernity upon the particular trajectories of Iranian engagements with modernity – merit our attention. Further studies along these lines may well give a fuller understanding of the presence of what Elleke Boehmer terms 'anti-imperial, cross border strategies' such as those that linked Irish and Indian anti-colonial movements against British imperialism. Through such a framework, Boehmer argues, we may be able to trace hitherto disregarded features of a 'globalized and constellated modernism' de-centred from the predominant narrative of Western modernity's influence on colonized societies.[36]

Predominant historical approaches to Iranian constitutionalism are too often produced within a framework that sets the national parameters as natural and tends to ignore or delegitimize those historical trends and trajectories that do not fit neatly into a nationalist perspective. The intermediary role played by the Iranian diaspora press in maintaining contacts with other reformist movements such as the Arab *Nahda* movement does not necessarily fit a nationalist paradigm, and thus tends to invite less interest by this mode of historiography. Rather than continuing within the limitations presented by the nationalist paradigm, we may instead view transformations to political discourse during this period as having emerged as a result of intercultural circulations – emerging from translations, or from the appropriation and circulation of textual materials across cultural boundaries.[37] This intercultural circulation brought about transformations in political and cultural discourse in both Iran and its diasporas, as well as in parts of the Arab world. These sources show a clear affinity between the Arab *Nahda* and the Iranian constitutional movement, an affinity promoted through the circulation of reformist and revolutionary discourses between the Arab *Nahda* press and Iranian diaspora publications in the Arab world at that time.

CHAPTER 21

The Iranian Constitutional Revolution as Reported in the Chinese Press

Yidan Wang

In the first decade of the twentieth century, a series of revolutionary movements was launched in different countries of Asia, including Iran, India, the Ottoman Empire, and China. As the first event of its kind in the East, the Iranian Constitutional Revolution evoked a significant echo in China at that time, and inspired the Chinese revolutionary democrats who played an important role in the Chinese Xinhai Revolution (1911–12) afterwards. The Iranian Constitutional Revolution has been regarded by Chinese scholars as the beginning of the Awakening of Asia, and the Chinese Xinhai Revolution as the high tide of it. In the past twenty years, some Chinese specialists have written articles on the Iranian Constitutional Revolution and tried to compare the two revolutions.[1]

In this chapter, I will discuss three Chinese periodicals that reported on the Iranian Constitutional Revolution while it was going on, and then make my own brief comparison of the Iranian Constitutional Revolution and the Chinese Xinhai Revolution.

Dongfang Zazhi (The Eastern Miscellany)

When skimming through the newspapers and journals published and distributed in the first decade of the twentieth century in China (the number of which exceeded two hundred), we find that the most detailed account of the Iranian Constitutional Revolution was given by *Dongfang Zazhi* (The Eastern Miscellany), a comprehensive monthly magazine that had a publication history of 45 years, from March 1904 to December 1948. This was the longest-lasting periodical and one that exerted a great influence on the modern history of China. Published by the famous Shangwu Yinshuguan (the Commercial Press), the longest-standing and most influential publishing house in China – which was founded in 1897 in Shanghai, moved to Beijing in 1954, and set up branches in Hong Kong and Singapore afterwards – *Dongfang Zazhi* was characterized by its large variety of information. Besides the editorials, which represented the editors' opinion and views, *Dongfang Zazhi* printed all kinds of news, reports, reviews, and commentaries selected from other periodicals or translated from the foreign presses, as well as official documents and correspondence such as the imperial edicts and memorials to the throne. Therefore it was very convenient for readers who did not have enough time to skim through all the newspapers and magazines. It was called 'a magazine of magazines' and became more and more popular among the people. Its low price and superb binding and layout were further reasons for its popularity. According to statistics, more than 10,000 copies of each issue were sold in 1911.[2] It might be helpful to note that most of the readers of *Dongfang Zazhi* were patriotic businessmen, enlightened gentry, educated persons, and students, who were, relatively speaking, quite interested in new knowledge and learning and more likely than others to concern themselves with state affairs and the destiny of the nation.

Shortly before the outbreak of the Iranian Constitutional Revolution, *Dongfang Zazhi* had published some news reports about Iran. In its third issue of 1904, there was a short article entitled 'The Coronation of the Persian Shah', recounting the ceremony at which Mozaffar al-Din Shah ascended the throne.[3] It was probably the first report on Iran in Chinese magazines. In its fifth issue (1904), it published a review entitled 'The Current Situation in the Persian Gulf', analyzing the competition between Russia and Great Britain in occupying the Persian Gulf, an area of great strategic significance.[4] Interestingly, in its ninth issue of 1904, *Dongfang Zazhi* published a mini-sized portrait of Mozaffar al-Din Shah (Figure 35).

35. Mozaffar al-Din Shah.

36. Mohammad Ali Shah.

After the outbreak of the Iranian Constitutional Revolution, and especially after 1909, *Dongfang Zazhi* paid much more attention to Iran than before, and published plenty of news reports tracking the development of the revolution. In its sixth issue of 1907, *Dongfang Zazhi* published a photo of the new Persian monarch, Mohammad Ali Shah (Figure 36), the successor of Mozaffar al-Din Shah. In 1909, when the Constitutional Revolution was spreading all over Iran and reaching its climax, *Dongfang Zazhi* published 44 news reports about Persia in its 12 issues of that year, providing Chinese readers with a very detailed and continuous account of the great event in progress in Iran. Most of these news reports were selected and translated from the British newspaper *The Times* [of London] (*Lundun Taiwushi Bao*) by a Chinese correspondent named Gan Yonglong. In addition to these news reports, *Dongfang Zazhi* frequently published commentaries on the Persian Revolution, such as 'Additional Remarks Concerning the History of the Persian Revolution',[5] 'How Regretful the Dethroned Persian King Is',[6] and 'How Unfortunate the Reigning Persian King Is'.[7]

After 1910, news reports about the Persian revolution declined, but several important analytical reviews indicated the magazine's ongoing interest in Iran's Constitutional Revolution. In 1910, there were two reviews: 'On the

Execution of a Treacherous Courtier Following the Death Sentence'[8] and 'Warning: Britain and Russia Are Carving up Persia';[9] in 1911, there were also two reviews: 'Brief Remarks on the Education of the Persian Shah' by Gan Yonglong,[10] and 'The Future of the Persian Gulf' by Kong Qinglai;[11] and in 1912, there was a remarkably long review entitled 'The Current Situation in Persia' by Qian Zhixiu.[12]

The editors and writers of *Dongfang Zazhi* were well known as constitutionalists in China at that time, which explains why they showed so much interest in the Iranian Constitutional Revolution. The title of the review 'Warning: Britain and Russia Are Carving up Persia' clearly exhibited the author's worry about Iran. In another review, the one entitled 'On the Execution of a Treacherous Courtier Following the Death Sentence', the author gave a very detailed description of how the bodyguard of Mohammad Ali Shah was sent to the gallows, discussed the cause of his death by hanging, and then reached the conclusion that those who perpetrate many injustices are doomed to self-destruction.[13] In the review 'The Future of the Persian Gulf', the author, Kong Qinglai, analysed the effect of the construction of the Baghdad railway on the political and economic situation of the Persian Gulf, especially its effect on the competition for spheres of influence between Britain and Germany.[14]

A review entitled 'Brief Remarks on the Education of the Persian Shah', by Gan Yonglong, appeared in the sixth issue of 1911. After reporting the news of the appointment of the American W. Morgan Shuster as financial adviser to the Iranian government by the National Assembly, the author discussed many other reforms undertaken by the Iranian constitutional government. Then, the author of the review concentrated on educational reform in Iran, regarding it as the most significant proof of the ideological progress of the Persians. Gan Yonglong, the author of the review, said:

> Today in Persia, the traditional private schools have been gradually transformed and new-style schools have been set up. Ahmad Shah, the Persian teenaged monarch, is fourteen years old now. The courses in the royal school arranged for him are all progressive and extensive, instead of the limited and traditional stick-in-the-mud ones. It reflects the progressive education policy of the new constitutional government. The royal regent of the Shah is a graduate of Oxford University, well nurtured by European-American culture. Ahmad Shah, who is the first monarch since the establishment of constitutionalism in Persia, will assume the reign of government upon coming of age. How will he be competent for this heavy responsibility if he has not received a good advanced education by then?[15]

Then, Gan Yonglong quoted an article from the American newspaper *American Review*, describing the circumstances under which Ahmad Shah was receiving his education:

In the imperial palace, there are twelve young men who graduated from universities in Paris and London or other capital cities in Europe. They are accompanying the Shah as his attendants, along with his teachers who teach him new kinds of learning and science. Besides, there are also several venerable persons teaching him traditional knowledge. To cultivate the Shah's qualities of republicanism, the constitutional government has specially selected twelve teenagers from different social classes and appointed them to study together with the Shah. In this way, the Shah cannot only find rivals in study, but also get acquainted with his people from different classes.[16]

It would be interesting for us to take a look at the photos of Ahmad Shah (Figure 37), the teenaged reigning Iranian monarch, and of two Qajar noblemen (Figure 38). Of the latter, one is Ala' al-Saltaneh[17] (Alan-Sadunnai), the Minister of Public Construction and the former Minister of Foreign Affairs, who had served as an envoy to Britain for more than twenty years and had also been sent on diplomatic missions to India, Turkey, and Russia, the other is Prince Mo'in al-Vezareh (Moyinnai Weixule), the son of Ala' al-Saltaneh, who entered the University of London at the age of 16, became a lawyer at the age of 21, and had seven foreign languages at his fingertips.

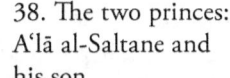

38. The two princes: A'lā al-Saltane and his son.

37. Ahmad Shah.

'The Current Situation of Persia', by Qian Zhixiu, an unusually long review, appeared in 1912. This eight-page review, as the author says, is a selected translation of an article by Edward Browne, which gives a description of the outrages committed by the Russian troops and Shoja' al-Dowleh, and of the miserable conditions in Persia, particularly in Tabriz, after the coup of December 1911.[18] The review analyses reasons for the failure of the Persian Revolution and points out that it was foreign interference, especially Russian armed intervention, that put an end to the Persian Constitutional Revolution, and that Great Britain played the part of an accomplice in helping Russia to kill the Persian revolution.[19]

The nine photos from *Dongfang Zazhi* included here are of special historical importance, as they show the real conditions of Persian society, mainly the Persian army, around 1911. The subjects of these photos are as follows: (1) The new Persian monarch Ahmad Shah (Figure 39); (2) The Persian land force (Figure 40); (3) The Persians praying before a battle, and a scene in front of the Persian telegraph office (Figure 41); (4) Five photos showing the current situation of the Persian army (Figure 42): (i) The Persian soldiers; (ii) The Cossack Brigade stationed in Persia; (iii) The hostel of the Persian trade caravan; (iv) The Persian soldiers as peddlers (they became peddlers because they did not receive their pay and provisions, so they had to sell things to survive); and (v) The Persian artillery.

Zhengyi Tongbao (Journal of Politics and Art)

Besides *Dongfang Zazhi*, there were also other periodicals which brought reports on the Iranian Constitutional Revolution, among which *Zhengyi Tongbao* (the Journal of Politics and Art) is worth mentioning. As one of the earliest periodicals in China, *Zhengyi Tongbao* started in 1902 in Shanghai and was published until 1908. The first information about Iran to appear in *Zhengyi Tongbao* was in its 17th issue of 1905, which reported a piece of news from St. Petersburg saying that Russia would soon dispatch more soldiers to Turkestan to augment its military strength in Persia.[20] In its later issues, *Zhengyi Tongbao* also paid special attention to the competition for spheres of influence in Persia between Russia and Britain. In its first issue of 1907, *Zhengyi Tongbao* reported the news of the death of Mozaffar al-Din Shah in January 1907.[21] Four months later, it provided news of the Iranian Constitutional Revolution. Generally speaking, *Zhengyi Tongbao* did not supply as much information about Iran as the above-mentioned *Dongfang Zazhi*. However, there was a remarkable review article, which deserves our notice. In 1907, after the establishment of constitutionalism in Persia, *Zhengyi Tongbao* published an article entitled 'Jiuwang Juelun Er (On the Ways of National Salvation, Part 2)' by Wang Deyuan.[22] In

39. Ahmad Shah.

40. The Persian land force.

this review, the author said, 'Nowadays, constitutionalism has been established even in the old-aged nation of Persia. With the establishment of the Persian constitutional government, the competition for spheres of influences in this country between Britain and Russia has been contained to a great extent.' He concluded that constitutionalism was the only way to save a nation from downfall, and therefore he appealed for the establishment of a constitutional government in China.[23]

41. (Left) In front of the Persian telegraph office.
(Right) The Persians praying before a war.

42. The current situation of the Persian army. (Upper left) The Persian soldiers. (Upper right) The Cossack Brigade stationed in Persia. (Middle) The hostel of the Persian trade caravan. (Below left) The Persian soldiers as peddlers. (Below right) The Persian artillery.

Minbao (A Magazine of the People)

Now we will deal with the most stirring and heart-warming article on the Iranian Constitutional Revolution, which was published by *Minbao*, the official periodical of the Chinese revolutionary party known as the 'United League of China' (Zhongguo Tongmenghui), the predecessor of the Guomindang (Kuomintang, the 'National Party of China'), of which Sun Zhongshan (Dr. Sun Yat-sen, 1866–1925), the forerunner of Chinese democracy, was the founder and leader. Created in November 1905 in Tokyo, Japan, *Minbao* was in great demand and very popular in China and abroad among the Chinese people, and had a circulation of more than 50,000.[24] Unlike *Dongfang Zazhi* and *Zhengyi Tongbao*, the two magazines mentioned earlier, *Minbao* was the official periodical of the United League of China. Naturally, its most important readers were the members of that party. Although the United League of China set up its head office in Tokyo, it had five home branches, in the cities of Shanghai, Chongqing, Hankou, Yantai, and Hongkong in China, as well as four overseas branches, in Singapore, Brussels, San Francisco, and Honolulu. In other words, the United League of China was so active that its members could be found not only all over China, but also in countries in the Southeast, Europe, North America, and Oceania, which means that the readers of *Minbao* were also very widespread in China and abroad. Besides the members of the United League of China, the readers of *Minbao* also consisted of progressive intellectuals, soldiers and junior officers of the New Army, peasants, workers, and businessmen. *Minbao* also exerted a great influence on Chinese merchants and students who were active abroad at that time.

Minbao did not report on any news concerning the Iranian Constitutional Revolution before 1907. But in the spring of 1910, after the convening of the Second Majles in Tehran, which opened a new phase in the Iranian Constitutional Revolution, *Minbao* published a special review of this great event. The article was entitled 'Bosi Geming (Persian Revolution)' and written by Minyi, the joint pen name of Wang Jingwei (1883–1944) and Hu Hanmin (1879–1936), the two core members of the United League of China. Wang Jingwei and Hu Hanmin had similar experiences in the early stages of their live: both had studied for several years in Japan, where they met Sun Zhongshan. In the autumn of 1905, they joined the United League of China, founded by Sun Zhongshan. From then on, they became faithful followers of Sun Zhongshan and took part in many armed revolts led by him against the Qing Dynasty (1644–1911), which presided over the last imperial government in the history of China.

Both Wang Jingwei and Hu Hanmin had, at different times, been the editor-in-chief of *Minbao*. They published many articles in that periodical under their real names, i.e., 'Jingwei' and 'Hanmin'. Having a very close relationship of cooperation, they also wrote, together, a series of reviews and articles such as 'Tu'erqi Geming (The Turkish Revolution)',[25] 'Xibanya zhi Lansha (The Massacre Occurred in Spain)',[26] etc., most often using the pen name Minyi, meaning 'the opinion of the people', for their jointly authored articles.

Later on, the article 'The Persian Revolution' was included in the *Collected Works of Wang Jingwei*,[27] which indicates that it was Wang Jingwei who did the actual writing of the article. Unfortunately, nothing in Wang Jingwei and Hu Hanmin's memoirs or autobiographies can be found that might tell us more about what they thought of the Iranian Constitutional Revolution; 'The Persian Revolution' was the one and only article they wrote about the Iranian Revolution. In any case, it was also a most important article, and reflected the reverberations of the Iranian Constitutional Revolution in the hearts of its Chinese contemporaries. In this article, the author praised highly the cause for which the Iranian constitutionalists were fighting, saying: 'It was the zeal for freedom, equality, and fraternity that aroused the fighting will of the Iranian constitutionalists and made them fearless in the struggle of resistance against power and force.'[28] He tried to work out the reasons why the Iranian constitutionalists had succeeded in establishing the Second National Assembly in November 1909, and believed that there were three reasons. First was the great bravery and the unyielding determination of the Persian constitutionalists, who were fighting a bloody battle against oppression and foreign intervention; second was the evenly matched trial of strength between Russia and Britain in Persia, which restrained unbridled Russian armed intervention to a certain extent; and third was Russia's domestic trouble, caused by the Russian Revolution in 1905–07, which weakened the power of Tsarist Russia.[29] He ended by drawing a conclusion from the Persian Constitutional Revolution:

> Enthusiasm for revolution is found today everywhere in the world. An autocrat and traitor to the people will not always have his way. It is the trend of the world. Now it is time for us to show determination and to rouse ourselves for vigorous efforts to make our country prosperous. We will succeed only when we do all we can. This is what the Persian Revolution has taught us.[30]

Obviously, the Chinese revolutionaries, who were dedicating themselves to a democratic revolutionary movement and taking part in revolts in different parts of China, felt very much encouraged by the Iranian Constitutional Revolution and as a result strengthened their own resolve to fight for democracy. One year later (in 1911), a thorough revolution led by Sun Zhongshan broke out in China, which finally led to the downfall of the Qing Dynasty and the establishment of the Republic of China.

Conclusion

While the Iranian Constitutional Revolution marked the beginning of the modern history of Iran, the Xinhai Revolution marked that of China. Both China and Iran are countries with ancient civilizations. Though conquered at times by great powers in the long process of their history, both of them have kept their traditional national cultures going. By the end of the nineteenth century, both countries were suffering from the misery of economic plunder and political dominance by foreign powers, especially Russia and Britain. At the same time, thoughts of democracy, freedom, independence, and equality were spreading from Europe into these two countries, thus awakening the national consciousness (or nationalism) and the patriotic enthusiasm of the intellectuals of both countries, who began to seek for ways to save their countries. This similar historical and social background was the main reason why the Chinese revolutionary democrats demonstrated so much interest in the Iranian Revolution when it broke out. Although the ways to achieve this goal were different in the two revolutions (the Chinese Xinhai Revolution abolished the monarchy and built up a republic, whereas the Iranian Revolution established a constitutional monarchy), the purpose of the two revolutions was the same: to drive out foreign powers and to build up a strong, prosperous, and independent fatherland. Therefore, the Chinese revolutionaries regarded the Iranian constitutionalists as their comrades, cherishing the same ideals and following the same path. To conclude very briefly, the Iranian Constitutional Revolution was a great inspiration to the Chinese revolutionaries, encouraging them to struggle more tenaciously for democracy, which finally led to the uprising of 1911 known in modern history as the 'Xinhai Revolution'.

CHAPTER 22

Japan and the Iranian Constitutional Revolution

Michael Penn

Although some scholarly attention has been given in the past to the impact of the Russo-Japanese War on would-be modernizers and reformers in Islamic West Asia and North Africa,[1] the broader picture of Japan's relationship with this region has yet to be drawn in convincing detail. Our purpose here is to inch us closer to that goal by examining the mutual perceptions and interactions of Japanese and Persians during the Iranian Constitutional Revolution of 1906–11. Utilizing sources from the Japanese newspaper press and the British Foreign Office archives, we discover that the parties had very different perceptions and attitudes towards each other, but that a handful of individuals were able to connect more authentically with the other side.

The outbreak of a political upheaval in Persia was first brought to the attention of the Japanese public by wire reports carried in their daily newspapers at the beginning of August 1906. For example, the *Tokyo Asahi Shinbun* carried its first report via Berlin on 2 August, and further wire reports were published at irregular intervals afterwards.

In their early reports, these short messages described the situation in Persia as a 'political upheaval' or 'breakdown of order' rather than as a revolution or a constitutional struggle. Later reports often focused on imperial rivalries among England, Russia, and Germany. However, there are two points of considerable significance that must be stated at the outset. First of all, although wire reports on the situation in Persia were relatively frequent, these reports were extremely short and cursory. In the main news columns of a paper such as the *Asahi*, for example, there were no attempts whatsoever to explain in any detail the nature of the struggle in Persia, nor any attempt to give context or assess the possible ramifications of these events for Japan itself. Secondly, the wire reports published in the Japanese dailies were largely written by European news services such as Reuters and simply translated into Japanese. As a result, they offer little insight into any uniquely Japanese viewpoints that might have been obtained in this manner.

The degree of indifference in the Japanese press to the events in Persia is rather remarkable. In 1906, there were no articles about Persia at all in the main news columns of the *Asahi*. In September and December of 1907 a total of four articles finally appeared, but three of these articles focused on the Anglo-Russian agreement, and only one on the domestic scene in Persia itself. Even the assassination of Amin al-Soltan, who had visited Tokyo in 1903 and had met the leading political figures of the country, passed without comment. In 1908, there were once again no articles at all about Persia.

What factors account for this indifference in the Japanese press? Four factors can be cited here. First of all, the Japanese newspaper press itself was not in one of its better periods overall. In the late 1880s and early 1890s, there was a proliferation of daily newspapers, each with its own perspective and attitudes. Although not all of these outfits were very professional or insightful, there was a vitality and maverick spirit in the news columns that could provide the historian with rich materials for consideration. By 1906, however, the maverick spirit of the Japanese press had been largely tamed. There were then fewer newspapers, with larger circulations. The main content of these papers in the first decade of the twentieth century had switched from serious issues of politics and culture to more domestic and commercial themes, and to the serialization of fictional short stories and light romances. Government censorship, the repression of feisty editors, and the more conservative political atmosphere in Japan following the victories over China and Russia had helped bring about these changes. Newspapers at this time were therefore more interested in making money than in making political statements. As a result, the poor coverage of events in Persia simply reflected the poor coverage of all serious political events in Japanese newspapers in this era.[2]

The second factor that could be mentioned is the influence of Westernization in Japan at this time. Ever since the mid-1880s, the political elite in Japan had made a conscious effort to remove Asian influences from Japanese culture and to 'enter' Europe as a fully equal, civilized power. The termination of the unequal treaties in 1899, Japan's alliance with Great Britain after 1902, and its great military victory over Tsarist Russia in 1905, seemed to indicate that Japan had finally arrived – although issues like the anti-Japanese-immigration movement in Pacific North America left the Westernizers with some lingering doubts. Be that as it may, the point is that Persians were regarded as Orientals, and the political and cultural elite of Japan had little use for Orientals, most of whom they regarded as being hopelessly backward and only half-civilized.

The third factor is that although business and trade might have formed an important connection between Japan and Persia in this era, direct trade links remained weak and underdeveloped. A Japanese trade mission had carried out an inspection of Persia as early as 1880, but little had come of these efforts in the decades that followed.³ Indirectly, Japan and Persia affected each other through the global market of products such as silk, but there was no direct steamship line between Japan and the Persian Gulf. That there were a handful of Japanese in Persia is attested to by this note written to the British Foreign Office by Percy Cox on 12 April 1908: 'I may mention that Japanese curiosity shops in Bombay from time to time send peddlers to Bushire to hawk goods, and that we have once or twice quite recently been called upon to give assistance to natives of that country.'⁴ On the other hand, in a different report written by British officials, in September 1906, they noted that, 'from Russian official data recently published ... Japan is not even named among countries trading with Persia, Japanese goods entering Southern Persia in considerable quantities on through second hands, mostly Indian traders.'⁵ The key point for our purposes is that Japanese trade with Persia was carried out indirectly, or through impoverished peddlers, and thus would not have attracted much attention from major Japanese traders back home. As a result, the Japanese business community, too, was rather indifferent to political affairs in Persia.

A fourth and final factor in the indifference in the Japanese press that could be cited is that Japanese academic expertise on Persia was also rather weak, so the newspapers may have had some difficulty finding knowledgeable authors for articles on Persian politics even had they desired to seek them out. This factor, however, could easily be exaggerated, because creative editors would have found knowledgeable and sympathetic Europeans in Yokohama who could have helped them, and there were indeed a few Japanese academic experts on the region, such as Hosuke Nagase.

At any rate, these four factors played the major role in ensuring that the Japanese public remained focused on domestic and local concerns rather than events in Persia. As far as most Japanese were concerned, they did not know what was happening in Persia – and, frankly, they did not care.

The great irony of this situation is that Persian public interest in Japan was higher than ever during these very same years. All close observers of the political scene in Persia agreed that the Japanese victories over Tsarist Russia – which they read about in considerable detail in newspapers such as *Habl al-Matin* – had a major effect on the public mood. As early as January 1905, British officials in Persia were becoming concerned, as can be perceived in this report by Evelyn Grant Duff: '[The] tone of communications addressed to legations here has been growing less civil for some time, and at court they are saying openly that Japan has shown Western Powers what Orientals can do,'⁶ and even in remote Sistan satisfaction was felt at the destruction of part of the Russian fleet. Later, when summarizing political events in Persia for the year 1905, the British legation in Tehran wrote as follows:

The victories of Japan and the subsequent revolutionary troubles in Russia have not only put the entire Persian question on an entirely different footing, but have raised new social, religious, and political questions in the country itself. The Persians are showing a new restlessness, a new impatience of the bad Government which they formerly seemed to accept so philosophically, and a general resentment of the present state of things, which, although still tentative, and only groping for expression in futile and often childish ways, may be traced all over the country, and in every department of public life.[7]

Evidence indicates that Japan was a major topic of political discussion in these years, with Persians debating the merits of Japanese modernization or making rueful comparisons between the state of their country and the presumed state of the Japanese nation.[8]

There is little doubt that the Persian public idealized Japan in an exaggerated manner, and was unaware of Japan's real attitudes towards Persia and the Persians. It is said that a group of constitutionalists led by Seyyed Mohammad Tabataba'i sent a telegram to the Emperor of Japan asking him to extend his benevolent protection to the Muslim community of Japan. In 1905 or 1906, however, such a community did not exist in Japan. The British legation in Tehran made an insightful observation on this point: 'The victories of the Japanese have undoubtedly diminished the prestige of all Europeans among the Persians, who only know that the Japanese are fellow Orientals, and are quite ignorant of the immense gulf separating the national characters of the two peoples.'[9]

Moreover, Tabataba'i had, on a different occasion, publicly regretted that Persia had never sent a diplomatic envoy to Tokyo, even though almost all other civilized powers had already done so. Despite the fact that Tabataba'i's lament was understandable, this point too reflected a mistaken evaluation of the Japanese government's intentions. Tokyo had been toying with the idea of setting up a legation in Persia since the 1870s, but had repeatedly shelved the suggestion out of indifference, self-interest, and a broad deference to the political sensitivities of Britain and Russia. In 1908, Percy Cox, the British Resident in the Persian Gulf, had himself taken the initiative to establish a consulate for Japan in Bushehr. However, when the British ambassador to Tokyo later brought this idea up with the Japanese foreign minister, the suggestion was politely dismissed. In other words, the Japanese themselves had ample opportunity to establish diplomatic representation in Persia, but had decided not to do so.

As we have seen, many Persians were amazed and excited over Japan's military victories in the Russo-Japanese War, and they feared and resented Tsarist Russia, which seemed to be the most direct threat to Persian national independence. An interesting illustration of both of these tendencies appeared in a July

1907 issue of *Habl al-Matin*, which was later translated into English by the British legation in Tehran:

> Is the Russian Minister, then, the only foreign Representative resident in Persia? Why do not the other Ministers behave in a similar manner? Is the might of Russia greater than that of England? Is the Russian army better than the German army? Is Russian justice greater than French justice? Why does the Russian Minister then not imitate his colleagues? Why does he not leave us alone? How long must we endure? Until when his patience? God knows these deeds will have a bad ending. ... All this prancing and blustering is unnecessary. Gently! Gently! The ships of Japan are swift. The army of Japan is ready. Square to the fight with her and recapture the Island of [Sakhalin]. In truth it was a great loss to Russia, this cowardly surrender of half a large island to the Japanese! Remove these Cossacks from the frontier of Astara and send them to the Manchurian frontier. Here an army is unnecessary. Japan is a foeman worthy of your steel. Surely Manchuria is more necessary than the protection of Haji Malik.[10]

Although the editors of *Habl al-Matin* surely enjoyed taunting the Russian legation with the humiliating defeat of the Russian army a couple of years earlier, ironically there had recently, between 1905 and 1907, been discussions in British diplomatic circles about the possibility of expanding the Anglo-Japanese Alliance to the frontiers of India, including Persia. The idea was that Japanese troops might supplement British forces in Afghanistan and Persia, if the need should arise. When these notions were informally raised with the Japanese side in late 1905, they were not particularly excited about the prospect, but did not entirely reject the proposals either. In the end, the British diplomats themselves withdrew the proposal because they feared that the introduction of Japanese troops to India would openly advertise British imperial decadence and would adversely affect the prestige of white Europeans in general. As a result, then, we can see that while the Iranians were imagining Japanese armies as being the standard-bearers of a reborn Asia in the struggle against Russian oppression, there was, in fact, a more serious possibility that Japanese armies may have been employed against Persia itself on behalf of British interests.[11]

And yet! And yet! For all of the misconceptions that the Persian constitutionalists had about the nature of modern Japan, they were not entirely wrong. The Japanese government and most of the political elite had little time for Persia, but even in Japan there were a handful of adventurers and eccentrics who took a serious interest in Persia, and some of them shared the Pan-Asian sentiment that the Persian newspapers were often appealing to.

The most interesting example was that of Tei Suzuki, a young man who decided to travel to Persia on the eve of the Constitutional Revolution, when the Japanese victories over Russia were being widely celebrated. The British consular reports on his movements and reception contain a good deal of interesting material.

Suzuki was in Persia between December 1905 and February 1906. He first came to the attention of the Foreign Office through Grant Duff's report from Tehran: 'The Japanese who passed through Tehran at the beginning of December, arrived at [Mashhad] on January 7, and is said to have excited much interest there. ... His name is Tei Suzuki, and he is a lieutenant in the Reserve and also a Buddhist priest.'[12]

Some detail about Suzuki's visit to Mashhad was given by Major P. Molesworth Sykes, the consul-general stationed there: 'I was visited by a Japanese priest of the Buddhist persuasion, named Tei Suzuki. He had recently come from America, via Batumi to Tehran, and was the bearer of a letter from His Britannic Majesty's Chargé d'Affaires. He was anxious to proceed to India across Afghanistan, and was rather sad at my saying it was out of the question.'[13]

In the following days, Major Sykes wrote more about the Japanese visitor: 'I sent the Japanese traveller to see both the Asaf al-Dowleh and the Karguzar, who were much pleased at seeing him. The whole of [Mashhad] is moved at his visit, and he is the recipient of many congratulations. The political effect is excellent. ... Tei Suzuki ... is correspondent for various newspapers in Japan, and an extremely nice man. I only hope that someday I shall be privileged to entertain a Japanese Minister or Military Attaché at Meshed. The effect would be excellent, as, even as it is, M. Tei's journey across Russia by himself, and his tiny stature, have evoked intense interest in Meshed, where the Russians are hated.'[14]

Suzuki next travelled to Torbat-e Heydarieh, where the local British officer, Captain John W. Watson, took somewhat less interest in him than had Major Sykes, writing, 'He is putting up with my Head Clerk, and has his meals with me. He speaks English, and is apparently touring for pleasure. He intends staying a week in Quetta, I do not know why, but I told him that he would find no Buddhists there.'[15]

Suzuki next appeared in the reports of Captain A. D. Macpherson, the consul in Sistan. He too included some interesting information about Suzuki and the Persian reactions to him: 'Suzuki was received very well throughout his stay at Birjand. The Shaukat-ul-Mulk asked him whether he had any connection with the Japanese Government, and the Mustansir-ul-Mulk asked him many questions on education and said he would try to persuade Persians to send their sons to Japan to be educated.'[16]

After some hesitation, the British authorities granted Suzuki's strong desire to travel overland to Quetta. Soon after he arrived back in Japan in June

1906, Suzuki published at least one account of conditions in Persia in a major Japanese newspaper, and may have written quite a bit more.[17]

In conclusion, we can say that the overall Japanese view of the Iranian Constitutional Revolution was, in general, remarkably unsympathetic. Even while most Persians were idolizing Japan as the protagonist of a rising Asia and a model for Persian political development, most Japanese were unconcerned and uninterested. Tokyo had its eyes firmly focused on Europe, and had come to see itself more as a European power in the East rather than as any kind of champion of Asia. The visions of Japan found in the *Habl al-Matin*, or in the excited political discussions of contemporary Persians, reflected ignorance of Japanese political conditions combined with a heavy dose of wishful thinking.

However, there were a handful of more sympathetic Japanese individuals, such as the aforementioned Tei Suzuki or the scholar Hosuke Nagase, who did take a genuine interest in Persian affairs. Later, in the 1930s, the liberal, Pan-Asianist sentiments of these few would combine with changes in Japanese elite politics to produce a more sustained Japanese interest in the Iran of Reza Shah; but at the time of the Constitutional Revolution, the Persians – as far as most Japanese were concerned – were on their own.

Appendix: Hosuke Nagase on 'The Persian Revolution'

As previously noted, one of the very few Japanese to take an interest in the Constitutional Revolution was the academic Hosuke Nagase. Presented here is an English translation of an article he published in the popular magazine *Taiyo* (The Sun) in February 1912.

There are several significant points to be made. First of all, this may be the only serious account of the Constitutional Revolution produced in Japan in that era. Nagase was practically the only scholar of the region at that time. Secondly, Nagase had actually travelled in the region during the previous decade, so he did have some first-hand knowledge to supplement what he had read in European accounts. Third, as he himself states directly, his own sympathies were with the revolutionary party, perhaps because Japan had itself faced political interference from European nations in the previous decades of its development. On the other hand, Nagase also makes clear that, in his analysis, Turkey (the Ottoman Empire) was a much stronger and more vital Islamic nation than Persia.

That said, at certain points he does seem to interact with the material sympathetically, and there is little doubt that he read the Persian experience through his own particular Japanese lens. For example, one can sense his pride that the Japanese victory over Russia in 1905 played such an important role in changing the attitudes of other Asian peoples yearning to cast off the European yoke.

We do not know exactly what sources Nagase used in compiling this account of the Constitutional Revolution, but we can safely assert that most other Japanese-language resources would have been useless to him. Also, he could not read Persian. Therefore, many of his facts must have come from either the European press, European scholars, or both.

The footnotes in this section of the paper will provide additional analysis of Nagase's views on the revolution. This English translation is by Yukie Suehiro and Michael Penn.

The Persian Revolution
by Hosuke Nagase, PhD

I

In recent years, the revolutionary movement in Persia has signified an awakening of the Islamic peoples as well as those of Turkey, and can be regarded as a remarkable event in the history of civilization. However, compared with Turkey, the level of Persian culture and the ability of the people are much lower. Moreover, the power of Persia as a country is extremely weak. Although its revolution succeeded three years ago, the Persian government still does not have the ability to fulfil its constitutional politics. Even now there are many political troubles in the country, and thus the Powers interfere in this country. They are faced with a national crisis.

According to my observations, the origin of this revolution is based on the existence of the Young Persia Party organized by patriotic people in Persia. The members of this party thought that the existence of Persia as an independent country had already passed in practical terms, and that their country would be divided by the Powers sooner or later. Therefore, they decided to destroy the old regime and form a constitutional government in order to restore the power of their country, and they firmly rose in revolt against the old regime. There were some incentives for raising the revolution. First, they were inspired by the success of the Young Turk Party. Moreover, the glorious victory of Japan as a constitutional country gave them motivation as well.[18] Therefore, I am interested in writing the history of this revolution, as I cannot help sympathizing with these people.

II

Before discussing the main theme, I would like to explain the two big social powers in Persia, or the relationship between the king and Islamic priests.

Successive Persian kings have called themselves 'Shah' since the age of the

Islamic Empire. They were believed to be endowed with a particular spiritual right. Thus they could control people with absolute and unlimited power. For example, they had the privilege to kill people, and this right made no distinction between ordinary people and the royal family. Thus, they were known as typical tyrants. Although there were several dynasties in the royal history of this country, the god-like power of the king was inherited and maintained its strength. Moreover, because Islam spread among the people rapidly, Persian kings could establish the basis of their regime through the doctrines of the Holy Qur'an. Therefore, they succeeded in establishing a strong relationship between royalty and the religion. In 1794, the Qajar royal family arose out of one of the Mongol nations and claimed itself to be descended from an officer of Genghis Khan. The royal family which founded the present dynasty inherited the honorific title 'the King of Kings'. This family also obtained and abused the absolute and unlimited power which has been handed down since the ancient age. However, the fourth king Naser al-Din and his son Mozaffar al-Din were influenced by Europeanization and they tried to reform the old political system, but they failed. This was because political conventions which had been maintained for a long time in this country prevented their plans from attaining success.

As for the Islamic priests, they already called themselves magi in the age of Zoroastrianism. At that time, they already had the second-highest social rank, below the king. Their power was so strong that even the king could not control it. Afterwards, they changed their faith to Islam and called themselves mullahs.[19] They had an influence not only on religious events but also political, legal, and other secular matters. Actually, they played an important role as lawyers and educators. They had a strong influence on the people and tremendous power in Persian society. Sometimes their power was strong enough to surpass that of the king, and they often became leaders of rebellion. During the recent revolution they stood on a platform and expressed ideas of liberalism, and they supported the revolutionary movement openly or secretly. In Turkey an emperor was also a sheykh of the Sunni sect of Islam, under the title of caliph. On the other hand, in Persia, a king was not a sheykh of the Shiite sect of Islam. A sheykh in Persia was the highest-ranking priest, who lived in Karbala,[20] which was located southwest of Baghdad. People looked up to him as a substitute for the founder, and a million people came to his mosque in order to pray with him every year. When the revolution broke out last year, it was said that this priest supported the revolutionists, and he proclaimed this movement as a jihad.

In short, in order to study both the causes of the Persian Revolution and the formation of this country, it is important for us to understand the fact that there were two conflicting social powers in Persia, and thus they came to be two main centres of the political conflict.

III

As for the above, the Persian kings Naser al-Din (who succeeded to the throne in 1848) and his son Mozaffar al-Din (who succeeded to the throne in 1896) had been to Europe twenty-three times. Therefore, they were influenced by Europeanization, and they tried to change their traditional regime into constitutional politics.[21] For example, they invited an Austrian military officer first and then a Russian officer to reform their military systems. Also, they employed a public officer of Belgium in order to establish both the postal system and the customs system (actually set up in 1899). They selected young people of noble families and made them study in Europe. Moreover, they constructed many technical schools and employed French people as teachers. However, it was difficult for them to get a good result because there was strong resistance by a group which supported the ancien régime. In addition to this opposition, there was an economic problem that stymied their reforms. Basically, the economic condition of this country was not stable and great sums of money were spent in order to invest in new enterprises. For example, it took several million yen to support the kings' travels to Europe. Because of these expenditures, foreign debt increased much more than previously. In order to pay off this debt, heavy taxes were imposed on the people, and creditor nations such as Britain and Russia were given some privileges from the Persian government. In this way, both countries started to interfere in the internal affairs of this country. People became dissatisfied with the king and expressed their complaints openly. In other words, the germ of the revolution was already seen at the time of the king Mozaffar al-Din. The members of the Young Persia Party who had received a modern education in Europe asserted the advantages of constitutional government loudly, and they demanded that the king establish the parliament. The Persian people agreed with this idea instantly because they tended to side with others easily.[22] They founded the National Constitutional Party and they engaged in political movements. Because of this, some rebellions broke out in various places and Persian society became unstable. Certainly, the higher Persian priests supported these movements willingly, and although they concealed their identity at first, they clearly demanded that the king establish the parliament (called Majles).

Finally, the king Mozaffar al-Din accepted the wish of the people on 10 August 1906. He published a temporary constitution immediately and he ordered the establishment of the parliament. He then carried out an election to choose members of the parliament. On 7 October of the same year, the king held the grand opening ceremony of the parliament in his palace. After that, the constitution was written and the king approved it. The Persian constitution was formally promulgated on 31 December. In making the constitution, Sa'd al-Dowleh was the most influential person. Once he lived in Belgium as the Persian minister and he knew the situation of that country very well. Because of that, it was said that Belgium was taken by him as a model for the Persian constitution.

In this way, the members of the Young Persia Party realized their dream. Persia became a constitutional country two years earlier than Turkey. Unfortunately, the king who supported progressivism fell sick and passed away on 9 January 1907, and then the prince Mohammad Ali succeeded to the throne. However, unlike the previous king, he was mediocre and had little knowledge about the international situation. Moreover, because of his weak character, he accepted the ideas of the conservative group easily, and thus he tried to abolish the constitutional government. Because of this, it is needless to say that he had the same fate as the Turkish king Abdülhamid.

IV

On 7 October 1906, the first session of parliament was held. In this meeting the first item on the agenda was a loan from Britain and Russia. The members of parliament thought that borrowing heavily from other countries would cause serious damage to the honour and benefit of their country. Therefore they decided to reject this subject unanimously. Instead of the loan, they made a plan to found a national bank in order to pay back their debts by issuing national bonds. They tried to take back some privileges which the branch banks of Britain and Russia had held in Persia. Next, they discussed the idea that the reform of their government was just nominal. First, they demanded that the king Mohammad Ali adopt a meritocracy. However, their behaviour was so rude that the king secretly proposed a plot to his close officers in order to abolish the constitutional government. There was severe conflict between the parliament and the government, which led to troubles between the officers and people in local areas. Finally, Prime Minister Ali Asghar Khan was assassinated, and there was a person who threw a bomb to kill the king.

Thus, the king reconciled with the parliament reluctantly. In January 1907, he promised again to respect the constitution in front of the speaker of the house of representatives. After that, the power of parliament increased even more, and the king became afraid. Unfortunately, it was then revealed that the king had concluded a secret treaty with Russia in order to ask for its protection. The conflict between the government and the National Constitutional Party broke out again, and there were some battles in the city of Tehran. The members of parliament blamed these struggles on the ministers of the conservative party and they strongly demanded that the king dismiss them. However, the king rejected this demand. He decided to attack the members of parliament using the Cossack Cavalry Brigade, led by the Russian colonel Liakhov, after having met with his close officers. Finally, the king succeeded in dissolving the parliament by force and abolished the constitution. This event caused a flutter among the people and led to a revolution. According to my observations, this is the first direct cause of the Persian Revolution.

V

The Persian king took oppressive measures to solve the problem, and he temporarily succeeded in putting down the resistance in Tehran. However, because of that, strong resistance arose among people in local areas, and thus many rebellions broke out all over the nation. There was a city which took the initiative in carrying out a rebellion among local cities. It was the capital city Tabriz of Azarbayjan which was the second largest city (population about 200,000) in Persia. In this city, the leader of the movement was Sattar Khan, who was a Persian of Mongol heritage as well as a famous rich merchant. He intended to raise a revolution and mobilized his army against the king with his friend Baqer Khan. They resisted the loyalist army and defeated it. Finally, they were able to occupy the palace and founded a temporary government, and thus they proclaimed their independence. There were some reasons why Tabriz came to be a main city of the revolutionary activities in those days, and even now the city has many rebellions. The first reason was that people in the city were full of independent spirit, and they intended to resist the central government. The second reason was that they had strong consciousness as Persians because their city was located on the border with Russia and Turkey. The third reason was that people in the city felt strong hostility towards Russia because there were conflicts with Russia. Another reason was that the people in this city were influenced by the revolutionary movements which broke out in Russia at that time.

As soon as the Persian patriots who lived in Turkey, Egypt, India, and Russia heard the news of the rebellion, they collected a great deal of money to support this revolutionary movement as if they were competing with each other. They sent their money to the revolutionaries in Tabriz. The Persian people who supported the revolution did these things for the sake of the independence of their motherland. Therefore, the ministers of Russia and Britain advised the Persian king to call the members of parliament together in order to restore peace to the country. Finally, the king accepted this advice and he promised to call the members of parliament together on 14 November in order to have an election on 20 December 1908. However, he did not want to keep this promise. He managed to make some excuses in order to break his promise. At this time, three hundred priests, officers, and merchants of the conservative group visited the king at the palace. They asked the king not to adopt the constitution because they thought that it was against their principles. Although it was not clear whether their visit was one of the king's strategies or not, he had his strong supporters and he decided to break his promise. Therefore, when the ministers of Britain and Russia demanded that the Persian king keep his promise again, he did not have any good excuses. Formally, the king founded a House of Councillors consisting of fifty members whom he appointed directly, and he held the parliament on 29 December of the same year. However, the 'constitutional party' was a kind of dummy group, and its members were only puppets of the king. Therefore, people could not trust their king any more, and that inspired them to revolution once again. Their movement increased in energy as if it were a fire burning out of control. According to my observations, that is the second direct cause [of the Persian Revolution].

VI

There were many rebellions all over the nation which spread from Azarbayjan in the north to each province of central and south Persia. Especially the Bakhtiyari nation, half-nomads who lived beside the Karun River in east Luristan, were brave and militant. About 25,000 cavalry of the Bakhtiyari were led by chief Samsam al-Saltaneh and they invaded Isfahan – an old city which had about 90,000 people, located in central Persia and in an important position for commerce or traffic – on 3 January. They killed the governor and officers of the state and occupied the governmental office, and then they founded their temporary government. The leader [Samsam] al-Saltaneh sent a telegram to his younger brother Sardar As'ad, who lived in Paris at that time. [Samsam] al-Saltaneh recalled his brother to Persia in order to raise a revolution with other rebellious people. Sardar As'ad was not only smart but also courageous. He was also educated in Europe, and he had enough knowledge. Moreover, he had an ambition that he would defeat the Qajar dynasty and the Bakhtiyari family would take the place of it. Later, Sardar As'ad became known as a hero in the revolutionary party.

At the end of January a rebellion also broke out in the important port of Bushehr in the Persian Gulf. Rebellious people killed the governor of the state and occupied the office, and then they proclaimed their independence. Many rebellions broke out in each region such as Larestan, Shiraz, Hamadan, and so on. In this way, the rebellious movement really spread all over the nation. At this time, the Russian government sent troops to the borders of Persia, and the Turkish government guarded this area, too. After that, the British government sent the cruiser *Fox* to the Persian Gulf and 100 soldiers landed at Bushehr. At the same time, 400 soldiers of Russia landed at Anzali on the coast of the Caspian Sea.

The Persian king had received news about the rebellion in Tabriz. The king commanded the previous prime minister, Prince 'Eyn al-Dowleh, to go to Tabriz in order to put down the rebellion with Rahim Khan. The loyalist army battled with the revolutionary army for a month near the city. The king's soldiers were often beaten back, and it was difficult for them to break the force of their enemy. During this war Rahim Khan attacked some villages around the city and plundered there. Finally, he occupied the road which led from the Russian border. Because of this, Tabriz was surrounded, and the traffic was shut down and food was short. People in the city were starving. Therefore, on 19 April, the Russian government ordered the Persian king to supply food to the representatives of other countries, foreigners, and to peaceful citizens in this area. If the king did not do so, the Russian government would interfere forcefully. The ministers of Britain and Russia sent a letter to the Persian king. In it, they utilized the difficult issue of debt payments. Their first condition was that he dismiss both the prime minister and the military minister, and the next was that he give amnesty to political prisoners. The third was that he respect the constitution. The fourth was that he reform the government. The fifth was that he construct a governmental system based on liberalism.

Finally, the king promised a six-day truce on 20 April and said he would supply food to the people in Tabriz. However, Prince 'Eyn al-Dowleh rejected this order and did not obey the king. Therefore the Russian government decided to interfere in Persia by force. On 26 April, the Russian General Snarsky approached Tabriz with his force of roughly 6,000 soldiers and occupied the city. At this time, the Persian king held to the truce and supplied food to the people in Tabriz.

The king did not seem to be fulfilling the plans of political reform proposed by Britain and Russia. As a result of this, the governments of both countries sent a final notice to the king on 30 April. In it they said that if the king did not carry out these reforms by 2 May, they would interfere in the country with strength. Finally, the king accepted this demand and consented to establish a new constitution. The king ordered the holding of an election to choose new members of parliament and he declared that he would call these members together on 19 July. The king also established a new government based on liberalism. Finally, he gave amnesty to political prisoners and withdrew his troops from Tabriz on 10 May. However, the timing of the king's obedience was so late that nobody believed in his declarations. The movements which sought a revolution in each region maintained their power.

VII

In those days the members of the revolutionary party became more and more passionately devoted to their movement, in part because the Russian troops occupied the northern area of Azarbayjan. They thought that the Russian government had tried to help the Persian king in order to destroy the constitutional party. Therefore, they criticized the intervention of Russia, and then they demanded that the king remove the Russian troops from their land. However, it was impossible for the government to fulfil this demand because it had no power to do so. Finally, the revolutionary party decided to advance on Tehran from each region in order to occupy it. This was the moment at which the highest-ranking priest in Karbala, who was mentioned above, sympathized with the members of the revolutionary party and proclaimed their movement a jihad.

Then Sepahdar, who was a leader of Gilan, appeared as a leader of the revolutionary party. He was also influenced by European civilization and one of the real brains in Persia. He believed in liberalism and he made an effort to establish a constitutional government. When the previous liberal government was formed, Sepahdar had been appointed governor of Gilan by the king. However, the king did not change his real way of thinking and eventually destroyed the constitutional government. Therefore, Sepahdar was so angry that he decided to be a leader of the revolutionary party and raised a rebellion in Qazvin. He cooperated with Sardar As'ad in Isfahan, and he inspired his brothers in local areas. He made a plan to advance on Tehran, and his brothers agreed with his idea, and thus they decided to raise a revolution together.

In Qom, Sardar and his soldiers of the Bakhtiyari nation left for Tehran. Sepahdar in Qazvin, who had also become a leader of militias gathering from Tabriz and other regions, left for Tehran, too. When the Persian king received news of these movements, he understood that his situation was extremely perilous. Because this bad news upset him greatly, he immediately proclaimed martial law in Tehran. On May 17, 1909, the Persian king fled to the palace in Soltanabad with his princes and royalists.

The revolutionary army gathering from each region defeated the royalist army and swept all before them. As the revolutionary party approached Tehran gradually, the situation of the king grew into a crisis. On 3 July, the Russian government sent a letter to the Powers. In this letter, Russia said that the present condition of Persia was very serious. The Persian government had accepted the advice of Britain and Russia, and Persia had established a constitutional government and begun to reform its administration. However, the revolutionary movements had not ended, and now rebellious troops were approaching Tehran. Moreover, there were people who welcomed these troops in Tehran.

The condition of the city was dire. Not only the legations of Russia and other European countries in Persia, but also people's lives and properties, might be faced with danger. In order to protect them, the Russian government sent a regiment of Cossack horsemen, a battalion of infantry, and a battery from Baku to Anzali. The Russian government said that it would like to take the opportunity to approach Tehran through Qazvin. Also, the government declared that it had no intention of interfering in Persia. Therefore, the expeditionary army of Russia landed at Anzali on 6 July, and the advance party arrived in Tehran with their vehicles three days later.

However, the soldiers of the revolutionary party gathering from each region also arrived near Tehran and formed one large group. This group defeated the loyalist army and invaded Tehran on 12 July. After the group fought with the loyalist army in the city for three days, it succeeded in occupying Tehran.

During this battle the Persian king depended exclusively on the Cossack Brigade in Persia. However, the Russian colonel then made peace with Sepahdar and ordered his soldiers to stop fighting. This is because Liakhov knew that the numbers of the revolutionary troops were bigger than his own army. Thus, the Persian king did not have any real resources any more, and he proclaimed the end of the war according to the demands of Britain and Russia. On the night of 16 July, he went to the Russian legation and asked for its protection. That night he fled to Russia protected by Russian soldiers.

VIII

Finally, the revolutionary troops gained victory. The new government was under the control of Sepahdar. He called the main members of the government to a meeting, and then they decided to dethrone King Mohammad Ali. In his place, they put the ten-year-old Prince Ahmad Mirza forward as king. Sepahdar took the posts of both minister of the army and governor of Tehran. Sardar As'ad took the position of minister of the interior. Naser al-Molk, who was a senior member of the royal family, became minister of foreign affairs. After that, a new election was carried out on 19 August. A new parliament was held on 5 November. In this way, the Persian revolution ended in success.

However, there have been a lot of troubles in Persia since then. Last year, the abolition of the monarchy was discussed again, and there was a conflict between Persia and Russia. It was ended without major trouble only because the Persian government obeyed Russia absolutely. The revolution of Persia could not bring a bright future to this country. The present situation of this country seems to be unstable, as before. I cannot help sympathizing with the tragic end of the Persian Empire.

Notes

Introduction

1. Walter F. Vella, *Chaiyo!: King Vajiravudh and the Development of Thai Nationalism* (Honolulu: The University Press of Hawaii, 1978), p. 70.

Prologue

1. Mohammad Taqi Bahar, *Divan*, ed. Mohammad Malekzadeh, third edition, vol. 1, (Tehran: Amir Kabir, 1975), pp. 26–31.
2. Ibid, pp. 33–35.
3. Ali Akbar Dehkhoda, *Majmu'eh-ye ash'ar*, ed. Mohammad Mo'in (Tehran: Zavvar, 1955), pp. 124–26.
4. Ibid, pp. 127–28.
5. Yahya Aryanpur, *Az Saba ta Nima*, vol. 2 (Tehran: Zavvar, 1993), p. 127.
6. Bahar, *Divan*, pp. 127–29.
7. *Divan-e Kamel-e Iraj Mirza*, ed. Mohammad Ja'far Mahjub ([Los Angeles]: Sherkat-e Ketab, 1986), pp. 12–13.
8. Aryanpur, *Az Saba ta Nima*, pp. 72–73.
9. Dehkhoda, *Majmu'eh-ye ash'ar*, pp. 1–4.
10. Homa Katouzian, *Tanz va tanzineh-ye Hedayat* (Stockholm, 2002), pp. 64–65.
11. *Javdaneh Seyyed Ashraf al-Din Gilani*, ed. Hoseyn Namini (Tehran: Ketab-e Farzan, 1984), pp. 177–78.
12. Bahar, *Divan*, pp. 146–48.
13. *Javdaneh*, p. 178.
14. Edward G. Browne, *The Press and Poetry of Modern Persia* (Cambridge: Cambridge University Press, 1914), pp. 208–10.
15. Ibid, pp. 213–15.
16. Bahar, *Divan*, pp. 148–50.
17. Browne, *Press and Poetry*, pp. 222–24.
18. Bahar, *Divan*, pp. 208–13.
19. Browne, *Press and Poetry*, pp. 247–48.
20. *Divan-e 'Aref-e Qazvini*, ed. Abdorrahman Seyf-e Azad (Tehran: Amir Kabir, 1948), pp. 365–66.
21. See further, Homa Katouzian, *State and Society in Iran: The Eclipse of the Qajars and the Emergence of the Pahlavis* (London: I.B.Tauris, 2005), chapter 3.
22. Bahar, *Divan*, pp. 225–28.
23. Aryanpur, *Az Saba ta Nima*, pp. 140–41.

24. Bahar, *Divan*, pp. 216–17.
25. Browne, *Press and Poetry*, pp. 229–30., pp. 224–25.
26. Ibid, pp. 224–25.

Chapter 1. Whose Revolution? Stakeholders and Stories of the 'Constitutional Movement' in Iran, 1905–11

1. See for example Reza Afshari, 'The Historians of the Constitutional Movement and the Making of the Iranian Populist Tradition', *International Journal of Middle East Studies* 25/3 (1993); Afsaneh Najmabadi, '"Is Our Name Remembered?": Writing the History of Iranian Constitutionalism as Though Women and Gender Mattered', *Iranian Studies* 29/1–2 (1996); Afsaneh Najmabadi, *The Story of the Daughters of Quchan: Gender and National Memory in Iranian History* (Syracuse: Syracuse University Press, 1998), 'Introduction' and 'Epilogue'; Afsaneh Najmabadi, *Women with Mustaches and Men Without Beards: Gender and the Sexual Anxieties of Iranian Modernity* (Berkeley: University of California Press, 2005), 'Introduction'; Houri Berberian, *Armenians and the Iranian Constitutional Revolution of 1905–1911: "The Love for Freedom Has No Fatherland"* (Boulder: Westview Press, 2001), pp. 3–5; Mansour Bonakdarian 'Edward G. Browne and the Persian Constitutional Struggle: From Academic Orientalism to Political Activism', *Iranian Studies* 26/1–2 (1993); Mansour Bonakdarian, *Britain and the Iranian Constitutional Revolution of 1906–1911: Foreign Policy, Imperialism, and Dissent* (Syracuse: Syracuse University Press, 2006), pp. xv–xxxii; Janet Afary, *The Iranian Constitutional Revolution, 1906–1911: Grassroots Democracy, Social Democracy, and the Origins of Feminism* (New York: Columbia University Press, 1996), pp. 1–3, 7–13, 145–47, 150, 177–78, 341–42; Mohammad Tavakoli-Targhi, *Refashioning Iran: Orientalism, Occidentalism, and Historiography* (Basingstoke: Palgrave, 2001), pp. 15–17, 142–43; Mangol Bayat, *Iran's First Revolution: Shi'ism and the Constitutional Revolution of 1905–9* (Oxford: Oxford University Press, 1991), pp. 3–10, 18–21.
2. Hitherto I have placed the term 'constitutional' within quotation marks when referring to the period from 1905 to 1911, or to movements of that time, in order to indicate that it is *a label attached to them retrospectively*, although used in that period itself to describe particular institutions and their supporters. I realize that this could be an annoying practice, and shall discontinue it, but remind readers that to choose this label for parts of the Iranian past expresses the perceptions and priorities of later commentators and historians rather than those of protagonists in the early twentieth century.
3. Georges Lefebvre, *The French Revolution: From its Origins to 1793* (London: Routledge, 1962); Alfred Cobban, *The Social Interpretation of the French Revolution* (Cambridge: Cambridge University Press, 1964); George Taylor, 'Non-capitalist Wealth and the Origins of the French Revolution', *American Historical Review* 72/2 (1967); François Furet, *Interpreting the French Revolution* (Cambridge: Cambridge University Press, 1981); Lynn Hunt, *Politics, Culture and Class in the French Revolution* (London: Methuen, 1986); Dorinda Outram, *The Body and the French Revolution: Sex, Class, and Political Culture* (New Haven: Yale Univer-

4. Nazem al-Eslam Kermani, *Tarikh-e bidari-ye Iraniyan* (1910, Tehran: Agah, 1983); Ahmad Kasravi, *Tarikh-e mashruteh-ye Iran* (1939, Tehran: Amir Kabir, 1977–78); Mehdi Malekzadeh, *Tarikh-e enqelab-e mashrutiyat-e Iran* (1948–50, Tehran: 'Elmi, 1984); Yahya Dowlatabadi, *Tarikh-e mo'aser ya hayat-e Yahya* (1952, Tehran: 'Attar, 1984).

sity Press, 1989); Gwyn Lewis, *The French Revolution: Rethinking the Debate* (London: Routledge, 1993).

5. Fereydun Adamiyat, *Fekr-e azadi va moqaddameh-ye nehzat-e mashrutiyat* (Tehran: Sokhan, 1961); Fereydun Adamiyat, *Andishehha-ye Mirza Aqa Khan Kermani* (Tehran: Sokhan, 1966); Fereydun Adamiyat, *Andishehha-ye Mirza Fath 'Ali Akhundzadeh* (Tehran: Tahuri, 1970); Fereydun Adamiyat, *Andishehha-ye taraqqi va hokumat-e qanuni* (Tehran: Khʷarazmi, 1973); Fereydun Adamiyat, *Fekr-e demokrasi-ye ejtema'i dar nehzat-e mashrutiyat-e Iran* (Tehran: Payam, 1975); Fereydun Adamiyat, *Ide'olozhi-ye nehzat-e mashrutiyat-e Iran* (Tehran: Payam, 1976–92); Mangol Bayat, *Mysticism and Dissent: Socio-Religious Thought in Qajar Iran* (Syracuse: Syracuse University Press, 1982), chapters 5 and 6; Bayat, *Iran's First Revolution*; Vanessa Martin, *Islam and Modernism: The Iranian Revolution of 1906* (London: I.B.Tauris, 1989); Nikki Keddie, 'Religion and Irreligion in Early Iranian Nationalism', *Comparative Studies in Society and History* 4/3 (April 1962); Nikki Keddie, 'The Origins of the Religious-Radical Alliance in Iran', *Past and Present* 34 (1966); Abdul-Hadi Hairi, *Shi'ism and Constitutionalism* (Leiden: Brill, 1977); Ervand Abrahamian, 'The Crowd in the Persian Revolution', *Iranian Studies* 2/4 (1969); Ervand Abrahamian, 'The Causes of the Constitutional Revolution in Iran', *International Journal of Middle East Studies* 10/3 (1979); Ervand Abrahamian *Iran Between Two Revolutions* (Princeton: Princeton University Press, 1982); Afary, *Constitutional Revolution*; Cosroe Chaqueri, *The Origins of Social Democracy in Modern Iran* (Seattle: University of Washington Press, 2001).

6. See Bayat, *First Revolution*, pp. 7–10; Nikki Keddie, 'Iranian Revolutions in Comparative Perspective', *American Historical Review* 88/3 (1983).

7. Abrahamian, *Iran Between Two Revolutions*; John Foran, *Fragile Resistance: Social Transformation in Iran from 1500 to the Revolution* (Boulder: Westview Press, 1993). The authors set out frameworks for their analyses on pp. 3–6 and 3–15 of their respective texts; their accounts of the Constitutional Revolution occupy pp. 69–110 (Abrahamian) and pp. 170–94 (Foran).

8. See Bayat, *Iran's First Revolution*, pp. 8–9; Foran, *Fragile Resistance*, pp. 3–5, 396–97, 415, and John Foran (ed.), *A Century of Revolution: Social Movements in Iran* (London: UCL Press, 1994), pp. xi–xiii and chapter 9; Afary, *Iranian Constitutional Revolution*, pp. 341–42; explicit comparisons are made in Keddie, 'Iranian Revolutions', and Joanna de Groot, 'The Formation and Re-formation of Popular Movements in Iran', in Kenneth Brown et al. (eds.), *Urban Crises and Social Movements in the Middle East* (Paris: L'Harmattan, 1989).

9. I refer here to the tradition of 'subaltern studies' scoped and debated by historians of India during the British Raj, now drawn on by scholars working on other areas; see Ranajit Guha and Gayatri Spivak (eds.), *Selected Subaltern Studies*

(Oxford: Oxford University Press, 1988); David Ludden (ed.), *Reading Subaltern Studies* (London: Anthem Press, 2002); Walter Mignolo, *Local Histories/Global Designs: Critical History, Contested Meaning and the Globalization of South Asia* (Princeton: Princeton University Press, 2000); Dipesh Chakrabarty, *Habitations of Modernity: Essays in the Wake of Subaltern Studies* (Chicago: Chicago University Press, 2002).

10. See Badr ol-Moluk Bamdad, *From Darkness into Light: Women's Emancipation in Iran*, trans./ed. F. R. C. Bagley (Hicksville NY: Exposition Press, 1977), chapter 3; Mangol Bayat, 'Women and Revolution in Iran, 1905–11', in Nikki Keddie and Lois Beck (eds.), *Women in the Muslim World* (Cambridge MA: Harvard University Press, 1978); Homa Nateq [Nategh], 'Negahi beh barkhi neveshtehha va mobarezat-e zanan dar dowran-e mashrutiyat', *Ketab-e Jom'eh* 30 (1980); idem, 'Mas'aleh-ye zan dar barkhi az modavenat-e chap az nehzat-e mashrutiyat ta 'asr-e Reza Khan', *Zaman–e Now* 1, (1983); Eliz Sanasarian, *The Women's Rights Movement in Iran: Mutiny, Appeasement and Repression from 1900 to Khomeini* (New York: Praeger, 1982), pp. 19–24; Roshanak Mansur, 'Chehreh-ye zan dar jarayed-e mashruteh', *Nimeh-ye Digar* 1 (1984); Janet Afary, 'On the Origins of Feminism in Early Twentieth-Century Iran', *Journal of Women's History* 1 (1989); 'Ta'ammoli dar tafakkor-e ejtema'i-siyasi dar enqelab-e mashruteh', *Nimeh-ye Digar* 17 (1993); Afary, *Iranian Constitutional Revolution*, chapter 7; idem, 'Steering Between Scylla and Charybdis: Shifting Gender Roles in Twentieth-Century Iran', *NWSA Journal* 8 (1996); Afsaneh Najmabadi, '*Zanhā-yi millat*: Women or Wives of the Nation?', *Iranian Studies* 26/1–2 (1993); idem, 'The Erotic *vatan* (Homeland) as Beloved and Mother: to Love, to Possess, and to Protect', *Comparative Studies in Society and History* 39/3 (July 1997); Parvin Paidar, *Women and the Political Process in Twentieth-Century Iran* (Cambridge: Cambridge University Press, 1995), chapter 2; Tavakoli-Targhi, *Refashioning Iran*, chapter 7; Joanna de Groot, '"Brothers of the Iranian Race": Manhood, Nationhood, and Modernity in Iran 1870–1914', in Stefan Dudink, Karen Hagemann, and John Tosh (eds.), *Masculinities in Politics and War: Gendering Modern History* (Manchester: Manchester University Press, 2004).
11. Najmabadi, '"Is Our Name Remembered?"'; Najmabadi, *Daughters of Quchan*, especially pp. 4–9, 35–45, 48–52, 59–60, 62–67, 76–87, 98–100, 106–11, 115–18, 128–33, 156–66, 167–83; see also her *Women with Mustaches*.
12. Mostafa Vaziri, *Iran as Imagined Nation: The Construction of National Identity*, (New York: Paragon House, 1993), notably chapters 7 and 8; Firoozeh Kashani-Sabet, *Frontier Fictions: Shaping the Iranian Nation, 1804–1946* (Princeton: Princeton University Press, 1999).
13. Afary, *Iranian Constitutional Revolution*, pp. 78–88, 95–109, 151–76, 211–24, 237–48, 264–69; Bayat, *Iran's First Revolution*, pp. 76–105, 148–53, 156–58, 161–63, 172–74, 204–05, 208–10, 236–43, 248–58; Chaqueri, *Origins of Social Democracy*, pp. 85–88, 114–19, 134–39, 147–72, 191–94, and Cosroe Chaqueri, 'Armenian Iranians and the Birth of Iranian Socialism', in Chaqueri (ed.), *The Armenians of Iran* (Cambridge, MA: Center for Middle Eastern Studies, 1998); Berberian, *Armenians*, pp. 48–55, 86–100, 116–56; Houri Berberian, 'The Dash-

naktsutiun and the Iranian Constitutional Revolution', *Iranian Studies* 29/1–2 (1996); Charles Kurzman, 'Weaving Iran into the Tree of Nations', *International Journal of Middle East Studies* 37/2 (2005); Charles Kurzman, *Democracy Denied 1905–1915: Intellectuals and the Fate of Democracy* (Cambridge, MA: Harvard University Press, 2008).

14. See, for example, Shaul Bakhash, *Iran: Monarchy and Bureaucracy under the Qajars* (London: Ithaca Press, 1978), chapter 6; Abdul-Hadi Hairi, 'European and Asian Influences on the Persian Revolution of 1906', *Asian Affairs* 62/2 (1975); Bayat, *Iran's First Revolution*, chapter 4.
15. Edward G. Browne, *The Persian Revolution 1905–1909* (1910, reprint/facsimile, Washington DC: Mage Publishers, 1995), pp. 2, 323; Kasravi, *Tarikh-e mashruteh*, vol. 1, pp. 174–76, 258, 263–66, and his *Tarikh-e hejdah saleh-ye Azarbayjan* (1937, Tehran: Amir Kabir, 1977–78), 'Introduction' (unpaginated).
16. Afshari, 'Historians', p. 483; Ali Gheissari and Vali Nasr, *Democracy in Iran: History and the Quest for Liberty* (Oxford: Oxford University Press, 2006); Fakhreddin Azimi, *The Quest for Democracy in Iran: A Century of Struggle Against Authoritarian Rule* (Cambridge, MA: Harvard University Press, 2008).
17. See for example Kasravi, *Tarikh-e mashruteh*, vol. 1, pp. 260–62.
18. Bayat, *Iran's First Revolution*, p. 267.
19. Afary, *Iranian Constitutional Revolution*, pp. 341–42.
20. I explore the value of this approach in Joanna de Groot, *Religion, Culture, and Politics in Iran: From the Qajars to Khomeini* (London: I.B.Tauris, 2007), chapter 6, and clarify my use of these particular terms on p. 201.
21. I refer here to the argument that popular protest over prices or food shortages expressed not just material need but *political* notions of just treatment and legitimate public action. The phrase was coined by E. P. Thompson in his 'Moral Economy of the Crowd', *Past and Present* 50 (1971).
22. See Kasravi, *Tarikh-e mashruteh*, vol. 1, p. 210, *Tarikh-e hejdah saleh-ye Azarbayjan*, vol. 1, p. 34; Afary, *Iranian Constitutional Revolution*, pp. 140–41, 145, 167, 224–25, 248–51; Bonakdarian, *Britain and the Iranian Constitutional Revolution*, pp. 130–31, 148–49, 152.
23. See Doktor Mohammad Ali Homayun Katuzian [Homa Katouzian], 'Seyyed Hasan Taqizadeh, seh zendegi dar yek 'omr', in *Hasht maqaleh dar tarikh va adab-e mo'aser* (Tehran: Nashr-e Ney, 2006), pp. 32–87.
24. Nazem al-Eslam Kermani, *Tarikh-e bidari*, vol. 1, pp. 309–24; Kasravi, *Tarikh-e mashruteh*, vol. 1, pp. 52–54.
25. Nazem al-Eslam Kermani, *Tarikh-e bidari*, vol. 1, pp. 9–10, 243–49; *Tarikh-e mashruteh*, vol. 1, pp. 133–35, 181; vol. 2, pp. 489–94; Ahmad Kasravi, *Zendegani-ye man* (Tehran: n.p., 1944), pp. 11–13, 26, 31–33, 46; Ervand Abrahamian, 'Kasravi: The Integrative Nationalist of Iran', in Elie Kedourie and Sylvia Haim (eds.), *Towards a Modern Iran: Studies in Thought, Politics, and Society* (London: Frank Cass, 1980).
26. Kasravi, *Tarikh-e mashruteh*, vol. 1, pp. 52, 53; Nazem al-Eslam Kermani, *Tarikh-e bidari*, vol. 1, pp. 309–11, 316.
27. Kasravi, *Tarikh-e mashruteh*, vol. 1, pp. 53, 54; Nazem al-Eslam Kermani,

Tarikh-e bidari, vol. 1, pp. 310, 314, 316, 318, 321–23; Great Britain, *Foreign Office Consular Diaries*, FO248, vol. 820, Kerman consular diary entries for first week of June and last week of July 1904.
28. Nazem al-Eslam Kermani, *Tarikh-e bidari* vol. 1, pp. 311, 314, 315.
29. Ibid., pp. 318, 322–23; Kasravi, *Tarikh-e mashruteh*, pp. 53–54.
30. Nazem al-Eslam Kermani, *Tarikh-e bidari*, pp. 310, 312, 315, 316; Great Britain, *Foreign Office Consular Diaries*, FO248, vol. 846, Kerman consular diary entries for week ending 17 June, 9–23 July, 23–30 July, 21–28 October, 28 October–4 November, 11–19 November 1905; vol. 878, diary entry for 10–24 March 1906.
31. Gianroberto Scarcia, 'Kerman 1905: la Guerra tra Šeihī e Bālāsarī', *Annali del Instituto Universitario Orientale di Napoli* N.S. 13 (1963). His main source is a series of articles on early twentieth-century politics in Kerman published in the newspaper *Ettehad-e Melli*, nos. 318–44, in 1953–54.
32. The former position is taken in Mohammad Ebrahim Bastani Parizi, *Peyghambar-e dozdan* (Tehran: Amir Kabir, 1977), pp. 33–52, the latter in Nazem al-Eslam Kermani, *Tarikh-e bidari*, vol. 2, pp. 186, 188, 218 and the British consular material 1908–12 *passim*.
33. Bastani Parizi, *Peyghambar-e dozdan*, pp. 34–35; FO248, vol. 946, Bam news, May 1907; vol. 948, diary for 19–26 March, 27 March–2 April, 26 June–7 July, 7–9 July, 10–16 July, 23–30 July 1908; vol. 969, diaries for 1–8 July, 8–15 July, 23–30 September, 9–16 December 1909; vol. 998, diaries for 10–17 February, 17–24 February 1910; vol. 1030, diaries for 24–31 August, 21–September, 28 September–5 October, 5–12 October, 2–9 November, 21–28 December 1911; vol. 1052, diaries for 15–22 February, 22–28 February, 29 March–4/5 April, 4–11 April, 11–18 April, 25 April–2 May, 16–23 May, 6–13 June 1912.
34. This view is offered by Homa Katouzian, 'Liberty and License in the Constitutional History of Iran', in his *Iranian History and Politics: The Dialectic of State and Society* (London: Routledge/Curzon, 2003); Homa Katouzian, 'Problems of Democracy and the Public Sphere in Modern Iran', *Comparative Studies of South Asia, Africa, and the Middle East* 18/2 (1998).
35. My 'Constitutional Politics in Kerman: Backwater or Breakthrough?' (in preparation) will take the 'Kerman narrative' further; see also Janet Afary, 'Peasant Rebellions of the Caspian Region During the Iranian Constitutional Revolution', *International Journal of Middle East Studies* 23/2 (1991); and Afary, *Iranian Constitutional Revolution*, pp. 73–81, 151–72, 212–24; Heidi Walcher, 'The Constitutional Revolution in Isfahan: From Hierocracy to Tribal Command', paper presented at the centennial conference on the Iranian Constitutional Revolution, held in the University of Oxford 30 July–2 August 2006.

Chapter 2. The Iranian Constitutional Revolution as *lieu(x) de mémoire*: Sattar Khan

1. There is, unfortunately, no article concerning Mozart as a *locus memoriae* in Etienne François and Hagen Schulze (eds.), *Deutsche Erinnerungsorte*, 3 vols. (Munich: C. H. Beck, 2002). Regarding the images usually evoked by the name Mozart, Hildesheimer has discussed and contradicted these in his famous biogra-

phy. Wolfgang Hildesheimer, *Mozart* (1977, Frankfurt a. M.: Suhrkamp, 1993).
2. On which, see Reza Sheikh's contribution to this volume.
3. Maurice Halbwachs, *The Collective Memory* (New York: Harper, 1980).
4. Stephan Egger, 'Auf den Spuren der "verlorenen Zeit": Maurice Halbwachs und die Wege des "kollektiven Gedächtnisses"', in Maurice Halbwachs, *Stätten der Verkündigung im Heiligen Land: Eine Studie zum kollektiven Gedächtnis*, ed. and trans. Stephan Egger, (Konstanz: UVK Verlagsgesellschaft, 2003), p. 228.
5. Jan Assmann, 'Erinnern, um dazuzugehören: Kulturelles Gedächtnis, Zugehörigkeitsstruktur und normative Vergangenheit', in Kirsten Platt and Mihran Dabag (eds.), *Generation und Gedächtnis: Erinnerungen und kollektive Identitäten* (Opladen: Leske + Budrich, 1995), especially pp. 51–75, 59–60.
6. Pierre Nora, 'Entre Mémoire et Histoire: La problématique des lieux', in Pierre Nora, *Les lieux de mémoire I: La République* (Paris: Galllimard, 1984), pp. 17–20.
7. Ibid., p. 20. For a discussion of the term 'collective memory' see Jay Winter and Emmanuel Sivan (eds.), *War and Remembrance in the Twentieth Century* (Cambridge: Cambridge University Press, 2000), 'Introduction' and chapter 1 'Setting the Framework'. Drawing, among others, from Nora as well as Halbwachs, they understand 'collective memory' as 'a matrix of interwoven individual memories'. Ibid., p. 28.
8. Klaus Große-Kracht, 'Gedächtnis und Geschichte: Maurice Halbwachs und Pierre Nora', *Geschichte in Wissenschaft und Unterricht* 47 (1996), p. 27.
9. Ibid., 28–29.
10. Aleida Assmann, *Erinnerungsräume: Formen und Wandlungen des kulturellen Gedächtnisses* (Munich: C. H. Beck, 1999), p. 133.
11. See, for example, Jan Assmann, *Das kulturelle Gedächtnis: Schrift, Erinnerung und politische Identität in frühen Hochkulturen* (München: C. H. Beck, 1992); Paul Ricoeur, *La mémoire, l'histoire, l'oubli* (Paris: Seuil, 2000).
12. François and Schulze, *Deutsche Erinnerungsorte*.
13. Ibid., vol. 1, p. 13.
14. Ibid.
15. Christoph Cornelißen, 'Was heißt Erinnerungskultur? Begriff – Methoden – Perspektiven', *Geschichte in Wissenschaft und Unterricht* 54/10 (2003): pp. 548–63, 555.
16. Firoozeh Kashani-Sabet, *Frontier Fictions: Shaping the Iranian Nation, 1804–1946* (Princeton: Princeton University Press, 1999), p. 101.
17. Mostafa Vaziri, *Iran as Imagined Nation: The Construction of National Identity* (New York: Paragon House, 1992), p. 172. See also *Encyclopaedia Iranica*, s.v. 'Constitutional Revolution. i. Intellectual Background'.
18. Reza Afshari, 'The Historians of the Constitutional Movement and the Making of the Iranian Populist Tradition', *International Journal of Middle East Studies* 25/3 (1993), p. 477.
19. Mehdi Bamdad, *Sharh-e hal-e rejal-e Iran dar qarn-e 12 va 13 va 14 hejri*, vol. 2 (Tehran: Zavvar, 1968), p. 60.
20. The most detailed accounts of Sattar Khan's life are to be found in Esma'il Amirkhizi, *Qiyam-e Azarbayjan va Sattar Khan* (Tabriz: Ketabforushi-ye Tehran,

1950); and Ebrahim Safa'i, *Rahbaran-e mashruteh*, 2 vols. (Tehran: Javidan, 1965). The two books complement one another well, because Amirkhizi – who had acted as Sattar Khan's adviser – was an enthusiastic supporter, whereas Safa'i is a very critical observer of the man. Unless indicated otherwise, the biographical data on Sattar Khan is drawn from these sources. See also my forthcoming article 'Sattar Khan Sardar-e Melli', in the *Encyclopaedia Iranica*.

21. Two of Esma'il's three sons were executed by the Russians after their occupation of Tabriz in the spring of 1909. Safa'i, *Rahbaran*, vol. 1, p. 388 n1; Karim Taherzadeh Behzad, *Qiyam-e Azarbayjan dar enqelab-e mashrutiyat-e Iran* (Tehran: Sherkat-e Nasabi-ye Haj Mohammad Hoseyn Eqbal, 1955), p. 442.

22. Safa'i, *Rahbaran*, vol. 1, p. 388. According to Amirkhizi's relating of the story, there exist two narratives. One recounts that Sattar was released from prison because a famous Tabrizi *mujtahid* by the name of Haji Mirza Javad told the crown prince it was against the shari'a to detain youngsters. Another account, however, conveys Sattar's flight from Narin Qal'eh after two years of imprisonment. Amirkhizi, *Qiyam-e Azarbayjan*, pp. 11–13. Safa'i interrelates the two versions by saying that Haji Mirza Javad put in a word for Sattar *after* he had escaped prison.

23. In the travelogue of a high-ranking Iranian pilgrim, who visited the Shiite holy sites in 1856/7, the same situation at the shrine in Samarra is lamented. See Adib al-Molk, 'Abd al-Ali Khan, *Safarnameh-ye Adib al-Molk beh 'atabat: Dalil al-za'erin*, ed. Mas'ud Golzari (Tehran: Dadju, 1985), p. 114. See also Anja Pistor-Hatam, 'Fürbitte und Gedenken: Stationen schiitischer Wallfahrt im Irak, beschrieben in persischen Pilgerberichten des 19. Jahrhunderts', in Angelika C. Messner and Konrad Hirschler (eds.), *Heilige Orte in Asien und Afrika: Räume göttlicher Macht und menschlicher Verehrung* (Schenefeld: eb-Verlag, 2006), p. 101.

24. Amirkhizi, *Qiyam-e Azarbayjan*, pp. 16–18; Safa'i, *Rahbaran*, vol. 1, pp. 389–90. Whereas Safa'i does not reveal the sources of his shortened version, the tale is extensively related by Amirkhizi, who claims to have heard it directly from Sattar Khan. Unfortunately, it is impossible to know whether the story (*qaziyeh-ye 'ajibi*) Sattar Khan told him is true and if all of it really happened the way he apparently told it. In any case, in this story Sattar Khan is presented as a hero who acted according to the wishes of one of the highest ranking Shiite clerics of his time and punished Sunnis for their mistreatment of Shiite pilgrims, playing the role of *luti* to perfection.

25. On Baqer Khan see *Encyclopaedia Iranica*, s.v. 'Baqer Khan Salar-e Melli' and the literature mentioned therein.

26. Amirkhizi, *Qiyam-e Azarbayjan*, pp. 28–29; Safa'i, *Rahbaran*, vol. 1, p. 391.

27. Ahmad Kasravi, *Tarikh-e mashruteh-ye Iran*, 13th edition, vol. 1 (Tehran: Amir Kabir, 1977), pp. 325–29.

28. Amirkhizi, *Qiyam-e Azarbayjan*, p. 58.

29. Kasravi, *Tarikh-e mashruteh*, vol. 2, p. 677; Safa'i, *Rahbaran*, vol. 1, p. 392; Mehdi Malekzadeh, *Tarikh-e enqelab-e mashrutiyat-e Iran*, vol. 5 (Tehran: Amir Kabir, 1954), pp. 11–12.

30. For the three stages see Janet Afary, *The Iranian Constitutional Revolution, 1906–1911: Grassroots Democracy, Social Democracy, and the Origins of Feminism* (New York: Columbia University Press, 1996), pp. 212–13.
31. For the biography of Seqat al-Eslam see Nosratollah Fathi, *Zendeginameh-ye shahid-e niknam Seqat al-Eslam Tabrizi* (Tehran: Chapkhane-ye Khorrami, 1975).
32. Bamdad, *Sharh-e hal*, vol. 2, p. 60; Fathi, *Zendeginameh*, pp. 359–60; Malekzadeh, *Tarikh-e enqelab*, vol. 5, p. 30; Taherzadeh, *Qiyam-e Azarbayjan*, p. 223.
33. Malekzadeh, *Tarikh-e enqelab*, vol. 5, p. 30. See also Kasravi, *Tarikh-e mashruteh*, vol. 2, pp. 693–94.
34. Amirkhizi, *Qiyam-e Azarbayjan*, pp. 111–21.
35. Mohammad Esma'il Rezvani, *Enqelab-e mashrutiyat-e Iran* (Tehran: Ebn-e Sina, 1966), p. 177.
36. Apparently, the governor of Azarbayjan, Mokhber al-Saltaneh, was also involved in Sattar Khan's appointment. See, for example, Ahmad Kasravi, *Tarikh-e hejdah saleh-ye Azarbayjan*, 9th edition, vol. 1 (Tehran: Amir Kabir, 1977), pp. 97–111. According to Hedayat, Sattar Khan went to Ardabil voluntarily. Mehdiqoli Hedayat, *Khaterat va khatarat*, 2nd edition (Tehran: Zavvar, 1965), p. 197. He thought of Sattar Khan as a courageous (*shoja'*) but, unfortunately, stupid (*bihush*) man who had been taken advantage of by the wrong people. See ibid., p. 197.
37. For detailed accounts of Sattar Khan's time in Ardabil see Kasravi, *Tarikh-e hejdah saleh*, vol. 1, pp. 88–97; Amirkhizi, *Qiyam-e Azarbayjan*, pp. 410–37.
38. Safa'i, *Rahbaran*, vol. 1, pp. 404–05. In his account, Amirkhizi writes that he had warned Sattar Khan, hinting at the difficult situation in Ardabil due to the ongoing conflict between the Heydari and Ne'mati factions. He also told his friend to refrain from antagonizing the inhabitants of Ardabil – evidently to no avail. Amirkhizi, *Qiyam-e Azarbayjan*, pp. 411–12.
39. As compensation for services rendered, Sattar Khan wished for a piece of land to cultivate. The garden, Baba Baghi, he asked for had formerly been the hunting grounds of Crown Prince Mohammad Ali Mirza. Kasravi, *Tarikh-e hejdah saleh*, vol. 1, p. 145.
40. On Mokhber al-Saltaneh's own assessment of the situation in Tabriz see his memoirs: Hedayat, *Khaterat*, pp. 197–99. For more information on Hedayat, who was thrice appointed governor of Azarbayjan, see *Encyclopaedia Iranica*, s.v. 'Hedayat, Mokber-al-Saltana, Mehdiqoli'.
41. Malekzadeh, *Tarikh-e enqelab*, vol. 6, p. 190.
42. For detailed accounts of the celebrations on the way to and in Tehran itself, as well as the political turmoil in which Sattar Khan and Baqer Khan later became involved, see Amirkhizi, *Qiyam-e Azarbayjan*, pp. 449–575; Malekzadeh, *Tarikh-e enqelab*, vol. 6, pp. 188–237; Safa'i, *Rahbaran*, vol. 1, pp. 407–10; Esma'il Ra'in, *Yeprem Khan Sardar* (Tehran: Zarrin, 1971), pp. 343–62; Yahya Dowlatabadi, *Tarikh-e mo'aser ya Hayat-e Yahya*, vol. 3 (Teheran: Ebn-e Sina, 1952), pp. 133–35.
43. On Behbahani's rather dubious role see Safa'i, *Rahbaran*, vol. 1, pp. 173–203;

and *Encyclopaedia Iranica*, s.v. 'Behbahani, Ayatollah Mohammad'.
44. Kasravi took part in the revolution as a young man and became a member of the Anjoman-e Ayalati in Tabriz. It is, therefore, not really surprising that his views are prejudiced. See, for example, Kasravi, *Tarikh-e hejdah saleh*, vol. 1, p. 145.
45. Afshari, 'Historians', pp. 478–86.
46. Ibid., p. 491.
47. Fathi, *Zendeginameh*.
48. Ra'in, *Yeprem Khan Sardar*.
49. Amirkhizi, *Qiyam-e Azarbayjan*. Safa'i claims that he makes all the leaders of the Constitutional Revolution known to the public without himself being biased on account of political fanaticism or interests. See Safa'i, *Rahbaran*, vol. 1, pp. 5–6.
50. Amirkhizi, *Qiyam-e Azarbayjan*, p. 24.
51. See for example Safa'i, *Rahbaran*, vol. 1, p. 411, who claims that Sattar Khan was a patriot who combated tyranny. However, because he did not grasp the meaning of 'constitution', he did not obey parliamentary orders after the revolution's victory. See also Asghar Fathi, 'The Role of the "Rebels" in the Constitutional Movement in Iran', *International Journal of Middle East Studies* 10/1 (1979), p. 57.
52. Amirkhizi, *Qiyam-e Azarbayjan*, pp. 24–25; Safa'i, *Rahbaran*, vol. 1, p. 391.
53. Safa'i, *Rahbaran*, vol. 1, p. 391. See also Amirkhizi, *Qiyam-e Azarbayjan*, pp. 24–26.
54. See, for example, Saïd Amir Arjomand, *The Shadow of God and the Hidden Imam: Religion, Political Order and Social Change in Shi'ite Iran from the Beginning to 1890* (Chicago: University of Chicago Press, 1984), who states that in the eleventh/twelfth centuries, justice emerged as the twin companion of kingship (p. 94).
55. *Encyclopaedia Iranica*, s.v. 'Constitutional Revolution', pp. 169–71.
56. Eric Hobsbawm, *Bandits*, 4th edition (London: Free Press, 2000), p. 19.
57. For a definition of the 'noble robber' see ibid., pp. 47–48.
58. Ibid., p. 19.
59. Ibid., p. 12.
60. Ibid., p. 114.
61. On these two factions, see *Encyclopaedia Iranica*, s.v. 'Haydari and Ne'mati' and John R. Perry, 'Artificial Antagonism in Pre-Modern Iran: The Haydari-Ne'mati Urban Factions', in Donald J. Kagay and L. J. Andrew Villalon (eds.), *The Final Argument: The Imprint of Violence on Society in Medieval and Early Modern Europe* (Woodbridge: The Boydell Press, 1998).
62. Willem M. Floor, 'The Lutis – A Social Phenomenon in Qajar Persia. A Reappraisal', *Die Welt des Islams* 13 (1971), p. 109; Willem M. Floor, 'The Political Role of the Lutis in Iran', in Günther Schweizer (ed.), *Interdisziplinäre Iran-Forschung: Beiträge aus Kulturgeographie, Ethnologie, Soziologie und Neuerer Geschichte* (Wiesbaden: Reichert, 1979), pp. 181–82.
63. Vanessa Martin, *The Qajar Pact: Bargaining, Protest and the State in Nineteenth-Century Persia* (London: I.B.Tauris, 2005), pp. 113–14.
64. Ibid., p. 117.

65. Ibid., pp. 119, 124.
66. Ibid., pp. 126, 113–14.
67. Floor, 'The Political Role', p. 186.
68. Fathi, *Zendeginameh*, p. 239. It is, however, doubtful whether Seqat al-Eslam can be described as the leader of Sattar Khan's '*luti* gang'. More to the point would be to see him as a high-ranking cleric who may not only have advised 'his' *luti*s but may also have used them to achieve his own political goals. For the status of the *lutibashi* see Martin, *Qajar Pact*, p. 117.
69. Fathi, *Zendeginameh*, p. 359.
70. Cf. Fathi, 'The Role of the "Rebels"', p. 61.
71. Ibid., pp. 62–63.
72. Kasravi, *Tarikh-e mashruteh*, vol. 1, p. 328. My own translation.
73. Malekzadeh, *Tarikh-e enqelab*, vol. 5, p. 17. My own translation.
74. Amirkhizi, *Qiyam-e Azarbayjan*, pp. 21–23.
75. Safa'i, *Rahbaran*, vol. 1, pp. 390–91; 395–36; 411.
76. Edward G. Browne, *The Persian Revolution 1905–1909* (Cambridge: Cambridge University Press, 1910), pp. 441–42.
77. Ibid., p. 441.
78. '[...] one might say that the intellectuals have ensured the survival of the bandits'. Hobsbawm, *Bandits*, p. 144.
79. Winter and Sivan, *War and Remembrance*, p. 8 on the difference between the work of professional historians and collective memory.
80. The first narrative to appear in this context was Kasravi's *Tarikh-e mashruteh* in 1940. Afshari, 'The Historians of the Constitutional Movement', p. 477.
81. Ricoeur, *La mémoire*, p. 537.
82. Jan Assmann states that it is more in the nature of human beings to forget than to remember. Therefore, the fact that they remember and are interested in the past at all presents the real mystery. Assmann, *Das kulturelle Gedächtnis*, p. 67.
83. For the concepts of official, that is functional memory (*Funktionsgedächtnis*) and counter-memory (*Gegenerinnerung*) see Assmann, *Erinnerungsräume*, pp. 137–39.
84. The photos printed in an Iranian textbook from the Mohammad Reza Shah period show Seyyed Mohammad Tabataba'i and Seyyed Abdollah Behbahani as the clerical leaders of the constitutionalists, and Sattar Khan, Baqer Khan, 'Sur-e Esrafil', and Malek al-Motekallemin as the '*mojahedin*, who gave their own blood to present the Iranian people with freedom'. *Ta'limat-e ejtema'i: Panjom-e dabestan* ([Tehran]: Vezarat-e Amuzesh va Parvaresh, 1978), 197–98.

Chapter 3. Introducing Georgian Sources for the Historiography of the Iranian Constitutional Revolution (1905–11)

1. Edward G. Browne, *The Persian Revolution of 1905–1909* (Cambridge: The University Press, 1910).
2. Tria, 'La Caucase et la Revolution persane', *Revue du Monde Musulman* 3 (1911), p. 13, Kraus Reprint (Nedeln/ Liechtenstein, 1974), p. 332.
3. The census was conducted in 1897 as part of the general census of the Russian Empire. See Nugzar Ter-Oganov, 'Two Iranian Authors on Tbilisi: Majd

os-Saltaneh and Yahya Dowlatabadi', in Florence Hellot-Bellier and Irene Natchkebia (eds.), *La Géorgie entre la Perse et l'Europe* (Paris: L'Harmattan, 2006), p. 210. In response to the increased numbers of Iranians in the country, in 1906 an Iranian school was established in Tbilisi through the efforts of Iranian merchants and Iran's official representation in Transcaucasia. The school was founded by the Iranian charitable organization *Ettefaq* in Tbilisi with the help of Iran's consulate-general in Tbilisi and the ambassador of Iran to Russia, Mirza Hasan Khan Moshir al-Dowleh. The school offered language classes – Persian, Arabic, Turkish, Georgian, French, Russian, as well as shariʿa, geography, music, etc. (see Ter-Oganov, 'Two Iranian Authors on Tbilisi', p. 214). At some point, the school had up to 120 Iranian students. The school continued to function after the establishment of communist rule in Georgia, until 1931. Persian printing houses such as 'Gheyrat' and 'Sharq' had functioned in Tbilisi since the turn of the twentieth century to satisfy the needs for printed materials in the Persian language (ibid., p. 210). The popular journal *Molla Nasreddin* was published by Jalil Mamed-Qulizade in Tbilisi from 1906 to 1912, and its issues were distributed in various cities of Georgia. However, as Javid points out, the Tsarist governor of Batumi (Western Georgia) issued a special order to confiscate and destroy all issues of the journal in the city (see Salamollah Javid, *Fadakaran-e faramush shodeh-ye azadi* [Tehran, 1980], pp. 82, 89–90). Nevertheless, the publication of the journal continued even after Mamed-Qulizade had temporarily left Tbilisi in 1912–14.

4. Anton Kelenjeridze, *Sergo Ordzhonikidze-Zhurnalist* (Tbilisi: Merani, 1969), p. 5.
5. Janet Afary, *The Iranian Constitutional Revolution, 1906–1911: Grassroots Democracy, Social Democracy, and the Origins of Feminism* (New York: Columbia University Press, 1996), p. 237; Ervand Abrahamian, *Iran Between Two Revolutions* (Princeton: Princeton University Press, 1982), pp. 98–99; Mangol Bayat, *Iran's First Revolution: Shiʿism and the Constitutional Revolution of 1905–1909* (New York: Oxford University Press, 1991), p. 252; Houri Berberian, *Armenians and the Iranian Constitutional Revolution of 1905–1911: The Love of Freedom Has no Fatherland* (Boulder: Westview, 2001), pp. 142–43; Cosroe Chaqueri, 'Armenian-Iranians and the Birth of Iranian Socialism, 1905 to 1911', in Cosroe Chaqueri (ed.), *The Armenians of Iran: The Paradoxical Role of a Minority in a Dominant Culture: Articles and Documents* (Cambridge, MA: Center for Middle Eastern Studies, 1998), pp. 89, 103; Ahmad Kasravi, *Tarikh-e hejdah saleh-ye Azarbayjan* (Tehran: Amir Kabir, 1979), p. 13; Giorgi Chipashvili, 'Iz Istorii Internatsional'noi Deiatel'nosti Zakavkazskikh Revoliutsionerov v Irane', in *Sakartvelos Metsnierebata Akademiis Matsne* 4 (Tbilisi: Sakartvelos Metsnierebata Akademiis Gamomtsemloba, 1981); Georgii Arutiunyan, *Iranskaya Revolyutsiya 1905–1911 gg. i Bolsheviki Zakavkazya* (Yerevan: Armianskoe Gosudarstvennoe Izadtelstvo, 1956); Mikhail Ivanov, 'Vliyanie Russkoi Revolutsii 1905 Goda Na Iranskuyu Revolutsiyu 1905–1911 gg.', *Uchebnie Zapiski* (Leningrad: Izdatelstvo Leningradskogo Universiteta, 1949); Arsen Guidor, 'The Hnchakist Party and the Revolutionary Movement in Persia (1908–1911)', in Chaqueri (ed.), *The*

Armenians of Iran, pp. 303–04; 'Vasso A. Khachaturian to Georgi Plekhanov (November 1908)', in Chaqueri (ed.), *The Armenians of Iran*, p. 325; Archavir Tchilinkirian, 'Persian Revolution (1909–1910)', in Chaqueri (ed.), *The Armenians of Iran*, p. 233; Tria, *Kavkazskie Sotsial-Demokraty v Persidskoi Revoliutsii* (Paris: Izdanie Tsentralnogo Organa RSDRP "Sotsialdemokrat', 1910), pp. 10, 11. To cite one of the modern scholars working on this issue, 'only the help coming from the Caucasian revolutionary coalition protracted the Tabriz resistance under Sattar Khan's leadership and made the defeat of government forces possible.' (Chaqueri, 'Armenian-Iranians', p. 79). The Transcaucasians stayed in Tabriz alongside the local constitutionalists until the takeover of the city by the Russian troops, which resulted in a massacre of the constitutionalist revolutionaries and their supporters. On the dynamics of the relations between the constitutionalists and the Russian troops in Tabriz, see J. D. Clark, 'Constitutionalists and Cossacks: The Constitutional Movement and Russian Intervention in Tabriz 1907–1911', *Iranian Studies* 39/2 (2006), pp. 199–225; also Pavel Strelianov (Kalabukhov), *Neizvestnyi Pokhod, Kazaki v Persii v 1909–1914 gg.* (Moscow: Reittar, 2001); and Afary, *The Iranian Constitutional Revolution*, pp. 337–42.

6. Afary, *The Iranian Constitutional Revolution*, p. 222.
7. Batumi is a city in western Georgia on the Black Sea. The Social Democrat committee of Batumi was very active in collaborating with the Tbilisi committee for the purpose of assisting the Iranian constitutionalists. Like most of the Georgian Social Democrat committees at the time of the Tabriz revolt, it was of Menshevik orientation. There are many natives of western Georgia recorded in the sources concerning the Georgian members of the Tabriz and Rasht constitutional resistance.
8. Mikhail Agajanov, 'Tbilisis "Humatis" Istoriis Zogierti Sakitkhi Pirveli Revolutsiis Tslebshi', *Proceedings of the GCPCC Institute of the History of the Party* 7 (Tbilisi: Sakartvelos Partiis Istoriis Instituti, 1971), p. 157; Anton Kelenjeridze, *Gurjebi* (Tbilisi: Sakartvelos KP Tsentraluri Komitetis Gamomtsemloba, 1975), p. 21.
9. SR ('Eser', in Russian) is the abbreviation used throughout the Russian Empire for members of the Socialist Revolutionary Party founded in 1901. Although the SRs opposed the Tsarist regime, their political platform differed from that of the Social Democrats, both Menshevik and Bolshevik. The Socialist Revolutionary Party played an active role in the 1905 Russian Revolution, but was banned by the Bolsheviks after 1918. Among the Georgian revolutionaries, Grigol (Grisha) Emkhvari was of 'Eser' convictions. *Himmat* was established in Baku in 1904 and was active among the Muslim nationalities of the region. It was affiliated with the Baku committee of the Russian Social Democrat Labour Party and had branches in Tbilisi, Ganjah, and other cities in Transcaucasia. Afary, *The Iranian Constitutional Revolution*, p. 81.
10. *Gorji* is the Persian word for 'Georgian'.
11. Apolon Japaridze's memoir in Chipashvili, *V.I. Lenini da Iraneli Khalkhis Ganmantavisuplebeli Brdzola*, attachment, (Tbilisi: Metsniereba, 1970), pp. 89–90; Mikheil Bogdanov-Mariashkin's memoirs in Anton Kelenjeridze, *Gurjebi*

(Tbilisi: Sakartvelos KP Tsentraluri Komitetis Gamomtsemloba, 1975), p. 27.
12. About this see Giorgi Chipashvili, *Sergo Gamdlishvili Da Misi Iranuli Dghiurebi* (Tbilisi: Metsniereba, 1983), p. 10.
13. Tchilinkirian, 'Persian Revolution (1909–1910)', p. 233.
14. Insufficient scholarly attention to the Transcaucasian contribution to the constitutional movement was pointed out by Afary in her *The Iranian Constitutional Revolution*, p. 341.
15. As mentioned, Tria's report, *Kavkazskie Sotsial-Demokraty v Persidskoi Revoliutsii*, was published in Paris, in Russian, in 1910. In 1911, the report was published again, in French (see endnote 2). The Georgian text of the report was published as an attachment to Giorgi Chipashvili, *V.I. Lenini da Iraneli Khalkhis Ganmantavisuplebeli Brdzola*, pp. 99–108. Being the most-used Georgian source, it is the one that was edited by the Russian Social Democrat Workers' Party (RSDWP) leadership for the International Socialist Congress in Copenhagen in 1910. The Russian scholar Vladimir Genis also used Gurji Sergo's letters; see his 'Kavkazskie Boeviki v Persii (1908–1911 gg.)', *Voprosy Istorii* 5 (Moscow: Voprosi Istorii, 1997).
16. About the Tabriz resistance see Vlasa Mgeladze's *Sparsetis Revolutsia* (published as the third volume of his *Mogonebebi* (Memoirs) (Paris: Imprimerie Cooperative Arpajonaise, 1974); Sergo Gagoshidze's memoir in Kelenjeridze, *Gurjebi*, pp. 47–63; Davit Japaridze's memoirs in Kelenjeridze, *Gurjebi*, pp. 118–20. Chipashvili and Kelenjeridze may claim much credit for interviewing and recording the recollections of several former members of the 'Gorjis' who were then still alive. On the subject of the Rasht resistance there is Sergo Gamdlishvili's memoir 'Sparsetis Modzraobis Istoriidan' (From the History of the Persian Movement), which appeared in 1910 in a Tbilisi newspaper, *Akhali Skhivi*, in several instalments beginning in issue no. 3 (6 February) and ending in no. 35 (17 March); Apolon Japaridze's memoir in Chipashvili, *V.I. Lenini da Iraneli Khalkhis Ganmantavisuplebeli Brdzola*, attachment, pp. 89–98; Mikheil Bogdanov-Mariashkin's memoirs abridged in Kelenjeridze, *Gurjebi*, pp. 27–46.
17. Letters of 'Gorji', an anonymous Georgian correspondent in Tabriz, appeared in the November and December 1908 issues of the Tbilisi newspaper *Ali* (Flame) entitled 'Tserilebi Tavrizidan' (Letters from Tabriz); see issues of 2, 8, 9, 11, 13, 20, and 25 November, and of 2 and 5 December 1908. Lengthy letters entitled 'Tserilebi Sparsetidan' (Letters from Persia) and signed 'Mgzavri' (Traveller) appeared in December 1908 issues of the same newspaper – see issues of 23 and 24 December. There are also numerous anonymous reports from various places in Iran such as Tabriz, Marand, Salmas, Khoi, Urmia, Tehran, and Julfa, simply marked by the editors of newspapers as 'From Our Special Correspondent'.
18. 'Opening of a hospital in Tabriz' in *Ali*, 13 December 1908 (signed: Isari); see also an anonymous report on the same topic in *Ali*, 2 December 1908. 'Funeral of a Caucasian Fighter' in *Ali*, 5 December 1908. 'Revolutionaries' Demonstration in Tabriz' in *Ali*, 14 December 1908.
19. Some of these correspondents, referred to by the newspaper editors as 'Our Special Correspondent', were also members of the resistance in Tabriz and Rasht.

For example, Sergo Orjonikidze, who was sent by the Social Democrats to Gilan to coordinate work with the local revolutionaries, wrote for various Tbilisi newspapers using the pseudonyms 'Kldispireli' and 'Kldisdzireli' (Vladimir Kirillov and Aleksei Sverdlov, *G.K. Ordzhonikidze (Sergo): Biografia* (Moscow: Gosudarstvennoe Izdatelstvo Politicheskoi Literaturi, 1962), p. 41; Kelenjeridze, *Sergo Ordzhonikidze-Zhurnalist*, pp. 13–14, 21, 22). Sergo Gamdlishvili, besides writing his memoirs/diary, wrote for several Georgian and Russian newspapers. He mentions his work as a correspondent in his diary: Gurji Sergo, 'Sparsetis Modzraobis Istoriidan', *Akhali Skhivi* 35 (17 March 1910). A. Kelenjeridze, who wrote before Chipashvili, attributed the authorship of 'From the History of the Persian Movement' to Sergo Orjonikidze, but Chipashvili argued that the work was written by Sergo Gamdlishvili (Chipashvili, *Sergo Gamdlishvili*, pp. 14–29). About this issue and related arguments see Iago Gocheleishvili, 'Georgian Sources on the Iranian Constitutional Revolution: Sergo Gamdlishvili's Memoirs of the Gilan Resistance', *Iranian Studies* 40/1 (2007), pp. 79–80.

20. By the beginning of the twentieth century, Georgia had well-developed and diverse printed media which were an integral and important part of the political and social life of the country, even, as it appears, in rural areas. Luigi Villari, an Italian historian and journalist who travelled in 1905 in western Georgia, reported that 'every village has its library and even those furthest from the Government post stations provide their own mail service so as to receive the daily papers from Tbilisi, Batumi and Russia.' See his *Fire and Sword in the Caucasus* (London: T. F. Unwin, 1906), p. 84. The Russian military in the region confirmed that the population of provincial western Georgia 'were all literate' and that there were 'masses of schools in the region'. Filipe Makharadze, *Ocherki Revoliutsionnogo Dvizhenia v Zakavkaz'e* (Essays on the Revolutionary Movement in Transcaucasia) (Tbilisi: Gosizdat Gruzii, 1927), p. 393. Mikhail Kalinin, the chairman of the Russian All-Union Executive Committee, stated that 'the population of the villages in western Georgia ... resembles that of the town population; the language is that of the towns; the percentage of intellectuals is considerable'. Quoted in Stephen F. Jones, *Socialism in Georgian Colors: The European Road to Social Democracy* (Cambridge, MA: Harvard University Press, 2005), p. 331 n48. The Russian military confirmed that inhabitants of provincial western Georgia 'were all literate' and that there were 'masses of schools' in the region. Makharadze, *Ocherki Revoliutsionnogo Dvizhenia v Zakavkaz'e*, p. 393. The accounts by these sources might be a little exaggerated, but there was, indeed, a high degree of literacy among the population of provincial Georgia. The 'Negative' effect of education and the printed word on the society of Georgia seemed to the Tsarist authorities unquestionable, and when the spread of revolutionary ideas in these areas gained alarmingly in scale, the Russian authorities responded by shutting down libraries and conducting massive arrests of the village teachers. (Jones, *Socialism in Georgian Colors*, p. 140). The leaders of the peasant revolt in the province of Guria (in western Georgia) included in their demands 'free, compulsory education up to the age of sixteen' (ibid., p. 151).

21. 'Persian Revolutionary Committee in Istanbul' in *Ali*, 9 November 1908; 'Situ-

ation of Europeans in Tabriz' in *Ekali*, 3 October 1908; 'Sattar Khan and the Committee of the Young Turks' in *Amirani*, 19 September 1908; 'Persian Immigrants Protest Against Russia and England' in *Ekali*, 5 October 1908; 'Threat from Turkey' in *Imedi*, 19 October 1908; 'Reaction in Persia and the Russian Influence' in *Ekali*, 25 September 1908; 'Anjoman Addresses Austria', in *Imedi*, 28 October 1908.

22. 'Developments in Astara' in *Droeba*, 12 January 1909; 'Reasons for the Revolutionaries to Withdraw from Khoi' in *Ali*, 23 November 1908; 'Developments on the Persian-Turkish Border' in *Amirani*, 19 July 1908; 'Letter of the People of Julfa' in *Ali*, 13 December 1908; 'Who Controls the Town of Marand' in *Ali*, 2 November 1908; 'Popular Uprising in Rasht' in *Chveni Sakme*, 19 February 1902.

23. 'Letter from Women to the Revolutionaries' in *Amirani*, 26 August 1908; 'Shah's Message to the Revolutionaries of Shiraz' in *Amirani*, 4–5 September 1908; 'Letter of the Clerics of Najaf' in *Amirani*, 4–5 September 1908.

24. 'Memoirs of Yeprem Khan' in *Sakhalkho Gazeti*, 12 July 1912; 'Activities of Rahim Khan in Persia' in *Sakhalkho Gazeti*, 21 May 1910; about 'Eyn al-Dowleh in *Ekali*, 3 October 1908 and *Imedi*, 17 October 1908; 'Conversation with Colonel Liakhov' in *Ali*, 4 December 1909; about 'Butcher of Marand' in *Imedi*, 18 October 1908.

25. From an interview with Bogdanov-Mariashkin that was recorded by Kelenjeridze years after the Constitutional Revolution, it appears that Bogdanov-Mariashkin, by habit, still referred to Apolon Japaridze as 'Misha'. Misha Japaridze is also mentioned in the work of Ebrahim Fakhra'i, *Gilan dar jonbesh-e mashrutiyat* (Tehran: Sazman-e Entesharat va Amuzesh-e Enqelab-e Eslami, 1992), p. 116. In some cases, only the alias, or only the first or the last name, of a revolutionary is known. For example, Bogdanov-Mariashkin mentions two individuals named Giorgi, one of whom died in the battle for Rasht, and the other in the battle for Qazvin (see Kelenjeridze, *Gurjebi*, p. 139). Their last names and identities remain unknown. Sandro Veshakuri (Tabriz), Grigol Emkhvari (Tabriz), Petre Pochua (Tabriz), Lado Dumbadze (Alinja), Valiko Bakradze (Alinja), Kajaia (Alinja), Chito Tsertsvadze (Tabriz), Pulsa (Tabriz), Nakhvaladze (Tabriz), Lazare Gachechiladze (Tabriz), Sasha Avlabreli (Tabriz), Tsverava (Tabriz), Gordeladze (Tabriz), Iakob Metreveli (Tabriz), Giorgi (alias 'Zinger') (Rasht), Shalva Dolidze (Rasht), Giorgi 'Metsaghe' (Qazvin) are only a few of those Gorjis killed in the Iranian resistance whose names, or at least aliases, are known. Unfortunately, the names and identities of many Georgian internationalists killed in the Iranian constitutional resistance remain unknown. Most of those who died in Tabriz were buried in the fraternal grave of the Georgian revolutionaries in Tabriz, next to the Armenian Church, and those killed during the takeover of Qazvin seem to have been buried in the Armenian cemetery of Qazvin.

26. The memoirs of Gurji Sergo, a participant in the Gilan resistance, were published in February–March of 1910 in Tbilisi; the essay of Tria, a participant in the Tabriz resistance, was published in 1910; the description of the uprising in Rasht by its Georgian participant Apolon Japaridze appeared in a Tbilisi newspaper in

February of 1909, i.e., shortly after the event occurred.
27. Kasravi, *Tarikh-e hejdah saleh-ye Azarbayjan*, p. 13. Indeed, the Tabriz and Rasht revolts started and developed in quite different ways – the Tabriz uprising was initiated and conducted by the local activists, and the Transcaucasian revolutionaries only joined it later as it progressed, while in Rasht the actual uprising and takeover of the governor's palace occurred only after and as a result of the Transcaucasians' arrival and interference in the situation in Rasht.
28. Sources in Georgian languages describing constitutional resistance in Gilan and referring to the local Armenian revolutionaries primarily refer to the Dashnaks. Dashnaktsutiun (Hay Heghapokhakan Dashnaktsutiun, the Armenian Revolutionary Federation) was founded in Tbilisi in 1890 for the cause of the 'political and economic freedom of Turkish Armenia'. Anahide Ter Minassian, 'Nationalism and Socialism in the Armenian Revolutionary Movement (1887–1912)', in Ronald Grigor Suny (ed.), *Transcaucasia, Nationalism, and Social Change: Essays in the History of Armenia, Azerbaijan, and Georgia* (Ann Arbor: The University of Michigan Press, 1996), p. 151. From its basis in the Caucasus, the military corps of Dashnaks, composed mostly of Russian Armenian subjects, carried out paramilitary expeditions into the Armenian-populated parts of Ottoman Turkey. Many of these Armenian fighters, including Yeprem, were apprehended by the Russian authorities and sent to exile in Russia. Some of them, however, again including Yeprem, managed to escape from exile and settled in Iran. Later, when the Constitutional Revolution in Iran started, the Dashnaks, led by Yeprem, joined it. Yeprem's background in the Caucasus, his exile to Russia, and his escape to Iran are discussed in Andre Amuriyan, *Hamaseh-ye Yeprem* (Tehran: Javidan, 1976).
29. Gurji Sergo, 'Sparsetis Modzraobis Istoriidan', *Akhali Skhivi* 6 (10 February 1910). Another participant in the Rasht resistance, Bogdanov-Mariashkin, provides a very similar description of this meeting. (Bogdanov-Mariashkin's memoirs, p. 34).
30. Gurji Sergo, 'Sparsetis Modzraobis Istoriidan', *Akhali Skhivi* 6 (10 February 1910).
31. Apolon Japaridze's memoirs, pp. 93–94; Bogdanov-Mariashkin's memoirs, pp. 34–35, 37–38. Right after the operation Apolon Japaridze sent a letter to a Tbilisi newspaper, *Chveni Sakme*, describing the uprising in Rasht. It was published on 9 February 1909.
32. For example, they depict the activities of the international members of the Constitutional Revolution at Manjil, Rudbar, Yuzbashchai, Pachenar, Ambu, Alinja, etc., which are not described in other sources.
33. Bogdanov-Mariashkin's memoirs, pp. 24, 27–46.
34. Tria, *Kavkazskie Sotsial-Demokraty v Persidskoi Revoliutsii*, p. 15.
35. By 1905 there were practically two different and hostile organizations in Transcaucasia, the Mensheviks and the Bolsheviks. Makharadze, *Ocherki Revolutsionnogo Dvizhenia v Zakavkaz'e*, p. 316.
36. Sergo Ordzhonikidze, 'Borba s Menshevikami' (1907) (Fighting the Mensheviks), in *25 Let Bakinskoi Organizatsii Bolshevikov* (Baku: Gosizdat, 1924), p. 42.

37. Vladimir Genis, 'Kavkazskie Boeviki v Persii (1908–1911 gg.)', *Voprosy Istorii* 5 (Moscow: Voprosi Istorii, 1997), p. 12. However, it should be noted that the position of Georgian Social Democrats – both the Bolsheviks and the Mensheviks – regarding the Iranian constitutional movement generally coincided, and that the confrontation was caused by their differences in views on the political future of their own motherland.
38. Gurji Sergo, 'Sparsetis Modzraobis Istoriidan', *Akhali Skhivi* 3 (6 February 1910).
39. Genis, 'Kavkazskie Boeviki v Persii', p. 7.
40. Ibid. Evgenii Sablin also wrote in his correspondence to St. Petersburg that the Russian consul general, Passek, saw many natives of the Caucasus on his journey from Rasht to Qazvin (ibid.). Sablin, a staunch opponent of the constitutional movement, believed that Russia should rely on its own forces in Iran, rather than on the 'worthless' Shah. He was appointed to the Russian mission to Tehran in 1908 and immediately became deeply involved in the events of the revolution. He tried to stop the advance of the Gilani and Bakhtiyari constitutionalists on Tehran by threatening with 'foreign intervention', and when the constitutionalists took over Tehran he urged the Shah to bomb the city. Vladimir Genis, *Vitse-Konsul Vvedenskii, Sluzhba v Persii I Bukharskom Khanstve (1906–1920 gg.)* (Moscow: Izdateltsvo Sotsialno-politicheskaya Misl, 2003), p. 274.
41. In Persian sources they are usually referred to as 'Caucasians'. Sometimes, those Iranians who had lived and worked in the Caucasus and later returned to Iran to participate in the revolution together with the Caucasian groups were also called 'Caucasians'. Another collective term was *Gorji*, which, though literally meaning 'Georgian', was used to refer to individuals of various ethnicities who arrived in Iran from Georgia or who were members of the Georgian corps in Iran.
42. Tria, *Kavkazskie Sotsial-Demokraty v Persidskoi Revoliutsii*, p. 9.
43. Guidor also points out on this matter that after the combat ended, the Georgians requested the disarming of various armed groups involved in the resistance, to prevent the possibility of the proliferation of commands, but their demands were rejected, and the Georgians left Iran (Guidor, 'The Hnchakist Party and the Revolutionary Movement in Persia', pp. 304–05). Another reason for these Transcaucasians to leave Iran was the occupation of Tabriz by the Russian troops, who demanded that the local Iranian revolutionaries send away the Caucasians or face harsher actions from the Russian army.
44. Tria, *Kavkazskie Sotsial-Demokraty v Persidskoi Revoliutsii*, p. 15.
45. Gagoshidze recalls that he arrived in Tabriz wearing his artillerist uniform under his cloak, but that when Sattar Khan saw it, he asked him very politely to remove the shoulder straps – 'It's revolution', he explained. Gagoshidze's memoirs, p. 54.
46. One of the most striking examples of the roughs' participation in the revolution was their attack on the constitutionalist Majles on the orders of the royalists, just a short time after they had been working for the constitutionalists: Vanessa Martin, *Islam and Modernism: The Iranian Revolution of 1906* (Syracuse: Syracuse University Press, 1989), p. 149. Eventually, these Baku *qochi*s found themselves in conflict with the Caucasian faction of the resistance as well as with the Iranian revolutionaries and the local Armenian Dashnaks, and were forced to

leave Rasht at the demands of the 'Gorjis'. They were not from the working class, but were usually made up of individuals from lower social strata of the city population who often acted as a criminal gang. They were hired by various parties as an armed force during periods of violence and sometimes also by wealthy individuals, as bodyguards. See Ronald Grigor Suny, 'Labor and Liquidators: Revolutionaries and the "Reaction" in Baku, May 1908–April 1912', *Slavic Review* 34/2 (1975), p. 320.

47. Bogdanov-Mariashkin's memoirs, pp. 22–23, 34, 35.
48. Gurji Sergo, 'Sparsetis Modzraobis Istoriidan', *Akhali Skhivi* 3 (6 February 1910).
49. Tria, *Kavkazskie Sotsial-Demokraty v Persidskoi Revoliutsii*, p. 16.
50. Talking to the local revolutionaries at a secret meeting held in Rasht, the leader of the Georgians in Gilan is reported to have said: 'We have come to Iran not as Georgians. We have come to Iran as internationalists, and, thus, as revolutionaries.' Gurji Sergo, 'Sparsetis Modzraobis Istoriidan', *Akhali Skhivi* 14 (19 February 1910).
51. The article was entitled 'Ehsasat-e chand nafar Gorji, naql az jarideh-ye Mosavat-e Tabriz' and included by Esma'il Amirkhizi in his *Qiyam-e Azarbayjan va Sattar Khan* (Tehran: Negah, 2000), pp. 285–86.
52. About this see Chipashvili, *Sergo Gamdlishvili*, p. 10.
53. Indeed, among the Caucasian members of the resistance there were Socialist Revolutionaries, Mensheviks, Bolsheviks, and Anarchists. Bogdanov-Mariashkin's memoirs, p. 24.
54. These groups maintained contact with their political organizations in the Caucasus and, as Apolon Japaridze's accounts reveal, actually received directives and instructions from there, which were then to be enforced or, at least, presented and defended at the meetings of the local revolutionary committee (Apolon Japaridze's memoirs, p. 92). This soon became a source of tension between the outside revolutionaries and the local revolutionaries. The latter were not pleased by the fact that the Caucasians were not subordinated to already existing local revolutionary committees. Javid points out the emergence of such tension in Tabriz, and states that even the Iranians who lived in the Caucasus did not obey the local Iranian revolutionary committees, acting instead under the authority of the Caucasians commanders. (Javid, *Fadakaran*, 27) Gurji Sergo, who provides the Caucasians' view of the situation, describes the development of tension between the local and outside revolutionaries in Rasht. He explains that because the local revolutionaries were too passive, the Transcaucasians created their own committee in order to start immediate preparations for the revolt. This, however, caused resentment among the local Dashnaks, who, according to Gurji Sergo, were displeased with the increasing influence of the outside revolutionaries and demanded not only the subordination of all Georgians to the Dashnak leadership, but also that the Georgians put everything they had brought with them from the Caucasus at the local Dashnaks' disposal; otherwise, they threatened, they would desert the movement. (Gurji Sergo, 'Sparsetis Modzraobis Istoriidan', *Akhali Skhivi* 6 [10 February 1910]). Eventually, the outside Caucasians were subordinated to the command of the local Iranian revolutionary committees,

but they still retained permanent contact with their organizations in the Caucasus and continued to receive instructions from there throughout the revolution. Tria's accounts demonstrate that, although the Caucasians now reported to the local committee in Iran, their dependence on the decisions of the organizations in the Caucasus was never terminated. See Tria, *Kavkazskie Sotsial-Democraty v Persidkoi Revolutsii*, p. 11.

55. Ibid., pp. 9–10
56. Apolon Japaridze's memoirs, p. 91. Valiko, as it appears from the accounts of Guidor and Bogdanov-Mariashkin, later became the de facto leader of the Caucasian revolutionaries in Rasht and was one of the most recognizable Caucasian figures in the resistance. (Bogdanov-Mariashkin's memoirs, p. 29; Guidor, 'The Hnchakist Party and the Revolutionary Movement in Persia', p. 304). Kasravi refers to him as 'Valikof-e Gorji' and names him as a member of the *Komiteh-ye Sattar* and the *Komisiun-e jang* in Gilan (Kasravi, *Tarikh-e hejdah saleh-ye Azarbayjan*, pp. 8, 12). Valiko Gurji led the attack on the governor's palace in Rasht which resulted in the takeover of the town and later, after the takeover of the town, was the one to whom Sepahdar offered the command of the Caucasian corps in Gilan.
57. Bogdanov-Mariashkin's memoirs, p. 45.
58. The Georgians arrived in Rasht and Tabriz not only from Tbilisi, Batumi, and other Georgian towns and cities, but also from Baku, where a considerable number of Georgian revolutionaries resided by the time of the Tabriz revolt. For example, Sergo Gamdlishvili, a member of the Rasht resistance, arrived in Gilan from Baku. Whether the Georgian revolutionaries were selected and sent by their political organizations in the Caucasus or were recruited by the Iranian activists working in Transcaucasia, whether they arrived together or separately, in small groups, without even having ever met each other – once in Iran, most of them eventually came under the united command designated from the Caucasus. To the credit of the Transcaucasians, despite the political and ethnic diversity within their contingent, they were able to form one of the most tightly organized and efficient military forces. Although their corps included Bolsheviks known for their violent tactics and the common practice of 'expropriation', the majority of the rank and file as well as the military command of the Gorjis was comprised of Menshevik Social Democrats, and the corps was to become one of the most disciplined and well-organized groups in the resistance. In Iran, as Gurji Sergo claims, the 'Gorjis' tried to act with all possible tact and cautiousness. According to him, after the takeover of Rasht, when the constitutionalists launched searches and arrests of the royalists in the town, the Georgian corps refused to participate in the searches of the houses, arrests, or even street patrolling, as they believed that such actions on part of foreigners could cause undesirable and negative consequences. Gurji Sergo, 'Sparsetis Modzraobis Istoriidan', *Akhali Skhivi*, 8 (12 February 1910).
59. Bogdanov-Mariashkin's memoirs, pp. 30–31.
60. Tria, *Kavkazskie Sotsial-Demokraty v Persidskoi Revoliutsii*, pp. 11–12.
61. However, the committee did include several Iranian members. According to

Sergo, the committee was set up with the purpose of persuading the local revolutionaries to start immediate preparation for the armed uprising and takeover of Rasht, which was of vital importance for the survival of the Tabriz resistance (Gurji Sergo, 'Sparsetis Modzraobis Istoriidan', p. 3). Echoing the words of Sergo, Bodganov-Mariashkin points out that the passiveness of the local revolutionaries might have delayed the uprising in Gilan for far too long, affecting the fate of the Tabriz revolt. Such efforts by the Transcaucasians were sometimes successful, as in the case mentioned above, but on other occasions, as in the case of the demand of the Georgian revolutionaries to disarm the revolutionary fighters after the takeover of Tehran, they failed.

62. In Rasht, the Caucasians urged the local constitutionalists to follow the example of Tabriz and resort to prompt armed uprising. The Transcaucasian revolutionaries considered the commencement of the uprising in northern Iran as a logical and, in the current situation, the most effective step towards saving the Tabriz resistance and thus the revolution itself, which, as Sergo claims, was the Caucasians' agenda in Iran. Sergo, 'Sparsetis Modzraobis Istoriidan', p. 3.
63. Tria, *Kavkazskie Sotsial-Demokraty v Persidskoi Revoliutsii*, pp. 11–12.
64. Ibid., pp. 15, 9, 16, 14; Bogdanov-Mariashkin's memoirs, pp. 32–33, 44–45.
65. Tria, *Kavkazskie Sotsial -Demokraty v Persidskoi Revoliutsii*, p. 9.
66. Bogdanov-Mariashkin's memoirs, p. 45.
67. Bogdanov-Mariashkin's accounts show that the average age of his fellow revolutionaries was 18 to 20. Bogdanov-Mariashkin himself was 19 years old; his fellow Socialist Revolutionary Grigor Emkhvari was 21; Gurji Sergo was 21.
68. After their arrival in Iran, some of the revolutionaries realized the scale of the difficulty, and, probably, the impossibility of all of Iran rising in revolt. This realization is reflected in the memoirs of Sergo, who speaks about the lack of revolutionary spirit 'in the rest of Persia' and especially in northern Iran (Gurji Sergo, 'Sparsetis Modzraobis Istoriidan', p. 3). It is interesting, that the conclusions of Sergo are very similar to those arrived at later by the leadership of the Russian revolutionaries, which maintained that 'there could be no question of revolution in northern Iran, ... where the most basic preconditions for any kind of socialist revolution do not exist'. The statements were made in 1921: see Vladimir Genis, *Krasnaya Persiia: Bolsheviki v Gilane, 1920–1921*, Dokumentalnaia Khronika (Moscow: Tsentr Strategicheskikh I Politicheskikh Issledovanii / MNPI, 2000), p. 185.
69. Kelenjeridze, *Gurjebi*, p. 45.
70. The uprising preceded both the 1905 Russian Revolution and the Iranian Constitutional Revolution. It resulted in the complete abolition of the Tsarist authorities' control over the area, termination of the landlords' economic dominance, and the formation of local peasant councils that administered local affairs. Eventually, a massive military expedition of Tsarist troops to Guria brought to an end the 'Gurian Republic'. (On the Gurian peasant republic see Jones, *Socialism in Georgian Colors*, pp. 129–58) Georgian Social Democrats, and especially their committees in western Georgia, were involved in this uprising and later continued to cooperate with the local councils in Guria.

71. Mgeladze, *Sparsetis Revolutsia*, p. 3.
72. Gurji Sergo, 'Sparsetis Modzraobis Istoriidan', p. 3.
73. Bogdanov-Mariashkin's memoirs, pp. 32–33.
74. The official position of the Caucasian revolutionaries regarding the Iranian clergy's role in the Iranian Constitutional Revolution, partly reflected in Tria's report, admits the significant role of the clergy in the beginning stages of the revolution but points out the change in the clergy's position as the movement progressed: Tria, *Kavkazskie Sotsial-Demokraty v Persidskoi Revoliutsii*, p. 15. On the reasons underlying the change of attitude among the Iranian ulema regarding the constitution and on the various aspects of the complex of relations between the ulema and constitutionalists in Iran during the Constitutional Revolution, see Martin, *Islam and Modernism*.
75. For the social dynamics of the Constitutional Revolution in Iran, where 'not a single class fought against [the regime]', see Homa Katouzian, *State and Society in Iran: The Eclipse of the Qajars and the Emergence of the Pahlavis* (London: I.B.Tauris, 2000), p. 50.
76. 'From Persian Astara to Rasht there were not even ten people who would undertake at least the accommodation of the Caucasians. Thanks to the group working in the Caucasus, three or four such individuals were found in the town of Rasht: Sardar Mohi (Mo'ezz al-Soltan), his brother Mirza Karim Khan, Seid Gusein (Kermai) and Mirza Ali Mamed Khan, who provided them with housing and food.' Gurji Sergo, 'Sparsetis Modzraobis Istoriidan', p. 3. Even after that, as the author notes, there was no coordination between the Caucasians, and they continued to live in separate places without contact with each other. Ibid.
77. Gurji Sergo, 'Sparsetis Modzraobis Istoriidan', p. 3.
78. The Iranians residing and working in the Caucasus played an important part in involving Transcaucasians in the Iranian revolution during the period under discussion. Heydar Khan was very active in Baku, working to involve the Transcaucasians in the resistance. He was affiliated with the Social Democrat organization and was one of the organizers of the 'Society of Azarbayjanis' in Iran; see Afary, *The Iranian Constitutional Revolution*, pp. 112, 428, and Abrahamian, *Iran Between Two Revolutions*, p. 87. Karim Khan was the brother of Mo'ezz al-Soltan, one of the revolutionary leaders in Gilan. They are both mentioned many times in the memoirs of Sergo, Bogdanov-Mariashkin, and Apolon Japaridze. Sergo describes how Karim Khan travelled to Baku to purchase arms for the Rasht resistance: Gurji Sergo, 'Sparsetis Modzraobis Istoriidan', p. 6.
79. Gagoshidze's memoirs, p. 49.
80. Gurji Sergo, 'Sparsetis Modzraobis Istoriidan', p. 3.
81. Tria, *Kavkazskie Sotsial-Demokraty v Persidskoi Revoliutsii*, pp. 9–10.
82. Bogdanov-Mariashkin's memoirs, pp. 28, 31.
83. On this see Jones, *Socialism in Georgian Colors*, p. 148.
84. Silovan Ivaniadze (1882–1913) was a Georgian revolutionary, a native of the village Didi Jikhaishi in western Georgia, and a participant in the Tabriz resistance.
85. About this see Chipashvili, *Sergo Gamdlishvili*, p. 10. Fakhra'i and Abrahamian

also note in their works the importance of the Caucasians' skills in using bombs and handling artillery for the military successes of the revolutionaries: Fakhra'i, *Gilan dar jonbesh-e mashrutiyat*, p. 116; Abrahamian, *Iran Between Two Revolutions*, pp. 98–99.

86. Bogdanov-Mariashkin, who had spent some time in Astara before crossing the border, dealt with such issues directly and his accounts are based on first-hand knowledge of the matter. Bogdanov-Mariashkin's memoirs, pp. 29–30.
87. The style of the original source is preserved in the translation. Gagoshidze's memoirs, pp. 53–54. Although phrases and words in Azeri and Persian are abundant in the memoirs of almost all the Georgian resisters, they usually appear with errors, as the Georgians did not speak either of the languages at all and simply tried to transliterate the words and phrases with the letters of the Georgian alphabet as accurately as they could.
88. The Hnchak (Hunchak) Party was founded in 1887 in Geneva by several Armenian students. The focus of the organization was the situation of Armenians in Ottoman Turkey. See Ter Minassian, 'Nationalism and Socialism', p. 149 and Louise Nalbandian, *The Armenian Revolutionary Movement: The Development of Armenian Political Parties Through the Nineteenth Century* (Berkeley: University of California Press, 1963), pp. 104–31.
89. Mgeladze, *Sparsetis Revolutsia*, pp. 26–28.
90. Bogdanov-Mariashkin's memoirs, pp. 22–23; Gurji Sergo, 'Sparsetis Modzraobis Istoriidan', p. 3.

Chapter 4. Constitutional Rights and the Development of Civil Law in Iran, 1907–41

1. I am grateful to Vanessa Martin for providing me with valuable editorial comments and to Ervand Abrahamian, Abbas Amanat, Saïd Amir Arjomand, Mohsen Ashtiany, Ali Banuazizi, Houchang Chehabi, and Hossein Modarressi for their helpful discussions and comments. For a Persian version of this essay with some modifications, see Ali Gheissari, 'Mafahim va nahadha-ye hoquq-e asasi dar Iran: Negahi be tadvin-e qanun-e madani va tahavvol-e qovveh-ye qaza'iyeh, az sadr-e mashrutiyat ta Shahrivar-e 1320' (Constitutional Rights Reconsidered: the Development of Civil Law and the Shaping of Iran's Judiciary, 1907–1941), tr. Kaveh Bayat, in *Goftogu*, Special Issue on the Iranian Constitutional Revolution, Touraj Atabaki (ed.), no. 51 (2008), pp. 47–61.
2. For Malkam Khan's influential periodical, *Qanun* (The Law), see Mirza Malkam Khan, *Ruznameh-ye Qanun*, London, reprinted with an Introduction by Homa Nateq (Tehran: Amir-Kabir, 1976). For Malkam's writings, see also Mirza Malkam Khan, *Kolliyat* (Collected Works), edited by Hashem Rabi'zadeh (Tehran: Majles, 1907); Mirza Malkam Khan, *Majmu'eh-ye asar* (Collected Works), edited by Mohammad Mohit Tabataba'i (Tehran: 'Elmi, 1948); and Mirza Malkam Khan Nazem al-Dowleh, *Resalehha*, edited by Hojjatollah Asil (Tehran: Nashr-e Ney, 2002). For studies on Malkam Khan see, for example, Hamid Algar, *Mirza Malkum Khan: A Biographical Study in Iranian Modernism* (Berkeley: University of California Press, 1973); and Shaul Bakhash, *Iran:*

Monarchy, Bureaucracy and Reform under the Qajars: 1858–1896 (London: Ithaca Press, 1978), pp. 305–74.

3. Mirza Mohammad Khan Sinaki (Majd al-Molk), *Kashf al-ghara'ib* (Unraveling Strange Matters), also referred to as *Resaleh-ye Majdiyeh* (The Majdiyeh Treatise), edited by Sa'id Nafisi (Tehran: Markazi, 1942), new edition edited by Fazlollah Gorgani (Tehran: Eqbal, 1979).

4. Yusef Khan Mostashar al-Dowleh, *Resaleh-y mowsumeh be yek kalameh* (A Treatise on One Word), written in Paris in 1287 AH (1870), reprinted, edited by Ali Reza Dowlatshahi (Tehran: Bal, 2007).

5. For an English translation of the Iranian Fundamental Law, see Edward G. Browne, *A Brief Narrative of Recent Events in Persia, followed by an Appendix on the Persian Constitution* (London: Luzac & Co, 1909), pp. 65–101, reprinted in Edward G. Browne, *The Persian Revolution of 1905–1909*, new edition with Introduction, Correspondence, and Reviews, edited by Abbas Amanat (Washington, DC: Mage Publishers, 1995), pp. 351–400.

6. As in, for example, the expression attributed to Louis XIV, '*l'état c'est moi*' (I am the State).

7. The parallel may also be seen in the modern maintenance of aristocratic country houses, where there is a noticeable shift from their unrestricted ownership by their original owners to having public organizations (such as the National Trust, in the case of Britain) run them while the original families become merely keepers and guardians. With regard to notions of pre-modern societies, arbitrary power, and the rise of the modern state and its institutions, see, for example, Max Weber, *Economy and Society*, edited by Gunther Roth and Claus Wittich, translated by Ephraim Fischoff, et al., 3 vols. (New York: Bedminster Press, 1968), vol. 1, p. 56; for a summary of Weber's definition, see Quentin Skinner, *The Foundations of Modern Political Thought*, Volume One: *The Renaissance* (Cambridge: Cambridge University Press, 1978), Preface, pp. ix–x. For studies on the ideas of rights, justice, and notions of state and individual in pre-modern Iran, see Ann K. S. Lambton, 'Quis custodiet custodes', *Studia Islamica* 5 (1955), and 6 (1956); idem, 'Justice in the Medieval Persian Theory of Kingship', *Studia Islamica* 22 (1970), pp. 181–92; idem, chapter 17, 'The State and the Individual', in A. K. S. Lambton, *State and Government in Medieval Islam: An Introduction to the Study of Islamic Political Theory: The Jurists* (Oxford: Oxford University Press, 1981), pp. 307–15; and idem, *Local Particularism and the Common People in Pre-Modern Iran*, Durham Middle East Papers No. 67 (December 2001). For a broader Islamic context, see Michael Cook, *Commanding Right and Forbidding Wrong in Islamic Thought* (Cambridge: Cambridge University Press, 2001).

8. Examples include Anushirvan's legendary bell for common people to seek justice and his 'Grievances Court' (Divan-e Mazalem), or the story of the old woman demanding justice from Sultan Sanjar. See *Encyclopaedia Iranica*, s.v. 'Dād'; and Linda T. Darling, '"Do Justice, Do Justice, For That is Paradise": Middle Eastern Advice for Indian Muslim Rulers', *Comparative Studies of South Asia, Africa and the Middle East* 22/1–2 (2002), pp. 3–19. For the administration of justice in medieval Iran, see, for example, Ann K. S. Lambton, *Continuity and Change in*

Medieval Persia: Aspects of Administrative, Economic and Social History, 11th–14th Century (New York: State University of New York Press, Bibliotheca Persica, 1988). For a broad range of references in Persian classical literature, see Charles-Henri de Fouchécour, *Moralia: Les notions morales dans la littérature persane du 3e/9e au 7e/13e siècles* (Paris: Editions Recherche sur les civilisations, 1986); see also Maria E. Subtelny, *Le monde est un jardin: aspects de l'histoire culturelle de l'Iran médiéval* (Paris: Association pour l'Avancement des Etudes Iraniennes, 2002). For a discussion on 'the circle of justice' and 'the just government' in the constitutional period, see Nader Sohrabi, 'Revolution and State Culture: The Circle of Justice and Constitutionalism in 1906 Iran', in George Steinmetz (ed.), *State/Culture: State-Formation after the Cultural Turn* (Ithaca, NY: Cornell University Press, 1999), pp. 253–88.

9. It can further be noted that in other languages, too, 'right' and 'rights' have similar connotations. Right as opposed to wrong; right as the correct way or system; and rights as the sum of what an individual or a company expects as part of its entity and also expects the government and society to respect and protect. It does also have financial implications, as in, for example, 'copyright'.

10. For a theoretical discussion on constitutions and constitutionalism, see Jan-Erik Lane, *Constitutions and Political Theory* (Manchester: Manchester University Press, 1996).

11. For a concise account and selective bibliography on *fiqh*, see *Encyclopaedia Iranica*, s.v. 'Feqh (Jurisprudence)'. With regard to Islamic views on public law, it has often been noted that in such views priority is given to 'the promotion of social objectives and the protection of collective rather than individual interest'; see Abdul Rahman I. Doi, 'Public Law', in John L. Esposito (ed.), *The Oxford Encyclopedia of the Modern Islamic World* (New York and Oxford: Oxford University Press, 1995), pp. 368–70, here p. 368. For a classical work on Islamic public law, see Ali b. Muhammad al-Mawardi, *Al-Ahkam al-sultaniya* (Cairo: Dar al-Fikr, 1983). Further discussion on private and public law in Islam can be found in Bernard Weiss, *The Spirit of Islamic Law* (Athens, GA: University of Georgia Press, 1998), chapter 8: 'Private and Public Dimensions of the Law', pp. 172–85. For additional contributions to the question of public law in Islam, see Chibli Mallat (ed.), *Islam and Public Law: Classical and Contemporary Studies* (London, Dordrecht, Boston: Graham and Trotman, 1993); and with regard to Islamic penal law, see Rudolph Peters, *Crime and Punishment in Islamic Law: Theory and Practice from the Sixteenth to the Twenty-first Century* (Cambridge: Cambridge University Press, 2005). Islamic concepts and traditions of public and especially international law in the medieval period and their influence on the West are discussed in Marcel A. Boisard, 'On the Probable Influence of Islam on Western Public and International Law', *International Journal of Middle East Studies* 11/4 (1980), pp. 429–50. For recent discussions on Islamic views on the public and private sphere and the theories of social contract, see respectively Mohsen Kadivar, 'Pishdaramadi bar bahs-e "omumi va khosusi" dar farhang-e eslami' (An Introduction to the Debate on "Public and Private" [sphere] in Islamic Culture) available at: http://kadivar.com/Index.asp?DocId=593&AC=1&AF=1&ASB=1

&AGM=1&AL=1&DT=dtv; and Shahrough Akhavi, 'Shiite Theories of Social Contract', in Abbas Amanat and Frank Griffel (eds.), *Shari'a: Islamic Law in the Contemporary Context* (Stanford: Stanford University Press, 2007), pp. 137–55.

12. Any fair and accurate assessment of the political history of the Qajar state in the nineteenth century should view it in a more global context, i.e., as operating in a time of aggressive and global performance by a number of strong imperial powers. Comparing Iran with other nations in the region, the country did remarkably well to survive and retain as much of its territory as it did. For a valuable contribution to this topic, see Vanessa Martin, *The Qajar Pact: Bargaining, Protest and the State in Nineteenth-Century Persia* (London: I.B.Tauris, 2005).

13. The origin of the term *mashrutiyat* (for constitutionalism) has been debated among historians. Iranians initially used the French term *constitution*. It is widely held that the term *mashrutiyat* was first coined in the Ottoman Empire and then reached Iran. For further discussion on this topic, see my *Iranian Intellectuals in the Twentieth Century* (Austin, TX: University of Texas Press, 1998), pp. 24–25.

14. Here *asasi* also has the connotation of 'foundational', i.e., the set of laws on which subsequent laws are built, a kind of secular scripture.

15. Empowerment of the individual was therefore interpreted in terms of checking the arbitrary powers of the state rather than giving priority to individual autonomy and human agency.

16. This approach to some extent resonated with the Ottoman Tanzimat reforms over half a century earlier which, in many ways, anticipated the future evolution of the state and national ideology in neighbouring Turkey. For the Ottoman Tanzimat, see Şerif Mardin, *The Genesis of Young Ottoman Thought* (Princeton: Princeton University Press, 1962); Stanford J. Shaw and Ezel Kural Shaw, *History of the Ottoman Empire and Modern Turkey*, Volume 2, *Reform, Revolution and the Republic* (Cambridge: Cambridge University Press, 1977); and Anja Pistor-Hatam, '*Tanzîmât* oder *Ittihâd*: Zwei Konzepte osmanisch-persischer Einigung', *Turcica* 24 (1994), pp. 247–61.

17. For studies on the Shiite ulema and their relation with the state before the constitutional movement, see Hamid Algar, *Religion and State in Iran, 1785–1906: The Role of the Ulama in the Qajar Period* (Berkeley: University of California Press, 1969); and Saïd Amir Arjomand, *The Shadow of God and the Hidden Imam: Religion, Political Order, and Societal Change in Shi'ite Iran from the Beginning to 1890* (Chicago: University of Chicago Press, 1984).

18. For Nuri, see Sheykh Fazlollah Nuri, *Lavayeh-e aqa Sheykh Fazlollah Nuri*, edited by Homa Rezvani (Tehran: Nashr-e Tarikh-e Iran, 1983); and Sheykh Fazlollah Nuri, *Rasa'el, e'lamiyehha,maktubat va ruznameh-ye sheykh-e shahid Fazlollah Nuri*, edited by Mohammad Torkaman (Tehran: Rasa, 1983). For studies on Nuri's position, see A. H. Hairi, 'Shaykh Fazl Allah Nuri's Refutation of the Idea of Constitutionalism', *Middle Eastern Studies* 13/3 (1977), pp. 327–39; Yann Richard, 'Le radicalisme islamique du sheykh Fazlollah Nuri et son impact dans l'histoire de l'Iran contemporain', *La Pensée et les Hommes*, n.s. 29/2 (*Les Intégrismes*, Dossier édité par Jacques Lemaire et Jacques Marx) (Brussels, 1986), pp. 60–86; Vanessa Martin, 'The Anti-Constitutionalist Arguments of Shaikh

Fazlallah Nuri', *Middle Eastern Studies* 22/2 (April 1986), pp. 181–96; Vanessa Martin, 'Shaikh Fazlallah Nuri and the Iranian Revolution 1905–09', *Middle Eastern Studies* 23/1 (January 1987), pp. 39–53; and Vanessa Martin, *Islam and Modernism: The Iranian Revolution of 1906* (Syracuse: Syracuse University Press, 1989).

19. For Khorasani, see Molla Mohammad Kazem Khorasani, *Siyasatnameh-ye Khorasani*, edited by Mohsen Kadivar (Tehran: Kavir, 2006); Mohsen Kadivar, 'Andisheh-ye siyasi-ye Akhund-e Khorasani', available at: http://kadivar.com/Index.asp?DocId=605&AC=1&AF=1&ASB=1&AGM=1&AL=1&DT=dtv; and Mohsen Kadivar, 'Jaygah-e din va hoquq-e mardom dar hokumat-e mashruteh az didgah-e Akhund Khorasani', available at: http://kadivar.com/Index.asp?DocId=1866&AC=1&AF=1&ASB=1&AGM=1&AL=1&DT=dtv. For Na'ini's tract, see Mirza Mohammad Hoseyn Na'ini, *Tanbih al-umma va tanzih al-milla*, edited by Seyyed Mahmud Taleqani, new edition (1955, Tehran: Enteshar, 1999). For a study of Na'ini's position, see Abdul-Hadi Hairi, *Shī'īsm and Constitutionalism in Iran: A Study of the Role Played by the Persian Residents of Iraq in Iranian Politics* (Leiden: Brill, 1977); see further Javad Tabataba'i, *Ta'ammoli darbareh-ye Iran*, volume 2: *Nazariyeh-ye hokumat-e qanun dar Iran*, part 2: *Mabani-ye nazariyeh-ye mashruteh-kh^{v}ahi* (Tabriz: Sotudeh, 2007), pp. 475–525. For the ulema of Najaf and Karbala, see further Meir Litvak, *Shi'i Scholars of Nineteenth-Century Iraq: The Ulama of Najaf and Karbala* (Cambridge: Cambridge University Press, 1998).

20. In this context, personal liberty can be viewed as a constitutive paradigm in modern political and legal theory which recognizes, protects, and promotes not only the rights and responsibilities of the individual vis-à-vis the state and society but also of the conditions in which the individual enjoys both the possibility and the ability to act according to his or her own will. It is therefore possible to distinguish and separate democracy and justice from secularism and liberty.

21. For example, a reformist such as Malkam Khan was, like a latter-day Hume, a secular sceptic who nevertheless knew the powerful impact of religion and also needed to be particularly careful in a world in which sceptics and atheists were still at risk; however, some of the others were genuine believers.

22. See *Encyclopaedia Iranica*, s.v. 'The Constitutional Revolution: iii. The Constitution'; and Janet Afary, 'Civil Liberties and the Making of Iran's First Constitution', *Comparative Studies of South Asia, Africa and the Middle East* 25/2 (2005), pp. 341–59.

23. For further discussion, see Ali Gheissari and Vali Nasr, *Democracy in Iran: History and the Quest for Liberty* (Oxford: Oxford University Press, 2006), pp. 30–32. For a selection of documents and state regulations aimed at legal reform in Iran prior to the Constitutional Revolution, see Mohammad Taqi Damghani, *Avvalin qavanin-e Iran qabl az mashrutiyat* (Tehran: Behzad, 1978). For an overview of the Qajar judicial system, see Willem Floor, 'Change and Development in the Judicial System of Qajar Iran (1800–1925)', in Edmund Bosworth and Carole Hillenbrand (eds.), *Qajar Iran: Political, Social, and Cultural Change 1800–1925* (Edinburgh: Edinburgh University Press, 1983), pp. 113–47.

24. For a general survey of legal reforms in Iran during the period under consideration, see Majid Mohammadi, *Judicial Reforms and Reorganization in 20th Century Iran: State-Building, Modernization and Islamization* (London: Routledge, 2008), pp. 55–108.
25. Mohammad Ali Forughi, *Hoquq-e asasi ya'ni adab-e mashrutiyat-e doval* (Tehran, 1907), new edition edited by Ali Asghar Haqdar (Tehran: Kavir, 2003); also reprinted in Changiz Pahlavan, *Rishehha-ye tajaddod* (Tehran: Nashr-e Qatreh, 2004), pp. 111–94.
26. Mostafa 'Adl (Mansur al-Saltaneh), *Hoquq-e asasi ya osul-e mashrutiyat va sharh-e qanun-e asasi* (Tehran, 1910).
27. Nosrat al-Dowleh Firuz, *Qanun-e jaza-ye 'orfi* (Tehran, 1916–17).
28. Mohammad Mosaddeq, *Hoquq-e parlemani dar Iran va Orupa* (Tehran, 1923). Prior to this work mention can also be made of Mohammad Mosaddeq's *Dastur dar mahakem-e hoquqi* (Procedure of Civil Courts) (Tehran, 1914). For Mosaddeq's additional writings, see also Iraj Afshar (ed.), *Mosaddeq va masa'el-e hoquq va siyasat* (Mosaddeq on Law and Politics) (Tehran: Zamineh, 1979).
29. The initial components of the Iranian constitutional laws included: the Royal Proclamation (of 5 August 1906), the Electoral Law (of 9 September 1906), the Fundamental Law (of 30 December 1906), and the Supplementary Fundamental Law (of 7 October 1907). To these was later added the New Electoral Law (of 1 July 1909). For an English translation of these documents, see E. G. Browne, *The Persian Revolution of 1905–1909*.
30. Amin Banani, *Modernization of Iran: 1921–1941* (Stanford: Stanford University Press, 1961), p. 69.
31. Ahmad Matin-Daftari, *A'in-e dadresi-y madani va bazargani* (Civil and Commercial Court Procedure) (Tehran, 1945), pp. 8–10 (2nd edition, Tehran: Majd, 2002), as quoted in Banani, *Modernization of Iran*, p. 69.
32. For a political biography of Hasan Pirniya (Moshir al-Dowleh), see Ebrahim Bastani Parizi, *Talash-e azadi: mohit-e siyasi va zendegani-ye Moshir al-Dowleh Pirniya* (first edition, 1961), fourth edition (Tehran: Novin, 1977).
33. Indeed, the transition from Qajar to Pahlavi rule, and from Ahmad Shah to Reza Shah, was a radical and fundamental change with profound implications. It was not simply about a new dynasty coming to power and one king replacing another – the new authoritarian regime was more a dictatorship with a constitutional façade than an absolutist monarchy. The change had broad implications for the structure and functions of the Iranian state and its relations with society.
34. For Mohsen Sadr (Sadr al-Ashraf), see his *Khaterat-e Sadr al-Ashraf* (Tehran: Vahid, 1985).
35. For Davar, see, for example, Baqer 'Aqeli, *Davar va 'adliyeh* (Tehran: 'Elmi, 1990); *Encyclopaedia Iranica*, s.v. 'Davar, Ali-Akbar'.
36. For bibliographic references, see respectively Abu Ja'far Muhammad b. Ya'qub b. Ishaq al-Kulayni, *Kitab al-Kafi*, 8 vols., ed. Ali Akbar Ghaffari (Tehran, 1968); Sheykh Abu-Ja'far Muhammad b. Hasan al-Tusi, *al-Fihrist*, reprinted *Fehrest-e mosannafat-e Shi'ah* (Tehran, n.d.); Sheykh Ja'far b. al-Hasan al-Muhaqqiq al-Hilli, *Sharayi' al-Islam wa al-ahkam*, Persian translation by Abolqasem Yazdi,

ed. Mohammad Taqi Daneshpazhuh (Tehran, 1967); Zayn al-Din Ali b. Ahmad al-'Amili (al-Shahid al-Thani), *Sharh-e al-lum'ah al-Dimishqiyah*, 2 vols. (Qom, 1986); Muhammad b. Hasan al-Hurr al-'Amili, *Wasa'il al-Shi'ah ila tahsil masa'il al-shari'ah*, 20 vols., eds. Sheykh 'Abd al-Rahim al-Rabbani al-Shirazi and Muhammad al-Razi (Tehran, 1956–69), 2nd edition, 20 vols., ed. Sheykh 'Abd al-Rahim al-Rabbani al-Shirazi (Beirut: Dar al-Ihya' al-Turath al-'Arabi, [4th printing] 1971); Sheykh Muhammad Hasan b. Baqir al-Najafi, *Jawahir al-kalam fi sharh sharayi' al-Islam*, 43 vols. (Tehran: Dar al-Kutub al-Islamiyah, 1979); Sheykh Morteza Ansari, *Kitab al-Makasib*, 3 vols. (Qom, 2003).

37. See Seyyed Mohammad Meshkat, *Mu'taqad al-Imamiyah*, Persian text, ed. Mohammad Taqi Daneshpazhuh (Tehran, 1960); Seyyed Mohammad Kazem Yazdi, *'Urwat al-wuthqa*, new edition, 5 vols., (Qom: Nashr-e Eslami, 1996). For a bibliographical survey on Shiite law, see Hossein Modarressi, *An Introduction to Shi'i Law: A Bibliographical Study* (London: Ithaca Press, 1984); further see, Hossein Modarressi, *Tradition and Survival*, Vol. 1: *A Bibliographical Survey of Early Shiite Literature* (Oxford: Oneworld, 2004). For further studies on Shiite jurisprudence, see Aqa Mohammad Sangelaji, *Zavabet-e mo'amelat va kolliyat-e 'oqud va iqa'at: Ketab-e qaza dar Islam* (General Rules of Transactions: Contracts and Unilateral Contracts in Islamic Jurisprudence) (Tehran, 1949); Mahmud Shehabi, *Advar-e feqh* (General Classification of *Fiqh*), 3 vols. (Tehran, 1950 and 1957), new edition (Tehran: Tehran University, 1975); Sheykh Mohammad 'Abdoh Borujerdi, *Kolliyat-e hoquq-e eslami* (A General Introduction to Islamic Law) (Tehran, 1960); Mohammad Mohsen Aqa Bozorg al-Tehrani, *Tabaqat-i a'lam al-Shi'ah* (Shi'a Index), 6 vols. (Qom, 1994); and Muhammad Baqir as-Sadr, *Lessons in Islamic Jurisprudence*, translated with an Introduction by Roy Parviz Mottahedeh (Oxford: Oneworld, 2003).

38. 'Abbas Mobarakian, *Chehrehha dar tarikhcheh-ye nezam-e amuzesh-e 'ali-ye hoquq va 'adliyeh-ye novin* (A Short History of Legal Education and the New Judiciary [in Iran]) (Tehran: Peydayesh, 1998), p. 497 n1. A major incentive for expediting legal reforms was the desire to abolish the Capitulation regime in which foreign states, in the absence of a uniform and standard legal system in Iran, maintained jurisdiction over their own nationals residing in Iran. This was a major source of contention among Iranian nationalists and statesmen. Following the reorganization of the ministry of justice and upon the ratification of the Civil Law, during the premiership of Mehdi Qoli Hedayat (Mokhber al-Saltaneh), on 10 May 1928 the Capitulation regime was abolished by the Majles. Article 5 of the Civil Law stipulated that 'All inhabitants of Iran, whether they are nationals of Iran or of foreign countries, are subject to Iranian laws, except in cases which are excepted by law.'

39. For additional information on the evolution of Iran's Civil Law, see *Encyclopaedia Iranica*, s.v. 'Civil Code'; and *Encyclopaedia Iranica*, s.v. 'Davar'. For early discussions on civil law see, for example, Mostafa 'Adl (Mansur al-Saltaneh), *Hoquq-e madani* (Civil Law), 3rd edition (Tehran, 1938); Seyyed Ali Shayegan, *Hoquq-e madani-ye Iran* (Iran's Civil Law) (Tehran, 1937); and Aqa Sheykh Mohammad Sangelaji, *Hoquq-e madani* (Civil Law) (Tehran, 1937). For later contributions,

see Seyyed Hasan Emami, *Hoquq-e madani* (Civil Law), 6 vols. (Tehran: Tehran University, 1954).
40. Banani, *Modernization of Iran*, p. 74.
41. For a general account of the evolution of modern law, see Ali Pasha Saleh, *Qovveh-ye moqanneneh va qovveh-ye qaza'iyeh* (Legislative and Judicial Branches) (Tehran: Tehran University, 1964); and Ali Pasha Saleh, *Sargozasht-e qanun: mabahesi az tarikh-e hoquq, durnama'i az ruzgaran-e pishin ta emruz* (The Story of Law: An Overview from Ancient Times to the Present), 2nd edition (Tehran: Tehran University, 2004). For a general index of Iranian laws from the First Session of the Majles (1906) until 1955, see Ashraf Mohajer, *Rahnama-ye qavanin az dowreh-ye avval-e qanungozari ta akher-e sal-e 1334* (An Introduction to [Iranian] Laws from the First Legislative Session to 1955) (Tehran, n.d.).
42. Shayegan, *Hoquq-e madani-ye Iran*, 3rd edition (Tehran, 1945), pp. 33–38, as quoted in Banani, *Modernization of Iran*, p. 74. For early discussions on Iran's penal code, see Mohammad Baheri, *Taqrirat darbareh-ye hoquq-e jaza* (Notes on Penal Law) (Tehran: Tehran University, n.d.); and Seyyed Ali Ha'eri Shahbagh, *Sharh-e qanun-e mojazat-e 'omumi* (On General Penal Law) (Tehran, n.d.); and Shams al-Din Amir-'Ala'i, *Mojazat-e e'dam* (Capital Punishment) (Tehran, 1950) (new edition, Tehran: Dehkhoda, 1978).
43. See, for example, Saleh, *Qovveh-ye moqanneneh*; Fereydun Adamiyat, *Ide'olozhi-ye nehzat-e mashrutiyat-e Iran* (Ideology of the Iranian Constitutional Movement) (Tehran: Payam, 1976), p. 408; and *Encyclopaedia Iranica*, s.v. 'The Constitutional Revolution: iii. The Constitution'. For the administrative history of Iran in the medieval period, see Lambton, *Continuity and Change in Medieval Persia*.
44. Whereas in liberalism priority is given to the preservation, protection, and promotion of individual liberties, in collectivism it is given to the interests of the community and society. In broad terms, early articulations of these divergent approaches in modern Western political theories can be found in, for example, the writings of John Locke (1632–1704) and Jean-Jacques Rousseau (1712–78), respectively. For a general and theoretical discussion of the question of civil liberties and constitutional government in Iran, see Youssef Aliabadi, 'The Idea of Civil Liberties and the Problem of Institutional Government in Iran', *Social Research* 67/2 (Summer 2000), pp. 345–76.
45. However, it should be noted that, at least in theory, subjects always had recognized rights and responsibilities as well, as depicted in the emblematic 'circle of justice'. See for example, Subtelny, *Le Monde est un jardin*, in particular chapter 2, p. 53.
46. As used by Jürgen Habermas, in his *Knowledge and Human Interests*, trans. Jeremy J. Shapiro (Boston: Beacon Press, 1971).
47. For an early discussion of procedural laws in Iran, see Sheykh Mohammad 'Abdoh Borujerdi, *Osul-e mohakemat-e hoquqi: osul-e qaza'i-ye hoquqi va jaza'i-ye divan-e 'ali-ye keshvar* (Code of Civil Trials: Civil and Penal Procedures of the Supreme Court) (Tehran, 1932). For a more detailed discussion, see Ahmad Matin-Daftari, *A'in-e dadresi-ye madani va bazargani* (Civil and Commercial Procedural Law), vol. 1 (Tehran, 1945); vol. 2 (Tehran, 1955). See also Moham-

mad Ali Hedayati, *A'in-e dadresi-ye keyfari* (Criminal Procedural Law) (Tehran: Tehran University, 1953). For an early discussion of the question of procedural laws from an Islamic point of view, see Aqa Sheykh Mohammad Sangelaji, *A'in-e dadresi dar eslam* (Procedural Law in Islam) (Tehran: Tehran University, 1950).

48. For a general study of the relation between the ulema and the state in early Pahlavi Iran, see Shahrough Akhavi, *Religion and Politics in Contemporary Iran: Clergy–State Relations in the Pahlavi Period* (Albany, NY: State University of New York Press, 1980).

Chapter 5. The Constitutional Revolution, Popular Politics, and State-Building in Iran

1. For a discussion of the forces shaping Western scholarship on modern Iran see Stephanie Cronin, 'Writing the History of Modern Iran: A Comment on Approaches and Sources', *Iran (Journal of the British Institute of Persian Studies)* 36 (1998), pp. 175–84.
2. See Stephanie Cronin (ed.), 'Introduction', *The Making of Modern Iran: State and Society under Reza Shah, 1921–1941* (London: RoutledgeCurzon, 2003); Homa Katouzian, *State and Society in Iran: The Eclipse of the Qajars and the Emergence of the Pahlavis* (London and New York: I.B.Tauris, 2000); Homa Katouzian, *Iranian History and Politics: The Dialectic of State and Society* (London: RoutledgeCurzon, 2003).
3. Stephanie Cronin, *The Army and the Creation of the Pahlavi State in Iran 1910–1925* (London: I.B.Tauris, 1997). For the First World War in Iran see Touraj Atabaki (ed.), *Iran and the First World War: A Battleground of the Great Powers* (London: I.B.Tauris, 2007); Oliver Bast (ed.), *La Perse et La Grande Guerre* (Tehran: Institut Français de Recherche en Iran, 2002).
4. Although scholarly attention has focused primarily on the state and the high politics of the Tehran elite, recently work has appeared which aims at shifting the spotlight downwards, towards the politics of 'subaltern' groups in Iran. See, for example, Vanessa Martin, *The Qajar Pact: Bargaining, Protest and the State in Nineteenth-Century Persia* (London: I.B.Tauris, 2005).
5. This era tended to produce, in Turkey and China as well as across the Middle East, including in Iran, not multi-party democracies but prolonged periods of disintegration followed by authoritarian modernizing regimes, whether of left or right. See Charles Kurzman's contribution in this volume.
6. See Janet Afary, *The Iranian Constitutional Revolution, 1906–1911: Grassroots Democracy, Social Democracy, and the Origins of Feminism* (New York: Columbia University Press, 1996); Cosroe Chaqueri, *The Russo-Caucasian Origins of the Iranian Left: Social-Democracy in Modern Iran* (Richmond, Surrey: Curzon, 2001); Stephanie Cronin (ed.), *Reformers and Revolutionaries in Modern Iran: New Perspectives on the Iranian Left* (London: Routledge, 2004).
7. The phrase was coined by Nikki Keddie. See N. R. Keddie, 'The Origins of the Religious-Radical Alliance in Iran', in N. R. Keddie, *Iran: Religion, Politics and Society* (London: Cass, 1980), pp. 53–65.
8. Nikki Keddie, *Religion and Rebellion in Iran: the Tobacco Protest of 1891–2*

(London: Cass, 1966).
9. Afary, *The Iranian Constitutional Revolution*, p. 55. For the tradition of sanctuary, see *Encyclopaedia Iranica*, s.v. 'Bast'; Abbas Khalesi, *Tarikhcheh-ye bast va bastneshini* (Tehran: 'Elmi, 1987).
10. For a discussion of these consequences see Cronin (ed.), *The Making of Modern Iran*, p. 6.
11. Stephanie Cronin, 'Importing Modernity: Foreign Military Missions to Qajar Iran', *Comparative Studies in Society and History* 50/1 (2008), pp. 197–226.
12. For the hostile popular response to this measure see Stephanie Cronin, 'Conscription and Popular Resistance in Iran (1925–1941)', in Erik Jan Zürcher (ed.), *Arming the State: Military Conscription in the Middle East and Central Asia 1775–1925* (London: I.B.Tauris, 1999), pp. 145–67.
13. Afary, *The Iranian Constitutional Revolution*, pp. 167–72.
14. See Martin, *The Qajar Pact*, pp. 183–91. The framing of protest in this way may be traced into the 1920s and beyond. See, for example, Stephanie Cronin, 'Resisting the New State: Peasants and Pastoralists in Iran, 1921–1941', *Journal of Peasant Studies* 32/1 (2005), pp. 1–47. For a discussion of the persistence of subaltern notions of natural justice see Stephanie Cronin (ed.), 'Introduction', *Subalterns and Social Protest: History from Below in the Middle East and North Africa* (Routledge: London 2007), pp. 3–4.
15. See Stephanie Cronin, 'Modernity, Change and Dictatorship in Iran: the New Order and Its Opponents', *Middle Eastern Studies* 39/2 (2003), pp. 1–36.
16. The modern study of the political 'crowd' was pioneered by social historians such as George Rude and E. P. Thompson and has since generated much debate and a considerable literature, particularly relating to the history of early modern and modern Europe. See, for example, George Rude, *The Crowd in History: A Study of Popular Disturbances in France and England* (New York: Wiley, 1964); George Rude, *Paris and London in the Eighteenth Century: Studies in Popular Protest* (London: Fontana, 1974); and E. P. Thompson, 'The Moral Economy of the English Crowd in the Eighteenth Century', *Customs in Common* (London: Merlin, 1991). For a recent discussion of the literature see the introduction in Tim Harris (ed.), *The Politics of the Excluded, c 1500–1850* (Basingstoke: Palgrave, 2001). The concepts developed by Rude et al. were quickly taken up and applied to Iran. See Ervand Abrahamian, 'The Crowd in the Persian Revolution', *Iranian Studies* 2/4 (1969), pp. 128–50; Stephen L. McFarland, 'Anatomy of an Iranian Political Crowd: The Tehran Bread Riot of December 1942', *International Journal of Middle East Studies* 17/1 (1985), pp. 51–65; Stephanie Cronin, 'Popular Protest, Disorder and Riot in Iran: The Tehran Crowd and the Rise of Riza Khan, 1921–1925', *International Review of Social History* 50/2 (2005), pp. 167–201; and Martin, *The Qajar Pact*. For a discussion of the Middle Eastern crowd, see Cronin (ed.), 'Introduction', *Subalterns and Social Protest*, pp. 5–8.
17. Donald Quataert has pointed out the 'everyday' character of popular protest in similar conditions in the Ottoman Empire. See his 'Rural Unrest in the Ottoman Empire', in Farhad Kazemi and John Waterbury (eds.), *Peasants and Politics in the Modern Middle East* (Miami: Florida International University Press, 1991), p. 40.

18. In Iran, as elsewhere, there were, of course, many different types of urban crowd, sometimes 'radical', sometimes 'conservative', often defying such ready categorizations. Crowds varied in both their social composition and their political objectives, and might be mobilized by opposing leaderships. For a discussion of the 'constitutional' and the 'conservative' crowd during the Constitutional Revolution, see Abrahamian, 'The Crowd in the Persian Revolution'. For an analysis of the complexity of the Tehran crowd during the early Pahlavi period, see Cronin, 'Popular Protest'.
19. For examples of petitions from merchants and guilds, see *Asnadi az anjomanha-ye baladi, tojjar va asnaf*, 2 volumes (Tehran: Sazeman-e Chap va Entesharat-e Vezarat-e Farhang va Ershad-e Eslami, 2001).
20. Vanessa Martin, 'Constitutional Revolution: Events', *Encyclopaedia Iranica*, pp. 176–87.
21. See Cronin, 'Popular Protest', p. 173.
22. Cronin, 'Popular Protest'. See also Vanessa Martin, 'Mudarris, republicanism and the rise to power of Reza Khan, Sardar-e Sipah', Cronin (ed.), *The Making of Modern Iran*, pp. 65–77.
23. See Cronin, 'Modernity, Change and Dictatorship'; Houchang Chehabi, 'Dress Codes for Men in Turkey and Iran', Touraj Atabaki and Erik Zürcher (eds.), *Men of Order: Authoritarian Modernization under Atatürk and Reza Shah* (London: I.B.Tauris, 2004), pp. 222–23; and Bianca Devos, *Kleidungspolitik in Iran: Die Durchsetzung der Kleidungsvorschriften für Männer unter Rizā Šāh* (Würzburg: Ergon Verlag, 2006).
24. Consul-General Daly to Knatchbull-Hugessen, 15 July, 1935, FO371/18994/E4871/4338/34.
25. Mansoureh Ettehadieh Nezam-Mafi, 'The Council for the Investigation of Grievances: A Case Study of Nineteenth Century Iranian Social History', *Iranian Studies* 22/1 (1989), pp. 51–61; and *Encyclopaedia Iranica*, s.v. 'Constitutional Revolution: Intellectual Background'.
26. See Cronin, *The Army and the Creation of the Pahlavi State*, p. 76; Katouzian, *State and Society in Iran*, pp. 121–63.
27. Cronin, 'Popular Protest'.
28. On elections in the Reza Shah period see *Asnadi az entekhabat-e majles-e shura-ye melli dar dowreh-ye Pahlavi-ye avval* (Tehran: Edareh-ye Koll-e Arshiv, Asnad va Muzeh-ye Daftar-e Ra'is-e Jomhur, 1378).
29. For a valuable discussion of the problems of security, especially in the rural areas, faced by the constitutional authorities, and the solutions they proposed, see Vanessa Martin and Morteza Nouraei, 'The Role of the *Karguzar* in the Foreign Relations of State and Society of Iran from the mid-nineteenth century to 1921: Part II: The *Karguzar* and Security, the Trade Routes of Iran and Foreign Subjects 1900–1921', *Journal of the Royal Asiatic Society*, Third Series, 16/1 (2006), pp. 29–41.
30. See Jean Calmard, 'Les réformes militaires sous les Qâjâr (1794–1925)', in Yann Richard (ed.), *Entre l'Iran et l'Occident* (Paris: Editions de la Maison des Sciences de l'Homme, 1989), pp. 17–42; Yann Richard, 'La fondation d'une armée

nationale en Iran', in Yann Richard (ed.), *Entre l'Iran et l'Occident*, pp. 43–60.
31. Cronin, 'Importing Modernity', pp. 197–98.
32. Ibid., p. 201.
33. For the early history of the Cossack Brigade see Firouz Kazemzadeh, 'The Origin and Early Development of the Persian Cossack Brigade', *American Slavic and East European Review* 15/3 (1956), pp. 351–63. This article is based on the memoirs of the first and fifth commandants of the brigade, Lieutenant Colonel Domantovich and Colonel Kossagovsky. The memoirs of Kossagovsky have been translated from Russian into Persian and published under the title *Khaterat-e Kolonel Kasakufski*, trans. by Abbas Qoli Jali (Tehran: Chapkhaneh-ye Kaviyan, 1965). See also Cronin, *The Army and the Creation of the Pahlavi State*; Reza Ra'iss Tousi, 'The Persian Army, 1880–1907', *Middle Eastern Studies* 24/2 (1988), pp. 206–29; Lt.-Col. H. P. Picot, *Report on the Organization of the Persian Army*, Durand to Salisbury, 18 January, 1900, FO881/7364.
34. Ahmad Amir Ahmadi, *Khaterat-e nakhostin sepahbod-e Iran*, vol. 1 (Tehran: Mo'asseseh-ye Pazhuhesh va Motale'at-e Farhangi, 1994), p. 47.
35. Colonel Douglas to Spring-Rice, 17 July, 1907, FO371/311/26050.
36. Military Report on Persia, 1911, compiled by the General Staff, Army Headquarters, India. IOL/Mil/17//15/5.
37. Ibid.
38. Khodayar Khodayari, later, major general in Reza Shah's army. For biographical details see Cronin, *The Army and the Creation of the Pahlavi State*, pp. 240–41.
39. Stephanie Cronin, 'Britain, the Iranian Military and the Rise of Reza Khan', in Vanessa Martin (ed.), *Anglo-Iranian Relations since 1800* (London: Routledge, 2005), pp. 99–127.
40. For a discussion of Sweden's motivation and role as a supplier of military advisers to foreign governments, including Iran, see Nils Palmstierna, 'Swedish Army Officers in Africa and Asia', *Revue Internationale d'Histoire Militaire*, 26 (1967), pp. 45–73.
41. For the Swedish officers see Markus Ineichen, *Die schwedischen Offiziere in Persien (1911–1916): Friedensengel, Weltgendarmen oder Handelsagenten einer Kleinmacht im ausgehenden Zeitalter des Imperialismus?* (Bern: Peter Lang, 2002). Two of the Swedish officers with the force have left memoirs. P. Nyström, *Fem Ar i Persien som Gendarmofficer* (Stockholm: n.p., 1925); Hjalmar Pravitz, *Frau Persien i Stiltje och Storm* (Stockholm: Karskrona Tryckort, 1918).
42. For the Government Gendarmerie see Cronin, *The Army*; Lt.-Col. Parviz Afsar, *Tarikh-e zhandarmeri-ye Iran* (Qom: n.p., 1953); Jahangir Qa'em Maqami, *Tarikh-e zhandarmeri-ye Iran* (Tehran: n.p., 1956); S.-Å. Persson, 'The Swedish Gendarmerie in Persia', in Andreas Ådahl (ed.), *Iran through the Ages: A Swedish Anthology* (Stockholm: A. B. P. A. Norstedt & Söner, 1972), pp. 129–36.
43. See Hassan Arfa, *Under Five Shahs* (London: John Murray, 1964), pp. 51–52.
44. See Paul Luft, 'The End of Czarist Rule in Iran', in Charles Melville (ed.), *History and Literature in Iran: Persian and Islamic Studies in Honour of P.W. Avery* (London: British Academic Press, Cambridge University, 1990), pp. 99–114.
45. See Cronin, *The Making of Modern Iran*, pp. 8–9, 157–210; Stephanie Cronin,

Tribal Politics in Iran: Rural Conflict and the New State, 1921–1941 (London: RoutledgeCurzon, 2006), pp. 16–17.

Chapter 6. Municipalities and Constitutionalism in Iran

1. Samuel P. Huntington, *Political Order in Changing Societies* (New Haven: Yale University Press, 1968), p. 266.
2. For examples, refer to *Vaqaye'-e Ettefaqiyeh* no. 315 (11 February 1957), p. 2; no. 322 (1 April 1857), p. 3; no. 336 (9 July 1857), p. 2.
3. Ibid.
4. *Vaqaye'-e Ettefaqiyeh* no. 244 (21 September 1856), pp. 1–2.
5. Mansureh Ettehadieh, *Inja Tehran ast: Majmu'eh-ye maqalati darbareh-ye Tehran 1269–1344 H.Q.* (Tehran: Nashr-e Tarikh-e Iran, 1998), p. 142.
6. Ali Akbar Dehkhoda, *Loghatnameh*, vol. 1 (Tehran: University Press, 1994), p. 898. See also Willem Floor, 'The office of *muhtasib* in Iran', *Iranian Studies* 18 (1985), pp. 53–74.
7. Ettehadieh, *Inja Tehran ast*, p. 144.
8. Ibid, p. 145.
9. Ibid.
10. Ibid, p. 151.
11. Mohammad Hoseyn, E'temad al-Saltaneh, *Ruznameh-ye khaterat*, Iraj Afshar (ed.) (Tehran: Amir Kabir, 1990), p. 128.
12. Ibid, p. 160.
13. Ibid, p. 575.
14. *Arshiv-e Sazman-e Asnad va Ketabkhaneh-ye Melli-ye Jomhuri-ye Eslami-ye Iran*, no. 69601300.
15. E'temad al-Saltaneh, *Ruznameh-ye khaterat*, p. 671.
16. Ibid.
17. Gholam Hoseyn Mirza Saleh (ed.), *Mozakerat-e Majles-e Avval* (Tehran: Maziyar, 2005). Session dated Sunday, 23 December 1906, p. 78.
18. Ibid.
19. *Arshiv-e Sazman-e Asnad*, no. 240026804, p. 1.
20. *Mozakerat-e Majles-e Avval*, Sunday, 17 February 1907, p. 140.
21. Ibid.
22. *Arshiv-e Sazman-e Asnad*, no. 240026804, p. 2.
23. Ibid, pp. 3–4.
24. Ibid.
25. *Mozakerat-e Majles-e Avval*, Sunday, 12 December 1907, p. 78.
26. Haj Seyyed Nasrollah Taqavi said in response to Aqa Sayyed Hoseyn: 'The regulations of the municipality have nothing to do with this matter. Those are the regulations of the provincial councils and have been written.' *Mozakerat*, Tuesday, 19 March 1907, p. 175.
27. *Ruznameh-ye Anjoman-e Moqaddas-e Melli-ye Isfahan [Newspaper of the Sacred Isfahan National Council]* Year 1, no. 20 (Sunday, 19 May 1907), p. 7.
28. Ibid., Year 1, no. 21 (Sunday, 25 May 1907), p. 6.
29. *Mozakerat* (Sunday, 17 February 1907), p. 140.

30. *Arshiv*, no. 240036804, p. 3.
31. Ibid., p. 10.
32. Ibid., p. 18.
33. Ibid., p. 20.
34. *Ruznameh-ye Anjoman-e Tabriz*, no. 147 (Monday, 28 Sha'ban 1325/6 October 1907), p. 2.
35. Ibid.
36. Ibid., p. 3.
37. Ibid., no. 106 (Tuesday, 1 July 1907), pp. 1–2.
38. Ibid., no. 146 (Sunday, 5 October 1907), p. 3.
39. *Ruznameh-ye Anjoman-e Moqaddas-e Melli-ye Isfahan*, Year 2, no. 15 (Saturday, 29 March 1908), p. 8.
40. *Arshiv*, no. 119/31/3–240.
41. Ibid., no. 29703507.
42. Ibid., no. 12/5591/1–290.
43. Ibid., no. 24002712–3.
44. Ibid.
45. Ibid., no. 240026804, 12.
46. *Mozakerat* (Thursday, 27 February 1908), p. 605.
47. Ibid. (Thursday, 2 Safar 1326/6 March 1908), p. 613.
48. *Ruznameh-ye Anjoman-e Moqaddas-e Melli-ye Isfahan*, Year 2, no. 16 (Monday, 14 April 1908), p. 3.
49. *Arshiv*, no. 119/31/1–240.
50. *Mozakerat-e Dowreh-ye Dovvom-e Taqniniyeh [Proceedings from the Second Legislature]*. Session 46, Saturday, 1 February 1910.
51. Ibid.
52. Ibid.
53. *Arshiv*, no. 45/34/1–293.
54. *Arshiv*, no. 29800669.
55. *Arshiv*, no. 19/13/1–293.
56. *Arshiv*, no. 240014543.
57. *Arshiv*, no. 240003758.
58. *Arshiv*, no. 240005098.
59. *Arshiv*, no. 24500844.
60. Ibid.
61. *Arshiv*, no. 240004958.
62. Reza Mokhtari Esfahani (ed.), *Asnadi az anjomanha-ye baladi: tojjar va asnaf (1300–1320 H. Sh.)*, vol. 1 (Tehran: Ministry of Islamic Guidance Publications, 2001), p. 1.
63. Ibid., vol. 2, p. 865.
64. Ibid., vol. 2, pp. 866–68.
65. Ibid., vol. 2, p. 869.
66. Ibid., vol. 2, p. 868.

Chapter 7. Merchants, Their Class Identification Process, and Constitutionalism

1. See Ahmad Ashraf, 'Marateb-e ejtema'i dar dowran-e Qajar', *Ketab Agah* (Tehran: Agah, 1981), p. 78; Charles Issawi, *Tarikh-e eqtesadi-ye Iran*, translated by Y. Azhand, (Tehran: Gostareh, 1983), p. 62.
2. Karl Marx, *The Poverty of Philosophy* (Chicago: C. H. Kerr, 1920), pp. 188–89, as quoted in Ervand Abrahamian, *Iran Between Two Revolutions* (Princeton: Princeton University Press, 1983), p. 33; Goran Therborn, 'The Rise of Social Scientific Marxism and the Problems of Class Analysis', in S. N. Eisenstadt and H. J. Helle (eds.), *Micro Sociological Theory*, vol. 1 (London: Sage, 1989).
3. Soheila Torabi Farsani, *Tojjar, mashrutiyat va dowlat-e modern* (Tehran: Nashr-e Tarikh-e Iran, 2005), pp. 69–83.
4. Soheila Torabi Farsani, 'Rahkarha-ye tojjar dar ruyaru'i ba sarmayehha-ye biganeh pish az enqelab-e mashruteh', *Farhang-e Esfahan* 22 (Winter 2001–2), pp. 52–61.
5. From Haj Ali Akbar Sarraf to Haj Lotf-Ali, 13 December 1894/14 Jumada II 1312 (Ettehadieh Archives); from Haj Ali Akbar Sarraf to Haj Lotf-Ali, 1 November 1898/27 Jumada II 1316, no. 11. (Ettehadiyeh Archives).
6. Mansureh Ettehadieh, 'Masa'el-e sarrafi az khelal-e sotur-e namehha-ye yek sarraf', in *Yadnameh-ye Ebrahim-e Fakhra'i* (Tehran: Talayeh, 1989), pp. 329-30.
7. From Haj Ali Akbar Sarraf to Haj Lotf-Ali, 12 May 1895/17 Dhu l'Qa'da 1312, no. 294 (Ettehadieh Archives).
8. *Sarf* or 'conversion' is the word from which the term *sarraf* is derived; it is the interest which *sarraf*s added to the amount of money they lent to merchants. The expression used for the rate of interest was *sarf-e qeran*, which can be literally translated as 'the conversion rate of qeran'. The *sarf-e qeran* was an issue over which *sarraf*s and merchants were in frequent dispute. At the point mentioned here the merchants tried to use the clerics to have it lowered and the *sarraf*s, on the other hand, were making efforts to either raise it or at least keep it at the going rate.
9. From Haj Ali Akbar Sarraf to Haj Lotf-Ali, 21 September 1898/5 Jumada I 1316, no. 13 (Ettehadieh Archives).
10. From Haj Ali Akbar Sarraf to Haj Lotf Ali, 10 January 1895/13 Rajab 1312, no. 261 (Ettehadieh Archives). (Gambling and anything that might have any resemblance to it is strictly forbidden by Islamic law, and thus merchants tried to persuade the religious authorities that *sarraf*s were conducting their transactions in an irreligious manner.)
11. Ibid.
12. From Haj Ali Akbar Sarraf to Haj Lotf-Ali, n.d., (Ettehadieh Archives).
13. From Haj Ali Akbar Sarraf to Haj Lotf-Ali, 5 October 1898/19 Jumada I 1316, no. 17 (Ettehadieh Archives).
14. Nazem al-Eslam Kermani, *Tarikh-e bidari-ye iraniyan*, ed. Ali Akbar Sa'idi Sirjani, vol. 1 (Tehran: Agah, 1983), p. 600.
15. Zahra Shaji'i, *Namayandegan-e Majles-e Showra-ye Melli dar bist-o-yek dowreh-ye taqniniyeh* (Tehran: Mo'asseseh-ye Motale'at va Tahqiqat-e Ejtema'i, 1965), p. 18.

16. *Khaterat-e Vahid*, no. 31, pp. 11 and 14; *Habl al-Matin*, vol. 7 (5 August 1909), p. 13.
17. Habl al-Matin, vol. 15, no. 5 (9 September 1907), pp. 20–21; vol. 15, no.19, pp. 20–22.
18. *Mozakerat-e Majles dar dowreh-ye avval-e taqniniyeh*, 4 November 1906/17 Ramadan 1324–22 July 1908/ 22 Jumada II 1326) (Tehran: Entesharat-e Majles, 1973), p. 537.
19. Ibid., 18 April 1907/5 Rabi' I 1325, p. 499; 20 and 22 April 1907/7 and 9 Rabi' I 1325, p. 505; 14 April 1908/12 Rabi' I 1326, p. 507; 16 April 1908/14 Rabi' I 1326, p. 509; 18 April 1908/16 Rabi' I 1326, p. 512.
20. *Neda-ye Vatan* no. 31 (28 April 1907/15 Rabi' II 1325), p. 5.
21. *Mozakerat-e Majles-e Avval*, 6 January 1908/2 Dhu l-Hajja 1325, p. 51.
22. *Habl al-Matin*, vol. 13, no. 26 (23 February1906), p. 17.
23. *Habl al-Matin*, vol. 15, no. 26 (20 January 1908), p. 9.
24. Ibid., vol. 14, no. 43 (24 June 1907), pp. 18–19; 'Maktub-e Eslambol', ibid., vol. 14, no. 46 (15 July 1907), pp. 21–22.
25. *Habl al-Matin* (Tehran) no. 145 (30 July 1907/19 Jumada II 1325), p. 3.
26. 'Resaleh-ye selseleh-ye tojjar-e Esfahan', quoted by Musa Najafi, *Motun, mabani va takvin-e andisheh-ye tahrim dar tarikh-e siyasi-ye Iran* (Mashhad: Bonyad-e Pazhuheshha-ye Eslami-ye Astan-e Qods-e Razavi, 1993), pp. 135–36.
27. Ahmad Ashraf, *Mavane'-e tarikhi-ye roshd-e sarmayehdari dar Iran* (Tehran: Zamineh, 1980), p. 102.
28. *Mozakerat-e Majles-e Avval*, 6 January 1908/2 Dhu l'Hajja 1325, pp. 50–52; 25 and 27 January 1908/21 and 23 Dhu l-Hajja 1325, pp. 77–79.
29. Ibid., 5 and 7 November 1906/18 and 20 Ramadan 1324, pp. 10–13; 29 and 30 October 1907/22 and 23 Ramadan 1325, p. 462.
30. Ibid., 10, 14, and 16 November 1906/23, 27 and 29 Ramadan 1324, pp. 3, 5, 7, 12, 15, and 6 December 1906/19 Shawwal 1324, pp. 10–18.
31. Ibid., 13 November 1907/7 Shawwal 1325, p. 382.
32. *Jarideh-ye Melli-e Anjoman-e Tabriz* no. 26 (5 January 1907/20 Dhu l-Qa'da 1324), pp. 1–2.
33. Mehdi Qoli Hedayat (Mokhber al-Saltaneh), *Khaterat va khatarat* (Tehran: Zavvar, 1982), pp. 166–67.
34. *Habl al-Matin*, vol. 15, no. 33 (16 March 1908), p. 16.
35. *Encyclopaedia Iranica*, s.v. 'Classes in the Qajar period', p. 670.
36. Vanessa Martin, *Islam and Modernism: The Iranian Revolution of 1906* (London: I.B.Tauris), pp. 40, 55.
37. *Sur-e Esrafil* no. 25 (13 March 1908/9 Safar 1326), p. 8.
38. *Habl al-Matin* (Tehran), vol. 1, no. 155 (7 November 1907/1 Shawwal 1325), p. 4.
39. Yahya Dowlatabadi, *Hayat-e Yahya*, vol. 2 (Tehran: Ferdowsi, 1992), pp. 192–93.
40. Ehtesham al-Saltaneh, *Khaterat*, ed. Seyyed Mohammad Mahdi Musavi (Tehran: Zavvar, 1988), pp. 601–05.
41. *Rahnama* no. 19 (22 February 1908), pp. 2–3.
42. *Ruznameh-ye Majles* no. 170 (2 September 1907), pp. 1–3.

43. Dowlatabadi, *Hayat-e Yahya*, vol. 2, p. 217.
44. A list of those who attempted to bring down the Atabak's government is given in Dossier Gh-516, (Markaz-e Asnad-e Bonyad-e Mostaz'afan).
45. Dowlatabadi, *Hayat-e Yahya*, vol. 2, pp. 136–38.
46. *Ruznameh-ye Majles* no. 170 (2 September 1907), pp. 1–3.
47. *Ruh al-Qodos* no. 6 (16 September 1907/8 Sha'ban 1325), p. 3.
48. *Habl al-Matin* (Tehran) no. 105 (1 September 1907), p. 23.
49. *Habl al-Matin*, vol. 15, no. 27 (27 June 1908), pp. 19–24. See also Martin, *Islam and Modernism*, pp. 145–48 for an account of these events.
50. *Ruznameh-e Anjoman-e Tabriz* no. 108 (26 Jumada I 1325), p. 3.
51. Hashem Mohit Mafi, *Tarikh-e enqelab-e Iran ya moqaddamat-e mashrutiyat*, ed. Majid Tafreshi and Javad Janfada (Tehran: Ferdowsi, 1984), p. 213.
52. Dowlatabadi, *Hayat-e Yahya*, vol. 2, pp. 301–03.
53. Ibid., pp. 318–19.
54. *Habl al-Matin* (Tehran), vol. 1, no. 145 (11 Ramadan 1325), p. 4.
55. *Ettehadiyeh-ye* Tojjar Documents (Amin al-Zarb Archives). For more information see Soheila Torabi Farsani, 'Hey'at-e Ettehadiyeh-ye Tojjar', *Majalleh-ye Goruh-e Tarikh* (Tehran University) 2/1 (1380/2001), pp. 293–317.

Chapter 8. Tribes of the Homeland: The Bakhtiyari in the Revolutionary Press

1. *The Encyclopedia of Islam*, new edition, s.v. 'Ilat'.
2. *Habl al-Matin* (Calcutta), 5 July 1909, year 7, number 1.
3. *Habl al-Matin* (Calcutta), 13 September 1909, year 7, number 10. '*Mellat-e azad kard jonbesh-e kh"ish ashkar/hami-ye mellat resid ba sepah-e Bakhtiyar.*' Translation: 'The nation rebelled/the protectors of the nation arrived with the cavalries of the Bakhtiyar.'
4. See Edward G. Browne, *The Persian Revolution, 1905–1909* (Cambridge: Cambridge University Press, 1910), p. 266. This emphasis on the Bakhtiyaris' devotion to the nationalist cause can also be found in the following works: Ali Qoli Khan Sardar As'ad and 'Abd al-Hoseyn Lesan al-Saltaneh Sepehr, *Tarikh-e Bakhtiyari*, ed. Jamshid Kiyanfar (Tehran: Asatir, 1997); Nurollah Daneshvar 'Alavi, *Tarikh-e Iran va jonbesh-e vatan parastan-e Esfahan va Bakhtiyari* (Tehran: Anzan, 1998); Mahdi Malekzadeh, *Tarikh-e enqelab-e mashrutiyat-e Iran*, 7 vols. (Tehran: 'Elmi, 1984); and Esfandiyar Ahanjedeh, *Bakhtiyari va mashruteh* (Arak: Zarrehbin, 1995). For first-person accounts by Bakhtiyaris on the Constitutional Revolution, see Eskandar Khan 'Akkasheh, *Tarikh-e Il-e Bakhtiyari*, ed. Farid Moradi (Tehran: Farhangsara, 1986); and Bibi Maryam Bakhtiyari, *Khaterat-e Sardar Maryam*, ed. Gholam Hoseyn Nowruzi Bakhtiyari (Tehran: Anzan, 2003).
5. Iraj Afshar, *Mobarezeh ba Mohammad Ali Shah* (Tehran: Tus, 1980), documents 31, 74.
6. David Fraser, *Persia and Turkey in Revolt* (Edinburgh: W. Blackwood, 1910), p. 88. This alarmist perspective on the Bakhtiyaris' emergence in the revolution can be read in the correspondence of Grahame, the British consul at Isfahan, for which see the correspondence from the city of Isfahan in the series FO 248/965.

In similar language, Morgan Shuster noted that the Bakhtiyari tribesmen in Tehran aimed to plunder the treasury, wreaked havoc, and were among the forces that brought about the demise of the constitutional movement in Iran. See Shuster, *The Strangling of Persia* (New York: Century, 1912). This view of tribalism as a source of 'chaos', disorder, and warlordism in national politics during the constitutional period is prevalent in more recent studies as well. In *The Turban for the Crown: The Islamic Revolution in Iran* (Oxford: Oxford University Press, 1988), Saïd Amir Arjomand highlights 'the rebellion of the tribes *against* the constitution' and attributes the Bakhtiyaris' support for *mashrutiyat* to the convictions of Sardar As'ad; see Arjomand, *The Turban for the Crown*, pp. 48–57.

7. Fraser, *Persia and Turkey in Revolt*, p. 200.
8. Noting that the Constitutional Revolution coincided with the exploration for oil at Masjed-e Soleyman, Abo'l Fath Ozhan, a Bakhtiyari historian, speculates that the ruling khans' acceptance of a 3-per-cent instead of a 10-per-cent share of the D'Arcy Oil Company was based on the British promise that they would back the tribe in the revolution. But this seems improbable, as Ozhan does not provide a source, instead basing his hunch on the coincidence of the discovery of oil at Masjed-e Soleyman in April 1908 and the Bakhtiyari's emergence in the revolution in January 1909. See Ozhan, *Tarikh-e Bakhtiyari* (Tehran: Vahid, 1966), p. 176. For a similarly unfounded view of the Bakhtiyari as the proxies of the British in the Constitutional Revolution, see Mehdi Bamdad, *Sharh-e hal-e rejal-e Iran dar qarn-e davazdah, sizdah, chahardah-e hejri*, vol. 2 (Tehran: Zavvar, 1978), p. 451. What is certain is that in 1908, after oil was struck at Masjed-e Soleyman, Sardar As'ad met with Charles Hardinge, the British Undersecretary for Foreign Affairs; Henry Lynch, the financier of the Bakhtiyari or Lynch Road; and members of the Persia Committee in London. Discussions centred on the Bakhtiyari oil fields but certainly touched upon political events and the Constitutional Revolution as well. Sardar As'ad promised personally to visit the oil fields when he returned to Iran and to see to it that the tribes did not threaten British engineers and company workers. He sought the removal of D. L. R. Lorimer, the unpopular and strict British consul at Ahvaz, and the Bengal Lancers that had been brought in to protect the oil company in 1907. There was also 'conversation about other matters', perhaps the Constitutional Revolution, though it remains unclear what, if any, assurances the Bakhtiyari received. This is certainly not the same as actually encouraging the Bakhtiyari's participation in the revolution, as Ozhan and Bamdad imply. Indeed, there still remained tensions over oil exploration and the Lynch Road that complicated relations between the Bakhtiyari tribes and the British Empire. See FO 248/923, 'Visit of the Bakhtiyari Khans to London and Conversation with Sir C. Hardinge', Louis Mallet to C. M. Marling, 6 July 1908. For literature in English on the British influence on the Bakhtiyari during the constitutional period, see Firuz Kazemzadeh, *Russia and Britain in Persia: A Study in Imperialism* (New Haven: Yale University Press, 1968), and Ira Klein, 'British Intervention in the Persian Revolution, 1905–1909', *The Historical Journal* 15/4 (December 1972), pp. 731–52. For a study of Bakhtiyari connections to the liberal Persia Commit-

tee in London, see Mansour Bonakdarian, 'Iranian Constitutional Exiles and British Foreign-Policy Dissenters, 1908–1909', *International Journal of Middle East Studies* 27/2 (May 1995), pp. 175–91.

9. Gene Garthwaite, *Khans and Shahs: A Documentary Analysis of the Bakhtiyari in Iran* (Cambridge: Cambridge University Press, 1983), pp. 112–25.
10. Mirza Mohammad Taqi Lesan al-Molk Sepehr, *Nasekh al-tavarikh*, ed. Jamshid Kiyanfar (Tehran: Asatir, 1998); Reza Qoli Khan Hedayat, *Rowzat al-safa-ye Naseri*, ed. Jamshid Kiyanfar (Tehran: Entesherat-e Asatir, 2001); Mirza Abo l-Hasan Sani' al-Molk Ghaffari, *Ruznameh-ye dowlat-e 'alliyeh-ye Iran* (Tehran: Ketabkhaneh-ye Melli-ye Iran, 1991); Government of Iran, *Ruznameh-ye Vaqaye'-e ettefaqiyeh* (Tehran: Ketabkhaneh-ye Melli-ye Iran, 1994); Mohammad Hasan Khan E'temad al-Saltaneh, *Mer'at al-boldan*, ed. 'Abd al-Hoseyn Nava'i (Tehran: Daneshgah-e Tehran, 1988).
11. *Habl al-Matin* (Tehran) 28 December 1908, year 16, number 24.
12. On Sattar Khan, see Anja Pistor-Hatam's chapter in this volume.
13. Sardar As'ad and Sepehr, *Tarikh-e Bakhtiyari*, p. 448.
14. *Habl al-Matin* (Tehran), 7 June 1909, year 16, number 45. 'Zendeh bad Haji 'Ali Qoli Khan / Payandeh bad hemmat-e mardan / Sar afraz bad mellat-e Iran'.
15. *Habl al-Matin* (Calcutta), 26 July 1909, year 7, no. 4. 'Zendeh bad Samsam al-Saltaneh va Sattar Khan, boland konandeh-ye nam-e nik-e Iran'.
16. Following the death of Esfandiyar Khan in 1903, various Bakhtiyari khans vied for control over the tribes. The promise of oil revenues following the Bakhtiyari Oil Agreement (1905) also raised the stakes of the competition between the khans. Among the khans vying for power and prestige was Najaf Qoli Khan Samsam al-Saltaneh, who rose to the *ilkhan*ship based on his reputation as traditional Lur leader and because of his bravery in raids and forays. Perhaps the most influential of the khans, however, was the *ilkhan*'s half-brother Ali Qoli Khan, who established himself as the tribes' man of letters, learning European languages and opening a tribal school in the mountains. In 1879, he had made the pilgrimage to Mecca, becoming Haji Ali Qoli Khan, and in 1900, he travelled to various European cities via India and Egypt, returning to Iran after residing in Europe for two years. During the reign of Mozaffar al-Din Shah (r. 1896–1907), Haji Ali Qoli Khan acquired the title of Sardar As'ad (Fortunate Commander). In late 1906, however, just before the coronation of Mohammad Ali Shah, who favoured Lotf Ali Khan Amir Mofakhkham, Sardar As'ad again left for Europe, to seek treatment for his failing eyesight. With the accession of Mohammad Ali Shah to the throne, Lotf Ali Khan Amir Mofakhkham (formerly Shoja' al-Soltan) of the Haji Ilkhani Bakhtiyari, who had served Mohammad Ali Shah during his days as crown prince and governor of Azarbayjan, was appointed as the head of the royal guard in the capital. Following the coup in 1908 and the subsequent revolt in Tabriz, the Shah ordered Amir Mofakhkham to gather a cavalry of Bakhtiyari horsemen to subdue it. In the autumn of 1908 Amir Mofakhkham sent his younger brother and tribal strongman Naser Khan Sardar Jang to quell the uprising in Tabriz at the head of five hundred Bakhtiyari horsemen.

17. *Jahad-e Akbar* (The Great Striving), Isfahan, Muharram 1327/1909. On Zargham al-Saltaneh and the Bakhtiyari's entry into Isfahan, also see 'Alavi, *Tarikh-e Iran va jonbesh-e vatan parastan-e Esfahan va bakhtiyari*, pp. 39–46.
18. Ibid., p. 49; Ahanjedeh, *Bakhtiyari va mashruteh*, pp. 117–18.
19. Sardar As'ad and Sepehr, *Tarikh-e Bakhtiyari*, p. 456.
20. See *Habl al-Matin* (Tehran) 11 January 1909, year 16, number 25.
21. See *Habl al-Matin* (Tehran), 11 January 1909, year 16, no. 25; *Habl al-Matin* (Tehran), 15 February 1909, year 16, no. 29.
22. *Chehreh Nama* (Cairo), 14 October 1909, year 6, no, 17.
23. Sardar As'ad and Sepehr, *Tarikh-e Bakhtiyari*, pp. 456–57.
24. *Habl al-Matin* (Tehran), 8 February 1909, year 16, no. 28.
25. Malekzadeh, *Tarikh-e enqelab-e mashrutiyat-e Iran*, vol. 6, p. 1090.
26. *Habl al-Matin* (Tehran), 8 February 1909, year 16, no. 28.
27. Ibid.
28. Ibid.
29. *Habl al-Matin* (Tehran), 22 February 1909, year 16, no. 30.
30. Sardar As'ad and Sepehr, *Tarikh-e Bakhtiyari*, p. 192.
31. See for instance the August 1909 edition of *Habl al-Matin*, in which an armed Samsam al-Saltaneh appears on the cover: *Habl al-Matin* (Calcutta), 23 August 1909, year 7, no. 7.
32. On *Farhang* of Isfahan, see Seyyed Farid Qasemi, *Avvalinha-ye matbu'at-e Iran* (Tehran: Nashr-e Abi, 2004), pp. 423–87.
33. These local newsletters can be found at the University of Isfahan Library and Archives. I would like to thank 'Abd al-Mahdi Rajayi, the gifted young scholar of Qajar Isfahan, for generously introducing me to this collection.
34. *Zayandeh Rud*, Isfahan, 1909, year 1, number 5. In Persian, the poem reads: *Sar bararad chon ke Samsam az niyam / Kar-e mellat mishavad tamam. Bakhtiyari asl-e gheyrat zendeh bad / Ta abad salar-e heshmat zendeh bad!*
35. *Kashkul* (Isfahan), Rabi' II 1327/1909, year 2, no. 8. This letter also appeared in *Jahad-e Akbar*.
36. *Kashkul* (Isfahan), Rabi' II 1327/1909, year 2, number 8.
37. Sardar As'ad and Sepehr, *Tarikh-e Bakhtiyari*, p. 182; Edward G. Browne, *The Persian Revolution*, p. 315.
38. Browne, *The Persian Revolution*, pp. 319–21.
39. The significance of the constitutional period in the making of Bakhtiyari history and identity is suggested by the writing of the tribal history *Tarikh-e Bakhtiyari*. This work was written and compiled during the constitutional period under the direction of Sardar As'ad and largely authored by 'Abd al-Hoseyn Lesan al-Saltaneh Sepehr, who completed the manuscript in 1911. It was the first written history of the Bakhtiyari and the first tribal ethnography in the Persian language. *Tarikh-e Bakhtiyari* was in part written to memorialize the tribes' role in the Constitutional Revolution and is invaluable as a Bakhtiyari narrative of *mashrutiyat*, providing a view of the Constitutional Revolution as experienced by one of the most powerful tribes on the peripheries of Iran.
40. On this theme see Peter Sahlins, *Boundaries: The Making of France and Spain in*

the Pyrenees (Berkeley: University of California Press, 1989), pp. 8, 197.
41. On this theme see the classic social histories written by Richard Cobb on revolutionary armies, *sans-culottes*, and ordinary people in the French Revolution. See Cobb, *Les armées révolutionnaires* (Paris: Mouton, 1961–63); *The Police and the People: French Popular Protest, 1789–1820* (Oxford: Oxford University Press, 1970); *Reactions to the French Revolution* (Oxford: Oxford University Press, 1972); and *Paris and Its Provinces, 1792–1802* (Oxford: Oxford University Press, 1975).
42. Haj Sayyah, *Khaterat-e Haj Sayyah va Dowreh-ye Khuf va Vahshat* (Tehran: Ketabkhaneh-ye Ebn-e Sina, 1967), pp. 625–26.
43. Sardar As'ad and Sepehr, *Tarikh-e Bakhtiyari*, p. 596; Garthwaite, *Khans and Shahs*, p. 123; Janet Afary, *The Iranian Constitutional Revolution, 1906–1911: Grassroots Democracy, Social Democracy, and the Origins of Feminism* (New York: Columbia University Press, 1996), pp. 333–34.
44. *Habl al-Matin* (Calcutta), 9 September 1912, no. 9, year 21; also see *Habl al-Matin* (Tehran) 2 June 1913, year 21, no. 2.
45. *Habl al-Matin* (Tehran), 3 May 1914, year 21, no. 40.
46. *Molla Nasreddin*, 12 Rabi' I 1330/1912, no. 8. Janet Afary generously guided me to the image of the Bakhtiyari in this issue of *Molla Nasreddin* and translated the caption as well.
47. Stephanie Cronin has recently explored similar themes in Bakhtiyari history during the Reza Shah period. See Cronin, *Tribal Politics in Iran: Rural Conflict and the New State* (London: Routledge, 2007). Also see Cronin, 'Riza Shah and the Disintegration of Bakhtiyari Power in Iran, 1921–1934', in Stephanie Cronin (ed.) *The Making of Modern Iran: State and Society under Riza Shah, 1921–1941* (London: RoutledgeCurzon, 2003), pp. 241–68.

Chapter 9. Revolution and a High-Ranking Sufi: Zahir al-Dowleh's Contribution to the Constitutional Movement

1. See his 'A Traveller's Narrative', translated by Hamid Algar, in Hamid Algar, *Mirza Malkum Khan: A Biographical Study of Iranian Modernism* (Berkeley: University of California Press, 1973), pp. 278–99.
2. See Mangol Bayat-Philipp, 'Mirza Aqa Khan Kirmani: A Nineteenth Century Persian Nationalist', in Elie Kedourie and Sylvia Haim (eds.), *Towards a Modern Iran: Studies in Thought, Politics, and Society* (London: Frank Cass, 1980), pp. 36–59.
3. For late nineteenth-century intellectuals who were critical of the Sufi tradition, see Lloyd Ridgeon, *Sufi Castigator: Ahmad Kasravi and the Iranian Mystical Tradition* (London: Routledge, 2006), p. 23. An example of the criticism voiced by clerics at the time of the Constitutional Revolution can be found in a treatise written by a mullah named Seyyed 'Abd al-'Azim 'Emad al-'Olama Khalkhali. See Hamid Dabashi, trans., 'On the Meaning of Constitutional Monarchy and its Benefits', in Said Amir Arjomand (ed.), *Authority and Political Culture in Shi'ism* (Albany: State University of New York Press, 1988), pp. 334–70.
4. For Kasravi's opinions of the Sufis, see his *Sufigari*, translated by Ridgeon, *Sufi*

Castigator, pp. 65–119.
5. Ahmad Kasravi, *Tarikh-e mashruteh-ye Iran* (Tehran, 1940–43), a partial translation of which has been published as Ahmad Kasravi, trans. Evan Siegel, *History of the Iranian Constitutional Revolution* (Costa Mesa, CA: Mazda Publishers, 2006); Nazem al-Eslam Kermani, *Tarikh-e bidari-ye Iraniyan* (Tehran: Chapkhaneh-ye Majles, 1953); Mehdi Malekzadeh, *Tarikh-e enqelab-e mashruteh-ye Iran*, 2nd edition (Tehran: 'Elmi, 1984).
6. Ebrahim Safa'i, *Rahbaran-e mashruteh, dowreh-e avval* (Tehran: Javidan, 1984).
7. During the constitutional period there were various forms of active Sufism, and the full role that the Sufis played in the revolution is yet to be written. The two main orders in Iran were the Dhahabis and the Ne'matollahis. The latter was split into the Soltan Ali Shahis, the Safi Ali Shahis and the Dhu al-Riyasateyn.
8. Safa'i himself wrote, 'In 1916 Mirza Fakr al-Din Mojtahedzadeh, judge at [the Ministry] of Justice (the father of the author), son of Mr. Najafi Mojtahed Mala'eri, commenced service (*khedmat*) to Zahir al-Dowleh in the way of poverty, and because of this he chose the family name Safa'i.' Safa'i, *Rahbaran*, p. 164 n2.
9. Mehdi Malekzadeh, *Tarikh-e enqelab*, p. 255.
10. Ibid. It is interesting to speculate on Malekzadeh's views here, and one is tempted to attribute his slight criticisms to the fact that his father, Malek al-Motakallemin, was executed in the wake of the bombardment of the Majles, whereas other supporters of the Constitutional Revolution quietly slipped away when real danger was immanent. See Mangol Bayat, *Iran's First Revolution: Shi'ism and the Constitutional Revolution of 1905–1909* (New York: Oxford University Press, 1991), pp. 228–30. It is interesting to note that Malekzadeh records how his radical father was a friend of Zahir al-Dowleh (ibid., p. 466).
11. Ahmad Kasravi, *Tarikh-e hejdah saleh-ye Azarbayjan,* 12th edition (Tehran: Amir Kabir, 1999–2000), p. 463.
12. Ibid.
13. Iraj Afshar (ed.), *Khaterat va asnad-e Zahir al-Dowleh* (1972, Tehran: Zarrin, 1988). These memoirs of Zahir al-Dowleh cover the constitutional period and the bombardment of the Majles by Mohammad Ali Shah in 1908. The book also contains Zahir al-Dowleh's treatise entitled *Tarikh-e sahih-e bi dorugh, ya koshteh shodan-e Naser al-Din Shah* (The Correct History with no Lie: Or the Assassination of Naser al-Din Shah). Of interest too is a collection of documents and telegrams (that pertain to 1908, and events after those discussed in this paper), see Iraj Afshar, *Zahir al-Dowleh dar hokumat-e Mazandaran* (Tehran: Nashr-e Qatreh, 2005).
14. Mehdi Bamdad, *Sharh-e hal-e rejal-e Iran* (Tehran: Zavvar, 1968).
15. Mo'ayyer al-Mamalek, *Rejal-e 'asr-e Naseri* (Tehran: Nashr-e Tarikh-e Iran, 1361/1982), pp. 109–14.
16. See Mohammad Hoseyni, 'Anjoman-e okhovvat: tariqat va siyasat', *Nashr-e Tarikh-e Iran* 6 (1998), pp. 7–54, and Mohammad Hoseyni, 'Enhedam va gharat-e Anjoman-e Okhovvat', *Nashr-e Tarikh-e Iran* 24 (Winter 2002), pp. 79–113. European scholarship on Sufism during the constitutional period is

inevitably behind that in Iran. The only substantial piece of work worthy of any mention is Bert G. Fragner, *Persische Memoirenliteratur als Quelle zur neueren Geschichte Irans* (Wiesbaden: Franz Steiner Verlag, 1979). Fragner's work has been translated into Persian: Majid Jalilvand Reza'i, trans., *Khaterat nevisi-ye Iraniyan* (Tehran: Sherkat-e Entesharat-e 'Elmi va Farhangi, 1998).

17. Bamdad, *Sharh-e hal*, vol. 4, pp. 13–14.
18. The dates given in this paragraph are those that appear in Safa'i, *Rahbaran*, p. 136.
19. *Tarikh-e sahih-e bi dorugh*, included in Iraj Afshar (ed.), *Khaterat va asnad-e Zahir al-Dowleh*, p. 20.
20. Ibid., p. 21.
21. Abbas Amanat, *Pivot of the Universe: Nasir al-Din Shah and the Iranian Monarchy, 1831–1896* (London: I.B.Tauris, 1997), p. 409.
22. For Safi Ali Shah's relation with the Shah see Mas'ud Homayuni, *Tarikh-e selselehha-ye tariqeh-ye Ne'matollahiyeh dar Iran* (Tehran: Entesharat-e Maktub-e 'Erfan-e Iran, n.d.), pp. 312–15.
23. See Mohammad Esma'il Rezvani (ed.), *Safarnameh-ye Zahir al-Dowleh* (Tehran: Ketabkhaneh-ye Mostowfi, 1992).
24. For a discussion of these secret societies, see Ervand Abrahamian, *Iran Between Two Revolutions* (New Jersey: Princeton University Press, 1982), pp. 69–81; and A. K. S. Lambton, 'The Secret Societies and the Persian Revolution of 1905–6', *St. Antony's Papers* 4 (London: Oxford University Press, 1958), pp. 43–60.
25. See *Encyclopaedia Iranica*, s.v. 'Anjoman-e Okowwat'.
26. Afshar (ed.), *Khaterat*, p. xxxix.
27. Safa'i, *Rahbaran*, p. 138.
28. For a discussion of titles under the Qajar dynasty, see the introduction to Karim Soleymani, *Alqab-e rejal-e dowreh-ye qajariyeh* (Tehran: Ney, 2001), pp. 7–21.
29. Matthijs Van den Bos, *Mystic Regimes: Sufism and the State in Iran, from the late Qajar Era to the Islamic Republic* (Leiden: Brill, 2002), p. 106.
30. Safa'i, *Rahbaran*, p. 139.
31. Ibid.
32. Cited in Homayuni, *Tarikh*, p. 331. The citation is from an unpublished work of Zahir al-Dowleh's entitled 'Ruh al-Arvah'.
33. *Khedmat* (service), as it is traditionally understood in Persian Sufi texts, may be to one's sheykh, to the brethren, or to the wider community. The concept is particularly strong within the tradition of *javanmardi* (often translated as chivalry), which promotes attributes of selflessness, bravery, courage, and loyalty.
34. *Zaher* and *baten* are Qur'anic terms, and in the Persian Sufi tradition, the former refers to outer, external manifestations of things, while the latter refers to inner manifestations. Zahir al-Dowleh wrote much poetry, and his verses reflect this *zaher/baten* nature of Sufism. Two examples are given in Ridgeon, *Sufi Castigator*, pp. 41–42. For a discussion of the *zaher/baten* dichotomy in Iranian culture, see M. C. Bateson, J. W. Clinton, J. B. M. Kassarjian, H. Safavi, and M. Soraya, 'Safa-yi Batin: A Study of the Interrelations of a Set of Iranian Ideal Character Types', in L. Carl Brown and Norman Itzkowitz (eds.), *Psychological Dimensions*

of Near Eastern Studies (Princeton: The Darwin Press, 1977), pp. 257–73.
35. For a discussion of the legacies of Safi Ali Shah and Zahir al-Dowleh on the Anjoman-e Okhovvat, see Ridgeon, *Sufi Castigator*, pp. 36–42.
36. This is not to say that overtly mystical themes are absent from the poetry and prose of these two Sufis. For example, see Zahir al-Dowleh's poem translated in Ridgeon, *Sufi Castigator*, p. 41, and the mystical experiences and visions that were told about Safi Ali Shah (see Homayuni, *Tarikh*, pp. 261–88).
37. Afshar (ed.), *Khaterat*, p. xlv.
38. *Encyclopaedia Iranica*, s.v. 'Freemasonry in the Qajar Period'.
39. *Encyclopaedia Iranica*, s.v. 'Anjoman-e Okowwat'.
40. Given that Freemasonry in Iran was identified with universal liberal ideas, its anticlericalism, and its secrecy and affiliation with Britain (and for that matter other European states), it is not difficult to see why Mohammad Ali Shah, the anti-constitutionalist monarch, was vehemently opposed to it. See *Encyclopaedia Iranica*, s.v. 'Freemasonry: i. Introduction'.
41. Kasravi, *Tarikh-e hejdah saleh*, p. 463.
42. This was probably one of the schools set up by the Alliance Israélite Universelle (an organization that was established in Paris in 1860, and which aimed to assist Jews in Islamic lands). Of particular use on the Alliance Israélite Universelle schools is Avraham Cohen, 'Iranian Jewry and the Educational Endeavours of the Alliance Israélite Universelle', *Jewish Social Studies* 48 (1986), pp. 5–44.
43. Surprising as this may seem, Cohen appears to endorse Zahir al-Dowleh's observations. Cohen (p. 22) states, 'The Jewish child in Shiraz, Hamadan, Sanandaj or Isfahan spoke a Judeo-Persian dialect at home. He was not even entirely fluent in Farsi, the language of his surrounding environment. When he came to school, teachers began speaking French to him, using this language to instruct him in arithmetic, reading, writing and later history, geography, science and so forth. Hebrew was studied as a means of learning the Bible, and Farsi was a second language.'
44. Afshar (ed.), *Khaterat*, p. 303. (Emphasis added).
45. Fragner, *Persische Memoirenliteratur*, p. 134 (*Khaterat nevisi*, p. 196).
46. Sheykh Fazlollah Nuri's treatise has been translated in Abdul-Hadi Hairi, 'Shaykh Fazl Allāh Nūrī's Refutation of the Idea of Constitutionalism', *Middle Eastern Studies* 13/3 (1977), pp. 329–38.
47. Literally, the 'Council for Public Benefit'.
48. For the Alliance school see above. (Afshar [ed.], *Khaterat*, pp. 159–60).
49. Afshar (ed.), *Khaterat*, p. 157. Afshar's edition also includes a photograph of the construction site, which clearly shows the bricks and the masses assembled at the site (the photograph is located between pp. 148–49).
50. Vanessa Martin, *Islam and Modernism: the Iranian Revolution of 1906* (London: I.B.Tauris, 1989), pp. 81–82.
51. Fragner, *Persische Memoirenliteratur*, p. 132 n69 (*Khaterat nevisi*, p. 193 n69).
52. Zahir al-Dowleh addressed him as 'brother', which suggests that he was also a member of the Anjoman-e Okhovvat. Ibid., pp. 134–35 (p. 197).
53. Ibid., p. 135 (p. 198).

54. Martin, *Islam and Modernism*, p. 77.
55. Afshar (ed.), *Khaterat*, pp. 94–95.
56. Martin, *Islam and Modernism*, p. 82.
57. Afshar (ed.), *Khaterat*, pp. 246–47.
58. Fragner, *Persische Memoirenliteratur*, p. 139 (*Khaterat nevisi*, p. 202).
59. Afshar (ed.), *Khaterat*, p. 103.
60. Fragner, *Persische Memoirenliteratur*, p. 139 (*Khaterat nevisi*, p. 202).
61. The Persian pronouns do not indicate gender, therefore I have left this ambiguity in my English translation.
62. Afshar (ed.), *Khaterat*, pp. 142–43.
63. Martin, *Islam and Modernism*, p. 90.
64. Afshar (ed.), *Khaterat*, p. 108. The date given is 21 July 1906.
65. Ibid., p. 301.
66. Telegram dated 2 October 1906, Afshar (ed.), *Khaterat*, p. 196.
67. Afshar (ed.), *Khaterat*, p. 151.
68. Ibid., p. 235.
69. Martin, *Islam and Modernism*, p. 83.
70. Moshir al-Dowleh was the title of Mirza Nasrollah Khan Na'ini who had served as foreign minister until 1906, and then served for six months as the prime minister under Mozaffar al-Din Shah, and then for two months under Mohammad Ali Shah. (See Bamdad, *Sharh*, vol. 4, pp. 351–60). Vanessa Martin notes that during the *bast* at Hazrat 'Abd al-'Azim from December 1905 to January 1906 (at the start of the chain of events that led to the granting of the constitution), Moshir al-Dowleh (then foreign minister) donated large sums of money to senior clerics sympathetic to the *bast*. (*Islam and Modernism*, p. 71). Martin also includes him in a group of 'reformist bureaucrats'; ibid., p. 79. Given this, it is difficult to pass judgement on the episode that passed between Zahir al-Dowleh and Moshir al-Dowleh; it may simply be an isolated episode that gives an indication of Zahir al-Dowleh's courage in dealing with other high officials.
71. Safa'i, *Rahbaran*, p. 145.
72. Ibid., p. 147.
73. Mangol Bayat, *Iran's First Revolution*, pp. 180–81.
74. Safa'i, *Rahbaran*, pp. 151–53.
75. Hoseyni, 'Enhedam', pp. 86–87.
76. Ibid., p. 88.
77. Janet Afary, *The Iranian Constitutional Revolution, 1906–1911: Grassroots Democracy, Social Democracy, and the Origins of Feminism* (New York: Columbia University Press, 1996), p. 84.
78. Ibid., pp. 84–85.
79. Ibid., p. 40.
80. For the situation in Gilan in this period see ibid., pp. 154–62.
81. Safa'i, *Rahbaran*, pp. 153–54.
82. Afshar (ed.), *Khaterat*, p. 340. Zahir al-Dowleh wrote to the Shah: 'Yesterday evening about 2,000 armed people, some of whom had put on military garb, spontaneaously set off for Tehran.'

83. Ibid., pp. 340–41. This argument is based on Zahir al-Dowleh's own telegram to the Shah, and so of course one could expect him to say that he had attempted to prevent the march on Tehran. See also Safa'i, *Rahbaran*, p. 156.
84. Hoseyni, 'Enhedam', p. 84.
85. Moshir al-Saltaneh (Mirza Ahmad Khan) had been governor of Gilan, and in 1907/8 was made prime minister. His second cabinet had been formed when the Majles was bombarded. See Bamdad, *Sharh*, vol. 1, pp. 100–03.
86. Afshar, *Khaterat*, p. 354.
87. Although the attack focused on Zahir al-Dowleh's house, the whole street suffered very badly from the plundering of the Cossacks. The studio of the famous photographer Sevruguin was next to Zahir al-Dowleh's house, and as a result of the damage in the attack, of more than 7,000 glass plates, only 2,000 could be salvaged. See http://www.asia.si.edu/archives/finding_aids/sevruguin.html.
88. Baqer 'Aqeli, *Khandanha-ye hokumatgar-e Iran* (Tehran: Namak, 2005–6), p. 122.
89. Qavam al-Dowleh (Mirza Mohammad Ali Khan, whose first title was Mo'aven al-Molk) served in three cabinets under Moshir al-Saltaneh during the constitutional period.
90. Malekeh-ye Iran explains that the problem concerned properties of Haji Zahir al-Dowleh that were endowed for his descendants, and were under the trusteeship of Zahir al-Dowleh. Afshar (ed.), *Khaterat*, p. 378.
91. Nayeb al-Saltaneh was the title given to Kamran Mirza, the third son of Naser al-Din Shah (and therefore Malekeh-ye Iran's brother), who occasionally acted as regent in the Shah's absence. See Bamdad, *Sharh*, vol. 3, pp. 149–60.
92. Afshar (ed.), *Khaterat*, p. 378.
93. Kasravi, *Tarikh-e mashruteh*, p. 57. The large property of Zell al-Soltan, the Ma'sudiyeh, was attacked, as were the houses of his sister (Banu-ye 'Ozma), and his son, Jalal al-Dowleh.
94. Hoseyni, 'Enhedam', pp. 79–80.
95. Mo'ayyer al-Mamalek, *Rejal*, p. 112.
96. See Abrahamian, *Iran Between Two Revolutions*, p. 78.
97. The others included the editor of *Sur-e Esrafil*, Mirza Jahangir Khan; Seyyed Mohammad Reza of Shiraz, the editor of *Mosavat*; Malek al-Motakallemin; Aqa Seyyed Jamal of Isfahan; Mirza Davud Khan; Haji Mirza Yahya Dowlatabadi, and Mirza Ali Mohammad ('Biradar'). Edward Granville Browne, *The Persian Revolution of 1905–1909* (1910, London: Frank Cass, 1966), p. 204.
98. Hosayni, 'Enhedam', p. 90. Strangely, Kasravi claims that it was a lie that Zahir al-Soltan was one of the constitutionalists; *Tarikh-e mashruteh*, p. 657.
99. Afshar (ed.), *Khaterat*, p. 358.
100. Browne, *The Persian Revolution*, p. 208.
101. It was claimed by Liakhov that the dervishes had thrown a bomb from the headquarters of the Anjoman-Okhovvat, which exploded and killed five Cossacks. (Afshar [ed.], *Khaterat*, p. 375). He also claimed that a sack of bombs was discovered in the building (which Malekeh-ye Iran herself seems to confirm; ibid.).

Strangely, Kasravi commented that the claim of a bomb from the headquarters was a lie (*Tarikh-e mashruteh*, p. 657.)

102. Entezam al-Saltaneh, otherwise known by his Sufi name of Binesh Ali Shah, was in the inner circle of dervishes within the Anjoman-e Okhovvat.
103. Telegram from Malekeh-ye Iran to Zahir al-Dowleh, dated 1 Jumada II, reproduced in Afshar (ed.), *Khaterat*, p. 377.
104. Telegram from Malekeh-ye Iran to Zahir al-Dowleh, dated 27 Jumada I. Afshar (ed.), *Khaterat*, p. 361.
105. See Bamdad, *Sharh*, vol. 1, pp. 374–76.
106. Ibid., pp. 371–74.
107. Ibid., p. lxxiii.
108. Contained in Afshar (ed.), *Khaterat*, pp. 380–81.
109. Ibid., p. xxxv.
110. Ibid., p. 449.

Chapter 10. The *Rowshanfekr* in the Constitutional Period: An Overview

1. Jacques Le Goff, *Les intellectuels au Moyen Age* (Paris: Seuil, 1985), p. 4.
2. Ibid, p. 48.
3. Ibid, p. 79.
4. Fazlur Rahman, *Islam* (New York: Holt, Rinehart and Winston, 1966), p. 78.
5. For more details on the history of religious movements in Qajar times, see Mangol Bayat, *Mysticism and Dissent: Socio-religious Thought in Qajar Iran* (Syracuse: Syracuse University Press, 1982).
6. See Bayat, *Mysticism and Dissent*, chapter 5.
7. Cited in Nikki R. Keddie, *Islamic Response to Imperialism* (Berkeley: University of California Press, 1968), p. 107.
8. See for instance Mohammad Mehdi Sharif-Kashani, *Vaqe'at-e ettefaqiyeh*, vol. 1 (Tehran: Nashr-e Tarikh-e Iran, 1983), pp. 48–49, 63–64.
9. Letters of Mozaffar al-Din Shah to the *mujtahid* Abdollah Behbahani in Hashem Mohit-Mafi, *Moqaddamat-e mashrutiyat* (Tehran: Ferdowsi, 1984), p. 113.
10. Cited in Mostafa Rahimi, *Qanun-e asasi-ye Iran va osul-e demokrasi*, 3rd edition (Tehran: Sepehr, 1978), p. 83.
11. Mohit-Mafi, *Moqaddamat*, pp. 186–88.
12. Ibid, p. 133.
13. Sharif-Kashani, *Vaqe'at*, vol. 1, pp. 93–95, 82.
14. Ibid, p. 109; see also Bayat, *Iran's First Revolution: Shi'ism and the Constitutional Revolution, 1905–1909* (Oxford: Oxford University Press, 1991), chapter 8 and sources cited there.
15. Sharif-Kashani, *Vaqe'at*, vol. 1, p. 119; see also the text of a pamphlet charging the ulema with corruption and failure to carry out their religious responsibilities, idem, pp. 55–58.
16. Ibid, pp. 121–22.
17. See Sharif-Kashani, *Vaqe'at*, vol. 1, pp. 162–63.
18. Eugen Weber, *Peasants into Frenchmen: The Modernization of Rural France, 1870–1914* (Stanford: Stanford University Press, 1976). See also his *My France*:

Politics, Culture, Myth (Cambridge, MA: Belknap Press of Harvard University Press, 1991). I have chosen to cite Weber rather than the much-quoted Benedict Anderson's by now classic analysis of nationalism. The two authors have much in common. However, Weber's historical, factual analysis of France seems to me more appropriate for my approach to the study of Iran at the turn of the century. Although other historians have challenged some of his findings, preferring to date the rise of nationalist identity to the French Revolution, the fact remains that forging this identity took much longer than commonly understood.

19. Ismail Ra'in, *Faramushkhaneh va faramasoneri dar Iran*, 3 vols., 3rd edition (Tehran: Amir Kabir, 1978); Mahmud Katira'i, *Faramasoneri dar Iran az aghaz ta tashkil-e lozh-e bidari* (Tehran: Eqbal, 1968); Hamid Algar, 'An introduction to the History of Freemasonry in Iran', *Middle Eastern Studies* 6 (1970), pp. 276–96. A more objective account is to be found in Paul Sabatiennes, 'Pour une histoire de la première loge maçonnique en Iran', *Revue de l'Université de Bruxelles* 3–4 (1977), pp. 415–42. For an analysis of the popularity of conspiracy theories see Houchang E. Chehabi, "The Paranoid Style in Iranian Historiography," in Touraj Atabaki (ed.), *Iran in the 20th Century: Historiography and Political Culture* (London: I.B.Tauris, 2009), pp. 155–76 and 294–303.
20. Pierre Chevallier, *Histoire de la Franc-Maçonnerie française*, vol. 2 (Paris: Fayard, 1974), p. 149.
21. Ibid, p. 488.
22. Ibid, p. 18.
23. Ibid, vol. 3, p. 65. For more details on French Freemasonry's role in the Third Republic see also: André Combes, *Histoire de la Franc-Maçonnerie au XIXe siècle* (Monaco: Editions du Rocher, 1999); Jacqueline Lalouette, *La Libre pensée en France, 1848–1940* (Paris: Albin Michel, 1997). For a more negative assessment of Freemasonry see Ghislaine Ottenheimer and Renaud Lecadre, *Les Frères invisibles* (Paris: Albin Michel, 2001).
24. For greater details on the Alliance's activities in Iran see Homa Nateq, *Karnameh-ye farhangi-ye farangi dar Iran.* (Paris: Khavaran, 1996), pp. 83–114. Nateq, however, does not link the Alliance with the Freemasons.
25. Grand Orient Archives 1871. Téhéran: Le Réveil de l'Iran.
26. Mohammad Sadeq confirmed in an interview with Ra'in that both he and his father were members of the Bidari lodge. Ra'in, *Faramushkhaneh*, vol. 2, p. 251.
27. The lists of the Grand Orient archives mention a total of 168 members in the lodge's sixteen years of existence. Ra'in lists 120 members in *Faramushkhaneh*, vol. 2, pp. 446–53. Although his work offers great detail based on interviews with many Iranian masons and other sources, Ra'in must be read with caution, so sweeping are his often unfounded generalizations and so hostile his attitude.
28. Ottenheimer and Lecadre, *Les Frères invisibles*, pp. 48–49.
29. Cited in Ra'in, *Faramushkhaneh*, vol. 2, pp. 61–63.
30. Morel to the General Secretary, 16 April 1909, and unsigned memo dated 24 May 1909. Réveil de l'Iran file.
31. Nateq, *Karnameh*, pp. 106–07. I have no evidence that Nicolas was also a Freemason. His name does not appear on the Bidari list.

32. Şükrü Hanioğlu, *The Young Turks in Opposition* (New York: Oxford University Press, 1995), pp. 18, 20, 21.
33. Niyazi Berkeş, *The Development of Secularism in Turkey* (Montreal: McGill University Press, 1964), p. 308 n20.
34. Paul Dumont, 'Une délégation Jeune-Turque à Paris', *Balkan Studies* 28/2 (1987), p. 316. See also Dehkhoda's letter to Mo'azed al-Saltaneh, 15 November 1908, in Iraj Afshar (ed.), *Namehha-ye siyasi-ye Dehkhoda* (Tehran: Ruzbahan, 1979), pp. 21–26; and the group photograph of its members wearing European-style clothes in Iraj Afshar (ed.), *Mobarezeh ba Mohammad Ali Shah: Asnadi az fa'aliyatha-ye azadikh"ahan-e Iran dar Orupa va Estanbol dar salha-ye 1326–1328* (Tehran: Tus, 1982), p. 24.
35. Dumont, 'Une délégation Jeune-Turque', p. 322.
36. *Sorush* 11, 20 October 1909.
37. Ibid., 2, 7 July, 1909.
38. Ibid.
39. Ibid., 3, July 1909.
40. Afshar (ed.), *Mobarezeh*, pp. 69–72, 74–75, 113.
41. 'Tabi'at-e saltanat chist?', *Sur-e Esrafil*, 2/1.
42. See also Nahid Mozaffari's contribution to this volume.
43. Letter of Dehkhoda to the *anjoman*, 18 March 1909, in Afshar (ed.), *Namehha-ye siyasi*, pp. 43–54.
44. Iraj Afshar (ed.), *Khaterat va asnad-e Mostashar al-Dowleh-ye Sadeq*, vol. 4 (Tehran: Ferdowsi, 1982), pp. 99–101.
45. Text of the decree in ibid, vol. 1, p. 290.
46. Cables of Taqizadeh and Mostashar al-Dowleh in ibid., vol. 2, pp. 161–95.
47. Cited in Bayat, *Iran's First Revolution*, p. 246.
48. 'Eyn al-Dowleh's letters to Taqizadeh in Iraj Afshar (ed.), *Owraq-e tazeh yab-e mashrutiyat* (Tehran: Javidan, 1980), 143–57.
49. Correspondence of Taqizadeh and Mostashar al-Dowleh's in Afshar (ed.), *Khaterat va asnad*, vol. 2 (1983), pp. 161–95.
50. Afshar (ed.), *Owraq*, pp. 36–40.
51. Lecomte report dated 13 August 1909. Archives du Ministère des Affaires Etrangères. Correspondences Politiques et Commerciales. Nouvelle Serie: Perse. Vol. 3, pp. 210–14.
52. Yahya Dowlatabadi, *Tarikh-e mo'aser ya Hayat-e Yahya*, new edition, vol. 3 (Tehran: 'Attar, 1982), p. 121.
53. Mehdi Malekzadeh, *Tarikh-e enqelab-e mashrutiyat-e Iran*, vol. 3 (Tehran: 'Elmi, 1984), pp. 1274–75.
54. Abbas Zaryab and Iraj Afshar (ed.), *Namehha-ye Edvard Braun beh Seyyed Hasan Taqizadeh* (Tehran: Ketabha-ye Jibi, 1984), pp. 22–25.
55. Dowlatabadi, *Tarikh-e mo'aser ya Hayat-e Yahya*, vol. 3, p. 129.

Chapter 11. An Iranian Modernist Project: Ali Akbar Dehkhoda's Writings in the Constitutional Period

1. For example, Ervand Abrahamian, *Iran Between Two Revolutions* (Princeton: Princeton University Press, 1982); Fereydun Adamiyat, *Fekr-e democrasi-ye ejtema'i dar nehzat-e mashruteh-ye Iran* (Tehran: Payam, 1976); Janet Afary, *The Iranian Constitutional Revolution, 1906–1911: Grassroots Democracy, Social Democracy, and the Origins of Feminism* (New York: Columbia University Press, 1996); Christophe Balaÿ and Michel Cuypers, *Aux sources de la nouvelle persane* (Paris: Editions Recherche sur les civilisations, 1983); Mangol Bayat, *Iran's First Revolution: Shi'ism and the Constitutional Revolution of 1905–1909* (New York: Oxford University Press, 1991); Mangol Bayat, 'The Cultural Implications of the Constitutional Revolution', in Edmund Bosworth and Carole Hillenbrand (eds.), *Qajar Iran: Political, Social, and Cultural Change, 1800–1925* (Costa Mesa, CA: Mazda Publishers, 1992); Mansureh Ettehadieh, *Peydayesh va tahavvol-e ahzab-e siyasi-e mashrutiyat* (Tehran: Nashr-e Gostareh, 1982); Khosrow Shakeri, *Pishine-hha-ye eqtesadi-ejtema'i-ye jonbesh-e mashrutiyat* (Tehran: Akhtaran, 2005); Khosrow Shakeri, *Naqsh-e aramaneh dar sosiyal demokrasi-ye Iran (1911–1905)* (Tehran: Shirazeh, 2003).
2. *Sur-e Esrafil* (Tehran) in thirty-two issues, from 30 May 1907 to 20 June 1908; three issues of *Sur-e Esrafil* published in exile in Yverdon, Switzerland and Paris, France, dated 23 January, 6 February, and 8 March 1909. *Sorush* (Istanbul) from July 1909 to October 1909.
3. Various sources state that Mirza Jahangir Khan was an Azali Babi who had become a secularist and a social democrat. See Sorour Soroudi, 'Sur-e Esrafil 1907–8: Social and Political Ideology', *Middle Eastern Studies* 24 (April 1988), p. 231; Bayat, *Iran's First Revolution*, p. 44.
4. See also Soroudi, 'Sur-e Esrafil 1907–8'.
5. For example, Khosrow Shakeri, 'Federalism and Republicanism: Lone Voices in Modern Iranian Intellectual History' (unpublished mnauscript). I would like to thank Dr. Shakeri for his generous advice and for sharing his considerable knowledge and written work on this subject.
6. The discussion in this paper is focused more on the relationship between French Enlightenment thought and Dehkhoda's political ideas. The elements of Russian social democratic thought that inspired Dehkhoda most can be seen in his programmes for economic and agricultural change. See Nahid Mozaffari, 'Crafting Constitutionalism: Ali Akbar Dehkhoda and the Iranian Constitutional Revolution' (PhD dissertation, Harvard University, 2001), chapter 4.
7. *Mostahdeseh* literally means 'newly come to be', and I think 'modern' is an appropriate translation of this often-used term.
8. *Sur-e Esrafil* no. 14 (19 September 1907), pp. 3–4. This is part of a long essay that Dehkhoda wrote directly addressed to the ulema, after major objections were made to his use of the word *kohneh-parast* to refer to those who resisted change. Henceforth, references to *Sur-e Esrafil* will appear as *SE*, with the number of the page following the number of the issue; for example, *SE* no. 1, p. 1. The translations from *Sur-e Esrafil* are all my own. The essays in both *SE* no. 12 (5 Septem-

ber 1907) and *SE* no. 14 (19 September 1907) are seminal and contain many of Dehkhoda's important ideas. They are discussed in different contexts below.
9. *SE* no. 1 (30 May 1907), p. 2.
10. Ibid.
11. This not-so-veiled reference is to Amin al-Soltan's opinion that Iran was not ready for constitutionalism. *SE* no. 1, p. 2. Since in this essay Dehkhoda was addressing Mohammad Ali Shah, and advising him to embrace constitutionalism, he concentrated the blame for despotic tendencies on Amin al-Soltan, in order to give the Shah a way to save face.
12. Dehkhoda is quoting Amin al-Soltan's comment here. Ibid.
13. These dates correspond with the assassination/execution of Julius Caesar, Charles I of Britain, and Louis XVI of France. Earlier in the essay, Dehkhoda argued that people kill their kings – in the abovementioned cases as well as that of Naser al-Din Shah – not because those kings had been personally guilty of great crimes but because they had heeded the bad advice of arrogant, ill-intentioned ministers who were not cognizant of their nation's level of maturity, and thereby crushed their demands for freedom. *SE* no. 1, pp. 2–3.
14. *SE* no. 2 (6 June 1907), p. 1.
15. Ibid., pp. 1–2.
16. Ibid.
17. *SE* no. 3 (13 June 1907), pp. 1–2.
18. Note that the Arabic word *uns/ons* is the root word for the Persian word *ensan* (humankind).
19. *SE* no. 2, p. 2.
20. Since Dehkhoda got into so much trouble with the use of this word, he actually declared in an essay that the word *kohneh-parast* is a translation of the French word *réactionnaire*, though in the Iranian context, he was clearly referring to the traditionalist religious and political points of view. He attributed the first use of this translation to Mirza Malkam Khan. See *SE* no. 14, pp. 4.
21. Ya'reb ibn Qahtan is considered to be the founder of the Yemeni tribes and the first person who spoke Arabic. See Seyyed Mohammad Dabirsiyaqi (ed.), *Maqalat-e Dehkhoda*, vol. 2 (Tehran: Tirazheh Press, 1989), p. 63 n2.
22. The term used here is *taziyaneh-ye tariqat*. *Tariqat* can refer to either religion in general or Sufi sects in particular. I believe that Dehkhoda left this deliberately vague in his choice of words.
23. *SE* no. 12 (5 September 1907), pp. 1–3.
24. *Malaz al-Islam*, a title for the ulema.
25. *SE* no. 12, p. 3.
26. *SE* no. 28 (4 Rabi' II 1326/26 May 1908), p. 2. From issue no.15, *Sur-e Esrafil* only published hijri lunar dates.
27. There are a number of references to Shapshal, Mohammad Ali Shah's Russian tutor and adviser, as a Jew (*yahudi*) in *Sur-e Esrafil*, where he is being criticized for corruption and exerting bad influence on Mohammad Ali Shah. See *Sur-e Esrafil* no. 31 (16 June 1908), where he is referred to as 'Shapshal-e yahudi' in an angry tone, along with Amir Bahador Jang, whose religious affiliation is not

deemed problematic enough to be worth mentioning. Also, in a critique of Ottoman Sultan Abdülhamid's hostile policies towards constitutionalist Iran and his repressive internal policies, one writer (Asef) in *Sur-e Esrafil* (no. 12, p. 5) wrote: 'He has taken away the rights of qualified people and snuffed out the light of their livelihood, and instead, has brought the wandering Jewish whores from Syria and keeps them publicly in the royal domain and decrees honours and medals for them. ... He has promoted the Jews of the provinces of Syria to the high ranks of general and colonel to mollify and please the two wandering [Jewish] girls.' On the whole, the secular constitutionalist intellectuals cultivated good relations with minorities and advocated for their rights publicly. The principles of common humanity and common nationality were seen as the main bond among people, but at the end of the day they were not immune from the sentiments and language of prejudice in society.
28. *SE* no. 19 (28 Shawwal 1328/1 November 1910), p. 2. Dehkhoda is referring to Jean Jaurès (1859–1914), the French socialist leader. The context of this discussion is land reform and peasant rights. He refers to the peasant uprisings around Rasht.
29. Referred to as *qavanin-e 'asr-e jadid*; see *SE* no. 6 (22 Jumada I 1325/2 July 1907), p. 3.
30. Adamiyat, *Fekr-e democrasi*, pp. 9, 11–12.
31. This is obvious from the frequent coverage and mention of such efforts in *Sur-e Esrafil*.
32. These translations were not formally published, but were used as texts.
33. Peter Gay, *The Enlightenment: An Interpretation* (New York: Norton Library, 1977), pp. 326–27.
34. Montesquieu, *The Spirit of the Laws* (Cambridge: Cambridge University Press, 1989), Book 3, pp. 21–30.
35. Ibid., Book 8, p. 112.
36. Ibid., p. 116.
37. Ibid., p. 119.
38. See Peter Gay's discussion on the unsettled 'great contest between rationalism and empiricism' in Montesquieu. *The Enlightenment*, p. 326.
39. Voltaire, 'A,B,C,' in *Philosophical Dictionary*, vol. 2, p. 500. As quoted in Gay, *The Enlightenment*, p. 326.
40. See *SE* Yverdon no. 1 (23 January 1909), p. 1.
41. The most eloquent such depictions can be found in the satire columns *charand parand*. See particularly *SE* no. 3 and no. 4.
42. 'Shar'-e gheyr-e mashub', *SE* Yverdon no. 1, p. 3.
43. For Montesquieu, 'Despotic government has fear as its principle, and not many laws are needed for timid, ignorant, beaten-down people.' Montesquieu, *The Spirit of the Laws*, Book 5, Chapter 14, p. 59. See also Book 3, Chapters 9–10, pp. 28–30.
44. Ironically, Montesquieu uses the system of rule in 'Persia' as a prime example of despotic government. He used Chardin's *Voyages* extensively as a source of information about how Iranian despotism functioned. *The Spirit of the Laws*, Book 3,

Chapter 10, p. 29.

45. The context of this essay is important to note. Dehkhoda wrote this essay in Yverdon, Switzerland, in the first issue of *Sur-e Esrafil* to be published after the coup in June 1908. This is a plea to his countrymen to withdraw their allegiance from Mohammad Ali Shah and expel him from power. In essence, in the three essays, one in each of the three issues of the Yverdon *Sur-e Esrafil*, he attempts to delegitimize Mohammad Ali's power from the constitutional, the religious, and the international points of view.
46. See, for example, the references to *mozare'eh* and *mozarebeh* in his economic discussions in *Sur-e Esrafil*, no. 17 to 19, 21 to 25, and 29 to 30 (from 14 Shawwal 1325/19 November 1907 through 24 Rabi' II 1326/25 April 1908).
47. *Sur-e Esrafil*'s editorial entitled 'Moslemin va sherk', no. 16, p. 1.
48. Montesquieu, *The Spirit of the Laws*, Book 24, Chapter 1, p. 459.
49. Ibid. See also pp. 476 and 493.
50. *Sur-e Esrafil* no. 16, p. 1. Emphasis added.
51. These are the titles of the leaders of the following religious communities respectively: Babi, Azali, Baha'i, and Sheykhi.
52. Dehkhoda can be excused for not knowing about the Mormons, a new religion born on American soil.
53. *Sur-e Esrafil*, no. 4.
54. See Soroudi, 'Sur-e Esrafil, 1907–8', p. 236.
55. *SE* no. 5, pp. 2–3.
56. Soroudi, 'Sur-e Esrafil, 1907–8', p. 247 n22.
57. See Abdul-Hadi Hairi, *Shi'ism and Constitutionalism in Iran* (Leiden: E. J. Brill, 1977), p. 75, quoting Sheykh Hadi's book *Tahrir al-'Oqala'*.
58. For a discussion of these issues see Mozaffari, 'Crafting Constitutionalism'.
59. *Sur-e Esrafil* no. 1, pp. 4–5.
60. European civilization impressed Dehkhoda; he admired Enlightenment thought and practice, and the scientific aspects of Western progress. However, his admiration was informed by a knowledge of history, and was not uncritical. He peppered his essays with criticism of Western claims of superiority and the practice of colonial encroachment. During the period of the First Majles, his views represented the position of the radical faction both inside and outside the Majles, which were consistent with the views of the Social Democratic party (Hemmat) in the critique of economic injustice and colonialism. See, for instance, *SE* no. 29, p. 1, and Dabirsiyaqi (ed.), *Maqalat*, vol. 1, pp. 8–9.

Chapter 12. Readership, the Press and the Public Sphere in the First Constitutional Era

1. The most celebrated reading room was of course the National Library, which had come into being in 1904, two years before the promulgation of the constitution. However, it was in the months that followed the constitution that an increasing number of advertisements were placed in the pages of the press heralding the opening of new reading rooms as well as the publication of a variety of new books on a range of subject matters. Examples abound. For a selection, see

Tarbiyat no. 418 (25 October 1906), p. 1; *Habl al-Matin* no. 9 (8 May 1907), p. 4; *Habl al-Matin* no. 68 (15 July 1907), p. 4.

2. Seyyed Farid Qasemi, *Rahnama-ye matbu'at-e Iran: 'asr-e Qajar 1253 q./1215–1304 sh.* (Tehran: Markaz-e Motale'at va Tahqiqat-e Rasanehha, 1993), p. 28. (Since Qasemi uses the lunar calendar in his study, he estimates that 73 years had passed between the introduction of the first Persian-language newspaper and the spate of publications in the aftermath of the constitution.)

3. More specifically, the first issue of the Tehran *Habl al-Matin* appeared on 29 April 1907. This newspaper was a branch of the respected Calcutta *Habl al-Matin* which had begun publication in Calcutta on a weekly basis in 1893. That the need was felt for a daily at this point had much to do with the changing times. That is, by the time the Calcutta weekly arrived in Tehran, it was usually one month out of date and therefore in no position to compete with all the other publications that had come into being in the aftermath of the constitution. As a result, Mirza Seyyed Hasan Kashani (the younger brother of Mo'ayyed al-Eslam, the editor of the Calcutta *Habl al-Matin*), who at the time not only happened to be in Tehran, but was also very active in constitutional politics, set up the daily *Habl al-Matin*. See Ahmad Kasravi, *Tarikh-e mashruteh-ye Iran*, 5th ed., (Tehran: Amir Kabir, 1961), pp. 276–77.

4. In November 1907, in an obituary for Zoka' al-Molk, *Sur-e Esrafil* paid tribute to *Tarbiyat* in the following way: 'In addition to … the beneficial [articles] that it published, among the services that this newspaper [*Tarbiyat*] carried out for our motherland (*vatan*), one is that by means of its engaging style. …, it appealed to the people of Iran who had [formerly] been annoyed with newspapers, and prompted them into becoming readers of newspapers.' *Sur-e Esrafil* no. 15 (5 November 1907), p. 5. In the studies that have been done on the Iranian press, *Tarbiyat* is furthermore considered as a pioneer in its own right in that it is said to have led to the publication of other privately owned newspapers in different parts of the country. See Go'el Kuhan, *Tarikh-e sansur dar matbu'at-e Iran*, vol. 1 (Tehran: Agah, 1984), p. 183.

5. In his diary, Mohammad Hasan Khan E'temad al-Saltaneh makes numerous references to Zoka' al-Molk cooperating with him in producing the state-sponsored *E'tela'* newspaper. At times, the latter is said to have co-written the newspaper, and at others, to have been in charge of copying (*paknevis*) what E'temad al-Saltaneh had written. For examples, see Mohammad Hasan Khan E'temad al-Saltaneh, *Ruznameh-ye khaterat-e E'temad al-Saltaneh*, ed. Iraj Afshar (Tehran: Amir Kabir, 1966), pp. 86, 129, 843.

6. For a brief biography of Mirza Mohammad Hoseyn Khan Forughi, Zoka' al-Molk, see Mohammad Sadr Hashemi, *Tarikh-e jarayed va majallat-e Iran*, vol. 2 (Isfahan: Kamal, 1984), pp. 122–24; Mehdi Bamdad, *Tarikh-e rejal-e Iran dar qarn-e davazdah, sizdah, chahardah*, vol. 3 (Tehran: Ketabforushi-ye Zavvar, 1968), pp. 384–88.

7. *Tarbiyat* no. 434 (14 March 1907), pp. 1–3.
8. *Tarbiyat* no. 130 (9 March 1899), p. 4.
9. *Tarbiyat* no. 45 (21 October 1897), p. 3.

10. *Tarbiyat* no. 373 (10 August 1905), p. 1.
11. For more on this initial feeling of optimism, see Negin Nabavi, 'Spreading the Word: Iran's First Constitutional Press and the Shaping of a "New Era"', *Critique: Critical Middle Eastern Studies* 14/3 (2005), pp. 307–21.
12. *Tarbiyat* no. 434 (14 March 1907), pp. 1–3.
13. The Association of Free Men (*Majma'-e azadmardan*) had come into being in June 1903. See Sadr Hashemi, *Tarikh-e jarayed*, vol. 3, p. 209. Following the granting of the constitution, Mirza Jahangir Khan Sur-e Esrafil, together with Seyyed Mohammad Reza Mosavat, joined the Revolutionary Committee (*Komiteh-ye Enqelab*), which had been set up with the aim of furthering the constitutional movement. It was, moreover, as a result of their journalistic activities that, following the coup d'état on 23 June 1908, they were persecuted together with Seyyed Hasan Kashani. That is, while Mirza Jahangir Khan Sur-e Esrafil was arrested and executed, Seyyed Hasan Kashani and Seyyed Mohammad Reza Mosavat were exiled to the Caucasus, after having taken refuge in the British legation.
14. *Majles* no. 6 (3 December 1906), p. 4.
15. These feelings enjoyed such prevalence that they were also reflected in the letters that were sent to the newspapers. One, for example, reads, 'The Iranians, today, have reached such a degree of perceptiveness and are so tireless in preserving their rights that they watch and scrutinize the actions and thoughts of every individual with the utmost care and attention. ... As has been made clear from the beginning, no mighty power can trample on and eliminate the rights of a nation that has woken up from the sleep of ignorance and learnt about its rights.' 'Maktub-e shahri', *Habl al-Matin* no. 23 (25 May 1907), p. 4.
16. 'We are the supporters (*havakh"ah*) of freedom (*horriyat*) and liberty (*azadi*), and love equality (*mosavat*) and brotherhood (*baradari*).' *Habl al-Matin* no. 1 (29 April 1907), p. 1. At times, these principles were translated into direct support for the underdog. In one issue, for example, after expressing outrage at the neglect that was suffered by widows in Iran, the editorial announced that *Habl al-Matin* would set up a charity (*daftar-e e'aneh*) to raise money for the widows who had assembled in Tupkhaneh Square for the duration of a month in protest at not being taken care of by the government. See *Habl al-Matin* no. 103 (29 August 1907), pp. 1–2.
17. *Habl al-Matin* no. 20 (21 May 1907), p. 2.
18. Soroud Soroudi, '*Sur-e Esrafil*, 1907–08: Social and Political Ideology', *Middle Eastern Studies* 24/2 (1988), p. 246. See also Nahid Mozaffari's chapter in this volume.
19. *Habl al-Matin* no. 1 (29 April 1907), p. 2.
20. For example, see 'Siyasi', *Habl al-Matin* no. 7 (6 May 1907), p. 3. 'O people of the dear motherland (*vatan*): the progress of Iran is dependent on the unity between the nation (*mellat*) and state (*dowlat*). Until there is unity and solidarity, it will not be possible to develop'.
21. *Gheyrat* is a difficult term to translate. It has connotations of honour, jealousy, and passion, and is often translated as 'zeal'. However, in the constitutional writ-

ings, *gheyrat* is construed as a quality that urges people not to remain passive but to take action. It is in an attempt to convey this sense that I have translated this term as 'strength of conviction'.

22. 'Mojassameh-ye gheyrat', *Habl al-Matin* no. 23 (25 May 1907), p. 3. In addition to articles, the point about the crucial role of *gheyrat* was also reflected in the letters that were published in newspapers. For example, a letter published in *Mosavat* on 24 November 1907, while expressing similar ideas, took them a little further. Addressing itself to the people of Iran, it read: 'Now is the time for strength of conviction (*gheyrat*). Your freedom and dignity are a result of conviction. Your honour and salvation are a result of conviction. Your wealth, independence, and nationality are a result of conviction. Other than strength of conviction, you have no solution.' 'Maktub-e shahri', *Mosavat* no. 6 (24 November 1907), p. 6.

23. This challenges the assumption made by some, like Yahya Aryanpur, who, with regard to the press of the constitutional era, was of the opinion that 'most of the writers did not know what they were writing or whom they were writing for.' See Yahya Aryanpur, *Az Saba ta Nima: tarikh-e sad-o panjah saleh-ye adab-e farsi*, vol. 2 (Tehran: Ketabha-ye Jibi, 1971), p. 25.

24. Whereas the price of each issue of the daily Tehran *Habl al-Matin* was two shahis, the weeklies *Sur-e Esrafil* and *Mosavat* cost their readers four shahis. This should be compared to *Tarbiyat*, which as a weekly published in 1896 cost five shahis per copy. Even though, in the short five-month period (between 3 April and 22 September 1898) when *Tarbiyat* became a daily, its price was reduced to two shahis per issue, in general, it seems that selling single issues at an affordable price became the policy of most other newspapers only after the promulgation of the constitution. For example, *Majles*, one of the first dailies to be published, and which sold for three shahis per copy, made a point of this policy, stating in its first issue: 'In the same manner as other dailies in the world, for those who are in search of particular issues, or are not able to subscribe on an annual basis, single issues will be sold in specific locations and on all streets at an affordable price.' *Majles* no. 1 (25 November 1906), p. 2. In the absence of exact figures for the average wage in 1906–07, it is difficult to assess how reasonably priced these newspapers truly were. However, in his memoirs, Mirza Qoli Hedayat estimates the average monthly salary of a schoolteacher in 1905 to have been 300 riyals (or 6,000 shahis), and that of a janitor (*farrash*), 60 riyals (or 1,200 shahis), which suggests that newspapers would not have been prohibitive for most. (See Mehdi Qoli Hedayat, *Khaterat va khatarat: tusheh'i az tarikh-e shesh padshah va gusheh'i az dowreh-ye zendegi-ye man* [Tehran: Zavvar, 1965], pp. 138–39.)

25. An earlier version of this section on certain aspects of readership can be found in Nabavi, 'Spreading the Word', pp. 317–20.

26. 'Maktub-e Anzali', *Mosavat* no. 4 (13 November 1907), p. 5.

27. 'Maktub-e Qom', *Mosavat* no. 3 (4 November 1907), p. 3.

28. The Russian newspaper *Novoe Vremya* is translated and cited in *Mosavat* as reporting that 'In Tehran, there are many cases of tailors or stitchmakers who both work and read newspapers. Among those who read newspapers, there are

a number who pass them onto the poor after they finish with them so that the latter, too, can benefit from reading them.' *Mosavat* no. 16 (8 March 1908), p. 6.
29. E. G. Browne, *The Persian Revolution, 1905–1909* (Reprint, Washington, DC: Mage Publishers, 1995), p. 143.
30. Janet Afary, *The Iranian Constitutional Revolution, 1906–1911: Grassroots Democracy, Social Democracy and the Origins of Feminism* (New York: Columbia University Press, 1996), p. 152.
31. 'Maktub-e shahri', *Habl al-Matin* no. 4 (2 May 1907), p. 3.
32. 'Maktub-e Qom', *Mosavat* no. 3 (4 November 1907), p. 7.
33. 'Towzih-e vazehhati keh ta konun dar Iran beh khiyal-e an nistand', *Sur-e Esrafil* no. 20 (16 January 1908), pp. 3–4.
34. See, for example, 'Layeheh-i dar bara'at-e zemmeh', *Habl al-Matin* no. 68 (15 July 1907), p. 6.
35. One writer who identified himself as Ali Asghar Tehrani, wrote towards the end of his letter, 'Being a member of the nation (*mellat*), I ask you to publish my letter in your newspaper for the time being. Perhaps, God willing, some sort of compassion will find its way into the hearts of our ministers, judges, and dignitaries, and they will pay attention to matters of justice and enable me to get my rights.' 'Tazallom-e yeki az hamvatanan', *Sur-e Esrafil* no. 30 (26 May 1908), p. 4.
36. 'Layeheh-ye yeki az khavatin', *Habl al-Matin* no. 105 (1 September 1907). There was another letter with a similarly critical tone towards Sheykh Fazlollah, also by a woman and published in *Sur-e Esrafil*, two months earlier, on 1 July 1907. See *Sur-e Esrafil*, no. 7–8 (1 July 1907), pp. 4–5. Neither of the two letters indicated the name of the author.
37. See Afsaneh Najmabadi, 'Zanhā-yi Millat: Women or Wives of the Nation?', *Iranian Studies* 26/1–2 (1993), p. 65.
38. 'Maktub-e yeki az khavatin', *Habl al-Matin* no. 65 (11 July 1907), p. 3.
39. 'Taghayyor', *Habl al-Matin* no. 64 (10 July 1907), p. 3. As a result of this protest, the original letter did get published the next day.
40. For example, on an occasion when the letter-writer was known to Zoka' al-Molk, an introduction would be given as in the following case: 'His Excellency the learned and erudite Mirza Seyyed Reza Khan, known as Sadiq al-Hokama, is among the well-known physicians of Tabriz, and a close friend of *Tarbiyat*.' *Tarbiyat* no. 376 (31 August 1905), p. 2.
41. See, for example, *Tarbiyat* no. 349 (26 January 1905), p. 4.
42. In one instance when the letter-writer was not known to Zoka' al-Molk, he justified the letter's publication in the following way: 'In the last days, a letter bearing the stamp of Ahmad al-Hoseyni has been received from Zanjan [and] addressed to me. I have no past with the respected writer. It is said [, however], that his Excellency Haji Seyyed Ahmad is the son of Haji Mir Bahador al-Din, one of the landowners of Khamseh who is [also] from the ranks of the ulema. ... In any case, since he talks of certain ills, and encourages the brothers to do good work, and there are no signs of ill intention, it will be published here. It is hoped that it will be of use.' *Tarbiyat* no. 420 (15 November 1906), p. 4.

43. Benedict Anderson, *Imagined Communities: Reflections on the Origin and Spread of Nationalism* (Revised ed., London and New York: Verso, 1991), p. 36.
44. See, for example, James L. Gelvin, *The Modern Middle East: A History* (New York and Oxford: Oxford University Press, 2005), p. 145.

Chapter 13. Writing in Tehran: The First Freedom of Press Law

1. *Oqyanus* (Tehran) no. 2 (25 May 1908), p. 1.
2. William Warner, 'Communicating Liberty: The Newspapers of the British Empire as a Matrix for the American Revolution', in *English Literary History* 72 (2005), pp. 339–61.
3. Sayyed Mohammad-e Hashemi (ed.), *Mozakerat-e Majles: Dowreh-ye avval-e taqniniyeh. Zamimeh-ye Ruznameh-ye Rasmi-ye Keshvar-e Shahanshahi-ye Iran* (Tehran: Majles, 1946), p. 584. See also Edward G. Browne, *The Persian Revolution of 1905–1909* (Cambridge: Cambridge University Press, 1910), p. 375 and Janet Afary, *The Iranian Constitutional Revolution, 1906–1911: Grassroots Democracy, Social Democracy, and the Origins of Feminism* (New York: Columbia University Press, 1996), p. 138.
4. Hashemi (ed.), *Mozakerat-e Majles*, pp. 587–91.
5. *Encyclopaedia Iranica*, s.v. 'Constitutional Revolution vi: The press'.
6. *Neda-ye Vatan* (Tehran) no. 92 (28 October 1907), p. 1.
7. Ibid.
8. *Oqyanus* (Tehran) no. 2 (25 May 1908), p. 1.
9. *Habl al-Matin* (Tehran) no. 58 (4 July 1907), p. 3.
10. For the debate over the slavery on the border with the Turkmens see Afsaneh Najmabadi, *The Story of the Daughters of Quchan: Gender and National Memory in Iranian History* (Syracuse: Syracuse University Press, 1998).
11. *Mohakemat* (Tehran) no. 45 (2 April 1908), p. 4.
12. *Neda-ye Vatan* (Tehran) no. 62 (22 September 1907), p. 1.
13. Ibid.
14. *Habl al-Matin* (Tehran) no. 59 (5 July 1907), p. 2.
15. *Eblagh* (Tabriz) no. 1 (not dated, but before February 1907), p. 1.
16. *Oqyanus* (Tehran) no. 2 (25 May 1908), p. 1.
17. *Neda-ye Vatan* (Tehran) no. 144 and 145 (6 January 1908), pp. 1–2.
18. *Neda-ye Vatan* (Tehran) no. 146 (7 January 1908), p. 1.
19. *Ruh al-Qodos* (Tehran) no. 15 (22 January 1908), p. 1.
20. *Mohakemat* (Tehran) no. 25 (18 November 1907), p. 1. See also see *Ruh al-Qodos*.
21. *Mohakemat* (Tehran) no. 26 (2 December 1907), p.1.
22. On which, see also Nahid Mozaffari's chapter in this volume.
23. Edward G. Browne, *The Press and Poetry of Modern Iran* (Los Angeles: Kalimat Press Reprint, 1983).
24. See Mohammad Sadr Hashemi, *Tarikh-e jarayed va majallat-e Iran*, vol. 1 (Tehran: n/a), pp. 253–57.
25. *Sobh-e Sadeq* (Tehran) no. 81 (27 May 1908), pp. 3–4.
26. *Habl al-Matin* (Tehran) no. 59 (5 July 1907), p. 2.
27. *Tamaddon* (Tehran) no. 48 (13 January 1908), p. 4; no. 49 (20 January 1908), p. 3.

28. *Tamaddon* (Tehran) no. 52 (March 1908), pp. 3–4.
29. *Mohakemat* (Tehran) no. 45 (2 April 1908), p. 4 for Afsah al-Motekallemin's case.
30. *Mohakemat* (Tehran) no. 15 (November 1908), p. 4 for Habl al-Matin's case before the Press Law.
31. *Habl al-Matin* (Tehran) no. 58 (4 July 1907), p. 3.
32. *Mosavat* (Tehran) no. 19 (5 April 1908), p. 1.
33. See Hashemi (ed.), *Mozakerat-e Majles*, pp. 587–91.
34. Ibid.
35. *Ruh al-Qodos* (Tehran) no. 17 (24 February 1908), p. 4. See also Hashemi (ed.), *Mozakerat-e Majles*, p. 589.

Chapter 14. The Constitutional Revolution and Persian Dramatic Works: An Observation on Social Relations Criticism in the Plays of the Constitutional Era

1. Peter J. Chelkowski (ed.), *Ta'zieh: Ritual and Drama in Iran* (New York: New York University Press, 1979); Sadeq Homayuni, *Ta'ziyeh dar Iran* (Shiraz: Navid, 1968).
2. Jamshid Malekpur, *Adabiyat-e namayeshi dar Iran*, vol. 1 (Tehran: Tus, 1984), pp. 130–31; Mohammad Baqer Mo'meni, 'Akhundzadeh va Namayeshnameh', *Tamsilat* (Tehran: Nashr-e Andisheh, 1970), pp. 27–43.
3. Fath-Ali Akhundzadeh, *Alefba-ye jadid va maktubat*, edited by Hamid Mohammadzadeh (Tabriz: Nashr-e Ehya, 1978), p. 182.
4. Fath-Ali Akhundzadeh, *Tamsilat*, translated by Mirza Ja'far Qarachehdaghi, (Lithography, Tehran, 1874); Malekpur, *Adabiyat*, vol. 1, pp. 136–37.
5. Akhundzadeh, *Alefba-ye jadid*, pp. 183–84, 333–34.
6. Ibid., pp. 389–92.
7. Malekpur, *Adabiyat*, vol. 1, p. 186; Yahya Aryanpur, *As Saba ta Nima*, vol. 1 (Tehran: Kh'arazmi, 1975), pp. 359–60, *Dare'at al-ma'aref-e bozorg-e Eslam*, s.v. 'Tabrizi, Mirza Aqa'; H. Sadiq, *Namayeshnamehha-ye Mirza Aqa Tabrizi* (Tehran: Tahuri, 1975).
8. Shiva Balaghi, 'The Iranian as Spectator and Spectacle: Theater and Nationalism in the Nineteenth Century', in Fatma Müge Göçek (ed.), *Social Constructions of Nationalism in the Middle East* (Albany, NY: State University of New York Press, 2001), p. 199.
9. Ibid.
10. Ibid., p. 200.
11. Malekpur, *Adabiyat*, vol. 1, p. 195; Hiva Guran, *Kusheshha-ye nafarjam: Seyri dar sad sal Tiyatr-e Iran* (Tehran: Agah, 1981), p. 54.
12. Sadiq, *Namayeshnamehha-ye Mirza Aqa Tabrizi*, pp. 8–9.
13. Malekpur, *Adabiyat*, vol. 1, pp. 185, 186, and 194; Mayel Bektash, 'Mirza Aqa Tabrizi', *Faslnameh-ye Tiyatr* 1/1 (1977), p. 23.
14. Malekpur, *Adabiyat*, vol. 2, pp. 74–77, 206.
15. It must be pointed out that some believe that the Anjoman-e Okhovvat had a direct relation with the Iranian Democrat party, their Sufi behaviour constitut-

ing only a cover for this relationship. Hasen Shirvani, *Honar-e namayesh* (Tehran: Farhang va Honar, 1976), pp. 29–30; Malekpur, *Adabiyat*, vol. 2, pp. 33–34.
16. On Zahir al-Dowleh see Iraj Afshar (ed.), *Khaterat va asnad-e Zahir al-Dowleh* (Tehran: Ketabha-ye Jibi, 1972) and Lloyd Ridgeon's essay in the present collection.
17. Malekpur, *Adabiyat*, vol. 2, pp. 74–77.
18. Ibid., p. 210.
19. Ibid., p. 213.
20. Ibid., pp. 211–12.
21. Ibid., p. 76.
22. On Na'ini, see the editors' introduction in Mohammad Golbon and Faramarz Talebi (eds.), Mirza Reza Na'ini, *Ruznameh-ye Tiyatr* (Tehran: Cheshmeh, 1987) pp. 50–51; Malekpur, *Adabiyat*, vol. 2, pp. 249–51; and *Dare'at al-ma'aref-e bozorg-e Eslam*, s.v. 'Tiyatr'.
23. Golbon and Talebi (eds.), Na'ini, *Ruznameh-ye Tiyatr*, pp. 50–51.
24. On As'adi see Ranjbar Fakhri, *Namayesh dar Tabriz* (Tehran: Sazeman-e Asnad-e Melli-ye Iran, 2004), passim.
25. Ibid., pp. 644–46.
26. Ibid.
27. Mohammad Sadr Hashemi, *Tarikh-e jarayed va majallat-e Iran*, vol. 4 (Isfahan: Kamal, 1985), pp. 209–10.
28. Mas'ud Kuhestaninezhad, *Gozideh-ye asnad-e namayesh dar Iran*, vol. 1 (Tehran: Sazeman-e Asnad-e Melli-ye Iran, 2002), pp. 177–91. The play was published in *Mosavat*, vol. 1, no. 22 (1908), pp. 4–8.

Chapter 15. National Identity and Photographs of the Constitutional Revolution

1. John Bloom, *Photography at Bay* (Albuquerque: University of New Mexico Press, 1993), p. 12.
2. Nazem al-Eslam Kermani, *Tarikh-e bidari-ye Iraniyan*, Ali Akbar Sa'idi Sirjani, ed., (Tehran: Agah, 1983).
3. Ahmad Kasravi, *Tarikh-e mashruteh-ye Iran* (Tehran: Amir Kabir, 1978).
4. The dialectics of idea and image lies at the crux of this study. Among the books that have inspired me are Shahrokh Meskub [Meskoob], *Hoviyat-e irani va zaban-e farsi* (Tehran: Bagh-e Ayene, 1994); Homi Bhabha, *The Location of Culture* (London: Routledge, 1994), particularly chapters 2 and 8; Mohamad Tavakoli-Targhi, *Refashioning Iran: Orientalism, Occidentalism and Historiography* (New York: Palgrave, 2001), particularly chapters 5, 6, and 7; Firoozeh Kashani-Sabet, *Frontier Fictions: Shaping the Iranian Nation: 1804–1946* (Princeton: Princeton University Press 1999); Richard Rudisill, *Mirror Image: The Influence of Daguerreotype on American Society* (Albuquerque: University of New Mexico Press 1971); and Wright Morris, *Time Pieces: Photographs, Writing and Memory* (New York: Aperture Foundation, 1989).
5. Research indicates that the first camera entered Iran in 1840. I am disregarding the first ten years of photography, which may be called the daguerreotype years,

for no daguerreotype from Iran has been found yet. A more realistic starting date for photography by Iranians is 1863, the year the first Court photographer was officially appointed.
6. Meskub, *Hoviyat*, p. 35.
7. Expression borrowed from Rudisill, *Mirror Image*, pp. 31–32.
8. For a critique of the photography of the period see Reza Sheikh, 'The Rise of the Kingly Citizen', in Parisa Damandan Nafisi (ed.), *Portrait Photographs of Isfahan: Faces in Transition 1920–1950* (London: Saqi Books, 2004).
9. For a critique of portrait photography within a socioeconomic context see John Tagg, *The Burden of Representation: Essays on Photographies and Histories* (London: Macmillan Education, 1988), and Gisèle Freund, *Photography and Society* (London: David R. Godine, 1980).
10. Photographs of modern schools, members of the Majles, syndicates, and societies (*anjoman*) abound next to those of a fledgling government bureaucracy.
11. Bloom, *Photography at Bay*, p. 12.
12. Here the analyst 'reads into them what he has already learned by other means, or what he believes he knows, and wants to "demonstrate"'. Underpinning this approach, Ginzburg continues, is 'the conviction that works of art, in a broad sense, furnish a mine of first-hand information that can explicate, without intermediaries, the mentality and emotive life of a distant age'. Ginzburg raises a profound methodological issue of pressing relevance to all those working with imagery and artifacts, and although this is ultimately an unsolvable problem, the manner in which many arguments about the 'political effect' of images overlay them with conclusions arrived at 'by other means' is especially striking and troubling. Carlo Ginzburg, 'From Aby Warburg to E. H. Gomrich: A Problem of Method', in *Clues, Myths, and Historical Method* (Baltimore: Johns Hopkins University Press 1989), p. 35, as quoted in Christopher Pinney and Nicolas Peterson (eds.), *Photography's Other Histories* (Durham, NC: Duke University Press 2003), p. 3. I should like to thank Corien Vuurman, photohistorian at Leiden University, for bringing Ginzburg's arguments to my attention and for her constructive criticism of this chapter.
13. Dowlatabadi published his article at a later date: Yahya Dowlatabadi, *Kongereh* (Istanbul: *Matbaʿeh-ye Shams*, 1912). The article had three sections: (a) the history of Iranians (*Sabeqeh-ye ahval-e Iraniyan*), (b) the mores and customs of Iranians (*Akhlaq va ʿadat-e Iraniyan*), and (c) the change in the Iranian government and the reasons for it (*Tabdil-e asas-e hokumat-e Iran va sabab-e an*).
14. For the account of Dowlatabadi's preparation and participation in the conference refer to his memoirs: Yahya Dowlatabadi, *Tarikh-e moʿaser ya hayat-e Yahya*, 2nd edition (Tehran: Ferdows, 1982), pp. 114–53.
15. The albums have been archived under the title of *Aksha-ye dowreh-ye Qajar*, numbers 1–12, in the Majles Library.
16. For a full account of the article and the photographs see Reza Sheikh, 'Sad ruz Dar al-Fonun: moʿarrefi-ye Iran dar avvalin kongereh-ye nezhadi 1911', *'Aksnameh* 4/14 (Summer 2004), pp. 2–11.
17. 1910 is the date of the collage of figure 8.

18. The author is indebted to the owners of the Mo'tazedi collection and to Nader Sohrabi of Columbia University for translations of the Ottoman text on the postcards.
19. The only book on Iranian postcards is Qasem Safi, *Kartpostalha-ye tarikhi-ye Iran* (Tehran: Mo'asseseh-ye Farhangi-ye Gostaresh-e Honar, 1999).
20. These postcards carry the following caption: 'Tauris en révolution'. Refer to figure 13.
21. There is practically no reliable data on the size of the market or number of postcards printed.
22. I am indebted to the owners of the Mo'tazedi collection for placing this album at my disposal for study.
23. 'How happy I am to see myself on top of this scaffold, I am exalted and the world is under my feet...a freedom fighter is hung without trial on 2 Safar 1327 HQ'. This translation and the ones in the following notes are my own.
24. 'The trace of your existence that is found on this sheet is the soul that adorns us (your creations), it is the picture of your face that is entwined in this world, this is why the whole world is (glowing) red'. Photograph of the three clerics of Najaf who endorsed the constitutional movement.
25. 'If you want justice to destroy one hundred links of injustice, you must wear the chain of dictatorship on your neck.' (The names of the prisoners shown here are then listed.)
26. 'This head which is the sign of leadership is today void of life, behold the sight and know that this is the result of love for the nation.'
27. 'The first political elite and educators (raising awareness) of the nation and martyrs on the road to freedom and *mojahed*s of the path to humanity.' The group of six, clockwise from top, are: Malek al-Motekallemin; Haji Mirza Ebrahim Aqa, the Majles deputy from Tabriz; Seyyed Jamal al-Din Va'ez; Seyyed Hasan Sharifzadeh; Seyyed Jamal al-Din Asadabadi; and Mirza Reza Kermani. The single photograph on the lower left shows Abbas Aqa Tabrizi; the one on the lower right shows Mirza Jahangir Khan Sur-e Esrafil.
28. Roland Barthes, *Image, Music, Text* (New York: Farrar, Straus and Giroux: 1977), pp. 32–52,
29. The newsletters were gathered and published once in 1943 and again in 1967. It was not until after the revolution in 1983 that the task was completed and portrait photographs were added to the introductory section of the book.
30. Interestingly, the first chapter of his book is entitled *Iraniyan cheguneh bidar shodand* (How Iranians wake up).
31. Kasravi, *Tarikh-e mashruteh*, pp. 3–6.
32. In his drive to replace as many Arabic words as possible, Kasravi replaced the word *aks* (picture) with *peykareh*, just as he coined the word *negareh* for painting. He made meticulous use of photographs and put much effort into formulating well-thought-out captions. Some valuable information extracted from the captions for the purposes of this study are: (a) not all portraits were taken at the time of the constitutional events; (b) at one point during the peaceful sit-ins at the British legation, the protesters within the compound communicated with the

outside and disseminated their thoughts by photographing their written communiqué. Copies were thus made and spread in the city, but this proved to be an expensive practice and was later stopped later; and (c) some photographs were 'staged' in the studio to depict what had happened outside.

33. Sohrab Yazdani, *Kasravi va tarikh-e mashruteh-ye Iran* (Tehran: Ney, 1367), p. 8.
34. Kasravi, *Tarikh-e mashruteh*, p. 3.
35. Prior to the twentieth century, by royal order, Qajar Court photographers carried out extensive photo expeditions across the country, and photographs of the royal realm were presented in elaborate albums to the king. Refer to the photo archive of the Golestan Palace in Tehran.
36. Of course, from another vantage point, it is the publicizing of portrait photographs of individuals with a public reputation that turns them into celebrities.
37. Sheikh, 'Rise of the Kingly Citizen,' pp. 235–37.
38. Morris, *Time Pieces*, p. 34.
39. Inspired by David Ellis, 'Images of D. H. Lawrence: On the Use of Photographs in Biography', in Graham Clarke (ed.), *The Portrait in Photography* (London: Reaktion Books, 1992), pp. 155–73.
40. 'A photograph is a *trace* of the real.' Susan Sontag, *On Photography* (London: Allen Lane, 1978), p. 154.
41. Barthes, 'Rhetoric of the Image', in *Image, Music, Text*, pp. 274–75.
42. There are a handful of photographs of dead bodies strewn on the battlefield and a set of men posing by lynched bodies, particularly in his original version of *Tarikh-e hejdah saleh-ye Azarbayjan*.
43. Ellis, 'Images of D. H. Lawrence', p. 171. As Sontag and Barthes would say, a photographic portrait is a *memento mori*. See Sontag, *On Photography*, and Roland Barthes, *Camera Lucida*, trans. Richard Howard (London: Vintage, 1981).
44. Rudisill, *The Mirror Image*, pp. 31–32
45. This is inspired by Rudisill's treatment of the daguerreotype in American photo-history.
46. Sheikh, 'Rise of the Kingly Citizen', pp. 245–49.
47. Mohammad Ali Akbari, *Tabar shenasi-ye hoviyat-e jadid-e irani: 'asr-e Qajariyeh va Pahlavi-ye avval* (Tehran: Sherkat-e Entesharat-e 'Elmi Farhangi, 2005), pp. 79–107
48. Homi Bhabha (ed.), *Nation and Narration* (London: Routledge, 1990), p. 292.
49. Ibid., p. 295. This is not to negate the 'conjunctive' use of photographs and text. I am simply emphasizing that photographs or images can also be viewed on their own in treating the topic of national identity.
50. Ibid.
51. Ibid.
52. For a study of the state-driven visual media campaign during the reign of Reza Shah Pahlavi refer to Sheikh, 'Rise of the Kingly Citizen', and for the years after the Islamic Revolution refer to Peter Chelkowski and Hamid Dabashi, *Staging a Revolution: The Art of Persuasion in the Islamic Republic of Iran* (New York: New York University Press, 1999).

53. We begin by faces lost in a crowd (set-ins). We then transition to a heightened sense of individuality in response to aggression after the coup. We finally regroup as civil servants and civic organizations. In between we witness the realignment of political figures facing the shifting circumstances.

Chapter 16. *Mashrutiyat, Meşrutiyet,* and Beyond: Intellectuals and the Constitutional Revolutions of 1905–12

1. This paper draws on Charles Kurzman, *Democracy Denied, 1905–1915* (Cambridge, MA: Harvard University Press, 2008). That work describes the Iranian *mashrutiyat* as a democratic revolution, with ideals and institutions comparable to countries that were considered leading 'democracies' at the time. For the purposes of the present volume, however, the more usual term 'Constitutional Revolution' is used instead.
2. Edward G. Browne, *The Persian Revolution of 1905–1909* (1910, Washington, DC: Mage, 1995), p. 120.
3. Mehdi Malekzadeh, *Tarikh-e enqelab-e mashrutiyat-e Iran*, vol. 1 (Tehran: 'Elmi, 1984), p. 87.
4. *Habl al-Matin* (Calcutta), 24 August 1906, p. 9.
5. Ali Gheissari, 'Despots of the World Unite! Satire in the Iranian Constitutional Press: The *Majalleh-ye Estebdad*, 1907–1908', *Comparative Studies of South Asia, Africa and the Middle East* 25/2 (2005), p. 368.
6. V. I. Lenin, 'The Right of Nations to Self-Determination' (1914), in Robert C. Tucker (ed.), *The Lenin Anthology* (New York: W. W. Norton, 1975), p. 162; James Bryce, *Modern Democracies* (New York: The Macmillan Company, 1922), pp. 501–02; *The Positivist Review* 228 (1 December 1911), p. 387.
7. John Foran, 'Dependency and Resistance in the Middle East, 1800–1925', *Political Power and Social Theory* 8 (1993), pp. 107–40; John Mason Hart, *Revolutionary Mexico: The Coming and Process of the Mexican Revolution* (Berkeley: University of California Press, 1987); Don C. Price, *Russia and the Roots of the Chinese Revolution, 1896–1911* (Cambridge, MA: Harvard University Press, 1971); Nader Sohrabi, 'Historicizing Revolutions: Constitutional Revolutions in the Ottoman Empire, Iran, and Russia, 1905–1908', *American Journal of Sociology* 100/6 (1995), pp. 383–447; Nader Sohrabi, 'Constitutionalism, Revolution and State: The Young Turk Revolution of 1908 and the Iranian Constitutional Revolution of 1906 with Comparisons to the Russian Revolution of 1905' (PhD dissertation, Department of Sociology, University of Chicago, 1996); Nader Sohrabi, 'Global Waves, Local Actors: What the Young Turks Knew about Other Revolutions and Why It Mattered', *Comparative Studies in Society and History*, 44/1 (2002), pp. 45–79; Ivan Spector, *The First Russian Revolution: Its Impact on Asia* (Englewood Cliffs, NJ: Prentice-Hall, 1962).
8. Charles Kurzman, 'Waves of Democratization', *Studies in Comparative International Development* 33/1 (1998), pp. 37–59.
9. 'Ali Akbar Velayati, *Tarikh-e ravabet-e khareji-ye Iran*, vol. 1 (Tehran: Daftar-e Motale'at-e Siyasi va Beyn-al-melali, 1991), p. 17.
10. Stephen Gwynn, *The Letters and Friendships of Sir Cecil Spring Rice: A Record*

(Boston, MA: Houghton Mifflin Company, 1929), p. 88.
11. F. H. Villiers, British ambassador in Lisbon, to Arthur Hardinge, British ambassador in Brussels (soon to succeed Villiers in Lisbon), 9 October 1910, Great Britain, Public Record Office, FO 371/1208.
12. Rose Louise Greaves, 'Some Aspects of the Anglo-Russian Convention and Its Working in Persia, 1907–1914', *Bulletin of the School of Oriental and African Studies* 31/2 (1968), p. 291.
13. Daniel M. Crane and Thomas A. Breslin, *An Ordinary Relationship: American Opposition to Republican Revolution in China* (Miami: University Presses of Florida, Florida International University Press, 1986), pp. 80–81.
14. Friedrich Katz, *The Secret War in Mexico: Europe, the United States, and the Mexican Revolution* (Chicago: University of Chicago Press, 1981), p. 89.
15. Arthur Hardinge, British ambassador in Lisbon, to Eyre Crowe, British assistant under-secretary of state, April 4, 1912, Great Britain, Public Record Office, FO 371/1463; J. D. Vincent-Smith, 'Britain and Portugal, 1910–16' (PhD dissertation, Department of History, London School of Economics and Political Science, University of London, 1971), p. 87.
16. J. M. Hone and Page L. Dickinson, *Persia in Revolution* (London: T. Fisher Unwin, 1910), p. 88.
17. James W. Long, 'Organized Protest Against the 1906 Russian Loan', *Cahiers du monde russe et soviétique* 13/1 (1972), pp. 31–32.
18. Katz, *The Secret War in Mexico*, pp. 107–08.
19. Marius B. Jansen, *The Japanese and Sun Yat-Sen* (Cambridge, MA: Harvard University Press, 1967), pp. 165–66, 188–89; Ernest P. Young, *The Presidency of Yuan Shih-k'ai* (Ann Arbor: The University of Michigan Press, 1977), pp. 119, 128.
20. Fernand Farjenel, *Through the Chinese Revolution* (London: Duckworth and Co., 1915), pp. 302–05.
21. K. N. Smirnov, *Zapiski Vospitatelia Persidskogo Shakha, 1907–1914 Gody* (Tel Aviv: Ivrus, 2002), pp. 75–76. I thank Zumrad Ahmedjanova for the translation.
22. Gene R. Garthwaite, *Khans and Shahs: A Documentary Analysis of the Bakhtiyari in Iran* (Cambridge, MA: Cambridge University Press, 1983), p. 122; G. P. Gooch and Harold Temperley (eds.), *British Documents on the Origins of the War, 1898–1914* (London: His Majesty's Stationery Office, 1936), vol. 10, part 1, p. 837; Robert A. McDaniel, *The Shuster Mission and the Persian Constitutional Revolution* (Minneapolis: Bibliotheca Islamica, 1974), p. 191; USSR, *Mezhdunarodnye Otnosheniia v Epokhu Imperializma: Dokumenti iz Arkhivov Tsarskogo i Vremennogo Pravitel'stva 1878–1917* (Moscow, USSR: Gosudarstvennoe Izdatel'stvo Politicheskoi Literatury, 1939), second series, vol. 19, part 1, pp. 50–51. I thank Veronica Gushin for the translation.
23. Gooch and Temperley, *British Documents*, vol. 10, part 1, p. 841.
24. Firuz Kazemzadeh, *Russia and Britain in Persia, 1864–1914: A Study in Imperialism* (New Haven: Yale University Press, 1968), p. 639.
25. Jean-Yves Veillard, 'L'affaire Dreyfus et l'opinion publique internationale', in Laurent Gervereau and Christophe Prochasson (eds.), *L'affaire Dreyfus et le tour-*

nant du siècle (1894–1910) (Paris: Bibliothèque de documentation internationale contemporaine, 1994), pp. 258–66.
26. *Habl al-Matin* (Tehran) 1/47 (22 June 1907), p. 2.
27. Mustafa Refik, 'Abdülhamid ve Dreyfüs Meselesi', *Osmanlı Mecmuası* 2/43 (1 September 1899), p. 2.
28. Jesús Jareño López, *El Affaire Dreyfus en España, 1894–1906* (Murcia: Editorial Godoy, 1981), p. 154.
29. Muhammad Rashid Rida, 'Al-Yahud fi Faransa wa fi Misr', *al-Manar* (Cairo) 1/2 (18 March 1898), p. 55.
30. Mahmud Khoja Behbudiy, 'Padarkush' (1911), in Edward A. Allworth, 'Murder as Metaphor in the First Central Asian Drama', *Ural-Altaischer Jahrbücher/Ural-Altaic Yearbook* 68 (1986), pp. 74–76, 81; Abdulhamid Sulayman Cholpan, 'Dokhtur Muhammadyor' (1914), *Sharq Yulduzi* 1 (1992), p. 136, translated by Adeeb Khalid and Ken Petersen in Charles Kurzman (ed.), *Modernist Islam, 1840–1940: A Sourcebook* (New York: Oxford University Press, 2002), p. 268.
31. Michael Confino, 'On Intellectuals and Intellectual Traditions in Eighteenth- and Nineteenth-Century Russia', *Daedalus* 101/102 (1972), p. 138.
32. *Min Bao* (Tokyo) 3 (3 April 1906), p. 1. I thank Mei Zhou for the translation.
33. Wolfgang Lippert, *Entstehung und Funktion einiger chinesischer marxistischer Termini* (Wiesbaden: Franz Steiner Verlag, 1979), p. 316; Vera Schwarcz, *The Chinese Enlightenment: Intellectuals and the Legacy of the May Fourth Movement of 1919* (Berkeley: University of California Press, 1986), p. 186.
34. A few Freemasons were involved in the constitutionalist movement in Iran, but Masonic influences such as organizational structures and rituals were widespread among constitutionalists, some of whom soon formed a Masonic lodge in 1907–08. See Esma'il Ra'in, *Faramushkhaneh va faramasoneri dar Iran* (Tehran: Amir Kabir, 1979), vols. 1–2; Thierry Zarcone, *Secret et sociétés secrètes en islam: Turquie, Iran et Asie centrale, XIXe–XXe siècles: franc-maçonnerie, carboneria et confréries soufies* (Milan: Archè, 2002); and Mangol Bayat's contribution to this volume. Freemasons were more prominent in some of the revolutions of the period, but not others.
35. Abraham Ascher, *The Revolution of 1905*, vol. 2 (Stanford, CA: Stanford University Press, 1992), pp. 51–52.
36. Vasco Pulido Valente, *O Poder e o Povo: A Revolução de 1910* (Lisbon: Publicações Dom Quixote, 1976), p. 98.
37. Alan Knight, *The Mexican Revolution*, vol. 1 (Cambridge: Cambridge University Press, 1986), pp. 166–67.
38. Edward Friedman, 'The Center Cannot Hold: The Failure of Parliamentary Democracy in China From the Chinese Revolution of 1911 to the World War in 1914' (PhD dissertation, Department of Government, Harvard University), pp. 163–64; see also Edward J. M. Rhoads, *China's Republican Revolution: The Case of Kwangtung, 1895–1913* (Cambridge, MA: Harvard University Press, 1975), pp. 235–36.
39. Alexander Blok, 'The People and the Intelligentsia' (1908), in Marc Raeff (ed.), *Russian Intellectual History: An Anthology* (Atlantic Highlands, NJ: Humanities

Press, 1978), p. 363.
40. Quoted in H. E. Chehabi, 'From Revolutionary Tasnīf to Patriotic Surūd: Music and Nation-Building in Pre-World War II Iran', *Iran* 37 (1999), p. 145.
41. Tarik Z. Tunaya, *Hürriyet İlanı: İkinci Meşrutiyetin Siyasî Hayatına Bakışlar* (Istanbul: Baha Matbaası, 1959), p. 64.
42. John Rutherford, *Mexican Society during the Revolution: A Literary Approach* (Oxford: Clarendon Press, 1971), p. 89.
43. Maria Filomena Mónica, *Educação e Sociedade no Portugal de Salazar* (Lisbon: Editorial Presença, 1978), p. 179.
44. Schwarcz, *The Chinese Enlightenment*, p. 13.
45. Abdul-Hadi Hairi, *Shīʿism and Constitutionalism in Iran* (Leiden: Brill, 1977), pp. 124, 158–59.
46. Ali Gheissari, *Iranian Intellectuals in the Twentieth Century* (London: I.B.Tauris, 1998), pp. 15–16.
47. For example, Rasul Jaʿfariyan, *Bast-neshini: mashruteh-kh"ahan dar sefarat-e Engelis* (Tehran: Moʾasseseh-ye Motalaʿat-e Tarikh-e Moʿaser-e Iran, 1999), pp. 58–63.
48. Asadollah Mamaqani, *Maslak al-imam fi salamat al-Islam* (Istanbul: Matbaʿeh-ye Shams, 1910), p. 60.
49. Yahya Dowlatabadi, *Hayat-e Yahya*, 6th edition, vol. 2 (Tehran: ʿAttar, Ferdowsi, 1992), p. 86.
50. *Qanun* (London) 1/6 (19 July 1890), p. 1. The terms *ʿoqala* and *daneshmandan* are treated as synonyms by Mangol Bayat, *Iran's First Revolution: Shiʿism and the Constitutional Revolution of 1905–1909* (New York: Oxford University Press, 1991), p. 34. I will argue that there is a distinction between them, since *daneshmandan* also included seminary scholars.
51. Mehdi Malekzadeh, *Tarikh-e enqelab-e mashrutiyat-e Iran*, 4th edition, vol. 2 (Tehran: ʿElmi, n.d.), pp. 241–43, translated in Charles Kurzman, 'Weaving Iran into the Tree of Nations', *International Journal of Middle East Studies* 37/2 (2005), p. 151.
52. *Tarbiyat* (Tehran) 1/60 (3 February 1898), p. 237.
53. Haj Mirza Mohammad Ali Moʿin al-Saltaneh, *Safarnameh-ye Shikago* (Paris: Georges Meunier et Cie., 1902), p. 102.
54. Mohammad Nazem al-Eslam Kermani, *Tarikh-e bidari-ye Iraniyan*, vol. 1 (Tehran: Entesharat-e Bonyad-e Farhang-e Iran, 1968), p. 6. Another underground constitutionalist group opened with an appeal to intellectuals as 'men of goodwill and enlightened thought' (*mardan-e kheyrkh"ah va rowshanfekr*) (Malekzadeh, *Tarikh*, vol. 2, p. 241), though this usage of *rowshanfekr* – which came to be the main term for 'intellectual' during the Pahlavi era – appears to be anachronistic. I have found no other use of the term during the constitutional era.
55. Ahmad Majd al-Eslam Kermani, *Tarikh-e enqelab-e mashrutiyat-e Iran*, vol. 1 (Isfahan: Daneshgah-e Esfahan, 1972), p. 87.
56. Dowlatabadi, *Hayat-e Yahya*, vol. 2, p. 84.
57. Jaʿfariyan, *Bast-neshini*, p. 61.

58. Heydar Khan 'Amuoghli, 'Varaqi az tarikh-e mashruteh-ye Iran', *Yadegar* 3/5 (1946–47), p. 80, translated in A. Reza Sheikholeslami and Dunning Wilson, 'The Memoirs of Haydar Khan 'Amu Ughlu', *Iranian Studies* 6/1 (1973), p. 37.
59. Nazem al-Eslam Kermani, *Tarikh-e bidari*, vol. 1, p. 514.
60. Ebrahim Safa'i (ed.), *Asnad-e mashruteh*, 2nd ed. (Tehran: Roshdiyeh, 1973), p. 78, translated in Cyrus Amir-Mokri, 'Redefining Iran's Constitutional Revolution' (PhD dissertation, Department of History, University of Chicago, 1992), p. 114, and in Vanessa A. Martin, *Islam and Modernism: The Iranian Revolution of 1906* (London: I.B.Tauris, 1989), p. 93.
61. Ervand Abrahamian, 'The Crowd in the Persian Revolution', *Iranian Studies* 2/4 (1969), p. 134; Ervand Abrahamian, *Iran Between Two Revolutions* (Princeton: Princeton University Press, 1982), p. 85; Bayat, *Iran's First Revolution*, p. 135; Edward G. Browne, *The Persian Revolution, 1905–1909* (Washington, DC: Mage Publishers, 1995), p. 122; Martin, *Islam and Modernism*, pp. 94–96.
62. Abrahamian, *Iran Between Two Revolutions*, p. 85; Ahmad Tafreshi Hoseyni, *Ruznameh-ye akhbar-e mashrutiyat va enqelab-e Iran* (Tehran: Amir Kabir, 1973), pp. 41–42.
63. Kurzman, 'Weaving Iran into the Tree of Nations', p. 151; Martin, *Islam and Modernism*, pp. 68–69.
64. Hairi, *Shī'ism and Constitutionalism in Iran*, pp. 98–100.
65. Nazem al-Eslam Kermani, *Tarikh-e bidari*, vol. 1, p. 547.
66. *Rahnema* (Tehran), 3 August 1907, p. 2. See also similar comments by Sheykh Esma'il Mahallati, discussed in Bayat's contribution to this volume.
67. *Mozakerat-e majles*, 8 January 1907 (Tehran: Chapkhaneh-ye Majles, 1946), vol. 1, p. 53.
68. *Majles* (Tehran) 1/27 (12 January 1907), p. 3.
69. *Habl al-Matin* (Tehran) 11/7 (4 September 1906), p. 12.
70. *Anjoman* (Tabriz) 1/99 (15 June 1907), p. 2.
71. *Mozakerat-e majles*, 11 July 1907, vol. 1, p. 209.
72. *Neda-ye vatan* (Tehran) 1/1 (27 December 1906), p. 7.
73. Mohammad Ali Khan [Forughi] bin Zoka' al-Molk, *Hoquq-e asasi, ya'ni adab-e mashrutiyat-e doval* (Tehran: Self-published, 1908), pp. 17–19, 37.
74. Saïd Amir Arjomand, 'The Ulama's Traditionalist Opposition to Parliamentarism, 1907–1909', *Middle Eastern Studies* 17/2 (1981), pp. 174–90.
75. Negin Nabavi, 'Spreading the Word: Iran's First Constitutional Press and the Shaping of a "New Era"', *Critique: Critical Middle Eastern Studies* 14/3 (2005), p. 311.
76. Willem Floor, 'Change and Development in the Judicial System of Qajar Iran (1800–1925)', in Edmund Bosworth and Carole Hillebrand (eds.), *Qajar Iran: Political, Social and Cultural Change, 1800–1925* (Edinburgh: Edinburgh University Press, 1983), pp. 113–47; James Greenfield, 'Die geistlichen Scharia-gerichte in Persien', *Zeitschrift für vergleichende Rechtswissenschaft* 48 (1934), pp. 157–67; Sohrabi, 'Constitutionalism, Revolution and State', 302–03. See also Ali Gheissari's contribution in this volume.
77. A. Reza Arasteh, *Education and Social Awakening in Iran, 1850–1968* (Leiden:

Brill, 1969), pp. 223–30; Ali Kani, *Sazman-e farhangi-ye Iran* (Tehran: Entesharat-e Daneshgah-e Tehran, 1954), pp. 21–22.
78. James W. Cunningham, *A Vanquished Hope: The Movement for Church Renewal in Russia, 1905–1906* (Crestwood, NY: St. Vladimir's Seminary Press, 1981).
79. John S. Curtiss, *Church and State in Russia: The Last Years of the Empire, 1900–1914* (New York: Columbia University Press, 1940), p. 79.
80. E. Morgado (ed.), *Legislação Republicana ou As Primeiras Leis e Disposições da República Portugueza* (Lisbon: Empreza do Almanach Palhares, 1910).
81. Alberto J. Pani, *Una Encuesta Sobre Educación Popular* (Mexico City: Poder Ejecutivo Federal, Departamiento de Aprovisionamientos Generales, Dirección de Talleres Gráficos, 1918), p. 149.
82. Sally Borthwick, *Education and Social Change in China: The Beginnings of the Modern Era* (Stanford, CA: Hoover Institution Press, 1983), p. 83.
83. M. Şükrü Hanioğlu, *The Young Turks in Opposition* (New York: Oxford University Press, 1995), pp. 200–03.
84. Namık Kemal, 'Wa shawirhum fi'l-amr', *Hürriyet* (London) 1/4 (20 July 1868), pp. 1–4, translated by M. Şükrü Hanioğlu in Kurzman (ed.), *Modernist Islam*, pp. 144–48.
85. Murtaza Korlaelçi, *Pozitivizmin Türkiye'ye Girişi ve İlk Etkileri* (Istanbul: İnsan Yayınları, 1986), pp. 252, 261.
86. Hüseyin Cahit Yalçın, *Siyasal Anılar* (Istanbul: Türkiye İş Bankası Yayınları, 1976), p. 123.
87. M. Şükrü Hanioğlu, *Preparation for a Revolution: The Young Turks, 1902–1908* (New York: Oxford University Press, 2001), p. 309.
88. *Şûra-yı ümmet* (Paris) 75 (20 May 1905), pp. 1–2, parts translated in Hanioğlu, *The Young Turks in Opposition*, p. 207. I thank Professor Hanioğlu for providing me with the original article, and Yektan Türkyılmaz for translation assistance.
89. İsmail Kara, *İslâmcıların Siyasî Görüşleri* (Istanbul: İz Yayıncılık, 1994), p. 75.
90. *Mosavat* 1/12 (9 February 1908), pp. 3–4, translated in Mohammad Tavakoli-Targhi, 'From Patriotism to Matriotism: A Tropological Study of Iranian Nationalism, 1870–1909', *International Journal of Middle East Studies* 34/2 (2002), p. 229.

Chapter 17. Erin and Iran Resurgent: Irish Nationalists and the Iranian Constitutional Revolution

1. This essay incorporates material from two forthcoming monographs on *Confluences of Nationalisms, Internationalisms, & Transnationalisms: India, Iran, and Ireland, 1905–1921* and *Global Networks of Anti-Imperialist Nationalist Resistance, 1905–1914*. My thanks to Houchang Chehabi for his editorial comments on an earlier draft of this essay.
2. See also the contributions of Charles Kurzman, Farzin Vejdani, Touraj Atabaki, and Yidan Wang in this volume.
3. On Irish and Gaelic Revivals, see John Hutchinson, *The Dynamics of Cultural Nationalism: The Gaelic Revival and the Creation of the Irish Nation State* (London: Allen & Unwin, 1987); P. J. Mathews, *Revival: The Abbey Theatre, Sinn Féin,*

the Gaelic League, and the Co-Operative Movement (Notre Dame, IN: University of Notre Dame Press, 2004); Timothy G. McMahon, *Grand Opportunity: The Gaelic Revival and Irish Society, 1893–1910* (Syracuse: Syracuse University Press, 2008); and Karen Steele, *Women, Press, and Politics during the Irish Revival* (Syracuse: Syracuse University Press, 2007).

4. The Irish Parliamentary Party was founded in 1882, supplanting the former Home Rule League established in 1873. Following the fragmentation in party ranks in 1890, the party was once again united under the leadership of John Redmond in 1900 with the Irish nationalist MPs unanimously decrying the British-instigated Boer War in southern Africa (1899–1902).

5. The Irish Republican Brotherhood was formed in 1858 and was led by Tom Clarke and Sean MacDermott in the years before the outbreak of the First World War.

6. In 1906, the eponymous newspaper *Sinn Féin* replaced the *United Irishman* (founded in 1899) as Griffith's organ of the Sinn Féin movement.

7. It should be mentioned that there also were other Irish individuals, including some unionists, who participated in the Iranian debate underway in the United Kingdom at the time, particularly in the aftermath of the conclusion of the 1907 Anglo-Russian Agreement, which, among other arrangements, divided Iran into British and Russian spheres of influence and resulted in an Anglo-Russian stand-off with Iranian constitutional/nationalist camps, eventually culminating in the termination of the Iranian revolution in December 1911. These other Irish individuals in the Iranian debate included the Liberal-Imperialist Henry Finnis Blosse Lynch of Irish descent, who was a co-founder and chairman of the Persia Committee (a lobby group founded in London in October 1908 by British critics of Anglo-Russian intervention in Iran who supported the Iranian revolution and Iran's independence). Lynch was a member of the imperialist Liberal League (1902–10), founded by a group of Liberal Party members primarily opposed to the implementation of Irish Home Rule. Other Irish participants in the Iranian debate included Émile Joseph Dillon, a journalist for various British and Russian papers and the regular foreign affairs correspondent for the *Contemporary Review* (London), who persistently reviled the Iranian constitutionalists/nationalists and their advocates in the United Kingdom.

8. On the reception of the Constitutional Revolution in Egypt see Kamran Rastegar's contribution to this volume.

9. For some examples of worldwide expressions of support and direct and indirect assistance to the Iranian revolutionary movement, see Mansour Bonakdarian, *Britain and the Iranian Constitutional Revolution of 1906–1911: Foreign Policy, Imperialism, and Dissent* (Syracuse: Syracuse University Press, 2006); Janet Afary, *The Iranian Constitutional Revolution, 1906–1911: Grassroots Democracy, Social Democracy, and the Origins of Feminism* (New York: Columbia, 1996); Salamollah Javid, *Nehzat-e mashrutiyat-e Iran va naqsh-e azadikh^{v}ahan-e jahan* (Tehran: Donya, 1968/69); Houri Berberian, *The Love for Freedom Has No Fatherland: Armenians and the Iranian Constitutional Revolution of 1905–1911* (Boulder: Westview, 2001); Iago Gocheleishvili, 'Georgian Sources on the

Iranian Constitutional Revolution (1905–1911): Sergo Gamdlishvili's Memoirs of the Gilan Resistance', *Iranian Studies*, 40/1 (March 2007), pp. 59–85; and Iago Gocheleishvili's contribution to this volume.

10. For a few examples, see Howard Brasted, 'Indian Nationalist Development and the Influence of Irish Home Rule, 1870–1886', *Modern Asian Studies* 14/1 (1980), pp. 37–63; Michael Silvestri, '"The Sinn Féin of India": Irish Nationalism and the Policing of Revolutionary Terrorism in Bengal', *Journal of British Studies* 39/4 (October 2000), pp. 454–86; Ganesh Devi, 'India and Ireland: Literary Relations', in Joseph McMinn (ed.), *The Internationalism of Irish Literature and Drama* (Gerrards Cross: Colin Smythe, 1982), pp. 294–308; Gauri Viswanathan, 'Ireland, India, and the Poetics of Internationalism', *Journal of World History* 15/1 (March 2004), pp. 7–30; Matthew Erin Plowman, 'Irish Republicans and the Indo-German Conspiracy of World War I', *New Hibernia Review* 7/3 (Autumn 2003), pp. 80–105; and Tadhg Foley and Maureen O'Connor (eds.), *Ireland and India: Colonies, Culture and Empire* (Dublin: Irish Academic Press, 2007).

11. On Iranian–Indian nationalist solidarities and collaborations from 1906 to 1918, see *Encyclopaedia Iranica*, s.v. 'India: ix. Political and Cultural Relations: Qajar Period, Early Twentieth Century'.

12. Increasingly after the start of the nineteenth century, the Irish had travelled to and published descriptions of Iran and served in the British diplomatic service as well as in British consular and military forces in Iran, as in the case of the Anglo-Irish Sir Gore Ouseley who served as a British representative to the Qajar Court from 1811 to 1814 or those serving in the British imperial military forces during the Anglo-Iranian wars of 1838 and 1856–57, among many other examples. Irish authors had compiled travel narratives of Iran, as well as historical, geographical, and other accounts, and had contributed to the dissemination of translations of Iranian literature in the English language. Additionally, the Persian language (by no means limited to the use of Persian in Iran) had been taught at Trinity College (University of Dublin) since the seventeenth century, and English translations of historical accounts of Iran and Iranian literature and poetry, among other works, were available to Irish readers. On the teaching of Persian and Iran-related courses at Trinity College, see also Menahem Mansoor, *The Study of Irish Orientalism* (Dublin: Hodges, Figgis & Co., 1944); and Mansour Bonakdarian, 'Iranian Studies in the United Kingdom in the Twentieth Century', *Iranian Studies* 43/2 (April 2010), pp. 280–81.

13. See also Declan Kiberd, *Inventing Ireland: The Literature of the Modern Nation* (Cambridge, MA: Harvard University Press, 1995).

14. See Joseph Lennon, *Irish Orientalism: A Literary and Intellectual History* (Syracuse: Syracuse University Press, 2004).

15. It should be pointed out that the pro-German stance of the IRB and Sinn Féin at the time led to their avoidance of criticism of German imperialism.

16. On the Persia Committee, see Bonakdarian, *Britain and the Iranian Constitutional Revolution*.

17. See, for example, *Iran-e now* (Tehran) no. 47 (16 December [misprinted as 17 December] 1910), p. 1.

18. At the 1910 gathering of the Nationalities and Subject Races conference in June 1910 (London), Bernard Temple presented a paper in defence of Iran's independence. See *Nationalities and Subject Races. Report of Conference Held in Caxton Hall, Westminster June 28–30, 1910* (London: P. S. King & Son, 1911), pp. 62–73; and *Labour Leader* (London), 2 June 1911, p. 339. On the 1910 conference, see also *Sinn Féin*, 9 July 1910, p. 1; ibid., 16 July 1910, p. 3; and ibid., 6 August 1910, p. 3.
19. *Freeman's Journal*, 28 January 1910, p. 7. This bungled execution was also mentioned in an article by Louise Kenny in *Sinn Féin*, 5 February 1910, p. 2.
20. British advocates of the Iranian revolution included those on the left of the British political spectrum, ranging from Radicals to Labour and socialists, as well as the likes of the exceptional conservative champion of 'Egypt for Egyptians', Wilfrid Scawen Blunt, and the indefatigable champion of Iran's independence, the Cambridge orientalist Edward Granville Browne. Blunt was among the rare critics of Anglo-Russian intervention in Iran who alluded to the Irish Question in his advocacy of the Iranian revolution.
21. Although many of these same critics repeatedly alluded to India in their discussion of Iranian developments, such references were frequently couched in the context of India's 'security', notwithstanding the Social Democratic Federation's or the Independent Labour Party's periodic expressions that the Iranian revolution could hasten Indian self-government (with the SDF having no representation in the Persia Committee). The general silence on the Irish Question on the part of Grey's critics in the Persia Committee did not stop some of Grey's supporters in the Iranian debate from alluding to Dillon's Irish nationalist politics as an alleged clear indication of his hostility to 'progress' or 'British' interests. For example, during a 1912 parliamentary debate, the Unionist Mark Sykes remarked: 'The hon. member [i.e., Dillon] cannot possibly forget anyone who brings order and prosperity to a distracted country. I can perfectly well understand it, because order and prosperity in countries like Ireland and Egypt are opposed to the kind of politics in which [Irish] Nationalists take a part.' *Parliamentary Debates* (Commons), 5th series, 1912, vol. 40, c. 1977.
22. *Manchester Guardian*, 22 January 1909, p. 7.
23. Edward Granville Browne, *The Persian Revolution of 1905–1909*. New edition (Washington, DC: Mage, 1995 [1910]), pp. 146–47.
24. *Gaelic American*, 22 September 1906, p. 4.
25. Ibid., 2 June 1906, p. 4.
26. Ibid., 21 July 1906, p. 2.
27. 'Persia and China', *Gaelic American*, 6 January 1912, p. 4.
28. Similar to the *Gaelic American*, *Sinn Féin* too was notorious for its anti-Jewish posturing, with Griffith in 1904 (at the time the editor of *United Irishman*) having publicly justified the Limerick pogrom, despite his later praise for the Zionist project in Palestine as a nationalist endeavour: 'Israel represents the triumph of Sinn Fein.' *Sinn Féin*, 16 March 1912, p. 2. On Irish anti-Semitism, see also Neil R. Davison, *James Joyce, Ulysses, and the Construction of Jewish Identity: Culture, Biography, and 'The Jew' in Modernist Europe* (Cambridge: Cambridge University

Press, 1996).
29. *Irish Review* 1/6 (August 1911), p. 269.
30. *Gaelic American*, 17 July 1909, p. 4.
31. *Gaelic American*, 14 September 1912, p. 4.
32. Ryan had earlier written for Griffith's *United Irishman* (1899–1906) under the pseudonym 'Irial' and, while based in Cairo along with his colleague William J. Maloney, periodically sent articles and reports on the developments in Egypt to the *Gaelic American* and *Sinn Féin*.
33. *Gaelic American*, 22 December 1906, p. 6. On subsequent Iranian constitutionalist/nationalist appeals for self-reliance, see for example an article in the Tehran *Majles* on 'national-made garments', no. 54 (22 February 1908), pp. 3–4.
34. *Gaelic American*, 8 December 1906, p. 2.
35. *Sinn Féin*, 23 March 1907, p. 3.
36. *Sinn Féin*, 10 October 1908, p. 3.
37. See, for example, *Gaelic American*, 13 March 1909, p. 7.
38. *Sinn Féin*, 26 November 1910, p. 3.
39. See Bonakdarian, *Britain and the Iranian Constitutional Revolution*, pp. 229–31; *Encyclopaedia Iranica*, s.v. 'India: ix. Political and Cultural Relations: Qajar Period, Early Twentieth Century'.
40. *Gaelic American*, 11 November 1911, p. 4.
41. *Sinn Féin*, 'Persicus Odi', 5 February 1910, p. 2.
42. See Lennon, *Irish Orientalism*, passim.
43. See Gauri Viswanathan, 'Ireland, India, and the Poetics of Internationalism', *Journal of World History* 15/1 (March 2004), pp. 7–30; Catherine Candy, 'Relating Feminisms, Nationalisms and Imperialisms: Ireland, India and Margaret Cousins's Sexual Politics', *Women's History Review* 3/4 (1994), pp. 581–94; and idem, 'Unreasonable Histories: Persia, America and the Decolonizing Occult in Margaret Cousins's Irish-Indian Mediations' (forthcoming).
44. See David Lloyd, 'James Clarence Mangan's Oriental Translations and the Question of Origins', *Comparative Literature* 38/1 (Winter 1986), p. 23.
45. Hanna Sheehy Skeffington, 'The Women's Movement – Ireland', *Irish Review* 2/17 (July 1912), p. 226.
46. *Sinn Féin*, 21 December 1912, p. 3. This poem also appeared in the London radical-liberal paper *Nation*.
47. See also Tony Ballantyne, *Orientalism and Race: Aryanism in the British Empire* (Houndmills: Palgrave, 2002).
48. For this translation, see Iraj Bashiri, *The Fiction of Sadeq Hedayat* (Lexington, Kentucky: Mazda Publishers, 1984), p. 55.
49. Clare O'Halloran, 'Irish Re-Creations of the Gaelic Past: The Challenge of Macpherson's Ossian', *Past and Present* 124 (August 1989), p. 82; Colin Kidd, 'Gaelic Antiquity and National Identity in Enlightenment Ireland and Scotland', *English Historical Review* 109(434) (November 1994), pp. 1197–1214; Joseph Lennon, 'Antiquarianism and Abduction: Charles Vallancey as Harbinger of Indo-European Linguistics', *European Legacy* 10/1 (February 2005), pp. 5–20; idem, *Irish Orientalism*, pp. 81–101 and passim; Thomas R. Trautmann, *Aryans*

and British India (Berkeley: University of California Press, 1997), pp. 93–97; and Ballantyne, *Orientalism and Race*, p. 36.
50. See, for example, Canon Isaac Taylor, 'The Origin and Primitive Seat of the Aryans', *Journal of the Anthropological Institute of Great Britain and Ireland* 17 (1888), pp. 238–75.
51. *Gaelic American*, 14 March 1908, p. 3. On Kuno Meyer, see also Seán Ó Lúing, *Kuno Meyer, 1858–1919: A Biography* (Dublin: Geography Publications, 1991).
52. O'Halloran, 'Irish Re-Creations of the Gaelic Past', p. 69.
53. Ibid., pp. 69–95.
54. *Gaelic American*, 14 March 1908, p. 3.
55. O'Halloran, 'Irish Re-Creations of the Gaelic Past', p. 82.
56. These Irish commentators frequently avoided the distinction made in prevailing Aryan racial theories between the northern 'Aryan' versus the southern 'Dravidian' racial attributes of India's population.
57. Michael de Nie, *The Eternal Paddy: Irish Identity and the British Press, 1798–1882* (Madison: University of Wisconsin Press, 2004); Robert J. C. Young, *Colonial Desire: Hybridity in Theory, Culture and Race* (New York: Routledge, 1995), pp. 68–89; Catherine Hall, 'The Nation Within and Without', in Catherine Hall, Keith McClelland, and Jane Rendall (eds.), *Defining the Victorian Nation: Class, Race, Gender and the Reform Act of 1867* (Cambridge: Cambridge University Press, 2000), pp. 204–20; Amy E. Martin, '"Becoming a Race Apart": Representing Irish Racial Difference and the British Working Class in Victorian Critiques of Capitalism', in Terrence McDonough (ed.), *Was Ireland a Colony? Economics, Politics and Culture in Nineteenth-Century Ireland* (Dublin: Irish Academic Press, 2005), pp. 186–211; Noel Ignatiev, *How the Irish Became White* (New York: Routledge, 1995); David R. Roediger, *The Wages of Whiteness: Race and the Making of the American Working Class* (New York: Verso, 1999).
58. Gustav Spiller (ed.), *Papers on Inter-Racial Problems. Communicated to the First Universal Races Congress Held at the University of London July 26–29, 1911* (London: P. S. King & Son, 1911), p. 153. Dowlatabadi also stated: 'The Persians of to-day will therefore be very happy if, after long centuries of separation from their ancient kinsfolk, they can again cement the broken ties and strengthen them from day to day.' Ibid, p. 145. Ironically, the assertion of 'Aryan'/'Indo-European' racial affinity was deployed by some British imperialists as an additional 'historical' *legitimization* of British imperial intervention in Iran and India. For example, G. N. Curzon had written: 'The future of Great Britain, according to this view [i.e., the 'Great Game'], will be decided not in Europe, not even upon the seas and oceans which are swept by her flag, or in the Greater Britain that has been called into existence by her offspring, but in the continent whence our emigrant stock first came, and to which as conquerors their descendants have returned.' George Nathaniel Curzon, *Persia and the Persian Question. Volume I.* (London: Longmans, Green, and Co., 1892), pp. 3–4. See also Mansour Bonakdarian, 'Negotiating Universal Values and Cultural and National Parameters: Iran and Turkey at the First Universal Races Congress (London, 1911)', *Radical History Review* 92 (Spring 2005), pp. 118–32.

59. *Gaelic American*, 2 February 1907, p. 5.
60. *Gaelic American*, 2 March 1907, p. 5. On the Pan-Aryan Association, in addition to other issues of the *Gaelic American*, see also 'Plea for India and Persia', *New York Times*, 15 January 1908, p. 16; Harald Fischer-Tiné, 'Indian Nationalism and the "world forces": transnational and diasporic dimensions of the Indian freedom movement on the eve of the First World War', *Journal of Global History* 2/3 (November 2007), pp. 325–44; Joan M. Jensen, *Passage from India: Asian Indian Immigrants in North America* (New Haven: Yale University Press, 1988), pp. 19, 168; and Aravind Ganachari, *Nationalism and Social Reform in the Colonial Situation* (Delhi: Kalpaz Publications, 2005), pp. 137–40, 152–53. Among the more ardent supporters of Irish and Indian nationalist activists in the United States at the time was the lawyer Myron Phelps, also a keen scholar of the Baha'i faith and the author of the 1903 *Life and Teachings of Abbas Effendi* (with an introduction by Edward G. Browne), among his other publications. On Phelps, see also Ganachari, *Nationalism and Social Reform*, pp. 149–59; Alan Raucher, 'American Anti-Imperialists and the Pro-India Movement, 1900–1932', *The Pacific Historical Review* 43/1 (February 1974), pp. 83–110. Phelps was at odds with Barakatullah over Indian nationalists' organizational and campaign tactics in the United States. Barakatullah, who was in regular contact with militant Irish nationalists while in the United States, would later join the Indian Ghadar Movement (founded in San Francisco in 1913) and serve as the prime minister of the German-backed 'provisional government of India' in Afghanistan during the First World War, which he helped set up in 1915, with the Iranian nationalist committee in Berlin during the war cooperating with the Berlin-based Indian Independence Committee and a number of Indian nationalists joining the German-backed Iranian anti-British (and anti-Russian) nationalist forces inside Iran. See also *Encyclopaedia Iranica*, s.v. 'India: ix. Political and Cultural Relations: Qajar Period, Early Twentieth Century'.
61. In this framework, the search for 'the essence of … a distant precolonial Celtic civilizational past' also 'designate[d] "India" as another archetypal alternative to modernity.' Candy, 'Relating Feminisms, Nationalisms and Imperialisms', p. 582.
62. See also Susan Johnston Graf, 'Heterodox Religions in Ireland: Theosophy, the Hermetic Society, and the Castle of Heroes', *Irish Studies Review* 11/1 (2003), p. 51.
63. He 'based his poem "His Bargain" on the one hundred and seventy-third poem of Hafiz's *Divan*. He quoted Hafiz's poem in a speech in *Diarmuid and Grania*, which he and George Moore wrote together in 1902: "Life of my life, I knew you before I was born, I made a bargain with this brown hair before the beginning of time and it shall not be broken through unending time."' Shamsul Islam, 'The Influence of Eastern Philosophy on Yeats's Later Poetry', *Twentieth Century Literature* 19/4 (October 1973), pp. 284–85.
64. On the Persia Society (founded in London in March 1911 by Lord Lamington, the president of the Persia Committee, and Mirza Mahdi Khan Moshir al-Molk, the Iranian minister in London, 1907–20), see Bonakdarian, *Britain and the*

Iranian Constitutional Revolution.
65. In Edward Granville Browne, *The Literature of Persia* (London: Persia Society, 1912 [published by John Hogg]), pp. 38–41.
66. See, for example, Partha Chatterjee, *The Nation and Its Fragments: Colonial and Postcolonial Histories* (Princeton: Princeton University Press, 1993); Gyan Prakash, *Another Reason: Science and the Imagination of Modern India* (Princeton: Princeton University Press, 1999); Farzin Vahdat, *God and Juggernaut: Iran's Intellectual Encounter with Modernity* (Syracuse: Syracuse University Press, 2002), pp. xvi, 27–29, 52–54, and passim; and Bonakdarian, 'Negotiating Universal Values and Cultural and National Parameters', pp. 125–26.
67. Ryan would also appear as one of the characters in James Joyce's *Ulysses* (1922). It also should be pointed out that the 'Orient', including Iran, operated as an heterotopic *real-yet-unreal* constructed imagined space in Joyce's writing, including in *Ulysses*. For example, one of the characters in James Joyce's 1904 short story 'The Sisters' related a dream: 'I felt that I had been very far away, in some land where the customs were strange – in Persia, I thought.' James Joyce, *Dubliners*, with an Introduction by Laurence Davies (Ware, Hertfordshire: Wordsworth, 2001), 4. 'The Sisters' first appeared in August 1904 in the *Irish Homestead Journal* and was later published in Joyce's collection of short stories *Dubliners* in 1914. See also Ian Almond, 'Tales of Buddha, Dreams of Arabia: Joyce and Images of the East', *Orbis Litterarum* 57(2002), pp. 18–30.
68. See also the reports on Maloney's and Ryan's work with the *Egyptian Standard* and *Egypt* appearing in the *Gaelic American*, 1 January 1909, p. 4; 3 August 1912, p. 4; 14 September 1912, p. 5.
69. *Majles*, second year, no. 43 (6 February 1908), p. 3.
70. See W. S. Blunt, *My Diaries*, pp. 631, 642, 656, 781; E. G. Browne, *The Persian Revolution*, pp. 275, 300, 303; William Morgan Shuster, *The Strangling of Persia* (Reprint, Washington, DC: Mage, 1987[1912]), p. 124. Browne mistakenly identified Maloney as 'an occasional correspondent to the *Manchester Guardian* and other papers', while Blunt and Shuster misspelled Maloney's name as 'Malony' and 'Moloney' respectively (although later in life Maloney himself appears to have used different variations of his surname's spelling).
71. Frederick Ryan, 'The Persian Struggle', *Irish Review* 1/6 (August 1911), p. 286.
72. *Irish Independent*, 29 December 1911, p. 4. See also the partial reproduction of this article in *Egypt* (London), no. 11, January 1912, p. 122.
73. *Irish Worker*, 12 September 1914.
74. *Sinn Féin*, 14 November 1914.
75. Roger Casement, *The Crime Against Europe: A Possible Outcome of the War of 1914* (Berlin: The Continental Press, 1915), p. 7. Some of the essays in this publication were written prior to the outbreak of the First World War.
76. Eamon De Valera, *India and Ireland* (New York: Friends of Freedom for India, 1920) (Speech delivered on 28 February 1920 at the Central Opera House, New York City), p. 24.
77. On Armenian Dashnaktsutiun and Hnchak assistance to Iranian revolutionaries, see Berberian, *The Love for Freedom Has No Fatherland*.

78. Joseph Maunsell Hone and Page L. Dickinson, *Persia in Revolution. With Notes of Travel in the Caucasus* (London: T. Fisher Unwin, 1910), pp. 90–91. The Irish MP mentioned in this quote was John Dillon. On the special liaison between the *Times* and the British Foreign Office, see Bonakdarian, *Britain and the Iranian Constitutional Revolution*, pp. 129–30, 132, 185.
79. On attempts by Iranian nationalists and their supporters in Britain to project a 'moderate' image of the Iranian constitutional movement in the British press, see ibid., pp. 129–31, 148–49, 203–04.
80. See also Peter Heehs, *The Bomb in Bengal: The Rise of Revolutionary Terrorism in India 1900–1910* (New Delhi: Oxford University Press, 2004 [1993]).
81. Other than occasional Irish travellers to Iran since the early nineteenth century, the Irish serving in British and 'Indian forces' stationed in Iran, or Irish members of British diplomatic and consular staff, or commercial agents, etc., direct Iranian contacts with Ireland were scant. Very few Iranians had actually visited Ireland, and there were only a few personal accounts of Ireland available to Iranian readers in Persian, among them the travelogue of the Indo-Iranian author Mirza Abu Talib Khan Esfehani (*Masir-e talebi fi belad-i afranji*, 1812; originally published in English in London in 1810 as *Travels of Mirza Abu Taleb in Asia, Africa and Europe*). Other early Iranian travellers to Ireland included the early nineteenth century Iranian envoy to Britain Mirza Abul Hassan Khan 'Ilchi' (Shirazi), who visited Ireland during his second mission to Britain in 1816–19, and the famed late nineteenth and early twentieth century traveller Mirza Mohammad Ali Mahallati ('Haji Sayyah').
82. The occasional Iranian press reports on the Irish Question after the late nineteenth century ranged from 'Monsieur Gladstone' in the Tehran *Sherafat* (no. 23, April/May 1898. pp. 153–54) – providing an account of the British prime minister, William Gladstone's, disestablishment of the Church of Ireland (1871) and agrarian reforms in Ireland (i.e., Irish Land Acts of 1870 and 1881) and adding that Gladstone had ultimately failed to introduce self-government in Ireland (i.e., the Irish Home Rule Bills of 1886 and 1894), with the paper maintaining that Gladstone's reforms had significantly removed 'danger' to 'British government' – to a translation of a speech on British rule in India by Marquis Okuma Shigenobu (the former Japanese foreign minister and a founder of the Constitutional Progressive Party of Japan) in the Tehran constitutionalist paper *Majles*, which included a reference to Britain's 'divide and rule' politics in Ireland, among other places (no. 73, 15 March 1908, p. 4). It also should be pointed out that the (higher education) curriculum at such institutions as Dar al-Fonun (founded in 1851) and the School of Political Science (founded in 1899), with some of the classes taught by European instructors, included general courses in European history.
83. In a letter to the Tabriz constitutionalist paper *Anjoman* on the benefits of education, pro-constitutional students from the Sa'adat school wrote: 'All the harm and injury we suffer[,] all the catastrophes and misery that befall us[,] are undoubtedly due to lack of knowledge and ignorance. It is knowledge that in a short time made the savages of America the most civilized in the world[.] It is knowledge

that enabled the tent-dwellers of Siberia [i.e., Russia] and the Irish Isles [i.e., the United Kingdom] to quickly overpower the six-thousand-year-old nations of Iran and India' 3/19 (9 November 1908), p. 2.

84. The article in the pre-revolutionary paper *Tarbiyat* (Tehran) was exemplary of this range of historicization of Ireland, leaving aside its omission of Wales from the designation 'Britain'. This article on 'The Size of the Population of Great Britain', stated: 'The territory of England [i.e., 'United Kingdom'], excluding its foreign possessions, consists of two islands that have been divided into provinces[:] England and Ireland and Scotland, and Great Britain implies England and Scotland.' 17 Rajab 1319/30 October 1901 [listed as '31' October 1901], p. 974.

85. See also Mansour Bonakdarian, 'A World Born through the Chamber of a Revolver: Revolutionary Violence, Culture, and Modernity in Iran, 1906–1911', *Comparative Studies of South Asia, Africa and the Middle East* 25/2 (2005), pp. 324–28.

86. See also *Encyclopaedia Iranica*, s.v. 'India: VI. Political and Cultural Relations: The Afsharid and Zand Periods'; 'India: viii. Political and Cultural Relations: Qajar Period, the Nineteenth Century'; and 'India: ix. Political and Cultural Relations: Qajar Period, Early Twentieth Century'.

87. See also Seyyed Mohammad Jamalzadeh, 'Dar-zadan-e Ser Roger Kezment' (The Hanging of Sir Roger Casement), *Kaveh* (Berlin) 1/11 (1916), pp. 71–73; Iraj Afshar (ed.), *Zendegi-ye Tufani: Khaterat-e Seyyed Hasan Taqizadeh*, 2nd edition (Tehran: 'Elmi, 1993/94), p. 497.

Chapter 18. Crafting Constitutional Narratives: Iranian and Young Turk solidarity 1907–09

1. See Charles Kurzman *Democracy Denied, 1905–1915* (Cambridge, MA: Harvard University Press, 2008), and his chapter in this volume.
2. Yahya Dowlatabadi, *Tarikh-e mo'aser ya Hayat-e Yahya*, vol. 3 (Tehran: Ebn-e Sina, 1951), p. 26.
3. Ibid., p. 27.
4. For a diplomatic history of the Ottoman–Iranian border dispute during the Constitutional Revolution, see Sinan Kuneralp, 'The Ottoman *Drang Nach Osten*: The Turco-Persian Border Problem in Azerbaican, 1905–1912', in Sinan Kuneralp, *Studies on Ottoman Diplomatic History IV* (Istanbul: ISIS press, 1990).
5. Şükrü Hanioğlu, *Preparation for a Revolution: the Young Turks, 1902–1908* (Oxford: Oxford University Press, 2001), p. 180.
6. 'Akhbar-e Kharejeh (Foreign News)', *Sur-e Esrafil* no. 24 (24 Muharram 1326/27 February 1908), p. 5. While these and similar uprisings prior to the 1908 revolution have been dismissed as nothing more than the manipulations of the CUP from Paris, an alternative reading might see opponents to Abdülhamid in Eastern Anatolia not as pawns moved from Paris, but rather as agents in their own right, negotiating their unique set of interests through the vocabulary constitutionalism. For the former perspective, see Hanioğlu, *Preparation for a Revolution*, p. 3. In this case, constitutionalism and a desire to avoid over-taxation need not

7. Asef [?], 'Harakat-e Majnuneh', *Sur-e Esrafil* no. 12 (5 September 1907), pp. 3–5.
8. Yusuf Hikmet Bayur, *Türk İnkilâbi Tarihi*, vol. 2, part 4 (Ankara: Türk Tarih Kurumu, 1963), pp. 101–02.
9. Fethi Tevetoğlu, *Ömer Nâci* (Istanbul: Millî Eğitim Basımevi, 1973), pp. 3–5, 7–11.
10. Ibid., p. 101.
11. Ibid., pp. 101–02.
12. Houri Berberian, *Armenians and the Iranian Constitutional Revolution of 1905–1911* (Boulder: Westview Press, 2001), p. 70.
13. Ibid., p. 38.
14. Erdal Aydoğan and İsmail Eyyüpoğlu, *Bahaeddin Şakir Bey'in bıraktığı vesikalara göre İttihat ve Terakki* (Ankara: Alternatif Yayınları, 2004), p. 298.
15. See Fereydun Bazargan, 'Sharh-e hal-e Sa'id Salmasi' *Yadegar* 3/10 (1947), p. 83. Tevetoğlu mistakenly identifies the school and the journal as being named *Serat al-Mostaqim*. See Tevetoğlu, *Ömer Nâci*, p. 102. For a fascinating study on this educational movement and its impact in the Central Asian context, see Adeeb Khalid, *The Politics of Muslim Cultural Reform: Jadidism in Central Asia* (Berkeley: University of California Press, 1998). On the attempt to deflect the suspicion of the Ottoman consulate, see Aydoğan and Eyyüpoğlu, *Bahaeddin*, p. 302; Tevetoğlu, *Ömer Nâci*, p. 102.
16. Bazargan, 'Sharh-e hal-e Sa'id Salmasi', pp. 79–80.
17. Tevetoğlu, *Ömer Nâci*, p. 103.
18. Mehdi Malekzadeh, *Tarikh-e enqelab-e mashrutiyat-e Iran* (Tehran: 'Elmi, 1984), p. 954.
19. Dowlatabadi, *Tarikh-e mo'aser*, p. 27.
20. Tevetoğlu, *Ömer Nâci*, p. 104. Another account says that Naci's release was due to an amnesty granted through the intercession of the British ambassador and the Shah's officer. See ibid., p. 17.
21. Tevetoğlu, *Ömer Nâci*, p. 104.
22. Ibid., p. 111.
23. Dowlatabadi, *Tarikh-e mo'aser*, p. 27.
24. Palmira Brummett discusses how the Ottoman press was interested in events in Iran during the Lesser Despotism, fearing that if the revolution could fail there it could also fail in the Ottoman Empire. See Palmira Johnson Brummett, *Images and Imperialism in the Ottoman Revolutionary Press, 1908–1911* (Albany: State University of New York Press, 2000), p. 91. For a discussion of *'ebrat* in Iranian historiography, see Abbas Amanat, 'The Study of History in Post-Revolutionary Iran: Nostalgia, or Historical Awareness?', *Iranian Studies* 22/4 (1989), pp. 3–18.
25. Tevetoğlu, *Ömer Nâci*, pp. 112–16.
26. See Anja Pistor-Hatam, *Iran und die Reformbewegung im osmanischen Reich: Persische Staatsmänner, Reisende und Oppositionelle unter dem Einfluß der Tanzimat* (Berlin: Klaus Schwarz, 1992) and Th. Zarcone and F. Zarinebaf (eds.), *Les Iraniens d'Istanbul* (Teheran: Institut Français de Recherches en Iran and Istanbul: Institut Français d'Etudes Anatoliennes, 1993).

27. For more on the Anjoman-e Sa'adat, see Hodjatollah Djoudaki, 'L'*Anjoman-e Sa'âdat* des Iraniens d'Istanbul', in Zarcone and Zarinebaf (eds.), *Les Iraniens d'Istanbul*. See also *Encyclopaedia Iranica*, s.v. 'Anjoman-e Sa'adat'.
28. Dowlatabadi, *Tarikh-e mo'aser*, p. 38. For more on Dowlatabadi, see *Encyclopaedia Iranica*, s.v. 'Dawlatabadi, Sayyed Yahya'.
29. Janet Afary, *The Iranian Constitutional Revolution, 1906–1911: Grassroots Democracy, Social Democracy and the Origins of Feminism* (New York: Columbia University Press, 1996), p. 232. For the original passage, see Iraj Afshar, *Owraq-e tazehyab-e mashrutiyat va naqsh-e Taqizadeh* (Tehran: Javidan, 1980), p. 403.
30. Ibid., pp. 402–03. Salmasi's emphasis on the Babi label in undermining more radical constitutionalists is absent from Dowlatabadi's account of the speech, which is not astonishing given Dowlatabadi's own Babi sympathies. See Dowlatabadi, *Tarikh-e mo'aser*, pp. 41–42.
31. Mansour Bonakdarian, 'Iranian Constitutional Exiles and British Foreign-Policy Dissenters, 1908–9', *International Journal of Middle East Studies*, 27/2 (May, 1995), p. 184; Berberian, *Armenians*, p. 73. Berberian's British sources are dated 1907, which predates the rise of the Young Turk government. I am unable to evaluate the Armenian source she includes; however, it is likely that if the book was written after the second constitutional period, when the CUP took a much more Turkish nationalist position vis-à-vis minorities, including the Armenians, that this could have skewed the narration of events for the period of 1908 to 1909, where it appears there was quite a bit more optimism for the prospect of Armenian-Young Turk cooperation than has been traditionally accepted.
32. Faruk Bilici, 'L'Iran dans deux journaux ottomans: *Beyân ül-Hak* et *Tanin* (1908–1912)', in Zarcone and Zarinebaf (eds.), *Les Iraniens d'Istanbul*, p. 71.
33. Hanioğlu, *Preparation for a Revolution*, p. 180; Bayur, *Türk Inkilâbi Tarihi*, pp. 100–01; Aydoğan and Eyyüpoğlu, *Bahaeddin*, pp. 299–300.
34. Malekzadeh, *Tarikh-e enqelab-e mashrutiyat-e Iran*, p. 954.
35. Ahmad Kasravi, *Tarikh-e mashruteh-ye Iran* (Tehran: Amir Kabir, 1980), p. 875.
36. Halil Paşa, *Halil Paşa: Ittihad ve Terakki'den Cumhuriyete Bitmeyen Savaş*, 2nd edition, edited by Taylan Sorgun (Istanbul: Kum Saati, 2003), p. 46.
37. FO 248 974, A. C. Wratislaw to G. H. Barclay 'Events at Urmi and Salmas – reports' Tabriz, 18 March 1909.
38. FO 248 944, Wratislaw, 'Situation', 26 December 1908.
39. Halil Paşa, *Halil Paşa*, pp. 47–51; Kasravi, *Tarikh-e mashruteh*, p. 876; Esma'il Amirkhizi, *Qiyam-e Azarbayjan va Sattar Khan* (Tehran: Negah, 2000), pp. 290–91.
40. Kasravi, *Tarikh-e mashruteh*, p. 876.
41. FO 248 974, A. C. Wratislaw to G. H. Barclay, 'Events at Urmi and Salmas – reports' Tabriz, 18 March 1909.
42. 'Naql az ruznameh-ye Mokafat', *Anjoman* no. 44, 21 April 1909, p. 1; Kasravi, *Tarikh-e mashruteh*, p. 876.
43. Kasravi, *Tarikh-e mashruteh*, p. 876.
44. Amirkhizi, *Qiyam-e Azarbayjan*, p. 291; Kasravi, *Tarikh-e mashruteh*, p. 876; 'Naql az ruznameh-ye Mokafat', *Anjoman* no. 44, p. 1; Halil Paşa, *Halil Paşa*, p.

50. Kasravi says Salmasi died on 21 March.
45. 'Naql az Ruznameh-ye Mokafat matba'-e Khoi', *Anjoman* no. 43, 17 Rabi' I/8 April 1909, p. 4.
46. 'Naql az ruznameh-ye Mokafat', *Anjoman*, no. 44, p. 1.
47. Halil Paşa, *Halil Paşa*, p. 51.
48. FO 248 944, 'Question of Bast', 1 July 1908.
49. There has been astonishingly little discussion of this *bast* and of its broader significance for Iranian–Ottoman relations in contemporary scholarship of the period. See Bayat, *Iran's First Revolution: Shi'ism and the Constitutional Revolution of 1905–1909* (New York: Oxford University Press, 1991), p. 235; Vanessa Martin, *Islam and Modernism: the Iranian Revolution of 1906* (Syracuse, NY: Syracuse University Press, 1989), pp. 170–71, 173–74; Saïd Amir Arjomand, *The Turban for the Crown: The Islamic Revolution in Iran* (New York: Oxford University Press, 1988), p. 54.
50. Malekzadeh, *Tarikh-e enqelab-e mashrutiyat-e Iran*, p. 979.
51. Nazem al-Eslam Kermani, *Tarikh-e bidari-ye Iraniyan* (Tehran: Agah, 1983), p. 342.
52. FO 881 9465, 44492, Sir G. Barclay to Sir Edward Grey, Tehran, 21 December 1908; Martin, *Islam and Modernism*, pp. 170–71.
53. Martin, *Islam and Modernism*, p. 171.
54. Dowlatabadi, *Tarikh-e mo'aser*, p. 62; Malekzadeh, *Tarikh-e enqelab-e mashrutiyat*, p. 979.
55. Malekzadeh, *Tarikh-e enqelab-e mashrutiyat*, p. 980; Mohammad 'Alaqband, *Tarikh-e mashrutiyat* (Tehran: Iran National Baha'i Archives, Private Printing, Volume 2, 132 B.E./1976), pp. 181–82.
56. 'Alaqband, *Tarikh-e mashrutiyat*, p. 183.
57. Kermani, *Tarikh-e bidari-ye Iraniyan*, pp. 296–97.
58. FO 881 9465, 45414, Sir Edward Grey to Sir G. Lowther, Foreign Office, 28 December 1908.
59. FO 881 9465, 1, Sir G. Lowther to Sir Edward Grey, Constantinople, 31 December 1908; Dowlatabadi, *Tarikh-e mo'aser*, p. 62.
60. Ibid., pp. 62–65; Malekzadeh, *Tarikh-e enqelab-e mashrutiyat*, pp. 979–80.
61. Nazem al-Eslam Kermani, *Tarikh-e bidari-ye Iraniyan*, p. 389.
62. HR.SYS 682/5/6, Tevfik Paşa to Turkhan Paşa, 29 November 1908.
63. FO 881 9465, 402017, Sir G. Lowther to Sir Edward Grey, Constantinople, 1 December 1908.
64. FO 881 9465, 42245, Sir G. Lowther to Sir Edward Grey, Constantinople, 3 December 1908.
65. FO 248 944, Wratislaw, 1 December 1908; FO 248 944, Wratislaw, 'German and Turkish officers', 12 November 1908 Confidential; FO 248 944, 1 December 1908; Wratislaw 'Turkish assistance to nationalists', 2 December 1908; FO 248 944, 1 December 1908, Wratislaw 'Germans at Tabriz' 7 December 1908; FO 248 944, 1 December 1908; FO 248 944, Gulhek, 28 June 1908, 'Situation Refugees to be discouraged'; FO 248 944, Stevens 'Tabriz Situation', 25 October 1908, Tabriz; FO 248 944, Wratislaw, 'German and Turkish officers', 12

November 1908 Confidential.
66. Dowlatabadi, *Tarikh-e mo'aser*, p. 103.
67. FO 248 974, 134, 'Russian Military authorities' Wratislaw, Tabriz, 30 May 1909.
68. Although it should be said that Sattar Khan was rather reluctant to take *bast*. It was only after the persuasion of Seqat al-'Olama' that he agreed to take *bast*. He even returned to his home during the *bast* on several occasions when he was not supposed to. See Amirkhizi, *Qiyam-e Azarbayjan*, pp. 334–35 and Karim Taherzadeh Behzad, *Qiyam-e Azarbayjan dar enqelab-e mashrutiyat-e Iran* (Tehran: Eqbal, 1955), pp. 299–300.
69. Kasravi, *Tarikh-e hejzdah saleh-ye Azarbayjan* (Tehran: Amir Kabir, 1961), p. 47.
70. Edward Granville Browne, *The Persian Revolution of 1905–1909* (Washington, DC: Mage Publishers, 1995), p. 304.
71. HR.SYS 682/5/18, 7 June 1909.
72. HR.SYS 682/5/20, Imperial Ambassador of Turkey in St. Petersburg [Turkan Pasha] to Rifat Pasha 16 June 1909.
73. Dowlatabadi, *Tarikh-e mo'aser*, p. 103.
74. FO 248 974, 157, Wratislaw, Tabriz, 17 June 1909. For the letter from the *bastis* to the Ottoman government complaining of Russian incursions in Iran, see Amirkhizi, *Qiyam-e Azarbayjan*, pp. 336–38.
75. HR.SYS 682/5/28, 12 July 1909. Dowlatabadi claims that the reason that Rifat Paşa was so sympathetic to the Russians was that his wife was Russian. See Dowlatabadi, *Tarikh-e mo'aser*, p. 103.
76. Ibid., p. 103; HR.SYS 682/5/31, 18 July 1909, Rifat Pasha to Turkhan Pasha.
77. Dowlatabadi, *Tarikh-e mo'aser*, p. 103; for Isvolsky's anger at the delays, see HR.SYS 682/5/32, 17 July 1909 Turkhan Pasha to Rifat Pasha.
78. On which see Juan R. I. Cole, 'Shaikh al-Ra'is and Sultan Abdülhamid II: The Iranian Dimension of Pan-Islam', in Israel Gershoni, Hakan Erdem, and Ursula Woköck (eds.), *Histories of the Modern Middle East: New Directions* (Boulder: Lynne Rienner, 2002), pp. 167–88; and Nejat Göyünç, 'Displays of Friendship between Persia and Turkey during the Time of Mozafaroddin Shah and Abdulhamit II', *Journal of the Regional Cultural Institute* 4 (1971), pp. 57–66.
79. On Ottoman Pan-Islamism in relation to Iran in this period see also Gökhan Çetinsaya, *Ottoman Administration of Iraq, 1890–1908* (London: Routledge, 2006), pp. 116–26.
80. Aydoğan and Eyyüpoğlu, *Bahaeddin*, p. 300.
81. FO 248 944, Barclay to Wratislaw (?), 1 December 1908.
82. FO 248 944, Stevens, 'Turkish freedom proclaimed' or 'Decypher', Tabriz, 4 August 1908.
83. For the original Arabic letter, see Nazem al-Eslam Kermani, *Tarikh-e bidari-ye Iraniyan*, pp. 232–33. For a translation of this text into English, see FO 881 9416 32619, Sir G. Lowther to Sir Edward Grey, Constantinople, 16 September 1908, Inclosure 3, 'Nedjef Mujteheds to Haji Ali Pasha, First Chamberlain of the Sultan', Undated.
84. Ha'iri, *Shi'ism and Constitutionalism in Iran: A Study of the Role Played by the Persian Residents of Iraq in Iranian Politics* (Leiden: Brill, 1977), pp. 88–89.

85. Bayat, *Iran's First Revolution*, p. 255.
86. There is, of course, a parallel to be drawn here with the fatwa supposedly issued by Hasan Shirazi during the Tobacco Rebellion. For a full treatment of this episode, see Nikki Keddie, *Religion and Rebellion in Iran* (London: Cass, 1966).
87. Abbas Amanat, 'In Between the Madrasa and the Marketplace: The Designation of Clerical Leadership in Modern Shi'ism', in Said Arjomand (ed.), *Authority and Political Culture in Shi'ism* (Albany, NY: State University of New York Press, 1988).
88. Malekzadeh, *Tarikh-e enqelab-e mashrutiyat*, p. 1015.
89. Feroz Ahmed, *The Young Turks: The Committee of Union and Progress in Turkish Politics 1908–1914* (Oxford: Oxford University Press, 1969), p. 13.
90. Alaqband, *Tarikh-e mashrutiyat*, pp. 183–84.
91. 'Telegrafat-e Akhireh', *Sorush* no. 4, 21 July 1909, pp. 6–7 and 'Telegrafat-e Akhireh', *Sorush* no. 5, 28 July 1909, pp. 4–5.
92. 'Surat-e majales-e jashn-e melli-ye Iraniyan dar Anjoman-e Sa'adat va mavaqe'-e digar va notqha va khatabehha-i keh qara'at shodeh', *Sorush* no. 5, 28 July 1909, pp. 5–6.
93. 'Untitled', *Sorush* no. 5, 28 July 1909, p. 7.
94. For the use of Pan-Turkism in Iran during the First World War, see Touraj Atabaki, 'Going East: The Ottomans' Secret Service Activities in Iran', in Touraj Atabaki (ed.), *Iran and the First World War: Battleground of the Great Powers* (London: I.B.Tauris, 2006).

Chapter 19. Constitutionalists *Sans Frontières*: Iranian Constitutionalism and its Asian Connections

1. I would like to extend my gratitude to Houchang Chehabi, Reza Jafari, and Vanessa Martin for their comments in preparing this paper. An earlier version of this article was published in *Comparative Studies of South Asia, Africa and the Middle East* 28/1 (2008).
2. Nader Sohrabi, 'Historicizing Revolutions: Constitutional Revolutions in the Ottoman Empire, Iran, and Russia, 1905–1908', *American Journal of Sociology* 100/6 (May 1995), pp. 1383–1447.
3. See Farzin Vejdani's chapter in this book and the references therein.
4. Dipesh Chakrabarty, *Provincializing Europe: Postcolonial Thought and Historical Difference* (Princeton, NJ: Princeton University Press, 2000), p. 7.
5. Ibid.
6. Colonel Yates to Foreign Office, 8 August 1894, cited in Nasereddin Parvin, *Tarikh-e ruznamehnegari-ye Iraniyan va digar parsi-nevisan*, vol. 1 (Tehran: Nashr-e Daneshgahi, 1998).
7. On *Akhtar* see Orhan Koloğlu, '*Akhtar*, journal persan d'Istanbul', in Thierry Zarcone and Fariba Zarinebaf (eds.), *Les Iraniens d'Istanbul* (Tehran: Institut Français de Recherches en Iran and Istanbul: Institut Français d'Etudes Anatoliennes, 1993), pp. 133–40 and Anja Pistor-Hatam, 'The Persian newspaper *Akhtar* as a transmitter of Ottoman political ideas', in ibid., pp. 141–48.
8. *Turkistanskie vedomosti* no. 48 (1898).

9. *Qanun* no. 17 (n.d.); no. 6 (1890); no. 21 (n.d.).
10. Hélène Carrère d'Encausse, *Islam and the Russian Empire: Reform and Revolution in Central Asia* (London: I.B.Tauris, 1988), p. 102.
11. *Habl al-Matin* no. 1 (1917); telegram of Russian Ministry of Foreign Affairs to the Governor General of the Caucasus, 22 April 1913, file 5259, fond 13, no. 13, Georgian State Archive, Tbilisi.
12. Seyyed Sa'd al-Din Hashemi, *Jonbesh-e mashruteh-kh"ahi dar Afghanestan* (Stockholm: Shura-ye Farhangi-ye Afghanestan, 2001), pp. 207–14.
13. Ibid., p. 242.
14. *Seraj al-Akhbar* no. 17 (1914). For the English translation, my sincere thanks go to Reza Jafari. For the original see the Appendix.
15. Carrère d'Encausse, *Islam and the Russian Empire*, p. 85.
16. *Seraj al-Akhbar* no. 2 (1913).
17. Ibid.
18. Abdollah Habibi, *Jonbesh-e mashrutiyat dar Afghanestan* (Kabul: n.p., 1993), p. 97.
19. For a summary of *Seraj al-Akhbar*'s coverage of Iran see May Schinasi, *Afghanistan at the Beginning of the Twentieth Century: Nationalism and Journalism in Afghanistan: A Study of Serâj ul-akhbâr (1911–1918)* (Naples: Istituto Universitario Orientale, 1979), pp. 179–81.
20. *Seraj al-Akhbar* no. 8 (1911).
21. *Bokhara-ye Sharif* no. 15 (1912).
22. *Bokhara-ye Sharif* no. 54 (1912); nos. 76–85 (1912).
23. More than two thousand years later, the dialogue, in somewhat adapted form, was employed in European culture. One finds it applied in diverse ways by illustrious men of letters such as François Fénélon (1651–1715) or Walter Landor (1775–1864). Fénélon, as a representative of the Age of Reason, presents his own contemporary criticism of Louis XIV's Court by bringing together famous figures from world history in his *Dialogue des morts*: Charon meets Mercury, Herodotus and Lucian converse together, and Socrates talks with Alcibiades. Landor, while operating within the more poetic mode of romanticism, also dramatizes imaginary conversations between historical celebrities, ranging from Hannibal to Queen Elizabeth I. The dialogue form in European literature has since had a long and varied life through the centuries.
24. For a detailed study of the adaptation of this new genre in the Persian language, see Touraj Atabaki, 'Dialogue: A Literary Form in Persian Nineteenth/Twentieth-Centuries Political Discourse', B. G. Fragner et al. (eds.), *Proceedings of the Second European Conference of Iranian Studies* (Rome: Istituto Italiano per il Medio ed Estremo Oriente, 1995).
25. 'Sheykh va vazir', in *Resalehha-ye Mirza Malkam Khan Nazem al-Dowleh*, ed. Hojatollah Asil (Tehran: Nashr-e Ney, 2002), p. 373.
26. 'Abd al-Ra'uf Fetrat Bokhara'i, *Monazereh-e modarres-e bokhara'i ba yek nafar farangi dar Hendustan* (Istanbul: Matba'a-i Islamiya, 1909).
27. 'Abd al-Ra'uf Fetrat Bokhara'i, *Hindistanda bir Farangi ila Bukharali bir muddares-in bir niche masalala ham usul-i jadida khususida qilgan*, trans. Mo'in

b. Shokrollah Samarkandi (Tashkent: Turkistan Kitabkhanesi, 1913).
28. Mirza Yusef Khan Mostashar al-Dowleh, *Yek Kalameh*, ed. Sadeq Sajjadi (Tehran: Nashr-e Tarikh-e Iran, 1985).
29. For a comprehensive study of Jadidis, see Adeeb Khalid, *The Politics of Muslim Cultural Reform: Jadidism in Central Asia* (Berkeley: University of California Press, 1998). See also *Encyclopaedia Iranica*, s.v. 'Jadidism'.
30. Fetrat Bokhara'i, *Hindistanda*, p. 25.
31. Mirza Asadollah Ghaffarzadeh, a prominent figure in the early twentieth-century Iranian revolutionary movement, was born in Ardabil and educated at Dar al-Fonun in Tehran. He left Iran for the Caucasus in 1903 and while there joined the Social Democratic Party of Russia. In 1917, together with other Social Democrats sympathetic to the Russian Bolsheviks, he formed the *Ferqeh-e 'Edalat* (Justice Party), which later evolved into the Communist Party of Iran. It was while he held the post of first secretary of the party that he was assassinated in Gilan, in 1918. See A. Agahi, 'Piramun-e nakhostin ashna'i-ye Iranian ba Marksism', *Donya* 3 (1962); and Ervand Abrahamian, *Iran between Two Revolutions* (Princeton, NJ: Princeton University Press, 1983), p. 115. In 1911, Habibollah Shirazi edited and published a volume in Tehran under the title of *Siyasat-e Talebi*. According to Shirazi the two articles in this volume, 'Maqaleh-e siyasi' and 'Maqaleh-e melki', were written by Abolrahim Talebov (1834–1911), and he could only publish them after the author's death. The second article, 'Maqaleh-e melki', is identical to *Mosahebeh-ye Iraniyeh* mentioned in the present work. In 1978 Iraj Afshar reprinted the *Siyasat-e Talebi* with other works of 'Abd al-Rahim Talebov in a new volume. Iraj Afshar, *Azadi va Siyasat* (Tehran: Sahar, 1978). The question that remains to be answered is why *Mosahebeh-ye Iraniyeh* was catalogued under the name of Mirza Abdollah Ghaffarzadeh.
32. An unidentified censor was apparently not pleased with the word 'Muscovite' and therefore crossed it out and substituted the word '*kharejeh*' (foreign).
33. The unidentified censor also removed 'Turkmanchai Treaty' and replaced it with the more general term 'foreign treaties'.
34. Carrère d'Encausse, *Islam and the Russian Empire*, p. 103.
35. Mirza Seraj al-Din Haji Mirza 'Abd al-Ra'uf, *Tohaf-e ahl-e Bokhara*, Mohammad Asadiyan, ed., (Tehran: Bu-Ali, 1990). Jan Rypka at al., *Iranische Literaturgeschichte* (Lepizig: VEB Otto Harrassowitz, 1959), pp. 410–11.
36. Jan Rypka, *The History of Iranian Literature* (Dordrecht, Netherlands: D. Reidl Publishing, 1968), p. 589.
37. *Encyclopedia Iranica*, s.v. 'Akhundzadeh'. See also Ali Miransari's contribution to this volume.
38. Gulam Memedli, *Azerbeyjan teatrlarin salnamesi* (Baku: Azerbaijan Devlet Nashriyati, 1975), p. 197.
39. Ibid.
40. Ibid., p. 305
41. *Ayneh* no. 38 (1914).
42. Memedli, *Azerbeyjan teatrlarin salnamesi*, p. 458.
43. For a study of this transition as it affected Bukhara see William L. Hanaway,

Jr., 'Farsi, the Vatan, and the Millat in Bukhara', in Edward Allworth (ed.), *The Nationality Question in Soviet Central Asia* (New York: Praeger, 1973), pp. 143–50.

Chapter 20. *Mashruteh* and *al-Nahda*: The Iranian Constitutional Revolution in the Iranian Diaspora Press of Egypt and in Arab Reformist Periodicals

1. For example, new studies have emphasized the roles of women, peasants, and religious minorities in the revolution, such as Houri Berberian, *Armenians and the Iranian Constitutional Revolution of 1905–1911: 'The Love for Freedom Has No Fatherland'* (Boulder: Westview Press, 2001), and Janet Afary, *The Iranian Constitutional Revolution, 1906–1911: Grassroots Democracy, Social Democracy, and the Origins of Feminism* (New York: Columbia University Press, 1996).
2. M. Reza Afshari, 'The Historians of the Constitutional Movement and the Making of the Iranian Populist Tradition', *International Journal of Middle East Studies* 25/3 (1993), pp. 477–94.
3. The paradigmatic example of this is clearly Ahmad Kasravi's influential history of the revolution, *Tarikh-e mashruteh-ye Iran* (Tehran: Seda-ye Moʻaser, 2001).
4. See, for example, Mehrzad Borujerdi, *Iranian Intellectuals and the West: The Tormented Triumph of Nativism* (Syracuse: Syracuse University Press, 1996).
5. Significant populations of Iranians lived outside of Iran at the end of the nineteenth century; their migration from Iran was due to a variety of reasons. In this study I will use the term 'diaspora' to describe the variety of Iranian communities living outside of Iran at this time. While I am unable to discuss in detail the merits and drawbacks of this term's usage in this context, I do find it generally more useful than similar terms such as 'exilic communities', which connote a political dynamic to the extraterritoriality of these communities, which is not sufficient to describe them.
6. I use the Arabic term *Nahda* largely to denote the cultural movement (often termed a 'renaissance') reviving and to an extent innovating upon the Arabic literary and cultural traditions in the late nineteenth and early twentieth centuries. I speak of reformism as a political trend both within Ottoman ruling classes and among elites in Arab states within the Ottoman domains – in particular, Egypt. Reformism is admittedly a somewhat vague term, but its merit is that it allows for a general grouping of often competing or discordant ideological positions that share certain key goals – i.e., the reconfiguration of key institutions and systems of governance, as well as the economy. For more on the Arab *Nahda*, see Peter Pormann, 'The Arab Cultural Awakening (Nahda) 1870–1950, and the Classical Tradition', *International Journal of the Classical Tradition* 13/1 (2002), pp. 4–20. Also see: Albert Hourani, *Arabic Thought in the Liberal Age* (Cambridge: Cambridge University Press, 2002); and on Ottoman reforms, see Roderic Davison, *Reform in the Ottoman Empire, 1856–1876* (Princeton: Princeton University Press, 1963). See also Fatimah Al-Sulaim, 'The Arab Nahda Projects and the Arab Intellectuals' Perspectives of Modernity and Social Change in the Arab World' (PhD dissertation, American University, 2004). Also: Albert Hourani, 'Ottoman Reform and the Politics of Notables', in Albert Hourani, P.S.

Khoury, and M. C. Wilson (eds.), *The Modern Middle East* (Berkeley: University of California Press, 1993), pp. 83–110.

7. See Anja Pistor-Hatam, *Iran und die Reformbewegung im osmanischen Reich: Persische Staatsmänner, Reisende und Oppositionelle unter dem Einfluß der Tanzimat* (Berlin: Klaus Schwarz, 1992); Thierry Zarcone and Fariba Zarinebaf (eds.), *Les Iraniens d'Istanbul* (Paris: Institut Français de Recherches en Iran, 1993); and Pardis Minuchehr, 'Homeland from Afar: the Iranian Diaspora and the Quest for Modernity, 1908–1909' (PhD dissertation, Columbia University, 1998). See also Mansour Bonakdarian, 'Iranian Constitutional Exiles and British Foreign-Policy Dissenters, 1908–9', *International Journal of Middle East Studies* 27/2 (1995), pp. 175–91.

8. For more on the Iranian community in Cairo, see Anja Luesink, 'The Iranian Community in Cairo at the Turn of the Century', in Zarcone and Zarinebaf (eds.) *Les Iraniens d'Istanbul*, pp. 193–202. It is significant that the protagonist of Zeyn al-'Abedin Maragheh'i's late nineteenth-century book *Siyahatnameh-ye Ebrahim Beyk* is a member of the Iranian community of Cairo, testifying to the significance of this community within the larger Iranian diaspora at the time. Even today businesses and shops in Cairo may be found bearing distinctly Iranian names, especially in the formerly Iranian Khan al-Khalili quarter.

9. Luesink, 'The Iranian Community in Cairo', p. 193.

10. Mohammad Yadegari, 'The Iranian Settlement in Egypt as Seen Through the Pages of the Community Newspaper, *Chihrinima*', in Elie Kedouri and Sylvia Haim (eds.), *Modern Egypt: Studies in Politics and Society* (London: Frank Cass, 1980), p. 99.

11. Luesink, 'The Iranian Community in Cairo', p. 194.

12. Yadegari, 'The Iranian Settlement in Egypt', pp. 109–10.

13. Luesink, 'The Iranian Community in Cairo', p. 200. Yadegari also reports in depth on the activities of the Iranian Charity Association, which served a number of purposes including providing educational and medical assistance as well as aid to the poor. Yadegari, 'The Iranian Settlement in Egypt', p. 108.

14. Yadegari comments that by 1935, knowledge of Persian among Iranian diaspora members in Egypt was poor enough for the Iranian ambassador to Egypt to have to give speeches to the community in Arabic. Yadegari, 'The Iranian Settlement in Egypt', p. 111.

15. For more on the history of this periodical, see 'Hekmat' in Mohammad Sadr Hashemi, *Tarikh-e jarayed va majallat-e Iran*, vol. 2 (Tehran: Kamal, 1984), pp. 228–30.

16. Hashemi, *Tarikh-e jarayed*, p. 229.

17. *Hekmat*, 'Jashn-e jolus-e a'lahazrat-e humayun-e soltani', 2 September 1898, p. 2.

18. *Hekmat*, 28 December 1898, p. 6.

19. For more on *Chehreh Nama*, see Yadegari, 'The Iranian Settlement in Egypt'. It is worth noting that the most complete collection of this periodical appears to be contained in the Egyptian National Library – the Dar al-Kutub – whose cataloguing shows a collection beginning in 1909 and continuing until 1953,

with an apparent gap of two years between 1922 and 1924. Unfortunately, this collection appears to lack the first five or so years of the periodical, as well as most of the post-revolutionary period – some of these are located in other collections. *Chehreh Nama* appears in the Dar al-Kutub periodicals catalogue as the first periodical in the category '*dawriyat farisi*'.
20. See 'Chehreh Nama' in Hashemi, *Tarikh-e jarayed*, pp. 190–99.
21. *Al-Hilal*, 6 January 1906, pp. 26–27.
22. For example, Hashemi lists the contents from issue 1, vol. 2 of *Chehreh Nama*, which include an article 'translated from *al-Muqtataf*'. Hashemi, *Tarikh-e jarayed*, p. 192.
23. *Chehreh Nama* no. 22 (1910), p. 12.
24. Both of these journals were published in Cairo by Syrian (Lebanese) Christians. For more on the publishers of both and how their identity related to the ideological grounding of these periodicals, see Donald M. Reid, 'Syrian Christians, the Rags-To-Riches Story, and Free Enterprise', *International Journal of Middle East Studies* 1/4 (1970), pp. 358–67.
25. For more on *al-Muqtataf*, see Martin Hartmann, *The Arabic Press of Egypt* (London: Luzac & Co, 1899), pp. 69–70; and Nadia Farag, '*Al-Muqtataf*, 1876–1900, a Study of the Influence of Victorian Thought on Modern Arabic Thought' (D.Phil. dissertation, University of Oxford, 1969). For more on the genre of these periodicals, see Stephen Sheehi, 'Arabic Literary-Scientific Journals: Precedence for Globalization and the Creation of Modernity', *Comparative Studies of South Asia, Africa and the Middle East* 25/2 (2005), pp. 439–49.
26. *Al-Muqtataf*, 'Mudhaffar al-Din Shah wa bilad Iran', February 1907, pp. 91–96.
27. Ibid., p. 94.
28. *Al-Muqtataf*, 'Al-Mar'a al-Iraniyya, wa ta'thiruha fi rijal al-islah bi-bilad Iran', July 1908, pp. 684–87.
29. *Al-Muqtataf*, 'Bilad al-Furs wa mustaqbilha', June 1909, pp. 527–28.
30. For more on Zaydan's translations see Kamran Rastegar, 'Literary Modernity Between Arabic and Persian Prose: Jurji Zaydan's *Riwayat* in Persian Translation', *Critical Comparative Studies* 4/3 (2007), pp. 359–78.
31. *Al-Hilal*, 1 October 1909, p. 38.
32. Ibid.
33. Ibid., p. 39.
34. Ibid., p. 42.
35. Rudi Matthee, 'Jamal al-Din al-Afghani and the Egyptian National Debate', *International Journal of Middle East Studies*, 21/2 (1989), pp. 151–69; Elie Kedourie, *Afghani and 'Abduh: An Essay on Religious Unbelief and Political Activism in Modern Islam* (London: Routledge, 1966).
36. Elleke Boehmer, *Empire, the National, and the Postcolonial, 1890–1920: Resistance in Interaction* (Oxford: Oxford University Press, 2002), pp. 5, 175.
37. These intercultural circulations are discussed at length in my book: Kamran Rastegar, *Literary Modernity Between the Middle East and Europe* (London: Routledge, 2007).

Chapter 21. The Iranian Constitutional Revolution as Reported in the Chinese Press

1. See Peng Shuzhi, 'Lun 1905–1911 nian Yilang Zichanjieji Geming (On the Iranian Bourgeois Revolution in 1905–1911)', *Southwest Asia Study* 4 (1987), pp. 57–66; Zhang Qizheng, 'Yilang Geming yu Xinhai Geming zhi Bijiao (A Comparative Study of the Iranian Revolution and the Chinese Xinhai Revolution)', *Journal of Hengyang Normal School* (Social Sciences) 1 (1994), pp. 53–58. Chinese scholars have generally designated the Iranian Constitutional Revolution as a 'bourgeois revolution'. Two specialists hold that peasants, petty bourgeois, handicraftsmen, and proletarians were the motive force of the Iranian Revolution, and they have pointed out that there were three reasons for the failure of the Iranian Revolution: 1) the lack of leadership from any real and strong revolutionary party; 2) the absence of the mass of people in the movement; 3) and the armed intervention of foreign armies, especially those of Russia and Britain. For obvious reasons, Chinese scholars have neglected the role religion played in the Iranian Constitutional Revolution.
2. Ding Shouhe (ed.), *Xinhai Geming Shiqi Qikan Jieshao* (An Introduction to the Periodicals published during the Xinhai Revolution), vol. 3 (Beijing: Renmin Publishing House, 1983), pp. 178–80, 219.
3. 'Bosiwang zhi Dengwei (The Coronation of the Persian Shah)', *Dongfang Zazhi* 1/3 (1904), p. 222.
4. 'Bosiwan zhi Jinzhuang (The Current Situation in the Persian Gulf)', *Dongfang Zazhi* 1/5 (1904), p. 24.
5. 'Bu Ji Bosi Geming zhi Lishi (Additional Remarks Concerning the History of the Persian Revolution)', *Dongfang Zazhi* 6/10 (1909), pp. 46–51.
6. 'Ke'ai Bosi zhi Fei-huang (How Regretful the Dethroned Persian King Is)', *Dongfang Zazhi* 6/11 (1909), p. 57.
7. 'Kelian Bosi zhi Jin-huang (How Unfortunate the Reigning Persian King Is)', *Dongfang Zazhi* 6/11 (1909), pp. 57–58.
8. 'Bosi Ningchen zhi Shou-sixing (On the Execution of a Treacherous Courtier Following the Death Sentence)', *Dongfang Zazhi* 7/12 (1910), pp. 59–60.
9. 'Ying-E Guafen Bosi zhi Jinggao (Warning: Britain and Russia Are Carving up Persia)', *Dongfang Zazhi* 7/12 (1910), pp. 67–68.
10. Gan Yonglong, 'Bosi Huangdi Dianxue Jilüe (Brief Remarks on the Education of the Persian Shah)', *Dongfang Zazhi* 8/6 (1911), pp. 1–2.
11. Kong Qinglai, 'Bosiwan zhi Weilai (The Future of the Persian Gulf)', *Dongfang Zazhi* 8/8 (1911), pp. 16–18.
12. Qian Zhixiu, 'Bosi zhi Jinzhuang (The Current Situation in Persia)', *Dongfang Zazhi* 9/9 (1912), pp. 12–20.
13. 'Bosi Ningchen zhi Shou-sixing', *Dongfang Zazhi*, pp. 59–60.
14. Kong Qinglai, 'Bosiwan zhi Weilai', *Dongfang Zazhi*, pp. 16–18.
15. Gan Yonglong, 'Bosi Huangdi Dianxue Jilüe', *Dongfang Zazhi*, p. 1.
16. Ibid., pp. 1–2.
17. About the life of this prince, see *Encyclopaedia Iranica*, s.v. 'Alā'-al-Saltana'.
18. Qian Zhixiu, 'Bosi zhi Jinzhuang (The Current Situation in Persia)', p. 12.

Compare with Edward G. Browne, *The Persian Crisis of December 1911, How It Arose and Whither It May Lead Us* (Cambridge: University Press, 1912).
19. Qian Zhixiu, 'Bosi zhi Jinzhuang', p. 16.
20. 'Wanguo Xianshi Xinshi: xili yiqian-jiubai-ling-wu-nian jiu-yue ershisan-ri (Foreign News on 23 September 1905)', *Zheng-yi Tongbao* 4/17 (1905).
21. 'Wanguo Xianshi Xinshi: xili yiqian-jiubai-ling-qi-nian yi-yue shisan-ri (Foreign News on 13 January 1907)', *Zheng-yi Tongbao* 6/1 (1907).
22. Wang Deyuan, 'Jiuwang Juelun Er (On the Ways of National Salvation, Part 2)', *Zheng-yi Congshu*, 'Dingwei Zheng-xue-wen Bian 6' (Taipei: Wenhai Publishing House, 1976), pp. 1484–85.
23. Ibid., p. 1485.
24. Ding Shouhe (ed.), *Xinhai Geming Shiqi Qikan Jieshao* (An Introduction to the Periodicals Published During the Xinhai Revolution), vol. 1 (Beijing: Renmin Publishing House, 1982), p. 504.
25. Minyi, 'Tu'erqi Geming (Turkish Revolution)', *Minbao* 25 (1910), pp. 1–7.
26. Minyi, 'Xibanya zhi Lansha (The Massacre Occurred in Spain)', *Minbao* 26 (1910), pp. 10–14.
27. Wang Jingwei, *Wang Jingwei Wencun* (Collected Works of Wang Jingwei), vol. 1 (Guangzhou: Minzhi Shuju, 1927, second edition), pp. 183–87.
28. Minyi, 'Bosi Geming (Persian Revolution)', *Minbao* 25 (1910), p. 8.
29. Ibid., pp. 8–12.
30. Ibid., p. 12.

Chapter 22. Japan and the Iranian Constitutional Revolution

1. For the case of Iran, see Abdul-Hadi Hairi, 'European and Asian Influences on the Persian Revolution of 1906', *Asian Affairs* 62 (1975), pp. 155–64; and Hashem Rajabzadeh, 'Russo-Japanese War as Told by Iranians', *Annals of Japan Association for Middle East Studies* 3/2 (1988).
2. The best scholarly account of the Japanese press in this period is James L. Huffman, *Creating a Public: People and Press in Meiji Japan* (Honolulu: University of Hawaii Press, 1997).
3. This is a reference to the Masaharu Yoshida mission of 1880–81 about which there are presently more than half a dozen scholarly articles available.
4. Foreign Office 371 / 505, p. 238, No. 555/1129, 12 Apr. 1908.
5. Foreign Office 371 / 114, p. 46, incl. by Cooke, 6 Sept. 1906, in Nicolson to Grey No. 594, 7 Sept. 1906.
6. Foreign Office 371 / 105, p. 54, No. 24 Tel., 25 Jan. 1906.
7. Foreign Office 371 / 106, p. 427, incl. in Grant Duff to Grey, No. 53, 27 Feb. 1906.
8. See Hashem Rajabzadeh, 'Japan as Seen by Qajar Travelers', in Elton L. Daniel (ed.), *Society and Culture in Qajar Iran: Studies in Honor of Hafez Farmayan* (Costa Mesa, CA.: Mazda, 2002), pp. 285–310; Anja Pistor-Hatam, 'Progress and Civilization in Nineteenth-Century Japan: The Far Eastern State as a Model for Modernization', *Iranian Studies* 29/1–2 (Winter/Spring 1996), pp. 111–26; Roxane Haag-Higuchi, 'A Topos and Its Dissolution: Japan in Some

20th Century Iranian Texts', *Iranian Studies* 29/1–2 (Winter/Spring 1996), pp. 71–84.
9. Foreign Office 371 / 106, p. 427, incl. in Grant Duff to Grey, No. 53, 27 Feb. 1906.
10. Foreign Office 371 / 311, p. 431, Spring Rice to Grey, No. 174, 11 Aug. 1907.
11. The scholarship on this issue still needs to be drawn out, but the issue is mentioned briefly in Ian Nish, *The Anglo-Japanese Alliance: The Diplomacy of Two Island Empires 1894–1907* (London: Athlone Press, 1966).
12. Foreign Office 371 / 105, p. 487, Grant Duff to Grey, No. 31, 1 Feb. 1906.
13. Foreign Office 371 / 107, p. 454, Mashad Diary, No. 2, to 13 Jan 1906.
14. Ibid, p. 454.
15. Foreign Office 371 / 107, p. 458, Turbat-i Haidari Diary to 14 Jan. 1906.
16. Foreign Office 371 / 107, p. 398, Report of Sistan Consul, No. 5, to 7 Feb. 1906.
17. Tei Suzuki's short travel account can be found in the *Asahi Shinbun* issue of June 30, 1906.
18. This is a reference, of course, to the Japanese victory in the Russo-Japanese War of 1904–05. Many people thought it significant that Japan, a country governed by a written constitution since 1889, had defeated Russia, which had yet to adopt a governing constitution.
19. This is an ingenious but probably not very accurate description of the conversion of Persia from Zoroastrianism to Islam. Nagase's way of explaining the relatively influential role of the ulema in Persia as compared to Ottoman lands was to emphasize what he saw as age-old patterns in Persian culture.
20. Nagase probably meant to say Najaf, not Karbala. Needless to say, Nagase's account of the Constitutional Revolution was not always perfectly accurate. More important than the facts he presents are the attitudes that he displays towards his subject.
21. Like most Japanese at that time, Nagase probably felt pride in the Meiji Constitution of 1889 which was seen as an important landmark in the political modernization of Japan. His attitude in this regard was similar to that of many Persian constitutionalists who perhaps overestimated the immediate political and military benefits of the promulgation of a constitution. It should be noted that contemporary European commentators, however, were pushing both Japanese and Persians towards this conclusion.
22. This is one of several points at which Nagase contends that Persians in general had 'weak characters'. Japan was heavily under the cultural influence of European orientalism at this time, and in addition had its own deep-rooted sense of superiority to all other countries. As he states directly, Nagase was genuinely sympathetic to the Persians, but at the same time he clearly felt that they ranked lower in the hierarchy of civilizations than Japan, or even Ottoman Turkey.

Index

Abbas Aqa Tabrizi, 267, 274, 460
Abbas Mirza, 85, 91, 95, 274
'Abd al-Hadi, 344
'Abd al-Hoseyn Lesan al-Saltaneh Sepehr *see* Lesan al-Saltaneh
'Abd al-Ra'uf Fetrat Bokhara'i, 348
'Abd al-Rahim Elahi, Mirza, 225, 227
'Abd al-Rahim Haqqverdiev *see* Haqqverdiev
'Abdollah Behbahani *see* Behbahani, Seyyed 'Abdollah
'Abdollah Mazandarani *see* Mazandarani, Sheykh 'Abdollah
'Abdollah Qajar, 238
Abdülhamid II, Sultan, 319–25, 327, 330, 336, 338, 360, 364–74, 391, 450, 476, 480
Abolqasem Khan Naser al-Molk *see* Naser al-Molk
Abozziya' *see* Shabestari, Seyyed Mohammad
Abrahamian, Ervand (as a historian), 16–18
Adamiyat, Fereydun (as a historian), 16, 18, 22, 23, 39
Adib al-Mamalek Farahani, 5, 10, 179
'Adl, Mostafa *see* Mansur al-Saltaneh
Afary Janet (as a historian), 16, 17, 18, 19, 20, 21, 24, 47
Afghan press, 342–47
Afghanistan, xxx, 200, 298, 299, 343–46, 352, 385, 386, 473
Afjeh'i, Seyyed Mohammad Reza, 75, 76
Afsah al-Motekallemin, 236
Afshari, Reza (as a historian), 22
Ahmad al-Hoseyni, Haji Seyyed, 455

Ahmad Danesh, 349
Ahmad Khan Vazir Hozur *see* Vazir Hozur
Ahmad Shah Qajar, 88, 140, 255, 273, 274, 339, 364, 372–75, 396, 424
Ahmed Rıza, 181, 321–23, 325
Ahvaz, 436
Akhtar, 342
Akhundzadeh, Fath-Ali, xviii, 143, 239–42, 248, 352–54
al-Afghani, Seyyed Jamal al-Din (Asadabadi), 169, 267, 327, 366
al-Hilal, 362, 364–66
al-Muqtataf, 361, 362–64, 366
al-Nahda, xxxi, 357–68
'Ala al-Saltaneh, Ahmad Khan, 373
Alexandria, 358–60
Ali Jenab, 139
Ali Khan Qajar Zahir al-Dowleh *see* Zahir al-Dowleh
Ali Reza Khan 'Azod al-Molk *see* 'Azod al-Molk
Alliance Française, 177, 180
Ameri, Mirza Javad Khan, 76
America, American, United States, 175, 207, 244, 246, 269, 293, 294, 298–302, 305–07, 309, 312, 361, 372, 377, 382, 386
Amin al-Soltan, Ali Asghar, 102, 127, 198, 216, 267, 274, 382, 449
Amin al-Tojjar, Mirza Mohammad, 122
Amin al-Zarb, Haj Mohammad Hoseyn, 74, 118, 125, 127, 178, 194, 195
Amin Aqdas, 102
Amir A'zam, 228, 236
Amir Bahador Jang, Hoseyn Pasha Khan, 160, 161, 233, 274

Amir Habibollah Khan, 343
Amir Kabir, Mirza Taqi Khan, 86, 177, 273
Amir Mofakhkham, Lotf Ali Khan, 437
Amirani, 49
Amirkhizi, Esma'il, 37, 38, 40, 42
Amol, 119
Amuoghli, Heydar Khan, 63, 160, 187
ancient relics, 254, 255, 273
Anglo-Iranian Agreement 1919, 90, 313
Anglo-Russian Agreement 1907, xxxii, 81, 156, 294–99, 301, 312, 313, 316, 331, 382, 468, 470
Anjoman, 234, 466, 475, 478, 479
Anjoman of Tabriz, 136, 184, 435
Anjoman-e Asnaf, 124–28, 129
Anjoman-e Ayalati (Tabriz), 38, 406
Anjoman-e Azarbayjan, 180
Anjoman-e baladiyeh, 139
Anjoman-e Esfahan, 135, 136, 138
Anjoman-e Eslami of Tabriz, 234
Anjoman-e Golestan, 38
Anjoman-e Haqiqat, 37
Anjoman-e Hemmat, 208, 234
Anjoman-e Ma'aref, 156
Anjoman-e Jonub, 126
Anjoman-e Makhfi, 27, 31
Anjoman-e Melli of Azarbayjan, 106, 322
Anjoman-e Okhovvat, xxvi, 144, 145, 148–51, 156, 158–60, 162, 244, 440–42, 444, 445, 457
Anjoman-e Sa'adat of Istanbul, 181–83, 326, 332, 338, 339
Anjoman-e Seraj al-Akhbar, 343–45
Anjoman-e Tejarat, 121–22
Anjoman-e Tojjar, 121–24
Anjoman-e Vatankh^{v}ahan-e Irani, 122
Anzali, 9, 158, 185, 236, 258, 394, 396
Aqa Khan Kermani *see* Kermani, Mirza Aqa Khan
Arab reformist periodicals, xxxi, 356–68
Arabia, 199
Ardabil, 36, 38, 43, 111
Aref-e Qazvini, 9
Armenia, Armenians, xxiii, 21, 39, 40, 46, 52, 53, 55, 59, 63, 66, 95, 126, 151, 201, 323, 326
army, 84–86, 91–92, 95–96, 104
Aryanism, 304, 306–08, 313
As'adi, Abbas Ali, xxviii, 242, 243, 244, 247
Asadollah Mamaqani *see* Mamaqani, Sheykh Asadollah
Asahi (*Tokyo Asahi Shinbun*), 381, 382
Asef al-Dowleh, 228
Ashraf al-Din, Seyyed, 4–6, 8, 9–11
asnaf, guilds, 117, 124–29, 323, 333
'Assar, Seyyed Mohammad Kazem, 76
Astanqul Beg, 345
Astara, 49, 65, 137, 385
Astarabad, 137
'*Atabat*, 6, 37, 41
Austria, Austrian, 33, 49, 92, 390
Ayineh-ye Gheyb Nama, 229, 231
azadi see freedom
azadi kh^{v}ahan, 37, 44, 338
Azerbaijan, Azerbaijani, xxxiii, 46, 53, 58, 59, 65, 66, 187, 293, 346, 351–54
Azarbayjan, Azarbayjani, xxx, xxxii, 26, 35, 41, 46, 48, 51, 52, 54, 55, 57, 64, 110, 135, 137, 140, 144, 180, 184, 232, 274, 314, 320, 321, 323, 324, 328, 331–33, 337, 352, 392, 393, 395, 405, 437
Azerbaijani dramatists, 352–55
Azimi, Fahreddin (as a historian), 23
'Azod al-Molk, Ali Reza Khan, 140

Babis, 175, 209, 285, 327, 448, 451, 478
Baha'is, 451, 473, 479
Bahaeddin Şakir, 321, 477, 478, 480
Bahar, Mohammad Taqi, 1, 2, 3, 5, 7–9, 11
Bakhtiyari, xxv, 39, 46, 95, 131–42, 182, 183, 185, 273, 274, 283, 311, 393, 395
Baku, 46, 47, 53–56, 63, 65, 66, 184, 186, 341, 343, 345, 346, 350, 352, 354, 396, 409, 414, 416, 418
Balasari, 29
Baluch, Baluchestan, 30, 31
Bam, 30, 31
Bamdad, 126, 127

bandits, xxii, 36, 40, 41, 43, 44
Baqer Khan, 39, 49, 267, 274, 300, 333, 335, 392, 405
Barakatullah, Mulavi Abdul Hafiz Mohammad, 307
Barforush (Babol), 273
bast, 3, 38, 86–88, 90, 97, 128, 154, 155, 161, 162; *bast* at the British Legation 1906, 84, 89, 121, 253, 281, 284, 286, 287, 298, 331; *bast* at the Ottoman Embassy 1908, 331–35
Batumi, 47, 49, 54, 63, 64, 386, 408, 409, 411, 416
Bayat, Mangol (as a historian), 16–19, 21, 23
bazaar, bazaaris, xxv, 23, 61, 71, 74, 84, 87, 88, 101, 107, 109, 117–21, 124–26, 128, 129, 136, 257
Behbahani, Seyyed 'Abdollah, 27, 28, 39, 74, 76, 103, 125, 126, 128, 154, 171, 173, 189, 209, 267, 274
Beijing, 369, 282
Beirut, 361
Bengal, 291, 292, 302
Berberian, Houri (as a historian), 21
Berlin, 241, 301, 318
Bidari-ye Iran, Lodge, 178–79
Birjand, 386
Blunt, Wilfred Scawen, 300, 302, 309
Bogdanov-Mariashkin, Mikheil, 48, 52, 53, 55, 57, 58, 59, 60, 61, 64, 65
Bokhara-ye sharif, 346, 347
Bolsheviks, xxiii, xxiii, 53, 54, 59, 161, 409, 413–16, 483
Boluri, Haji Mirza Aqa, 234
Bombay, 122, 383
bonakdar, 118
Bonakdar, Haj Mohammad Taqi, 122
Borujerdi, Sheykh Mohammad 'Abdoh, 76
Britain, British (with regard to foreign policy towards Iran, otherwise throughout), xxix, xxxi, 28, 30, 55, 71, 81, 82, 90, 92, 96, 119, 132, 136, 171, 190, 278, 282, 294, 298, 302, 317, 331, 332, 335
Browne, Edward Granville (as a historian), 22; and the Persia Committee, 184, 297, 300–11, 291–318, 374
Brussels, 293, 377
Bucharest, 194
Bukhara, 282, 341–50, 352, 483
Bulgaria, 293, 317
Bushire, 383

Calcutta, 343, 348
capitulations, 358
Caucasus, xxiii, xxx, 36, 46–48, 50, 51, 53, 56, 58, 60, 61, 63, 64, 185, 189, 201, 240, 242, 244, 314, 341, 342, 343, 345, 350–53, 355
Cemaleddin *şeyhülislam*, 338
censorship, xxviii, 148, 214, 226, 232–36, 240, 241, 284, 382
Central Asia, xiii, xxx, xxxi, 283, 298, 341, 342, 343, 345, 346, 348, 351–55, 367
Chamber of Commerce *see* Anjoman-e Tejarat
Chaqueri, Cosroe (as a historian), 17, 21
Chehreh Nama, xxxi, 31, 136
China, Chinese, xxix, xxxi, xxxii, 21, 83–85, 155, 187, 200, 278–85, 290, 291, 298, 369–79, 382, 427, 487
Chinese press, xxxi, 369–79
Chinese revolution (1911), 21, 277, 298
Chinese Revolutionary Party, 377
church and state, 167, 176, 181
citizen, xxiv, xxvi, 20, 25, 26, 43, 70, 77, 79, 103, 108, 112, 171, 189, 202, 214, 222, 227, 228, 234, 237
civil courts, 74
civil law, xxiii, xxiv, 69–79, 106
civilizational discourse, 307
class, xxiii, xxiv xxix, 18, 19, 22, 23, 25, 26, 29, 55, 57, 61, 62, 82, 83, 84, 99, 103, 111, 112, 117–30, 142, 189, 193, 195, 243–45, 252, 267, 277, 283–85, 351, 155, 358, 362, 363, 373
clerc, 166, 168, 169, 173
clergy *see* ulema
Colum, Padraic, 304
Committee for the Assistance to the

Persian Revolution, 47
Communist Party of Iran, 483
companies, 118, 123
Comtean positivism, xxix, 283
constitution, meaning of as a term, 71
Constitution of 1906, 1, 38, 45, 73, 74, 76, 77, 81, 85, 87, 88, 132, 134
constitutionalism (throughout)
constitutional narrative, 319–40
consultation, 290
Cossack Brigade, xxiv, 45, 63, 85, 91–96, 129, 140, 159–61, 324, 374, 376, 396, 430
Coup d'état of June 1908, 1, 4, 35, 85, 94, 95, 174, 180, 184, 194, 222, 242, 244, 245, 247, 253, 274, 280, 282, 285, 289, 300, 324, 330, 437, 451, 453, 462
Court (royal), xxiv, xxviii, 92, 99, 102, 140, 144, 146, 148–50, 158, 162, 171, 177, 205, 241, 243–45, 248, 252, 281, 353, 360, 362, 459, 461
cultural critique, 204
CUP (Committee of Union and Progress)
Curios, 254
Curzon, George Nathaniel, 317

daneshmandan, xxix, 277, 283, 286–89
D'Arcy Oil Company, 436
Dar al-Fanun, 177, 254, 255, 274
Dashnaks, 40, 56, 63, 66, 323, 324, 325, 413–15
Davar, Ali Akbar, 75, 77, 78
Dehkhoda, Ali Akbar, xvii, 2, 4, 11, 132, 179, 181–84, 187, 188, 193–212
Democrat Party, 86, 187, 244
Denis, Monsieur, 102
despotism, 195, 203–05, 217, 229, 242, 281, 290, 311, 325, 336
Dhu al-Riyasateyn, 440
dialogue (*monazereh, mokalemeh*), 347–51
diaspora, xxxi, 292, 357–68
Dillon, John, 294–97, 299, 308, 309, 313–15
dowlat, 168, 170, 171, 217, 251

Dowlatabadi, Yahya, xxii, 187, 189, 254, 255, 257, 260, 267, 268, 273, 285, 306, 327, 332, 334, 445, 408, 459, 472, 478, 480
drama, 239–48, 304, 352–55
Dreyfus affair, 283

Eblagh, 230
Ebrahim Khan Hakim al-Molk *see* Hakim al-Molk
'edalat see justice
'edalatkhaneh, 71, 89, 145, 152, 153
education, 18, 29, 103, 107, 109, 145, 155, 158, 161, 162, 168, 176, 177, 187, 189, 194–96, 201, 204, 209, 210, 212, 215, 220, 230, 242, 244, 247, 272, 283, 285, 286, 289, 346, 372, 386, 390, 411, 475, 485
Eftekhar al-Tojjar, 15, 128
Egypt, Egyptian, xxxi, 91, 230, 283, 291, 293, 294, 296, 298–300, 308–10, 313, 315, 317, 322, 357–68, 392, 437, 468, 470, 471, 484, 485
Egyptian Standard (al-Liwa), 309, 310
Ehtesab al-Molk, Taqi Khan, 102
ehtesabiyeh, 100–02
Ehtesham al-Saltaneh, Mirza Mahmud Khan, 103, 126
Eiravani, Sheykh Mohammad Reza, 75
Electoral Law 1907, 89, 215
elite, xxviii, 2, 24, 29, 69, 71, 73, 82, 86, 89, 92, 125, 132, 149, 162, 167, 173, 177, 178, 185, 188, 248, 249, 250, 252, 257, 267, 271, 273, 359, 382, 385
Emperor of Japan, 384
Enlightenment, xxvi, xxvii, 165–67, 174, 175, 182, 193, 195, 202, 204, 211, 212, 277
Entezam al-Saltaneh, 149, 160, 178
Enver Paşa, 328, 330
Eqbal al-Dowleh, 135, 136
Eqbal al-Saltaneh Maku'i, 223, 224
equality, 144, 171, 175, 179, 197, 212, 214, 216, 218, 289, 379
Erzurum, 323, 325
Esfahan, 139
Eskandari, Mahmud, 230

E'tela al-Dowleh, Mirza Hoseyn Khan, 139
E'temad al-Saltaneh, Mirza Hasan Khan, 101, 102
'Eyn al-Dowleh, 'Abd al-Majid Mirza, 50, 332, 394

factories, 53, 119, 146, 257
Farhang, 138
Fars, 110, 136, 137, 146, 228
Faryad, 234, 236
Fatemi Qomi, Seyyed Mohammad, 75, 76
Fath-Ali Shah Qajar, 246
Fathi, Asghar (as a historian), 41
Fazlollah Nuri, Sheykh *see* Nuri, Sheykh Fazlollah
financial institutions, 118, 120
Finland, 291, 296
fiqh, 71, 75, 76, 78, 79
Firuzkuhi, Sheykh Ali Baba, 76
First World War, xxi, xxx, 1, 75, 83, 86, 130, 190, 195, 265, 278, 291–95, 312, 313, 318, 340, 354, 355, 473
Foran, John (as a historian), 16, 18, 19, 23
France, French, xxix, 70, 92, 151, 167, 174–82, 189–91, 194–98, 210, 225, 244, 260, 273, 279, 282, 283, 286, 288, 290, 309, 310
fraternity, 122, 175, 179, 289
freedom (*azadi*), xxi, xxviii, 1, 5, 22, 23, 27, 29, 30, 31, 42, 66, 72, 136, 140, 144, 149, 175, 176, 184, 185, 187, 193, 200–02, 279, 299, 327, 330, 338, 364, 365, 378, 379
freedom of expression, 209, 231–32
Freemasonry, xxvi, 150, 151, 166, 174–78, 190

Gaelic American, 298–302, 305–07, 309, 312
Gagoshidze, Sergo, 48, 56, 64, 65
Gamdlishvili, Sergo, 48, 64
Gan Yonglong, 371, 372
Gendarmerie, xxiv, 36, 83, 85, 91, 95, 96

gender *see* women
Geneva, 175
Georgia, Georgians, xxiii, 46, 47, 48, 53, 56, 58, 59, 64, 66, 185
Georgian Bolsheviks, 53
Georgian press, 49–50
Georgian Social Democrats, 47, 53, 53
Germany, German, 200, 241, 281, 301, 305, 313, 318, 333, 372, 381, 385
Ghaffarzadeh, Asadollah, 351, 483
Ghanizadeh Delmaqani, Mahmud, 234
Gheissari, Ali (as a historian), 23
gheyrat (in the sense of activism), 217, 221
Gilan, 46–48, 51, 52, 54, 59, 62, 64–66, 137, 140, 145, 156, 158, 161, 185, 228, 236, 274, 395
Gorjis, 45–48, 54, 55, 57, 64
Grand Orient de France, 176–81
Grey, Edward, 295–97, 299, 300, 302, 312, 314–17, 332
guilds *see asnaf*
Guomindang, 377
Guria, 61, 64
Gurji, Sergo, 52, 54, 55, 56, 57, 59, 61, 62, 63, 64
Gwynn, Stephen Lucius, 295

Habib Orumiyeh, Mirza, 234
Habl al-Matin of Calcutta, 343, 344, 348, 383, 387
Hadi Najmabadi, *see* Najmabadi, Haj Sheykh Hadi
Hadid, 233
Ha'eri Yazdi, Ayatollah 'Abdolkarim, 76
Hafez, 274
Hairi, Abdul-Hadi (as a historian), 17
Haji Sayyah *see* Mahallati, Mirza Mohammad Ali
Hajibekov Uzeir, 354
Hakim al-Molk, Ebrahim Khan, 178, 180
Halil Bey, 328
Hamadan, 145, 150–56, 162, 393
Haqiqat, 346
haqq, hoquq, 42, 70, 71, 197, 198, 251, 288

Haqqverdiev, 'Abd al-Rahim, 353, 354
Hasan Khan Moshir al-Molk *see* Moshir al-Molk
Hasan Shirazi, Mirza *see* Mirza Hasan Shirazi
Hashrud, Central Asia, battle of, 329, 330, 334
Hedayat, Sadeq, , xiii, 304
Hekmat, xxxi, 131, 359, 360
Herat, 343
Hey'at-e Ettehadiyeh-ye Tojjar, 130
Heydar Khan Amuogli *see* Amuogli
Himmat, 47
historiography, xxi, xxii, xxiii, xxviii, xxxi, 15–66, 81, 132, 142, 265, 341, 357, 365–68
Hnchakists, 66
Hong Kong, 369
horriyat, 136, 197, 216, 218, 219, 251, 339
humanism, humanists, 166, 167, 175, 201, 202, 205, 212
Hoseyn Pasha Khan, Amir Bahador Jang *see* Amir Bahador Jang

ijtihad, 78
image and identity, 249–74
Imamate, doctrine of, 149
Imedi, 49, 50
Imperial Bank, 129
imperialism, 71, 132, 190, 300, 309, 311, 322, 367
India, Indians, xxi, xxix, 122, 242, 273, 278, 282, 291–96, 298, 300–04, 306–08, 313, 315–17, 343, 345, 348, 349, 358, 361, 367, 369, 373, 383, 385, 386, 392, 416, 473
intellectuals and revolution, 277–90
intelligentsia (per se), xxvi, 17, 23, 165, 171, 172, 174, 175, 178, 179, 182, 183, 187, 190, 283, 284, 289, 351
intercultural contexts, 366–68
international socialism, 355
internationalism, 53, 60
Iraj Mirza, 3
Iran-e now, 186, 187, 189, 234
Iraq, xv, 37, 41, 148

Ireland, Irish, 22, 291–98, 304–05, 307, 312–18
Irish national politics, 292–94
Isfahan, 5, 88, 104, 107, 109, 110, 123, 131–42, 151, 204, 301, 353, 393, 395
Islamic law *see shari'a*
Islamic Revolution, xxii, 19, 77, 251, 266
Islamic rhetoric, 166
Istanbul, 49, 122, 136, 176, 177, 181, 183, 194, 195, 254, 258, 290, 310, 324, 326–27, 330, 335, 337, 338, 342, 348, 352, 358, 364, 365, 411
Italy, Italian, 76, 92, 311

Jahad-e akbar, 132–35, 139, 140
Jahangir Khan, Mirza, 4, 179, 194, 216, 274, 330, 444, 448, 453, 460
Jahanshah Khan, 233
Jalal al-Din Mo'ayyed al-Eslam Kashani *see* Mo'ayyed al-Eslam
Jalal al-Dowleh, Soltan Hasan Mirza, 159
Jamal al-Din al-Afghani *see* al-Afghani
Jamal al-Din Va'ez Esfahani, Seyyed, 179, 180, 209, 267, 274, 287
Japan, Japanese, xxxii, 64, 93, 200, 282, 283, 319, 377, 381–96, 475, 489
Japanese press, 382, 383
Japanese victory over Russia 1905, 319
Japaridze, Apolon, 48, 50, 52, 53, 58
Javad, Haj Mirza, 404
Javad Khan *see* Sa'd al-Dowleh
Jerusalem, 175
Jews, 46, 53, 59, 66, 151, 157, 159, 175
journalism, 215, 216, 233, 243, 248, 267, 342–47
Jugashvili, Soso (Stalin), 54
Julfa, 49, 61, 65
justice, xxiii, xxv, 1, 20, 22, 24, 26, 40, 41, 42, 70, 71–73, 75, 78, 86, 89, 104, 142, 145, 146, 152, 153, 155, 171, 188, 195, 196, 199, 203, 209–12, 216, 219, 220, 222, 227, 228, 231, 234, 273, 278, 303, 309

Kabul, 343, 345

kadkhoda, 100, 101, 106
kalantar, 100, 101, 105, 106, 112
Kalkhorian, 131
Kamran Mirza Nayeb al-Saltaneh *see* Nayeb al-Salataneh
Karaj, 55
Karim Khan, 418
Kashan, 109, 140
Kashani Sabet, Firoozeh (as a historian), 21
Kashani, Mohammad Ali, 75
Kashani, Seyyed Hasan, 216
Kashkul, 132, 134, 138–41, 150, 339
Kasravi, Ahmad (and as a historian), xxii, 16–18, 20, 22, 23, 27–29, 33, 39, 250, 254, 260, 265, 266, 269, 271
Kazimayn, 37
Keddie, Nikki (as a historian), 17, 18
Kerman, 27–31, 137, 270, 274
Kermani, Mirza Aqa Khan, 199
Kermani, Mirza Reza, 267, 274, 327
Kermanshah, 136, 156
Ketabcheh-ye gheybi, 347
Khamseh, 131
Kheyr al-kalam, 236
Khoi, 49
Khomeini, Ayatollah Ruhollah, 24, 191
Khorasan, 137, 146, 194, 228, 273
Khorasani, Mohammad Kazem, 72, 136, 139, 332
Khorshid, 234
Kong Qinglai, 372
Kuchek Khan Jangali, 267
Kurdistan, Kurds, 255
Kurzman, Charles (as a historian), 21

Lahuti, Abolqasem, 11
Lahore Panjabee, 301
Lalla Rookh, 303
Larestan, 137, 393
law, law courts, legality, 22, 23, 25, 166–68, 171, 173, 176, 177, 179, 184, 198, 199, 202, 203, 205, 206–09, 311–12, 348, 349, 355
law and Islam, xxiv, xxvi, 289–91
legitimacy, legitimate, 69, 88, 90, 96, 105, 165–69, 171, 178, 195, 204, 205, 208, 210, 290, 323, 364
Leonozov fish factory, 65
Lesan al-Saltaneh Sepehr, 'Abd al-Hoseyn, 435
letters to the editor, xxvii, 218–23
Liakhov, Colonel Vladimir, 50, 60, 93–95, 159, 161, 324, 392, 396, 412, 444
lieu(x) de memoire, xxii, xxiii, 33–44
Loft Ali Khan Amir Mofakhkham *see* Amir Mofakhkham
Loghatnameh, 195
London, xvii, 132, 183, 385, 254, 255, 268, 292, 293, 295, 298–302, 306, 309, 313, 316, 317, 343, 371, 373
Loqman al-Mamalek, Zeyn al-Abedin, 177
lutis, 31, 38, 41
Lynch, Henry Finnis, 296

Ma'sud Mirza Zell al-Soltan *see* Zell al-Soltan
Mahabad, 110
Mahallati, Haji Sayyah, 178
Mahmud Khan Ehstesham al-Saltaneh *see* Ehtesham al-Saltaneh
Mohammad Khan Zoka' al-Molk, *see* Zoka' al-Molk
Majalleh-ye estebdad, 278
Majd al-Eslam, 28, 139, 227, 228, 233
Majles (assembly – throughout)
Majles, 209, 210
Majles-e vokala-ye tojjar, 119
Majma'-e Azadmardan, 216, 248
Malayer, 246
Malek al-Motekallemin, Haj Mirza Nasrollah, 157, 160, 179, 180, 209, 235, 236, 267, 274, 330
Malekeh-ye Iran (Tuman Agha), 146, 159–61
Malekzadeh, Mehdi (as a historian), 16, 17, 23
Malkam Khan, Mirza, 69, 143, 152, 201, 241, 242, 274, 343, 348
Maloney, William J., 294, 309, 310, 314
Mamaqani, Sheykh Asadollah, 76, 337
man on the street, xxviii, 249, 257
Manchuria, 65, 282, 385

Mangan, Clarence James, 303
Mansur al-Saltaneh, Seyyed Mostafa 'Adl, 74, 75
Maragheh'i, Zeyn al-Abedin, 352, 485
Marand, 49, 50, 66
Martin, Vanessa (as a historian), 17, 18, 23
Masaharu Yoshida, 488
Mashhad, 36, 88, 89, 234, 245, 270, 343, 344, 386
mashrutiyat (as a term), 70, 71, 138, 140, 170, 172, 173, 193, 195, 196, 202, 277–90, 367
Matin al-Saltaneh, 109
Matin Daftari, Ahmad, 76
Mazandaran, 137, 161, 273
Mazandarani, Sheykh 'Abdollah, 136, 332
Mecca, 175
Mehdi Khan, Moshir al-Molk, 359
Mehdi Khan Za'im al-Dowleh *see* Za'im al-Dowleh
Mehdi Qoli Hedayat *see* Mokhber al-Saltaneh
Mehmed V Reshad, Sultan, 336, 339
Mehrabad, 3
Meiji Constitution of 1886, 489
mellat, 18, 132, 136, 140, 171, 208, 209, 217, 241, 251, 339, 344
Mensheviks, 53, 54, 59
merchants, xxv, xxviii, 20, 31, 41, 47, 56, 64, 65, 71, 84, 99, 101, 104, 109, 111, 112, 117–30, 151, 245, 252, 253, 267, 274, 279, 284, 286, 287, 332, 333, 358, 360, 363, 377, 393
meşrutiyet, xxix, 2, 277–89, 329
Mesopotamia, 199, 200
Mexico, Mexican, 21, 279–82, 284, 289
Mexican Revolution, 21, 277, 279, 284, 291
Mgeladze, Vlasa (Tria), 46, 48, 53–56, 61, 64, 66
Midhat Paşa, 330
Minbao, 377, 378
minorities, 209, 222, 359, 450, 478
Mir Qasem Khan, 344
Mirza Aqa Tabrizi, 179, 240, 242, 248, 408, 433
Mo'azed al-Saltaneh, 179, 180, 187
Mo'ayyed al-Ashraf, 139
Mo'ayyed al-Eslam Kashani, Jalal al-Din, 273, 343, 348, 452
Modarres, Seyyed Hasan, 88
Moderate Party, moderates, 166, 171, 172, 179, 181, 184–90, 195, 216, 244, 301
modernity, modern (selective), xxi, xxii, xxiv, xxvi, xxvii, xxix, 18, 20, 35, 70, 71, 77–79, 82, 86, 88–89, 92, 97, 100, 101, 103, 108, 113, 117–20, 125, 129, 131, 150, 174, 188, 202, 210, 226, 230, 238, 307, 309, 342, 357, 365, 367
Mo'ezz al-Soltan, 62, 63
Mohakemat, 233
Mohammad Ali Foroughi *see* Zoka' al-Molk
Mohammad Ali (Haji Sayyah), 375
Mohammad Ali Khan Qavam al-Dowleh *see* Qavam al-Dowleh
Mohammad Ali Shah Qajar, xxviii, xxx, 1, 2, 38, 45, 51, 93, 94, 132, 139, 140, 145, 148, 153, 154, 156, 157, 158, 161, 172, 173, 195, 198, 204, 233, 242, 244–47, 253, 255, 265, 267, 274, 282, 296, 320, 324, 327, 328, 330, 332, 333, 335–38, 364, 365, 371, 372, 437, 440, 442, 443, 449, 451
Mohammad Hashem Asef *see* Rostam al-Hokama
Mohammad Hoseyn Na'ini *see* Na'ini, Mirza Mohammad Hoseyn
Mohammad Iman, 331
Mohammad Ja'far, Mirza, 232
Mohammad Kazem Khorasani *see* Khorasani, Mohammad Kazem
Mohammad Naser Khan Qajar *see* Qajar, Mohammad Naser Khan
Mohammad Nazem al-Eslam Kermani *see* Nazem al-Eslam Kermani
Mohammad Reza, Haji Mirza, xxviii, 19, 27, 28
Mohammad Qoli Hedayat *see* Mokhber al-Molk, Mohammad Qoli Hedayat

Mohammad Tabataba'i *see* Tabataba'i, Seyyed Mohammad
Mohamamadzadeh, Mirza Rahim, 242, 243
Mohsen Khan Mozaffar al-Molk *see* Mozaffar al-Molk, Mohsen Khan
Mohsenieh Association, 242, 243, 247
mohtaseb, 101
Mo'in al-Tojjar, 123, 125
Mo'in al-Vezareh, 373
Mojahed, 233, 234
mojahedin, 37–39, 41–43, 47, 95, 137, 140, 184, 185, 189, 257, 265, 274, 323, 329–30, 333, 334, 407
Mojir al-Dowleh, 232, 345
Mokhber al-Molk, Mohammad Qoli Hedayat, 74
Mokhtar al-Molk, 149
Mokhber al-Saltaneh, Mehdi Qoli Hedayat, 38, 74, 405, 425, 434
Molla Ebrahim Khalil the Alchemist, 239, 240
Molla Nasreddin, 142, 341, 345, 408, 439
Momtaz al-Dowleh, 179, 187
monavvar al-fekr, xxvi, 165, 173, 277, 283, 285, 289
moneylenders *see sarraf*
Monsieur Jordan the Herbalist, 239, 240
Monte Forte, Comte Antoine di, 100
Montesquieu, Charles de Secondat, 203–04, 206
Morel, Paul Henri, 177, 178, 180
Morocco, 309
Morteza Qoli Khan Sani' al-Dowleh *see* Sani' al-Dowleh
Mosaddeq, Mohammad, 74
Mosahebeh-ye molla va tajer, 347
Mosahebeh-e Iraniyeh, 350, 351, 483
Mosavat, 57, 209, 214, 216, 219, 220, 233, 236, 237, 243, 248
mosavat see equality
Mosavat, Seyyed Mohammad Reza, xxxviii, 216, 242–44, 248
Moshir al-Dowleh, Mirza Nasrollah Khan, 73–75, 155, 156, 179
Moshir al-Saltaneh, 158, 159
Mostashar al-Dowleh, Sadeq Khan, 184, 187, 242
Mostashar al-Dowleh, Yusef Khan, 69, 349
Movaqqar al-Saltaneh, 127
Mozaffar al-Din Shah Qajar, 1, 33, 36, 73, 92, 131, 148, 152, 153, 158, 170, 171, 193, 213, 214, 242, 326, 336, 349, 362, 364, 370, 371, 374, 389, 390, 437, 443
Mozaffar al-Molk, Mohsen Khan, 158
mujtahids, 29, 39, 41, 74, 120, 125, 126, 128
mullas *see* ulema
Municipal Law 1907, xxiv, 102–05, 107, 108, 112, 113
municipal revenue, 108–11
municipalities, xxiv, 99–113
Muslim League, 302, 315
Mustansir al-Mulk, 386
mysticism, 168, 169, 230, 303, 308

Naci, Ömer, 322–25, 328, 330
Na'ini, Mirza Mohammad Hoseyn, 72, 285
Na'ini, Mirza Reza, 242–44, 246
Nader Shah Afshar, 204, 273, 274, 278, 353, 354
Nagase, Hosuke, 383, 387, 388
Najaf, 37, 49, 72, 128, 136, 189, 195, 208, 233, 234, 267, 274, 287, 332, 337, 353, 460
Najaf Qoli Khan Samsam al-Saltaneh *see* Samsam al-Saltaneh, Najaf Qoli Khan
Najmabadi, Afsaneh (as a historian), 16, 20, 24
Najmabadi, Haj Sheykh Hadi, 194, 195, 208
Namık Kemal, 290, 235
Naqus, 139
Narimanov, Nariman, 47, 353, 354
Naser al-Din Shah Qajar, 71, 92, 100, 101, 118, 143, 145, 146, 148, 161, 240–42, 267, 274, 327, 353, 389, 390, 440, 444, 449
Naser al-Molk, Abolqasem Khan, 9,

242, 255, 273, 274, 396
Naser Khan Sardar-e Jang *see* Sardar-e Jang
Nasim-e Shomal, 4
Nasir, Jamal 'Abd al-, 359
Nasr, Vali (as a historian, 23
Nasrollah Khan Moshir al-Dowleh *see* Moshir al-Dowleh
Nasrollah Malek al-Motekallemin *see* Malek al-Motekallemin
National Bank, 118, 123, 126, 127, 391
nation (as a distinct entity), 171–74, 180, 182, 184, 186, 187, 189, 198, 203
nation building, 217, 218, 225, 230, 232, 241, 449, 453
national identity, xxviii, xxix, 174, 249–74, 461
nationalism, xxi, xxii, xxiii, xxx, xxxiii, 10, 21, 25, 26, 44, 72, 86, 96, 158, 174, 187, 189, 241, 282, 303, 311, 317, 353, 355, 367, 379
Nayeb al-Saltaneh, Kamran Mirza, 101, 102, 159
Nazem al-Dowleh, 149
Nazem al-Eslam Kermani, Mirza Mohammad, xxii, 17, 22, 27, 28, 39, 179, 250, 265
Nazem Beg, 181
Nazm al-Molk, 102
Ne'matollahi Sheykhs, 148
Neda-ye vatan, 121, 227, 232
New Theatre, 243, 248
nezamnameh-ye anjomanha-ye tejarati, 122
Nightmare of Autocracy or the Sinners, 242–44, 284
Nimr, Faris, 362
Niyazi Bey, 330
North Africa, 91, 179, 341, 381
Norway, 291
Nosrat al-Dowleh Firuz, 74
Nosrat al-Soltan, 149, 160
nostalgia, 260–65
Nuri, Sheykh Fazlollah, xxvi, 3, 5, 6, 28, 72, 128, 166, 173, 220, 274
Nurollah, Aqa Sheykh, 104, 135

Odessa, 161, 436, 437
oil, 53, 89, 90, 110, 132
'oqala, 165, 196, 277, 285, 287
Oqyanus, 225, 227, 230
Orientalism, 295, 303, 304, 310
Orjonikidze, Grigol (comrade Sergo), 54, 411
'Orvat al-Vosqa, 139
Ottoman constitutional revolution, 277, 279, 322, 327, 338, 339, 364
Ottoman Empire, Ottomans, Turkey, Turks, xxx, xxxi, 83–85, 122, 136, 181, 185, 279, 280, 281, 283, 319–26, 328, 330, 331–32, 334–38, 341, 345, 366
Ottoman–Iranian border crisis, 328–29
Ouseley, Gore, 469

Pahlavi literature, 347
Pahlavi Mohammad Reza *see* Mohammad Reza Shah
Pahlavi, Reza Shah *see* Reza Shah
Pahlavis, xxi, xxiii, xxv, 1, 21, 69, 75, 77, 78, 82, 83, 86, 88–90, 96, 97, 117, 123, 125, 130, 251, 271, 424, 465
Paidar, Parvin (as a historian), 20
Palestine, 199, 470
Pan-Aryanism, 304, 306, 307, 313
Pan-Asianism, 385–87
Pan-Islam, Pan-Islamism, xxx, 21, 169, 327, 331–33, 336, 339, 340, 360, 366
Pantomime, xxvi, 145, 149, 156, 157, 162, 244
Pan-Turanism, 355
Pan-Turkism, xxx, 320, 340, 355
Paris, 139, 177–82, 186, 195, 282, 290, 320, 322, 323, 328, 373, 393
Party-Games, 184–90
Parvaneh, 139, 197
patriotism, 26, 42, 86, 151, 175, 180, 311
peasants, 20, 23, 30, 61
Persia Committee, 184, 295, 296, 300, 302, 308, 310, 317, 436, 468, 470, 473
Persian Gulf, 370, 372, 383, 384, 393, 394

photo collections, 250, 254, 255
photographic portraiture, 250, 270
photography, photographs, xxiii, xxviii, xxix, 33, 44, 136, 146, 147, 157, 249–74, 362
poetry, xxi, 1–12, 210, 262, 303, 336, 441, 442, 469
police (formation of force), 37, 56, 65, 85, 88, 101, 102, 104, 111
political drama, 242–44
political parties, xxxiii, 53, 59, 95, 186, 189, 201, 244
popular politics, xxii, 20, 26, 81–97
Portugal, Portuguese, xxix, 277–89
Portuguese revolution, 277–89
Poshtekuhian, 131
Postal service, 111
pre-Islamic past, 41, 148, 303, 347
press, xxv, xxvi, 10, 25, 89, 90, 95, 97, 131–42, 213–23, 225–38
private law, 70–71, 78, 79
progress, xxii, 2, 17, 18, 21, 23, 25, 27, 47, 202, 205, 209, 213, 214, 219, 222, 230, 234, 348, 350, 360, 371, 372, 435
public health, 284
public law, 70, 71, 76–79
public opinion, xxvii, 12, 89, 174, 178, 195, 217, 220, 290
public sphere, xxvi, xxvii, 211, 213–23, 227, 228

Qajar, Mohammad Naser Khan, 146
Qarachehdaghi, Mirza Ja'far, 240
Qaradagh, 36
Qasem Khan Ref'at Nezam *see* Ref'at-e Nezam, Mirza Qasem Khan
Qashqa'i, 131, 134, 136, 137
Qasida, 215, 242
Qavam al-Dowleh, Mirza Mohammad Ali Khan, 159, 444
Qavam al-Molk, 228, 444
Qazvin, 39, 48, 58, 104, 142, 184, 185, 194, 273, 395, 396
Qian Zhixiu, 372, 374
Qing dynasty, 83, 85, 377, 378
*qochi*s (roughs), 56

Qom, 76, 84, 88, 111, 185, 273, 274, 287, 395
Quetta, 386

ra'iyat, 171
racial theories, 303–08, 310, 311
Rafiq va vazir, 347, 348
Ra'is al-Tojjar, 118
Rasht, 46–59, 61, 63, 64, 66, 104, 118, 144, 158, 184, 236, 258, 270, 274, 409, 412–18, 450
Rasulzadeh, Amin, 186, 234
reactionaries, 60, 195, 200, 201, 205, 267
readership, xxvii, xxxi, 213–23, 241, 342, 359, 361
Redmond, John, 295, 299, 313, 468
Ref'at-e Nezam, Mirza Qasem Khan, 27, 30
religious dissidents, 23, 166
Republic of Plato, 347
Revolutionary Committees, 49, 52, 58, 59, 64, 65, 140, 160, 194, 195, 411, 415, 453
Reza Shah Pahlavi (Reza Khan) *see* Pahlavi, Reza Shah
Richard, Joseph, 177
Rifat Paşa, 332, 334, 335, 338
rights of the nation, xxiii, 69, 72, 265
rights, constitutional, 69–79, 299
rights, political, 70, 301
Rome, 167, 175
Rosen, Friedrich, 241
Roshdiyeh, Mirza Hasan, 177
Rostam al-Hokama, Mohammad Hashem Asef, 15, 16, 19
rowshanfekran, 165–91
rowzeh-kh"ani, 28
Ruh al-qodos, 232–33, 238
Russia, Russians, Soviet Union xxiii, xxiv, xxvii, xxix, xxxii, 9, 11, 38, 43, 46, 54–56, 58–60, 62–65, 83–85, 90, 92, 119, 123, 143, 151, 154, 157, 158, 190, 193, 201, 205, 208, 211, 236, 260, 261, 277–78, 293, 305, 331–36, 351–53, 363, 365
Russian policy towards Iran, xxxi,

49–51, 56, 59, 60, 71, 81, 92–96, 111, 140, 142, 182–87, 195, 202, 295, 299, 300–03, 312–17, 331–36, 370
Russian Revolution of 1905, xxix, 21, 58, 277–90, 291, 378
Russian ultimatum of 1911, 1, 83, 141, 142, 190, 345

Saʻd al-Dowleh, Javad Khan, 74, 391
Saʻid Salmasi, 323, 324, 329
Saʻidiyeh, 323
Sabahaddin, Prince, 321–23, 326
Sablin, Evgenii, 55, 414
Sadeq Hazrat, 109
Sadeq Khan Mostashar al-Dowleh *see* Mostashar al-Dowleh
Sadr, Mohsen *see* Sadr al-Ashraf
Sadr al-Ashraf Mohsen Sadr, 75, 76
Safaʼi, Ebrahim (as a historian), 39
Safavid, Safavids, 72, 257, 353
Safi Ali Shah, 148–50
Salar al-Dowleh, 156, 159, 255
Salmas, 37, 324, 328, 329, 410
saltanat, 137, 140, 168, 170–72
Samarra, 37, 404
Samsam al-Saltaneh Bakhtiyari, Najaf Qoli Khan, 3, 135–39, 141, 142, 393
Sanandaj, 442
Saniʻ al-Dowleh, Morteza Qoli Khan, 74, 109, 110, 134, 273
sanitation, 100–02, 105, 106, 108, 111
Sardar Asʻad Bakhtiyari, 95, 132, 135, 139–42, 182, 393, 395, 396
Sardar-e Jang, Naser Khan, 437
Sarraf Yaqub, 362
sarraf, xxv, 117, 119, 120, 124, 129, 433
Sasanian, 138
satire, xxvii, 2, 194, 196, 210, 288, 450
Sattar Khan, xxii, xxv, 33–44, 49, 56, 59, 66, 135, 136, 267, 274, 300, 328, 329, 331, 333–35, 393, 404–07, 409, 414, 480
Savojbolagh (Mahabad), 110, 321
Schneider, Justin, 177, 278
scholasticism, 167
Secret Centre, 158
secularism, 17, 19, 35, 73, 174, 206, 326,
423
Sedq al-Molk, Haji, 233
Sepah, Salar, Mirza Hoseyn Khan, 139
Seqat al-Eslam, Aqa Nurollah, 135
Seqat al-Eslam, Sheykhi cleric, 38, 39, 41, 106
Seraj al-akbar, 343–45
Seraj al-Din, Haji Mirza, ʻAbd al-Raʼuf a.k.a. Doktor Shaber, 352
Sevruguin (photographer), 147, 157
Shabestari, Seyyed Mohammad, 233, 234
shabnameh, 18, 87, 221
Shah ʻAbd al-ʻAzim Shrine, 28, 128, 257, 273
Shahnameh, of Ferdowsi, 219
Shahrdar, Habibollah, 242–44
Shahsavan, 93, 131, 234
Shanghai, 369, 374, 377
Shapshal, 449
shariʻa, Islamic law, xxiii, xxiv, 69, 71, 73, 74, 76–78, 170, 172, 173, 201, 290, 338
Sheykh Ali Mirza the Governor of Tuyserkan, 242, 243, 246
Sheykh va Vazir, 348
Sheykhis, 29, 38–41
Shiism, Shiite, 19, 37, 40, 41, 44, 69, 72, 73, 75, 79, 122, 125, 136, 143, 158, 168–70, 173, 174, 208, 226, 234, 241, 285, 301, 317, 330, 337, 389, 404
Shiraz, 49, 88, 110, 122, 148, 152, 177, 270, 293
Shirazi, Mirza Hasan, 37, 148
Shoʻaʻ al-Dowleh, 179
Shojaʻ al-Saltaneh, 66
Shuster, Morgan, 1, 9, 300, 372, 436
Singapore, 369, 377
Sinn Fein, 292, 313, 314
Sinn Fein, 298, 300–04, 309, 312–14
Sistan, 383, 386
Siyahatnameh-ye Ebrahim Beyk, 352
Skeffington, Hannah Sheehy, 304
Sobh-e sadeq, 234
social democracy, xxvii, 22, 193, 195, 211
Social Democrats, 47, 53, 54, 56, 58,

62, 158, 166, 184, 187, 341, 409, 411, 414, 416, 417, 483
social relations criticism, 239–48
socialists, 187, 292, 317, 470
Soltan al-'Olama Khorasani *see* Torbati
Soltan Ali Shahi, 440
Sorayya, 131
Sorush, xxvii, 181, 183, 189, 193–95, 211
South Africa, 299, 316, 468
Spain, Spanish, 167, 283, 378
state-building, xxxiii-xxxv, 69, 81–97
Sufis, Sufism, dervishes, xxvi, 143–62, 208, 243, 244, 354, 439, 440–42, 444, 445, 449, 450
Sun Yat-sen (Sun Zhongshan), 377, 378
Sunnis, 37, 317, 377, 389, 404
superstition, 182, 205, 208–10, 240, 241, 243, 246, 247
Supplementary Fundamental Law 1907, xxviii, 74, 153, 226, 232, 237, 289
Sur-e Esrafil, xxvii, 4, 132, 182, 183, 194–96, 199, 201, 202, 204, 207–09, 211, 214, 216, 220, 233, 267, 274, 289, 330, 343, 344, 351, 448
Sweden, Swedish, 95, 96, 291, 430
Swinny, Shapland Hugh, 195, 302
Switzerland, Yverdon, 183
Syria, Syrian, 199, 361, 450, 486

ta'ziyeh, 240, 241
Tabataba'i, Abolqasem, 331
Tabataba'i, Seyyed Mohammad, 27, 28, 74, 104, 125, 126, 152–55, 158, 161, 162, 171, 173, 174, 179, 209, 267, 274, 287, 331, 304, 407
Tabataba'i, Seyyed Sadeq, 174, 179
Tabriz, xxiii, xxv, 27, 31, 36–39, 41–43, 45–49, 51–59, 62–66, 84 ,88, 105–07, 109, 135–37, 158, 172, 177, 180, 184, 187, 230, 233, 234, 247, 253, 260, 261, 266, 270, 274, 300, 325, 327, 328, 331, 333–36, 365, 374, 392, 394, 395, 409–12, 412–28
Tabrizi, Mirza Aqa, xxviii, 179, 240–42, 248
tahzib-e akhlaq, 240
Taiwan, 280

Taiyo, 287
Tajer Esfahani, Aqa Mirza Aqa, 122
Tajer, Mirza Ebrahim, 122
Tajikistan, 352
Talat Paşa, 332, 335
Talebov, 'Abd al-Rahim, 202, 242–44, 260, 261, 273, 274, 483
Tamaddon, 236
Taqavi, Haj Seyyed Nasrollah, 74–76, 179, 187, 431
Taqizadeh, Seyyed Hasan, xxii, 26, 74, 103, 160, 161, 174, 179, 180, 184–90, 241
Tarbiyat, 209, 214–16, 218, 221
Tarzi, Mahmud, 345
Tashkent, 348, 355
Tatars, 341, 355
Tavakoli Targhi, Mohamad (as a historian), 16, 20
Tehran, xxv, xxviii, 1, 6, 24, 26, 28, 31, 36–39, 43, 46, 48, 49, 51, 55, 57, 74, 84, 87, 90, 94, 95, 104–10, 112, 119, 121–23, 128–31, 133, 136, 139, 142, 145, 148, 153–60, 172, 177, 178, 180, 182, 184–86, 194, 214–16, 219, 220, 225–48, 254–60, 267, 270–74, 278, 324, 331–35, 383–86, 391, 392, 395, 396
Tei Suzuki, 385, 387
Tholozan, Dr Joseph-Désiré, 177
Tiyatr, 243, 246
Tibet, 298, 299
Times, 132, 314, 315, 371
Tobacco Protest 1891, 84, 87
Tokyo, 377, 382, 384, 387
Torbat-e Heydarieh, 386
Torbati, Sheykh Ahmad, 232
towhid, 206, 212
trade, xxxii, 77, 101, 106, 107, 108, 122–23, 151, 334, 374, 376, 382, 383
Transcaucasian, xxxii, 21, 45–64, 66, 182, 184, 409, 410, 413–18
transnational, xxix, xxx, 24, 277, 294, 323, 327, 340, 473
travel diaries, xxx, 352
Tria *see* Mgeladze, Vlasa
tullab, 24, 29, 207

Tuman Aqa *see* Malekeh-ye Iran
Turkey *see* Ottoman
Turkmanchai, Treaty of, 351, 483
Turkmen, Turkmenistan, 36, 131, 228, 273, 274

ulema (mullas, clergy), xxv, xxvi, xxix, 6, 17–19, 23, 24, 26, 27, 29, 61, 62, 72–73, 76, 78, 87–89, 94, 104, 111, 117, 123, 125, 126, 136, 137, 158, 165–74, 189, 190, 195, 199–201, 203, 205, 206, 208, 210–12, 226, 234, 267, 274, 286–90, 297, 301, 310, 327, 331–33, 337, 338, 351, 418
Urmia, 156, 234–36, 321, 328, 410

Van, 323, 330
Vaqaye'-e ettefaqiyeh, 100, 134
Varamin, 159
vatan, 42, 137, 151, 197, 217, 221
vatan-parasti see patriotism
Vazir Hozur, Ahmad Khan, 178
Vaziri, Mostafa (as a historian), 21
Vienna, 194

Wang Deyuan, 374
Wang Jingwei, 377, 378
Western-style drama, 239
women, gender, xxii, xxvii, xxxi, 20, 23–26, 29, 31, 49, 97, 104, 138, 144, 187, 206, 209, 220–22, 257, 260, 268, 274–79, 302, 363

Yalta, 352
Yamin al-Mamalek, 149
Yazd, 109, 123

Yazdi, Seyyed Mohammad, 75
Yeats, William Butler, 303, 307, 308
Yeprem Khan, 40, 50, 66, 95, 158, 185, 274
Yokohama, 383
Young Turk Revolution, 1908 166, 291, 310, 314, 320, 323, 325, 327, 337, 338, 341
Young Turks, xxvi, 49, 168, 181–83, 298, 314, 317, 320–23, 327, 330, 345, 365
Yusef Khan Mostashar al-Dowleh *see* Mostashar al-Dowleh
Yushij, Nima, 11
Yusufzadeh, Mirza Jalal, 346

Zahir al-Dowleh, Ali Khan Qajar, xxvi, xxviii, 143–62, 242–45, 248, 274, 441, 443, 444
Zahir al-Soltan, 160
Za'im al-Dowleh, Mehdi Khan, 359
Zargham al-Saltaneh, Ebrahim Khan, 135, 136
Zayandeh rud, 132, 134, 139, 140
Zaydan, Jurji, 361, 362, 364
Zell al-Soltan, Ma'sud Mirza, 135, 138, 159, 179, 274
Zeyn al-'Abedin Maragheh'i *see* Maragheh'i, Zeyn al-'Abedin
Zhengyi Tongbao (Journal of Politics), 374–77
Zoka' al-Molk, Mahmud Khan, 273
Zoka' al-Molk, Mohammad Ali Forughi, 74, 179, 214–16, 218, 221, 452, 455
Zoroastrianism, 307, 389, 489

www.ingramcontent.com/pod-product-compliance
Lightning Source LLC
Chambersburg PA
CBHW052111010526
44111CB00036B/1622